EYEWITNESS TRAVEL

GREAT BRITAIN

EYEWITNESS TRAVEL

GREAT
BRITAIN

Main Contributor **Michael Leapman**

LONDON, NEW YORK,
MELBOURNE, MUNICH AND DELHI
www.dk.com

Art Editor Stephen Bere

Project Editor Marian Broderick

Editors Carey Combe, Sara Harper, Elaine Harries,
Kim Inglis, Ella Milroy, Andrew Szudek,
Nia Williams

Designers Susan Blackburn, Elly King, Colin Loughrey, Andy Wilkinson

Contributors Josie Barnard, Christopher Catling, Juliet Clough, Lindsay Hunt,
Polly Phillimore, Martin Symington, Roger Thomas

Maps Jane Hanson, Phil Rose, Jennifer Skelley (Lovell Johns Ltd),
Gary Bowes (Era-Maptec Ltd)

Photographers Joe Cornish, Paul Harris, Rob Reichenfeld, Kim Sayer

Illustrators Gary Cross, Richard Draper, Jared Gilby (Kevin Jones Assocs), Paul Guest, Roger
Hutchins, Chris Orr & Assocs, Maltings Partnership, Ann Winterbotham, John Woodcock

Printed and bound by South China Printing Co. Ltd., China

First published in the UK in 1995 by Dorling Kindersley Limited
80 Strand, London WC2R 0RL, UK

14 15 16 17 10 9 8 7 6 5 4 3 2 1

**Reprinted with revisions 1996, 1997, 1998, 1999, 2000, 2001, 2002, 2003,
2004, 2005, 2006, 2008, 2009, 2010, 2011, 2013, 2014**

Copyright 1995, 2014 © Dorling Kindersley Limited, London

A Penguin Random House Company

MIX
Paper from
responsible sources
FSC
www.fsc.org
FSC™ C018179

Front cover main image: View over Blackmore Vale from Gold Hill, Shaftesbury,
Dorset, England

 River Manifold Valley near Ilam, Peak District National Park, Derbyshire

Contents

A 14th-century illustration
of two knights jousting

Introducing
Great Britain

Beefeater at the Tower of London

London

Eilean Donan Castle on Loch Duich in the Scottish Highlands

Jacobean "Old House" in Hereford

HOW TO USE THIS GUIDE

This guide helps you to get the most from your holidays in Great Britain. It provides both detailed practical information and expert recommendations. *Introducing Great Britain* maps the country and sets it in its historical and cultural context. The six regional chapters, plus *London*, describe important sights, using maps, pictures and illustrations. Features cover topics from houses and famous gardens to sport. Hotel, restaurant, and pub recommendations can be found in *Travellers' Needs*. The *Survival Guide* has practical information on everything from transport to personal safety.

London at a Glance

The centre of London has been divided into four sight-seeing areas. Each has its own chapter, which opens with a list of the sights described. The last section, *Further Afield*, covers the most attractive suburbs. All sights are numbered and plotted on an area map. The information for each sight follows the map's numerical order, making sights easy to locate within the chapter.

1 Area Map
For easy reference, the sights in each area are numbered and located on an area map.

Colour-coding on each page makes the area easy to find in the book.

A locator map shows you where you are in relation to surrounding areas. The area of the *Street-by-Street Map* is highlighted.

Numbered circles pinpoint all the listed sights on the area map.

Stars indicate the sights that no visitor should miss.

2 Street-by-Street Map
This gives a bird's-eye view of the heart of each sightseeing area. The numbering of the sights ties in with the area map and the fuller descriptions on the pages that follow.

A suggested route for a walk takes in the most attractive and interesting streets in the area.

3 Detailed information
The sights in London are described individually. Addresses, telephone numbers, opening hours, admission charges, tours and wheelchair access are also provided, as well as public transport links.

1 Introduction
The landscape, history and character of each region is outlined here, showing how the area has developed over the centuries and what it has to offer the visitor today.

Great Britain Area by Area

Apart from London, Great Britain has been divided into 14 regions, each of which has a separate chapter. The most interesting towns and places to visit have been numbered on a Regional Map.

Each area of Great Britain can be identified quickly by its colour coding, shown on the inside front cover.

2 Regional Map
This shows the main road network and gives an illustrated overview of the whole region. All entries are numbered and there are also useful tips on getting around the region by car, train and other forms of transport.

3 Detailed information on each sight
All important sights in each area are described in depth in this section. They are listed in order, following the numbering on the Area Map. Practical information on opening hours, telephone numbers, websites, admission charges and facilities available is given for each sight. The key to the symbols used can be found on the back flap.

Story boxes explore related topics.

The Visitors' Checklist provides the practical information you will need to plan your visit.

4 Great Britain's major sights
These are given two or more full pages in the sightseeing area in which they are found. Historic buildings are dissected to reveal their interiors; and museums and galleries have colour-coded floor plans to help you find important exhibits.

INTRODUCING GREAT BRITAIN

DISCOVERING GREAT BRITAIN

The tours on the next six pages have been designed to take in as many of Britain's myriad highlights as possible, while keeping long-distance travel to a minimum. First comes a two-day taste of London; this connects with the week-long tour of the Southeast that follows. The latter, in turn, links with a seven-day circuit through the West Country, and there are three further seven-day trips covering the North, Scotland, and Wales and the West. Scotland and the North can be easily combined into a fortnight-long drive. Each itinerary comes with extra suggestions for travellers who wish to extend their stay. Select and splice the tours that take your fancy, or simply dip in and out and be inspired.

Idyllic scene
Ponies roam freely at Haytor in Dartmoor National Park.

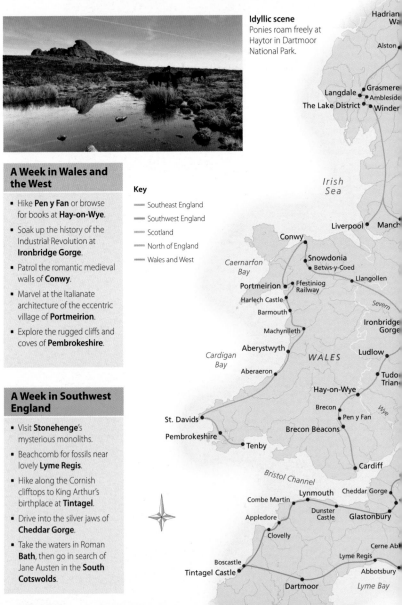

A Week in Wales and the West

- Hike **Pen y Fan** or browse for books at **Hay-on-Wye**.
- Soak up the history of the Industrial Revolution at **Ironbridge Gorge**.
- Patrol the romantic medieval walls of **Conwy**.
- Marvel at the Italianate architecture of the eccentric village of **Portmeirion**.
- Explore the rugged cliffs and coves of **Pembrokeshire**.

A Week in Southwest England

- Visit **Stonehenge**'s mysterious monoliths.
- Beachcomb for fossils near lovely **Lyme Regis**.
- Hike along the Cornish clifftops to King Arthur's birthplace at **Tintagel**.
- Drive into the silver jaws of **Cheddar Gorge**.
- Take the waters in Roman **Bath**, then go in search of Jane Austen in the **South Cotswolds**.

Key
— Southeast England
— Southwest England
— Scotland
— North of England
— Wales and West

Hadrian Wa
Alston

Langdale Grasmere
The Lake District Ambleside
Winder

Irish Sea

Liverpool Manch

Conwy
Snowdonia
Caernarfon Betws-y-Coed
Bay Llangollen
Portmeirion Ffestiniog Railway
Harlech Castle
Barmouth Ironbridge Gorge
Machynlleth *Severn*
Aberystwyth Ludlow
Cardigan Bay *WALES*
Aberaeron Tudo Trian
Hay-on-Wye
Brecon
St. Davids Pen y Fan
Pembrokeshire Brecon Beacons
Tenby *Wye*
Cardiff

Bristol Channel Cheddar Gorge
Combe Martin Lynmouth
Appledore Dunster Castle Glastonbury
Clovelly
Cerne Ab
Boscastle Lyme Regis
Tintagel Castle Abbotsbury
Dartmoor *Lyme Bay*

A Week in Scotland

- Investigate Sherlock Holmes, Jekyll and Hyde and other literary legends in **Edinburgh**.
- Visit **Balmoral**, summer retreat of the royal family.
- Cross the mighty **Cairngorm Mountains**.
- Go in search of the Loch Ness monster on a cruise through the Great Glen from **Inverness**.
- Visit the art galleries of revitalized **Glasgow**.

Travelling in style
This horse-drawn carriage up the Long Walk at Windsor Castle travels at a relaxed pace.

A Week in the North of England

- Catch up with the latest in contemporary art at **Tate Liverpool**.
- Hike the sensational scenery of the **Lake District**.
- Watch archaeologists dig up real Roman history beside the remarkable 2nd-century ramparts of **Hadrian's Wall**.
- Ride back in time on a vintage tram to a working pit village at **Beamish**.
- Eat Britain's best fish and chips on the harbour at **Whitby**.
- Come face to face with the Vikings in **York**, and wander along streets barely changed since medieval times.

A Week in Southeast England

- Take the sea air in buzzing Georgian **Brighton**.
- Examine King Arthur's Round Table in historic **Winchester**.
- Soak up idyllic riverside views on a cruise along the Thames to **Henley**.
- Visit **Windsor Castle**, then take a stately carriage ride in Windsor Great Park.
- Search for Harry Potter among the colleges of **Oxford**.
- Watch a play at the Royal Shakespeare Theatre in **Stratford-upon-Avon**.

Two Days in London

Two years would barely be enough to see the sights of London, but this itinerary scoops up the very best of the city's history, pageantry and art.

- **Arriving** London's main international airport is Heathrow, 14 miles (22 km) west of the city centre and served by the Heathrow Express train service, which connects in 15 minutes with London's excellent underground network at Paddington Station.

- **Moving on** An extensive rail network links London's mainline stations to provincial towns and cities. Coach connections are generally cheaper (and slower); many depart from Victoria Coach Station.

Day 1

Morning Begin where London did, beside the surviving chunk of Roman wall outside Tower Hill underground station. It's a five-minute walk from here to the **Tower of London** *(pp122–3)*, where two hours should be enough to take in an enthralling guided tour with a Beefeater, and drop in on either the Tudor weaponry in the White Tower or the Crown Jewels. Stop at the Tower's Armoury Café for a snack, then walk 10 minutes west to **Monument** *(p120)*, Sir Christopher Wren's 17th-century column, to learn the history of the Great Fire of London. The view (via 311 spiral steps) over the City of London includes the dome of St Paul's Cathedral, the Gherkin and the Shard. Next, cross London Bridge for an iconic photo of **Tower Bridge** *(p120)*, peek into **Southwark Cathedral** *(p124)*, and forage for lunch among the cosmopolitan food stalls at **Borough Market** *(p124)* (open Thu–Sat). The charismatic **George Inn** *(p124)* is a great alternative: an authentic coaching tavern from 1676, it serves hearty pub meals.

The London Eye on the South Bank, offering great views across the city

Afternoon Spend the afternoon on Bankside, choosing between the colossal (and free) modern art installations in the Turbine Hall at **Tate Modern** *(p125)* and an entertaining auditorium tour at the spectacularly recreated **Shakespeare's Globe** *(p124)* next door. Better still, do both. Cross the Millennium Bridge for a look at **St Paul's Cathedral** *(pp118–19)*, and perhaps have dinner at the One New Change complex nearby, where celebrity chefs Jamie Oliver and Gordon Ramsay both have restaurants. Take in a play at the Globe, or board an evening riverboat cruise from Bankside Pier (Apr–Oct).

Day 2

Morning Start the day either by mingling with some of Britain's famous monarchs (and seeing where William and Kate were married) on a self-guided tour around **Westminster Abbey**

A street entertainer in the bustling Piazza, Covent Garden

(pp96–7) or by crossing Westminster Bridge and taking a panoramic spin on the **London Eye** *(p85)*. To beat the crowds, book the first ride on the Eye (9:30am). Next, wander through Parliament Square into serene St James's Park, and skirt the lakeside to reach Horse Guards Parade, where mounted sentries trot in at 11am (10am on Sun) for the Changing of the Guard. Stroll on through Trafalgar Square into the West End, and join the queue for half-price theatre tickets at the official booth in Leicester Square.

Afternoon After a dim sum lunch in Chinatown, visit the **National Gallery** *(pp86–7)*, packed with masterpieces. The neighbouring **National Portrait Gallery** *(p85)* is a fine place to enjoy an English high tea – its third-floor restaurant is knee-high with Nelson's Column. If there is time before the show, walk 10 minutes east to **Covent Garden** *(pp82–3)* for supper or a drink in the piazza while watching the area's celebrated street entertainers.

> ### To extend your trip...
> Devote a third day to a scenic stroll in **Kensington Gardens** *(p105)*, dropping in to visit the area's titanic trio of museums: the **Natural History Museum** *(p104)*, the **Science Museum** *(p104)* and the **Victoria and Albert** *(pp102–3)*. All offer free admission.

A Week in Southeast England

- **Airports** Heathrow is the main hub in the Southeast, a 90-minute drive from Brighton. However, Gatwick Airport is closer, just 45 minutes away. The nearest major airport to Cambridge is Stansted.

- **Transport** A car is necessary to cover this tour in full, although main cities and towns are linked by rail.

Day 1: Brighton
Popularized two centuries ago by the Prince Regent, **Brighton** (pp178–9) was Britain's first sea-bathing resort and retains a certain glamour. Tour the **Royal Pavilion** (pp182–3), with its onion domes, then stroll along the Victorian pier or head to the Lanes for some shopping. Next, drive east along the coast road to Seaford, gateway to one of England's most iconic viewpoints: along the chalk cliffs of the **Seven Sisters** (p184).

Day 2: Winchester
The drive west to Winchester winds through some of southern England's most bucolic country-side. Stop off at **Steyning** (p178), with its chequered church tower and tipsy Tudor houses, or at **Petworth House** (p176), whose treasure trove of art runs from Greek sculpture to Gainsborough. The Horse Guards Inn, in nearby Tillington, is lovely for lunch. Upon reaching **Winchester** (pp174–5), ancient capital of the Saxons, drop into the Great Hall to see King

Arthur's (alleged) Round Table, then tour the Norman cathedral and find Jane Austen's grave.

Day 3: Touring the Thames
Workaday Reading is the starting point for a day along a lazy stretch of the **River Thames** (pp238–9). Take a cruise to the town of Henley, whose River & Rowing Museum celebrates the famous Henley Regatta. Back in the car, drive on to riverside Marlow for lunch at the Michelin-starred Hand & Flowers pub. Other highlights include Cookham, with its gallery showcasing the art of Stanley Spencer, and the National Trust gardens at **Cliveden** (p166). End the day in **Windsor** (p239).

Day 4: Windsor and Eton
Windsor Castle (pp240–41) is the favourite weekend retreat of the Queen – and the world's oldest occupied royal abode. Storm its Round Tower and swoon over the State Apartments, then take a carriage tour (weekends only in winter) in adjacent Windsor Great Park. Across the river and open for tours (Apr–mid-Oct) is **Eton College** (p239), England's most exclusive school, whose old boys include Princes William and Harry.

Day 5: Oxford and Blenheim
Home to England's oldest university, **Oxford** (pp226–31) demands a full day. Visit **Christ Church** (p230), where *Alice in Wonderland* was written and *Harry Potter* filmed. Next, leaf through the **Bodleian Library** (p231), climb one of the famous dreaming spires at **St Mary the Virgin Church** (p229) or hire a

Punting on the River Cam past King's College Chapel, Cambridge

punt at Magdalen Bridge. It's a 20-minute drive north to stately **Blenheim Palace** (pp232–3), the birthplace of Winston Churchill.

Day 6: The Cotswolds and Stratford
Spend the morning exploring classic Village England with the **Midlands Garden Tour** (pp324–5), in the North Cotswolds. Stanton, Snowshill and Chipping Campden are especially idyllic, with good lunching pubs. Then it's on to **Stratford-upon-Avon** (pp328–9). Join the throng for a peek into Shakespeare's Birthplace museum, and take in a play at the Royal Shakespeare Theatre – be sure to book in advance.

Day 7: Cambridge
The week ends in **Cambridge** (pp214–19), more compact than Oxford, and with one stand-out attraction – a chauffeured punting ride along **The Backs** (p214), to peek into the back gardens of a parade of majestic colleges, including **King's College** (pp216–17), with its 500-year-old chapel. The city's other highlights include the **Fitzwilliam Museum** (p216), for its mummies and Old Masters.

To extend your trip...
From Cambridge, continue east into East Anglia, heading north to the beautiful **Norfolk Coast** (pp200–1) via **Ely** (pp198–9), or south to the civilized Suffolk coast at **Southwold** (p206) via **Constable Country** (p208).

The promenade and Palace Pier in Brighton

A Week in Southwest England

- **Airports** Many overseas visitors to Southwest England will arrive at Heathrow, but the provincial airports at Bristol and Exeter are in the region.
- **Transport** A car is necessary for this tour.

Day 1: Stonehenge and Salisbury

Journey back 5,000 years at **Stonehenge** (pp266–7), the grandest gathering of prehistoric stones in Europe. To step inside the stone circle itself, it's necessary to book ahead for an early morning ticket. Spend the afternoon in nearby **Salisbury** (pp268–9), home of England's tallest cathedral. Don't miss a roof tour, up to a viewing gallery under the famous spire.

Day 2: Wessex

Aim southwest and tour ancient Wessex, immortalized in the novels of Thomas Hardy. The market town of **Dorchester** (p273), the setting for The Mayor of Casterbridge, is hemmed by a countryside of stone villages and soft-focus hills. Essential stops include the rather lewd **Cerne Abbas** giant (p273) and Hardy's childhood home at Higher Bockhampton. Head west to **Abbotsbury** (p272), with its medieval Swannery and gardens, then follow the coast to Lyme Regis, where you can relax by eating ice cream on the quayside and looking for fossils along the beach.

Day 3: Dartmoor and Tintagel

Rise early for a long drive west into Devon. It's worth it, especially with a diversion for lunch on **Dartmoor** (pp298–9), a landscape of brooding hills, woods and waterfalls, pierced with romantic granite tors. The Rock Inn at Haytor Vale is well placed for a romp on **Haytor Rocks** (p299). Spend the afternoon sampling the craggy Cornish coast at **Boscastle** (p289) – from there it's a 4-mile (6-km) hike along the Southwest Coast Path to the cliff-hanging ruins of **Tintagel Castle** (p289), said to be the birthplace of King Arthur.

Day 4: The Exmoor Coast

Exmoor (pp254–5) is Dartmoor's softer sister, where heathery hills tumble to meet the sea in a succession of pretty villages. Break your journey with a cream tea in the cobbled alleyways of **Clovelly** (p290) or among the charming fishermen's nooks in **Appledore** (p291). Paddle in the cove at **Combe Martin** (p292); trundle up the cliffs on the water-powered funicular railway at **Lynmouth** (p292); and rampage across the ramparts at dreamy **Dunster Castle** (p255).

Day 5: Glastonbury and Wells

Now known for its music festival, **Glastonbury** (p257) has been a tourist magnet since the Middle Ages, when the local monks enticed pilgrims with tales of King Arthur and the Holy Grail. Climb Glastonbury Tor for breezy views across the Somerset Levels. Spend the afternoon in **Wells** (pp256–7), dominated by a vast cathedral and busy with independent shops. If there's time, drive on to **Cheddar Gorge** (p258), a great silver gulch gouging through the Mendip Hills.

Day 6: Bath

Bath (pp262–3) is an irresistibly beautiful city founded by the Romans; a visit to their immaculately restored open-air **baths** (pp264–5) is an engrossing window on life in imperial Britain in the 1st century. Those who wish to bathe in the thermal waters can do so at nearby **Thermae Bath Spa** (p265) – turn up and swim, or book ahead for treatments. Today's townscape, lined with Palladian terraces and crescents, looks much as it did when Jane Austen lived here 200 years ago.

Day 7: The South Cotswolds

Follow Jane Austen east to discover **Lacock** and **Corsham** (p259), two Cotswold villages so impeccably unspoilt that they often star in costume-drama adaptations of Austen's work. Both Lacock's Rising Sun and the Methuen Arms, in Corsham, are great lunch choices. Spend your final afternoon driving the Wiltshire Downs to **Avebury** (p267), a village surrounded by a stone circle and dotted with prehistoric remains.

To extend your trip…
Continue west from Dartmoor into deepest Cornwall, and visit the **Eden Project** (pp286–7) and the arty seaside enclave of **St Ives** (p281). Or top off your tour with a day in cosmopolitan **Bristol** (pp260–61).

Stonehenge – Britain's most famous and dramatic prehistoric monument

For practical information on travelling around Great Britain see pp636–43

A misty scene at Rydal Water in the Lake District

A Week in the North of England

- **Airports** This itinerary begins and ends at Manchester Airport, but flying out from Newcastle or Leeds-Bradford may increase flexibility.

- **Transport** A car is necessary for this tour.

Day 1: Liverpool
Both **Manchester** (pp376–7) and **Liverpool** (pp380–81) jostle for a full day's attention. If time is tight, choose the latter. Begin beside the Mersey at **Albert Dock** (p381), where the Victorian warehouses have been rescued from dereliction and filled with contemporary art at Tate Liverpool, history at the Merseyside Maritime Museum, and music at the kitschy but fun Beatles Story. Pop pilgrims will want a picture on stage at the Cavern Club, still a live music venue today.

Day 2: The Lake District
England's most spectacular national park deserves to be lingered over. Start with **Windermere** (p371), the largest of the district's many lakes, for a steamboat tour or a lazy hour feeding the swans. Skip the touristy lakeside town of Bowness and take a car-ferry hop over the water to the picture-postcard village of Hawkshead. Stop en route to look for bunny rabbits in the rustic gardens at **Hill Top** (p371),

once home to Beatrix Potter, now a National Trust property open to the public.

Day 3: Langdale and Grasmere
It's a short drive north to **Ambleside** (p370), gateway to some of the area's most rugged mountain scenery. Pick up a picnic at Lucy's Deli in Church Street and press on into **Langdale** (p369). For an easy-going taste of the area's walking possibilities, hike south from quaint **Elterwater** (p369) to view the lake of the same name; then wander beside nearby **Grasmere** (p370), home of the Romantic poet William Wordsworth.

Day 4: Hadrian's Wall
Cross the Pennines to visit **Hadrian's Wall** (pp426–7). Break the drive in Alston, 304 m (1,000 ft) up in the hills, which

Whitby Harbour and St Mary's Church, Yorkshire

claims to be the nation's highest market town. The best surviving stretch of Emperor Hadrian's 2nd-century Roman rampart lies in the lonesome countryside between Housesteads Fort and Vindolanda, where in summer it is possible to watch a live archaeological dig unfold.

Day 5: Durham
Newcastle (pp428–9) is enjoying a renaissance, especially around its vibrant quayside, overlooked by the **Baltic Centre for Contemporary Art** (p428) in Gateshead. Follow the **North Pennines Tour** (p431) via Stanhope to reach the 1,000-year-old university town of **Durham** (pp432–3), with its striking Norman castle and cathedral on the River Wear. The reimagined 1913 colliery town at **Beamish Open Air Museum** (pp428–9) offers an unusual diversion en route.

Day 6: Whitby and the Moors
Whitby (p400) is a charismatic seaside town, its red-roofed fishermen's cottages huddled around a busy quayside. Breeze along the beach, explore the Captain Cook Museum, and climb the 199 steps to Whitby Abbey, with its spooky Dracula connections. After a fish-and-chip lunch at the Magpie Café, drive across the enigmatic **North York Moors** (p399) to Grosmont for a scenic steam-train ride.

Day 7: York
The tangled alleyways of the Shambles quarter in **York** (pp408–13) have changed little since medieval times. Walk the city walls, delve beneath the streets to discover the old Viking city at the **Jorvik centre** (p412), then soak up the sacred history of **York Minster** (pp410–11), the grandest medieval Gothic cathedral in northern Europe.

To extend your trip...
Link this itinerary with a week in **Scotland** (see p17) or, with an extra day or two, drive further north into Northumberland for beautiful unspoilt beaches and **Alnwick Castle** (p424).

A Week in Wales and the West

- **Airports** Cardiff Airport is the largest in Wales, but Bristol, Birmingham and Manchester are also viable starting points for this tour.
- **Transport** A car is essential.

Day 1: Cardiff

A century ago, **Cardiff** (pp474–5) was the world's busiest coal port; today, it offers a rich seam of attractions, from the Neo-Gothic **castle** (pp476–7) and art-filled **National Museum** (p475) to the newly transformed docklands district, with its hands-on science museum **Techniquest** (p474). The **Cardiff Bay Visitor Centre** (p474) is a good starting point. Consider capping the day with a performance at the **Wales Millennium Centre** (p474), a hotbed of music, dance and comedy.

Day 2: Brecon Beacons

This wild and wonderful national park has the highest mountain in southern Britain, **Pen y Fan** (pp472–3), which dominates the drive north along the A470; the Storey Arms outdoor centre is the trailhead for the short, sharp climb. The Georgian market town of Brecon is worth an hour's investigation, or stop off at the nearby Felin Fach Griffin pub, for lunch on the

Buildings and boats lining the shore at the seaside resort of Tenby

lawn. While away the afternoon in **Hay-on-Wye** (p465), a bucolic border town in the Black Mountains that is famous for its 30 or so bookshops.

Day 3: Ludlow and Ironbridge

Drive onward into the Welsh Marches, diverting, if there's time, to go through the famed "Tudor triangle" west of **Leominster** (p317). Weobley, Pembridge and Eardisland are the stand-out villages here, lined with tipsy timber-framed cottages in black and white. Have lunch in **Ludlow** (pp316–17), pinned to a hilltop by its storybook Norman castle and known for its sophisticated dining; the Green Café, beside the tumbling River Teme, is a great choice. Nearby **Ironbridge Gorge** (pp318–19), once the crucible of the Industrial Revolution, is now an attractive living museum.

Day 4: Snowdonia

North Wales is all about by the slatey scenery of Snowdonia. A drive towards the mountains could pause in the canal town of **Llangollen** (p454), for a boat ride through the sky across the spectacular 38-m (124-ft) arches of Pontcysyllte Aqueduct, built by Thomas Telford (p451) in 1805. The best base in the national park is **Betws-y-Coed** (p454), hemmed in by tall peaks – a walk through the wooded glen to Swallow Falls makes an inspiring outing. If you have more time, continue north to **Conwy** (pp450–51), guarded from the sea by its imperious 13th-century fortress and ring of medieval walls.

Day 5: Portmeirion

Perhaps Britain's most extravagant folly, **Portmeirion** (pp458–9) is a madcap Italian-style village on a peninsula above Tremadog Bay. Eccentric and elegant in equal parts, it's a charming place to fritter away a morning. Not far south, **Harlech Castle** (p458) commands a crag-top spot above the ocean – but those tired of medieval masonry may prefer to head

Winter at Swallow Falls in the Snowdonia mountain range, North Wales

to the panoramic **Ffestiniog Railway** instead (pp456–7).

Day 6: The Cardigan Coast

The roads swerving south alongside Cardigan Bay constitute some of Britain's greatest scenic drives: en route, there is Barmouth for beaches, **Machynlleth** (p466) for Welsh revolutionary history, and **Aberystwyth** (pp466–7) for pubs and partying, activities buoyed by its lively student population. Conclude the coastal tour at **Aberaeron** (p467), with its pastel-painted Georgian townhouses lined up prettily around the harbour.

Day 6: Pembrokeshire

This southwest corner of Wales is a honeypot for summer holidaymakers, and no wonder: the rugged cliffs, endless white beaches and cute seaside villages are packed with promise. Those who prefer history to beaches can make for **St Davids** (pp468–9) – its grand 12th-century cathedral and Bishop's Palace were built to honour the province's patron saint, born nearby. But the coastline west of **Tenby** (p470) is loveliest of all, a fittingly dramatic finale to this tour.

> **To extend your trip...**
> The Wye Valley around **Tintern** (p479) is a wooded wonderland, especially beautiful in autumn. Or, in the north, there's the town of **Chester** (pp314–15), with its Roman walls.

A Week in Scotland

- **Airports** This itinerary is a circuit from Edinburgh Airport. Glasgow Airport, just an hour away, is an alternative.

- **Transport** A car is essential for touring in Scotland.

Day 1: Edinburgh
Scotland's capital, **Edinburgh** (pp508–15) is a powerhouse of the arts, and it spills over with world-class theatre, music and comedy at the **Edinburgh Festival** (p513) every August. The medieval Old Town clusters chaotically around hilltop **Edinburgh Castle** (pp510–11), while below, the **National Gallery of Scotland** (p508) shows off its world-class art collection. Stroll down the famous **Royal Mile** (pp512–15) to visit the **Palace of Holyroodhouse** (p514); take a late-night literary tour in search of Sherlock Holmes and Jekyll and Hyde; or climb the city's extinct volcano, Arthur's Seat.

Day 2: Stirling
The grand Renaissance halls of **Stirling Castle** (pp500–1) rise romantically atop vertiginous cliffs, and there's more than enough pomp and history to fill a morning here. Afterwards, wander down into the cobbled wynds of Stirling's Old Town, its bagpipe shops and bars still cradled among 16th-century walls. If there's time, continue north to **Doune Castle** (p502), an intact Stuart stronghold famously featured in the film Monty Python and the Holy Grail.

Day 3: Royal Deeside
Get ready for a majestic drive into the teeth of the Grampians, pausing perhaps in **Dunkeld** (p545) or **Pitlochry** (p545), both swaddled in frothy woodland; Dunkeld features in Shakespeare's Macbeth, while Pitlochry offers beautiful walks on its doorstep along pine-lined Loch Faskally. Don't linger long, however: the target for the day is the baronial estate at Balmoral, summer home of the Windsors and the undisputed highlight of the **Royal Deeside Tour** (pp544–5).

Day 4: The Cairngorms
Climbing across the **Cairngorms** (pp548–9), the A939 road is packed with drama all the way to Speyside. The latter is a great place to sample whisky, Scotland's most famous export, ideally at the Glenlivet Distillery (tours Mar–Oct). The **Inverness Museum and Art Gallery** (p540) gives a fine primer on the history of the Highlands; its exhibits include a tress of Bonnie Prince Charlie's hair (p539). To see where his attempt on power perished, drive out to nearby **Culloden** (p541), the moorland setting for the last battle fought on British soil, in 1746.

Day 5: The Great Glen
Slicing through Scotland's most spectacular mountains, the Great Glen is perhaps best seen on a morning cruise from Inverness. Afterwards, gaze out in search of Nessie, the mythical Loch Ness monster, from the lochside road south-west to Fort William, via the **Loch Ness Exhibition Centre** (p540) and the romantically ruined **Urquhart Castle** (p540). The view of Ben Nevis is the best thing about Fort William, so keep going into gorgeous **Glencoe** (p547), where hill-walking options range from gentle to gargantuan, and the Clachaig Inn serves up near-legendary Highland hospitality.

Day 6: Loch Lomond
An awe-inspiring coastal road follows Loch Linnhe to Connel, then head inland to **Loch Awe** (p551), where lightning-blasted Kilchurn Castle decays delectably beside the water. It's south from here to **Inveraray** (p552), where a rather grander castle is still home to the Clan Campbell. Tour the family portrait collection and vicious-looking weaponry display in the Armoury Hall, then aim east to **Loch Lomond** (p498), Britain's largest freshwater lake. The best views are from the top of Ben Lomond, on its eastern banks.

Day 7: Glasgow
Scotland's biggest city, **Glasgow** (pp520–25) was built on Victorian industry, but it offers plenty for the 21st-century visitor. The well-to-do West End district is the hub of things, busy with bars and restaurants and home to Kelvingrove Park, with its twin art galleries, the **Hunterian** (p523) and the **Kelvingrove** (p523). Quirkier attractions include the **Tenement House** (p521), a working-class time capsule from Edwardian Glasgow, and Charles Rennie Mackintosh's **Willow Tea Room** (p522), a glamorous interior from 1904.

> **To extend your trip...**
> For more wild scenery and a salty scent of the islands, take the **Road to the Isles Tour** (pp550–51) from Fort William, and cast off for **Skye** (pp538–9) and the **Western Isles** (p533).

Edinburgh Castle in all its glory

Putting Great Britain on the Map

Lying in northwestern Europe, Great Britain is bounded by the Atlantic Ocean, the North Sea and the English Channel. The island's landscape and climate are varied, and it is this variety that even today affects the pattern of settlement. The remote shores of the West Country peninsula and the inhospitable mountains of Scotland and Wales are less populated than the relatively flat and fertile Midlands and Southeast, where the vast majority of the country's 63 million people live. Due to this population density, the south is today the most built-up part of the country.

Key

— Motorway
— Major road
- - Ferry route
⋯ Channel Tunnel
— National border

For map symbols *see back flap*

Shetland Islands

Unst

Yell

Mainland

Foula

Lerwick

Fair Isle

Orkney Islands

Westray

Sanday

Mainland
Stromness

Stronsay

Kirkwall

Hoy

Scrabster

Wick

A9

Aberdeen ↓

NORWAY

SWEDEN

DENMARK

North Sea

REP. OF IRELAND

GREAT BRITAIN

NETHERLANDS

London

GERMANY

POLAND

BELGIUM

CZECH REPUBLIC

SLOVAKIA

Atlantic Ocean

FRANCE

SWITZ.

AUSTRIA

HUNGARY

SLOV.

CROATIA

BOSNIA HERZ.

SERBIA

MONTEN.

KOS.

ITALY

MAC

ALBANIA

GREECE

PORTUGAL

SPAIN

ALGERIA

A1

Newcastle upon Tyne

69

Sunderland

A1(M)

56

North Sea

Esbjerg →

A1(M)

ford

Leeds

York

A165

M62

Kingston upon Hull

62

Huddersfield

M180

Grimsby

Manchester

Sheffield

A16

A6

M1

ENGLAND

Groningen

toke-on-Trent

Nottingham

A7

A28

Derby

NETHERLANDS

A6

A1

Zwolle

mingham

Peterborough

A47

Norwich

Amsterdam

A4

rwick

Northampton

A11

A12

Utrecht

A1

Stratford-upon-Avon

Cambridge

M40

M1

A1(M)

M11

Ipswich

The Hague

A12

Arnhem

ucester

Harlow

Harwich

Rotterdam

A15

A3

Oxford

A12

A59

M4

Windsor

London

A58

Eindhoven

M3

M2

Ramsgate

Zeebrugge

A1

Salisbury

M25

Canterbury

Ostend

A14

Antwerp

A2

A61

A36

M23

Dover

Dunkirk

N9

Brussels

hampton

Brighton

Folkestone

Calais

BELGIUM

Aachen

Portsmouth

Newhaven

Boulogne

Lille

A16

Liege

A15

emouth

Isle of Wight

Strait of Dover

A25

A14

A4

A26

A2

A26

annel

A16

Abbeville

Amiens

LUXEMBOURG

Dieppe

N27

A28

FRANCE

A26

N51

Luxembourg

Cherbourg

Le Havre

N15

Rouen

A16

A1

A31

St Malo

N13

Caen

A13

A13

A4

Reims

A4

Metz

Regional Great Britain: London, the South, the Midlands and Wales

Great Britain has airline connections with most cities in the world. London is the main transport hub with three major international airports, including Heathrow, the world's busiest. The most populous area, Southern Britain, is divided within this book, into four regions – Southeast England, the West Country, Wales and the Midlands – with a separate chapter for London. Road and rail links to the North and Scotland *(see pp22–3)* are plentiful, as are links between all main towns.

Key to colour-coding

- London

Southeast England
- The Downs and Channel Coast
- East Anglia
- Thames Valley

The West Country
- Wessex
- Devon and Cornwall

Wales
- North Wales
- South and Mid-Wales

The Midlands
- The Heart of England
- East Midlands

Key

- ═══ Motorway
- ─── Major road
- ─── Railway line
- ─ ─ ─ Ferry route
- ▪▪▪▪ Channel Tunnel

For map symbols *see back flap*

Greater London

Watford · Barnet · Enfield

Edgware · Finchley

Ruislip · Walthamstow

Wembley · Hampstead · Stratford · Barking · Dagenham

Uxbridge · Ealing · LONDON · London City Airport · Greenwich

Heathrow · Richmond · Dulwich · Bexley · Dartford

Staines · Kingston-upon-Thames · Wimbledon · Bromley · Orpington

Croydon · Epsom

0 km · 20
0 miles · 20

Newcastle upon Tyne
Durham
Darlington
Bradford · Leeds · York
Doncaster
Sheffield · Worksop
Lincoln · Skegness
Boston
Derby · Nottingham · Cromer
East Midlands · Loughborough · King's Lynn · Norwich · Great Yarmouth
Leicester · Stamford · Swaffham · Lowestoft
Corby · Peterborough · Thetford · Southwold
Warwick · Coventry · Northampton · Huntington · Bury St Edmunds · Aldeburgh
Stratford-upon-Avon · Milton Keynes · Cambridge · Ipswich · Felixstowe
Banbury · Bedford · Harwich
Cheltenham · Woburn · Stevenage · Colchester
Oxford · Luton · Stansted · Chelmsford · Clacton-on-Sea
St Albans · See inset above · Esbjerg, Hoek van Holland
High Wycombe · Watford · London City Airport · Southend-on-Sea
Marlborough · Windsor · Heathrow · LONDON · Margate · Ostend
Newbury · Reading · Ramsgate
Basingstoke · Guildford · Sevenoaks · Maidstone · Canterbury · Dunkirk
Gatwick · Royal Tunbridge Wells · Dover
Winchester · Crawley · Folkestone · Calais
Southampton · Chichester · Brighton · Lewes · Rye · Channel Tunnel
Lymington · Portsmouth · Newhaven · Hastings · Boulogne
Cowes · Eastbourne
Isle of Wight · Le Touquet

0 kilometres · 75
0 miles · 75

Channel Islands, St Malo · Cherbourg · Caen, Le Havre, Cherbourg · Dieppe

Regional Great Britain: The North and Scotland

This part of Great Britain is divided into two sections in this book. Although it is far less populated than the southern sector of the country, there are good road and rail connections, and ferry services link the islands with the mainland.

Key to colour-coding

The North Country

- Lancashire and the Lakes
- Yorkshire and Humber Region
- Northumbria

Scotland

- The Lowlands
- The Highlands and Islands

Mileage chart

London

Distance in miles
Distance in kilometres

London										
111 179	Birmingham									
150 241	102 164	Cardiff								
74 119	185 298	228 367	Dover							
372 599	290 466	373 600	442 711	Edinburgh						
389 626	292 470	374 602	466 750	45 72	Glasgow					
529 851	448 721	530 853	600 966	158 254	167 269	Inverness				
184 296	81 130	173 278	257 414	213 343	214 344	371 597	Manchester			
274 441	204 328	301 484	343 552	107 172	145 233	265 426	131 211	Newcastle		
112 180	161 259	235 378	167 269	360 579	383 616	517 832	185 298	260 418	Norwich	
212 341	206 332	152 261	287 462	427 784	426 785	545 1038	250 451	427 655	324 521	Plymouth

For map symbols *see back flap*

Orkney and Shetland Islands

Shetland Islands

Unst
Yell

Mainland

Foula

Lerwick

Fair Isle

Westray

Mainland

Sanday

Stronsay

Stromness

Kirkwall

Orkney Islands

Hoy

Scrabster

Thurso

Wick

Aberdeen ↓

Stromness
Scrabster
Thurso
Wick

A836
A895
A897
A9

Kirkwall,
Lerwick

Elgin
Fraserburgh
Peterhead

A98
A96
A97
A92
A939
A95
A97
A96
A92

Aberdeen
Aberdeen

Braemar

A93
A93.9
A93
A94
A90
A92

Forfar
Montrose

A926
A932
A90
A92

Arbroath

Perth
Dundee
St Andrews

A9
A90
A91
A915

Kirkcaldy
Dunfermline

A91
A985
A92

Edinburgh
Edinburgh

M8
A71
A70
A68
A1

Berwick-upon-Tweed

Holy Island

Galashiels
Peebles

Farne Islands

A7
A698
A1

Bamburgh

Hawick
Jedburgh
Alnwick
Warkworth

A72
A708
A701
A710
A75

A68
A697
A696

Morpeth

Carlisle

Hexham
Newcastle
Newcastle Upon Tyne
Durham
Sunderland

Amsterdam →

A69
A69
A1(M)
A19

Cockermouth
Keswick
Penrith

Hartlepool

A66
A595
A596

Barnard Castle
Appleby-in-Westmorland

A689
A66

Middlesbrough

aven
Grasmere

A689
A685

Darlington

Whitby

Hawkshead
Windermere
Kendal

A6
A591
A590
A66

Richmond

A19

Scarborough

A684
A171
A170

Helmsley

Barrow-in-Furness

Heysham

Thirsk
Ripon

Flamborough Head

A608

Lancaster

A65

Skipton
Harrogate
York

Bridlington

A59
A61
A1(M)
A166
A165

Blackpool

Leeds Bradford
Burnley
Bradford
Leeds

Beverley

A59
A64
A1079
A63

Southport
Preston

Blackburn
Rochdale
Halifax
Huddersfield

Wakefield

Kingston upon Hull

M55
M6
M65
M62

Bolton
Wigan

Barnsley
Doncaster

Scunthorpe

Grimsby

A580
A628
M180

Rotterdam,
Zeebrugge →

Liverpool
Liverpool

Manchester
Manchester
Stockport

Sheffield

A46
A631
A15

Chester

A57
A61
A1

Lincoln

A55
A56
A54
A53

A158
A15
A153

Key to map

Motorway
Major road
Railway line
Ferry route

A PORTRAIT OF GREAT BRITAIN

Britain has been assiduous in preserving its traditions, but offers the visitor much more than stately castles and pretty villages. A diversity of landscape, culture, literature, art and architecture, as well as its unique heritage, results in a nation balancing the needs of the present with those of its past.

Britain's character has been shaped by its geographical position as an island. Never successfully invaded since 1066, its people have developed their own distinctive traditions. The Roman invasion of AD 43 lasted 350 years but Roman culture and language were quickly overlain with those of the northern European settlers who followed. Ties with Europe were loosened further in the 16th-century when the Catholic church was replaced by a less dogmatic established church.

Although today a member of the European Union, Britain continues to delight in its non-conformity, even in superficial ways such as driving on the left-hand side of the road instead of the right. The Eurotunnel has opened up links to France, with journey times from Folkestone to Calais taking only 35 minutes.

The British heritage can be seen in its ancient castles, cathedrals and stately homes with their gardens and Classical parklands. Age-old customs are renewed each year, from royal ceremonies to traditional Morris dancers performing on village greens.

For a small island, Great Britain encompasses a surprising variety in its regions, whose inhabitants maintain distinct identities. Scotland and Wales are separate countries from England with their own legislative assemblies.

Walking along the east bank of the River Avon, Bath

◄ A cricket match played at Charterhouse School, Godalming, Surrey

Widecombe-in-the-Moor, a Devon village clustered round a church and set in hills

They have different customs, traditions, and, in the case of Scotland, different legal and educational systems. The Welsh and Scots Gaelic languages survive and are sustained by their own radio and television networks. In northern and West Country areas, English itself is spoken in a rich variety of dialects and accents, and these areas maintain their own regional arts, crafts, architecture and food.

The landscape is varied, too, from the craggy mountains of Wales, Scotland and the north, through the flat expanses of the Midlands and eastern England to the soft, rolling hills of the south and west. The long, broad beaches of East Anglia contrast with the picturesque rocky inlets along much of the west coast.

Scottish coat of arms at Edinburgh Castle

Despite the spread of towns and cities over the last two centuries, rural Britain still flourishes. Nearly three-quarters of Britain's land is used for agriculture. The main commercial crops are wheat, barley, sugar beet and potatoes, though what catches the eye in early summer are the fields of bright yellow rape or slate-blue flax.

The countryside is dotted with farms and charming villages, with picturesque cottages and lovingly tended gardens – a British passion. A typical village is built around an ancient church and a small, friendly pub. Here the pace of life slows. To drink a pint of ale in a cosy, village inn and relax before a fire is a time-honoured British custom. Strangers will be welcomed cordially, though perhaps with caution; for even if strict formality is a thing of the past, the British have a tendency to be reserved.

In the 19th and early 20th centuries, trade with the extensive British Empire, fuelled by abundant coal supplies, spurred manufacturing and created wealth. Thousands of people moved from the countryside to towns and cities near mines, mills and factories. By 1850 Britain was the world's strongest industrial nation. Now many of these old industrial centres have declined, and today manufacturing

Lake and gardens at Petworth House, Sussex

employs only 10 per cent of the labour force, while 75 per cent work in the growing service sector. These service industries are located mainly in the southeast, close to London, where modern office buildings bear witness to comparative prosperity.

Society and Politics

British cities are melting-pots for people not just from different parts of the country but also from overseas. Irish immigration has long ensured a flow of labour into the country, and since the 1950s hundreds of thousands have come from former colonies in Africa, Asia and the Caribbean. Today, EU membership has led to another wave of immigration to Britain, mostly from Eastern Europe. Nearly six per cent of Britain's 60 million inhabitants are from non-white ethnic groups – and about half of these were

Crowds at Petticoat Lane market in London's East End

born in Britain. The result is a multicultural society that can boast a wide range of music, art, food and religions. However, prejudice does exist and in some inner-city areas where poorer members of different communities live, racial tensions can occasionally arise. Even though discrimination in housing and employment on the grounds of race is against the law, it does occur. Britain's class structure still intrigues and bewilders many visitors, based as it is on a subtle mixture of heredity and wealth. Even though many of the great inherited fortunes no longer exist, some old landed

Bosses in Norwich Cathedral cloisters

families still live on their large estates, and many now open them to the public. Class divisions are further entrenched by the education system. While more than 90 per cent of children are educated free by the state, richer parents often opt for private schooling, and the products of these private schools are disproportionately represented in the higher echelons of government and business.

The monarchy's position highlights the dilemma of a people seeking to preserve its most potent symbol of national unity in an age that is suspicious of inherited privilege. Without real political power, though still head of the Church of England, the Queen and her family are subject to increasing public scrutiny and some citizens advocate the abolition of the monarchy.

Democracy has deep foundations in Britain: there was even a parliament of sorts in London in the 13th century.

Priest in the Close at Winchester Cathedral

Yet with the exception of the 17th-century Civil War, power has passed gradually from the Crown to the people's elected representatives. A series of Reform Acts between 1832 and 1884 gave the vote to all male citizens, though women were not enfranchised on an equal basis until 1928. Margaret Thatcher – Britain's first woman Prime Minister – held office for 12 years from 1979. During the 20th century, the Labour (left wing) and Conservative (right wing) parties have, during their periods in office, favoured a mix of public and private ownership for industry and ample funding for the state health and welfare systems.

The position of Ireland has been an intractable political issue since the 17th century. It was divided in 1920, with the north becoming part of the UK. In the 1970s, 80s and much of the 90s, Northern Ireland was a battleground, with both Loyalist and Republican paramilitary groups waging bombing campaigns. The Good Friday Agreement of 1998 was a huge step forward, and the path to lasting peace now seems possible. The power-sharing Sinn Féin and DUP government is addressing the final stumbling blocks of policing and justice.

Afternoon tea on the back lawn at the Thornbury Castle Hotel, Avon

The House of Lords, in Parliament

Culture and the Arts

Britain has a famous theatrical tradition stretching back to the 16th century and William Shakespeare. His plays have been performed on stage almost continuously since he wrote them, and the works of 17th- and 18th-century writers are also frequently revived. Contemporary British playwrights such as Tom Stoppard, Alan Ayckbourn and David Hare draw on this long tradition with their vivid language and by using comedy to illustrate serious themes. British actors such as Helen Mirren, Judi Dench, Colin Firth, Ian McKellen, Kate Winslet and Anthony Hopkins have international reputations.

While London is the focal point of British theatre, fine drama is to be seen in many other parts of the country. The Edinburgh Festival and its Fringe are the high point of Great Britain's cultural calendar with theatre and music to suit all tastes. Other music festivals are held across the country, chiefly in summer, while there are annual festivals of literature at Hay-on-Wye and Cheltenham. Poetry has had an enthusiastic following since Chaucer wrote the *Canterbury Tales* in the 14th century: poems from all eras can even be read on the London Underground, where they are interspersed with the advertisements in the carriages and on the station platforms.

In the visual arts, Britain has a strong tradition in portraiture, caricature, landscape and watercolour. Modern British artists David Hockney and Lucian Freud, and sculptors Henry Moore and Barbara Hepworth, have enjoyed worldwide recognition. British architects including Christopher Wren, Inigo Jones, John Nash and Robert Adam all created

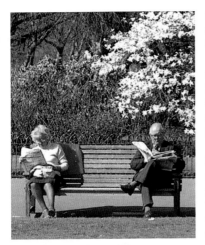

Reading the newspaper in Kensington Gardens

radio networks and 10 digital television channels, as well as an additional 17 digital radio stations.

The British are great sports fans, and soccer, rugby, cricket and golf are popular. Nationwide, fishing is the most popular sporting pastime, and the British make excellent use of their national parks as keen walkers.

British food used to be derided for its lack of imagination, but many chefs – such as Fergus Henderson at St John – are revitalizing the nation's standing, combining top-notch traditional ingredients with a variety of culinary influences and techniques from around the world. Other home-grown British chefs such as Heston Blumenthal and Angela Hartnett have also helped elevate British cuisine. Furthermore, there is a great appetite for Indian, Spanish, Chinese, Italian and Thai food, among many others.

In this, as in other respects, the British are doing what they have done for centuries: accommodating their own traditions to influences from other cultures, while leaving elements of their national character intact.

styles that define British cities; and today, Norman Foster and Richard Rogers carry the standard for Post-Modernism. Britain is famous for its innovative fashion designers, such as Vivienne Westwood and Matthew Williamson, many of whom now show their spring and autumn collections in Paris.

The British are avid newspaper readers. There are nine national newspapers published from London on weekdays: the standard of the serious newspapers, such as *The Independent* and *The Guardian*, is very high, and *The Times* is read the world over because of its reputation for strong reporting. The best selling, however, are the tabloids, which are packed with celebrity gossip, crime and sport.

The indigenous film industry has produced international hits such as *The Queen* and *Slumdog Millionaire*, though blockbusters such as the Harry Potter films are often backed by the US. Acclaimed British film directors include Danny Boyle and Mike Leigh. British television is famous for the quality of its news, current affairs and drama programmes. The publicly funded British Broadcasting Corporation (BBC), which controls five national

Whitby harbour and St Mary's Church, Yorkshire

Gardens through the Ages

Styles of gardening in Britain have expanded alongside architecture and other evolving fashions. The Elizabethan knot garden became more elaborate and formal in Jacobean times, when the range of plants greatly increased. The 18th century brought a taste for large-scale "natural" landscapes with lakes, woods and pastures, creating the most distinctively English style to have emerged. In the 19th century, fierce debate raged between supporters of natural and formal gardens, developing into the eclecticism of the 20th century when "garden rooms" in differing styles became popular.

Monumental column

A grotto and cascade brought romance and mystery.

"Capability" Brown (1715–83) was Britain's most influential garden designer, favouring the move away from formal gardens to man-made pastoral settings.

Blackthorn

Classical temples were a much appreciated feature in 18th-century gardens and were often exact replicas of buildings that the designers had seen in Greece.

Elaborate parterres were a feature of aristocratic gardens of the 17th century, when the fashion spread from Europe. This is the Privy Garden at Hampton Court Palace, restored in 1995 to its design under William III.

Maple

Winding paths were carefully planned to allow changing vistas to open out as visitors strolled around the garden.

Ideal Landscape Garden

Classical Greece and Rome inspired the grand gardens of the early 18th century, such as Stourhead and Stowe. In-formal clumps of trees played a critical part in the serene, manicured landscapes.

Design and Formality

A flower garden is a work of artifice, an attempt to tame nature rather than to copy it. Growing plants in rows or regular patterns, interspersed with statues and ornaments, imposes a sense of order. Designs change to reflect the fashion of the time and the introduction of new plants.

Medieval gardens usually had a herber (a turfed sitting area) and a vine arbour. A good reconstruction is Queen Eleanor's Garden, Winchester.

Tudor gardens featured edged borders and sometimes mazes. The Tudor House Garden, Southampton, also has beehives and heraldic statues.

Herbaceous borders, full of lush plants, are the glory of the summer garden. Gertrude Jekyll (1843–1932), was high priestess of the mixed border, with her eye for seductive colour combinations.

Cedar of Lebanon

Yew

The Palladian bridge was a favourite feature, often decorative rather than practical.

Rhododendron

Knot Gardens were in vogue in the 1500s. Intersecting lines of lavender or box were filled with flowers, herbs or vegetables, as in this restoration at Pitmedden in Scotland.

VISITORS' CHECKLIST

Practical Information
The "yellow book", Gardens of England and Wales, the annual guide to the National Gardens Scheme, lists gardens open to the public.

Development of the Modern Pansy

All garden plants derive from wild flowers, bred over the years to produce qualities that appeal to gardeners. The story of the pansy, one of our most popular flowers, is typical.

 The wild pansy (Viola tricolor) native to Britain is commonly known as heartsease. It is a small-flowered annual which can vary considerably in colour.

 The mountain pansy (Viola lutea) is a perennial. The first cultivated varieties resulted from crossing it with heartsease in the early 19th century.

The Show Pansy was bred by florists after the blotch appeared as a chance seedling in 1840. It was round in form with a small, symmetrical blotch.

The Fancy Pansy, developed in the 1860s, was much larger. The blotch covered all three lower petals save for a thin margin of colour.

Modern hybrids of pansies, violas and violettas, developed by selective breeding, are varied and versatile in a wide range of vibrant new colours.

17th-century gardening was more elaborate. Water gardens like those at Blenheim were often combined with parterres of exotic foreign plants.

Victorian gardens, their formal beds a mass of colour, were a reaction to the landscapes of "Capability" Brown. Alton Towers has a good example.

20th-century gardens mix historic and modern styles, as at Hidcote Manor, Gloucestershire. Growing wild flowers is a popular choice.

Stately Homes

The grand country house reached its zenith in the 18th and 19th centuries, when the old landed families and the new captains of industry enjoyed their wealth, looked after by a retinue of servants. The earliest stately homes date from the 14th century, when defence was paramount. By the 16th century, when the opulent taste of the European Renaissance spread to England, houses became centres of pleasure and showplaces for fine art (see pp306–07). The Georgians favoured chaste Classical architecture with rich interiors, the Victorians flamboyant Gothic. Due to 20th-century social change many stately homes have been opened to the public, some administered by the National Trust.

The saloon, a domed rotunda based on the Pantheon in Rome, was designed to display the Curzon family's Classical sculpture collection to 18th-century society.

The Drawing Room, the main room for entertaining, contains the most important pictures and some exquisite plasterwork.

The Marble Hall is where balls and other social functions took place among Corinthian columns of pink alabaster.

The Family Wing is a self-contained "pavilion" of private living quarters; the servants lived in rooms above the kitchen. The Curzon family still live here.

**The M...
Roo...
decorated
musical the
Music was the
entertainmen
social occas...

1650	1700	1750
Colen Campbell (1676–1729) designed Burlington House (see p85)	**William Kent** (1685–1748) built Holkham Hall (see p201) in the Palladian style	**John Carr** (1723–1807) designed the Palladian Harewood House (see p414)	**Robert Adam** (1728–92), who often worked with his brother James (1730–94) was as famous for decorative details as for buildings	**Henry Holland** (1745–180... designed the Neo-Classica... south range of Woburn Abbey (see p234)
Sir John Vanbrugh (see p402) was helped by **Nicholas Hawksmoor** (1661–1736) on Blenheim Palace (see pp232–3)	Castle Howard (1702) by Sir John Vanbrugh		Adam fireplace, Kedleston Hall, adorned with Classical motifs	

National Trust

National Trust
oak leaf design

At the end of the 19th century, there were real fears that burgeoning factories, mines, roads and houses would obliterate much of Britain's historic landscape and finest buildings. In 1895 a group that included the social reformer Octavia Hill formed the National Trust, to preserve the nation's valuable heritage. The first building acquired by the trust was the medieval Clergy House at Alfriston in Sussex, in 1896 (see p184). Today the National Trust is a charity that runs many historic houses and gardens, and vast stretches of countryside and coastline (see p623). It is supported by more than two million members nationwide.

A corridor links the kitchen to the main house.

The 13th-century church is all that is left of Kedleston village, moved in 1760 to make way for the new house and its grounds.

Kedleston Hall

This Derbyshire mansion (see p340) is an early work of the influential Georgian architect Robert Adam, who was a pioneer of the Neo-Classical style derived from ancient Greece and Rome. It was built for the Curzon family in the 1760s.

Life Below Stairs by Charles Hunt (c.1890)

Life below stairs

A large community of resident staff was essential to run a country house smoothly. The butler was in overall charge, ensuring that meals were served on time. The housekeeper supervised uniformed maids who made sure the place was clean. The cook ran the kitchen, using fresh produce from the estate. Ladies' maids and valets acted as personal servants.

1800	1850	

Norman Shaw (1831–1912) was an exponent of Victorian Gothic, as in Cragside (above), and a pioneer of the Arts and Crafts movement (see p332)

Philip Webb (1831–1915) was a leading architect of the influential. Arts and Crafts movement (see p332), whose buildings favoured the simpler forms of an "Old English" style, instead of flamboyant Victorian Gothic

Sir Edwin Lutyens (1869–1944) designed the elaborate Castle Drogo in Devon (see p299), one of the last grand country houses

Dining Room, Cragside, Northumberland

Standen, West Sussex (1891–94) by Philip Webb

Heraldry and the Aristocracy

The British aristocracy has evolved over 900 years from the feudal obligations of noblemen to the Norman kings, who conferred privileges of rank and land in return for armed support. Subsequent monarchs bestowed titles and property on their supporters, establishing new aristocratic dynasties. The title of "earl" dates from the 11th century; that of "duke" from the 14th century. Soon the nobility began to choose their own symbols, partly to identify a knight concealed by his armour: these were often painted on the knight's coat (hence the term "coat of arms") and also copied onto his shield.

The College of Arms, London: housing records of all coats of arms and devising new ones

Royal Coat of Arms

The most familiar British coat of arms is the sovereign's. It appears on the royal standard, or flag, as well as on official documents and on shops that enjoy royal patronage. Over nearly 900 years, various monarchs have made modifications. The quartered shield in the middle displays the arms of England (twice), Scotland and Ireland. Surrounding it are other traditional images including the lion and unicorn, topped by the crown and the royal helm (helmet).

Edward III (1327–77) was the founder of the chivalric Order of the Garter. The garter, bearing the motto, Honi soit qui mal y pense (evil be to him who thinks of evil), goes round the central shield.

The lion is the most common beast in heraldry.

The red lion is the symbol of Scotland.

The unicorn is a mythical beast, generally regarded as a Scottish royal beast in heraldry.

Henry II (1154–89) formalized his coat of arms to include three lions. This was developed by his son Richard I to become the "Gules three lions passant guardant or" seen on today's arms.

The royal helm with gold protective bars was introduced to the arms by Elizabeth I (1558–1603).

Dieu et mon droit (God and my right) has been the royal motto since the reign of Henry V (1413–22).

Henry VII (1485–1509) devised the Tudor rose, joining the white and red roses of York and Lancaster.

Admiral Lord Nelson

When people are ennobled they may choose their own coat of arms if they do not already have one. Britain's naval hero (1758–1805) was made Baron Nelson of the Nile in 1798 and a viscount in 1801. His arms relate to his life and career at sea; but some symbols were added after his death.

A seaman supports the shield.

The motto means "Let him wear the palm (or laurel) who deserves it".

A tropical scene shows the Battle of the Nile (1798).

The San Joseph was a Spanish man o'war that Nelson daringly captured.

Tracing your Ancestry

For records of births, deaths and marriages in England and Wales since 1837, contact the General Register Office (0845 603 7788; **www.gro.gov.uk**), and in Scotland New Register House, 3 West Register St, Edinburgh EH1 3YT (0131 334 0380; **www.gro-scotland.gov.uk**). For help in tracing family history, consult the Society of Genealogists, 14 Charterhouse Bldgs, London EC1 (020 7251 8799).

Inherited titles

usually pass to the eldest son or the closest male relative, but some titles may go to women if there is no male heir.

The Duke of Edinburgh (born 1921), husband of the Queen, is one of several dukes who are members of the Royal Family.

The Marquess of Salisbury (1830–1903), Prime Minister three times between 1885 and 1902, was descended from the Elizabethan statesman Robert Cecil.

Earl Mountbatten of Burma (1900–79) was ennobled in 1947 for diplomatic and military services.

Viscount Montgomery (1887–1976) was raised to the peerage for his military leadership in World War II.

Lord Byron (1788–1824), the Romantic poet, was the 6th Baron Byron: the 1st Baron was an MP ennobled by Charles I in 1625.

Peers of the Realm

There are nearly 1,200 peers of the realm. In 1999 the process began to abolish the hereditary system in favour of life peerages that expire on the death of the recipient (see left and below). Ninety-two hereditary peers are entitled to sit in the House of Lords, including the Lords Spiritual – archbishops and senior bishops of the Church of England – and the Law Lords. In 1958 the Queen expanded the list of life peerages to honour people who had performed notable public service. From 1999 the system of "peoples peerages" began to replace inherited honours.

Key to the Peers

- 25 dukes
- 35 marquesses
- 175 earls and countesses
- 98 viscounts
- 800+ barons and baronesses

The Queen's Honours List

Twice a year several hundred men and women nominated by the Prime Minister and political leaders for outstanding public service receive honours from the Queen. Some are made dames or knights; a few receive the prestigious OM (Order of Merit); far more receive lesser honours such as OBEs or MBEs (Officers or Members of The Most Excellent Order of the British Empire).

Mother Teresa received the OM in 1983 for her work in India.

Terence Conran, founder of Habitat, was knighted for services to industry.

The Beatles were given MBEs in 1965. Paul McCartney was knighted in 1997.

Rural Architecture

For many, the essence of British life is found in villages. Their scale and serenity nurture a way of life envied by those who live in towns and cities. The pattern of British villages dates back some 1,500 years, when the Saxons cleared forests and established settlements, usually centred around a green or pond. Most of today's English villages existed at the time of the *Domesday Book* in 1086, though few actual buildings survive from then. The settlements evolved organically around a church or manor; the cottages and gardens were created from local materials. Today, a typical village will contain structures of various dates, from the Middle Ages onward. The church is usually the oldest, followed perhaps by a tithe barn, manor house and cottages.

Abbotsbury, in Dorset – a typical village built up around a church

A steep-pitched roof covers the whole house.

Timbers are of Wealden oak.

Eaves are supported by curved braces.

Wealden Hall House in Sussex is a medieval timber-framed house, of a type found in southeast England. It has a tall central open hall flanked by bays of two floors and the upper floor is "jettied", overhanging the ground floor.

A tiled roof keeps the grain dry.

The entrance is big enough for ox-wagons.

Holes let in air–and birds.

Walls and doors are weatherboarded.

The medieval tithe barn stored produce for the clergy – each farmer was required to donate one tenth (tithe) of his annual harvest. The enormous roofs may be supported by crucks, large curved timbers extending from the low walls.

The Parish Church

Slender spire from the Georgian era

The church is the focal point of the village and, traditionally, of village life. Its tall spire could be seen – and its bells heard – by travellers from a distance. The church is also a chronicle of local history: a large church in a tiny village indicates a once-prosperous settlement. A typical church contains architectural features from many centuries, occasionally as far back as Saxon times. These may include medieval brasses, wall paintings, misericords *(see p345)*, and Tudor and Stuart carvings. Many sell informative guide books inside.

West Elevation

Pinnacled towers dating from the 15th century are situated at the west end.

Buttresses support old walls.

Bells summon the congregation.

Norman arches are rounded.

Stone cottages such as this Pennine longhouse are built from hard, local granite, keeping out the severe winter weather. Farm animals were housed in the barn *(on right)*, and the family home was at the other end *(see far right)*.

Chimneys come in various shapes.

The roof is made from slabs of Lake District stone.

Windows were often small in cold areas.

The roof is surfaced with tiles.

Type of stone used depends on locality. In Cumbria blue-grey Pennine stone was used.

Building materials

The choice of materials depended on local availability. A stone cottage in east Scotland or Cornwall would be granite, or in the Cotswolds, limestone. Timber for beams was often oak. Flint and pebble were popular in the chalky south and east. Slate is quarried in Wales and brick was widely used from Tudor times.

Weatherboard houses were built chiefly in southeast England in the 18th and 19th centuries; the timber boarding acted as cladding to keep out the cold and rain.

Bay windows add light and space.

Welsh slate, making a durable roof

Tiles made from fired clay

Thatch is made from reeds or straw.

Flint and pebble – common in Norfolk

Wood planks used for weatherboarding

Thatched cob cottages of the 17th century have a cob covering a timber frame. The cob is made from a mixture of wet earth, lime, dung, chopped reed, straw, gravel, sand and stones.

Walls are 1 m (3 ft) thick.

Brick, widely used since Tudor times

Local hard granite from South Wales

South Elevation

The nave is often the oldest part of the building, with extensions added in later centuries.

Pointed arches date from the 13th century.

Many pulpits are Jacobean.

A screen separates nave from chancel.

The chancel houses the choir and altar.

Towers are often later additions, due to their tendency to collapse.

Ropes used by bell-ringers.

The font, where babies are baptized, is often a church's oldest feature.

The Countryside

For its size, Britain contains an unusual variety of geological and climatic conditions that have shaped diverse landscapes, from treeless windswept moorland to boggy marshes and small hedged cattle pastures. Each terrain nurtures its typical wildlife and displays its own charm through the seasons. With the reduction in farming and the creation of footpaths and nature reserves, the countryside is becoming more of a leisure resource.

Indigenous Animals and Birds

There are no large or dangerous wild animals in Britain but a wealth of small mammals, rodents and insects inhabit the countryside, and the rivers and streams are home to many varieties of fish. For bird-watchers there is a great range of songbirds, birds of prey and seabirds.

Livestock graze on low pastures.

Trees provide shelter and protection for wildlife.

Higher land is uncultivated.

Bushes and trees grow between rocks.

The highest ground is often covered in snow until spring.

Streams flow over a stony bed from mountain springs.

Wooded Downland

Chalk downland, seen here at Ditchling Beacon on the Downs *(see p185)*, has soil of low fertility and is grazed by sheep. However crops are sometimes grown on the lower slopes. Distinctive wild flowers and butterflies thrive here, while beech and yew predominate in the woods.

Spear thistle has pink heads in summer that attract several species of butterfly.

The dog rose is one of Britain's best-loved wild flowers; its pink single flower is widely seen in hedgerows.

Hogweed has robust stems and leaves with large clusters of white flowers.

Wild Hillside

Large tracts of Britain's uplands remain wild terrain, unsuitable for crops or forestry. Purple heather is tough enough to survive in moorland, the haunt of deer and game birds. The highest craggy uplands, such as the Cairngorms *(see p548–9)* in Scotland, pictured here, are the habitat of birds of prey, such as the golden eagle.

Ling, a low-growing heather with tiny pink bell-flowers, adds splashes of colour to peaty moors and uplands.

Meadow cranesbill is a wild geranium with distinctive purple flowers.

Tormentil has small yellow flowers. It prefers moist, acid soil and is found near water on heaths and moors in summer.

Swallows, swifts and house martins are all summer visitors.

Kestrels are small falcons that prey on mammals such as voles.

Rabbits are often spotted feeding at the edge of fields or near woods.

Robins, common in gardens and hedgerows, have distinctive red breast feathers.

Foxes, little bigger than domestic cats, live in hideaways in woods, near farmland.

Cereal crops ripen in small fields.

Hedgerows provide refuge for wildlife.

Small mixed woods break up the field pattern.

Sheep graze on salty marshes.

Culverts drain water from the field.

Reed beds edge the water.

Traditional Fields

The patchwork fields here in the Cotswolds *(see p308)* reflect generations of small-scale farming. A typical farm would produce silage, hay and cereal crops, and keep a few dairy cows and sheep in enclosed pastures. The tree-dotted hedgerows mark boundaries that may be centuries old.

Marshland

Flat and low-lying wetlands, criss-crossed with dykes and drainage canals, provide the scenery of Romney Marsh *(see also p186)* as well as much of East Anglia. Some areas have rich, peaty soil for crops, or salty marshland for sheep, but there are extensive uncultivated sections, where reed beds shelter wildlife.

Sea lavender is a saltmarsh plant that is tolerant of saline soils. It flowers in late summer.

The oxeye daisy is a larger relative of the common white daisy, found in grassland from spring to late summer.

Orchids are among the rarer wild flowers. This species is the Common Spotted Orchid.

Cowslips belong to the primrose family. In spring they are often found in the grass on open meadowlands.

Poppies glow brilliant red in cornfields.

Buttercups are among the most common wild flowers. They brighten meadows in summer.

Walkers' Britain

Walkers of all levels of ability and enthusiasm are well served in Britain. There is an unrivalled network of long-distance paths through some spectacular scenery, which can be tackled in stages with overnight stays en route, or dipped into for a single day's walking. For shorter walks, Britain is dotted with signposts showing public footpaths across common or private land. You will find books of walk routes in local shops and a large map will keep you on track. Choose river routes for easy walking or take to the hills for a greater challenge.

The West Highland Way is an arduous 95 mile (153 km) route from Milngavie, near Glasgow, to north of Fort William, across mountainous terrain with fine lochs and moorland scenery *(see p498).*

The Pennine Way was Britain's first designated long-distance path. The 268 mile (431 km) route from Edale in Derbyshire to Kirk Yetholm on the Scottish border is a challenging upland hike, with long, lonely stretches of moorland. It is only for experienced hill walkers.

Offa's Dyke Footpath follows the boundary between Wales and England. The 168 mile (270 km) path goes through the beautiful Wye Valley *(see p465)* in the Welsh borders.

Pembrokeshire Coastal path is 186 miles (299 km) of rugged cliff-top walking from Amroth on Carmarthen Bay to the west tip of Wales at Cardigan.

Ordnance Survey maps

The best maps for walkers are published by the Ordnance Survey, the official mapping agency (08456 050505). Out of a wide range of maps the most useful are the Explorer series, which include the more popular regions and cover a large area, on a scale of 1:25,000, and the Landranger series, on a scale of 1:50,000.

The Southwest Coastal Path offers varied scenery from Minehead on the north Somerset coast to Poole in Dorset, via Devon and Cornwall– in all a marathon 630 mile (1,014 km) round trip.

Fort William

Glasgow   Kirk Yet

St Bees Head
Windermere

Prestatyn

St Dogmaels
Amroth
Chepstow

Minehead

Signposts

Long-distance paths are well signposted, some of them with an acorn symbol (or with a thistle in Scotland). Many shorter routes are marked with coloured arrows by local authorities or hiking groups. Local councils generally mark public footpaths with yellow arrows. Public bridleways, marked by blue arrows, are paths that can be used by both walkers and horse riders – remember, horses churn up mud. Signs appear on posts, trees and stiles.

Tips for Walkers

Be prepared: The weather can change very quickly: dress for the worst. Always take a compass, a proper walking map and get local advice before undertaking any ambitious walking. Pack some food and drink if the map does not show a pub en route.
On the walk: Always keep to the footpath and close gates behind you. Never feed or upset farm animals, leave litter, pick flowers or damage plants.
Where to stay: The International Youth Hostel Federation (see pp622–3) has a network of hostels which cater particularly for walkers. Bed-and-breakfast accommodation is also available near most routes (see p557).
Further information: The Ramblers' Association (020 7339 8500; www.ramblers.org.uk) is a national organization for walkers, with a guide to accommodation.

The Coast to Coast Walk crosses the Lake District, Yorkshire Dales and North York Moors, on a 190 mile (306 km) route. This demanding walk covers a spectacular range of North Country landscapes. All cross-country routes are best walked from west to east to take advantage of the prevailing wind.

Robin Hood's Bay

Dales Way runs from Ilkley in West Yorkshire to Bowness-on-Windermere in the Lake District, 81 miles (130 km) of delightful flat riverside walking and valley scenery.

The Ridgeway is a fairly easy path that follows an ancient track once used by cattle drovers. Starting near Avebury (see p267) it covers 85 miles (137 km) to Ivinghoe Beacon.

Peddars Way and the Norfolk Coast Path together make 94 miles (151 km) of easy lowland walking, from Thetford, north to the coast then east to Cromer.

Sheringham

Thetford

Icknield Way, the most ancient prehistoric road in Britain, is 105 miles (168 km) long and links the Ridgeway to Peddars Way.

Ivinghoe

mble

Avebury

London

rnham

Dover

hester

Eastbourne

e Harbour

The Thames Path follows the river for 213 miles (341 km) from central London to Kemble, its source in Gloucestershire.

The South Downs Way is a 101 mile (162 km) walk from Eastbourne on the south coast to Winchester (see pp174–5). It can be completed in a week.

The Isle of Wight Coastal Path circles the entire island on an easy 65 mile (105 km) footpath.

The North Downs Way is an ancient route through 141 miles (227 km) of low-lying hills from Farnham in Surrey to Dover or Folkestone in Kent.

THE HISTORY OF GREAT BRITAIN

Britain began to assume a cohesive character as early as the 7th century, with the Anglo-Saxon tribes absorbing Celtic and Roman influences and finally achieving supremacy. They suffered repeated Viking incursions and were overcome by the Normans at the Battle of Hastings in 1066. Over centuries, the disparate cultures of the Normans and Anglo-Saxons combined to form the English nation, a process nurtured by Britain's position as an island. The next 400 years saw English kings involved in military expeditions to Europe, but their control over these areas was gradually wrested from them. As a result they extended their domain over Scotland and Wales. The Tudor monarchs consolidated this control and laid the foundations for Britain's future commercial success. Henry VIII recognized the vital importance of sea power and under his daughter, Elizabeth I, English sailors ranged far across the world, often coming into conflict with the Spanish.

The total defeat of the Spanish Armada in 1588 confirmed Britain's position as a major maritime power. The Stuart period saw a number of internal struggles, most importantly the Civil War in 1641. But by the time of the Act of the Union in 1707 the whole island was united and the foundations for representative government had been laid. The combination of this internal security with continuing maritime strength allowed Britain to seek wealth overseas. By the end of the Napoleonic Wars in 1815, Britain was the leading trading nation in the world. The opportunities offered by industrialization were seized, and by the late 19th century, a colossal empire had been established across the globe. Challenged by Europe and the rise of the US, and drained by its leading role in two world wars, Britain's influence waned after 1945. By the 1970s almost all the colonies had become independent Commonwealth nations.

Contemporary map showing the defeat of the Armada (1588), making Britain into a world power

◀ Henry VIII, founder of the British navy, seen here with his son, Edward, and wife Jane Seymour

Kings and Queens

All English monarchs since the Norman Conquest in 1066 have been descendants of William the Conqueror. Scottish rulers, until James VI and the Union of Crowns in 1603 *(see pp486–7),* have been more diverse. When the Crown passes to someone other than the monarch's eldest son, the name of the ruling family usually changes. The rules of succession have been precisely laid down and strongly favour men over women, but Britain has still had six queens since 1553. In Norman times the monarchy enjoyed absolute power, but today the position is largely symbolic.

1413–22 Henry V

1509–47 Henry VIII

1399–1413 Henry IV

1485–1509 Henry VII

1553– Mar

1483–5 Richard III

1066–87 William the Conqueror

1087–1100 William II

1100–35 Henry I

1135–54 Stephen

1327–77 Edward III

1050	1100	1150	1200	1250	1300	1350	1400	1450	1500
Norman		Plantagenet					Lancaster	York	Tudor
1050	1100	1150	1200	1250	1300	1350	1400	1450	1500

1154–89 Henry II

1189–99 Richard I

1199–1216 John

1216–72 Henry III

1307–27 Edward II

1272–1307 Edward I

1461–70 and 1471–83 Edward IV

1547–53 Edward VI

1422–61 and 1470–1 Henry VI

1377–99 Richard II

Matthew Paris's 13th-century chronicle showing clockwise on top left Richard I, Henry II, John and Henry III.

1483 Edward V

1901–10 Edward VII

1936 Edward VIII

1689–1702 William III and Mary II

1685–8 James II

1702–14 Anne

1660–85 Charles II

1714–27 George I

1603–25 James I

1837–1901 Victoria

1727–60 George II

1952– Elizabeth II

1600	1650	1700	1750	1800	1850	1900	1950	2000	2050
Stuart		Hanover			Saxe-Coburg	Windsor			
1600	1650	1700	1750	1800	1850	1900	1950	2000	2050

1830–37 William IV

1649–60 The Commonwealth, established by Oliver Cromwell

1820–30 George IV

1936–52 George VI shown on the George Medal

1910–36 George V

1625–49 Charles I

58–1603 zabeth I

1760–1820 George III

Prehistoric Britain

Britain was part of the European landmass until the end of the last Ice Age, around 6000 BC, when the English Channel was formed by melting ice. The earliest inhab-itants lived in limestone caves: settlements and farming skills developed gradually through the Stone Age. The magnificent wooden and stone henges and circles are masterworks from around 3000 BC, but their significance is a mystery. Flint mines and ancient pathways are evidence of early trading and many burial mounds (barrows) survive from the Stone and Bronze Ages.

Axe Heads
Stone axes, like this one found at Stone-henge, were used by Neolithic men.

Cup and ring marks
were carved on standing stones, such as this one at Ballymeanoch.

Mapping the Past

Monuments from the Neolithic (New Stone), Bronze and Iron Ages, together with artifacts found from these periods, provide a wealth of information about Britain's early settlers, before written history began with the Romans.

Neolithic Tools
Antlers and bones were made into Neolithic leather-working tools. These were found at Avebury *(see p267)*.

Pottery Beaker
The Beaker People, who came from Europe in the early Bronze Age, take their name from these drinking cups often found in their graves.

Gold Breast Plate
Made by Wessex goldsmiths, its spectacular pattern suggests it belonged to an important chieftain.

Pentre Ifan, an impressive Neolithic burial chamber in South Wales, was once covered with a huge earth mound.

Mold Cape
Gold was mined in Wales and Cornwall in the Bronze Age. This intricately worked warrior's cape was buried in a grave at Mold, Clwyd.

This gold cup, found in a Cornish barrow, is evidence of the wealth of Bronze Age tribes.

6000–5000 As the Ice Age comes to an end, sea levels rise, submerging the land-link between Britain and the Continent

Neolithic flint axes

6000 BC	5500 BC	5000 BC	4500 BC	4000 BC	3500 BC

A gold pendant and button (1700 BC), found in Bronze Age graves

3500 Neolithic Age begins. Long barrows and stone circles built around Britain

Skara Brae is a Neolithic village of about 2500 BC *(see p533)*.

Maiden Castle
An impressive Iron Age hill fort in Dorset, its concentric lines of ramparts and ditches follow the contours of the hill top *(see p273)*.

Iron Age Brochs, round towers with thick stone walls, are found only in Scotland.

Iron Age Axe
The technique of smelting iron came to Britain around 700 BC, brought from Europe by the Celts.

Castlerigg Stone Circle is one of Britain's earliest Neolithic monuments *(see p365)*.

Uffington White Horse
Thought to be 3,000 years old, the shape has to be "scoured" to keep grass at bay *(see p225)*.

Where to See Prehistoric Britain

Wiltshire, with Stonehenge *(p266)* and Avebury *(p267)*, has the best group of Neolithic monuments, and the Uffington White Horse is nearby *(p225)*. The Scottish islands have many early sites and the British Museum *(pp110–11)* houses a huge collection of artefacts.

A circular bank with over 180 stones encloses the Neolithic site at Avebury *(see p267)*.

A chalk figure, thought to be a fertility goddess, was found at Grimes Graves *(see p198)*.

This bronze Celtic helmet (50 BC) was found in the River Thames, London.

Snettisham Torc
A torc was a neck ring worn by Celtic men. This one, found in Norfolk, dates from 50 BC and is made from silver and gold.

Stonehenge was begun around 3,500 years ago *(see pp266–7)*.

3000 BC	2500 BC	2000 BC	1500 BC	1000 BC	500 BC

500 Temples, or henges, are built of wood or stone

1650–1200 Wessex is at the hub of trading routes between Europe and the mines of Cornwall, Wales and Ireland

1000 First farmsteads are settled

550–350 Migration of Celtic people from southern Europe

500 Iron Age begins. Hill forts are built

2100–1650 The Bronze Age reaches Britain. Immigration of the Beaker People, who make bronze implements and build ritual temples

Chieftain's bronze sceptre (1700 BC)

1200 Small, self-sufficient villages start to appear

150 Tribes from Gaul begin to migrate to Britain

Roman Britain

Throughout the 350-year Roman occupation, Britain was ruled as a colony. After the defeat of rebellious local tribes, such as Boudicca's Iceni, the Romans remained an unassimilated occupying power. Their legacy is in military and civil construction: forts, walls, towns and public buildings. Their long, straight roads, built for easy movement of troops, are still a feature of the landscape.

Cavalry Sports Helmet
Found in Lancashire, it was used in tournaments by horsemen. Cavalry races and other sports were held in amphitheatres near towns.

Main baths

Silver Jug
This 3rd-century jug, the earliest known silver item with Christian symbols, was excavated near Peterborough.

Fishbourne Palace was built beside a natural harbour, so ships could moor nearby.

Entrance hall

Hadrian's Wall
Started in 120 as a defence against the Scots; it marked the northern frontier of the Roman Empire and was guarded by 17 forts housing over 18,500 foot-soldiers and cavalry.

Mithras
This head of the god Mithras was found on the London site of a temple devoted to the cult of Mithraism. The sect demanded of its Roman followers loyalty and discipline.

54 BC Julius Caesar lands in Britain but withdraws

Julius Caesar (c.102–44 BC)

AD 61 Boudica rebels against Romans and burns their towns, including St Albans and Colchester, but is defeated *(see p199)*

AD 70 Romans conquer Wales and the North

Boudica (1st century), Queen of the Iceni

140–143 Romans occupy southern Scotland and build Antonine Wall to ma the frontier

55 BC | **AD 1** | **AD 50**

AD 43 Claudius invades; Britain becomes part of the Roman Empire

AD 78–84 Agricola advances into Scotland, then retreats

120 Emperor Hadrian builds a wall on the border with Scotland

Flavian Mosaic
Roman floors of the 1st century used patterns in black and white stone. More mosaics survive at Fishbourne than at any other British site.

Courtyard

Guest apartment

Box hedges

Aisled hall

Where to See Roman Britain

Many of Britain's main towns and cities were established by the Romans and have Roman remains, including York *(see pp408–13)*, Chester *(see pp314–15)*, St Albans *(see p236)*, Colchester *(see p209)*, Bath *(see pp262–5)*, Lincoln *(see pp344–5)* and London *(see pp74–159)*. Several Roman villas were built in southern England, favoured for its mild climate and proximity to Europe.

The Roman baths in Bath *(see pp262–5)*, known as Aquae Sulis, were built between the 1st and 4th centuries around a natural hot spring.

Fishbourne Palace

Built in the late 1st century for Togidubnus, a pro-Roman king, the palace (here reconstructed) featured advanced technology such as under-floor heating and indoor plumbing for baths (see p175).

Chi-Rho Symbol
This early Christian symbol is from a 3rd-century fresco at Lullingstone Roman villa in Kent.

Battersea Shield
Found in the Thames near Battersea, the shield bears Celtic symbols and was probably made at about the time of the first Roman invasion. Archaeologists suspect it may have been lost by a warrior while crossing the river, or offered as a sacrifice to one of the many river gods. It is now at the British Museum *(see pp110–11)*.

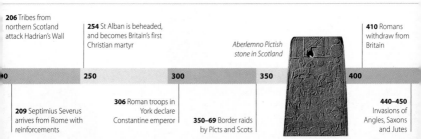

206 Tribes from northern Scotland attack Hadrian's Wall

254 St Alban is beheaded, and becomes Britain's first Christian martyr

Aberlemno Pictish stone in Scotland

410 Romans withdraw from Britain

0 | **250** | **300** | **350** | **400**

209 Septimius Severus arrives from Rome with reinforcements

306 Roman troops in York declare Constantine emperor

350–69 Border raids by Picts and Scots

440–450 Invasions of Angles, Saxons and Jutes

Anglo-Saxon Kingdoms

By the mid-5th century, Angles and Saxons from Germany had started to raid the eastern shores of Britain. Increasingly they decided to settle, and within 100 years Saxon kingdoms, including Wessex, Mercia and Northumbria, were established over the entire country. Viking raids throughout the 8th and 9th centuries were largely contained, but in 1066, the last invasion of England saw William the Conqueror from Normandy defeat the Anglo-Saxon King Harold at the Battle of Hastings. William then went on to assume control of the whole country.

Viking Axe
The principal weapons of the Viking warriors were spear, axe and sword. They were skilled metal-workers with an eye for decoration, as seen in this axe-head from a Copenhagen museum.

Vikings on a Raiding Expedition
Scandinavian boat-building skills were in advance of anything known in Britain. People were terrified by these large, fast boats with their intimidating figureheads, which sailed up the Thames and along the coasts.

Anglo-Saxon Calendar
These scenes from a chronicle of seasons, made just before the Norman invasion, show life in late Anglo-Saxon Britain. At first people lived in small farming communities, but by the 7th century towns began to spring up and trade increased. Saxon kings were supported by nobles but most of the population were free peasants.

St Augustine (d.604)

c.470–495 Saxons and Angles settle in Essex, Sussex and East Anglia

c.556 Saxons move across Britain and set up seven kingdoms

635 St Aidan establishes a monastery on Lindisfarne

730–821 Supremacy of Mercia, whose king, Offa (d.796), builds a dyke along the Mercia–Wales border

450	500	550	600	650	700

450 Saxons first settle in Kent

563 St Columba lands on Iona

597 St Augustine sent by Rome to convert English to Christianity

617–85 Supremacy of Northumbrian kingdom

Mercian coin which bears the name of King Offa

Ox-drawn plough for tilling

Alfred Jewel
This 9th-century
gold ornament in
the Ashmolean
Museum *(see p228)* has
the inscription: "Alfred
ordered me made". This may refer
to the Saxon King Alfred.

Where to See Anglo-Saxon Britain

The best collection of Saxon
artefacts is from a burial ship
unearthed at Sutton Hoo in
Suffolk in 1938 and now on
display at the British Museum
(see pp110–11). There are fine
Saxon churches at Bradwell in
Essex and Bosham in Sussex
(see p175). In York the Viking
town of Jorvik has been
excavated *(see p412)* and
actual relics are shown
alongside models of people
and dwellings.

The Saxon church of St
Laurence *(see p259)* was built
in the late 8th century.

Minstrels entertaining at a feast

Edward the Confessor
In 1042, Edward – known as
"the Confessor" because of
his piety – became king. He
died in 1066 and William of
Normandy claimed the throne.

Hawks, used to kill game

Harold's Death
This 14th-century illustration
depicts the victorious William of
Normandy after King Harold was
killed with an arrow in his eye.
The Battle of Hastings *(see p185)*
was the last invasion of Britain.

Legend of King Arthur
Arthur is thought to have been
a chieftain who fought the Saxons
in the early 6th century. Legends
of his knights' exploits appeared
in 1155 *(see p289)*.

An invading Norman ship

802–839 After the
death of Cenwulf (821),
Wessex gains control
over most of England

867 Northumbria falls to the Vikings

878 King Alfred defeats
Vikings but allows them to
settle in eastern England

1016 Danish King
Canute *(see p175)*
seizes English crown

800	850	900	950	1000	1050	1100

843 Kenneth McAlpin
becomes king of all Scotland

926 Eastern England,
the Danelaw, is
reconquered by
the Saxons

1042 The Anglo-
Saxon Edward
the Confessor
becomes king
(d.1066)

1066 William of Normandy
claims the throne, and
defeats Harold at the Battle
of Hastings. He is crowned
at Westminster

c.793 Lindisfarne sacked by
Viking invaders; first Viking raid
on Scotland about a year later

The Middle Ages

Remains of Norman castles on English hill tops bear testimony to the military might used by the invaders to sustain their conquest – although Wales and Scotland resisted for centuries. The Normans operated a feudal system, creating an aristocracy that treated native Anglo-Saxons as serfs. The ruling class spoke French until the 13th century, when it mixed with the Old English used by the peasants. The medieval church's power is shown in the cathedrals that grace British cities today.

Magna Carta
To protect themselves and the church from arbitrary taxation, the powerful English barons compelled King John to sign a "great charter" in 1215 (see p239). This laid the foundations for an independent legal system.

Craft Skills
An illustration from a 14th-century manuscript depicts a weaver and a copper-beater – two of the trades that created a wealthy class of artisans.

Becket is received into heaven.

Henry II's knights murder Becket in Canterbury Cathedral.

Murder of Thomas Becket

The struggle between church and king for ultimate control of the country was brought to a head by the murder of Becket, the Archbishop of Canterbury. After Becket's canonization in 1173, Canterbury became a major centre of pilgrimage.

Ecclesiastical Art
Nearly all medieval art had religious themes, such as this window at Canterbury Cathedral (see pp190–91) depicting Jeroboam.

Black Death
A plague swept Britain and Europe several times in the 14th century, killing millions of people. This illustration, in a religious tract, produced around 100 years later, represents death taking its heavy toll.

1071 Hereward the Wake, leader of the Anglo-Saxon resistance, defeated at Ely

1154 Henry II, the first Plantagenet king, demolishes castles, and exacts money from barons instead of military service

1170 Archbishop of Canterbury, Thomas à Becket, is murdered by four knights after quarrelling with Henry II

1100 **1150** **1200** **1250**

1086 The *Domesday Book*, a survey of every manor in England, is compiled for tax purposes

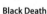

Domesday Book

1215 Barons compel King John to sign the *Magna Carta*

1256 First Parliament to include ordinary citizens

Battle of Agincourt
In 1415, Henry V took an army to France to claim its throne. This 15th-century chronicle depicts Henry beating the French army at Agincourt.

This casket (1190), in a private collection, is said to have contained Becket's remains.

Becket takes his place in Heaven after his canonization.

Two clergymen look on in horror at Becket's murder.

Where to See Medieval Britain

The university cities of Oxford (pp226–31) and Cambridge (pp214–19) contain the largest concentrations of Gothic buildings. Magnificent cathedrals rise high above many historic cities, among them Lincoln (pp344–5) and York (pp408–13). Both cities still retain at least part of their ancient street pattern. Military architecture is best seen in Wales (pp442–3) with the formidable border castles of Edward I.

All Souls College in Oxford (see p230), which only takes graduates, is a superb blend of medieval and later architecture.

Richard III
Richard, shown in this 16th-century painting, became king during the Wars of the Roses: a bitter struggle for power between two factions of the royal family – the houses of York and Lancaster.

Castle Life
Every section of a castle was allotted to a baron whose soldiers helped defend it. This 14th-century illustration shows the coats of arms (see p34) of the barons for each area.

John Wycliffe (1329–84)
This painting by Ford Madox Brown (1821–93) shows Wycliffe with the Bible he translated into English to make it accessible to everyone.

82–3
ward I
nquers
ales

1296 Edward I invades Scotland but Scots resist stoutly

Edward I (1239–1307)

1314 Scots defeat English at the Battle of Bannockburn (see p486)

1348 Europe's population halved by Black Death

1381 Peasants' revolt after the imposition of a poll tax on everyone in the country over 14

1300

1350

1387 Chaucer starts writing the *Canterbury Tales* (see p190)

1415 English victory at Agincourt

1400

Geoffrey Chaucer (c.1345–1400)

1485 Battle of Bosworth ends Wars of the Roses

1453 End of Hundred Years' War against France

1450

Tudor Renaissance

After years of debilitating civil war, the Tudor monarchs established peace and national self-confidence, reflected in the split from the church of Rome – due to Henry VIII's divorce from Catherine of Aragon – and the consequent closure of the monasteries. Henry's daughter, Mary I, tried to re-establish Catholicism but under her half-sister, Elizabeth I, the Protestant church secured its position. Overseas exploration began, provoking clashes with other European powers seeking to exploit the New World. The Renaissance in arts and learning spread from Europe to Britain, with playwright William Shakespeare adding his own unique contribution.

Curtains behind the queen are open to reveal scenes of the great English victory over the Spanish Armada in 1588.

Sea Power
Henry VIII laid the foundations of the powerful English navy. In 1545, his flagship, the *Mary Rose* (see p173), sank before his eyes in Portsmouth harbour on its way to do battle with the French.

Theatre
Some of Shakespeare's plays were first seen in purpose-built theatres such as the Globe (see p124) in south London.

The globe signifies that the queen reigns supreme far and wide.

Monasteries
With Henry VIII's split from Rome, England's religious houses, like Fountains Abbey (see pp394–5), were dissolved. Henry stole their riches and used them to finance his foreign policy.

1497 John Colet denounces the corruption of the clergy, supported by Erasmus and Sir Thomas More

1533–4 Henry VIII divorces Catherine of Aragon and is excommunicated by the Pope. He forms the Church of England

1542–1567 Mary, Queen of Scots rules Scotland

1490

1510

1530

1497 John Cabot (see p260) makes his first voyage to North America

1513 English defeat Scots at Flodden (see p486)

Henry VIII (1491–1547)

1535 Act of Union with Wales

1536–40 Dissolution of the Monasteries

1549 First Book of Comr Prayer introdu

Mary, Queen of Scots
As great-granddaughter of Henry VII, she laid claim to the English throne in 1559. But in 1567, Elizabeth I had her imprisoned for 20 years until her execution for treason in 1587.

Jewels symbolize triumph.

Where to See Tudor Britain

Hampton Court Palace *(p177)* has been altered over the centuries but remains a Tudor showpiece. Part of Elizabeth I's former home at Hatfield *(p235)* still survives. In Kent, Leeds Castle, Knole *(pp192–3)* and Hever Castle *(p193)* all have connections with Tudor royalty. Burghley House *(pp346–7)* and Hardwick Hall *(p306)*, both Midlands mansions, retain their 16th-century character.

This astronomical clock at Hampton Court *(see p177)*, with its intriguing zodiac symbols, was installed in 1540 by Henry VIII.

Defeat of the Armada

Spain was England's main rival for supremacy on the seas, and in 1588 Philip II sent 100 powerfully armed galleons towards England, bent on invasion. The English fleet – under Lord Howard, Francis Drake, John Hawkins and Martin Frobisher – sailed from Plymouth and destroyed the Spanish navy in a famous victory. This commemorative portrait of Elizabeth I by George Gower (d.1596) celebrates the triumph.

Protestant Martyrs
Catholic Mary I reigned from 1553 to 1558. Protestants who opposed her rule were burned, such as these six churchmen at Canterbury in 1555.

William Shakespeare (1564–1616)

1570 Sir Francis Drake's first voyage to the West Indies

1584 Sir Walter Raleigh tries to colonize Virginia after Drake's first unsuccessful attempt

1591 First play by Shakespeare performed

1600 East India Company founded, beginning British involvement on the Indian continent

1553 Death of Edward VI; throne passes to the Catholic Mary I

1558 Elizabeth I ascends the throne

1559 Mary, Queen of Scots lays claim to English throne

1587 Execution of Mary, Queen of Scots on the orders of Elizabeth I

1588 Defeat of the Spanish Armada

Sir Walter Raleigh (1552–1618)

1603 Union of Crowns. James VI of Scotland becomes James I of England

Stuart Britain

The end of Elizabeth I's reign signalled the start of internal turmoil. The throne passed to James I, whose belief that kings ruled by divine right provoked clashes with Parliament. Under his son, Charles I, the conflict escalated into Civil War that ended with his execution. In 1660 Charles II regained the throne, but after his death James II was ousted for Catholic leanings. Protestantism was reaffirmed with the reign of William and Mary, who suppressed the Catholic Jacobites *(see p487).*

Science
Sir Isaac Newton (1642–1727) invented this reflecting telescope, laying the foundation for a greater understanding of the universe, including the law of gravity.

Charles I stayed silent at his trial.

Oliver Cromwell
A strict Protestant and a passionate champion of the rights of Parliament, he led the victorious Parliamentary forces in the Civil War. He became Lord Protector of the Commonwealth from 1653 to 1658.

The headless body kneels by the block.

On the way to his death, the king wore two shirts for warmth, so onlookers should not think he was shivering with fright.

Theatre
After the Restoration in 1660, when Parliament restored the monarchy, theatre thrived. Plays were performed on temporary outdoor stages.

Execution of Charles I

Cromwell was convinced there would be no peace until the king was dead. At his trial for treason, Charles refused to recognize the authority of the court and offered no defence. He faced his death with dignity on 30 January 1649, the only English king to be executed. His death was followed by a republic known as the Commonwealth.

1605 "Gunpowder Plot" to blow up Parliament thwarted

1614 "Addled Parliament" refuses to vote money for James I

1620 Pilgrim Fathers sail in the *Mayflower* to New England

1642 Civil War breaks out

1653–8 Cromwell rules as Lord Protector

1600

1625

1650

1611 New translation of Bible published, known as King James Version

James I (1566–1625)

1638 Scots sign National Covenant, opposing Charles I's Catholic leanings

1649 Charles I executed outside Banqueting House and Commonwealth declared by Parliament

1660 Restorat of the monar under Charle

Restoration of the Monarchy

This silk embroidery celebrates the fact that Charles II escaped his father's fate by hiding in an oak tree. There was joy at his return from exile in France.

The axeman holds the severed head of Charles I.

Plague

Bills of mortality showed the weekly deaths as bubonic plague swept London in 1665. Up to 100,000 Londoners died.

Hatfield House (p235) is a splendid Jacobean mansion.

Onlookers soaked up the king's blood with their handkerchiefs to have a memento.

Anatomy

By dissecting corpses, physicians began to gain an understanding of the working of the human body – a crucial step towards modern surgery and medicine.

Pilgrim Fathers

In 1620 a group of Puritans sailed to America. They forged good relations with the native Indians; here they are shown being visited by the chief of the Pokanokets.

1665–6 Great Plague

The Great Fire of London

1707 Act of Union with Scotland

1666 Great Fire of London

1688 The Glorious Revolution: Catholic James II deposed by Parliament

1675

1700

1690 Battle of the Boyne: William's English/Dutch army defeats James II's Irish/French army

1692 Glencoe Massacre of Jacobites (Stuart supporters) by William III's forces

William III (1689–1702)

Georgian Britain

The 18th century saw Britain, now recovered from the trauma of its Civil War, develop as a commercial and industrial powerhouse. London became a centre of banking, and a mercantile and professional class grew up. Continuing supremacy at sea laid the foundations of an empire; steam engines, canals and railways heralded the Industrial Revolution. Growing confidence was reflected in stately architecture and elegant fashions but, as cities became more crowded, conditions for the underclass grew worse.

Slate became the preferred tile for Georgian buildings. Roofs became less steep to achieve an Italian look.

A row of sash windows is one of the most characteristic features of a Georgian house.

Oak was used in the best dwellings for doors and stairs, but pine was standard in most houses.

Battle of Bunker Hill
In 1775 American colonists rebelled against British rule. The British won this early battle in Massachusetts, but in 1783 Britain recognized the United States of America.

The saloon was covered in wallpaper, a cheaper alternative to hanging walls with tapestries or fabrics.

The drawing room was richly ornamented and used for entertaining visitors.

Watt's Steam Engine
The Scottish engineer James Watt (1736–1819) patented his engine in 1769 and then developed it for locomotion.

The dining room was used for all family meals.

Lord Horatio Nelson
Nelson (see p35) became a hero after his death at the Battle of Trafalgar fighting the French.

Steps led to the servants' entrance in the basement.

1720 "South Sea Bubble" bursts: many speculators ruined in securities fraud

1746 Bonnie Prince Charlie (see p539), Jacobite claimant to throne, defeated at the Battle of Culloden

| 1700 | 1715 | 1730 | 1745 | 1760 |

1714 George, Elector of Hanover, succeeds Queen Anne, ending the Stuart dynasty and giving Britain a German-speaking monarch

1721 Robert Walpole (1646–1745) becomes the first Prime Minister

George I (1660–1727)

Satirical engraving about the South Sea Bubble, 1720

1757 Britain's first canal completed

Canal Barge (1827) Canals were a cheap way to carry the new industrial goods but were gradually superseded by railways during the 19th century.

The attics were where children and servants slept.

The master bedroom often had a mahogany four- poster bed.

Where to See Georgian Britain

Bath (see pp262–5) and Edinburgh (see pp508–15) are two of Britain's best-preserved Georgian towns. The Building of Bath Museum in Bath (see p265) has a real Georgian flavour and Brighton's Royal Pavilion (see pp182–3) is a Regency extravaganza by John Nash.

Charlotte Square (see p508) in Edinburgh has fine examples of Georgian architecture.

Chippendale Armchair (1760) Thomas Chippendale (1718–79) designed elegant furniture in a style still popular today.

Furniture was often carved, depicting animal heads and legs.

Georgian Town House

Tall, terraced dwellings were built to house wealthy families. The main architects of the time were Robert Adam (see p32) and John Nash (see p109).

The servants lived and worked in the basement during the day.

Kitchen

Hogarth's Gin Lane Conditions in London's slums shocked William Hogarth (1697–1764), who made prints like this to urge social reform.

1788 First convict ships are sent to Australia

1776 American Declaration of Independence

1811–17 Riots against growing unemployment

1805 The British, led by Lord Nelson, beat Napoleon's French fleet at Battle of Trafalgar

1815 Duke of Wellington beats Napoleon at Waterloo

Caricature of Wellington (1769–1852)

1775	1790	1805	1820

Silver tureen, 1774

1783 Steam-powered cotton mill invented by Sir Richard Arkwright (1732–92)

1807 Abolition of slave trade

1825 Stockton to Darlington railway opens

1811 Prince of Wales made Regent during George III's madness

1829 Catholic Emancipation Act passed

Victorian Britain

When Victoria became Queen in 1837, she was only 18. Britain was in the throes of its transformation from an agricultural country to the world's most powerful industrial nation. The growth of the Empire fuelled the country's confidence and opened up markets for Britain's manufactured goods. The accelerating growth of cities created problems of health and housing and a powerful Labour movement began to emerge. But by the end of Victoria's long and popular reign in 1901, conditions had begun to improve as more people got the vote and universal education was introduced.

Florence Nightingale *(1820–1910)* Known as the Lady with the Lamp, she nursed soldiers in the Crimean War and pioneered many improvements in army medical care.

Glass walls and ceiling

Prefabricated girders

Newcastle Slum *(1880)* Rows of cheap houses were built for an influx of workers to the major industrial cities. The awful conditions spread disease and social discontent.

As well as silk textiles exhibits included carriages, engines, jewels, glass, plants, cutlery and sculptures.

Union Banner Trade unions were set up to protect industrial workers against unscrupulous employers.

Ophelia by Sir John Everett Millais *(1829–96)* The Pre-Raphaelite painters chose Romantic themes, reflecting a desire to escape industrial Britain.

Vase made for the Great Exhibition

1832 Great Reform Bill extends the vote to all male property owners

1841 London to Brighton railway makes resort accessible

1851 Great Exhibition

1867 Second Reform Act gives the vote to all male householders in towns

1830   **1840**   **1850**   **1860**

1834 Tolpuddle Martyrs transported to Australia for forming a union

1833 Factory Act forbids employment of children for more than 48 hours per week

1854–6 Britain victorious against Russia in Crimean War

1863 Opening of the London Underground

Triumph of Steam and Electricity

This picture from the *Illustrated London News* (1897) sums up the feeling of optimism engendered by industrial advances.

Elm trees were incorporated into the building along with sparrows, and sparrow hawks to control them.

Where to See Victorian Britain

The industrial cities of the Midlands and the North are built around grandiose civic, commercial and industrial buildings. Notable Victorian monuments include the Manchester Museum of Science and Industry (*see p378*) and, in London, the Victoria and Albert Museum (*see pp102–3*) and St Pancras train station.

The Rotunda, Manchester is a stately Victorian building.

Great Exhibition of 1851

The brainchild of Prince Albert, Victoria's consort, the exhibition celebrated industry, technology and the expanding British Empire. It was the biggest of its kind held up until then. Between May and October, six million people visited Joseph Paxton's lavish crystal palace, in London's Hyde Park. Nearly 14,000 exhibitors brought 100,000 exhibits from all over the world. In 1852 it was moved to south London where it burned down in 1936.

Cycling Craze

The bicycle, invented in 1865, became immensely popular with young people, as illustrated by this photograph of 1898.

1872 The Ballot Act introduces secret voting

1874 Benjamin Disraeli becomes Prime Minister

1870 Education Act makes school compulsory for children up to the age of 11

1877 Queen Victoria created Empress of India

1884 Telephones introduced

Early telephone

1892 First Labour MP elected

1893 Gladstone's Irish Home Rule Bill defeated

1901 Queen Victoria dies

1899–1902 Britain defeats South African Dutch settlers in Boer War

Cartoon of Gladstone, Vanity Fair (1869)

1870 | 1880 | 1890 | 1900

Britain from 1900 to 1950

When Queen Victoria's reign ended in 1901, British society threw off many of its 19th-century inhibitions, and an era of gaiety and excitement began. This was interrupted by World War I. The economic troubles that ensued, which culminated in the Depression of the 1930s, brought misery to millions. In 1939 the ambitions of Germany provoked World War II. After emerging victorious from this conflict, Britain embarked on an ambitious programme of social, educational and health reform.

Welwyn Garden City was based on the Utopian ideals of Sir Ebenezer Howard (1850–1928), founder of the garden city movement.

Suffragettes
Women marched and chained themselves to railings in their effort to get the vote; many went to prison. Women over 30 won the vote in 1919.

The Roaring Twenties
Young flappers discarded the rigid social codes of their parents and instead discovered jazz, cocktails and the Charleston.

New towns
A string of new towns was created on the outskirts of London, planned to give residents greenery and fresh air. Welwyn Garden City was originally founded in 1919 as a self-contained community, but fast rail links turned it into a base for London commuters.

Wireless
Invented by Guglielmo Marconi, radios brought news and entertainment into homes for the first time.

World War I
British troops in Europe dug into deep trenches protected by barbed wire and machine guns, only metres from the enemy, in a war of attrition that cost the lives of 17 million.

1903 Suffragette movement founded

1911 MPs are given a salary for the first time, allowing working men to be elected

1914–18 World War I

1924 First Labour government

1900	1905	1910	1915	1920

Henry Asquith (1852–1928), Prime Minister

1908 Asquith's Liberal government introduces old age pensions

1918 Vote given to all women over 30

1922 First national radio service begins

Marching for Jobs
These men were among thousands who marched for their jobs after being put out of work in the 1920s. The stock market crash of 1929 and the ensuing Depression caused even more unemployment.

Garden cities all had trees, ponds and open spaces.

World War II
German night-time air raids targeted transport, military and industrial sites and cities, such as Sheffield, in what was known as the "Blitz".

Modern Homes
Labour-saving devices, such as the vacuum cleaner, invented by William Hoover in 1908, were very popular. This was due to the virtual disappearance of domestic servants, as women took jobs outside the home.

Family Motoring
By the middle of the century, more families could afford to buy mass-produced automobiles, like the 1950s Hillman Minx pictured in this advertisement.

Cheap housing and the promise of a cleaner environment attracted many people to these new cities.

1926 General Strike

Edward VIII (1894–1972) and Wallis Simpson (1896–1986)

1936 Abdication of Edward VIII

1944 Education Act: school leaving age raised to 15; grants provided for university students

1947 Independence for India and Pakistan

1948 National Health Service introduced

1925 — 1930 — 1935 — 1940 — 1945

1929 Stock market crashes

1928 Votes for all men and women over 21

1936 First scheduled television service begins

1939–45 Winston Churchill leads Britain to victory in World War II

Food ration book

1945 Majority Labour government; nationalization of railways, road haulage, civil aviation, Bank of England, gas, electricity and steel

Britain Today

With the deprivations of war receding, Britain entered the Swinging Sixties, an explosion of youth culture characterized by the mini-skirt and the emergence of pop groups. The Age of Empire came to an end as most colonies gained independence by the 1970s – although Britain went to war again in 1982 when Argentina sought to annexe the tiny Falkland Islands.

People were on the move; immigration from the former colonies, though not always embraced by the locals, enriched British culture, and increasing prosperity allowed millions of people to travel abroad. Britain joined the European Community in 1973, and forged a more tangible link when the Channel Tunnel opened in 1994.

1982 British troops set sail to drive the Argentinians from the British-owned Falkland Islands

1970s The outlandish clothes, hair and make-up of Punk Rockers shock the country

1981 Charles, Prince of Wales, marries Lady Diana Spencer in "fairytale" wedding at St Paul's Cathedral

1960s The miniskirt takes British fashion to new heights of daring – and Flower Power arrives from California

1951 Winston Churchill comes back as Prime Minister as Conservatives win general election

1965 Death penalty is abolished

1950	1960	1970	1980
1950	1960	1970	1980

1953 Elizabeth II crowned in first televised Coronation

1963 The Beatles pop group from Liverpool captures the spirit of the age with numerous chart-topping hits

1975 Drilling begins for North Sea oil

1984 Year-long miners' strike fails to stop pit closures and heralds decline in trade union power

1951 Festival of Britain lifts postwar spirits

1959 First motorway, the M1, built from London to the Midlands

VOTE!
...GET BRITAIN OUT

1957 First immigrants arrive from the Caribbean by boat

1973 After years of negotiation, Britain joins the European Community

1979 The "Iron Lady" Margaret Thatcher becomes Britain's first woman Prime Minister; her right-wing Conservative Government privatizes several state-owned industries

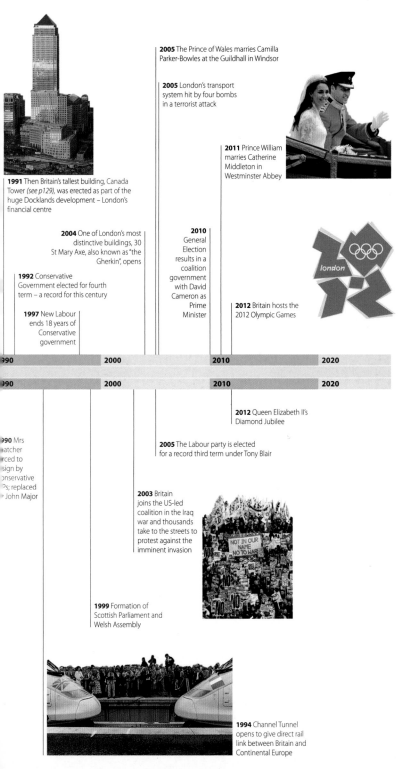

2005 The Prince of Wales marries Camilla Parker-Bowles at the Guildhall in Windsor

2005 London's transport system hit by four bombs in a terrorist attack

2011 Prince William marries Catherine Middleton in Westminster Abbey

1991 Then Britain's tallest building, Canada Tower (*see p129*), was erected as part of the huge Docklands development – London's financial centre

2004 One of London's most distinctive buildings, 30 St Mary Axe, also known as "the Gherkin", opens

2010 General Election results in a coalition government with David Cameron as Prime Minister

2012 Britain hosts the 2012 Olympic Games

1992 Conservative Government elected for fourth term – a record for this century

1997 New Labour ends 18 years of Conservative government

| 990 | 2000 | 2010 | 2020 |

| 990 | 2000 | 2010 | 2020 |

2012 Queen Elizabeth II's Diamond Jubilee

2005 The Labour party is elected for a record third term under Tony Blair

990 Mrs
atcher
rced to
sign by
onservative
Ps; replaced
John Major

2003 Britain joins the US-led coalition in the Iraq war and thousands take to the streets to protest against the imminent invasion

1999 Formation of Scottish Parliament and Welsh Assembly

1994 Channel Tunnel opens to give direct rail link between Britain and Continental Europe

GREAT BRITAIN THROUGH THE YEAR

Every British season has its particular charms. Most major sights are open all year round, but many secondary attractions may be closed in winter. The weather is changeable in all seasons and the visitor is as likely to experience a crisp, sunny February day as to be caught in a cold, heavy shower in July. Long periods of adverse weather and extremes of temperature are rare. Spring is characterized by daffodils and bluebells, summer by roses and autumn by the vivid colours of changing leaves. In wintertime, country vistas are visible through the bare branches of the trees. Annual events and ceremonies, many stemming from age-old traditions, reflect the attributes of the seasons.

Bluebells in spring in Angrove woodland, Wiltshire

Spring

As the days get longer and warmer, the countryside starts to come alive. At Easter many stately homes and gardens open their gates to visitors for the first time, and during the week before Whit Sunday, or Whitsun (the seventh Sunday after Easter), the Chelsea Flower Show takes place.

This is the focal point of the gardening year and spurs on the nation's gardeners to prepare their summer displays. Outside the capital, many music and arts festivals mark the middle months of the year.

March
Ideal Home Show
(second week), Earl's Court, London. New products and ideas for the home.
Crufts Dog Show, National Exhibition Centre, Birmingham.
St Patrick's Day *(17 March)*. Musical events in major cities celebrate the feast day of Ireland's patron saint.
Oxford and Cambridge Boat Race *(late Mar or early Apr)*, River Thames, London.

April
Maundy Thursday (Thursday before Easter), the Queen gives money to pensioners.
St George's Day *(23 April)*, English patron saint's day.
Antiques for Everyone *(last week)*, National Exhibition Centre, Birmingham.

Water garden exhibited at the Chelsea Flower Show

May
Furry Dancing Festival *(8 May)*, Helston, Cornwall. Spring celebration *(see p284)*.
Well Dressings *(Ascension Day)*, Tissington, Derbyshire *(see p341)*.
Chelsea Flower Show *(May)*, Royal Hospital, London.
Brighton Festival *(last three weeks)*. Performing arts.
Glyndebourne Festival Opera Season *(mid-May– end Aug)*, near Lewes, East Sussex. Opera productions.
International Highland Games *(last weekend)*, Blair Atholl, Scotland.

Summer

Life moves outdoors in the summer months. Cafés and restaurants place tables on the pavements and pub customers take their drinks outside. The Queen holds garden parties for privileged

Yeomen of the Guard conducting the Maundy money ceremony

guests at Buckingham Palace while, more modestly, village fêtes – which include traditional games and local stalls – are organized. Beaches and swimming pools become crowded and office workers picnic in city parks at lunch. The rose, England's national flower, bursts into bloom in millions of gardens. Cultural treats include open-air theatre performances, outdoor concerts, the Proms in London, the National Eisteddfod in Wales, Glyndebourne's opera festival, and Edinburgh's festival of the performing arts.

Glastonbury music festival, a major event attracting thousands of people

June

Hay Festival (end May–early June), Hay-on-Wye, Wales. Family-friendly literature and music festival.

Bath International Music Festival (late May–early Jun), various venues. Arts events.

Royal Academy of Arts Summer Exhibition (Jun–Aug). Large and varied London show of new work by many artists.

Trooping the Colour (Sat closest to 10 Jun), Whitehall, London. The Queen's official birthday parade.

Isle of Wight Music Festival (mid-Jun). International headlining pop stars and rock groups feature in this historic music festival.

Deck chair at Brighton

Glastonbury Festival (late June), Somerset.

Aldeburgh Festival (second and third weeks), Suffolk. Arts festival with concerts and opera.

Royal Highland Show (third week), Ingliston, near Edinburgh. Agricultural show.

Leeds Castle (last week Jun–early Jul). Open-air concerts.

Glasgow Jazz Festival (last weekend Jun–early Jul). Various venues.

July

Henley Royal Regatta (late Jun–Jul), Henley-on-Thames. Rowing regatta on the Thames.

International Eisteddfod (first week), Llangollen, North Wales. International music and dance competition (see p454).

Hampton Court Flower Show (early July), Hampton Court Palace, Surrey.

Cambridge Folk Festival (last weekend). Music festival attracting top international artists.

Royal Welsh Show (last weekend), Builth Wells, Wales. Agricultural show.

Sidmouth Folk Week (late Jul–early Aug), Sidmouth, Devon (see p293).

August

Royal National Eisteddfod (early in month). Traditional arts competitions, in Welsh (see p439). Various locations.

Henry Wood Promenade Concerts (mid-Jul–mid-Sep), Royal Albert Hall, London. Famous concert series popularly known as the Proms.

Edinburgh International Festival (mid-Aug–mid-Sep). The largest festival of theatre, dance and music in the world (see p485).

Edinburgh Festival Fringe. Alongside the festival, there are 400 shows a day.

Brecon Jazz (mid-Aug), jazz festival in Brecon, Wales.

International Beatleweek (last weekend), Liverpool. Music and entertainment related to the Fab Four (see p381).

Notting Hill Carnival (last weekend), London. A West Indian street carnival featuring floats, bands, Caribbean food and stalls.

Assessment of sheep at the Royal Welsh Show, Builth Wells

Reveller in bright costume at the Notting Hill Carnival

Boxes of apples from the autumn harvest

Autumn

After the heady escapism of summer, the start of the new season is marked by the various party political conferences held in October and the royal opening of Parliament. All over the country on 5 November, bonfires are lit and fireworks let off to celebrate the foiling of an attempt to blow up the Houses of Parliament by Guy Fawkes and his co-conspirators in 1605. Cornfields become golden, trees turn fiery yellow through to russet and orchards are heavy with apples

Shot putting at Braemar

and other autumn fruits. In churches throughout the country, thanksgiving festivals mark the harvest. The shops stock up for the run-up to Christmas, their busiest time of the year.

September
Blackpool Illuminations (*beg Sep–end Oct*). A 5 mile (8 km) spectacle of lighting along Blackpool's seafront.
The Braemar Gathering (*first Sat*), Braemar, Scotland. Kilted clansmen from all over the country toss cabers, shot putt, dance and play the bagpipes. The royal family usually attends.
International Sheepdog Trials (*Jul–Sep*), all over Britain, with venues changing from year to year.
Great Autumn Flower Show, Harrogate, N Yorks. Displays by nurserymen and national flower organizations.
St Ives Festival (*second and third weeks*), Cornwall. Open studios, exhibitions, live music, poetry and theatre take place in civic buildings, galleries, pubs and the streets of this picturesque and historic fishing village and artists' community.

October
Harvest Festivals (*whole month*), all over Britain especially in farming areas.
Horse of the Year Show (*6–10 Oct*), NEC, Birmingham.
Nottingham Goose Fair (*first week*). One of Britain's oldest traditional fairs now has a funfair.
Canterbury Festival (*second and third weeks*). Music, drama and the arts.
Brighton Early Music Festival (*end Oct*), Sussex. Choral performances in venues across Brighton and Hove.

Procession leading to the state opening of Parliament

November
State Opening of Parliament (*Oct or Nov*). The Queen goes from Buckingham Palace to Westminster in a state coach, to open the new parliamentary session.
London Film Festival (*end Oct–beg Nov*). Forum for new films, various venues.
Lord Mayor's Show (*second Sat*). Parade in the City, London.
Remembrance Day (*second Sun*). Services and parades at the Cenotaph in Whitehall, London, and all over Britain.
RAC London to Brighton Veteran Car Rally (*first Sun*). A 7am start from Hyde Park, London to Brighton, East Sussex.
Guy Fawkes Night (*5 Nov*), fireworks and bonfires all over the country.
Regent Street Christmas Lights (*mid-Nov*), London.

Fireworks over Edinburgh on Guy Fawkes Night

Winter landscape in the Scottish Highlands, near Glencoe

Winter

Brightly coloured fairy lights and Christmas trees decorate Britain's principal shopping streets as shoppers rush to buy their seasonal gifts. Carol services are held in churches across the country, and pantomime, a traditional entertainment for children deriving from the Victorian music hall, fills theatres in major towns.

Many offices close between Christmas and the New Year. Shops reopen for the January sales on 27 December – a paradise for bargain-hunters.

Brightly lit Christmas tree at the centre of Trafalgar Square

December

Christmas Tree *(first Thu)*, Trafalgar Square, London. The tree is donated by the people of Norway and is lit by the Mayor of Oslo; this is followed by carol singing.
Carol concerts *(whole month)*, all over Britain.
Harrods Christmas Parade *(beg Dec)*, London. Parade with floats to celebrate myth of Santa Claus.
The Burning of the Clocks *(21 Dec)*, Brighton, Sussex. Parades and fireworks on Brighton beach celebrating the winter solstice.
Midnight Mass *(24 Dec)*, in churches everywhere around Britain.

Sprig of holly

Public holidays

New Year's Day (1 Jan).
2 Jan (Scotland only).
Easter weekend (March or April). In England it begins on **Good Friday** and ends on **Easter Monday**; in Scotland there is no Easter Monday holiday.
May Day (usually first Mon in May).
Late Spring Bank Holiday (last Mon in May).
Bank Holiday (first Mon in August, Scotland only).
August Bank Holiday (last Mon in August, except Scotland).
Christmas and Boxing Day (25–26 December).

January

Hogmanay and **New Year** *(31 Dec, 1 Jan)*, Scottish celebrations. **Burns Night** *(25 Jan)*. Scots everywhere celebrate poet Robert Burns' birth with poetry, feasting and drinking.

February

Chinese New Year *(late Jan or early Feb)*. Lion dances, firecrackers and processions in Chinatown, London.

Morris dancing on May Day in Midhurst, Sussex

The Sporting Year

Many of the world's major competitive sports, including soccer, cricket and tennis, were invented in Britain. Originally devised as recreation for the wealthy, they have since entered the arena of mass entertainment. Some, however, such as the Royal Ascot race meeting and Wimbledon tennis tournament, are still valued as much for their social prestige as for the sport itself. Other delightful sporting events in Britain take place at a local level: village cricket, point-to-point racing and the Highland Games are all popular amateur events.

Royal Ascot is the f
day social highlight of
horse racing year. The
class of the thoroughb
is matched by the h
style of the fashions, w
royalty attend

Oxford and Cambridge Boat Race, first held in 1829 at Henley, has become a national event, with the two university eights now battling it out between Putney and Mortlake on the Thames.

The FA Cup Final is the apex of the football season.

Derby Day horse races, Epsom

January	February	March	April	May	June

Cheltenham Gold Cup steeplechase (see p332)

Grand National steeplechase, Aintree, Liverpool (see p380)

Rugby League Cup Final, Wembley

Embassy World Snooker Championships, Sheffield

Wimbledon Lawn Tennis Tournment is the world's most prestigious lawn tennis championship.

Six Nations Rugby Union is an annual contest between England, France, Italy, Ireland (left), Scotland (right) and Wales. This league-based competition runs through winter ending in March.

Henley Royal Regatta (see p238) is an international rowing event on the Thames (first held in 1839). It is also a glamorous social occasion.

London Marathon attracts thousands of long-distance runners, from the world's best to fancy-dressed fund raisers.

sh Grand Prix, held at Silverstone, tain's round of the Formula World Championship.

Tickets and Touts

For many big sporting events, the only official source of tickets is the club concerned. Booking agencies may offer hard-to-get tickets – though often at high prices. Unauthorized touts may lurk at popular events but their expensive tickets are not always valid. Check carefully.

Tickets for the Grand Prix

British Open Golf Championship, a major golf event, is held at one of several British courses. Here, Luke Donald swings.

The LV= County Championship is the domestic first-class cricket competition in England and Wales. It takes place at Lord's *(see p159).*

Oxford versus Cambridge rugby union, Twickenham

Cowes week *(see p172)*, a yachting festival, covers all classes of racing.

Horse of the Year Show brings together top show-jumpers to compete on a tough indoor course *(see p68).*

ly	**August**	**September**	**October**	**November**	**December**

European Show jumping Championships at Hickstead

Braemar Highland Games *(see p68)*

British Figure Skating and Ice Dance Championships are a feast of elegance on ice (various venues).

Winmau World Masters Darts Championships

Gold Cup Humber powerboat race, Hull

Cartier International Polo, at the Guards Club, Windsor *(see p239)*, is one of the main events for this peculiarly British game, played mainly by royalty and army officers.

Key to Sport Seasons

- Cricket
- River fishing
- Football (soccer)
- Hunting and shooting
- Rugby (union and league)
- Flat racing
- Jump racing
- Athletics – track and field
- Road running and cross-country
- Polo

The Climate of Great Britain

Britain has a temperate climate. No region is far from the sea, which exerts a moderating influence on temperatures. Seldom are winter nights colder than -15°C, even in the far north, or summer days warmer than 30°C in the south and west: a much narrower range than in most European countries. Despite Britain's reputation, the average annual rainfall is quite low – 108 cm (42 inches) – and heavy rain is rare. The Atlantic coast is warmed by the Gulf Stream, making the west slightly warmer, though wetter, than the east.

Inverness

The Highlands and Islands

Edinbu
Glasgow

The Lowlar

Lancash
and
the Lake

Liverp
North
Wales
Caernarfon

South
and
Mid-
Wales

Cardiff

Wesse

Exeter
Devon and
Cornwall

LANCASHIRE AND THE LAKES

°C				
	12 / 5	19 / 13	14 / 8	6 / 2
☀	5.5 hrs	6 hrs	3 hrs	1.5 hrs
☂	53 mm	85 mm	104 mm	90 mm
month	Apr	Jul	Oct	Jan

THE HEART OF ENGLAND

°C				
	12 / 5	20 / 13	13 / 8	6 / 2
☀	4.5 hrs	5.5 hrs	3 hrs	1.5 hrs
☂	53 mm	69 mm	69 mm	74 mm
month	Apr	Jul	Oct	Jan

Average monthly maximum temperature

Average monthly minimum temperature

Average daily hours of sunshine

Average monthly rainfall

SOUTH AND MID-WALES

°C				
	13 / 5	20 / 13	14 / 8	7 / 2
☀	5.5 hrs	6 hrs	3.5 hrs	1.5 hrs
☂	65 mm	89 mm	109 mm	108 mm
month	Apr	Jul	Oct	Jan

NORTH WALES

°C				
	11 / 5	17 / 11	14 / 8	6 / 1
☀	3 hrs	3.5 hrs	2.5 hrs	1.5 hrs
☂	144 mm	206 mm	261 mm	252 mm
month	Apr	Jul	Oct	Jan

DEVON AND CORNWALL

°C				
	13 / 6	19 / 13	15 / 9	8 / 4
☀	6 hrs	6.5 hrs	3.5 hrs	2 hrs
☂	53 mm	70 mm	91 mm	99 mm
month	Apr	Jul	Oct	Jan

WESSEX

°C				
	14 / 6	21 / 14	15 / 9	7 / 2
☀	5.5 hrs	6.5 hrs	3.5 hrs	2 hrs
☂	49 mm	65 mm	85 mm	74 mm
month	Apr	Jul	Oct	Jan

THAMES VALLEY

°C				
	14 / 5	22 / 13	15 / 7	7 / 1
☀	5.5 hrs	6 hrs	3 hrs	1.5 hrs
☂	41 mm	55 mm	64 mm	61 mm
month	Apr	Jul	Oct	Jan

rthumbria
● Newcastle upon Tyne

Yorkshire
● York

chester

East Midlands

Birmingham
: of
nd

● Norwich

● Cambridge

East Anglia

Thames Valley

Oxford

London

Downs and Channel Coast

● Dover

● Portsmouth

THE HIGHLANDS AND ISLANDS

°C	Apr	Jul	Oct	Jan
max	11	17	13	7
min	3	10	7	1
☀	4.5 hrs	3.5 hrs	2 hrs	1 hrs
☂	111 mm	137 mm	215 mm	200 mm
month	Apr	Jul	Oct	Jan

THE LOWLANDS

°C	Apr	Jul	Oct	Jan
max	11	19	14	6
min	4	11	7	1
☀	5 hrs	5.5 hrs	3 hrs	1.5 hrs
☂	38 mm	69 mm	56 mm	47 mm
month	Apr	Jul	Oct	Jan

NORTHUMBRIA

°C	Apr	Jul	Oct	Jan
max	11	18	13	6
min	5	13	8	2
☀	5 hrs	5.5 hrs	3 hrs	1.5 hrs
☂	38 mm	64 mm	61 mm	62 mm
month	Apr	Jul	Oct	Jan

YORKSHIRE

°C	Apr	Jul	Oct	Jan
max	13	21	14	6
min	5	12	7	1
☀	5 hrs	5.5 hrs	3 hrs	1.5 hrs
☂	41 mm	62 mm	56 mm	59 mm
month	Apr	Jul	Oct	Jan

EAST MIDLANDS

°C	Apr	Jul	Oct	Jan
max	13	21	14	6
min	4	12	6	0
☀	5 hrs	5.5 hrs	3 hrs	1.5 hrs
☂	38 mm	58 mm	56 mm	56 mm
month	Apr	Jul	Oct	Jan

THE DOWNS AND CHANNEL COAST

°C	Apr	Jul	Oct	Jan
max	14	22	14	6
min	4	12	6	0
☀	5.8 hrs	7.3 hrs	4 hrs	2 hrs
☂	38 mm	58 mm	56 mm	56 mm
month	Apr	Jul	Oct	Jan

LONDON

°C	Apr	Jul	Oct	Jan
max	13	22	16	8
min	7	15	10	4
☀	5 hrs	6 hrs	3.5 hrs	1.5 hrs
☂	39 mm	45 mm	50 mm	44 mm
month	Apr	Jul	Oct	Jan

EAST ANGLIA

°C	Apr	Jul	Oct	Jan
max	14	22	15	7
min	4	12	6	1
☀	5 hrs	6 hrs	3.5 hrs	1.5 hrs
☂	37 mm	58 mm	51 mm	49 mm
month	Apr	Jul	Oct	Jan

LONDON

London at a Glance

The largest city in Europe, London is home to over seven million people and covers 625 sq miles (1,600 sq km). The capital was founded by the Romans in the first century AD as a convenient administrative and comm-unications centre and a port for trade with Continental Europe. For a thousand years it has been the principal residence of British monarchs as well as the centre of business and government, and it is rich in historic buildings and treasures from all periods. In addition to its diverse range of museums, galleries and churches, London is an exciting contem-porary city, packed with a vast array of entertainments and shops. The attractions on offer are virtually endless but this map highlights the most important of those described in detail on the following pages.

Buckingham Palace *(pp90–91)* is London home and office to the monarchy. The Changing of the Guard takes place on the palace forecourt.

Regen and Bloc *(see pp1*

West West *(see p*

South Kensington and Hyde Park *(see pp98–105)*

Hyde Park *(p79)*, the largest central London park, boasts numerous sports facilities, restaurants, an art gallery and Speakers' Corner. The highlight is the Serpentine Lake.

0 kilometres 1
0 miles 0.5

Greater London

Watford
Enfield
Barnet
Harrow
Wembley Hampstead
Hackney **London City Airport**
Ealing Acton **LONDON** Romford
Heathrow Airport
Richmond Greenwich *Thames*
Kingston upon Thames Wimbledon Dulwich Dartford
Beckenham
Sutton Bromley
Epsom Croydon

0 kilometres 15
0 miles 15

The Victoria and Albert Museum *(pp102–3)* is the world's largest museum of decorative arts. This German cup is 15th century.

◀ View of the River Thames across Tower Bridge, with The Shard in the background

The British Museum's *(pp110–11)* vast collection of antiquities from all over the world includes this Portland Vase from the 1st century BC.

The National Gallery's *(pp86–7)* world-famous collection of paintings includes works such as *Christ Mocked* (c.1495) by Hieronymus Bosch.

The City and Southwark *(see pp112–125)*

Thames

St Paul's *(pp118–19)* huge dome is the cathedral's most distinctive feature. Three galleries around the dome give spectacular views of London.

Westminster Abbey *(pp96–7)* has glorious medieval architecture and is crammed with impressive tombs and monuments to some of Britain's greatest public figures.

The Tower of London *(pp122–3)* is most famous as the prison where enemies of the Crown were executed. The Tower houses the Crown Jewels, including the Imperial State Crown.

Tate Britain *(p95)* displays an outstanding collection of British art ranging from stylized Elizabethan portraiture, such as *The Cholmondeley Ladies,* to cutting edge installation and film.

London's Parks and Gardens

London has one of the world's greenest city centres, full of tree-filled squares and large expanses of grass, some of which have been public land since medieval times. From the elegant terraces of Regent's Park to the Royal Botanic Gardens at Kew, every London park and garden has its own charm and character. Some are ancient crown or public land, while others were created from the grounds of private houses or disused land. Londoners make the most of these open spaces: for exercise, listening to music, or simply escaping the bustle of the city.

Holland Park *(see pp126–7)* offers acres of peaceful woodland, an open-air theatre *(see p157)* and a café.

Kew Gardens *(see p130)* are the world's premiere botanic gardens. An amazing variety of plants from all over the world is complemented by an array of temples, monuments and a landscaped lake.

Richmond Park *(see p130)*, London's largest Royal Park, remains unspoiled with roaming deer and magnificent river views.

0 kilometres

0 miles   0.5

Seasonal Best

As winter draws to a close, spectacular drifts of crocuses, daffodils and tulips are to be found peeping above the ground in Green Park and Kew. Easter weekend marks the start of outdoor events with funfairs on many commons and parks. During the summer months the parks are packed with picnickers and sunbathers and you can often catch a free open-air concert in St James's or Regent's parks. The energetic can play tennis in most parks, swim in Hyde Park's Serpentine or the ponds on Hampstead Heath, or take rowing boats out on the lakes in Regent's and Battersea parks. Autumn brings a different atmosphere, and on 5 November firework displays and bonfires celebrate Guy Fawkes Night *(see p68)*. Winter is a good time to visit the tropical glasshouses and the colourful outdoor winter garden at Kew. If the weather gets really cold, the Round Pond in Kensington Gardens may be fit for ice-skating.

Winter in Kensington Gardens, adjoining Hyde Park

Hampstead Heath *(see p128)* is a breezy open space embracing a variety of landscapes.

Regent's Park *(see p107)* has a large boating lake, an open-air theatre *(see p157)* and London Zoo. Surrounded by Nash's graceful buildings, it is one of London's most civilized retreats.

St James's Park, in the heart of the city, is a popular escape for office workers. It is also a reserve for wildfowl.

Green Park, with its shady trees and benches, offers a cool, restful spot in the heart of London.

Thames

Battersea Park is a pleasant riverside site with a man-made boating lake.

Greenwich Park *(see p129)* is dominated by the National Maritime Museum. There are fine views from the Old Royal Observatory on the hill top.

Hyde Park and Kensington Gardens *(see p105)* are both popular London retreats. There are sporting facilities, a lake and art gallery in Hyde Park. This plaque is from the ornate Italian Garden in Kensington Gardens.

Historic Cemeteries

In the late 1830s, a ring of private cemeteries was established around London to ease the pressure on the monstrously overcrowded and un-healthy burial grounds of the inner city. Today the cemeteries, notably **Highgate** *(see p128)* and **Kensal Green**, are well worth visiting for their flamboyant Victorian monuments.

Kensal Green cemetery on the Harrow Road

WEST END AND WESTMINSTER

The West End is the city's social and cultural centre and the London home of the royal family. Stretching from the edge of Hyde Park to Covent Garden, the district bustles all day and late into the night. Whether you're looking for art, history, street- or café-life, it is the most rewarding area in which to begin an exploration of the city. Westminster has been at the centre of political and religious power for a thousand years. In the 11th century, King Canute founded Westminster Palace and Edward the Confessor built Westminster Abbey, where all English monarchs have been crowned since 1066. As modern government developed, the great offices of state were established in the area.

Sights at a Glance

Historic Streets and Buildings

1 The Piazza and Central Market
3 Royal Opera House
9 Piccadilly Circus
11 Ritz Hotel
13 The Mall
14 *Buckingham Palace pp90–91*
16 Royal Mews
17 Cabinet War Rooms and Churchill Museum
18 Downing Street
19 Banqueting House
20 *Houses of Parliament pp94–5*

7 *National Gallery pp86–7*
8 National Portrait Gallery
10 Royal Academy
15 The Queen's Gallery
22 Tate Britain

Churches

12 Queen's Chapel
21 *Westminster Abbey pp96–7*

Museums and Galleries

2 London Transport Museum
4 Somerset House

Attractions

5 London Dungeon
6 London Eye

See also Street Finder maps 10, 11, 18, 19

For keys to symbols *see back flap*

Street-by-Street: Covent Garden

Until 1973, Covent Garden was an area of decaying streets and warehouses, which only came alive after dark when the fruit and vegetable market traders packed up for the day. Since then the Victorian market and elegant buildings nearby have been converted into stylish shops, restaurants, bars and cafés, creating an animated district which attracts a lively young crowd, night and day.

Seven Dials is a replica of a 17th-century monument marking the crossroads.

Covent Garden

Neal Street and Neal's Yard are lined with many specialist shops converted from former warehouses.

St Martin's Theatre *(see p157)* is home to the world's longest running play, *The Mousetrap*.

Stanfords map shop

The Lamb and Flag, built in 1623, is one of London's oldest pubs.

New Row is lined with little shops and cafés.

SEVEN SHORTS GARDENS

DIALS

EARLHAM STREET

NEAL STREET

MONMOUTH STREET

UPPER ST MARTIN'S LANE

SHELTON STREET

LONG ACRE

FLORAL STREET

ROSE ST

GARRICK STREET

ST MARTIN'S LANE

KING STREET

BEDFORD STREET

NEW ROW

BEDFORDBURY

HENRI

St Paul's Church was designed in 1633 by Inigo Jones *(see p57)*, in the style of the Italian Renaissance architect, Andrea Palladio. Jones also designed the original Covent Garden Piazza.

❸ Royal Opera House Some of the world's greatest opera singers and ballet dancers have performed at the Royal Opera House.

Locator Map
See Street Finder map 11

Key

— Suggested route

| 0 metres | 100 |
| 0 yards | 100 |

❷ London Transport Museum
This museum's intriguing collection brings to life the history of the city's tubes, buses and trains. It also has fine examples of 20th-century commercial art.

Jubilee Market

❶ ★ Piazza and Central Market
Shops and cafés fill the piazza and market.

❶ The Piazza and Central Market

Covent Garden WC2. **Map** 11 C2.
Ⓔ Covent Garden. ♿ cobbled streets. Street performers in Piazza: 10am–dusk daily.
Ⓦ **coventgardenlondonuk.com**

The 17th-century architect Inigo Jones (see p57) planned the Piazza in Covent Garden as an elegant residential square, modelled on the piazza in the Tuscan town of Livorno, which he had seen under construction during his travels in Italy. For a brief period, the Piazza became one of the most fashionable addresses in London, but it was superseded by the even grander St James's Square (see p89) which lies to the southwest.

Decline accelerated when a fruit and vegetable market developed. By the mid-18th century, the Piazza had become a haunt of prostitutes and most of its houses had turned into seedy lodgings, gambling dens, brothels and taverns.

Meanwhile the wholesale produce market became the largest in the country and in 1828 a market hall was erected to ease congestion. The market, however, soon outgrew its new home and despite the construction of new buildings, such as Floral and Jubilee halls, the congestion grew worse. In 1973 the market moved to a new site in south London, and over the next two decades Covent Garden was redeveloped. Today only St Paul's Church remains of Inigo Jones's buildings, and Covent Garden, with its many small shops, cafés, restaurants, market stalls and street entertainers, is one of central London's liveliest districts.

A mid-18th-century view of Covent Garden's Piazza

METRO-LAND *PRICE TWO-PENCE*

Poster by Michael Reilly (1929),
London Transport Museum

❷ London Transport Museum

The Piazza, Covent Garden WC2.
Map 11 C2. **Tel** 020 7379 6344.
⊖ Covent Garden. **Open**
10am–6pm Sat–Thu, 11am–6pm Fri.
▨ ♿ 🛈 phone in advance. 🖼
🖳 ☒ ltmuseum.co.uk

This collection of buses, trams
and underground trains ranges
from the earliest horse-drawn
omnibuses to a present-day
Hoppa bus. Housed in the
Victo-rian Flower Market of
Covent Garden built in 1872,
the museum is particularly
good for children, who can sit
in the driver's seat of a bus or
an underground train, operate
signals and chat to an actor
playing a 19th-century tube-
tunnel miner.

London's bus and train
companies have long been

prolific patrons of artists,
and the museum holds a fine
collection of 19th- and
20th-century commercial art.
Copies of some of the best
works by distinguished artists,
such as Paul Nash and Graham
Sutherland, are on sale in the
shop. Original works can be
seen at the museum's depot
in Acton.

❸ Royal Opera House

Covent Garden WC2. **Map** 11 C2.
Tel 020 7304 4000. ⊖ Covent Garden.
Open for performances and guided
tours (phone to check). ▨
☒ roh.org.uk

The first theatre on this site was
built in 1732, and staged plays
as well as concerts. However,
the building was destroyed by
fire in 1808 and again in 1856.
The present structure was
designed in 1858 by E M Barry.
John Flaxman's portico frieze,
depicting tragedy and comedy,
survived from the previous
building of 1809.

The Opera House is home
to the Royal Opera and Royal
Ballet companies. After two
years of renovation the
building reopened in the new
millennium, complete with a
second auditorium and new
rehearsal rooms. Backstage
tours are available, and once a
month visitors can watch the
Royal Ballet rehearse.

❹ Somerset House

Strand WC2. **Map** 11 C2. **Tel** 020 7845
4600. ⊖ Temple. **Open** most areas
10am–6pm daily; check website for
more specific info. **Closed** 1 Jan,
24–26 Dec. Ice rink **Open** two months
in winter. ▨ 🖳 Courtauld Institute
of Art Gallery. ▨ ▨ 🛈 ♿ Tom's
Kitchen: **Tel** 020 7845 4646.
☒ somersethouse.org.uk

Designed in 1770 by William
Chambers, Somerset House
presents two great collections
of art, the **Courtauld Institute
of Art Gallery** and the
Embankment Galleries.

The courtyard forms an
attractive piazza (which
becomes an ice rink in winter),
and the riverside terrace has a
café. Tom's Kitchen is also highly
regarded, and Tom's Deli is a
great spot for lunch. Located
in Somerset House but famous
in its own right is the Courtauld
Institute of Art Gallery, which
includes important Impressionist
and Post-Impressionist works by
artists such as Manet, Renoir and
Cezanne. In 2008 the riverside
Embankment Galleries were
launched. Occupying 750 sq m
(900 sq yd) of exhibition space
on the two lower floors, the
changing programme covers
a broad range of contemporary
arts, including photography,
design, fashion and architecture.

❺ London Dungeon

Riverside Building, County Hall,
Westminster Bridge Rd, SE1. **Map** 11
C5. **Tel** 0871 423 2240. ⊖ Waterloo,
Westminster. **Open** 10am–5pm Mon–
Fri (from 11pm Thu), 10am–6pm Sat &
Sun; open till later at holiday times.
Closed 25 Dec. ▨ book in advance
to avoid queues. ♿ one wheelchair
user per tour.
☒ thedungeons.com/london

This museum is a great hit with
adults and children, illustrating
many of the most blood-thirsty
events in 1,000 years of
London's history within a
90-minute tour. Guy Fawkes's
attempt to blow up the Houses
of Parliament, Jack the Ripper's
reign of terror, and Great
Plague-carrying rats are all
covered. There are also two

Soho and Chinatown

Lion dancer in
February's Chinese
New Year celebrations

Soho has been renowned for pleasures of the table,
the flesh and the intellect ever since it was first
developed in the late 17th century. At first a
fashionable residential area, it declined when high
society shifted west to Mayfair and immigrants from
Europe moved into its narrow streets. Furniture-
makers and tailors set up shop here and were joined
in the late 19th century by pubs, nightclubs,
restaurants and brothels. In the 1960s, Hong Kong
Chinese moved into the area around Gerrard and
Lisle streets and they created an aromatic
Chinatown, packed with many restaurants and
food shops. Soho's raffish reputation has long attracted artists and
writers, ranging from the 18th-century essayist Thomas de Quincey to
poet Dylan Thomas and painter Francis Bacon. Although strip joints
and peep shows remain, Soho has enjoyed something of a renaissance,
and today is full of stylish and lively bars and restaurants.

For hotels and restaurants in this area see pp560–73 and pp582–603

The opulent Palm Court of the Ritz Hotel

state-of-the-art thrill rides. Henry's Wrath is a boat trip towards execution, as ordered by a virtual Henry VIII; and Drop Dead sees visitors plunged three storeys in the pitch dark.

❻ London Eye

Jubilee Gardens, South Bank, SE1. **Map** 12 D2. **Tel** 0870 990 8883 (information); 0871 423 2240 (booking – recommended in summer as tickets sell out days in advance). ⊖ Waterloo, Westminster. 🚌 11, 24, 211. **Open** Sep–Mar: 10am–8:30pm daily; Apr–Sep: 10am–9pm daily (Jul & Aug: to 9:30pm). **Closed** mid-Jan (for maintenance) and 25 Dec. 🅿 Pick up tickets at County Hall (adjacent to Eye) at least 30 mins before boarding time. 📷 🎦 ♿ **londoneye.com**

The London Eye is a 135-m (443-ft) observation wheel that was installed on the South Bank to mark the Millennium. Its enclosed passenger capsules offer a gentle, 30-minute ride as the wheel makes a full turn, with breathtaking views over London and for up to 42 km (26 miles) around. Towering over one of the world's most familiar riverscapes, it has under-standably captured the hearts of Londoners and visitors alike, and is one of the city's most popular attractions. Trips on the wheel are on the hour and half-hour.

❼ National Gallery

See pp86–7.

❽ National Portrait Gallery

2 St Martin's Place WC2. **Map** 11 B3. **Tel** 020 7312 2463. ⊖ Charing Cross, Leicester Sq. **Open** 10am–6pm Sat–Wed, 10am–9pm Thu & Fri. **Closed** 24–26 Dec. ♿ 🎦 📷 🎦 📷 ♿ **npg.org.uk**

This museum celebrates Britain's history through portraits, photographs and sculptures; subjects range from Elizabeth I to David Beckham. The 20th-century section contains paintings and photographs of the royal family, politicians, rock stars, designers, artists and writers.

❾ Piccadilly Circus

W1. **Map** 11 A3. ⊖ Piccadilly Circus.

Dominated by garish neon advertising hoardings, Piccadilly Circus is a hectic traffic junction surrounded by shopping malls. It began as an early 19th-century crossroads between Piccadilly and John Nash's *(see p109)* Regent Street. It was briefly an elegant space, edged by curving stucco façades, but by 1910 the first electric advertisements had been installed. For years people have congregated at its centre, beneath the delicately poised figure of Eros, erected in 1892.

❿ Royal Academy

Burlington House, Piccadilly W1. **Map** 10 F3. **Tel** 020 7300 8000. ⊖ Piccadilly Circus, Green Park. **Open** 10am–6pm Sat–Thu, 10am–10pm Fri. **Closed** 24–26 Dec, Good Fri. ♿ ♿ 🎦 📷 by appointment. 🎦 📷 ♿ **royalacademy.org.uk**

Founded in 1768, the Royal Academy is best known for its summer exhibition, which has been an annual event for over 200 years and comprises a rewarding mix of around 1,200 new works by established and unknown painters, sculptors and architects. During the rest of the year, the gallery shows prestigious touring exhibitions from around the world, and the courtyard in front of Burlington House, one of the West End's few surviving mansions from the early 18th century, is often filled with people waiting to get in. Quite apart from its aesthetic delights, the Royal Academy provides the weary traveller with a little lacuna of tranquillity. Its interior decoration inspires calm, and seems to be cut off from the stresses and strains of modern city life.

The Statue of Eros

⓫ Ritz Hotel

Piccadilly W1. **Map** 10 F3. **Tel** 020 7493 8181. ⊖ Green Park. 🎦 ♿ *See Where to Stay p560.* 🎦 **theritzlondon.com**

Cesar Ritz, the Swiss hotelier who inspired the word "ritzy", had virtually settled down to a quiet retirement by 1906 when this hotel was built and named after him. The colonnaded front of the château-style building was erected in 1906 to suggest just the merest whiff of Paris, where the grandest hotels were to be found at the turn of the century. It still maintains its Edwardian air of *fin de siècle* opulence and sophisticated grandeur, and is a popular venue for afternoon tea (reservations are required). A touch of *soigné* danger may be found in the casino.

❼ National Gallery

The National Gallery is London's leading art museum, with over 2,300 paintings, most on permanent display. It has flourished since 1824, when the House of Commons agreed to purchase 38 major paintings. These became the core of a national collection of European art that now ranges from Cimabue in the 13th century to 19th-century Impressionists. The gallery's particular strengths are in Dutch, Italian Renaissance and 17th-century Spanish painting. To the left of the main gallery lies the Sainsbury Wing, financed by the grocery family and completed in 1991. It houses the Early Renaissance collection.

The Adoration of the Kings *(1564)*
This unusual work is by Flemish artist Pieter Bruegel the Elder (c.1525–69).

★ **'The Burlington House Cartoon'** *(c.1499–1500)*
The genius of Leonardo da Vinci glows through this picture of the Virgin and Child, St Anne and St John the Baptist.

Pigott Education Centre entrance

Stairs to lower floor

Learning gallery

Link to main building

Stairs to lower floors

Key to floorplan

- Painting 1250–1500
- Painting 1500–1600
- Painting 1600–1700
- Painting 1700–1900
- Special exhibitions
- Non-exhibition space

The Arnolfini Portrait
Jan van Eyck (c.1385–1441), one of the pioneers of oil painting, shows his mastery of colour, texture, and minute detail in this portrait of 1434.

Entrance Sainsbury Wing

The Annunciation
This refined work of the early 1450s, by Fra Filippo Lippi, forms part of the gallery's exceptional Italian Renaissance collection.

★ 'The Rokeby Venus'
This is Velázquez's only surviving female nude (1647–51).

airs and lift to
wer galleries

Central Hall

VISITORS' CHECKLIST

Practical Information
Trafalgar Sq WC2. **Map** 11 B3.
Tel 020 7747 2885.
W nationalgallery.org.uk
Open 10am–6pm daily (9pm Fri).
Closed 1 Jan, 24–26 Dec. via
Sainsbury Wing and Getty
entrances.

Transport
Charing Cross, Leicester Sq,
Piccadilly Circus. 3, 6, 9, 11,
12, 13, 15, 23, 24, 29, 53, 87,
88, 91, 139, 159, 176, 453.
Charing Cross.

★ **The Hay Wain** (1821)
The great age of 19th-century landscape painting is represented by Constable and Turner (see p95). This picture shows how Constable caught changing light and shadow.

Getty
entrance

Trafalgar Square
entrance

The Ambassadors
The strange shape in the foreground of this Hans Holbein portrait (1533) is a distorted skull, a symbol of mortality.

The Neo-Classical façade is made of Portland stone.

At the Theatre (1876–7)
Renoir was one of the greatest painters of the Impressionist movement. The theatre was a popular subject among artists of the time.

Gallery Guide

Most of the collection is housed on one floor. The paintings hang chronologically, with the earliest works, 1250–1500, in the Sainsbury Wing. Lesser paintings of all periods are displayed on the lower floor of the main building. There is a restaurant on the first floor in the Sainsbury Wing.

Street-by-Street: Piccadilly and St James's

As soon as Henry VIII built St James's Palace in the 1530s, the surrounding area became the centre of fashionable court life. Today Piccadilly forms a contrast between the bustling commercial district full of shopping arcades, eateries and cinemas, with St James's, to the south, which is still the domain of the wealthy and the influential.

St James's Church was designed by Sir Christopher Wren in 1684.

🔟 ★ **Royal Academy**
The permanent art collection here includes this Michelangelo relief of the Madonna and Child (1505).

Fortnum & Mason
(see p152) was founded in 1707.

⓫ **The Ritz**
César Ritz founded one of London's most famous hotels in 1906.

Burlington Arcade, an opulent covered walk, has fine shops and beadles on patrol.

St James's Palace was built on the site of a leper hospital.

To the Mall and Buckingham Palace *(see pp90–91)*

Spencer House, restored to its 18th-century splendour, contains fine period furniture and paintings. This Palladian palace was completed in 1766 for the 1st Earl Spencer, an ancestor of the late Princess of Wales.

9 ★ Piccadilly Circus
The crowds and dazzling neon lights make this the West End's focal point.

Locator Map
See Street Finder map 10, 11

Key

— Suggested route

0 metres	100
0 yards	100

Piccadilly

Jermyn Street has elegant shops selling antiques, unusual gifts and men's clothing.

St James's Square has long been the most fashionable address in London.

Pall Mall is a street of gentlemen's clubs, which admit only members and their guests.

12 Queen's Chapel
This was the first Classical church in England.

Royal Opera Arcade is lined with quality shops. Designed by John Nash, it was completed in 1818.

12 Queen's Chapel

Marlborough Rd SW1. **Map** 11 A4.
Tel 020 7930 4832. Green Park.
Open to the public Sun services:
8:30am, 11:15am **royal.gov.uk**

The sumptuous Queen's Chapel was designed by Inigo Jones for the Infanta of Spain, the intended bride of Charles I (see pp56–7). Work started in 1623 but ceased when the marriage negotiations were shelved. The chapel was finally completed in 1627 for Charles's eventual queen, Henrietta Maria. It was the first church in England to be built in a Classical style, with a coffered ceiling based on a reconstruction by Palladio of an ancient Roman temple.

Interior of Queen's Chapel

13 The Mall

SW1. **Map** 11 A4. Charing Cross, Green Park.

This broad triumphal approach from Trafalgar Square to Buckingham Palace was created by Aston Webb when he redesigned the front of the palace and the Victoria Monument in 1911. The spacious tree-lined avenue follows the course of an old path at the edge of St James's Park. The path was laid out in the reign of Charles II, when it became London's most fashionable and cosmopolitan promenade. The Mall is used for royal processions on special occasions. Flag-poles down both sides fly the national flags of foreign heads of state during official visits. The Mall is closed to traffic on Sundays.

⚙ Buckingham Palace

Opened to visitors for the first time in 1993 to raise money for repairing fire damage to Windsor Castle *(see pp240–41)*, the Queen's official London home and office is an extremely popular attraction in August and September. John Nash *(see p109)* began converting the 18th-century Buckingham House into a palace for George IV in 1826 but was taken off the job in 1831 for overspending his budget. The first monarch to occupy the palace was Queen Victoria, just after she came to the throne in 1837. The tour takes visitors up the grand staircase and through the splendour of the State Rooms, but not into the royal family's private apartments.

Music Room
State guests are presented and royal babies christened in this room.

Green Drawing Room

White Drawing Room

Blue Drawing Room

Grand Staircase

State Dining Room

The Queen's Gallery
Masterpieces from the Royal Collection, such as Vermeer's *The Music Lesson* (c.1660), are displayed here in a series of changing exhibitions.

KEY

① **The Royal Standard** flies while the Queen is in residence.

② **The East Wing** façade was added by Aston Webb in 1913.

③ **The Changing of the Guard** takes place on the palace forecourt.

Throne Room
The Queen carries out many formal ceremonial duties here, under the richly gilded ceiling.

View over the Mall
On special occasions the Royal Family wave to crowds from the balcony.

⑮ The Queen's Gallery

Buckingham Palace Rd SW1. **Map** 10 F5. **Tel** 020 7766 7300. St James's Park, Victoria. **Open** 10am–5:30pm daily (last adm: 4:30pm). **Closed** 25, 26 Dec and other days through the year; visit the website for more details. royalcollection.org.uk

The Queen's art collection is one of the finest and most valuable in the world, rich in the works of old masters such as Rembrandt and Leonardo. The gallery hosts a rotating programme of exhibitions, enabling the year-round display of many masterpieces, drawings and decorative arts from the Queen's collection.

Detail: The Gold State Coach (1762), Royal Mews

⑯ Royal Mews

Buckingham Palace Rd SW1. **Map** 10 E5. **Tel** 020 7766 7302. Victoria. **Open** Feb–Mar, Nov–Dec: 10am–4pm Mon–Sat; Apr–Oct: 10am–5pm daily. Subject to closure at short notice. **Open** 9:30am–5pm daily all year **Closed** 25, 26 Dec. royalcollection.org.uk

Lovers of horses and royal pomp should not miss this working stable and coach house. Designed by John Nash in 1825, it houses horses and state coaches used on official occasions. Among them is the glass coach used for royal weddings and foreign ambassadors. The star exhibit is the ornate gold state coach, built for George III in 1762, which was used by the Queen during the Golden Jubilee celebrations in 2002. The shop sells interesting merchandise.

The Changing of the Guard

Dressed in brilliant scarlet tunics and tall furry hats called bearskins, the palace guards stand in sentry boxes outside the Palace. Crowds gather to watch the colourful and musical military ceremony as the guards march from Wellington Barracks to Buckingham Palace, parading for half an hour while the palace keys are handed by the old guard to the new.

Street-by-Street: Whitehall and Westminster

The broad avenues of Whitehall and Westminster are lined with imposing buildings that serve the historic seat of both government and the established church. On weekdays the streets are crowded with civil servants whose work is based here, while at weekends the area takes on a different atmosphere with a steady flow of tourists.

⓲ Downing Street
Sir Robert Walpole was the first Prime Minister to live here in 1732.

⓱ Cabinet War Rooms and Churchill Museum
Now open to the public, these were Winston Churchill's World War II headquarters.

St Margaret's Church is a favourite venue for political and society weddings.

㉑ ★ Westminster Abbey
The abbey is London's oldest and most important church.

Central Hall (1911) is a florid example of the Beaux Arts style.

Richard I's Statue is an 1860 depiction of the king, killed in battle in 1199.

KING CHARLES STREET

STOREY'S GATE

GREAT GEORGE STREET

BROAD   SANCTUARY

PARLIAMENT SQUARE

ST MARGARET STREET

ABINGDON STREET

GREAT COLLEGE STREET

Dean's Yard is a secluded grassy square surrounded by picturesque buildings from different periods, many used by Westminster School.

The Burghers of Calais is a cast of Auguste Rodin's 1886 original in France.

19 Banqueting House
Inigo Jones designed this elegant building in 1622.

Locator Map
See Street Finder map 11

The Cenotaph
(1920) is a war memorial by Sir Edwin Lutyens.

RICHMOND TERRACE

WHITEHALL

VICTORIA EMBANKMENT

Horse Guards is a parade ground protected by a guard, changed twice each day.

Westminster Pier is the main starting point for river trips (pp78–9).

Westminster

STREET

20 ★ Houses of Parliament
The seat of government is dominated by the clock tower, holding the 14-tonne bell Big Ben, hung in 1858. Its deep chimes are broadcast daily on BBC radio.

Key

— Suggested route

| 0 metres | 100 |
| 0 yards | 100 |

17 Cabinet War Rooms and Churchill Museum

Clive Steps, King Charles St SW1.
Map 11 B5. **Tel** 020 7930 6961.
Westminster. **Open** 9:30am–6pm daily (last adm: 5pm). **Closed** 24–26 Dec.
iwm.org.uk

This warren of cellars below a government office building is where the War Cabinet – first under Neville Chamberlain, then Winston Churchill from 1940 – met during World War II when German bombs were falling on London. The rooms include living quarters for ministers and military leaders and a Cabinet Room, where strategic decisions were taken. They are laid out as they were when the war ended, complete with Churchill's desk, communications equipment, and maps for plotting battles and strategies. The Churchill Museum records and illustrates Churchill's life and career.

Telephones in the Map Room, Cabinet War Rooms

18 Downing Street

SW1. **Map** 11 B4. Westminster.
Closed to the public.

Number 10 Downing Street has been the official resid-ence of the British Prime Minister since 1732. It contains a Cabinet Room in which government policy is decided, an impressive State Dining Room and a private apartment; outside is a well-protected garden.

Next door at No. 11 is the official residence of the Chancellor of the Exchequer, who is in charge of the nation's financial affairs. In 1989, iron gates were erected at the Whitehall end of Downing Street for security purposes.

⓳ Banqueting House

Whitehall SW1. **Map** 11 B4. **Tel** 020 3166 6154. 🚇 Charing Cross. **Open** 10am–5pm daily. **Closed** pub hols & for functions. Call in advance. 🏛 📷 🔊 ♿ partial. 🌐 hrp.org.uk

Completed by Inigo Jones (see p57) in 1622, this was the first building in central London to embody the Palladian style of Renaissance Italy. In 1629 Charles I commissioned Rubens to paint the ceiling with scenes exalting the reign of his father, James I. They symbolize the divine right of kings, disputed by the Parliamentarians, who executed Charles I outside the building in 1649 (see pp56–7).

Panels from the Rubens ceiling (1629–34), Banqueting House

⓴ Houses of Parliament

SW1. **Map** 11 C5. **Tel** 020 7219 3000. 🚇 Westminster. Visitors' Galleries: **Open** phone ahead for information on debate times. Access to the Visitors' Galleries is by queueing system; or UK residents may apply in advance to local MP. **Closed** frequently for parliamentary recesses. ♿ 📷 🏛 🌐 parliament.uk/visiting

There has been a Palace of Westminster here since the 11th century, though only Westminster Hall remains from that time. The present Neo-Gothic structure by Sir Charles Barry was built after the old palace was destroyed by fire in 1834. Since the 16th century it has housed the two Houses of Parliament, the Lords and the Commons. The House of Commons consists of elected Members of Parliament (MPs).

The party with most MPs forms the Government, with its leader as Prime Minister. The House of Lords comprises mainly appointed life peers, but also hereditary peers and Church of England bishops.

㉑ Westminster Abbey

See pp96–7.

The House of Commons' original chamber was destroyed by a bomb in 1941.

Central Lobby

Victoria Tower

Royal Gallery

Cromwell Green entrance

The House of Lords is a lavishly decorated Gothic Hall designed by Pugin in 1836–7.

Members' entrance

Big Ben has kept exact time for the nation almost continuously since 1859.

Westminster Hall

㉒ Tate Britain

Millbank SW1. **Map** 19 B2. **Tel** 020 7887 8888. ⊖ Pimlico. 🚌 87, 88, C10. 🚆 Victoria, Vauxhall. 🚤 to Tate Modern every 40 mins. 🅿 **Open** 10am–6pm daily (to 10pm Fri). **Closed** 24–26 Dec. 🅿 for major exhibitions. ♿ Atterbury St. 📷 ✎ 🚻 🍴 W tate.org.uk

Formerly the Tate Gallery, Tate Britain is the national gallery of British art, and includes works from the 16th to the 21st century. Displays draw on the huge Tate Collection, which also includes the international modern art seen at Tate Modern (p125). A river boat, Tate to Tate, takes visitors between the two galleries.

The collection is arranged chronologically, an approach that gives a clear overview of the range of art being produced at any one historical moment. It also allows fascinating juxtapositions to emerge – for example, a Gainsborough landscape hangs side by side with Hogarth's satires; Alma Tadema's frolicking female nudes of A Favourite Custom (1909) are seen next to Walter Sickert's gritty modernist icon La Hollandaise (1906). There are also permanent galleries devoted to two of the greatest figures in British art: William Blake and Henry Moore. Located in the Clore Galleries

The First Marriage (A Marriage of Styles I) (1962) by David Hockney

Recumbent Figure (1938) by Henry Moore

are works from the Turner Bequest (see below).

The section on the years 1500–1800 covers a period of dramatic change in British history, from the Tudors and Stuarts through to the age of Thomas Gainsborough.

The years 1800 to 1900 saw dramatic expansion and change in the arts in Britain. This section shows the new themes that began to emerge. Included are the "Victorian Narrative" painters such as William Powell Frith, and the work of the Pre-Raphaelites, such as John Everett Millais and Dante Gabriel Rossetti. The period 1900–1960 includes the work of Jacob Epstein, that of

Wyndham Lewis and his Vorticist group, and the celebrated modernist works of Henry Moore, Barbara Hepworth, Ben Nicholson, Francis Bacon and Lucian Freud.

The displays in the outstanding Tate collection of British art from 1960 to the present are changed on a regular basis. From the 1960s, Tate's funding for the purchase of works began to increase substantially, while artistic activity continued to pick up speed, encouraged by public spending. As a result, Tate Britain's collection is particularly rich in this period. Works range from the 1960s Pop artists David Hockney, Richard Hamilton and Peter Blake, through the works of Gilbert and George and the landscape artist Richard Long, to the 1980s paintings of Howard Hodgkin and R B Kitaj.

The Turner Bequest

The Turner Bequest comprises some 300 oil paintings and 20,000 watercolours and drawings, received by the nation from the great landscape painter J M W Turner some years after his death in 1851. Turner's will had specified that a gallery be built to house his pictures and this was finally done in 1987 with the opening of the Clore Galleries. Most of the oils are on view in the main galleries, and the watercolours are the subject of changing displays.

Shipping at the Mouth of the Thames (c.1806–7)

㉑ Westminster Abbey

Westminster Abbey has been the burial place of Britain's monarchs since the 11th century and the setting for many coronations and royal weddings. It is one of the most beautiful buildings in London, with an exceptionally diverse array of architectural styles, ranging from the austere French Gothic of the nave to the astonishing complexity of Henry VII's chapel. Half national church, half national museum, the abbey aisles and transepts are crammed with an extraordinary collection of tombs and monuments honouring some of Britain's greatest public figures, ranging from politicians to poets.

North Entrance
The mock-medieval stonework is Victorian.

Statesmen's Aisle

★ Nave
At a height of 31 m (102 ft), the nave is the highest in England. The ratio of height to width is 3:1.

Coronation Chair
Constructed in 1301, this chair has been used at every coronation since 1308.

KEY

① **Flying buttresses** help redistribute the great weight of the roof.

② **The Sanctuary** was built by Henry III and has been the scene of 38 coronations.

③ **The Pyx Chamber** is where the coinage was tested in medieval times.

④ **The Museum** has many of the abbey's treasures including wood, plaster and wax effigies of monarchs.

Coronation

The coronation ceremony is over 1,000 years old and since 1066, with the crowning of William the Conqueror on Christmas Day, the abbey has been its sumptuous setting. The coronation of Queen Elizabeth II, in 1953, was the first to be televised.

★ Henry VII Chapel
The chapel, built in 1503–19, has superb late Perpendicular vaulting and choir stalls dating from 1512.

WILLIAM SHAKESPEARE 1564–1616 BURIED AT STRATFORD-ON-AVON

Poets' Corner
A host of great poets are honoured here, including Shakespeare, Chaucer and T S Eliot.

★ Chapter House
A beautiful octagonal room, remarkable for its 13th-century tile floor. It is lit by six huge stained glass windows showing scenes from the abbey's history.

Cloisters
Built mainly in the 13th and 14th centuries, the cloisters link the Abbey church with the other buildings.

Historical Plan of The Abbey

The first abbey church was established as early as the 10th century, but the present French-influenced Gothic structure was begun in 1245 at the behest of Henry III. Because of its unique role as the coronation church, the abbey escaped Henry VIII's onslaught on Britain's monastic buildings (see pp54–5).

Key
- ▢ Built between 1055–1272
- ▢ Added from 1376–1420
- ▢ Built between 1500–1512
- ▢ Completed 1745
- ▢ Restored after 1850

SOUTH KENSINGTON AND HYDE PARK

This exclusive district embraces one of London's largest parks and some of its finest museums, shops, restaurants and hotels. Until the mid-19th century it was a genteel, semi-rural backwater of large houses and private schools lying to the south of Kensington Palace. In 1851, the Great Exhibition, until then the largest arts and science event ever staged *(see pp60–61)*, was held in Hyde Park, transforming the area into a celebration of Victorian learning and self-confidence. The brainchild of Queen Victoria's husband, Prince Albert, the exhibition was a massive success and the profits were used to buy 35 ha (87 acres) of land in South Kensington. Here, Prince Albert encouraged the construction of a concert hall, museums and colleges devoted to the applied arts and sciences; most of them survive. The neighbourhood soon became modish, full of flamboyant red-brick mansion blocks, garden squares and the elite shops still to be found in Knightsbridge.

Sights at a Glance

Historic Buildings
7 Kensington Palace

Churches
2 Brompton Oratory

Shops
1 Harrods

Parks and Gardens
6 Hyde Park and Kensington Gardens

Museums and Galleries
3 *Victoria and Albert Museum pp102–3*
4 Science Museum
5 Natural History Museum

See also Street Finder maps 8, 9, 16, 17

Street-by-Street: South Kensington

The numerous museums and colleges created in the wake of the Great Exhibition of 1851 *(see pp60–61)* con-tinue to give this neighbourhood an air of leisured culture. Visited as much by Londoners as tourists, the museum area is liveliest on Sundays and on summer evenings during the Royal Albert Hall's famous season of classical "Prom" concerts *(see p158)*.

The Royal Albert Hall opened in 1870 and was modelled on Roman amphitheatres.

The Memorial to the Great Exhibition is surmounted by a bronze statue of its instigator, Prince Albert.

The Royal College of Music, founded in 1882, exhibits historic musical instruments such as this harpsichord dating from 1531.

❹ ★ **Science Museum** Visitors can experiment with over a thousand interactive displays.

Entrance to South Kensington tube

❺ ★ **Natural History Museum** The Creepy Crawlies exhibition has proved highly popular.

Key

— Suggested route

| 0 metres | 100 |
| 0 yards | 100 |

The Albert Memorial was built in memory of Queen Victoria's husband who died in 1861.

Locator Map
See Street Finder maps 8, 16, 17

REGENT'S PARK & BLOOMSBURY

WEST END & WESTMINSTER

SOUTH KENSINGTON & HYDE PARK

❸ ★ Victoria and Albert Museum
The museum has a fine collection of applied arts and photography from around the world.

❷ Brompton Oratory
This ornate Baroque church is famous for its splendid musical tradition.

Brompton Square (1821)

To Knightsbridge and Harrods
→

GARDENS

NCES GARDENS

DENS

BROMPTON ROAD

Harrods Food Hall

❶ Harrods

87–135 Brompton Rd SW1. **Map** 9 B5. **Tel** 020 7730 1234. 🚇 Knightsbridge. **Open** 10am–8pm Mon–Sat, 11:30am–6pm Sun. ♿ 🚻 📷 *See Shops and Markets pp152–5.* 🌐 **harrods.com**

In 1849 Henry Charles Harrod opened a small grocery shop on Brompton Road, which soon became famous for its impeccable service and quality. The store moved into these extravagant premises in Knightsbridge in 1905.

❷ Brompton Oratory

Brompton Rd SW7. **Map** 17 B1. **Tel** 020 7808 0900. 🚇 South Kensington. **Open** 6am–8pm daily. ♿ 📷 🌐 **bromptonoratory.com**

The Italianate Oratory is a lavish monument to the 19th-century English Catholic revival. It was established as a base for a community of priests by John Henry Newman (later Cardinal Newman), who introduced the Oratorian movement to England in 1848. The church was opened in 1884, and the dome and façade added in the 1890s.

The sumptuous interior holds many fine monuments. The 12 huge 17th-century statues of the apostles are from Siena Cathedral, the elaborate Baroque Lady Altar (1693) is from the Dominican church at Brescia, and the 18th-century altar in St Wilfred's Chapel is from Rochefort in Belgium.

❸ Victoria and Albert Museum

The Victoria and Albert Museum (the V&A) contains one of the world's widest collections of art and design, ranging from early Christian devotional objects and the mystical art of southeast Asia to cutting-edge furniture design. Originally founded in 1852 as the Museum of Manufactures to inspire students of design, it was renamed by Queen Victoria in 1899 in memory of Prince Albert. The museum has undergone a dramatic redisplay of its collection, including work on the Fashion and Photographs gallery, Ceramics galleries, Sackler Education Centre and Medieval and Renaissance galleries, which span three levels. The Dr Susan Weber Gallery for furniture also opened here in 2012.

Silver galleries
Radiant pieces such as the Burgess Cup (Britain, 1863) fill these stunning galleries.

★ British Galleries
The Great Bed of Ware has been a tourist attraction since 1601, when Shakespeare sparked interest in it by making reference to it in *Twelfth Night*.

★ Fashion gallery
In this gallery, European fashion, fabrics and accessories from 1750 to the present day are displayed, such as these floral 1920s' Lilley & Skinner shoes.

Key to Floorplan

- Level 0
- Level 1
- Level 2
- Level 3
- Level 4
- Level 6
- Henry Cole Wing
- Non-exhibition space

Exhibition Road entrance

Gallery Guide

The V&A has a 7-mile (11-km) layout spread over six levels. Level 1, houses the China, Japan and South Asia galleries, as well as the Fashion gallery and the Cast Courts. The British Galleries are on levels 2 and 4. Level 3 contains the 20th Century galleries and displays of silver, jewellery, ironwork, paintings, photography and works of 20th-century design. The glass display is also on upper level 4. The Ceramics and Furniture galleries are on level 6. The Henry Cole Wing houses the Sackler Education Centre, RIBA Architecture Study Rooms and the Prints and Drawings Study Rooms.

Architecture gallery
Features highlights from the world class collection of drawings, models, photographs and architectural fragments of the V&A and RIBA collections, such as this 19th-century model.

VISITORS' CHECKLIST

Practical Information
Cromwell Rd SW7. **Map** 17 A1.
Tel 020 7942 2000.
w vam.ac.uk
Open 10am–5:45pm daily
(10am–10pm last Fri of each month). **Closed** 24–26 Dec.

Transport
South Kensington. 14, 74, 414, C1.

★ Medieval and Renaissance galleries
The stunning Burghley Nef (France, 1527) is located in these galleries in rooms 62–4.

The John Madejski Garden

China gallery
This magnificent ancestor portrait is among the many exquisite pieces on show in this gallery.

Aston Webb's façade (1909) is decorated with 32 sculptures of English craftsmen and designers.

★ Islamic Middle East gallery
On display are fantastic objects representing the finest in Islamic art and design, such as this 16th-century Ottoman table.

Main entrance

Newcomen's Steam Engine (1712), Science Museum

❹ Science Museum

Exhibition Rd SW7. **Map** 16 F1.
Tel 0870 870 4868. 🚇 South Kensington. **Open** 10am–6pm daily.
Closed 24–26 Dec. 🎬 for IMAX, special exhibitions and simulators only. 🚻 ♿ 🛍 📷 🍴
🖥 sciencemuseum.org.uk

Centuries of continuing scientific and technological development lie at the heart of the Science Museum's massive collections. The hardware displayed is magnificent: from steam engines to aeroengines; spacecraft to the very first mechanical computers. Equally important is the social context of science – what discoveries and inventions mean for day-to-day life – and the process of discovery itself. There are many interactive and hands-on displays which are very popular with children.

The museum is spread over seven floors and includes the high-tech Wellcome Wing at the west end of the museum. The basement features the excellent hands-on galleries for children, including The Garden. The Energy Hall dominates the ground floor, and is dedicated to steam power, with the still-operational Harle Syke Mill Engine of 1903. Here too are Space and Making the Modern World, a highlight of which is the display of the scarred Apollo 10 spacecraft, which carried three astronauts to the moon and back in May 1969. In Challenge of Materials, located on the first floor, our

expectations of materials are confounded with exhibits such as a bridge made of glass and a steel wedding dress.

The Flight gallery on the third floor is packed with early flying contraptions, fighter planes, aeroplanes and the Launchpad. The fourth and fifth floors house the medical science galleries, where Science and the Art of Medicine has a 17th-century Italian vase for storing snake bite treatment.

The high-tech Wellcome Wing offers four floors of interactive technology, including "Who Am I?", a fascinating exhibition exploring the science of you. With an IMAX 3D Cinema and the SimEx simulator ride, it is a breath-taking addition to the museum. The museum cafés and shop are particularly good.

❺ Natural History Museum

Cromwell Rd SW7. **Map** 16 F1. **Tel** 020 7942 5000. 🚇 South Kensington. **Open** 10am–5:50pm daily (to 10:30pm last Fri of month). **Closed** 24–26 Dec. 🚻 ♿ 🛍 📷 🖥
🖥 nhm.ac.uk

This cathedral-like building's richly sculpted stonework conceals an iron and steel frame; this construction technique was revolutionary when the museum opened in 1881. The imaginative displays tackle fundamental issues such as the ecology and evolution of the planet, the origin of species and the development of human beings – all explained through a dynamic combination of the latest technology, interactive techniques and traditional displays.

Relief from a decorative panel in the Natural History Museum

The museum is divided into four sections: the Blue Zone, Green Zone, Red Zone and the Orange Zone. In the Blue Zone, the Ecology exhibition explores the complex web of the natural world through a replica of a moonlit rainforest buzzing with the sounds of insects. One of the most popular exhibits is the Dinosaur Gallery, which includes life-like animatronic models of dinosaurs. The Vault, located in the Green Zone, contains a dazzling collection of the finest gems, crystals, metals and meteorites from around the world. The Darwin Centre is the largest curved structure in Europe. The eight-storey-high cocoon houses the museum's vast collection of insects and plants.

The Tuojiangasaurus skeleton (about 150 million years old), Natural History Museum

For hotels and restaurants in this area see pp560–73 and pp582–603

Statue of the young Queen Victoria outside Kensington Palace, sculpted by her daughter, Princess Louise

❻ Hyde Park and Kensington Gardens

W2. Map 9 B3. Tel 0300 061 2000. Hyde Park 🚇 Hyde Park Corner, Knightsbridge, Lancaster Gate, Marble Arch. Open dawn–midnight daily. ♿ 🚻 Kensington Gardens. Tel 0300 061 2000. 🚇 Queensway, Lancaster Gate. Open dawn–dusk daily. ♿ 🚻 See also pp78–9. Diana, Princess of Wales Memorial Playground: Open 10am–dusk daily. 🚻 🌐 royalparks.org.uk

The ancient manor of Hyde was part of the lands of Westminster Abbey seized by Henry VIII at the Dissolution of the Mona-steries in 1536 (see pp54–5). James I opened the park to the public in the early 17th century, and it was soon one of the city's most fashionable public spaces. Unfortunately it also became popular with duellists and highwaymen, and consequently William

III had 300 lights hung along Rotten Row, the first street in England to be lit up at night. In 1730, the Westbourne River was dammed by Queen Caroline in order to create the Serpentine, an artificial lake that is today used for boating and swimming, and Rotten Row for horse riding. The park is also a rallying point for political demonstrations, while at Speaker's Corner, in the northeast, anyone has had the right to address the public since 1872. Sundays are particularly lively, with many budding orators and a number of eccentrics revealing their plans for the betterment of mankind.

Adjoining Hyde Park is Kensington Gardens, the former grounds of Kensington Palace. Three great attractions for children are the innovative Diana, Princess of Wales Memorial Playground, the bronze statue of J M Barrie's fictional Peter Pan (1912), by George Frampton, and the Round Pond where people sail model boats. Also worth seeing is the dignified Orangery (1704), once used by Queen Anne as a "summer supper house" and now a summer café.

Detail of the Coalbrookdale Gate, Kensington Gardens

❼ Kensington Palace

Kensington Palace Gdns W8. Map 8 D4. Tel 0844 482 7777. 🚇 High St Ken, Queensway. Open Nov–Feb: 10am–5pm daily; Mar–Oct: 10am–6pm daily (last adm: 1 hr before close). Closed 1 Jan, 24–26 Dec. ♿ 🚻 🌐 hrp.org.uk

Kensington Palace was the principal residence of the royal family from the 1690s until 1760, when George III moved to Buckingham Palace. Over the years it has seen a number of important royal events. In 1714 Queen Anne died here from a fit of apoplexy brought on by over-eating and, in June 1837, Princess Victoria of Kent was woken to be told that her uncle William IV had died and she was now queen – the beginning of her 64-year reign.

Half of the palace still holds royal apartments, but the other half is open to the public. Among the highlights are the 18th-century state rooms with ceilings and murals by William Kent (see p32). After the death of Princess Diana in 1997, the palace became a focal point for mourners who gathered in their thousands at its gates and turned the area into a field of bouquets.

REGENT'S PARK AND BLOOMSBURY

Cream stuccoed terraces built by John Nash (see p109) fringe the southern edge of Regent's Park in London's highest concentration of quality Georgian housing. The park, named for the Prince Regent, was also designed by Nash, as the culmination of a triumphal route from the Prince's house in St James's (see pp88–9). Today it is the busiest of the royal parks and boasts a zoo, an open air theatre, boating lake, rose garden, cafés and London's largest mosque (see p128) with its popular market, shops and cafés, reached by walking, or taking a boat, along the picturesque Regent's Canal. Bloomsbury,

an enclave of attractive garden squares and Georgian brick terraces, was one of the most fashionable areas of the city until the mid-19th century, when the arrival of large hospitals and railway stations persuaded many of the wealthier residents to move west to Mayfair, Knightsbridge and Kensington. Home to the British Museum since 1753 and the University of London since 1828, Bloomsbury has long been the domain of artists, writers and intellectuals, including the Bloomsbury Group (see p167), George Bernard Shaw, Charles Dickens and Karl Marx. Traditionally a centre for the book trade, it remains a good place for literary browsing.

Sights at a Glance

Historic Streets

⑤ Bloomsbury

Museums and Galleries

① Madame Tussaud's
② Sherlock Holmes Museum
③ Wallace Collection
④ British Museum pp110–11

See also Street Finder
maps 1, 2, 3

❶ Madame Tussauds

Marylebone Rd NW1. **Map** 2 D5.
Tel 0870 400 3000. ⊖ Baker St. **Open**
9:30am–5:30pm Mon–Fri, 9am–6pm
Sat, Sun & school hols. **Closed** 25 Dec.
🏠 🐾 ♿ phone first. 📷
🌐 **madametussauds.com**

Madame Tussaud began her
wax-modelling career making
death masks of victims of the
French Revolution. She moved
to England and in 1835 set up
an exhibition of her work in
Baker Street, near the
present site, where
today's guests can
have photos taken
with some of the
world's most
famous faces.
The main sections
of the exhibition
are: A-List, where
visitors get to
feel what it is
like to be at
a celebrity
party;
Interactive
Music Zone,
devoted to the
giants of the
entertainment industries; and
the World Stage, a collection of
various royalty, statesmen, world
leaders, writers and artists.

Wax figure of
Elizabeth II

The Marvel Super Heroes 4D
Experience, an exclusive short
film complete with water, wind
and vibration effects, puts you
right in the heart of the action.
In the Spirit of London finale,
visitors travel in stylized taxi-
cabs through the city's history
to "witness" events, from the
Great Fire of 1666 to the

Wax model of Luciano Pavarotti (1990),
Madame Tussauds

Conan Doyle's fictional detective
Sherlock Holmes

Swinging 1960s. Ticket prices
also include entry to temporary
exhibitions featuring media
icons of the moment.
Educational tours are also
available for groups.

❷ Sherlock Holmes Museum

221b Baker St NW1. **Map** 1 C4. **Tel**
020 7224 3688. ⊖ Baker St. **Open**
9:30am–6pm daily. **Closed** 25 Dec. 🏠
🏠 🌐 **sherlock-holmes.co.uk**

Sir Arthur Conan Doyle's fictional
detective was supposed to live
at 221b Baker Street, which did
not exist. The museum, labelled
221b, actually stands between
Nos. 237 and 239, and is the
only surviving Victorian lodging
house in the street. There is a
reconstruction of Holmes's front
room, and memorabilia from
the stories decorate every room.
Visitors can buy plaques,
Holmes hats, Toby jugs and
meerschaum pipes.

❸ Wallace Collection

Hertford House, Manchester Sq W1.
Map 10 D1. **Tel** 0207563 9500. ⊖
Bond St, Baker St. **Open** 10am–5pm
daily. **Closed** 1 Jan, Good Fri, 24–26
Dec ♿ phone first. 📷 ✏ 🏠
🌐 **wallacecollection.org**

One of the world's finest
private collections of European
art, it has remained intact since
1897. The product of
passionate collecting by four
generations of the Seymour-
Conway family who were

Marquesses of Hertford,
it was bequeathed to the state
on the condition that it would
go on permanent public
display with nothing added
or taken away. Hertford House
still retains the atmosphere
of a grand 19th-century house,
and the Centenary Project in
1997 created more gallery
space and a stunning high-
level glass roof for the central
courtyard, which now contains
a sculpture garden and an
elegant restaurant.

The 3rd Marquess (1777–
1842), a flamboyant London
figure, used his Italian wife's
fortune to buy works by Titian
and Canaletto, along with
numerous 17th-century Dutch
paintings including works by
Van Dyck. The collection's
particular strength is 18th-
century French painting,
sculpture and decorative arts,
acquired by the 4th Marquess
(1800–70) and his natural son,
Sir Richard Wallace (1818–90).
The Marquess had a taste for
lush romanticism, and notable
among his acquisitions are
Watteau's *Champs Elysées*
(1716–17), Fragonard's *The
Swing* (1766) and Boucher's
*The Rising and Setting of the
Sun* (1753).

Other highlights at the
Wallace Collection include
Rembrandt's *Titus, the Artist's
Son* (1650s), Titian's *Perseus and
Andromeda* (1554–6) and Hals's
famous *Laughing Cavalier*
(1624). There is also an
important collection of
Renaissance armour, and superb
examples of Sèvres porcelain
and Italian majolica.

A 16th-century Italian majolica dish
from the Wallace Collection

For hotels and restaurants in this area see pp560–73 and pp582–603

John Nash's Regency London

John Nash, the son of a Lambeth millwright, was designing houses from the 1780s. However, it was not until the 1820s that he also became known as an inspired town planner, when his "royal route" was completed. This took George IV from his Pall Mall palace, through Piccadilly Circus and up the elegant sweep of Regent Street to Regent's Park, which Nash bordered with rows of beautiful Neo-Classical villas, such as Park Crescent and Cumberland Terrace. Though many of his plans were never completed, this map of 1851, which unusually places the south at the top, shows Nash's overall architectural impact on London. His other work included the revamping of Buckingham Palace (see pp90–91), and the building of several theatres and churches.

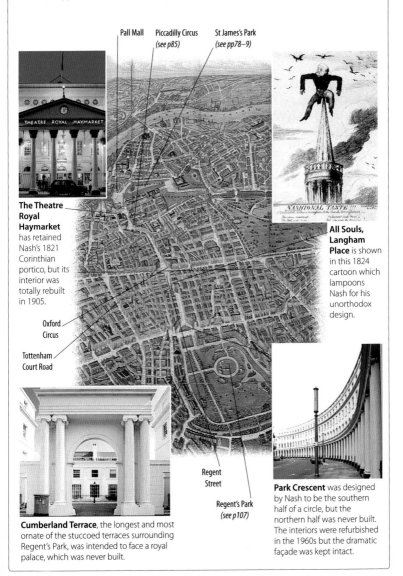

Pall Mall   Piccadilly Circus (see p85)   St James's Park (see pp78–9)

The Theatre Royal Haymarket has retained Nash's 1821 Corinthian portico, but its interior was totally rebuilt in 1905.

Oxford Circus

Tottenham Court Road

All Souls, Langham Place is shown in this 1824 cartoon which lampoons Nash for his unorthodox design.

Regent Street

Regent's Park (see p107)

Cumberland Terrace, the longest and most ornate of the stuccoed terraces surrounding Regent's Park, was intended to face a royal palace, which was never built.

Park Crescent was designed by Nash to be the southern half of a circle, but the northern half was never built. The interiors were refurbished in the 1960s but the dramatic façade was kept intact.

❹ British Museum

The oldest public museum in the world, the British Museum was established in 1753 to house the collections of the physician Sir Hans Sloane (1660–1753). Sloane's collection has been added to by gifts and purchases from all over the world, and the museum now contains objects spanning millions of years. The main part of the building (1823–50) is by architect Robert Smirke, but the architectural highlight is the modern Great Court, with the Reading Room at its centre.

★ **Egyptian Mummies**
Animals such as this cat (30 BC) were preserved alongside humans by the ancient Egyptians.

Upper floors

Bronze Figure Shiva Nataraja
This statue of the Hindu God Shiva Nataraja (c.1100) from South India forms part of the fine collection of Oriental art.

Montague Place entrance

★ **Parthenon Sculptures**
These reliefs from the Parthenon in Athens were brought to London by Lord Elgin around 1802 and are housed in a special gallery.

Gallery Guide

The Greek and Roman, and Middle Eastern collections are found on all three levels of the museum, predominantly on the west side. The African collection is located on the lower floor, while Asian exhibits are found on the main and upper floors on the north side of the museum. The Americas collection is located in the northeast corner of the ground floor. Egyptian artifacts are found in the large gallery to the west of the Great Court and on the first floor.

Ground floor

Key to floorplan

- Asian collection
- Enlightenment
- Coins and medals
- Greek and Roman collection
- Egyptian collection
- Middle Eastern collection
- Europe collection
- Temporary exhibitions
- Non-exhibition space
- Africa, Oceania and the Americas

The Great Court is London's largest covered square, with shops, cafés, a restaurant, display areas and educational facilities.

First floor

65
53
64
54
52
55
51
50
49
41
46
40 39 47
36 38
37
70
68
69
69a

Paul Hamlyn Library

1

2

Reading Room

Main entrance

6

The Egyptian Gallery on the main floor houses the Rosetta Stone, the inscription that enabled 19th-century scholars to decipher Egyptian hieroglyphs.

Mildenhall Treasure
The Great Dish was among the 34 pieces of 4th-century Roman silver tableware ploughed up in Suffolk in 1942.

★ **Lindow Man**
The skin on this 2,000-year-old human body was preserved by the acids of a peat-bog in Cheshire. He was probably killed in an elaborate ritual.

Private gardens of Bedford Square

❺ Bloomsbury

WC1. **Map** 3 B4. Russell Sq,
Tottenham Court Rd. Charles Dickens
Museum 48 Doughty St WC1. **Tel** 020
7405 2127. **Open** 10am–5pm daily.
w dickensmuseum.com

Home to numerous writers and artists, Bloomsbury is a traditional centre of the book trade. It is dominated by the British Museum and the University of London and characterized by several fine Georgian squares. These include **Russell Square**, where the poet T S Eliot (1888–1965) worked for a publisher for 40 years; **Queen Square**, which contains a statue of Queen Charlotte, wife of George III; and **Bloomsbury Square**, laid out in 1661. A plaque here commemorates members of the Bloomsbury Group *(see p167)*. One of London's best-preserved 18th-century oases is **Bedford Square**. Charles Dickens *(see p193)* lived at 48 Doughty Street during a brief but critical stage in his career, and it was here that

Queen Charlotte (1744–1818)

he wrote *Oliver Twist* and *Nicholas Nickleby*, both completed in 1839.

His former home is now the **Charles Dickens Museum**, which has rooms laid out as they were in Dickens's time, with objects taken from his other London homes and first editions of many of his works.

THE CITY AND SOUTHWARK

Dominated today by glossy office blocks, the City is the oldest part of the capital. The Great Fire of 1666 obliterated four-fifths of its buildings. Sir Christopher Wren rebuilt much of it and many of his churches survived World War II *(see pp62–3)*. Commerce has always been the City's lifeblood, and the power of its merchants and bankers secured it a degree of autonomy from state control. Humming with activity in business hours, it empties at night.

In the Middle Ages Southwark, on the south bank of the Thames, was a refuge for pleasure-seekers, prostitutes, gamblers and criminals. Even after 1550, when the area fell under the jurisdiction of the City, its brothels and taverns thrived. There were also several bear-baiting arenas in which plays were staged until the building of theatres such as the Globe (1598), where many of Shakespeare's works were first performed. Relics of old Southwark are mostly on the water-front, which has been imaginatively redeveloped and provided with a pleasant walkway.

Sights at a Glance

Historic Sights and Buildings
- ❸ Temple
- ❼ Lloyd's Building
- ❽ Monument
- ❾ Tower of London *pp122–3*
- ❿ Tower Bridge
- ⓬ HMS Belfast
- ⓮ The Old Operating Theatre

Pub
- ⓯ George Inn

Museums and Galleries
- ❹ Sir John Soane's Museum
- ❻ Museum of London
- ⓫ Design Museum
- ⓭ The Shard
- ⓲ Shakespeare's Globe
- ⓳ Tate Modern

Market
- ⓰ Borough Market

Churches and Cathedral
- ❶ St Stephen Walbrook
- ❷ St Paul's Cathedral *pp118–19*
- ❺ St Bartholomew-the-Great
- ⓱ Southwark Cathedral

See also Street Finder maps 12, 13, 14

　　　　　　　　　　　　For keys to symbols *see back flap*

Street-by-Street: The City

This is the financial heart of London and has been ever since the Romans set up a trading post here 2,000 years ago. For years it was London's main residential area but today very few people live here. The City was severely bombed in World War II and the main clues to its past are streets named after vanished inns and markets. Its numerous churches, many built after the Great Fire of 1666 by the architect Sir Christopher Wren *(see p118)*, are now dwarfed by lavish banks and post-modern developments.

St Mary-le-Bow takes its name from the bow arches in the Norman crypt. Anyone born within earshot of its bells is said to be a true Cockney.

New Change replaces Old Change, a 13th-century street destroyed in World War II.

St Paul's station

Statue of Queen Anne

St Nicholas Cole Abbey was the first church Wren built in the City (in 1677). It had to be restored after World War II bomb damage.

Mansion House station

St James Garlickhythe contains unusual sword rests and hat stands, beneath Wren's elegant spire of 1717.

2 ★ St Paul's Cathedral
Built after the Great Fire, Wren's cathedral is a masterpiece of Baroque design.

COLLEGE · OF · ARMS

The College of Arms is the official repository of the coats of arms and pedigrees of British families *(see p34)*. It was rebuilt here, on its former site, in the 1670s after the Great Fire.

For hotels and restaurants in this area see pp560–73 and pp582–603

Mansion House *(1753)*, designed by George Dance the Elder, is the official home of the Lord Mayor. The Palladian façade is a familiar City landmark.

Locator Map
See Street Finder map 13

Bank of England Museum

The Royal Exchange was founded in 1565 by Sir Thomas Gresham as a centre for commerce. The current building dates from 1844.

Bank station

Lombard Street, named after bankers who came here from Lombardy in the 13th century, retains its traditional banking signs.

Key

— Suggested route

St Mary Abchurch owes its unusually spacious feel to Wren's large dome. The altar carving is by Grinling Gibbons.

0 metres 100
0 yards 100

❶ ★ **St Stephen Walbrook**
This fine Wren church contains a striking white stone altar by Henry Moore.

Skinners' Hall is an 18th-century Italianate building constructed for the ancient guild that controlled trade in fur and leather.

❶ St Stephen Walbrook

39 Walbrook EC4. **Map** 13 B2. **Tel** 020 7626 9000. 🚇 Bank, Cannon St. **Open** 10am–4pm Mon–Fri. **Closed** public hols. ✝ 12:45am Thu. 🌐 ststephenwalbrook.net

The Lord Mayor's parish church was built by Sir Christopher Wren in the 1670s and is among the finest of all his City churches. The bright, airy interior is flooded with light by a huge dome that appears to float above the eight columns and arches that support it. The dome, deep and coffered with ornate plasterwork, was a forerunner of St Paul's. Original fittings, such as the highly decorative font cover and pulpit canopy, contrast with the stark simplicity of Henry Moore's massive white stone altar (1987). The best time to see the church is during one of its free organ recitals from 12:30 to 1:30pm on Fridays.

❷ St Paul's

See pp118–19.

Effigies in Temple Church

❸ Temple

Inner Temple, King's Bench Walk EC4. **Tel** 020 7797 8250. **Map** 12 E2. 🚇 Temple. **Open** 6am–8pm Mon–Fri, all day Sat & Sun (grounds only). ♿ Middle Temple Hall, Middle Temple Ln EC4. **Tel** 020 7427 4800. **Open** for lunch (book ahead). ♿ 🌐 middletemplehall.org.uk Temple Church. **Tel** 020 7353 3470. **Open** 11am–1pm & 2–4pm Mon–Fri; Sun service. 📷 book ahead.

A cluster of atmospheric squares form the Inner and Middle Temples, two of London's four Inns of Court, where law students are trained. The name Temple derives from the medieval Knights Templar, a religious order which protec- ted pilgrims to the Holy Land and was based here until 1312. Marble effigies of knights lie on the floor of the circular Temple Church, part of which dates from the 12th century. Middle Temple Hall has a fine Elizabethan interior.

❺ St Bartholomew-the-Great

West Smithfield EC1. **Map** 12 F1. **Tel** 020 7248 2294. 🚇 Barbican, St Paul's. **Open** 8:30am–5pm (4pm in winter) Mon–Fri, 10:30am–4pm Sat, 8:30am–8pm Sun. **Closed** 1 Jan, 25, 26 Dec. 🐕 ♿ by appt. 📷 🎫 Concerts. 🌐 greatstbarts.com

The historic area of Smithfield has witnessed a number of bloody events over the years, among them the execution of rebel peasant leader Wat Tyler in 1381, and, in the reign of Mary I (1553–58), the burning of scores of Protestant martyrs.

❹ Sir John Soane's Museum

13 Lincoln's Inn Fields WC2. **Map** 12 D1. **Tel** 020 7405 2107. 🚇 Holborn. **Open** 10am–5pm Tue–Sat, 6–9pm 1st Tue of month. **Closed** public hols, 24 Dec. ♿ call ahead of your visit. 📷 see website for details. 🌐 soane.org

One of the most eccentric museums in London, this house was left to the nation by Sir John Soane in 1837, with a stipulation that nothing should be changed. The son of a bricklayer, Soane became one of Britain's leading late Georgian architects developing a restrained Neo-Classical style of his own. After marrying the niece of a wealthy builder, whose fortune he inherited, he bought and re-constructed No. 12 Lincoln's Inn Fields. In 1813 he and his wife moved into No. 13 and in 1824 he rebuilt No. 14, adding a picture gallery and the mock medieval Monk's Parlour. Today, true to Soane's wishes, the collections are much as he left them – an eclectic gathering of beautiful, instructional and often simply peculiar artifacts. There are casts, bronzes, vases, antique fragments, paintings and a selection of bizarre trivia which ranges from a giant fungus from Sumatra to a scold-bridle, a device designed to silence nagging wives. Highlights include the sarcophagus of Seti I, Soanes's own designs, including those for the Bank of England, models by leading Neo-Classical sculptors and the *Rake's Progress* series of paintings (1734) by William Hogarth, which Mrs Soane bought for £570.

The building itself is full of architectural surprises and illusions. In the main ground floor room, cunningly placed mirrors play tricks with light and space, while an atrium stretching from the basement to the glass-domed roof allows light on to every floor.

A glass dome lets light on to all the floors.

A vast sarcophagus (1300 BC) stands on the floor of the crypt.

Hidden in a quiet corner behind Smithfield meat market (central London's only surviving wholesale food market), this is one of London's oldest churches. It once formed part of a priory founded in 1123 by a monk, Rahere, whose tomb is here. He was Henry I's court jester until he dreamed that St Bartholomew had saved him from a winged monster.

The 13th-century arch, now topped by a Tudor gatehouse, used to be the entrance to the church until the old nave was pulled down during the Dissolution of the Monasteries (see pp54–5). The painter William Hogarth was baptized here in 1697. The church featured in the films *Four Weddings and a Funeral* and *Shakespeare in Love*.

Delft plate made in London 1600, Museum of London

◀ Bartholomew's gatehouse

❻ Museum of London

150 London Wall EC2. **Map** 13 A1. **Tel** 020 7001 9844. ⊖ Barbican, St Paul's. **Open** 10am–6pm daily. **Closed** 24–26 Dec. 🎫 ♿ 🚻 📷 🎦
ⓦ **museumoflondon.org.uk**

This museum traces life in London from prehistoric times to the outbreak of World War I. Displays of archaeological finds and domestic objects alternate with reconstructed street scenes and interiors. There is also a working model of the Great Fire of 1666 in the London's Burning section. The Roman London gallery has a brightly coloured 2nd-century fresco from a Southwark bath house.

Visitors can discover the city's many incarnations in the London Before London, Roman London and Medieval London galleries. The London Before London collection includes the remains of the Shepperton woman, thought to be between 5,100 and 5,640 years old. The Galleries of Modern London retell London's history from 1666 to the present day with over 4,000 objects and interactive exhibits.

Every wall is covered and every room filled with artifacts from Soane's voluminous collection.

In the picture gallery, panels covered with paintings unfold to reveal more works of art hidden behind them.

The Monk's Parlour is full of grotesque Gothic casts.

❷ St Paul's Cathedral

The Great Fire of London in 1666 left the medieval cathedral of St Paul's in ruins. Wren was commissioned to rebuild it, but his design for a church on a Greek Cross plan (where all four arms are equal) met with considerable resistance. The authorities insisted on a conventional Latin cross, with a long nave and short transepts, which was believed to focus the congregation's attention on the altar. Despite the compromises, Wren created a magnificent Baroque cathedral, which was built between 1675 and 1710 and has since formed the lavish setting for many state ceremonies.

★ West Front and Towers
Inspired by the Italian Baroque architect, Borromini, the towers were added by Wren in 1707.

The Nave
An imposing succession of massive arches and saucer domes open out into the vast space below the cathedral's main dome.

KEY

① **The West Portico** consists of two storeys of coupled Corinthian columns, topped by a pediment carved with reliefs showing the Conversion of St Paul.

② **The balustrade** along the top of the dome was added in 1718 against Wren's wishes.

③ **The lantern** weighs a massive 700 tonnes.

④ **The Golden Gallery** has splendid views over London.

⑤ **The oculus** is an opening through which the cathedral floor can be seen.

⑥ **Stone Gallery**

⑦ **The High Altar** canopy was made in the 1950s, based on designs by Wren.

⑧ **Entrance to crypt,** which has many memorials to the famous.

⑨ **The South Portico** was inspired by the porch of Santa Maria della Pace in Rome.

⑩ **West Porch**

Main entrance approached from Ludgate Hill

★ **Dome**
At 111 m (360 ft), the elaborate dome is one of the highest in the world.

★ **Whispering Gallery**
The dome's unusual acoustics mean that words whispered against the wall can be heard clearly on the opposite side.

Choir
Jean Tijou, a Huguenot refugee, created much of the fine wrought iron-work in Wren's time, including these choir screens.

Entrance to Golden, Whispering and Stone galleries

Christopher Wren

Trained as a scientist, Sir Christopher Wren (1632–1723) began his impressive architectural career at the age of 31. He became a leading figure in the rebuilding of London after the Great Fire of 1666, building a total of 52 new churches. Although Wren never visited Italy, his work was influenced by Roman, Baroque and Renaissance architecture, as is apparent in his masterpiece, St Paul's Cathedral.

Choir Stalls
The 17th-century choir stalls and organ case were made by Grinling Gibbons (1648–1721), a wood-carver from Rotterdam. He and his team of craftsmen worked on these intricate carvings for two years.

Richard Rogers's Lloyd's building

❼ Lloyd's Building

1 Lime St EC3. **Map** 13 C2. **Tel** 020 7327 1000. ⊖ Monument, Bank, Aldgate.

Lloyd's was founded in the late 17th century and soon became the world's main insurers, issuing policies on everything from oil tankers to Betty Grable's legs. The present building, designed by Richard Rogers, dates from 1986 and is one of the most interesting modern buildings in London. Its exaggerated stainless-steel external piping and high-tech ducts echo Rogers' forceful Pompidou Centre in Paris. Lloyd's is well worth seeing floodlit at night.

❽ Monument

Monument St EC3. **Map** 13 C2. **Tel** 020 7626 2717. ⊖ Monument. **Open** 9:30am–5:30pm daily. **Closed** 1 Jan, 24–26 Dec. ♿ 🚻 **themonument.info**

This doric column, designed by Wren to commemorate the Great Fire of London that devastated the original walled city in September 1666, was, in 1681, the tallest isolated stone column in the world. Topped with a bronze flame, the Monument is 62 m (205 ft) high; the exact distance west to Pudding Lane, where the fire is believed to have started. Reliefs around the column's base show Charles II restoring the city after the tragedy.

The now restored column has 311 tightly spiralled steps that lead to a tiny viewing platform. (In 1842, it was enclosed with an iron cage to prevent suicides.) The steep climb is well worth the effort as the views from the top are spectacular and visitors are rewarded with a certificate.

❾ Tower of London

See pp122–3.

❿ Tower Bridge

SE1. **Map** 14 D3. **Tel** 020 7403 3761. ⊖ Tower Hill. The Tower Bridge Exhibition: **Open** Apr–Sep: 10am–6pm daily; Oct–Mar: 9:30am–5:30pm daily (last adm: 4pm). **Closed** 24–26 Dec. ♿ 🔊 access lift. 🚻 📷 **towerbridge.org.uk**

This flamboyant piece of Victorian engineering, designed by Sir Horace Jones, was completed in 1894 and soon became a symbol of London. Its two Gothic towers contain the mechanism for raising the roadway to permit large ships to pass through. The towers are made of a supporting steel framework clad in stone, and are linked by two high-level walkways which were closed between 1909 and 1982 due to their popularity with suicides and prostitutes. The bridge now houses The Tower Bridge Exhibition, with interactive displays bringing the bridge's history to life. There are fine river views from the walkways, and a look at the steam engine room that powered the lifting machinery until 1976, when the system was electrified.

Walkways, open to the public, give panoramic views over the Thames and London.

The roadway, when raised, creates a space 40 m (135 ft) high and 60 m (200 ft) wide, big enough for large cargo ships.

Engine room

South Bank

Lifts and 300 steps lead to the top of the towers.

The Victorian winding machinery was originally powered by steam.

Entrance

North Bank

⓫ Design Museum

Butlers Wharf, Shad Thames SE1.
Map 14 E4. **Tel** 020 7403 6033.
🚇 Tower Hill, London Bridge.
Open 10am–5:45pm daily (last adm:
5:15pm). **Closed** 25 & 26 Dec. 🅿️ ♿
🍴 Blueprint Café: 020 7940 8785 for
reservations. ♿ 🎁 🛒 📷
🌐 **designmuseum.org**

This museum was the first in the
world to be devoted solely to
modern and contemporary
design when it was founded
in 1989. A frequently changing
programme of exhibitions
explores landmarks in modern
design history and the most
exciting innovations in
contemporary design set
against the context of social,
cultural, economic and
technological changes. The
Design Museum embraces every
area of design, from furniture
and fashion, to household
products, cars, graphics,
websites and architecture in
exhibitions and new design
commissions. Each spring the
museum hosts Designer of the
Year, a national design prize,
with an exhibition at which the
public can vote for the winner.

The museum is arranged
over three floors, with major
exhibitions on the first floor.
There is a choice of smaller
displays on the second, which
also houses an Interaction
Space, where visitors can play
vintage video games and learn
about the designers featured in
the museum in the Design at
the Design Museum online
research archive. The shop and
café are on the ground floor. On
the first floor is the **Blueprint
Café** restaurant, which has
stunning views of the Thames
(booking ahead recommended).

Exterior of the Design Museum

The familiar sight of the naval gunship
HMS *Belfast* on the Thames

⓬ HMS Belfast

The Queen's Walk, SE1. **Map** 13 C3.
Tel 020 7940 6300. 🚇 London Bridge,
Tower Hill. **Open** 10am–6pm daily
(Nov–Feb: to 5pm) (last adm: 1 hr
before closing). **Closed** 24–26 Dec.
🅿️ ♿ limited. 🛒 📷 🌐 iwm.org.
uk/visits/hms-belfast

Originally launched in 1938
to serve in World War II, the
11,500-ton warship HMS
Belfast was instrumental in the
destruction of the German
battle cruiser *Scharnhorst* in
the battle of North Cape, and
also played an important role
in the Normandy Landings.

After the war, the warship,
designed for offensive action
and for supporting amphibious
operations, was sent to work for
the United Nations in Korea. The
ship remained in service with
the British navy until 1965.

Since 1971, *Belfast* has been
a floating museum, part of the
Imperial War Museums. Some
of it has been atmospherically
recreated to show what the
ship was like in 1943, when it
participated in sinking the
German battle cruiser. Other
displays portray life on board
during World War II, and there
are also general exhibits which
relate to the history of the Royal
Navy, as well as an interactive
Operations Room.

As well as being a great family
day out, on selected weekends
it is also possible for children
to participate in activities
and events that take place
on board the ship.

⓭ The Shard

London Bridge St, SE1. **Map** 13 B4.
Tel 0844 499 7111 (bookings). 🚇
London Bridge. **Open** 9am–10pm
daily. **Closed** 25 Dec. 🅿️ ♿ 📷
🌐 **theviewfromtheshard.com**

Designed by Italian architect
Renzo Piano, The Shard is the
tallest building in Western
Europe. At 310 m (1,016 ft) tall,
it dominates the London
skyline, its appearance changing
with the weather due to the
crystalline façade that reflects the
sunlight and sky. The building's
95 floors are home to offices, top
restaurants, the 5-star Shangri-
La hotel, and apartments, as
well as observation gallery The
View, which allows visitors
360-degree panoramas
covering 40 miles (64 km). There
are also multi-media displays on
the top four floors.

The Shard dominating the skyline

⓮ The Old
Operating Theatre

9a St Thomas St SE1. **Map** 13 B4.
Tel 020 7188 2679. 🚇 London Bridge.
Open 10:30am–5pm daily.
Closed 15 Dec– 5 Jan. 🅿️ 📷 ♿
partial. 🌐 **thegarret.org.uk**

St Thomas's Hospital stood here
from its foundation in the 12th
century until it was moved west
in 1862. At this time most of its
buildings were demolished to
make way for the railway. The
women's operating theatre (The
Old Operating Theatre Museum
and Herb Garret) survived only
because it was located away
from the main buildings, in a
garret over the hospital church.
It lay, bricked up and forgotten,
until the 1950s. Britain's oldest
operating theatre, dating back
to 1822, it has now been fitted
out as it would have been in the
early 19th century.

❾ Tower of London

Soon after William the Conqueror became king in 1066, he built a fortress here to guard the entrance to London from the Thames Estuary. In 1097 the White Tower was completed in sturdy stone; other fine buildings have been added over the centuries. The tower has served as a royal residence, armoury, treasury and, most famously, as a prison. Some were tortured here and among those who met their death were the "Princes in the Tower", the sons and heirs of Edward IV. Today the tower is a popular attraction, housing the Crown Jewels and other exhibits, such as the displays about the Peasants' Revolt of 1381, the only time the Tower's walls were breached. The most celebrated residents are the ravens; legend has it that the kingdom will fall if they desert the tower. All guided tours are led by the colourful Beefeaters.

★ **Jewel House**
Among the magnificent Crown Jewels is the Sceptre with the Cross (1660), which contains the world's biggest diamond.

Beauchamp Tower
Many high-ranking prisoners were held here, often with their own retinues of servants. The tower was built by Edward I around 1281.

Queen's House
This Tudor building is the sovereign's official residence at the Tower.

Main entrance from Tower Hill

KEY

① **Two 13th-century curtain walls** protect the tower.

② **Tower Green** was the execution site for favoured prisoners, away from crowds on Tower Hill, where many had to submit to public execution. Seven people died here, including two of Henry VIII's six wives, Anne Boleyn and Catherine Howard.

The Crown Jewels

The world's best-known collection of precious objects, now displayed in a splendid exhibition room, includes the gorgeous regalia of crowns, sceptres, orbs and swords used at coronations and other state occasions. Most date from 1661, when Charles II commissioned replacements for regalia destroyed by Parliament after the execution of Charles I (see pp56–7). Only a few older pieces survived, hidden by royalist clergymen until the Restoration – notably, Edward the Confessor's sapphire ring, said to be incorporated into the Imperial State Crown (see p77). The crown was made for Queen Victoria in 1837 and has been used at every coronation since.

The Sovereign's Orb (1661), a hollow gold sphere encrusted with jewels

"Beefeaters"
Thirty-seven
Yeomen Warders
guard the Tower
and live here.
Their uniforms
date back to
Tudor times.

★ **White Tower**
When the tower was finished in
1097, it was the tallest building
in London at 27 m (90 ft) high.

VISITORS' CHECKLIST

Practical Information
Tower Hill EC3. **Map** 14 D3.
Tel 0844 482 7799 for advance
booking. **W** hrp.org.uk
Open Mar–Oct: 9am–5:30pm
daily (from 10am Sun & Mon);
Nov–Feb: 9am–4:30pm daily
(from 10am Sun & Mon).
Closed 1 Jan, 24–26 Dec.
limited, except Jewel House.
Ceremony of the Keys:
9:30pm daily (book in advance).

Transport
Tower Hill; Tower Gateway
(DLR). RV1, 15, X15, 25, 42,
78, 100, D1, D9, D11.
Fenchurch Street.

★ **Chapel of St John**
This austerely beautiful Romanesque
chapel is a particularly fine
example of Norman architecture.

Traitors' Gate
The infamous entrance was used
for prisoners brought from trial in
Westminster Hall.

Bloody Tower
A permanent display
explores the mysterious
disappearance of Edward
IV's two sons, who were
put here by their uncle,
Richard of Gloucester
(later Richard III), after
their father died in 1483.
The princes disappeared,
and Richard was crowned
later that year. In 1674 the
skeletons of two children
were found nearby.

The George Inn, owned by the National Trust

⑮ George Inn

77 Borough High St SE1. **Map** 13 B4. **Tel** 020 7407 2056. 🚇 London Bridge, Borough. **Open** 11am–11pm Mon–Sat, noon–10:30pm Sun **Closed** 25 & 26 Dec. 🚫 NT

Dating from the 17th century, this building is the only traditional galleried coaching inn left in London and is mentioned in Dickens's *Little Dorrit*. It was rebuilt after the Southwark fire of 1676 in a style that dates back to the Middle Ages. There were originally three wings around a courtyard, where plays were staged in the 17th century. In 1889 the north and east wings were demolished, so there is only one wing remaining.

The inn is still a popular pub with a comfortable atmosphere, perfect on a cold, damp day. In the summer, the yard fills with picnic tables, and patrons are occasionally entertained by actors and morris dancers. The house bitter is highly recommended.

⑯ Borough Market

8 Southwark St SE1. **Map** 13 B4. **Tel** 020 7407 1002. 🚇 London Bridge. Retail market: **Open** 10am–3pm Mon–Wed, 11am–5pm Thu, noon–6pm Fri, 8am–5pm Sat.

Borough Market was until recently a wholesale fruit and vegetable market, which had its origins in medieval times, and moved to its current position beneath the railway tracks in 1756.

This hugely popular fine-food market has now become well established, selling gourmet foods from Britain and abroad, as well as quality fruit and vegetables, to locals and tourists alike.

Shakespeare window (1954), Southwark Cathedral

⑰ Southwark Cathedral

Montague Close SE1. **Map** 13 B3. **Tel** 020 7367 6700. 🚇 London Bridge. **Open** 8am–6pm daily (from 8:30am Sat & Sun); limited access during services. 📷 📅 ♿ 🚻 W **cathedral. southwark.anglican.org**

Although some parts of this building date back to the 12th century, it became a cathedral only in 1905. Many original features remain, notably the tomb of the poet John Gower (c.1325–1408), a contemporary of Chaucer *(see p176)*. There is a monument to Shakespeare, carved in 1912, and a memorial window *(above)* installed in 1954.

⑱ Shakespeare's Globe

21 New Globe Walk SE1. **Map** 13 A3. **Tel** 020 7902 1500. Box office: 020 7401 9919. 🚇 Southwark, London Bridge. Exhibition: **Open** Late Apr–early Oct: 9am–5:30pm daily; early Oct–late Apr: 10am–5:30pm daily. **Closed** 24, 25 Dec. 📷 ♿ 🚻 every 30 mins. (Rose Theatre tours for groups of 15 or more by appt only). Performances late Apr–early Oct. ♿ limited. 🚫 📷 📅 W **shakespearesglobe.com**

Opened in 1997, this circular building is a faithful reproduction of an Elizabethan theatre, close to the site of the original Globe where many of Shakespeare's plays were first performed. It was built using handmade bricks and oak laths, fastened with wooden pegs rather than metal screws, and has the first thatched roof allowed in London since the Great Fire of 1666. The theatre was erected thanks to a heroic campaign by the American actor and director Sam Wanamaker. Open to the elements (although the seats are protected), it operates only in the summer, and seeing a play here can be a thrilling experience, with top-quality acting under the artistic direction of Mark Rylance among others.

Beneath the theatre, Shakespeare's Globe Exhibition is open all year and covers many aspects of Shakespeare's work and times. Groups of 15 or more may book to see the foundations of the nearby Rose Theatre.

Shakespeare's *Henry IV* (performed at the Globe Theatre around 1600)

⑲ Tate Modern

Holland St, SE1. **Map** 13 A3. **Tel** 020 7887 8888. 🚇 Blackfriar's, Southwark. 🚌 to Tate Britain every 40 mins. **Open** 10am–6pm Sun–Thu, 10am–10pm Fri & Sat. **Closed** 24–26 Dec. 🎟 major exhibitions. ♿ ✍ 📷 📷 🌐 **tate.org.uk/modern**

Looming over the southern bank of the Thames, Tate Modern occupies the converted Bankside power station, a dynamic space for one of the world's premier collections of contemporary art. Tate Modern draws its main displays from the expansive Tate Collection, also shown at the other Tate galleries: Tate St Ives *(p277)*, Tate Liverpool *(p377)* and Tate Britain *(p91)*. The displays change frequently and works are sometimes moved temporarily, loaned out or removed for restoration. Works shown on these pages are examples of what might be on display. A river boat, *Tate to Tate*, transports visitors between Tate Modern and Tate Britain.

The gallery's west entrance leads straight into the massive Turbine Hall. Each year an artist is commissioned to install in this space. Louise Bourgeois was the first to do so, creating three giant towers and a gargantuan spider, *Maman* (2000). In 2010, Ai Weiwei's *Sunflower Seeds* filled part of the Turbine Hall with 100 million hand-crafted porcelain seeds.

An escalator whisks visitors from the Turbine Hall, up to level 2 where the main galleries are located. In a break with convention, Tate Modern organizes its displays by theme rather than chronology or school – a practice that cuts across movements and mixes up media. Four themes based on traditional genres reveal how traditions have been confronted, extended or rejected by artists throughout the 20th and into the 21st centuries.

Tate Modern's displays are arranged into two thematic wings on levels 3, 4 and 5. The collection focuses on key periods of twentieth-century art history including: Cubism; Surrealism; Abstract Expressionism; Constructivism; and Minimalism. At the centre of each of the four exhibitions is a focal display, from which all the other displays rotate.

Inverno from *Quattro Stagioni* (1993–4) by Cy Twombly

The Turbine Hall is used for temporary exhibitions of large-scale work

The collection includes works such as the iconic paintings *The Snail* by Henri Matisse and *Quattro Stagioni* by Cy Twombly, as well as the sculpture, *Fish* by Constantin Brancusi and other important pieces by the likes of Francis Picabia and Mark Rothko. To complement its permanent collection, Tate Modern presents a dynamic programme of temporary exhibitions, including three large-scale shows per year. Major live events are staged each year, taking their inspiration from the Collection. A striking new extension is currently being added to the south side of the gallery, which will double exhibition space. Three oil tanks, from the original power station, will form the foundations.

Fish (1926) by Constantin Brancusi

Bankside Power Station

This forbidding fortress was designed in 1947 by Sir Giles Gilbert Scott, the architect of Battersea Power Station, Waterloo Bridge and London's famous red telephone boxes. The power station is of a steel-framed brick skin construction, comprising over 4.2 million bricks. The Turbine Hall was designed to accommodate huge oil-burning generators and three vast oil tanks are still in situ, buried under the ground just south of the building. The tanks are to be employed in a future stage of Tate Modern development. The power station itself was converted by Swiss architects Herzog and de Meuron who designed the two-storey glass box, or lightbeam, which runs the length of the building. This serves to flood the upper galleries with light and also provides wonderful views of London.

The façade, chimney and light beam of Tate Modern

FURTHER AFIELD

Over the centuries London has steadily expanded to embrace the scores of villages that surrounded it, leaving the City as a reminder of London's original boundaries. Although now linked in an almost unbroken urban sprawl, many of these areas have maintained their old village atmosphere and character. Hampstead and Highgate are still distinct enclaves, as are artistic Chelsea and literary Islington. Greenwich, Chiswick and Richmond have retained features that hark back to the days when the Thames was an important artery for transport and commerce, while just to the east of the City the wide expanses of the for-mer docks have, in the last 20 years, been imaginatively rebuilt as new commercial and residential areas.

Sights at a Glance

1. Chelsea
2. Holland Park
3. Notting Hill and Portobello Road
4. Hampstead
5. Hampstead Heath
6. Highgate
7. Camden and Islington
8. East End and Docklands
9. Greenwich
10. Chiswick
11. Richmond and Kew

Key

- Main sightseeing areas
- Greater London
- Parks
- Motorway
- Major road
- Minor road

❶ Chelsea

SW3. ⊖ Sloane Square. **Map** 17 B2.

Riverside Chelsea has been fashionable since Tudor times when Sir Thomas More, Henry VIII's Lord Chancellor (see p54), lived here. The river views

Statue of Sir Thomas More (1478–1535), Cheyne Walk

attracted artists and the arrival of the historian Thomas Carlyle and essayist Leigh Hunt in the 1830s began a literary connection. Blue plaques on the houses of **Cheyne Walk** celebrate former residents such as J M W Turner (see p95) and writers George Eliot, Henry James and T S Eliot.

Chelsea's artistic tradition is maintained by its galleries and antique shops, many of them scattered among the clothes boutiques on **King's Road**. This begins at **Sloane Square**, named after the physician Sir Hans Sloane, who bought the manor of Chelsea in 1712. Sloane expanded the **Chelsea Physic Garden** (1673) along Swan Walk to cultivate plants and herbs.

Wren's **Royal Hospital**, on Royal Hospital Road was built in 1692 as a retirement home for old soldiers and still houses 400 Chelsea Pensioners.

Arab Hall, Leighton House (1866)

❷ Holland Park

W8, W14. ⊖ Holland Park. **Map** 7 B5.

This park is more intimate than the large royal parks such as Hyde Park (see p105). It was opened in 1952 on the grounds of **Holland House**, a centre of social and political intrigue in its 19th-century heyday.

Around the park are some magnificent late Victorian houses. **Linley Sambourne House** was built about 1870 and has received a much-needed facelift, though it remains much as Sambourne furnished it, in the Victorian manner, with china ornaments and heavy velvet drapes. He was a political cartoonist for the satirical magazine *Punch* and drawings cram the walls.

Leighton House, built for the Neo- Classical painter Lord Leighton in 1866, has been preserved as an extraordinary monument to the Victorian Aesthetic movement. The highlight is the Arab Hall, which was added in 1879 to house Leighton's stupendous collection of 13th- to 17th- century Islamic tiles. The best paintings include some by Leighton himself and by his contemporaries Edward Burne-Jones and John Millais.

Linley Sambourne House
18 Stafford Terrace W8. **Tel** Mon–Fri: 020 7602 3316; Sat & Sun: 020 7938 1295. ⊖ High St Ken. **Open** Wed, Sat & Sun (tours only, from 11:15am). 🚻 📷 compulsory. 📷

Leighton House
12 Holland Park Rd W14. **Tel** 020 7602 3316. ⊖ High St Ken. **Open** 10am–5:30pm Wed–Mon. **Closed** public hols. 🚻 📷 Wed & Sun. 🔍 📷

❺ Notting Hill and Portobello Road

W11. ⊖ Notting Hill Gate. **Map** 7 B2.

In the 1950s and 60s, Notting Hill became a centre for the Caribbean community and today it is a vibrant cosmo-politan part of London. It is also home to Europe's largest street carnival *(see p67)* which began in 1965 and takes over the entire area on the August bank holiday weekend, when costumed parades flood through the crowded streets.

Nearby, Portobello Road market *(see pp152–3)* has a bustling atmosphere with hundreds of stalls and shops selling a variety of collectables.

❹ Hampstead

NW3, N6. ⊖ Hampstead. ⊟ Hampstead Heath.

On a high ridge north of the metropolis, Hampstead is essentially a Georgian village with many perfectly maintained mansions and houses. It is one of London's most desirable residential areas, home to a community of artists and writers since Georgian times.

Situated in a quiet Hampstead street, **Keats House** (1816) is an evocative tribute to the life and work of the poet John Keats (1795–1821). Keats lived here for two years before his tragic death from consumption at the age of 25, and it was under a plum tree in the garden that he wrote his celebrated *Ode to a Nightingale*.

Georgian house, Hampstead

Mementoes of Keats and of Fanny Brawne, the neighbour to whom he was engaged, are on show. Extensive displays include paintings, prints, artifacts and the engagement ring that Keats gave to Fanny Brawne.

The **Freud Museum**, which opened in 1986, is dedicated to the dramatic life of Sigmund Freud (1856–1939), the founder of psychoanalysis. At the age of 82, Freud fled from Nazi persecution in Vienna to this Hampstead house where he lived and worked for the last year of his life. His daughter Anna, pioneer of child psychoanalysis, continued to live here until her death in 1982. Inside, Freud's rich Viennese-style consulting rooms remain unaltered, and 1930s home movies show moments of Freud's life, including scenes of the Nazi attack on his home in Vienna.

Keats House
Keats Grove NW3. **Tel** 020 7332 3868. ⊖ Hampstead, Belsize Pk. **Open** 1–5pm Tue–Sun (Nov–Feb: Fri–Sun). 🦽 partial. 📷 🌐 keatshouse.cityoflondon.gov.uk

Freud Museum
20 Maresfield Gdns NW3. **Tel** 020 7435 2002. ⊖ Finchley Rd. **Open** noon–5pm Wed–Sun. 🚻 🔍 🦽 limited. 📷 🌐 freud.org.uk

Antique shop on Portobello Road

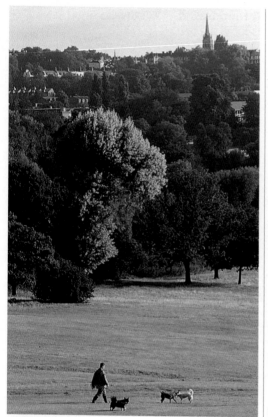

View east across Hampstead Heath to Highgate

❻ Highgate

N6. ⊖ Highgate, Archway.

A settlement since the Middle Ages, Highgate, became a fashionable aristocratic retreat in the 16th century. Today, it still has an exclusive rural feel, aloof from the urban sprawl below, with a Georgian high street and many expensive houses.

Highgate Cemetery *(see p79)*, with its monuments and hidden corners, has an extraordinary, magical atmosphere. Tour guides (daily in summer, weekends in winter) tell of the many tales of intrigue, mystery and vandalism connected with the cemetery since it opened in 1839. In the eastern section is the tomb of Victorian novelist George Eliot (1819–80) and of the cemetery's most famous incumbent, Karl Marx (1818–83).

🏛 **Highgate Cemetery**
Swains Lane N6. **Tel** 020 8340 1834.
⊖ Archway, Highgate. **Open** daily;
Western Cemetery by guided tour only. **Closed** during burials, 25–26 Dec. 🚫 📷 ♿
ⓦ highgate-cemetery.org

❼ Camden and Islington

NW1, N1. Camden: ⊖ Camden Town, Chalk Farm. Islington: ⊖ Angel, Highbury & Islington.

Camden is a lively area packed with restaurants, shops and a busy **market** *(see p152–3)*. Thousands of people come here each weekend to browse among the stalls or simply to soak up the atmosphere of the lively cobbled area around the canal, which is enhanced by the buskers and street performers.

Neighbouring Islington was once a fashionable spa but the rich moved out in the late 18th century and the area deteriorated rapidly. In the 20th century, writers such as Evelyn Waugh, George Orwell and Joe Orton lived here. Islington has been rediscovered and is now fashionable, being one of the first areas in London to become "gentrified", with many residents renovating the old houses.

❺ Hampstead Heath

N6. ⊖ Hampstead, Highgate.
🚇 Hampstead Heath.

Separating the hill-top villages of Hampstead and Highgate, the open spaces of Hampstead Heath are a precious retreat from the city. There are meadows, lakes and ponds for bathing and fishing, and fine views over the capital from **Parliament Hill**, to the east.

Situated in landscaped grounds high on the edge of the Heath is the magnificent **Kenwood House**, where classical concerts *(see p158)* are held by the lake in summer. The house was remodelled by Robert Adam *(see p32)* in 1764 and most of his interiors have survived, the highlight of which is the library. The mansion is filled with Old Master paintings, such as works by Van Dyck, Vermeer, Turner *(see p95)* and Romney; the star attraction is Rembrandt's self-portrait of 1663.

🏛 **Kenwood House**
Hampstead Lane NW3. **Tel** 020 8348 1286. **Open** 10am–5pm daily. ♿ 📷 🏠 EH ⓦ english-heritage.org.uk

Handmade crafts and antiques, Camden Lock indoor market

❽ East End and Docklands

E1, E2, E14. East End: 🔵 Aldgate East, Liverpool St, Bethnal Green. Docklands: 🔵 Canary Wharf.

In the Middle Ages the East End was full of craftsmen practising noxious trades such as brewing, bleaching and vinegar-making, which were banned within the City. The area has also been home to numerous immigrant communities since the 17th century, when French Huguenots, escaping religious persecution moved into Spitalfields and made it a silk-weaving centre. Textiles continued to dominate in the 1880s, when Jewish tailors and furriers set up workshops here, and in the 1950s, when Bengali machinists worked in cramped conditions.

A good way to get a taste of the East End is to explore its Sunday street markets *(see p153)* and sample freshly baked bagels and spicy Indian food. By way of contrast, anyone interested in contemporary architecture should visit the **Docklands**, an ambitious redevelopment of disused docks, dominated by the Canada Tower. Other attractions include the **V&A Museum of Childhood**, a delightful toy museum with lots of activities, **Dennis Severs' House**, in which you are taken on a historic journey from the 17th to the 19th centuries, and the **Museum of London, Docklands** that explores the history of London's river and port. See p117 for the website.

Canada Tower, Canary Wharf

Royal Naval College framing the Queen's House, Greenwich

🏛 **V&A Museum of Childhood**
Cambridge Heath Rd E2. **Tel** 020 8983 5200. **Open** 10am–5:45pm daily (9pm first Thu of month). **Closed** 1 Jan, 25 & 26 Dec. ♿ 🖥 📷 **w** vam.ac.uk/moc

🏛 **Dennis Severs' House**
18 Folgate St E1. **Tel** 020 7247 4013. **Open** noon–2pm Mon after 1st & 3rd Sun of month, Mon eve (by candle-light), noon–4pm Sun. 🚫 💳
w dennissevershouse.co.uk

❾ Greenwich

SE10. 🚆 Greenwich, Maze Hill. 🔵 Cutty Sark (DLR).

The world's time has been measured from the **Royal Observatory Greenwich** (now housing a museum) since 1884. The area is full of maritime and royal history, with Neo-Classical mansions, a park, antique shops and markets *(see pp152–3)*.

The **Queen's House**, designed by Inigo Jones for James I's wife, was comp-leted in 1637 for Henrietta Maria, the queen of Charles I. Its highlights include the perfectly cubic main hall and the spiral "tulip staircase".

An 18th-century compass, National Maritime Museum

The adjoining **National Maritime Museum** has exhibits that range from primitive canoes, through Elizabethan galleons, to modern ships. The **Old Royal Naval College** was designed by Christopher Wren *(see p118)* in two halves so that the Queen's House kept its river view. The Rococo chapel and the 18th-century *trompe l'oeil* Painted Hall are open to the public.

The majestic **Cutty Sark** was built in 1869 as a tea carrier and made its final voyage in 1938. In 2007 the ship was seriously damaged by fire. It was re-opened in 2012 following major renovations.

🏛 **Royal Observatory Greenwich**
Greenwich Park SE10. **Tel** 020 8858 4422. **Open** 10am–5pm daily. **Closed** 24–26 Dec. 📷
w rog.nmm.ac.uk

🏛 **Queen's House and National Maritime Museum**
Romney Rd SE10. **Tel** 020 8858 4422. **Open** daily. **Closed** 24–26 Dec. ♿ 🖥 📷 **w** nmm.ac.uk

🏛 **Old Royal Naval College**
King William Walk, SE10. **Tel** 020 8269 4799. **Open** 10am–5pm daily. **Closed** public hols. 🚫 🖥 📷

🏛 **Cutty Sark**
King William Walk, SE10. **Tel** 020 8858 4422. **Open** 10am–5pm daily. **Closed** 25 & 26 Dec. 🚫 ♿ 🖥 📷

⑩ Chiswick

W4. 🚇 Chiswick.

Chiswick is a pleasant suburb of London, with pubs, cottages and a variety of birdlife, such as herons, along the picturesque riverside. One of the main reasons for a visit is **Chiswick House**, a magnificent country villa inspired by the Renaissance architect Andrea Palladio. It was designed in the early 18th century by the 3rd Earl of Burlington as an annexe to his larger house (demolished in 1758), so that he could display his art collection and entertain friends.

Heron

🏛 Chiswick House

Burlington Lane W4. **Tel** 020 8995 0508. **Open** Feb & Mar: Sat & Sun; Apr–Oct: Sun–Wed & bank hols. Garden: **Open** dawn–dusk daily. 🏛 for house. ♿ call ahead. 🖥 📷 🅦 chgt.org.uk

⑪ Richmond and Kew

SW15. 🚇 🚆 Richmond.

The attractive village of Richmond took its name from a palace built by Henry VII (the former Earl of Richmond in Yorkshire) in 1500, the remains of which can be seen off the green. Nearby is the expansive **Richmond Park**, which was once Charles I's royal hunting ground. In summer, boats sail down the Thames from Westminster Millennium Pier,

making a pleasant day's excursion from central London.

The nobility continued to favour Richmond after royalty had left, and some of their mansions have survived. The Palladian villa, **Marble Hill House**, was built in 1724–9 for the mistress of George II and has been restored to its original appearance. On the opposite side of the Thames, the brooding **Ham House**, built in 1610, had its heyday later that century when it became the home of the Duke and Duchess of Lauderdale. Elizabeth Countess of Dysart inherited the house from her father, who had been Charles I's "whipping boy" – meaning that he was punished whenever the future king misbehaved. He was rewarded as an adult by being given a peerage and the lease of Ham estate.

A little further north along the Thames, **Syon House** has been inhabited by the Dukes and Earls of Northumberland for over 400 years. Numerous attractions here include a butterfly house, a museum of historic cars and a spectacular conservatory built in 1830. The lavish Neo-Classical interiors of the house, created by Robert Adam in the 1760s *(see p32)*, remain the highlight.

On the riverbank to the south, **Kew Gardens**, the world's most complete botanic gardens,

Brewers Lane, Richmond

feature examples of nearly every plant that can be grown in Britain. There are also conservatories displaying thousands of exotic tropical blooms.

🏛 Marble Hill House

Richmond Rd, Twickenham. **Tel** 020 8892 5115. **Open** prebooked tours only. 🏛 ♿ limited. ∥ 🖥 📷 🇪🇭

🏛 Ham House

Ham St, Richmond. **Tel** 020 8940 1950. **Open** Apr–Oct: Sat–Thu. Gardens: **Open** daily. 🏛 ♿ 🖥 📷 🇳🇹

🏛 Syon House

London Rd, Brentford. **Tel** 020 8560 0882. House: **Open** mid-Mar–Oct: Wed, Thu, Sun & pub hols. Gardens: **Open** daily (winter: Sat & Sun only). 🏛 📷 ♿ gardens only. 🖥 📷 🅦 syonpark.co.uk

🌿 Kew Gardens

Royal Botanic Gdns, Kew Green, Richmond. **Tel** 020 8332 5655. **Open** daily. **Closed** 1 Jan, 24–25 Dec. 🏛 ♿ 📷 ∥ 🖥 📷 🅦 kew.org

Chiswick House

LONDON STREET FINDER

The map references given with the sights, hotels, restaurants, shops and entertainment venues based in central London refer to the following four maps. All the main places of interest within the central area are marked on the maps in addition to useful practical information, such as tube, railway and coach stations. The key map below shows the area of London that is covered by the Street Finder. The four main city-centre areas (colour-coded in pink) are shown in more detail on the inside back cover.

Key

Major sight	Police station
Other sight	Church
Other building	Synagogue
Underground station	Railway line
Railway station	Motorway
Coach/bus station	Pedestrian street
River boat boarding point	«56 House number (main street)
Tourist information	
Hospital with casualty unit	

Scale of Map Pages

0 metres   200
0 yards   200   **1:11,000**

WESTWAY A40(M)

LORD HILLS BRIDGE
Royal Oak

NORTH WHARF RD

Paddington

LONDON STREET

WYNYARD ST

1

OURNE PARK VILLAS

STBOURNE PARK ROAD

WESTBOURNE

BRIDGE

ROAD

EASTBOURNE

TERRACE

WESTBOURNE GDNS

GLOUCESTER TERRACE

GLOUCESTER

PORCHESTER ROAD

PORCHESTER SQ

ORSETT TERRACE

GLOUCESTER TERRACE

TERRACE

CLEVELAND TERRACE

EASTBOURNE MEWS

WESTBOURNE

CHILWORTH MEWS

Paddington

PRAED ST

9

DURHAM TERRACE

ALEXANDER STREET

SUNDERLAND TER

NEWTON ROAD

BURDETT MEWS

QUEENSWAY

BISHOP'S

HALLFIELD ESTATE

GLOUCESTER

TERRACE

CLEVELAND

GARDENS

GLOUCESTER MEWS WEST

CLEVELAND

CHILWORTH

STREET

GLOUCESTER MEWS

TERRACE

CRAVEN

TERRACE

ROAD

SPRING STREET

CONDUIT

MEWS

WESTBOURNE GROVE

GARWAY ROAD

GARDENS SQUARE

KENSINGTON

REDAN PL

REDAN PLACE

PORCHESTER

SALEM RD

LEINSTER PL

LEINSTER GARDENS

PORCHESTER

GARDENS

QUEENSWAY

CLEVELAND SQUARE

CLEVELAND SQUARE

PORCHESTER TERRACE

QUEEN'S GARDENS

DEVONSHIRE TERRACE

CRAVEN HILL

BROOK MEWS NORTH

CRAVEN HILL GARDENS

CRAVEN

TERRACE

CRAVEN

MEWS

WESTBOURNE CRESCENT

LANCASTER TERRACE

2

PRINCE'S SQUARE

ILCHESTER GDNS

PRINCE'S SQUARE

PORCHESTER

Bayswater

INVERNESS MEWS

QUEENSBOROUGH MEWS

PORCHESTER TERRACE

CRAVEN HILL GARDENS

LANCASTER

GATE

LANCASTER

GATE

LANCASTER

GATE

Lancaster Gate

LANCASTER TERRACE

SQUARE

MOSCOW

ST PETERSBURGH PLACE

CHAPEL SIDE

BARK PLACE

INVERNESS PLACE

QUEENSBOROUGH TERRACE

LEINSTER TERRACE

LANCASTER

CAROLINE PL

INVERNESS TERRACE

BAYSWATER

ROAD

PALACE COURT

OSSINGTON STREET

ORME LANE

ORME COURT

Queensway

LANCASTER WALK

The Fountains

3

KENSINGTON

GARDENS MEWS

KENSINGTON PALACE GARDENS

KENSINGTON

Diana, Princess of Wales Memorial Playground

THE BROAD WALK

Peter Pan Statue

GARDENS TERRACE

VICARAGE GATE

Round Pond

Kensington Palace

PALACE AVENUE

LANCASTER WALK

4

DUKE'S LANE

YORK HOUSE PLACE

PALACE GREEN

GARDENS

CHURCH

OLD COURT PLACE

HOLLAND STREET

STREET

YOUNG STREET

DERRY ST

KENSINGTON

STREET

GH

Kensington Roof Gardens

High Street Kensington

WRIGHT'S LANE

SQUARE

KENSINGTON COURT

VICTORIA ROAD

CAMBRIDGE PLACE

DE VERE GARDENS

PALACE GATE

KENSINGTON GATE

THE FLOWER

WALK

Albert Memorial

9

KENSINGTON

HYDE PARK GATE

ROAD

Royal College of Art

Royal Albert Hall

5

KENSINGTON COURT PLACE

DOURO PL

CANNING PLACE

HYDEPARK GATE

QUEEN'S GATE

QUEEN'S GATE MEWS

BREMNER RD

JAY MEWS

ALBERT COURT

Royal College of Music

Museum of Instruments

ST ALBANS GROVE

PRINCE CONSORT ROAD

CALLENDAR RD

SHOPS AND MARKETS

London is one of the great shopping cities of Europe, with bustling, lively street markets, world-famous department stores and a wide variety of eclectic shops selling clothes, antiques, crafts and much more. The best shopping areas range from up-market districts such as Knightsbridge and Bond Street, which sell expensive designer clothes, to the busy, chaotic stretch of Oxford Street. The vibrant markets of Covent Garden, Berwick Street and Brick Lane are also popular. The city is best known, however, for its huge range of clothes shops selling everything from traditional tweeds to the latest zany designs of the ever-changing high-street fashion trends.

When to Shop

In central London, most shops stay open from 10am to about 5.30–6pm Monday to Saturday. Many department stores, however, have longer hours. The "late night" shopping until 7 or 8pm is on Thursday and Friday in Oxford Street and the rest of West End; and on Wednesday in Knightsbridge and Chelsea. Some shops in tourist areas, such as Covent Garden and the Trocadero, are open until 7pm or later every day, including Sunday. Some street markets and a number of other shops are usually open on Sundays as well.

Twice-yearly Sales

The traditional sale season is from January to February and from June to July, when shops slash prices and sell off left-over stock. The department stores have some of the best reductions – queues for the famous Harrods sale start to form long before it opens.

Shopping Areas

London's best shopping areas range from the up-market Knightsbridge, where porcelain, jewellery and couture come at the highest prices, to colourful markets, where getting the cheapest bargains is what it's all about.

The city beckons specialist shoppers with its treasures and collectibles crammed into inviting antiques shops, and streets full of antiquarian booksellers and art galleries.

Best of the Department Stores

Harrods is the king of the city's department stores with over 300 departments and a staff of 5,000. The spectacular food hall with Edwardian tiles displays fish, cheese, fruit and vegetables. Other specialities include fashion, china and glass, kitchenware and electronics. Londoners also often head for the nearby **Harvey Nichols**, which stocks the best of everything. The clothing department is particularly strong, with an emphasis on talented British, European and American names. The food hall, opened in 1992, is one of London's most stylish.

Selfridges, on Oxford Street, has expanded its range in recent years. It has arguably the widest choice of labels, a great lingerie department and a section devoted to emerging designers. It also has a food hall that features delicacies from all over the world.

Originally a drapery, **John Lewis**, to this date, has a good selection of fabrics and haberdashery. Its china, glass and household items make this store and its Sloane Square partner, **Peter Jones**, equally popular with Londoners.

Liberty, near Carnaby Street, has been famous ever since 1875 for its beautiful silks and other Oriental goods. Don't forget to check out the famous scarf department.

Fortnum and Mason's is best known for its ground-floor food department. It has everything from Fortnum's tins of biscuits and tea to cured meats and lovely wicker hampers. In fact, these exquisite delicacies are so engrossing that the upper floors filled with classic fashion and luxury items often remain free of crowds.

Harrods at night, illuminated by 11,500 lights

Markets

Whatever you're looking for, it's definitely worth visiting one of London's colourful markets. Many of them mix English traditions with those of more recent immigrants, creating an exotic atmosphere and a truly fascinating array of merchandise. At some, the seasoned hawkers have honed their sales patter to an entertaining art, which reaches fever pitch just before closing, when the plummeting prices at the end of the day are announced. Keep your wits about you, your hand on your purse and join in the fun.

Among the best of the West End markets are **Grays Antiques** and **Jubilee and Apple** markets in Covent Garden. Although it is somewhat touristy, **Piccadilly Crafts** is also very popular. In Soho, the spirited costermongers of **Berwick Street** peddle some of the cheapest and freshest fruit and vegetables in the area.

In the East End, **Petticoat Lane** is probably the most famous of London's street markets. Those in search of the

Bustling Petticoat Lane market, officially known as Middlesex Street

latest street fashions make a beeline for **Old Spitalfields**, while **Brick Lane** is massively popular due to its trendy location. Here you can find everything from shellfish to trainers. Nearby, **Columbia Road** is perfect for greenery and blossoms.

South of the river, **East Street** also has a flower market, but the majority of its traders sell clothes. **Bermondsey Market** is a gathering point for London's antiques traders. Collectors set off early to scrutinize the fine paintings and old jewellery. **Borough** (see p124) caters to the restaurant trade with its fine

food and farmer's market. **Brixton Market** stocks a superb assortment of Afro-Caribbean foods, often to the pounding beat of reggae music.

In north London, **Camden Lock Market** offers a vibrant atmosphere and stalls selling everything from vintage clothes to lovely crafts. In nearby Islington, **Camden Passage** is a quiet cobbled street where charming cafés nestle among quaint antiques shops.

In Notting Hill, **Portobello Road** is actually a bunch of markets rolled into one, and an entire afternoon can be spent browsing there.

DIRECTORY

Department Stores

Fortnum & Mason
181 Piccadilly W1. **Map** 11 A3. **Tel** 020 7734 8040.

Harrods
87–135 Brompton Rd SW1. **Map** 9 C5. **Tel** 020 7730 1234.

Harvey Nichols
109–125 Knightsbridge SW1. **Map** 9 C5. **Tel** 020 7235 5000.

John Lewis
278–306 Oxford St W1. **Map** 10 E1. **Tel** 020 7629 7711.

Liberty
210–20 Regent St W1. **Map** 10 F2. **Tel** 020 7734 1234

Peter Jones
Sloane Sq, SW1. **Map** 18 D2. **Tel** 020 7730 3434.

Selfridges
400 Oxford St W1. **Map** 10 D2. **Tel** 0800 123 400.

Markets

Bermondsey Market
Long Lane & Bermondsey St SE1. **Map** 13 C5. **Open** 4am–1pm Fri.

Berwick Street
Berwick St W1. **Map** 11 A2. **Open** 9am–6pm Mon–Sat.

Borough
8 Southwark St SE1. **Map** 13 B4. **Open** 10am–3pm Mon–Wed, 11am–5pm Thu, noon–6pm Fri, 8am–5pm Sat.

Brick Lane
Brick Lane E1. **Map** 6 E5. **Open** 9am–5pm Sun.

Brixton Market
Electric Ave SW9. **Open** 8am–6pm Mon–Sat (to 3pm Wed).

Camden Lock Market
Chalk Farm Rd NW1. ⊖ Camden Town, Chalk Farm. **Open** 9:30am–6pm daily.

Camden Passage
Camden Passage N1. **Map** 4 F1. **Open** 9am–6pm Wed & Sat.

Columbia Road
Columbia Rd E2. **Map** 6 D3. ⊖ Shoreditch, Old St. **Open** 8am–3pm Sun.

East Street
East St SE17. ⊖ Elephant & Castle. **Open** 8am–5pm Tue–Sun (to 6:30pm Sat and 2pm Sun).

Grays Antiques
58 Davies St, Mayfair. **Map** 10 E2. **Open** 10am–6pm Mon–Fri; 11am–5pm Sat.

Greenwich
College Approach SE10. **Open** 10am–5:30pm Tue–Sun.

Jubilee and Apple
Covent Gdn Piazza WC2. **Map** 11 C2. **Open** 9am–6pm daily.

Old Spitalfields
Commercial St E1. ⊖ Liverpool St. **Map** 6 D1. **Open** 10am–5pm Mon–Wed & 9am–5pm Sun (General Market), 9am–5pm Thu (Antiques & Vintage), 10am–4pm Fri (Fashion & Art), 11am–5pm Sat (Themed Market).

Petticoat Lane
Middlesex St E1. **Map** 14 E2. **Open** 10am–4:30pm Mon–Fri, 9am–2pm Sun.

Piccadilly Crafts
St James's Church, Piccadilly W1. **Map** 11 A3. **Open** 10am–6pm Wed–Sat.

Portobello Road
Portobello Rd W10. **Map** 7 C3. **Open** daily (main market Sat).

Clothes

British tailoring and fabrics are world-renowned for their high quality. **Henry Poole & Co, H Huntsman & Sons** and **Gieves & Hawkes** are among the most highly respected tailors on Savile Row.

A new generation of trend-conscious tailors who specialize in modern cuts and fabrics has firmly established itself on the fashion scene. The line-up includes **Richard James** and **Ozwald Boateng**. Several stalwarts of classic British style have also reinvented themselves as fashion labels. **Burberry** is the best example, although it still does a brisk trade in its famous trenchcoats, and distinctive accessories. Designers **Margaret Howell** and **Nicole Farhi** create trend-setting versions of British country garments for men as well as women.

London designers are known for their eclectic, irreverent style. *Grande dames* of fashion, Zandra Rhodes and **Vivienne Westwood** have been on the scene since the 1970s. Many other British designers of international stature also have their flagship stores in the capital, including **Stella McCartney**, the late **Alexander McQueen**, **Paul Smith** and **Matthew Williamson**. Designer clothes, however, are not just the preserve of the rich. If you want to flaunt a bit of British design but can't afford the high prices, it's worth visiting **Debenhams**, which has harnessed the talents of numerous leading designers. Cheaper versions of all the latest styles appear in the shops almost as soon as they have been sashayed down the catwalk. **Topshop** and **Oasis** have both won celebrity fans for their up-to-the-minute ensembles of hip and youthful fashions for women; young professionals head to **French Connection**. The up-market chains **Jigsaw** and **Whistles** are more expensive, with their emphasis on beautiful fabrics and shapes. Fashion-conscious young men can turn to **Reiss** and **Ted Baker** for trendy clothing.

Exterior of Harrods department store, with shoppers passing by

Shoes

Some of the most famous names in the footwear industry are based in Britain. If you can spare a few thousand pounds, you can have a pair custom-made by the Royal Family's shoemaker, **John Lobb**. Readymade, traditional brogues and Oxfords are the mainstay of **Church's Shoes**. **Oliver Sweeney** gives classics a contemporary edge. **The British Boot Company** in Camden has the widest range of funky Dr Martens, appropriated by rock'n'rollers and the grunge set. **Jimmy Choo** and **Manolo Blahnik** are two all-time favourites of most fashionable women all over the world. Less expensive, yet good quality designs can be found in **Hobbs** or **Pied à Terre**, while **Jones Bootmaker** and **Office** turn out young, voguish styles.

Gifts and Souvenirs

The market in Covent Garden Piazza stocks uniquely British pottery, knitwear and other crafts, and **Neal's Yard Remedies** sells organic health and beauty treats. To buy all your gifts under one roof, visit Liberty *(see p152)*, where all kinds of exquisite items can be found in every department.

Leading museums such as the Victoria and Albert *(see pp102–3)*, Natural History and Science Museums *(see p104)* sell unusual mementos. Try **Hamley's** for gifts and toys.

Books and Magazines

The bookshops in London rank among its most illustrious specialities. Charing Cross Road is a treasure-trove for those hunting for antiquarian, second-hand and new volumes. It is the home of **Foyles**, famous for its massive stock. Large branches of chains such as **Waterstones** co-exist with many specialist stores. **Hatchards** in Piccadilly is the city's oldest bookshop and one of its finest, offering an extensive and varied choice of titles.

Vintage Magazines in Soho stocks publications dating back to the early 1900s.

Art and Antiques

Art and antiques shops abound in London, and you are sure to find something of beauty and value within your means.

Cork Street is the centre of Britain's contemporary art world. **Waddington Custot Galleries** is the best known, while **Redfern Art Gallery** and **Flowers** exhibit unusual modern art.

Visit **Roger's Antiques Galleries** and Grays Antiques *(see p152)* for striking vintage jewellery and objets d'art.

The East End is a growing area for contemporary art. The cutting-edge **White Cube Gallery** is there, as is the internationally renowned **Whitechapel Art Gallery**.

For photography, visit the **Photographers' Gallery**, which has the largest collection of originals for sale in Britain. **Hamiltons Gallery** also hosts interesting exhibitions.

DIRECTORY

Clothes

Alexander McQueen
4–5 Old Bond St W1.
Map 10 F3.
Tel 020 7355 0088.

Burberry
21–23 New Bond St W1.
Map 10 F2.
Tel 020 7980 8425.
One of several branches.

Debenhams
334–348 Oxford St W1.
Map 10 E2.
Tel 08445 616 161.

French Connection
249–251 Regent St W1.
Map 10 F2.
Tel 020 7493 3124.
One of several branches.

Gieves & Hawkes
1 Savile Row W1.
Map 10 F3.
Tel 020 7432 6403.

H Huntsman & Sons
11 Savile Row W1.
Map 10 F3.
Tel 020 7734 7441.

Henry Poole & Co
15 Savile Row W1.
Map 10 F3.
Tel 020 7734 5985.

Jigsaw
6 Duke of York Sq,
Kings Rd SW3.
Map 17 C2.
Tel 020 7730 4404.

Margaret Howell
34 Wigmore St W1.
Map 10 E1.
Tel 020 7009 9009.

Matthew Williamson
28 Bruton St W1.
Map 10 E3.
Tel 020 7629 6200.

Nicole Farhi
158 New Bond St W1.
Map 10 E2.
Tel 020 7499 8368.

Oasis
12–14 Argyll St W1.
Map 10 F2.
Tel 020 7434 1799.

Ozwald Boateng
30 Savile Row &
9 Vigo St W1.
Map 10 F3.
Tel 020 7437 2030.

Paul Smith
Westbourne House
120 & 122 Kensington
Park Rd W11.
Map 7 B2.
Tel 020 7229 8982.

Reiss
Kent House, 14–17
Market Place W1.
Map 10 F1.
Tel 020 7637 9112.
One of several branches.

Richard James
29 Savile Row W1.
Map 10 F2.
Tel 020 7434 0605.

Stella McCartney
30 Bruton St W1.
Map 10 E3.
Tel 020 7518 3100.

Ted Baker
9–10 Floral St WC2.
Map 11 C2.
Tel 020 7836 7808.
One of several branches.

Topshop
Oxford Circus W1.
Map 10 F1.
Tel 08448 487 487.
One of several branches.

Vivienne Westwood
44 Conduit St W1.
Map 10 F2.
Tel 020 7439 1109.

Whistles
12–14 St Christopher's Pl
W1. **Map** 10 E2.
Tel 020 7487 4484.

Shoes

The British Boot Company
5 Kentish Town Rd NW1.
Map 2 F1.
Tel 020 7485 8505.

Church's Shoes
201 Regent St W1.
Map 10 F2.
Tel 020 7734 2438.

Hobbs
112–115 Long Acre WC2.
Map 11 C2.
Tel 020 7836 0625.
One of several branches.

Jimmy Choo
27 New Bond St W1.
Map 10 F2.
Tel 020 7493 5858.

John Lobb
9 St James's St SW1A.
Map 10 F4.
Tel 020 7930 3664.

Jones Bootmaker
Old Broad St EC2M.
Map 13 C1.
Tel 020 7256 7309.

Manolo Blahnik
49–51 Old Church St,
Kings Road SW3.
Map 17 A4.
Tel 020 7352 8622.

Office
57 Neal St WC2.
Map 11 B1.
Tel 020 7379 1896.
One of several branches.

Oliver Sweeney
5 Conduit St W1.
Map 10 F2.
Tel 020 7491 9126.

Pied à Terre
19 South Molton St W1.
Map 10 E2.
Tel 020 7629 1362.

Gifts and Souvenirs

Hamley's
188–196 Regent St W1.
Map 10 F2.
Tel 0871 7041977.

Neal's Yard Remedies
15 Neal's Yard WC2.
Map 11 2C.
Tel 020 7379 7222.

Books and Magazines

Foyles
113–119 Charing Cross
Rd WC2.
Map 11 B1.
Tel 020 7437 5660.

Hatchards
187 Piccadilly W1.
Map 10 F3.
Tel 020 7439 9921.

Vintage Magazines
39–43 Brewer St W1.
Map 11 A2.
Tel 020 7439 8525.

Waterstones
203–205 Piccadilly W1.
Map 11 A3.
Tel 020 7851 2400.
One of several branches.

Art and Antiques

Flowers
21 Cork St W1.
Map 10 F3.
Tel 020 7439 7766.

Hamiltons Gallery
13 Carlos Place W1.
Map 10 E3.
Tel 020 7499 9493.

Photographers' Gallery
16–18 Ramillies St W1.
Map 10 F2.
Tel 0845 262 1618.

Redfern Art Gallery
20 Cork St W1.
Map 10 F3.
Tel 020 7734 1732.

Roger's Antiques Galleries
65 Portobello Road W11.
Map 7 A1.
Tel 07885 723 433.

Waddington Custot Galleries
11, 12, 34 Cork St W1.
Map 10 F3.
Tel 020 7851 2200.

White Cube Gallery
144–152 Bermondsey
Street SE1 & 25–26
Mason's Yard SW1.
Map 13 C5.
Tel 020 7930 5373.

Whitechapel Art Gallery
77–82 Whitechapel
High St E1.
Map 14 E1.
Tel 020 7522 7888.

ENTERTAINMENT IN LONDON

London has the enormous variety of entertainment that only the great cities of the world can provide. The historical backdrop and the lively bustling atmosphere add to the excitement. Whether dancing the night away at a famous disco or making the most of London's varied arts scene, the visitor has a bewildering choice. A trip to London is not complete without a visit to the theatre which ranges from glamorous West End musicals to experimental Fringe plays. There is world-class ballet and opera in fabled venues such as Sadler's Wells and the Royal Opera House. The musical menu covers everything from classical, jazz and rock to rhythm and blues performed in atmospheric basement clubs, old converted cinemas and outdoor venues such as Wembley. Movie buffs can choose from hundreds of films each night. Sports fans can watch cricket at Lord's or participate in a host of activities from water sports to ice skating.

Time Out, published every Tuesday, is a free comprehensive guide to what is on in London, with detailed weekly listings and reviews. *The Evening Standard, The Guardian* (Saturday) and *The Independent* also have reviews and information on events. If you buy tickets from booking agencies rather than direct from box offices, do compare prices; it is also possible to purchase tickets online.

West End and National Theatres

Palace Theatre poster (1898)

The glamorous, glittering world of West End theatreland, emblazoned with the names of world-famous performers, offers an extraordinary range of entertainment.

West End theatres (see Directory for individual theatres) survive on their profits and rely on financial backers, known as "angels". Consequently, they tend to stage commercial productions with mass appeal: musicals, classics, comedies and plays by bankable contemporary playwrights.

The state-subsidized **National Theatre** is based in the Southbank Centre *(see p158)*. It has three auditoriums – the large, open-staged Olivier, the proscenium-arched Lyttelton, and the small studio space of the Cottesloe.

The **Royal Shakespeare Company** (RSC) regularly stages Shakespeare plays, but its repertoire includes Greek tragedies, Restoration comedies and modern works. Based at Stratford-upon-Avon *(see pp329–31)*, its major productions perform at London West End theatres. The RSC ticket hotline has information. **The Old Vic** has been rejuvenated under the artistic directorship of Kevin Spacey, whose exciting programme of drama attracts wide audiences.

Theatre tickets generally cost from £5 to £90 (for a top price West End show) and can be bought direct from box offices, by telephone or post. The "tkts" discount theatre ticket booth in Leicester Square sells tickets for a wide range of shows on the day of performance. It is open Monday to Saturday (10am–7pm) for matinees and evening shows, and Sundays (noon–3pm) for matinees only.

Off-West End and Fringe Theatres

Off-West End theatre is a middle category bridging the gap between West End and Fringe theatre. It includes venues that, regardless of location, have a permanent management team and often provide the opportunity for established directors and actors to turn their hands to more adventurous works in a smaller, more intimate, environment. Fringe theatres, on the other hand, are normally venues hired out to visiting companies. Both offer a vast array of innovative productions, serving as an outlet for new, often experimental writing.

Venues (too numerous to list – see newspaper listings), range from tiny theatres or rooms above pubs such as the Gate, which produces neglected European classics, to theatres

The Old Vic, the first home of the National Theatre from 1963

Open-air theatre at Regent's Park

such as the Donmar Warehouse, which attracts major directors and actors.

Open-Air Theatre

In summer, a performance of one of Shakespeare's airier creations such as *A Midsummer Night's Dream*, takes on an atmosphere of enchantment among the green vistas of Regent's Park (0870-060 1811). Lavish summer opera productions are staged at Holland Park (0207602 7856). Shakespeare's Globe *(see p124)* offers open-air theatrical performances in a beautifully recreated Elizabethan theatre.

Cinemas

The West End abounds with multiplex cinema chains (MGM, Odeon, UCI) which show big budget Hollywood films, usually in advance of the rest of the country, although release dates tend to lag well behind the US and many other European countries.

The Odeon Marble Arch has the largest commercial screen in Europe, while the Odeon Leicester Square boasts London's biggest auditorium with almost 2,000 seats.

Londoners are well-informed cinema-goers and even the larger cinema chains include some low-budget and foreign

BFI IMAX Cinema, at Waterloo

films in their repertoire. The majority of foreign films are subtitled, rather than dubbed. A number of independent cinemas, such as the Renoir and Prince Charles in central London, and the Curzon in Mayfair, show foreign-language and art films.

The largest concentration of cinemas is in and around Leicester Square although there are local cinemas in most areas. Just off Leicester Square, the Prince Charles is the West End's cheapest cinema. Elsewhere in the area you can expect to pay as much as £10 for an evening screening – almost twice the price of the local cinemas. Monday and afternoon performances in the West End are often cheaper. The BFI Southbank, at the Southbank Centre, is London's flagship repertory cinema. Subsidized by the British Film Institute, it screens a wide range of films, old and new, from all around the world. Nearby at Waterloo is the BFI IMAX, with one of the world's largest screens.

DIRECTORY

Adelphi
Strand. **Map** 11 C3.
Tel 0844 811 0053.

Aldwych
Aldwych. **Map** 11 C2.
Tel 0844 847 1712.

Apollo Victoria
Shaftesbury Ave. **Map** 11 B2. **Tel** 0844 871 7627.

Cambridge
Earlham St. **Map** 11 B2.
Tel 0844 412 4652.

Criterion
Piccadilly Circus. **Map** 11 A3. **Tel** 0844 847 1778.

Dominion
Tottenham Court Rd. **Map** 11 A1. **Tel** 0844 847 1775.

Duchess
Catherine St. **Map** 11 C2.
Tel 0844 482 9672.

Duke of York's
St Martin's Lane. **Map** 11 B2. **Tel** 0844 871 7627.

Fortune
Russell St. **Map** 11 C2.
Tel 0844 871 7626.

Garrick
Charing Cross Rd. **Map** 11 B2. **Tel** 0844 579 1974.

Gielgud
Shaftesbury Ave. **Map** 11 B2. **Tel** 0844 482 5130.

Harold Pinter
Panton St. **Map** 11 A3.
Tel 0844 871 7622.

Her Majesty's
Haymarket. **Map** 11 A3.
Tel 0844 412 2707.

Lyceum
Wellington St. **Map** 11 C2.
Tel 0844 871 7627.

Lyric
Shaftesbury Ave. **Map** 11 B2. **Tel** 0844 482 9674.

National
South Bank. **Map** 12 D3.
Tel 020 7452 3000.

New London
Drury Lane. **Map** 11 C1.
Tel 0871 230 1547.

Noel Coward
St Martin's Lane. **Map** 11 B2. **Tel** 0844 482 5141.

Novello Theatre
Aldwych. **Map** 12 D2.
Tel 0844 482 5120.

The Old Vic
Waterloo Rd SE1.
Map 12 E4.
Tel 0844 871 7628.

Palace
Cambridge Circus W1. **Map** 11 B2. **Tel** 0844 482 9676.

Phoenix
Charing Cross Rd. **Map** 11 B2. **Tel** 0870 060 6629.

Piccadilly
Denman St. **Map** 11 A2.
Tel 0844 412 6666.

Prince Edward
Old Compton St. **Map** 11 D5. **Tel** 0844 482 5151.

Prince of Wales
Coventry St. **Map** 11 A3.
Tel 0844 482 5115.

Queen's
Shaftesbury Ave. **Map** 11 B2. **Tel** 0844 800 1110.
RSC w rsc.org.uk.

Shaftesbury
Shaftesbury Ave. **Map** 11 B2. **Tel** 020 7379 5399.

St Martin's
West St. **Map** 11 B2.
Tel 0844 499 1515.

Theatre Royal: Drury Lane
Catherine St. **Map** 11 C2.
Tel 0844 412 4648.

Theatre Royal: Haymarket
Haymarket. **Map** 11 A3.
Tel 020 7930 8800.

Vaudeville
Strand. **Map** 11 C3.
Tel 0844 482 9675.

Wyndham's
Charing Cross Rd. **Map** 11 B2. **Tel** 0844 482 5120.

Royal Festival Hall, South Bank Centre

Classical Music, Opera and Dance

London is one of the world's great centres for classical music, with five symphony orchestras, internationally renowned chamber groups such as the Academy of St-Martin-in-the-Fields and the English Chamber Orchestra, as well as a number of contemporary groups. There are performances virtually every week by major international orchestras and artists, reaching a peak during the summer Proms season at the **Royal Albert Hall** (see p67). **Wigmore Hall** has excellent acoustics and is a fine setting for chamber music, as is the converted Baroque church (1728) of **St John's, Smith Square**. Although televised

and outdoor performances by major stars have greatly increased the popularity of opera, prices at the **Royal Opera House** (see p84) are still aimed at corporate entertainment but the policy now is to keep a few cheaper seats. The refurbished building is elaborate and productions are often extremely lavish. English National Opera, based at the **London Coliseum**, has more adventurous productions, appealing to a younger audience (nearly all operas are sung in English). Tickets range from £5 to £200 and it is advisable to book in advance.

The Royal Opera House is also home to the Royal Ballet, and the London Coliseum to the English National Ballet, the two leading classical ballet companies in Britain. Visiting ballets also perform in both.

There are numerous young contemporary dance companies, and **The Place** is a dedicated contemporary dance theatre where many companies perform. Other major dance venues are **Sadler's Wells**, the **ICA**, the **Peacock Theatre** and the **Chisenhale Dance Space**.

The **Barbican Concert Hall** and **Southbank Centre** (comprising the Royal Festival Hall, Queen Elizabeth Hall and Purcell Room) host an impressive variety of events ranging from touring opera and classical music performances to free foyer concerts.

Elsewhere in London many outdoor musical events take place in summer (see pp66–7) at venues such as **Kenwood House**. Events to look out for are: the London Opera Festival (June) with singers from all over the world; the City of London Festival (July) which

Kenwood House on Hampstead Heath (see p128)

DIRECTORY

Classical Music, Opera and Dance

Barbican Concert Hall
Silk St EC2. **Map** 5 A5.
Tel 020 7638 8891.
ⓦ barbican.org.uk

Chisenhale Dance Space
64–84 Chisenhale Rd E3.
Ⓔ Bethnal Green, Mile End. **Tel** 020 8981 6617.
ⓦ chisenhaledance space.co.uk

ICA
The Mall SW1. **Map** 11 A4.
Tel 020 7930 3647.
ⓦ ica.org.uk

Kenwood House
Hampstead Lane NW3.
Tel 020 8348 1286. Ⓔ

London Coliseum
St Martin's Lane WC2.
Map 11 B3. **Tel** 020 7845 9300. ⓦ eno.org

Peacock Theatre
Portugal St WC2. **Map** 12 D1. **Tel** 020 7863 8198.

The Place
17 Duke's Rd WC1. **Map** 3 B3. **Tel** 020 7121 1100.
ⓦ theplace.org.uk

Royal Albert Hall
Kensington Gore SW7.
Map 8 F5. **Tel** 020 7589 8212. ⓦ royal

alberthall.com

Royal Opera House
Floral St WC2. **Map** 11 C2.
Tel 020 7304 4000.
ⓦ roh.org.uk

Sadler's Wells
Rosebery Ave EC1.
Tel 020 7863 8198.
ⓦ sadlerswells.com

St John's, Smith Sq
Smith Sq SW1. **Map** 19 B1. **Tel** 020 7222 1061.
ⓦ sjss.org.uk

Southbank Centre
SE1. **Map** 12 D3.
Tel 0844 875 0073.
ⓦ southbankcentre. co.uk

Wigmore Hall
Wigmore St W1. **Map** 10 D1. **Tel** 020 7935 2141.
ⓦ wigmore-hall.org.uk

Rock, Pop, Jazz and Clubs

100 Club
100 Oxford St W1. **Map** 10 F1. **Tel** 020 7636 0933.
ⓦ the100club.co.uk

333
333 Old St EC1.
Tel 020 7739 1800.

Brixton Academy
211 Stockwell Rd SW9.
Ⓔ Brixton. **Tel** 0844 477 2000. ⓦ brixton-academy.co.uk

hosts a range of varied musical events; and contemporary dance festivals Spring Loaded (February–April) and Dance Umbrella (October) – *see Time Out* and newspaper listings.

Rock, Pop, Jazz and Clubs

London features scores of concerts, ranging from rock and pop, to jazz, Latin, world, folk and reggae. Among the city's largest venues are **The O2** and the **Royal Albert Hall**; smaller venues include **Brixton Academy** and **The Forum**.

There are a number of live jazz venues. Best of the old crop is **Ronnie Scott's**, although the **100 Club, Jazz Café** and **Vortex Jazz Club** have good reputations. The **Hippodrome** (on Leicester Square) also hosts jazz as well as cabaret nights.

London's club scene is one of the most innovative in Europe. It is dominated by big- name DJs, who host different nights in different clubs (see *Time Out* and newspaper listings). The West End venues **Ruby Blue** and the **Café de Paris** are glitzy, expensive and very much on the tourist circuit. The New York-style **Ministry of Sound**, the camp cabaret of **Madame Jojo's**, the trendy Shoreditch clubs **333** and **Cargo**, and a host of other

venues ensure that you will never be short of choice. Alternatives are the great laser and light shows at **Heaven**, the glamorous super-club **Pacha London**, or the live music venue **Koko** in Camden, which also hosts a variety of club nights. **Heaven** and the **Queen of Hoxton** are among the most popular of London's gay clubs.

Opening times are usually 10pm–3am, but on weekends many clubs open until 6am.

Sports

An impressive variety of public sports facilities are to be found in London, and they are generally inexpensive to use.

Swimming pools, squash courts, gyms and sports centres, with an assortment of keep-fit classes, can be found in most districts, and tennis courts hired in most parks. Water sports, ice skating and golf are among the variety of activities on offer. Spectator sports range from football and rugby at various club grounds to cricket at **Lord's** or the **Oval**, and tennis at the **All England Lawn Tennis Club**, Wimbledon. Tickets for the most popular matches can often be hard to come by (*see p71*). More traditional sports include polo at **Guards**, croquet at **Hurlingham** (private members only) and medieval "real tennis" at **Queen's Club**. See pages 614–617 for more on sporting activities.

Booth selling discounted tickets in Leicester Square

Café de Paris
3 Coventry St W1. **Map** 4 D5. **Tel** 020 7734 7700.

Cargo
83 Rivington St EC2. Old St. **Tel** 020 7739 3440.

Heaven
Under the Arches, Villiers St WC2. **Map** 11 C3. **Tel** 020 7930 2020.

Jazz Café
3–5 Parkway NW1. Camden Town. **Tel** 020 7688 8899.

Koko
1A Camden High St NW1. Mornington Crescent **Tel** 0870 432 5527.

Madame Jojo's
8–10 Brewer St W1. Map 11 A2. **Tel** 020 7734 3040.

Ministry of Sound
103 Gaunt St SE1. Elephant & Castle. ministryofsound.com

Pacha London
Terminus Place, SW1. **Map** 18 F1. **Tel** 0845 371 4489. pachalondon.com

Queen of Hoxton
1 Curtain Rd EC2. Shoreditch High St. **Tel** 020 7422 0958.

Ronnie Scott's
47 Frith St W1. **Map** 11 A2. **Tel** 020 7439 0747. ronniescotts.co.uk

Ruby Blue
Leicester Sq WC2. **Map** 4 E5. **Tel** 020 7287 8050.

The Forum
9–17 Highgate Rd NW5. Kentish Town. **Tel** 020 7428 4099

The O2 Arena
Peninsula Square SE10. North Greenwich. **Tel** 020 8463 2000.

Vortex Jazz Club
11 Gillett Sq N16. Dalston Kingsland. **Tel** 020 7254 4097.

Sports

All England Lawn Tennis Club
Church Rd, Wimbledon

SW19. Southfields. **Tel** 020 8944 1066.

Guards Polo Club
Windsor Great Park. Egham. **Tel** 01784 434212.

Hurlingham Club
Ranelagh Gdns SW6. **Map** 18 D3. **Tel** 020 7610 7400.

Lord's Cricket Ground
St John's Wood NW8. St John's Wood. **Tel** 020 7432 1000.

Oval Cricket Ground
Kennington SE11. Oval. **Tel** 020 7820 5700.

Queen's Club
Palliser Rd W14. Barons Court. **Tel** 020 7386 3400.

SOUTHEAST
ENGLAND

Southeast England at a Glance

The old Saxon kingdoms covered the areas surrounding London, and today, while their accessibility to the capital makes them a magnet for commuters, each region retains a character and history of its own. The attractions include England's oldest universities, royal palaces, castles, stately homes and cathedrals, many of which played critical roles in the nation's early history. The landscape is soft, with the green and rounded hills of the south country levelling out to the flat fertile plains and fens of East Anglia, fringed by broad, sandy beaches.

Blenheim Palace *(see pp232–3)* is a Baroque masterpiece. The Mermaid Fountain (1892) is part of the spectacular gardens.

Banbury

Bedfor

BEDFC SHIF

Lut

BUCKINGHAM-SHIRE

Oxford

THAMES VALLEY *(See pp220–41)*

Wat

OXFORD-SHIRE

High Wycombe

BERKSHIRE

Windsor

Reading

Newbury

Basingstoke

Guildford

HAMPSHIRE

SU

THE DOWNS A CHANNEL COA *(See pp168–93)*

Winchester

WEST SUSSE

Southampton

Chiche

Lymington

Portsmouth

Oxford University's buildings *(see pp226–31)* amount to a textbook of English architecture from the Middle Ages to the present. Christ Church College (1525) is the largest in the university.

Windsor Castle *(see pp240–41)* is Britain's oldest royal residence. The Round Tower was built in the 11th century when the palace guarded the western approaches to London.

Winchester Cathedral *(see pp174–5)* was begun in 1097 on the ruins of a Saxon church. The city has been an important centre of Christianity since the 7th century. The cathedral's northwest door is built in a characteristic medieval style.

◀ The Radcliffe Camera, Oxford

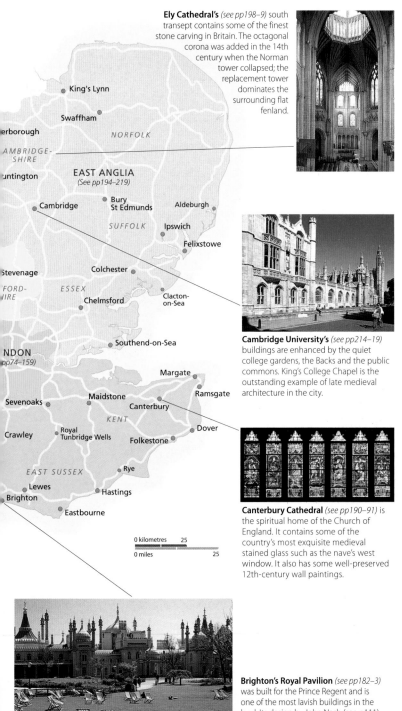

Ely Cathedral's *(see pp198–9)* south transept contains some of the finest stone carving in Britain. The octagonal corona was added in the 14th century when the Norman tower collapsed; the replacement tower dominates the surrounding flat fenland.

King's Lynn

Swaffham

erborough

NORFOLK

AMBRIDGE-
SHIRE

EAST ANGLIA
(See pp194–219)

untington

Cambridge

Bury
St Edmunds

Aldeburgh

SUFFOLK

Ipswich

Felixstowe

Stevenage

Colchester

FORD-
IRE

ESSEX

Chelmsford

Clacton-
on-Sea

NDON
pp74–159)

Southend-on-Sea

Margate

Sevenoaks

Maidstone

Canterbury

Ramsgate

KENT

Crawley

Royal
Tunbridge Wells

Folkestone

Dover

EAST SUSSEX

Rye

Lewes

Hastings

Brighton

Eastbourne

0 kilometres 25

0 miles 25

Cambridge University's *(see pp214–19)* buildings are enhanced by the quiet college gardens, the Backs and the public commons. King's College Chapel is the outstanding example of late medieval architecture in the city.

Canterbury Cathedral *(see pp190–91)* is the spiritual home of the Church of England. It contains some of the country's most exquisite medieval stained glass such as the nave's west window. It also has some well-preserved 12th-century wall paintings.

Brighton's Royal Pavilion *(see pp182–3)* was built for the Prince Regent and is one of the most lavish buildings in the land. Its design by John Nash *(see p111)* is based on Oriental themes, and it has been restored to its original splendour.

The Garden of England

With its fertile soil, mild climate and regular rainfall, the Kentish countryside has flourished as a fruit-growing region ever since its first orchards were planted by the Romans. Wine-making has also been established here, as the vine-covered hillsides around Lamberhurst show, and several vineyards may be visited. The orchards are dazzling in the blossom season, and in the autumn the branches sag with ripening fruit – a familiar sight which inspired William Cobbett (1762– 1835) to describe the area as "the very finest as to fertility and diminutive beauty in the whole world". Near Faversham, the fruit research station of Brogdale is open to the public, offering orchard walks, tastings and informative displays.

Hops and Hopping

Hop-picking, a family affair

Oast houses, topped with distinctive angled cowls, are a common feature of the Kentish landscape, and many have now been turned into houses. They were originally built to dry hops,

Seasonal Fruit

This timeline shows the major crops in each month of the farming year. The first blossoms may appear when the fields are still dusted with snow. As the petals fall, fruit appears among the leaves. After ripening in the summer sun, the fruit is harvested in the autumn.

Peach blossom is usually to be found on south-facing walls, as its fruit requires warm conditions.

Orchards are used to grow plums, pears and apples. The latter (blossoming above) remain Kent's most important orchard crop.

Raspberries are a luscious soft fruit. Many growers allow you to pick your own from the fields, and then pay by weight.

March	April	May	June	July

Sour cherry blossom is the earliest flower. Its fruit is used for cooking.

Pear blossom has creamy white flowers which appear two or three weeks before apple blossom.

Cherry plum blossom is one of the most beautiful blossoms; the plum is grown more for its flowers than its fruit.

Srawberries are Britain's favourite and earliest soft fruit. New strains allow them to be picked all summer.

Gooseberries are not always sweet enough to eat raw, though all types are superb in pies and other desserts.

an ingredient in brewing beer (see pp578–9). Many are still used for that, for although imports have reduced domestic hop-growing, more than four million tonnes are produced in Britain annually, mostly in Kent.

In summer, the fruiting plants can be seen climbing the rectangular wire frames in fields by the roadside. Until the middle of the 20th century thousands of families from London's East End would move to the Kentish hop fields every autumn for working holidays harvesting the crop and camping in barns. That tradition has faded, because now the hops are picked by machine.

The cowls turn in the wind, providing air which is controlled by trap-doors below.

Oast House

Hops are dried above a fan which blows hot air from the underlying radiators.

After drying, the hops are cooled and stored.

A press packs the hops into bags, ready for the breweries.

Plums are often served stewed, in pies, or dried into prunes. The Victoria plum (left) is the classic English dessert plum and is eaten raw. The Purple plum is also popular.

Greengages are green plums. They have a distinctive taste and can be made into jam.

Cherries are the sweetest of Kent's fruit: two popular varieties are Stella (top) and Duke.

Bramley Seedling is one of the best cooking apples, but it is not sweet enough to eat raw.

Pears, such as the William (left), should be eaten at the height of ripeness. The Conference keeps better.

August	September	October	November

Currants are among the most assertively flavoured fruit and are used in desserts and jams.

Peaches, grown in China 4,000 years ago, came to England in the 19th century.

Dessert apples, such as Cox's Orange Pippin (right), are some of England's best-loved fruits. The Discovery variety is easier to grow.

The Kentish cob, a variety of hazelnut, is undergoing a revival, having been eclipsed by European imports. Unlike many nuts, it is best picked fresh from the tree.

Vineyards are now a familiar sight in Kent (as well as Sussex and Hampshire). Most of the wine produced, such as Lamberhurst, is white.

Houses of Historical Figures

Visiting the homes of artists, writers, politicians and royalty is a rewarding way of gaining an insight into their private lives. Southeast England, near London, boasts many historic houses that have been preserved as they were when their illustrious occupants were alive. All these houses, from large mansions such as Lord Mountbatten's Broadlands to the more modest dwellings, like Jane Austen's House, contain exhibits relating to the life of the famous people who lived there.

Florence Nightingale (1820–1910), the "Lady with the Lamp", was a nurse in the Crimean War *(see p60)*. She stayed at Claydon House, Winslow, with her sister, Lady Verney.

Nancy Astor (1879–1964) was the first woman to sit in Parliament in 1919. She lived at Cliveden House, near Maidenhead, until her death.

The Duke of Wellington (1769 –1852) was given Stratfield Saye, Basingstoke, by the nation in 1817, as thanks for leading the British to victory at Waterloo *(see p59)*.

St N

Bedford

Banbury

Milton Keyn

Luton

Aylesbury

Oxford   THAMES VALLEY   St Alban
          (See pp220–41)

Watford

High Wycombe

Maidenhead

Reading   Windsor

Newbury

Woking

Basingstoke   Guildf

Farnham

0 kilometres   20

0 miles   20

Jane Austen (1775–1817) wrote three of her novels, including *Emma*, and revised the others at a house in Chawton, where she lived for eight years until shortly before her death *(see p176)*.

Winchester   THE DOWNS /
              CHANNEL CO
Romsey   *(See pp168–9*

Southampton

Chichester

Lymington   Portsmouth

Cowes

Lord Mountbatten (1900–79), a British naval commander and statesman, was the last Viceroy of India in 1947. He lived at Broadlands, near Southampton, all his married life and remodelled the original house considerably.

Queen Victoria (1819–1901) and her husband, Prince Albert, built Osborne House on the Isle of Wight *(see p172)* in 1855 as a seaside retreat for their family because they never truly warmed to the Royal Pavilion in Brighton.

Bloomsbury Group

A circle of avant-garde artists, designers and writers, many of them friends as students, began to meet at a house in Bloomsbury, London, in 1904 and soon gained a reputation for their Bohemian lifestyle. When Duncan Grant and Vanessa Bell moved to Charleston in 1916 *(see p184)*, it became a Sussex outpost of the celebrated group. Many of the prominent figures associated with the circle, such as Virginia Woolf, EM Forster, Vita Sackville-West and JM Keynes paid visits here. The Bloomsbury Group was also known for the Omega Workshops, which made innovative ceramics, furniture and textiles.

Vanessa Bell at Charleston by Duncan Grant (1885–1978)

Thomas Gainsborough (1727–88), one of Britain's greatest painters, was born in a house in Sudbury *(see Lavenham, p210)*. He was best known for his portraits, such as this one of *Mr and Mrs Andrews*.

Charles Darwin (1809–82), who developed the theory that man and apes have a common ancestor, wrote his most famous book, *On the Origin of Species*, while living at Down House, Downe.

Charles Dickens (1812–70), the prolific and popular Victorian novelist *(see p193)*, had many connections with Kent. He took holidays in Broadstairs, at Bleak House, later named after his famous novel.

Winston Churchill (1874–1965), Britain's inspirational Prime Minister in World War II *(see p193)*, lived at Chartwell, in Westerham, for 40 years until his death. He relaxed by rebuilding parts of the house.

Vanessa Bell (1879–1961), artist and member of the Bloomsbury Group, lived at Charleston, in Lewes, until her death in 1961. The 18th-century farmhouse reflects her decorative ideas and is filled with murals, paintings and painted furniture *(see p184)*.

Rudyard Kipling (1865–1936), the poet and novelist, was born in India but lived at Batemans, in Burwash, near Hastings, for 34 years until his death. His most famous works include *Kim*, the two *Jungle Books* and the *Just So Stories*.

THE DOWNS AND CHANNEL COAST

Hampshire · Surrey · East Sussex · West Sussex · Kent

When settlers, invaders and missionaries came from Europe, the southeast coast was their first landfall. The wooded chalk ridges and lower-lying weald beyond them made an ideal base for settlement and proved to be productive farmland.

The Romans were the first to build major fortifications along the Channel Coast to discourage potential attackers from the European mainland. The remains of many of these can be seen today, and some, like Portchester Castle just outside Portsmouth, were incorporated into more substantial defences in later centuries. There also exists substantial evidence of Roman domestic buildings, such as Fishbourne Palace, in coastal areas and further inland.

The magnificence of cathedrals such as Canterbury and Winchester bear witness to their role as important bases of the medieval church, then nearly as powerful as the state. Many Kent and Sussex ports grew prosperous on trade with the Continent – as did the hundreds of smugglers who operated from them. From Tudor times on, monarchs, noblemen and courtiers acquired estates and built manor houses in the countryside between London and the coast, appreciating the area's moderate climate and proximity to the capital. Many of these survive and are popular attractions for visitors. Today the southeast corner of England is its most prosperous and populous region. Parts of Surrey and Kent, up to 20 miles (32 km) from the capital, are known as the Stockbroker Belt: the area has many large, luxurious villas belonging to wealthy people prominent in business and the professions, attracted by the same virtues that appealed to the Tudor gentry.

The fertile area of Kent has long been known as the Garden of England, and despite the incursion of bricks and mortar, it is still a leading area for growing fruit (*see pp164–5*), being in a prime position for the metropolitan market nearby.

Aerial view of the medieval and moated Leeds Castle

◀ People walking on the cliff top near Beachy Head, East Sussex

Exploring the Downs and Channel Coast

The North and South Downs, separated by the lower-lying Weald are ideal walking country as well as being the site of many stately homes. Covering 618 sq miles (1,600 sq km), the South Downs National Park is steeped in English culture and history. From Tudor times, wealthy, London-based merchants and courtiers built their country residences in Kent, a day's ride from the capital, and many are open to the public. On the coast are the remains of sturdy castles put up to deter invaders from across the Channel. Some of Britain's earliest beach resorts were developed along this coast, and sea bathing is said to have been invented in Brighton.

Oast houses at Chiddingstone near Royal Tunbridge Wells

0 kilometres 20
0 miles 10

View of Brighton Pier from the promenade

For additional map symbols *see back flap*

Sights at a Glance

Getting Around

The area is well served, with a network of motorways and A roads from London to the major towns. The A259 is a scenic coast road which offers fine views over the English Channel. Bus and rail transport is also good, with a number of coach companies providing regular tours to the major sites. An InterCity train service runs to all the major towns.

Key

≡ Motorway
— Major road
— Secondary road
··· Minor road
— Scenic route
–•– Main railway
---- Minor railway
△ Summit

Canterbury Cathedral's spire, dominating the skyline

The Victorian Osborne House, Isle of Wight

❶ Isle of Wight

Isle of Wight. 🚶 138,000. 🚢 from Lymington, Southampton, Portsmouth. 🛈 Bus station, Ryde Esplanade (01983 813813). 🅆 **islandbreaks.co.uk**

A visit to **Osborne House**, the favoured seaside retreat of Queen Victoria and Prince Albert *(see p164)*, is alone worth the ferry ride from the mainland. Furnished much as they left it, the house provides a marvellous insight into royal life and is dotted with family mementos.

The **Swiss Cottage** was built for the royal children to play in. It is now a museum attached to Osborne House. Adjacent to it you can see the bathing machine used by the queen to preserve her modesty while taking her to the edge of the sea *(see p373)*.

The other main sight on the island is **Carisbrooke Castle**, built in the 11th century. A walk on its outer wall and the climb to the top of its keep provides spectacular views. It was here that Charles I *(see p56–7)* was held prisoner in 1647; an attempt to escape was foiled when he got stuck between the bars of a window.

The island is a base for ocean sailing, especially during Cowes Week *(see p71)*. The scenic highlight is the **Needles** – three towers of rock jutting out of the sea at the island's western end. This is only a short walk from Alum Bay, famous for its multi-coloured cliffs and sand.

🏛 **Osborne House**
East Cowes. **Tel** 01983 200022. **Open** 10am–6pm (5pm winter) daily (Nov–Mar: Sat & Sun). 🅿 🛗 limited. 🚭 (also 🖥 in Swiss Cottage Apr–Oct only). 🏠 EH

🏰 **Carisbrooke Castle**
Newport. **Tel** 01983 522107. **Open** daily (Nov–Mar: Sat & Sun). **Closed** 1 Jan, 24–26 Dec. 🅿 🛗 limited. 🛒 in summer. 🏠

❷ Beaulieu

Brockenhurst, Hampshire. **Tel** 01590 612345. 🚆 Brockenhurst then taxi. **Open** daily. **Closed** 25 Dec. 🏠 🅿 🛗 🚭 by appt. 🖥 🅆 **beaulieu.co.uk**

Palace House, once the gatehouse of Beaulieu Abbey, has been the home of Lord Montagu's family since 1538. It now contains the finest collection of vintage cars in the country at the **National Motor Museum**, along with boats used in the James Bond films.

There is also an exhibition of monastic life in the ruined ancient **abbey**, founded in 1204 by King John *(see p52)*

for Cistercian monks. The original refectory now serves as the parish church.

Environs
Just south is the maritime museum at **Buckler's Hard**, telling the story of ship-building in the 18th century. The yard employed 4,000 men at its peak but declined when steel began to be used. Boat trips are available.

🏛 **Buckler's Hard**
Beaulieu. **Tel** 01590 616203. **Open** daily. **Closed** 25 Dec. 🅿 🛗 ltd. 🖥 🏠

❸ New Forest

Hampshire. 🚆 Brockenhurst. 🚌 Lymington then bus. 🛈 main car park, Lyndhurst (023 8028 2269). **Open** 10am–5pm daily. **Closed** 1 Jan, 24–26 Dec. 🅆 **thenewforest.co.uk**

This unique expanse of heath and woodland is, at 145 sq miles (375 sq km), the largest area of unenclosed land in southern Britain.

Despite its name, this is one of the few primeval oak woods in England. It was the popular hunting ground of Norman kings, and in 1100 William II was fatally wounded here in a hunting accident.

Today it is enjoyed by up to seven million visitors a year, who share it with the New Forest ponies, unique to the area, and over 1,500 fallow deer.

❹ Southampton

Hampshire. 🚶 220,000. ✈ 🚆 🚌 🚢 🅆 **visit-southampton.co.uk**

For centuries this has been a flourishing port. The *Mayflower* sailed from here to America in 1620 with the Pilgrim Fathers, as did the *Titanic* on its maiden

A 1909 Rolls-Royce Silver Ghost at Beaulieu's National Motor Museum

The luxurious liner the *Titanic*, which sank in 1912

and ultimately tragic voyage in 1912.

Sea City Museum's galleries focus on the lives and times of those who have sailed from the port of Southampton over the past 2,000 years.

There is a walk around the remains of the medieval city wall. At the head of the High Street stands the old city gate, **Bargate**, the most elaborate gate to survive in England. It still has its 13th-century drum towers and is decorated with intricate, 17th-century armorial carvings.

Ⅲ Sea City Museum
Havelock Rd. **Tel** 023 8083 3007. **Open** 10am–5pm daily. 🅿️ ♿ 📷 💻
w seacity.co.uk

❺ Portsmouth

Hampshire. 🗺️ 207,000. ✈️ 🚢 🚌 ℹ️
D-Day Museum (023 9282 6722). 🚢
Thu–Sat. **w** visitportsmouth.co.uk

Once a vital naval port, Portsmouth is a vibrant waterfront city with a fascinating English naval history.

Under the banner of **Portsmouth Historic Dockyard**, the city's historic dockyard is the hub of Portsmouth's most important sights. Among these is the hull of the *Mary Rose*, the favourite of Henry VIII *(see p54)*, which capsized on its maiden voyage as it left to fight the French in 1545. It was recovered from the sea bed in 1982 and has been reunited, in the **Mary Rose Museum**, with many of the 19,000 16th-century objects that have been raised from the wreck in an ongoing £35-million project. This museum gives an absorbing insight into life at sea in Tudor times.

Nearby is HMS *Victory*, the English flagship on which Admiral Nelson was killed at Trafalgar *(see p35)* and now restored to its former glory. You can also visit the National Museum of the Royal Navy which deals with naval history from the 16th century to the Falklands War, the 19th-century HMS *Warrior*, and galleries telling the story of Nelson.

Portsmouth's other military memorial is the **D-Day Museum**. This is centred on the *Overlord Embroidery*, a masterpiece of needlework commissioned in 1968 from the Royal School of Needlework, depicting the World War II Allied landing in Normandy in 1944. **Portchester Castle**, on the north edge of the harbour, was fortified in the third century and is the best example of Roman sea defences in northern Europe. The Normans later used

The figurehead on the bow of HMS *Victory* at Portsmouth

the Roman walls to enclose a castle – only the keep survives – and a church. Henry V used the castle as a garrison before the Battle of Agincourt *(see p53)*. In the 18th–19th centuries it was a prisoner-of-war camp.

Among less warlike attractions is the **Charles Dickens Birthplace Museum** *(see p193)*, the house where the author was born in 1812.

The striking **Spinnaker Tower** rises to 170 m (558 ft) above Portsmouth; the views over the harbour and beyond are quite magnificent.

Ⅲ Portsmouth Historic Dockyard
Victory Gate, HM Naval Base. **Tel** 023 9283 9766. **Open** daily (last tickets: 4pm). **Closed** 24–26 Dec. 🅿️ ♿ partial. 📷 💻 📷

Ⅲ Mary Rose Museum
Portsmouth Historic Dockyard. **Tel** 023 9281 2931. **Open** daily (last tickets: 4pm). **Closed** 24–26 Dec. 🅿️ 📷 📷

Ⅲ D-Day Museum
Museum Rd. **Tel** 023 9282 7261. **Open** daily. **Closed** 24–26 Dec. 🅿️ ♿ 💻 📷

🏰 Portchester Castle
Church Rd, Porchester. **Tel** 023 9237 8291. **Open** phone for details. **Closed** 1 Jan, 24–26 Dec. 🅿️ ♿ 📷 📷 🔊

Ⅲ Charles Dickens Birthplace Museum
393 Old Commercial Rd. **Tel** 023 9282 7261. **Open** Apr–Sep: Tue–Sun; also 7 Feb (Dickens's birthday). 🅿️ 📷 📷

🗼 Spinnaker Tower
Gunwharf Quays. **Tel** 023 9285 7520. **Open** daily. 🅿️ 📷 💻

A wild pony and her foal roaming freely in the New Forest

❻ Winchester

Hampshire. 🚇 36,000. 🚆 🚌 ℹ️
Guildhall, High St (01962 840500). 🏪
Wed–Sat. 🆆 **visitwinchester.co.uk**

Capital of the ancient kingdom
of Wessex, the city of
Winchester was also the
headquarters of the Anglo-
Saxon kings until the Norman
Conquest *(see p51)*.

William the Conqueror built
one of his first English castles
here. The only surviving part of
the castle is the **Great Hall**,
erected in 1235 to replace the
original. It is now home to the
legendary Round Table. The story

behind the table is a mix of
history and myth. King Arthur *(see
p289)* had it shaped so no knight
could claim precedence. It was
said to have been built by the
wizard Merlin but was actually
made in the 13th century.

The **Westgate Museum** is
one of the two surviving 12th-
century gatehouses in the city
wall. The room (once a prison)
above the gate has a
16th-century painted ceiling.
It was moved here from
Winchester College, England's
oldest fee-paying, or "public"
school. Winchester has been an
ecclesiastical centre for many

The 13th-century Round Table, Great
Hall, Winchester

centuries. **Wolvesey Castle**
(built around 1110) was the
home of the **cathedral's**
bishops after the Conquest.

The Library has over 4,000 books.
This "B" from Psalm 1 is found in the
Winchester Bible, an exquisite work
of 12th-century illumination.

**The Norman chapter
house** ceased to be
used in 1580. Only the
Norman arches survive.

Author Izaac Walton
(1593–1683) is depicted in
the stained glass Anglers'
Window made in 1914.

The Lady Chapel
was rebuilt by
Elizabeth of York
(c.1500) after her
son was baptized
in the cathedral.

These magnificent choir-stalls
(c.1308) are England's oldest.

The Perpendicular nave is
the highlight of the building.

Jane Austen's
grave

Main
entrance

Visitors'
centre

Winchester Cathedral

The Close. **Tel** 01962 857200.
Open daily. 🅿️ ♿ ✏️ 📷
🆆 **winchester-cathedral.org.uk**

The first church was built here in 648, but the
present building was begun in 1079. Originally
a Benedictine monastery, much of the Norman
architecture remains despite continual
modifications until the early 16th century.

The 12th-century
black Tournai
marble font

The **Hospital of St Cross** is an almshouse built in 1446.

Weary strangers may claim the "Wayfarer's Dole" a horn (cup) of ale and bread, given out since medieval times.

🏛 **Great Hall & Visitor Centre**
Castle Ave. **Tel** 01962 846476.
Open daily. **Closed** 25, 26 Dec. 🚻

🏛 **Westgate Museum**
High St. **Tel** 01962 869864.
Open Sat & Sun. 📷

🏛 **Hospital of St Cross**
St Cross Rd. **Tel** 01962 878218.
Open Mon–Sat (daily in summer).
Closed Good Fri, 25 Dec. 🅿 🚻
🌐 stcrosshospital.co.uk

The Close originally contained the domestic buildings for the monks of the Priory of St Swithun – the name before it became Winchester Cathedral. Most of the buildings, such as the refectory and cloisters, were destroyed during the Dissolution of the Monasteries (*see p54*).

Prior's Hall

❼ Chichester

West Sussex. 🚶 26,000. 🚆 🚌 *i*
The Novium, Tower St (01243 775888).
🏪 Wed, alternate Fri (Farmers' market), Sat. 🌐 **visitchichester.org**

This wonderfully preserved market town, with an elaborate early 16th-century market cross at its centre, is dominated by its **cathedral**, consecrated in 1108. The cathedral's graceful spire dominates the town and is said to be the only English cathedral spire visible from the sea. Also of interest is the cathedral's unique detached bell tower dating from 1436.

There are two carved stone panels in the choir, dating from 1140. Modern works include paintings by Graham Sutherland (1903–80) and a stained-glass window by Marc Chagall (1887–1985).

Environs

Just west at Bosham is the Saxon **Holy Trinity Church**, thought to have been used by King Canute (*see p50*). Myth has it that this was where Canute failed to stop the incoming tide and so proved to his courtiers that his powers had limits. The church appears in the *Bayeux Tapestry*, held in France, because Harold heard mass here in 1064 before he was shipwrecked off Normandy and then rescued by William the Conqueror (*see p51*).

The refurbished **Fishbourne Roman Palace** (*see p49*), between Bosham and Chichester, is the largest Roman villa in Britain. It covers 3 ha (7 acres) and was discovered in 1960 by a workman. Constructed from AD 75, it was destroyed by fire in 285. The north wing has some of the

Chagall's stained-glass window (1978), Chichester Cathedral

finest mosaics in Britain, including one of Cupid.

To the north is the 18th-century **Goodwood House**. Its magnificent art collection features works by Canaletto (1697–1768) and Stubbs (1724–1806). Home to the Earl of March, it has a motor racing circuit, where the popular Festival of Speed is held in July, and a horseracing course on the Downs.

⛪ **Chichester Cathedral**
West St. **Tel** 01243 782595.
Open daily. **Closed** for Mass.
🚻 📷 🛍 📷

🏛 **Fishbourne Roman Palace**
Fishbourne. **Tel** 01243 785859. **Open**
Feb–mid-Dec: daily; mid-Dec–Jan (café closed): Sat, Sun. 🅿 🚻 📷 📷
📷 🌐 **sussexpast.co.uk**

🏛 **Goodwood House**
Goodwood. **Tel** 01243 755048. **Open**
mid-Mar–mid-Oct: Sun–Mon (pm); Aug: Sun–Thu (pm). **Closed** special events, last-minute closures. Call ahead. 🅿 🚻
📷 📷

William Walker

At the beginning of the 20th century, the cathedral's east end seemed certain to collapse unless its foundations were underpinned. But because the water table lies only just below the surface, the work had to be done under water. From 1906 to 1911, Walker, a deep-sea diver, worked six hours a day laying sacks of cement beneath the unsteady walls until the building was safe.

William Walker in his diving suit

The dominating position of Arundel Castle, West Sussex

❽ Arundel Castle

Arundel, West Sussex. **Tel** 01903
882173. 🚂 Arundel. **Open** Apr–Oct:
10am–5pm Tue–Sun. **Closed** public
hols. 🅿️ ♿ ✅ by arrangement. ⚡
📷 🏠 🌐 arundelcastle.org

Dominating the small riverside
town below, this vast, grey hill-
top castle, surrounded by
castellated walls, was first built
by the Normans.

During the 16th century it
was acquired by the powerful
Dukes of Norfolk, the country's
senior Roman Catholic family,
whose descendants still live
here. They rebuilt it after the
original was virtually destroyed
by Parliamentarians in 1643 *(see
p56),* and restored it again in the
19th century.

In the castle grounds is the
parish church of **St Nicholas**.
The small Catholic Fitzalan chapel
(c.1380) was built into its east
end by the castle's first owners,
the Fitzalans, and can only be
entered from the grounds.

❾ Petworth House

Petworth, West Sussex. **Tel** 01798
342207. 🚂 Pulborough then bus.
House **Open** Mar–Nov: Sat–Wed. Park
Open daily. 🅿️ 🚻 ♿ limited. ⚡ 📷 NT
🌐 nationaltrust.org.uk/petworth

This late 17th-century house
was immortalized in a series of
famous views by the painter J M
W Turner *(see p95).* Some of his
best paintings are on display here
and are part of Petworth's outstanding art collection, which also
includes works by Titian (1488–

1576), Van Dyck (1599–1641) and
Gainsborough *(see p167).* Also
extremely well represented is
ancient Roman and Greek
sculpture, such as the 4th-century
BC *Leconfield Aphrodite,* widely
thought to be by Praxiteles.

The Carved Room is decor-
ated with intricately carved
wood panels of birds, flowers
and musical instruments, by
Grinling Gibbons (1648–1721).

The large deer park includes
some of the earliest work of
"Capability" Brown *(see p30).*

The Restoration clock on the Tudor
Guildhall, Guildford

❿ Guildford

Surrey. 🅐 63,000. 🚂 🚌 ℹ️ 115
High St (01483 444333). 🗓️ Fri, Sat.
🌐 visitguildford.com

The county town of Surrey,
settled since Saxon times,
incorporates the remains of
a small refurbished Norman
castle. The high street is lined
with Tudor buildings, such as

the impressive **Guildhall**, and
the huge modern red-brick
cathedral, completed in 1954,
dominates the town's skyline.

Environs
Guildford stands on the end of
the North Downs, a range of
chalk hills that are popular for
walking *(see p41).* The area also
has two famous beauty spots:
Leith Hill – the highest point in
southeast England – and **Box
Hill**. The view from the latter is
well worth the short, gentle
climb from West Humble.

To the north of Guildford is
RHS Wisley with 97 ha (240
acres) of beautiful gardens.
To the south of the town is
Clandon Park, an 18th-century
house with a sumptuous
interior. Its Marble Hall boasts
an intricate Baroque ceiling.

Southwest is Chawton, where
Jane Austen's House *(see p166)*
is located. This red-brick house
is where Austen wrote most of
her popular, witty novels,
including *Pride and Prejudice,*
exploring middle-class manners
in Georgian England.

🏛️ **RHS Wisley**
Off A3. **Tel** 0845 260 9000. **Open** daily.
🅿️ 🚻 💺 ⚡ 📷 🌐 rhs.org.uk

🏛️ **Clandon Park**
West Clandon, Surrey. **Tel** 01483
222482. **Open** Mar–Oct: Tue–Thu, Sun;
public hols. 🅿️ ✅ 🚻 call 01483
224462. ⚡ 📷 NT

🏛️ **Jane Austen's House**
Alton, Hants. **Tel** 01420 83262.
Open Jan–mid-Feb: Sat & Sun; mid-
Feb–Dec: daily. **Closed** 25 & 26 Dec.
🅿️ 🚻 limited. 📷

⑪ Hampton Court

East Molesey, Surrey. **Tel** 0844 482 7777. 🚂 Hampton Court. **Open** daily. **Closed** 24–26 Dec. 🅿️ ♿ 🛍️ 🚻 🍴 📷 **w** hrp.org.uk

The powerful chief minister and Archbishop of York to Henry VIII (see pp54–5), Cardinal Wolsey, leased a small manor house in 1514 and transformed it into a magnificent country residence. In 1528, to retain royal favour, Wolsey gave it to the king. After the royal takeover, Hampton Court was extended twice, first by Henry himself and in the 1690s by William and Mary, who used Christopher Wren (see p118) as the architect. From the outside the palace is a harmonious blend of Tudor and English Baroque; inside there is a striking contrast between Wren's Classical royal rooms, which include the King's Apartments, and Tudor archi-tecture, such as the Great Hall. Many of the state apartments are deco-rated with paintings and furnishings from the Royal Collection. The Baroque gardens, with their radiating avenues of majestic limes, collections of rare plants and formal plant beds, have been painstakingly restored.

Ceiling decoration, Hampton Court

The Baroque maze is one of the garden's most famous features; visitors often become lost in it.

The Queen's Apartments, including the Presence Chamber and Bedchamber, are arranged around the the north and east sides of Fountain Court.

Fountain Court

The Fountain Garden still has a few of the original yews planted by William and Mary (see p57). Only one fountain remains out of the original 13 built.

Great Hall

Main entrance

Anne Boleyn's Gateway is at the entrance to Clock Court.

River Thames

The Mantegna Gallery houses Andrea Mantegna's nine canvasses depicting *The Triumphs of Caesar* (1490).

Long Water

Broad Walk

The Pond Garden, a sunken water garden, was part of Henry VIII's elaborate designs. The small pond in the middle contains a single-jet fountain.

The Tudor Chapel Royal was completed by Henry VIII. But the superb woodwork, including the massive reredos by Grinling Gibbons, all date from a major refurbishment by Queen Anne (c.1711).

⑫ Steyning

West Sussex. 🏠 5,000 ☷ *i* 9 The Causeway, Horsham (01403 211661).

This lovely little town in the lee of the Downs is packed with timber-framed houses from the Tudor period and earlier, with some built of flint and others in sandstone.

In Saxon times, Steyning was an important port and ship-building centre on the River Adur: King Ethelwulf, father of King Alfred *(see p51)*, was buried here in 858; his body was later moved to Winchester. The *Domesday Book (see p52)* records that Steyning had 123 houses, making it one of the largest towns in the south. The 12th-century church is spacious and splendid, evidence of the area's ancient prosperity; the tower, of chequered stone and flint, was added around 1600.

In the 14th century the river silted up and changed course away from the town, putting an end to its days as a port. Later it became an important coaching stop on the south coast road: the **Chequer Inn** recalls this prosperous period, with its unusual 18th-century flint and stone façade.

Environs

The remains of a **Norman castle** can be visited at Bramber, east of Steyning. This small, pretty village also contains the timber-framed **St Mary's House** (1470). It has fine panelled rooms, including the Elizabethan Painted Room, and one of the oldest trees in the country, a *Ginkgo biloba*.

Chanctonbury Ring and **Cissbury Ring**, on the hills west of Steyning, were Iron Age forts and the latter has the remains of a Neolithic flint mine. Worthing is the resort where Oscar Wilde (1854–1900) wrote *The Importance of Being Earnest*.

🏠 **St Mary's House**
Bramber. **Tel** 01903 816205. **Open** May–Sep: Sun (pm), Thu (pm), public hols (pm). ♿ 🖥 🏠

⑬ Street-by-Street: Brighton

As the nearest south coast resort to London, Brighton is perennially popular, but has always been more refined than its boisterous neighbours further east, such as Margate *(see p187)* and Southend. The spirit of the Prince Regent *(see p183)* lives on, not only in the magnificence of his Royal Pavilion, but in the city's reputation as a venue for adulterous weekends in discreet hotels. Brighton has always attracted actors and artists – Laurence Olivier made his final home here.

KING'S ROAD

BLACK L

GRAND JUNCTION RO

Old Ship Hotel
Built in 1559, it was later bought by Nicholas Tettersells, with the money given to him by Charles II as a reward for taking him to France during the Civil War *(see p56)*.

★ **Brighton Pier**
Built in 1899, this typical late-Victorian pier now caters for today's visitors with amusement arcades.

Key

— Suggested route

| 0 metres | 100 |
| 0 yards | 100 |

★ Royal Pavilion
The Prince Regent's fantastic Oriental palace helped turn Brighton into a fashionable resort, and is today its principal attraction.

VISITORS' CHECKLIST

Practical Information
East Sussex. 🏛 249,000.
ℹ 01273 290 337. 🕐 Mon–Sat.
🎭 International Arts Festival: May.
🌐 visitbrighton.com

Transport
🚆 Brighton. 🚌 Pool Valley.

Many new plays are first staged in the charming Theatre Royal, established in 1807, before they move to the West End of London.

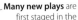

Art Deco
This 1920s Art Deco bronze lamp is on display at the Brighton Museum and Art Gallery.

Brighton Dome, an Indian-style building opposite the Royal Pavilion and once George IV's stables, is now a major arts venue.

The Lanes

BLACK LION ST · PRINCE ALBERT ST · UNION ST · MEETING HOUSE LA · MEETING HOUSE LA · NILE ST · MEETING HOUSE LANE · BRIGHTON PL · BARTHOLOMEWS · REGENT ARCADE · MARKET ST · NORTH ST · EAST ST

Sea Life Centre
Built in 1872 as a menagerie, it became an aquarium in 1929. Don't miss the sharks and other British marine life.

Eastbourne

The Lanes
Today a maze of antique and independent shops, the Lanes were the original streets of the village of Brighthelm-stone.

LANES

Brighton: Royal Pavilion

As sea bathing became fashionable in the mid-18th century, Brighton was transformed into England's first seaside resort. Its gaiety soon appealed to the rakish Prince of Wales, who became George IV in 1820. When, in 1785, he secretly married Mrs Fitzherbert, it was here that they conducted their liaison. He moved to a farmhouse near the shore and had it enlarged by Henry Holland *(see p32)*. As his parties grew more lavish, George needed a suitably extravagant setting for them, and in 1815 he employed John Nash *(see p109)* to transform the house into a lavish Oriental palace. Completed in 1823, the exterior has remained largely unaltered. Queen Victoria sold the Pavilion to the town of Brighton in 1850.

★ Great Kitchen
The Prince's epic banquets required a kitchen of huge proportions. The vast ranges and long shelves of gleaming copper pans were used by famous chefs of the day.

★ Banqueting Room
Fiery dragons feature in many of the interior schemes. This colourful one dominates the centre of the Banqueting Room's extraordinary ceiling, and has a huge crystal chandelier suspended from it.

KEY

① **The exterior** is partly built in Bath stone.

② **Standard Lamps** More dragons, along with dolphins and lotus flowers, figure on the Banqueting Room's eight original standard lamps, made of porcelain, ormolu and gilded wood.

③ **The banqueting table**, which seats 24 people, is laid as for a splendid feast.

④ **Banqueting Room Gallery**.

⑤ **South Galleries**

⑥ **The eastern façade of the Pavilion**

⑦ **Central Dome** Nash adopted what he called the Hindu Style, as in this delicate tracery on one of the imposing turban domes.

⑧ **Music Room Gallery**

⑨ **Yellow Bow Rooms**

⑩ **The Music Room**, with its crimson and gold murals, was where a 70-piece orchestra played to the Prince's guests.

⑪ **The domes** are made of cast iron.

Saloon
The original farmhouse that stood on the site was transformed into a villa by architect Henry Holland. The saloon, decorated with Chinese wallpaper, was the central room of the villa.

Prince of Wales and Mrs Fitzherbert

The Prince of Wales was only 23 years old when he fell in love with Maria Fitzherbert, a 29-year-old Catholic widow, and secretly married her. They lived in the farmhouse together and were the toast of Brighton society until George's official marriage took place to Caroline of Brunswick in 1795. Mrs Fitzherbert moved into a small house nearby.

VISITORS' CHECKLIST

Practical Information
Old Steine, Brighton. **Tel** 03000 290900. **Open** Apr–Sep: 9:30am–5:45pm; Oct–Mar: 10am–5:15pm (last adm: 45 mins before closing); daily.
Closed 25, 26 Dec. 🅿 ♿ limited. 🎫 📷 🍴 🛍
Ⓦ brighton-hove-pavilion. org.uk

Queen Victoria's Bedroom
This reproduction four-poster is on display in the upper floor apartments that were used by Queen Victoria (*see pp60–61*).

Long Gallery
Mandarin figures, which can nod their heads, line the pink and blue walls of this 49 m (162 ft) gallery.

⑪
⑨
⑩
⑧

Plan of the Royal Pavilion

Both Holland and Nash made additions and changes to the original farmhouse. The upper floor contains bedrooms, such as the Yellow Bow Rooms, which George's brothers used. The shaded areas represent the artwork above.

Plan labels: Exit · Entrance · Stairs to upper floor · King's Apartments · Shop · Octagon Hall · Great Kitchen · Banqueting Room · Saloon · Long Gallery · Music Room · Deckers Room · Banqueting Room Gallery · Music Room Gallery

Upstairs interior of Anne of Cleves House, Lewes

⑭ Lewes

East Sussex. 16,000. 187 High St (01273 483448). Glyndebourne Festival: May–Aug.

The ancient county town of Sussex was a vital strategic site for the Saxons, because of its high vantage point looking out over the coastline. William the Conqueror built a wooden castle here in 1067 but this was soon replaced by a large stone structure whose remains can be visited today.

In 1264 it was the site of a critical battle in which Simon de Montfort and his barons defeated Henry III, enabling them to establish the first English Parliament.

The Tudor **Anne of Cleves House** is a museum of local history, although Anne of Cleves, Henry VIII's fourth wife, never actually lived here.

On Guy Fawkes Night *(see p68)* lighted tar barrels are rolled to the river and various effigies, including of the Pope and Guy Fawkes, are burned. This commemorates the town's 17 Protestant martyrs burnt at the stake by Mary I *(see p55).*

Environs
Nearby are the 16th-century **Glynde Place**, a fine courtyard house, and the charming **Charleston**, home to the Bloomsbury Group *(see p167).*

Anne of Cleves House
Lewes. **Tel** 01273 474610. **Open** daily (Feb–Oct: phone for details). **Closed** 24–26 Dec.

Glynde Place
Lewes. **Tel** 01273 858224. **Open** May–Aug: pm Wed, Thu, Sun.

Charleston
Lewes. **Tel** 01323 811626. **Open** Apr–Oct: pm only, Bank Hol Mon. **charleston.org.uk**

⑮ Eastbourne

East Sussex. 93,000. Cornfield Rd (0871 663 0031). Wed. **visiteastbourne.com**

This Victorian seaside resort is a popular place for retirement, as well as a first-rate centre for touring the Downs. The South Downs Way *(see p41)* begins at **Beachy Head**, the spectacular 163 m (536 ft) chalk cliff just on the outskirts of the town. From here it is a bracing walk to the cliff top at Birling Gap, with views to the **Seven Sisters**, the chalk hills that end abruptly as they meet the sea.

Environs
To the west of Eastbourne is **Seven Sisters Country Park**, a 285 ha (700 acre) area of chalk cliffs and Downland marsh that is open all year. The **Park Visitor's Centre** contains information on the local area, history and geology.

Just north is the pretty village of **Alfriston**, with an ancient market cross and a 15th-century inn, **The Star**, in its quaint main street. Near the church is the 14th-century **Clergy House** that, in 1896, became the first National Trust property *(see p33).* To the east is the huge prehistoric chalk carving, the **Long Man of Wilmington** *(see p225).*

Park Visitor's Centre
Exceat, Seaford. **Tel** 0345 608 0193. **Open** Apr–Oct: daily; Feb, Mar, Nov: Sat & Sun. **Closed** Jan, Dec.

Clergy House
Alfriston. **Tel** 01323 870001. **Open** Sat–Mon, Wed, Thu. **Closed** Jan.

The lighthouse (1902) at the foot of Beachy Head, Eastbourne

The meandering River Cuckmere flowing through the South Downs to the beach at Cuckmere Haven

⑯ The Downs

East Sussex. 🚆 🚌 Eastbourne, Petersfield, Chichester & others. 𝒊 Cornfield Rd, Eastbourne (0871 663 0031). 🆆 southdowns.gov.uk

The North and South Downs are parallel chalk ridges that run from east to west all the way across Kent, Sussex and Surrey, separated by the lower-lying and fertile Kent and Sussex Weald.

The South Downs were given National Park status in 2011. The area features great biodiversity and encompasses a multitude of bustling towns and villages.

The smooth Downland hills are covered with springy turf, kept short by grazing sheep, making an ideal surface for walkers. The hill above the precipitous Devil's Dyke, just north of Brighton, offers spectacular views across the Downs. The legend is that the Devil cut the gorge to let in the sea and flood the

countryside, but was foiled by divine intervention. The River Cuckmere runs through one of the most picturesque parts of the South Downs.

Located at the highest point of the Downs is Uppark House, a neat square National Trust-owned building that has been meticulously restored to its mid-18th-century appearance.

⑰ Hastings

East Sussex. 🅰 83,000. 🚆 🚌 𝒊 Priory Meadow, Queens Square (01424 451111). 🆆 visithastings.com

This fascinating seaside town was one of the first Cinque Ports (see p186) and is still a thriving fishing port. The town is characterized by the unique tall wooden "net shops" on the beach, where for hundreds of years fishermen have stored their nets. In the 19th century,

the area to the west of the Old Town was built up as a seaside resort, which left the narrow, characterful streets of the old fishermen's quarter intact. There are two cliff railways and smugglers' caves displaying where contraband used to be stored (see p284).

Environs

Seven miles (11 km) from Hastings is Battle. The centre square of this small town is dominated by the gatehouse of **Battle Abbey**. William the Conqueror built this on the site of his great victory, reputedly placing the high altar where Harold fell, But the abbey was destroyed in the Dissolution (see p54). There is an evocative walk around the actual battlefield.

🏛 Battle Abbey

High St, Battle. **Tel** 01424 775705. **Open** Easter–Sep: daily; Oct–Easter: Sat & Sun. **Closed** 1 Jan, 24–26 Dec.
🅿 ♿ 🅿 📷 EH

Battle of Hastings

In 1066, William the Conqueror's (see p51) invading army from Normandy landed on the south coast, aiming to take Winchester and London. Hearing that King Harold and his army were camped just inland from Hastings, William confronted them. He won the battle after Harold was mortally wounded by an arrow in his eye. This last successful invasion of England is depicted on the Bayeux Tapestry in Normandy, France.

King Harold's death, Bayeux Tapestry

The wooden net shops, on Hastings' shingle beach

The fairy-tale 14th-century Bodiam Castle surrounded by its moat

🔞 Bodiam Castle

Nr Robertsbridge, E Sussex. **Tel** 01580 830196. 🚂 Robertsbridge then taxi. **Open** mid-Feb–Oct: daily; Nov–23 Dec: Wed–Sun; 27 Dec–mid-Feb: Sat, Sun. **Closed** 24–26 Dec. 🅿 ♿ ltd. 🖵 📷 NT

Surrounded by its wide, glistening moat, this late 14th-century castle is one of the most romantic in England.

It was previously thought to have been built as a defence against French invasion, but is now believed to have been intended as a home for a Sussex knight. The castle saw action during the Civil War (see p56), when it was damaged in an assault by Parliamentary soldiers. They removed the roof to reduce its use as a base for Charles I's troops.

It has been uninhabited since, but its grey stone has proved indestructible. With the exception of the roof, it was restored in 1919 by Lord Curzon who gave it to the nation.

Environs

To the east is **Great Dixter**, a 15th-century manor house restored by Sir Edwin Lutyens in 1910. The late Christopher Lloyd created a magnificent garden with a blend of terraces and borders, and a great nursery, too.

🏠 **Great Dixter**
Northiam, Rye. **Tel** 01797 252878. **Open** Apr–Oct: 2–5:30pm Tue–Sun & public hols. 🅿 📷 W greatdixter.co.uk

🔞 Rye

See pp188–9.

🔟 Romney Marsh

Kent. 🚂 Ashford. 🚌 Ashford, Hythe. ℹ Dymchurch Rd, New Romney (01797 369487). **Open** Easter–Sep: Thu–Mon; Oct–Easter: Fri–Mon.

Until Roman times Romney Marsh and its southern neighbour Walland Marsh were entirely covered by the sea at high tide. The Romans drained the Romney section, and Walland Marsh was gradually reclaimed during the Middle Ages. Together they formed a large area of fertile land, particularly suitable for the Romney Marsh sheep bred for the quality of their wool.

Dungeness, a desolate and lonely spot at the southeastern tip of the area, is dominated by a lighthouse and two nuclear power stations. It is also the southern terminus of the

Coastal Defence and the Cinque Ports

Before the Norman Conquest (see pp50–51), national government was weak and, with threats from Europe, it was important for Saxon kings to keep on good terms with the Channel ports. So, in return for keeping the royal fleet supplied with ships and men, five ports – Hastings, Romney, Hythe, Sandwich and Dover – were granted the right to levy taxes; others were added later. "Cinque" came from the old French word for five. The privileges were revoked during the 17th century. In 1803, in response to the growing threat from France, 74 fixed defences were built along the coast. Only 24 of these Martello towers still exist.

The cliff-top position of Dover Castle

A Martello tower, built as part of the Channel's defences

popular **Romney, Hythe and Dymchurch Light Railway** which was opened in 1927. During the summer this takes passengers 14 miles (23 km) up the coast to Hythe on trains a third the conventional size.

The northern edge of the marsh is crossed by the Royal Military Canal, built to serve both as a defence and supply line in 1804, when it was feared Napoleon was planning an invasion *(see p59)*.

The Kent Wildlife Trust Visitor Centre explores the history of the Marsh and its wildlife. For more information visit www.kentwildlifetrust.org.uk

㉑ Dover

Kent. 🚶 30,000. 🚢 🚌 🚆 ℹ️ Dover Museum, Market Sq (01304 201066). 🗓 Tue. 🌐 whitecliffscountry.org.uk

Its proximity to the European mainland makes Dover the leading port for cross-Channel travel. Its famous white cliffs exert a strong pull on returning travellers.

Dover's strategic position and large natural harbour mean the town has always had an important role to play in the nation's defences.

Built on the original site of an ancient Saxon fortification, **Dover Castle**, has helped defend the town from 1198, when Henry II first built the keep, right up to World War II, when it was used as the command post for the Dunkirk evacuation. Exhibits in the castle and in the labyrinth of tunnels beneath made by prisoners in the Napoleonic Wars *(see p59)* cover all these periods.

Environs

One of the most significant sites in England's early history is the ruin of **Richborough Roman Fort**. Now a large grassy site two miles (3 km) inland, this was where, in AD 43, Claudius's Roman invaders *(see p48)* made their first landing. For hundreds of years afterwards, Rutupiae, as it was known, was one of the most important ports of entry and military bases in the country.

🏰 **Dover Castle**
Castle Hill. **Tel** 01304 211067. **Open** daily (Nov–Jan: Sat & Sun). **Closed** 1 Jan, 24–26 Dec. 🅿️ 🎧 of the tunnels, by appt. 🔊 📷 📸 EH

🏰 **Richborough Roman Fort**
Richborough. **Tel** 01304 612 013. **Open** Oct: Wed–Sun; Nov–Mar: Sat & Sun. 🅿️ 🔊 📸 EH

㉒ Margate

Kent. 🚶 40,000. 🚢 🚌 ℹ️ The Droit House, Stone Pier (01843 577577). 🌐 visitthanet.co.uk

A boisterous seaside resort on the Isle of Thanet, Margate has long been a popular destination. Nowadays **Turner Contemporary** is the big draw, both architecturally and for its exhibitions, including a look at Turner's fascination with light.

Environs

Just south is a 19th-century gentleman's residence, **Quex Park**, with two unusual towers in its grounds. The adjoining **Powell-Cotton Museum** has a fine collection of predominantly African art and artifacts, as well as unique wildlife dioramas. To the west is a Saxon church, built

Visitors relaxing on Margate's popular sandy beach

within the remains of the bleak Roman coastal fort of **Reculver**. Dramatic twin towers, known as the Two Sisters, were added to the church in the 12th century. The church now stands at the centre of a very pleasant, if rather windy, 37 ha (91 acre) camp site.

🖼 **Turner Contemporary**
Rendezvous. **Tel** 01843 233 000. **Open** Tue–Sun. 📷 📸 🌐 turnercontemporary.org

🏛 **Quex Park & Powell-Cotton Museum**
Birchington. **Tel** 01843 842168. **Open** Tue–Sun. House pm only. 🅿️ 🔊 📷 for groups. 🅿️ 📸 🌐 quexpark.co.uk

🏰 **Reculver Fort**
Reculver. **Tel** 01227 740 676 (Herne Bay Tourist Information). **Open** daily (exterior only). EH

A drainage dyke running through the fertile plains of Romney Marsh

⑲ Street-by-Street: Rye

This ancient and charming fortified town was added to the original Cinque ports *(see p186)* in the 12th–13th century. A huge storm in 1287 diverted the River Rother so that it met the sea at Rye, and for more than 300 years it was one of the most important Channel ports. However, in the 16th century the harbour began to silt up and the town is now 2 miles (3 km) inland. Rye was frequently attacked by the French, culminating in 1377 when it was burnt to the ground.

★ Mermaid Street
This delightful cobbled street, its huddled houses jutting out at unlikely angles, has hardly altered since it was rebuilt in the 14th century.

The Mint
Site of 12th-century Mint in the time of King Stephen.

The Mermaid
Inn, rebuilt c.1420, is Rye's largest medieval building. In the 1750s it was the headquarters of notorious and bloodthirsty smugglers called the Hawkhurst gang.

View over the River Tillingham

Strand Quay
The brick and timber warehouses survive from the prosperous days when Rye was a thriving port.

Lamb House
This fine Georgian house was built in 1722. George I stayed here when stranded in a storm, and author Henry James (1843–1916) lived here.

St Mary's Church
The turret clock (1561) is claimed to be the oldest working clock in the country.

↑ Hastings and railway station

CINQUE PORT STREET

TOWER STREET

CONDUIT HILL

HIGH STREET

HILDERS CLIFF

LION STREET

EAST STREET

MARKET STREET

The 16th-century Flushing Inn

This cistern was built in 1735; horse-drawn machinery was used to raise water to the highest part of the town.

...UARE

Gun Garden, Ypres Tower

Key
— Suggested route

| 0 metres | 50 |
| 0 yards | 50 |

★ Ypres Tower
Built as a castle in 1250, it was turned into a house in 1430. It is now used as the museum.

VISITORS' CHECKLIST

Practical Information
East Sussex. 🚇 4,500. ℹ 4/5 Lion Street (01797 229049). 🛒 Wed, Thu. 🎭 Rye Festival: Sep.
🌐 visit1066country.com/rye

Transport
🚆 🚌 Station Approach.

Land Gate
Built in the 14th century this is the only survivor of the old fortified town's four gates.

Environs

Just 2 miles (3 km) to the south of Rye is the small town of **Winchelsea**. At the behest of Edward I, it was moved to its present position in 1288, when most of the old town on lower land to the southeast, was drowned by the same storm that diverted the River Rother in 1287.

Winchelsea is probably Britain's first coherently planned medieval town. Although not all of it was built as originally planned, its rectangular grid survives today, as does the **Church of St Thomas Becket** (begun c.1300) at its centre. Several raids during the 14th century by the French damaged the church and burned down scores of houses. The church has three tombs, and there are also two well-preserved medieval tombs in the chantry. The three windows (1928–33) in the Lady Chapel were designed by Douglas Strachan as a memorial to those who died in World War I. Just beyond the edges of present-day Winchelsea are the remains of three of the original gates – showing just how big a town was first envisaged. The beach below is one of the finest on the southeast coast.

Camber Sands, to the east of the mouth of the Rother, is another excellent beach. Once used by fishermen, it is now popular with swimmers and edged with seaside bungalows and a bustling holiday camp. Camber Sands is also a favourite spot in the UK for kite- and windsurfing.

The ruins of **Camber Castle** are west of the sands, near Brede Lock, Rye. This was one of the forts built along this coast by Henry VIII when he feared an attack by the French. When the castle was built it was on the edge of the sea but it was abandoned in 1642 when it became stranded inland as the river silted up.

🏛 **Camber Castle**
Camber, Rye.
Tel 01797 223862. **Open** Jul–Sep: Sat, Sun pm for 📷 only. EH

Jesus on Christ Church Gate,
Canterbury Cathedral

❷❸ Canterbury

Kent. 🚉 50,000. 🚢 🚌 ℹ️ The
Beaney House of Knowledge, 18 High
St (01227 378100). 🗓️ Wed, Fri.
🌐 canterbury.co.uk

Its position on the London to
Dover route meant Canterbury
was an important Roman town
even before the arrival of St
Augustine in 597, sent by the
pope to convert the Anglo-
Saxons to Christianity. The town
soon became the centre of the
Christian Church in England.

With the building of the
cathedral and the martyrdom
of Thomas Becket *(see p52)*,
Canterbury's future as a
religious centre was assured.
Today, the town is a UNESCO
World Heritage Site.

Adjacent to the ruins of St
Augustine's Abbey, destroyed in
the Dissolution *(see p54)*, is St
Martin's Church, the oldest in
England, where St Augustine first
worshipped. It has impressive
Norman and Saxon work.

The Westgate Towers, built
in 1381, make for an imposing
medieval gatehouse.

For a glimpse into the city's
ancient past, visit the **Canterbury
Roman Museum**.

The Poor Priests' Hospital,
founded in the 1100s, is now the
Canterbury Heritage Museum.

🏛️ **Canterbury Roman Museum**
Longmarket, Butchery Lane. **Tel** 01227
785575. **Open** 10am–5pm daily. 🐾
♿ 🌐 canterbury-museums.co.uk

🏛️ **Canterbury Heritage Museum**
Stour St. **Tel** 01227 475202. **Open**
10am–5pm daily. 🐾 📷
🌐 canterbury-museums.co.uk

Canterbury Cathedral

To match Canterbury's growing ecclesiastical rank as a major
centre of Christianity, the first Norman archbishop, Lanfranc,
ordered a new cathedral to be built on the ruins of the Anglo-
Saxon cathedral in 1070. It was enlarged and rebuilt many
times and as a result embraces examples of all styles of
medieval architecture. The most poignant moment
in its history came in 1170 when Thomas Becket
was murdered here *(see p52)*. Four years after his
death a fire devastated the cathedral and the
Trinity Chapel was built to
house Becket's remains.
The shrine quickly became
an important religious site
and until the Dissolution
(see p54) the cathedral was
one of Christendom's chief
places of pilgrimage.

Main entrance

KEY

① **The South West Porch** (1426)
may have been built to
commemorate the victory at
Agincourt *(see p53)*.

② **The nave** at 60 m (188 ft)
makes Canterbury one of the
longest medieval churches.

③ **Great Cloister**

④ **Chapter House**

⑤ **The circular Corona Chapel**

⑥ **Trinity Chapel**

⑦ **St Augustine's Chair**

⑧ **The quire** (choir), completed
in 1184, is one of the longest in
England.

⑨ **The Great South Window** has
four stained glass panels (1958) by
Erwin Bossanyi.

★ **Medieval
Stained Glass**
This depiction of
the 1,000-year-old
Methuselah is a detail
from the southwest
transept window.

Geoffrey Chaucer

Considered to be the first great English poet, Geoffrey Chaucer (c.1345–1400), a customs official by profession, wrote a rumbustious and witty account of a group of pilgrims travelling from London to Becket's shrine in 1387 in the *Canterbury Tales*. The pilgrims represent a cross-section of 14th-century English society and the tales remain one of the greatest and most entertaining works of early English literature.

Wife of Bath, *Canterbury Tales*

VISITORS' CHECKLIST

Practical Information
11 The Precincts, Canterbury.
Tel 01227 762862. **Open**
9am–5:30pm Mon–Sat (5pm winter), 12:30–2pm Sun. Contact advised. **Closed** for services & concerts; Good Friday, 24 & 25 Dec. 🕒 🕇 8am daily; 5:30pm Mon–Fri; 3:15pm Sat, Sun; 11am Sun. ♿ 📷
w canterbury-cathedral.org

Bell Harry Tower
The central tower, dominating the skyline, was built in 1498 to house a bell donated by Henry of Eastry 100 years before. The fan vaulting is a superb example of the late Perpendicular style.

★ Site of the Shrine of St Thomas Becket
This Victorian illustration (anon) portrays Becket's canonization. The Trinity Chapel was built to house his tomb which stood here until it was destroyed in 1538. The spot is now marked by a lighted candle.

★ Black Prince's Tomb
This copper effigy is on the tomb of Edward III's son, who died in 1376.

The keep of Rochester Castle, dominating Rochester and the Medway Valley

㉔ Leeds Castle

Maidstone, Kent. **Tel** 01622 765400.
🚉 Bearsted then bus. **Open**
10:30am–5:30pm daily. **Closed** for
concerts & 25 Dec. 🅿️ ♿ 🚫 🛍 📷
W leeds-castle.com

Surrounded by a lake that
reflects the warm buff stone of
its crenellated turrets, Leeds is
often considered to be the most
beautiful castle in England.
Begun in the early 12th century,
it has been continuously
inhabited and its present
appearance is a result of
centuries of rebuilding and
extensions, most recently in
the 1930s. Leeds has royal
connections going back to 1278,
when it was given to Edward I
by a courtier seeking favour.

Henry VIII loved the castle and
visited it often, escaping from the
plague in London. It contains a
life-sized bust of Henry from the
late 16th century. Leeds passed
out of royal ownership when
Edward VI gave it to Sir Anthony
St Leger in 1552 as a reward for
helping to pacify the Irish.

㉕ Rochester

Kent. 🅰 145,000. 🚉 🚌 🚐 👁 95 High
Street (01634 843666).

Clustered at the mouth of the
River Medway are the towns
of Rochester, Chatham and
Gillingham, all rich in naval
history, but none more so than
Rochester, which occupied a
strategic site on the London
to Dover road.

England's tallest Norman keep
is at **Rochester Castle**, worth
climbing for the views over the
Medway. The town's medieval
history is still visible, with the
original city walls – which
followed the lines of the Roman
fortifications – on view in the
High Street, and some well-
preserved wall paintings in the
cathedral, built in 1088.

Environs
In Chatham, the **Historic
Dockyard** is now a museum of
shipbuilding and nautical crafts.
Fort Amherst nearby was built in
1756 to protect the dockyard and
river entrance from attack, and
has 1,800 m (5,570 ft) of tunnels
to explore that were hewn by
Napoleonic prisoners of war.

🏰 **Rochester Castle**
Castle Hill. **Tel** 0870 333 1181. **Open**
10am–4pm (6pm Apr–Sep) daily
(last adm: 45 mins before close).

Closed 1 Jan, 24–26 Dec. 🅿️ ♿
grounds only. 📷 EH

🏛 **Historic Dockyard**
Dock Rd, Chatham. **Tel** 01634 823807.
Open daily. 🅿️ ♿ 🚫 🛍 📷
W thedockyard.co.uk

🏰 **Fort Amherst**
Dock Rd, Chatham. **Tel** 01634 847747.
Open call for details. 🅿️ 🛍

㉖ Knole

Sevenoaks, Kent. **Tel** 01732 462100.
🚉 Sevenoaks then taxi. House
Open Mar–Jul: Tue–Sun (pm);
Aug: daily; Sep–Oct: Wed–
Sun (pm), Good Fri & pub hols.
Park **Open** daily. 🅿️ ♿ 🚫 by appt.
🛍 📷 NT

This huge Tudor mansion was
built in the late 15th century,
and was seized by Henry VIII
from the Archbishop of
Canterbury at the Dissolution
(*see p54*). In 1566 Queen
Elizabeth I gave it to her
cousin Thomas Sackville. His
descendants have lived here
ever since, including the writer
Vita Sackville-West,
(1892–1962). The
house is well known
for its 17th-century
furniture, such as the
elaborate bed made for James
II. The 405-ha (1,000-acre) park
has deer and lovely walks.

A gladiator, Knole

Environs
A small manor house, **Ightham
Mote**, east of Knole, is one of the
finest examples of English

medieval architecture. Its 14th-century timber-and-stone building encloses a central court and is encircled by a moat.

At Sissinghurst Castle Garden are gardens created by Vita Sackville-West and her husband Harold Nicolson in the 1930s.

🖿 Ightham Mote

Ivy Hatch, Sevenoaks. **Tel** 01732 810378. **Open** Mar–Oct: Thu–Mon; Nov & Dec: Thu–Sun. 🅿️ ♿ ✏️ 📷 🅽🆃

🌿 Sissinghurst Castle Garden

Cranbrook. **Tel** 01580 710700. **Open** Mar–Dec: daily. 🅽🆃 🅿️ ♿ limited. ✏️ 📷 📷

The façade of Chartwell, Winston Churchill's home

㉗ Hever Castle

Edenbridge, Kent. **Tel** 01732 865224. 🚉 Edenbridge Town. **Open** Apr–Oct: daily; Nov, Dec, Mar: Wed–Sun (phone for times). 🅿️ ♿ limited. ✏️ 📷 groups by arrangement. 📷 🆆 **hevercastle.co.uk**

This small, moated castle is famous as the 16th-century home of Anne Boleyn, the doomed wife of Henry VIII, executed for adultery. She lived here as a young woman and the king often visited her while staying at Leeds Castle. In 1903 Hever was bought by William Waldorf Astor, who undertook a restoration programme, building a Neo-Tudor village alongside it to accommodate guests and servants. The moat and gatehouse date from around 1270.

Environs

To the northwest of Hever is **Chartwell**, the family home of Sir Winston Churchill (*see p63*). It remains furnished as it was when he lived here. Some 140 of his paintings are on display.

🖿 Chartwell

Westerham, Kent. **Tel** 01732 868381. House: **Open** Mar–Oct: daily. Gardens & exhibitions vary; phone for details. 🅿️ ♿ limited. ✏️ 📷 🅽🆃

Charles Dickens

Charles Dickens (1812–70), a popular writer in his own time, is still widely read today. He was born in Portsmouth but moved to Chatham aged five. As an adult, Dickens lived in London but kept up his Kent connections, taking holidays in Broadstairs, just south of Margate – where he wrote *David Copperfield* – and spending his last years at Gad's Hill, near Rochester. The town celebrates the famous connection with an annual Dickens festival.

㉘ Royal Tunbridge Wells

Kent. 🅰️ 55,000. 🚉 🚌 🛈 Old Fish Market, The Pantiles (01892 515 675). 🗓️ 2nd & 4th Sat. 🆆 **visittunbridgewells.com**

Helped by royal patronage, the town became a popular spa in the 17th and 18th centuries after mineral springs were discovered in 1606. The Pantiles – the colonnaded and paved promenade – was laid out in the 1700s.

Environs

Nearby manor house **Penshurst Place**, built in the 1340s, has an 18-m- (60-ft-) high Great Hall.

🖿 Penshurst Place

Tonbridge, Kent. **Tel** 01892 870307. **Open** Apr–Oct: daily; Mar: Sat & Sun: House: **Open** noon–4pm; Gardens: **Open** 10:30am–6pm; Toy Museum: noon–4pm. 🅿️ ♿ limited. ✏️ 📷 📷

An early 18th-century astrolabe to measure the stars, Hever Castle garden

EAST ANGLIA

Norfolk · Suffolk · Essex · Cambridgeshire

The bulge of land between the Thames Estuary and the Wash, flat but far from featureless, sits aside from the main north – south axis through Britain, and for that reason it has succeeded in maintaining and preserving its distinctive architecture, traditions and rural character in both cities and countryside.

East Anglia's name derives from the Angles, the people from northern Germany who settled here during the 5th and 6th centuries. East Anglians have long been a breed of plain-spoken and independent people. Two pro-minent East Anglians – Queen Boudica in the 1st century and Oliver Cromwell in the 17th century – were famous for their stubbornness and their refusal to bow to constituted authority. During the Civil War, East Anglia was Cromwell's most reliable source of support. The hardy people who made a difficult living hunting and fishing in the swampy fens, which were drained in the 17th century, were called the Fen Tigers. After draining, the peaty soil proved ideal for arable farming, and today East Anglia grows about a third of Britain's vegetables. The rotation of crops, heralding Britain's agricultural revolution, was perfected in Norfolk in the 18th century. Many of the region's towns and cities grew prosperous on the agricultural wealth, including Norwich. The sea also plays a prominent role in East Anglian life. Coastal towns and villages support the many fishermen who use the North Sea, rich in herring in former days but now known mainly for flat fish.

In modern times, the area has become a centre of recreational sailing, both off the coast and on the inland waterway system known as the Norfolk Broads. East Anglia is also home to one of Britain's top universities: Cambridge.

Lavender fields in full bloom in July, Heacham, Norfolk

 Punts lined up along the River Cam, Cambridge

Exploring East Anglia

As you move away from London, you soon reach the countryside immortalized by the painter Constable *(see p208)*, scattered with churches, windmills and medieval agricultural barns. Nature lovers will find it fruitful territory, especially North Norfolk with its bird reserves and seal colonies. Boating enthusiasts, too, are well catered for in this, Britain's driest and sunniest region. The local architecture ranges from a mix of medieval to modern. The distinctive pink-washed cottages in Suffolk, flint cottages in Norfolk and thatched roofs everywhere, are also much in evidence.

Punting on the River Cam in Cambridge

For additional map symbols *see back flap*

Key

— Motorway
— Major road
— Secondary road
--- Minor road
···· Scenic route
—•— Main railway
— Minor railway

Getting Around

The region's more isolated sights can be very difficult to reach by public transport and, for a few people, car rental may be a cheaper and more efficient method of travelling around. The M11 motorway runs from London to Cambridge. The coast road from Aldeburgh to King's Lynn takes you through some of the best countryside in the area. There are frequent main-line trains to Norwich, Ipswich and Cambridge although the local trains are more sporadic. There are international and domestic airports at Stansted (see p634) and Norwich.

Beach huts on Wells-next-the-Sea beach, north Norfolk

0 kilometres 10
0 miles 10

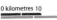

Sights at a Glance

1 Peterborough
2 Ely
3 Grimes Graves
4 Swaffham
5 Fens
6 King's Lynn
7 Sandringham
9 Blickling Hall
10 Norwich
11 Broads
12 Great Yarmouth
13 Lowestoft
14 Southwold
15 Dunwich
16 Aldeburgh
17 Framlingham Castle
18 Ipswich
20 Colchester
21 Coggeshall
22 Lavenham
23 Bury St Edmunds
24 Newmarket
25 Anglesey Abbey
26 Huntingdon
27 *Cambridge pp214–19*
28 Audley End
29 Epping Forest
30 Maldon

Walks and Tours

8 North Norfolk Tour
19 Constable Walk

❶ Peterborough

Cambridgeshire. 156,000. 🚉 🚌
🛈 9 Bridge Street (01733 452336).
🛒 Tue–Sat.
🌐 visitpeterborough.com

Although one of the oldest settlements in Britain, Peter-borough was designated a New Town in 1967, and is now a mixture of ancient and modern.

The city centre is dominated by the 12th-century **St Peter's Cathedral** which gave the city its name. The interior of this classic Norman building, with its vast yet simple nave, was badly damaged by Cromwell's troops *(see p56)*, but its unique painted wooden ceiling (1220) has survived intact. Catherine of Aragon, the first wife of Henry VIII, is buried here, although Cromwell's troops also destroyed her tomb.

Environs: The oldest wheel in Britain (1,300 BC) was found preserved in peat at **Flag Fen Bronze Age Centre**. The site provides a fascinating glimpse into prehistory.

🏛 **Flag Fen Bronze Age Centre**
The Droveway, Northey Rd. **Tel** 01733 313414. **Open** Apr–Sep: daily; Oct–Mar: contact for details. ♿ 📷 💻 🌐 flagfen.com

❸ Grimes Graves

Lynford, Norfolk. **Tel** 01842 810656.
🚉 Brandon then taxi. **Open** Apr–Sep: daily; Oct, Mar: Wed–Mon. ♿ 📷 ♿ exhibition area only. 🏛

One of the most important Neolithic sites in England, this was once an extensive complex of flint mines – 433 shafts have been located – dating from before 2000 BC.

Using antlers as pickaxes, Stone Age miners hacked through the soft chalk to extract the hard flint below to make weapons and tools. The flint may have been transported long distances around England on the prehistoric network of paths. You can descend 9 m (30 ft) by ladder into one of the shafts and see the galleries where the flint was mined. During excavations, unusual chalk models of

❷ Ely

Cambridgeshire. 18,000. 🚉 🛈 29 St Mary's St (01353 662062). **Open** daily. 🛒 Thu (general), Sat (craft & antiques); farmers' market every 2nd & 4th Sat. 🌐 visitely.org.uk

Built on a chalk hill, this small city is thought to be named after the eels in the nearby River Ouse. The hill was once an inaccessible island in the then marshy and treacherous Fens *(see p200)*. It was also the last stronghold of Anglo-Saxon resistance, under Hereward the Wake *(see p52)*, who hid in the cathedral until the Normans crossed the Fens in 1071.

Today this small prosperous city, totally dominated by the huge **cathedral**, is the market centre for the rich agri-cultural area surrounding it.

The lantern's glass windows admit light into the dome.

Stained glass museum

This painted wooden angel is one of hundreds of bosses that were carved all over the south and north transepts in the 13th and 14th centuries.

Octagon is made of wood, was built in 1322 when the Norman tower collapsed. Its roof, the lantern, took an extra 24 years to build and weighs 200 tonnes.

The tomb is that of Alan de Walsingham, designer of the unique Octagon.

Ely Cathedral

Ely. **Tel** 01353 667735. **Open** daily.
Closed special events. 📷 ♿ 📷 ♿ 💻 📷

Begun in 1083, the cathedral took 268 years to complete. It survived the Dissolution *(see p54)* but was closed for 17 years by Cromwell *(see p56)* who lived in Ely for a time.

a fertility goddess *(see p47)* and a phallus were discovered.

Environs
Nearby, at the centre of the once fertile plain known as the Breckland, is the small market town of **Thetford**.

Once a prosperous trading town, its fortunes dipped in the 16th century, when its priory was destroyed *(see p54)* and the surrounding land deteriorated due to excessive sheep grazing. The area was later planted with pine trees. A mound in the city marks the site of a pre-Norman castle.

The revolutionary writer and philosopher Tom Paine, author of *The Rights of Man*, was born here in 1737.

The huge cathedral dominates the flat Fens countryside surrounding Ely.

Painted ceiling, 19th century

The south aisle has 12 classic Norman arches at its foot, with pointed Early English windows above.

The Prior's Door (c.1150)

Area of cutaway

Oxburgh Hall surrounded by its medieval moat

❹ Swaffham

Norfolk. 🅼 6,700. 🚌 ℹ️ 4 London St (01760 722255). 🛒 Sat.
🌐 aroundswaffham.co.uk

The best-preserved Georgian town in East Anglia and a fashionable resort during the Regency period, Swaffham is at its liveliest on Saturdays when a market is held in the square around the market cross of 1783. In the centre of the town is the 15th-century **Church of St Peter and St Paul**, with a small spire added in the 19th century. It has a magnificent Tudor north aisle, said to have been paid for by John Chapman, the Pedlar of Swaffham. He is depicted on the two-sided town sign near the market place. Myth has it that he went to London and met a stranger who told him of hidden treasure at Swaffham. He returned, dug it up and used it to embellish the church, where he is shown in a window.

Environs
Castle Acre, north of the town, has the remains of a massive

Cluniac **priory**. Founded in 1090, its stunning Norman front still stands.

A short drive south is **Oxburgh Hall and Garden**, built by Sir Edmund Bedingfeld in 1482. The hall, entered through a huge 24 m (80 ft) fortified gatehouse, displays the velvet Oxburgh Hangings, embroidered by Mary, Queen of Scots *(see p515)*.

🏰 **Castle Acre Priory**
Castle Acre. **Tel** 01760 755394. **Open** daily (Nov–Mar: Sat & Sun. **Closed** 1 Jan, 24–26 Dec. 🅿️ ♿ ltd. 📷 EH

🏡 **Oxburgh Hall & Garden**
Oxborough. **Tel** 01366 328258. **Open** Mar–Oct: Sat–Wed (Aug: daily). Garden **Open** Nov–Dec: Sat, Sun. 🅿️ ♿ ltd. 🚫 📷 NT

Swaffham town sign

Boudica and the Iceni

When the Romans invaded Britain, the Iceni, the main tribe in East Anglia, joined forces with them to defeat the Catuvellauni, a rival tribe. But the Romans then turned on the Iceni, torturing Queen Boudica (or Boadicea). In AD 61, she led a revolt against Roman rule: her followers burned down London, Colchester and St Albans. The rebellion was put down and the queen took poison rather than submit. At Cockley Cley, near Swaffham, an Iceni camp has been excavated.

Illustration of Queen Boudica leading her Iceni followers

A windmill on Wicken Fen

❺ The Fens

Cambridgeshire/Norfolk. 🚊 Ely.
ℹ️ 29 St Mary's St, Ely (01353
662062). 🅦 visitely.org.uk

This is the open, flat, fertile
expanse that lies between
Lincoln, Cambridge, Bedford
and King's Lynn. Up until the
17th century it was a swamp,
and settlement was possible
only on "islands", such as Ely
(see p198).

Through the 17th century,
speculators, recognizing the
value of the peaty soil for farmland, brought in Dutch experts
to drain the fens. However,
as the peat dried, it
contracted, and the
fens have slowly been
getting lower. Powerful
electric pumps now
keep it drained.

Nine miles (14 km)
from Ely is Wicken Fen,
243 ha (600 acres) of
undrained fen
providing a habitat for
a wide range of water
life, wildfowl and
wild flowers.

Trinity Guildhall,
King's Lynn

❻ King's Lynn

Norfolk. 🅰 42,000. 🚉 🚌 ℹ️
Custom House, Purfleet Quay (01553
763044). 🚉 Tue, Fri, Sat.
🅦 visitwestnorfolk.com

Formerly Bishop's Lynn, its name
was changed at the Reformation
(see p54) to reflect the changing
political reality. In the Middle
Ages it was one of England's
most prosperous
ports, shipping grain
and wool from
the surrounding
countryside to Europe.
There are still a few
warehouses and
merchants' houses
by the River Ouse
surviving from this
period. At the north
end of the town is
True's Yard, a relic of the
old fishermen's quarter.

❼ North Norfolk Coastal Tour

This tour takes you through some of the most beautiful
areas of East Anglia; nearly all of the north Norfolk coast has
been designated an Area of Outstanding Natural Beauty.
The sea has dictated the character of the area. With
continuing deposits of silt, once busy ports are now far
inland and the shingle and sand banks that have been built
up are home to a huge variety of wildlife. Do bear in mind
when planning your journey that this popular route can
get congested during summer.

Tips for Drivers

Tour length: 28 miles (45 km).
Stopping-off points: Holkham
Hall makes a pleasant stop for a
picnic lunch. There are some
good pubs in Wells-next-the-Sea.
(See also pp636–7.)

② Hunstanton Cliffs
These magnificent cliffs
tower 18 m (60 ft) above
the beach. Their three
bands of colour are made
from car- stone and red
and white chalk.

• Holme-
next-the-Sea

Brancaster

Burnham
Market

Hunstanton

Norwich

Heacham

King's
Lynn

① Norfolk Lavender
The largest producer of
English Lavender, this whole
area is at its best in July and
August when the fields are a
blaze of purple.

③ Lord Nelson pub
Nelson (p54), born near
Burnham Market, dined
here before he went to
sea for the last time.

The **Trinity Guildhall**, located in the Saturday Market Place, dates back to the 15th century and was formerly a prison. The handsome **Custom House**, overlooking the river, was built in the 17th century as a merchant exchange. It is now a museum dedicated to the town's colourful maritime history. The Tourist Information Centre is also located here. **St Margaret's Church**, on the Market Place, dates back to 1101, and the interior includes a fine Elizabethan screen. In 1741 the tall spire on the southwest tower collapsed in a storm.

🖼 Custom House
Purfleet Quay. **Tel** 01553 763044. **Open** daily. ♿ ground floor.

Sandringham House, where the Royal Family spend every Christmas

❼ Sandringham

Norfolk. **Tel** 01485 545408. 🚌 from King's Lynn. **Open** Easter–Oct: daily. **Closed** one wk Jul. 🎨 ♿ 📷 📹 all year. 📷 all year.
🌐 sandringhamestate.co.uk

This sizeable Norfolk estate has been in royal hands since 1862 when it was bought by the Prince of Wales, who later became Edward VII. The 18th-century house was elaborately embellished and refurbished by the prince and now retains an appropriately Edwardian atmosphere.

The large stables are now a museum and contain several trophies that relate to hunting, shooting and horse racing – all favourite royal activities. A popular feature is a display of royal motor cars spanning nearly a century. In the park there are scenic nature trails.

④ Holkham Hall
This Palladian home is magnificent. Set in a beautiful landscaped park, it houses an impressive collection of art and Classical sculptures.

Key

━━ Tour route
═══ Other roads

⑦ Cley Windmill
This famous landmark over-looks Cley Marshes which became, in 1926, the first nature and bird reserve in Britain.

The Run

Holkham Bay

Bob Hall's Sands

Cromer

⑥

Blakeney ⑦

④

⑤

A149

Glaven

B1105

B1388

B1156

Stiffkey

Fakenham

Holt

0 kilometres   5

0 miles   3

⑤ Wells-next-the-Sea
Due to silting, this port is now a mile (1.5 km) from the sea. Its long sandy beach is popular and lined with colourful beach huts.

⑥ Blakeney Marshes
In the 13th century, Blakeney was a substantial trading port. Today, the marsh is inhabited by a seal colony and hundreds of sea birds.

For **additional map symbols** see back flap

The symmetrical red-brick façade of the 17th-century Blickling Hall

❾ Blickling Hall

Aylsham, Norfolk. **Tel** 01263 738 030.
🚂 Norwich, then bus. House:
Open Mar–Oct: Wed–Mon;
Nov–Feb: check website. Garden:
Open dawn–dusk daily. Park:
Open daily. 🅿️ ♿ 📷 🍴 NT
W nationaltrust.org.uk

Approached from the east, its symmetrical Jacobean front framed by trees and flanked by two yew hedges, Blickling Hall offers one of the most impressive vistas of any country house in the area.

Anne Boleyn, Henry VIII's tragic second queen, spent her childhood here, but very little of the original house remains. Most of the present structure dates from 1628, when it was home to James I's Chief Justice Sir Henry Hobart. Later in 1767 the 2nd Earl of Buckinghamshire, John Hobart, celebrated the Boleyn connection with reliefs in the Great Hall depicting Anne and her daughter, Elizabeth I. The Long Gallery is the most spectacular room to survive from the 1620s. Its ceiling depicts symbolic representations of learning.

The Peter the Great Room marks the 2nd earl's service as ambassador to Russia and was built to display a huge spectacular tapestry (1764) of the tsar on horseback, a gift from, Catherine the Great. It also has portraits (1760) of the ambassador and his wife by Gainsborough (*see p167*).

❿ Norwich

See pp204–5.

⓫ The Broads

Norfolk. 🚂 Hoveton, Wroxham.
🚌 Norwich, then bus. ℹ️ Station Rd,
Hoveton (01603 782281) Apr–Oct,
or Yare House, Thorpe Rd,
Norwich (01603 610 734).
W broads-authority.gov.uk

These shallow lakes and waterways south and northeast of Norwich, joined by six rivers – the Bure, Thurne, Ant, Yare, Waveney and Chet – were once thought to have been naturally formed, but in actual fact they are medieval peat diggings which flooded when the water level rose in the 13th century.

In summer the 125 miles (200 km) of open waterways, uninterrupted by locks, teem with thousands of boating enthusiasts. You can either hire a boat yourself or take one of the many trips on offer to view the plants and wildlife of the area. Look out for Britain's largest butterfly, the swallowtail. Wroxham, the unofficial capital of the Broads, is the starting point for many of these excursions.

The waterways support substantial beds of strong and durable reeds, much in demand for thatching (*see p37*). They are cut in winter and carried to shore in the distinctive Broads punts.

For a more detailed look at the origins of the Broads and their varied wildlife, visit the **Norfolk Wildlife Trust** – a large thatched floating information centre on Ranworth Broad, with displays on all aspects of the area, and a bird-watching gallery.

In the centre of Ranworth is **St Helen's Church** which has a painted medieval screen, a well-preserved 14th-century illuminated manuscript and spectacular views over the entire area from its tower.

🦋 **Norfolk Wildlife Trust**
Norwich. **Tel** 01603 625540.
Open Apr–Oct: daily. ♿ 📷

Sailing boat, Wroxham Broad, Norfolk

⑫ Great Yarmouth

Norfolk. 🚇 90,000. 🚆 🚌
ℹ️ Marine Parade (01493 846346).
📅 Wed, Fri (summer), Sat.
🌐 great-yarmouth.co.uk

Herring fishing was once the major industry of this port, with 1,000 boats engaged in it just before World War I. Over-fishing led to a depletion of stocks and, for the port to survive, it started to earn its living from servicing container ships and North Sea oil rigs.

It is also the most popular seaside resort on the Norfolk coast and has been since the 19th century, when Dickens *(see p193)* gave it useful publicity by setting part of his novel *David Copperfield* here.

The **Elizabethan House Museum** has a large, eclectic display which illustrates the social history of the area.

In the old part of the town, around South Quay, are a number of charming houses including the 17th-century **Old Merchant's House**. It retains its original patterned plaster ceilings as well as examples of old ironwork and architectural fittings from nearby houses, which were destroyed during World War II. The guided tour of the house includes a visit to the adjoining cloister of a 13th-century friary.

Fishing trawlers at Lowestoft's quays

🏛️ **Elizabethan House Museum**
4 South Quay. **Tel** 01493 855746.
Open Apr–Oct: daily (pm only weekends). 🅿️ 📷 NT

🏛️ **Old Merchant's House**
South Quay. **Tel** 01493 857900.
Open Apr–Sep: Mon–Fri. 🅿️ 📷 EH

Windmills on the fens and broads

The flat, open countryside and the stiff breezes from the North Sea made windmills an obvious power source for East Anglia well into the 20th century, and today they are an evocative and recurring feature of the landscape. On the Broads and Fens, some were used for drainage, while others, such as that at Saxtead Green, ground corn. On the boggy fens they were not built on hard foundations, so few survived, but elsewhere, especially on the Broads, many have been restored to working order. The seven-storey Berney Arms Windmill is the tallest on the Broads. Thurne Dyke Drainage Mill is the site of an exhibition about the occasionally idiosyncratic mills and their more unusual mechanisms.

Corn mill at Saxtead Green, near Framlingham

Herringfleet Smock Mill, near Lowestoft

⑬ Lowestoft

Suffolk. 🚇 55,000. 🚆 🚌 ℹ️ East Point Pavilion, Royal Plain (01502 533600). 📅 Tue–Sat.
🌐 visit-lowestoft.co.uk

The most easterly town in Britain was long a rival to Great Yarmouth, both as a holiday resort and a fishing port. Its fishing industry has only just survived. The coming of the railway in the 1840s gave the town an advantage over other resorts, and the solid Victorian and Edwardian boarding houses are evidence of its popularity.

Lowestoft Museum, in a 17th-century house, has a good display of the fine porcelain made here in the 18th century, as well as exhibits on local archaeology and domestic life.

Environs
Somerleyton Hall is built in Jacobean style on the foundations of a smaller mansion. Its gardens are a real delight, and there is a genuinely baffling yew hedge maze.

🏛️ **Lowestoft Museum**
Oulton Broad. **Tel** 01502 511457.
Open Apr–Oct: 1–4pm daily (from 2pm Sun). 📷 ltd. 📷 by appt.
🌐 lowestoftmuseum.org

🏛️ **Somerleyton Hall**
On B1074. **Tel** 01502 734901. **Open** Easter Sun–Oct: Tue, Thu & pub hols (Jul–Aug: also Sun). 🅿️ 📷 ♿ 📷 by appt. 📧 🌐 somerleyton.co.uk

⓾ Norwich

In the heart of the fertile East Anglian countryside, Norwich, one of the best-preserved cities in Britain, is steeped in a relaxed provincial atmosphere. The city was first fortified by the Saxons in the 9th century and still has the irregular street plan of that time. With the arrival of Flemish settlers in the early 12th century and the establishment of a textile industry, the town soon became a prosperous market and was the second city of England until the Industrial Revolution in the 19th century *(see pp60–61)*.

The quaintly cobbled medieval street of Elm Hill

One of over a thousand carved bosses in the cathedral cloisters

Exploring Norwich

The oldest parts of the city are Elm Hill, one of the finest medieval streets in England, and Tombland, the old Saxon market place by the cathedral. Both have well-preserved medieval buildings, which are now incorporated into pleasant areas of small shops.

With a trading history spanning hundreds of years, the colourful market in the city centre is well worth a visit. A good walk meanders around the surviving sections of the 14th-century flint city wall.

🏛 Norwich Cathedral

The Close. **Tel** 01603 218300. **Open** daily. Donations. 🗎 🖂 🖋 📷

W cathedral.org.uk

This magnificent building was founded in 1096 by Bishop Losinga and built with stone from Caen in France and Barnack.

The precinct originally included a monastery, and the surviving cloister is the most extensive in England. The thin cathedral spire was added in the 15th century, making it, at 96 m (315 ft), the second tallest in England after Salisbury (see

pp268–9). In the majestic nave, soaring Norman pillars and arches support a 15th-century vaulted roof whose stone bosses, many of which illustrate well-known Bible stories, have been beautifully restored.

Easier to appreciate at close hand is the elaborate wood carving in the choir – the canopies over the stalls and the misericords beneath the seats, one showing a small boy being smacked. Not to be missed is the 14th-century Despenser Reredos in St Luke's Chapel. It was hidden for years under a carpenter's table to prevent its destruction by Puritans.

Two gates to the cathedral close survive: **St Ethelbert's**, a 13th-century flint arch, and the **Erpingham Gate** at the west end, built by Sir Thomas Erpingham, who led the triumphant English archers at the Battle of Agincourt in 1415 *(see p53)*.

Beneath the east outer wall is the grave of Edith Cavell, the Norwich-born nurse who was arrested and executed in 1915 by the Germans for helping Allied soldiers escape from occupied Belgium.

🏛 Castle Museum

Castle Meadow. **Tel** 01603 495897. **Open** daily (Sun pm only). **Closed** 1 Jan, 25 & 26 Dec. 🗎 🖂 📷

W museums.norfolk.gov.uk

The brooding keep of this 12th-century castle has been a museum since 1894, when it ended 650 years of service as a prison. The most important Norman feature is a carved

A view of Norwich Cathedral's spire and tower from the southeast

Colman's Mustard

It was said of the Colmans that they made their fortune from what diners left on their plate. In 1814 Jeremiah Colman started milling mustard at Norwich because it was at the centre of a fertile plain where mustard was grown. Today at 15 Royal Arcade a shop sells mustard and related items, while a small museum illustrates the history of the company.

It's nicer with
MUSTARD

A 1950s advertisement for Colman's Mustard

door that used to be the main entrance.

Exhibits include significant collections of archaeology, natural history, fine art as well as the world's largest collection of ceramic teapots.

The art gallery is dominated by works from the Norwich School of painters. This group of early 19th century landscape artists painted directly from nature, getting away from the stylized studio landscapes that had been fashionable up to then. Chief among the group were John Crome (1768–1821), whom many compare with Constable *(see p208),* and John Sell Cotman (1782–1842), known for his watercolours. There are also regular exhibitions held here.

🏛 Church of St Peter Mancroft
Chantry Rd. **Tel** 01603 610443. **Open** 10am–4pm Mon–Sat (winter: to 3:30pm Sat); Sun (services only). Donations. &

This imposing Perpendicular church, built around 1455, so dominates the city centre that many visitors assume it is the cathedral. John Wesley *(see p283)* wrote of it, "I scarcely ever remember to have seen a more beautiful parish church".

The large windows make the church very light, and the dramatic east window still has most of its 15th-century glass. The roof is unusual in having wooden fan tracery – it is normally in stone – covering the hammerbeam construction. The famous peal of 13 bells rang out in 1588 to celebrate the defeat

of the Spanish Armada *(see p55)* and is still heard every Sunday. Its name derives from the Latin *magna crofta* (great meadow) which described the area in pre-Norman times.

🏛 Bridewell Museum
Bridewell Alley. **Tel** 01603 629127. **Open** 10am–4:30pm Tue–Sat. 🏛 &

One of the oldest houses in Norwich, this 14th-century flint-faced building was used for years as a jail for women and beggars. It now houses an exhibition of local industries, with displays of old machines and reconstructed shops. There is also a section about the people of Norwich.

🏛 Guildhall
Gaol Hill. **Tel** 01603 305575. 📷
Above the city's ancient market place is the imposing 15th-century flint and stone Guildhall with its gable of checkered flushwork (now a café).

🏛 Strangers' Hall
Charing Cross. **Tel** 01603 493625. **Open** Mar–Dec: Wed & Sat (tickets: call 01603 667229). **Closed** 24 Dec–mid-Feb. 🏛

This 14th-century merchant's house gives a glimpse into English domestic life through the ages. The house was lived in by immigrant weavers – the "strangers". It has a fine 15th-century Great Hall and a costume display featuring a collection of underwear.

🏛 The Sainsbury Centre for Visual Arts
University of E Anglia (on B1108). **Tel** 01603 593199. **Open** 10am–5pm Tue–Sun. **Closed** 23 Dec–20 Jan. & 📷 by arrangement. 📷
🔲 scva.ac.uk

This important art gallery was built in 1978 to house the collection of Robert and Lisa Sainsbury given to the University of East Anglia in 1973.

The collection's strength is in its modern European paintings, including works by Modigliani, Picasso and Bacon, and in its sculptures by Giacometti and Moore. There are also displays of ethnographic art from Africa, the Pacific and the Americas.

The centre, designed by Lord Norman Foster, one of Britain's most innovative architects, was among the first to display its steel structure openly.

Back of the New Mills (1814) by John Crome of the Norwich School

Purple heather in flower on Dunwich Heath

❶ Southwold

Suffolk. 🅼 3,900. 🚌 **ℹ** High Street (01502 724721). 🅰 Fri am.
W visit-southwold.co.uk

This picture-postcard seaside resort, with its charming white-washed villas clustered around small greens, has, largely by historical accident, remained unspoiled. The railway line which connected it with London was closed in 1929, which effectively isolated this Georgian town from an influx of day-trippers.

This was also once a large port, as testified by the size of the 15th-century **St Edmund King and Martyr Church**, worth a visit for the 16th-century painted screens. On its tower is a small figure dressed

Jack o'the Clock, Southwold

in the uniform of a 15th-century soldier and known as Jack o'the Clock. **Southwold Museum** tells the story of the Battle of Sole Bay, which was fought offshore between the English and Dutch navies in 1672.

Environs
The pretty village of **Walberswick** lies across the creek. By road it is a long detour and the only alternatives are a rowing-boat ferry across the harbour (summer only) or a footbridge across the river half a mile inland. Further inland at Blythburgh, the 15th-century **Holy Trinity Church** dominates the surrounding land. In 1944 a US bomber blew up over the church, killing Joseph Kennedy Jr, brother of the future American president.

🏛 **Southwold Museum**
9–11 Victoria St. **Tel** 01502 726097. **Open** Easter–Oct: 2–4pm daily (also am in Aug). 🐾 🚻

❶ Dunwich

Suffolk. 🅼 1,400.

This tiny village is all that remains of a "lost city" consigned to the sea by erosion. In the 7th century Dunwich was the seat of the powerful East Anglian kings. In the 13th century it was still the biggest port in Suffolk and some 12 churches were built. But the land was being eroded at about a metre (3 ft) a year, and the last original church collapsed into the sea in 1919.

Dunwich Heath, to the south, runs down to a sandy beach and is an important nature reserve. **Minsmere Reserve** has observation hides for watching a huge variety of birds.

🦋 **Dunwich Heath**
Nr Dunwich. **Tel** 01728 648501. **Open** dawn–dusk. 🚻 📷 **NT**

🦋 **Minsmere Reserve**
Minsmere, Westleton. **Tel** 01728 648281. **Open** daily. **Closed** 25, 26 Dec. 🐾 🚻 📷 **W** rspb.org.uk

❶ Aldeburgh

Suffolk. 🅼 3,840. 🚌 **ℹ** High St (01728 453637).

Best known today for the music festivals at Snape Maltings, Aldeburgh has been a port since Roman times (the Roman area is under water). Erosion has resulted in the fine

Intricate carving on the exterior of the Tudor Moot Hall, Aldeburgh

Tudor **Aldeburgh Museum**, once far inland, today being close to the beach. Its ground floor, originally the market, is now a museum. The large timbered court room above can only be reached by the original outside staircase.

The **church**, also Tudor, contains a large stained-glass window placed in 1979 as a memorial to the composer, Benjamin Britten. **The Red House** was Britten's home from 1957 to 1976.

🏛 **Aldeburgh Museum**
Moot Hall, Market Cross Pl. **Tel** 01728 454666. **Open** Apr–Oct: daily (pm). 🗓
🏠 w aldeburghmuseum.org.uk

🏛 **The Red House**
Golf Lane. **Tel** 01728 451700.
Open 2–5pm Tue–Sat. 📷

⑰ Framlingham Castle

Framlingham, Suffolk. **Tel** 01728 724189. 🚆 Wickham Market then taxi. **Open** call to check times. **Closed** 1 Jan, 24–26 Dec. ♿ partial. 🏠 🗓 EH

Perched on a hill, the small village of Framlingham has long been an important strategic site, even before the present castle was built in 1190 by the Earl of Norfolk.

Little of the castle from that period survives except the powerful curtain wall and its towers; walk round the top of it for fine views of the town.

Mary Tudor, daughter of Henry VIII, was staying here in 1553 when she heard she was to become queen.

Environs
To the southeast, on the coast, is the 27 m (90 ft), 16-sided keep of **Orford Castle**, built for Henry II as a coastal defence at around the same time as Framlingham. A short climb to the top of the castle gives fantastic views.

🏰 **Orford Castle**
Orford. **Tel** 01394 450472. **Open** daily (Nov–Mar: Sat & Sun). **Closed** 26 Dec. 📷 🏠 EH

Aldeburgh Music Festival

Composer Benjamin Britten (1913–76), born in Lowestoft, Suffolk, moved to Snape in 1937. In 1945 his opera *Peter Grimes* – inspired by the poet George Crabbe (1754–1832), once a curate at Aldeburgh – was performed in Snape. Since then the area has become the centre of musical activity. In 1948, Britten began the Aldeburgh Music Festival, held every June *(see p67)*. He acquired the Maltings at Snape and converted it into a music venue opened by the Queen in 1967. It has since become the focus of an annual series of East Anglian musical events in churches and halls throughout the entire region.

Benjamin Britten in Aldeburgh

⑱ Ipswich

Suffolk. 🅰 120,000. 🚆 🚌 🛈 St Stephen's Lane (01473 258070). 📅 Tue, Thu–Sat. 🎭 Ip-art (music & arts): last 2 wks Jun–1st 2 wks Jul.
w **visit-ipswich.com**

Suffolk's county town has a largely modern centre but several buildings remain from earlier times. It rose to prominence after the 13th century as a port for the rich Suffolk wool trade *(see p211)*. Later, with the Industrial Revolution, it began to export coal.

The **Ancient House** in Buttermarket has a superb example of pargeting – the ancient craft of ornamental façade plastering. The town's museum and art gallery,

Pargeting on the Ancient House in Ipswich

Christchurch Mansion, is a Tudor house from 1548, where Elizabeth I stayed in 1561. It also boasts the best collection of Constable's paintings out of London *(see p208)*, including four marvellous Suffolk landscapes, as well as paintings by Gainsborough *(see p167)*.

Ipswich Museum contains replicas of the Mildenhall and Sutton Hoo treasures, the originals being in the British Museum *(see pp110–11)*.

In the centre of the town is **St Margaret's**, a 15th-century church built in flint and stone with a double hammerbeam roof and 17th-century painted ceiling panels. **Wolsey's Gate**, a Tudor gateway of 1527, provides a link with Ipswich's most famous son, Cardinal Wolsey *(see p177)*. He started to build an ecclesiastical college in the town, but fell from royal favour before it was finished.

🏛 **Christchurch Mansion**
Soane St. **Tel** 01473 433554. **Open** 10am–5pm Tue–Sun. **Closed** 1 Jan, Good Fri, 24–27 Dec. ♿ limited. 📷 by appt. 🖥 📷

🏛 **Ipswich Museum**
High St. **Tel** 01473 433551. **Open** Tue–Sat. 🏠 ♿

⑲ Constable Walk

This walk in Constable country follows one of the most picturesque sections of the River Stour. The route taken would have been familiar to the landscape painter John Constable (1776–1837). Constable's father, a wealthy merchant, owned Flatford Mill, which was depicted in many of the artist's important paintings. Constable claimed to know and love "every stile and stump, and every lane" around East Bergholt.

The River Stour, used as a backdrop for Constable's *Boatbuilding* (1814)

Tips for Walkers

Starting point: Park off Flatford Lane, East Bergholt (charge to park). ℹ️ 01206 299460; NTS Bridge Cottage (01206 298260). **Getting there:** A12 to East Bergholt, then follow signs to Flatford. 🚆 Manningtree is within walking distance of Flatford. 🚌 from Ipswich or Colchester. **Stopping-off point:** Dedham. **Length:** 3 miles (5 km). **Difficulty:** Flat trail along riverside footpath with kissing gates.

⑤ Viewpoint
The view over the valley from the top of the hill shows Constable country at its best.

① Car Park
Follow the signs to Flatford Mill then cross the footbridge.

A12

Dedham Mill •

Stour

B1029 🅿

④ Dedham ◊

B1029

③

⑤ 🚶

Gosnalls Farm •

East Bergholt

🅿 ①

③ Fen Bridge
This modern footbridge replaced one that Constable used as a focus for many of his paintings.

Ram Lock •

Flatford Mill •
②

④ Dedham Church
The tall church tower appears in many of Constable's pictures including the *View on the Stour near Dedham* (1822).

0 metres	500
0 yards	500

Key

■■ Route
══ B road
═══ Minor road

② Willy Lott's Cottage
This cottage remains much the same as it did when featured in Constable's painting *The Hay-Wain* (see p87).

⑳ Colchester

Essex. 🗺 160,000. 🚌 🚆 ℹ Queen St (01206 282920). 🖪 Fri, Sat.
ⓦ visitcolchester.com

The oldest recorded town in Britain, Colchester was the effective capital of south-east England when the Romans invaded in AD 43, and it was here that the first permanent Roman colony was established.

After Boudica (see p199) burnt the town in AD 60, a 2 mile (3 km) wall was built, 3 m (10 ft) thick and 9 m (30 ft) high, to deter future attackers. You can still see these walls and the surviving Roman town gate, the largest in Britain.

During the Middle Ages Colchester developed into an important weaving centre. In the 16th century, a number of immigrant Flemish weavers settled in an area west of the castle, known as the **Dutch Quarter**, which still retains the original tall houses and steep, narrow streets.

Colchester was besieged for 11 weeks during the Civil War (see p56) before being captured by Cromwell's troops.

🏛 Hollytrees Museum
Castle Park. **Tel** 01206 282940. **Open** Tue–Sat. **Closed** 1 Jan, 24–27 Dec. 🚻 🏛 ⓦ cimuseums.org.uk

This elegant Georgian townhouse was built in 1719. Now a charming museum of social history, you can experience the day-to-day lives of Colchester people and changing technology over 300 years. Clock-making was an important craft in Colchester, and it is celebrated in displays here.

Young visitors especially will enjoy exploring the miniature world of the doll's house, and learning about the origin of the famous nursery rhyme "Twinkle, twinkle, little star", which was written in Colchester.

🏛 Castle Museum
Castle Park. **Tel** 01206 282939. **Open** 10am–5pm daily (from 11am Sun). **Closed** 1 Jan, 24–27 Dec. 🏛 🚻 🏛 ⓦ cimuseums.org.uk

This is the oldest and largest Norman keep still standing in

The Norman keep of the Castle Museum, Colchester

England. Twice the size of the White Tower at the Tower of London (see pp122–3), it was built in 1076 on the platform of a Roman temple dedicated to Claudius (see p48), using stones and tiles from other Roman buildings. The museum's displays relate the story of the town from prehistoric times to the Civil War. There is also a medieval prison.

🏛 Layer Marney Tower
Off B1022. **Tel** 01206 330784. **Open** Apr–Sep: Wed & Sun (Jul & Aug: Sun–Thu). 🚻 🏛 limited. 🚻 by appt. 🚻 🏛 ⓦ layermarneytower.co.uk

This remarkable Tudor gatehouse is the tallest in Britain: its pair of six-sided, eight-storey turrets reach to 24 m (80 ft). It was intended to be part of a larger complex, but the designer, Sir Henry Marney, died before it was completed. The brickwork and terracotta ornamentation around the roof and windows are models of Tudor craftsmanship.

🌿 Beth Chatto Garden
Elmstead Market. **Tel** 01206 822007. **Open** Mar–Oct: 9am–5pm daily (pm only Sun); Nov–Feb: 9am–4pm daily (from 10am Sun). **Closed** 22 Dec–5 Jan. 🚻 🏛 🚻 🖥 ⓦ bethchatto.co.uk

One of Britain's most eminent gardening writers, Beth Chatto began this experiment in the 1960s to test her belief that it is possible to create a garden in the most adverse conditions. The dry and windy slopes, boggy patches, gravel beds and wooded areas support an array of plants best suited to that particular environment.

㉑ Coggeshall

Essex. 🗺 4,000. 🖪 Thu.
ⓦ coggeshall-pc.gov.uk

This town has two of the most important medieval and Tudor buildings in the country. Dating from 1140, **Coggeshall Grange Barn** is the oldest surviving timber-framed barn in Europe. Inside is a display of historic farm wagons. The half-timbered merchant's house, **Paycocke's**, was built around 1500 and has a beautifully panelled interior. There is a display of Coggeshall lace.

🏛 Coggeshall Grange Barn
Grange Hill. **Tel** 01376 562226. **Open** Apr–Oct: Wed–Sun & public hols (pm). **Closed** Good Fri. 🚻 🏛 NT

🏛 Paycocke's
West St. **Tel** 01376 561305. **Open** Apr–Oct: Wed–Sun & public hols. **Closed** Good Fri. 🚻 🏛 NT

Beth Chatto Garden, Colchester, in full summer bloom

㉒ Lavenham

Suffolk. 1,800. Lady St (01787 248207).

Often considered the most perfect of all English small towns, Lavenham is a treasure trove of beautiful timber-framed houses ranged along streets whose pattern is virtually unchanged from medieval times. For 150 years, between the 14th and 16th centuries, Lavenham was the prosperous centre of the Suffolk wool trade. It still has many outstanding and well-preserved buildings; indeed no fewer than 350 of the town's buildings are Grade 2 listed, including the magnificent **Little Hall**.

Environs
Gainsborough's House, Sudbury, is a museum on this painter (see p167).

Little Hall Tel 01787 247 019. **Open** Mon: am; Tue–Thu, Sat & Sun: pm; public hols.

Gainsborough's House Sudbury. **Tel** 01787 372958. **Open** Mon–Sat. **Closed** 24 Dec–2 Jan, Good Fri. **w** gainsborough.org

Little Hall

The **solar bedroom** was the best and sunniest room in the house.

Dormitory

The **crown-post roof** is a superb feat of medieval engineering.

Bronze of Egyptian Goddess Cat Bastet

Library

Entrance

Dining room

The **herringbone-style** timber on the exterior was used often in the 14th century.

㉓ Bury St Edmunds

Suffolk. 34,000. 6 Angel Hill (01284 764667). Wed, Sat. **w** stedmundsbury.gov.uk

St Edmund was the last Saxon king of East Anglia, decapitated by Danish raiders in 870. Legend has it that a wolf picked up the severed head – an image that appears in a number of medieval carvings. Edmund was canonized in 900 and buried in Bury, where in 1014 King Canute (see p175) built an **abbey** in his honour, the wealthiest in England until its destruction in the Dissolution of the Monasteries (see p355). The abbey ruins now lie in the town centre.

Nearby are two large 15th-century churches, built when the wool trade made the town wealthy. **St James's** was designated a cathedral in 1914. The best features of **St Mary's** are the north porch and the hammer-beam roof over the nave. A stone slab in the northeast corner marks the tomb of Mary Tudor (see pp54–5).

Just below the **market cross** in Cornhill – remodelled by Robert Adam (see p32) in 1714 – stands the large 12th-century **Moyse's Hall**, a merchant's house that serves as the local history museum, displaying archaeology from the area.

Illustration of St Edmund

Environs
Three miles (5 km) southwest of Bury is the late 18th-century **Ickworth House**. This eccentric Neo-Classical mansion features

The 18th-century rotunda of Ickworth House, Bury St Edmunds

an unusual rotunda with a domed roof flanked by two huge wings. The art collection includes works by Reynolds and Titian. There are also fine displays of silver, porcelain and sculpture, for example, John Flaxman's (1755–1826) moving *The Fury of Athamas*. The house is set in a large park.

Moyse's Hall
Cornhill. **Tel** 01284 706183. **Open** daily (last adm: 4pm). **Closed** public hols, 24 Dec.

Ickworth House
Horringer. **Tel** 01284 735270. **Open** Mar–Oct: Thu–Tue.

❷ Newmarket

Suffolk. 🔼 17,000. 🚌 🚉 **i** 63 The Guineas (01638 719749). 🚩 Tue, Sat. **w** forest-heath.gov.uk

A walk down the short main street tells you all you need to know about this busy and wealthy little town. The shops sell horse feed and all manner of riding accessories; the clothes on sale are tweeds, jodhpurs and the soft brown hats rarely worn by anyone except racehorse trainers.

Newmarket has been the headquarters of British horse racing since James I decided that its open heaths were ideal for testing the mettle of his fastest steeds against those of his friends. The first ever

The stallion unit at the National Stud, Newmarket

recorded horse race was held here in 1622. Charles II shared his grandfather's enthusiasm and after the Restoration *(see p57)* would move the whole court to Newmarket, every spring and summer, for the sport – he is the only British king to have ridden a winner.

The modern racing industry began to take shape here in the late 18th century. There are now over 2,500 horses in training in and around the town, and two racecourses staging regular race meetings from around April to October *(see pp70–71)*. Training

A horse being exercised on Newmarket Heath

stables are occasionally open to the public but you can view the horses being exercised on the heath in the early morning. Tattersall's, the auction house for thoroughbreds, is in the centre of Newmarket.

The **National Stud** can also be visited. You will see the five or six stallions on stud, mares in foal and if you are lucky a newborn foal – most likely in April or May.

The **National Horseracing Museum** tells the history of the sport and contains many offbeat exhibits such as the skeleton of Eclipse, one of the greatest horses ever, unbeaten in 18 races and the ancestor of most of today's fastest performers. It also has a large display of sporting art.

National Stud
Newmarket. **Tel** 01638 666789. **Open** mid-Feb–Sep: tours only. **w** nationalstud.co.uk

National Horseracing Museum
99 High St, Newmarket. **Tel** 01638 667333. **Open** Mar–Dec: daily. **w** nhrm.co.uk

St Mary's Church, Stoke-by-Nayland, southeast of Bury St Edmunds

The Rise and Fall of the Wool Trade

Wool was a major English product from the 13th century and by 1310 some ten million fleeces were exported every year. The Black Death *(see p52)*, which swept Britain in 1348, perversely provided a boost for the industry: with labour in short supply, land could not be cultivated and was grassed over for sheep. Around 1350 Edward III decided it was time to establish a home-based cloth industry and encouraged Flemish weavers to come to Britain. Many settled in East Anglia, particularly Suffolk, and their skills helped establish a flourishing trade. This time of prosperity saw the construction of the sumptuous churches, such as the one at Stoke-by-Nayland, that we see today – East Anglia has more than 2,000 churches. The cloth trade here began to decline in the late 16th century with the development of water-powered looms. These were not suited to the area, which never regained its former wealth. Today's visitors are the beneficiaries of this decline, because the wool towns such as Lavenham and Bury St Edmunds never became rich enough to destroy their magnificent Tudor halls and houses and construct new buildings.

The façade of Anglesey Abbey

㉕ Anglesey Abbey

Lode, Cambridgeshire. **Tel** 01223 810080. 🚃 Cambridge then bus. House **Open** Mar–Oct: Wed–Sun; Garden **Open** daily year round. 📷 🚻 limited. 🚻 🏛 **NT**

The original Abbey was built in 1135 for an Augustinian order. But only the crypt – also known as the monks' parlour – with its vaulted ceiling on marble and stone pillars, survived the Dissolution (see p54).

This was later incorporated into a manor house whose treasures include furniture from many periods and a rare seascape by Gainsborough (see p210). The superb garden was created in the 1930s by Lord Fairhaven as an ambitious, Classical landscape of trees, sculptures and borders.

㉖ Huntingdon

Cambridgeshire. 🗺 18,000. 🚃 🚌 ℹ Princes St (01480 388588). 🔵 Wed, Sat.

More than 300 years after his death, Oliver Cromwell (see p56) still dominates this small town. Born here in 1599, a record of his baptism can be seen in the County Records Office in Huntingdon. You can see his name and traces of ancient graffiti scrawled all over it which says "England's plague for five years". **Cromwell Museum**, his former school, traces his life with pictures and mementoes, including his death mask.

Cromwell remains one of the most disputed figures in British history. An MP before he was 30, he became embroiled in the disputes between Charles I and Parliament over taxes and religion. In the Civil War (see p56) he proved an inspired general and, after refusing the title of king, was made Lord Protector in 1653, four years after the King was beheaded. Just two years after his death the monarchy was restored by popular demand, and his body was taken out of Westminster Abbey (see pp96–7) to hang on gallows.

There is a 14th-century bridge across the River Ouse which links Huntingdon with Godmanchester, the site of a Roman settlement.

🏛 Cromwell Museum
Grammar School Walk. **Tel** 01480 375830. **Open** Tue–Sun (Nov–Mar: pm only except Sat). **Closed** 1 Jan, 24–27 Dec, some public hols. 🚻 📷

㉗ Cambridge

See pp214–19.

㉘ Audley End

Saffron Walden, Essex. **Tel** 01799 522842. 🚃 Audley End then taxi. House **Open** Apr–Oct: pm daily. Garden **Open** Apr–Oct: daily; Nov–Mar: Sat & Sun. **Closed** 24 Dec–Jan. 📷 🚻 limited. 🚻 🚻 💻 📷 **EH** 🌐 english-heritage.org.uk

This was the largest house in England when built in 1603–14 for Thomas Howard, Lord Treasurer and 1st Earl of Suffolk. James I joked that Audley End was too big for a king but not for a Lord Treasurer. Charles II, his grandson, disagreed and bought it in 1667. He seldom went there, however, and in 1701 it was given back to the Howards, who demolished two thirds of it.

What remains is a Jacobean mansion, retaining its original hall and many fine plaster ceilings. Robert Adam (see p32) remodelled some of the interior in the 1760s, and these rooms have been restored to his original designs. At the same time, "Capability" Brown (see p30) landscaped the magnificent 18th-century park

Stained glass window, installed in 1771, represents the Last Supper.

The Chapel was completed in 1772 to a Gothic design. The furniture was made to complement the wooden pillars and vaulting which are painted to imitate stone.

Jacobean wooden screen (c.1605)

Main entrance

The Great Hall, hung with family portraits, is the highlight of the house, with the massive oak screen and elaborate hammerbeam roof surviving in their Jacobean form.

㉙ Epping Forest

Essex. 🚋 Chingford. 🚇 Loughton, Theydon Bois. 🛈 High Beach, Loughton (020–8508 0028) & Highbridge St, Waltam Abbey (01992 660336).

As one of the large open spaces near London, the 2,400 ha (6,000 acre) forest is popular with walkers, just as, centuries ago, it was a favourite hunting ground for kings and courtiers – the word forest denoted an area for hunting. Henry VIII had a lodge

A depiction of the Battle of Maldon (991) on the *Maldon Embroidery*

built in 1543 on the edge of the forest. His daughter Elizabeth I often used the lodge and it soon became known as **Queen Elizabeth's Hunting Lodge**.

This three-storey timbered building has been fully renovated and now houses an exhibition explaining the lodge's history and other aspects of the forest's life.

The tracts of open land and woods interspersed with a number of lakes, make an ideal habitat for a variety of plant, bird and animal life: deer roam the northern part, many of a special dark strain introduced by James I. The Corporation of

Epping Forest contains oaks and beeches up to 400 years old

London bought the forest in the mid-19th century to ensure it remained open to the public.

🏛 **Queen Elizabeth's Hunting Lodge**
Rangers Rd, Chingford. **Tel** 020 8529 6681. **Open** daily. **Closed** 25 Dec. 🚻 limited. 📷 by appt. 🅿 🛒

㉚ Maldon

Essex. 🏠 21,000. 🚋 Chelmsford then bus. 🛈 Wenlock Way (01621 856503). 🗓 Thu, Sat. 🌐 **visitmaldon.co.uk**

This delightful old town on the River Blackwater, its High Street lined with shops and inns from the 14th century on, was once an important harbour. One of its best-known industries was the production of Maldon sea salt, panned in the traditional way.

A fierce battle here in 991, when Viking invaders defeated the Saxon defenders, is told in *The Battle of Maldon*, one of the earliest known Saxon poems. The battle is also celebrated in the *Maldon Embroidery* on display in the **Maeldune Centre**. This 13-m- (42-ft-) long embroidery, made by locals, depicts the history of Maldon from 991 to 1991.

Environs

East of Maldon at Bradwell-on-Sea is the sturdy Saxon church of **St Peter's- on-the-Wall**, a simple stone building that stands isolated on the shore. It was built in 654, from the stones of a former Roman fort, by St Cedd, who used it as his cathedral. It was restored in the 1920s.

🏛 **Maeldune Centre**
Market Hill. **Tel** 01621 851628. **Open** Feb: Sat; Mar: Thu–Sat; Apr–Nov: Tue–Sat; Dec: call ahead. 📷 🌐 **maelduneheritagecentre.co.uk**

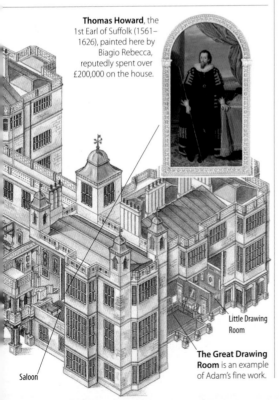

Thomas Howard, the 1st Earl of Suffolk (1561–1626), painted here by Biagio Rebecca, reputedly spent over £200,000 on the house.

Little Drawing Room

The Great Drawing Room is an example of Adam's fine work.

Saloon

㉗ Street-by-Street: Cambridge

Cambridge has been an important town since Roman times as it was sited at the first navigable point on the River Cam. In the 11th century religious orders began to be established in the town and, in 1209, a group of religious scholars broke away from Oxford University (*see pp226–31*) after academic and religious disputes and came here. Student life dominates the city but it is also a thriving market centre serving a rich agricultural region.

Round Church
The 12th-century Church of the Holy Sepulchre has one of the few round naves in the country. Its design is based on the Holy Sepulchre in Jerusalem.

Newmarket ◀

BRIDGE STREET

Magdalene Bridge carries Bridge Street across the Cam from the city centre to Magdalene College.

St John's College has superb Tudor and Jacobean architecture.

ST JOHN'S STREE

Kitchen Bridge

★ **Bridge of Sighs**
Built in 1831 and named after its Venetian counterpart, it is best viewed from the Kitchen Bridge.

Trinity College

Trinity Bridge

TRIN

| 0 metres | 75 |
| 0 yards | 75 |

Key

— Suggested route

Clare College

Clare Bridge

Grantchester

The Backs
This is the name given to the grassy strip lying between the backs of the big colleges and the banks of the Cam – a good spot to enjoy this classic view of King's College Chapel.

Great St Mary's Church
This clock is over the west door of the university's official church. Its tower offers fine views.

Gonville and Caius
(pronounced "keys"), founded in 1348, is one of the oldest colleges.

★ King's College Chapel
This late medieval masterpiece took 70 years to build (see pp216–17).

Market square

Bus and Coach station

King's College
Henry VIII, king when the chapel was completed in 1515, is commemorated in this statue near the main gate.

Queens' College
Its Tudor courts are among the university's finest. This 18th-century sundial is over the old chapel – now a reading room.

Corpus Christi College

To London and railway station

Mathematical Bridge
It is a myth that this bridge over the Cam at Queens' College was first built without nuts or bolts.

TRINITY STREET

KING'S PARADE

SILVER STREET

CAM

Fitzwilliam Museum

Trumpington St. **Tel** 01223 332900.
Open Tue–Sun; public hols. **Closed**
24–27 Dec, 1 Jan, Good Fri. Donation.
☐ ☐ by arrangement. ☐ ☐
w fitzmuseum.cam.ac.uk

One of Britain's oldest public museums, this massive Classical building has works of exceptional quality and rarity, especially antiquities, ceramics, paintings and manuscripts.

The core of the collection was bequeathed in 1816 by the 7th Viscount Fitzwilliam. Other gifts have since greatly added to the exhibits.

Works by Titian (1488–1576) and the 17th-century Dutch masters, including Hals, Cuyp and Hobbema's *Wooded Landscape* (1686), stand out among the paintings. French Impressionist gems include Monet's *Le Printemps* (1866) and Renoir's *La Place Clichy* (1880), while Picasso's *Still Life* (1923) is notable among the modern works. Most of the important British artists are represented, from Hogarth in the 18th century through Constable in the 19th to Ben Nicholson in the 20th.

The miniatures include the earliest surviving depiction of Henry VIII. In the same gallery are some dazzling illuminated manuscripts, notably the 15th-century *Metz Pontifical*, a French liturgical work.

The impressive Glaisher collection of European earthenware and stoneware includes a unique display of English delftware from the 16th and 17th centuries.

Handel's bookcase contains folios of his work, and nearby is Keats's original manuscript for *Ode to a Nightingale* (1819).

Portrait of Richard James (c.1740s)
by William Hogarth

Cambridge: King's College

Henry VI founded this college in 1441. Work on the chapel – one of the most important examples of late medieval English architecture – began five years later, and took 70 years to complete. Henry himself decided that it should dominate the city and gave specific instructions about its dimensions: 88 m (289 ft) long, 12 m (40 ft) wide and 29 m (94 ft) high. The detailed design is thought to have been by master stonemason Reginald Ely, although it was altered in later years.

★ **Fan Vaulted Ceiling**
This awe-inspiring ceiling, supported by 22 buttresses, was built by master stone-mason John Wastell in 1515.

KEY

① **The Fellows' Building** was designed in 1724 by James Gibbs, as part of an uncompleted design for a Great Court.

② **One of four octagonal turrets**

③ **Side chapels**

④ **Organ** The massive 17th-century organ case above the screen is decorated with two angels playing trumpets.

⑤ **The screen** is a superb example of Tudor woodwork and divides the chapel into antechapel and choir.

⑥ **Gothic gatehouse, 19th-century**

⑦ **Henry VI's statue** This bronze statue of the college's founder was erected in 1879.

Crown and Tudor Rose
This detail of Tudor heraldry on the west door of the Chapel reflects Henry VII's vision of English supremacy

King's College Choir

When he founded the chapel, Henry VI stipulated that a choir of six lay clerks and 16 boy choristers – educated at the College school – should sing daily at services. This still happens in term time but today the choir also gives concerts all over the world. Its broadcast service of carols has become a much-loved Christmas tradition.

Choristers in King's College Chapel

VISITORS' CHECKLIST

Practical Information
King's Parade. **Tel** 01223 331212.
Open Oct–Sep: daily (pm only on Sun during term time).
Closed for events ring first. 🅿
✝ term-time: 5:30pm Mon–Sat, 10:30am & 3:30pm Sun 🔊 📷
🅆 kings.cam.ac.uk

Stained-Glass Windows
The 16th-century windows in the chapel all depict biblical scenes. This one shows Christ baptizing his followers.

★ **Altarpiece by Rubens**
Painted in 1634 for the convent of the White Nuns in Belgium, The Adoration of the Magi was privately donated to King's in 1961.

Main entrance

Exploring Cambridge University

Cambridge University has 31 colleges *(see also pp214–15)*, the oldest being Peterhouse (1284) and the newest being Robinson (1979). Clustered around the city centre, many of the older colleges have peaceful gardens backing onto the River Cam, which are known as the "Backs". The layout of the older colleges, as at Oxford *(see pp230–31)*, derives from their early connections with religious institutions, although few escaped heavy-handed modification in the Victorian era. The college buildings are generally grouped around squares called courts and offer an unrivalled mix of over 600 years of architecture from the late medieval period through Wren's masterpieces and up to the present day.

The nave of the Wren Chapel at Pembroke College

The imposing façade of Emmanuel College

Emmanuel College
Built in 1677 on St Andrew's Street, Sir Christopher Wren's *(see p118)* chapel is the highlight of the college. Some of the intricate interior details, particularly the plaster ceiling and Amigoni's altar rails (1734), are superb. Founded in 1584, the college has a Puritan tradition. One notable graduate was the clergyman John Harvard, who emigrated to America in 1636 and left all his money to the Massachusetts college that now bears his name.

Senate House
King's Parade is the site of this Palladian edifice (built 1722–30), which is used primarily for university ceremonies. It was designed by James Gibbs in 1722 as part of a grand square of university buildings – which was never completed.

Corpus Christi College
Just down from Senate House, this was founded in 1352 by the local trade guilds, anxious to ensure that education was not the sole prerogative of church and nobility. Its Old Court is remarkably well

preserved and looks today much as it would have done when built in the 14th century.

The college is connected by a 15th-century gallery of red brick to St Bene't's Church (short for St Benedict's), whose large Saxon tower is the oldest structure in Cambridge.

King's College
See pp216–17.

Pembroke College
The college chapel was the first building completed by Wren *(see pp118–19)*. A formal classical design, it replaced a 14th-century chapel that was turned into a library. The college, just off Trumpington Street, also has fine gardens.

Jesus College
Although established between 1496 and 1516, some of its buildings on Jesus Lane are older, as the college took over St Radegond's nunnery, built in the 12th century. There are traces of Norman columns, windows and a well-preserved hammerbeam roof in the college dining hall.

The chapel keeps the core of the original church but the stained glass windows are modern and contain work by William Morris *(see pp224–5)*.

Queens' College
Built in 1446 on Queens' Land, the college was endowed in 1448 by Margaret of Anjou, queen of Henry VI, and again in 1465 by Elizabeth Woodville, queen of Edward IV, which explains the position of the apostrophe. Queens' has a marvellous

Punting by the King's College "Backs"

Punting on the Cam
Punting captures the essence of carefree college days: a student leaning on a long pole, lazily guiding the flat-bottomed river craft along, while others stretch out and relax. Punting is still popular both with students and visitors, who can hire punts from boatyards along the river – with a chauffeur if required. Punts do sometimes capsize, and novices should prepare for a dip.

collection of Tudor buildings, notably the half-timbered President's Gallery, built in the mid-16th century on top of the brick arches in the charming Cloister Court. The Principal Court is 15th century, as is Erasmus's Tower, named after the Dutch scholar.

Pepys Library in Magdalene College

The college has buildings on both sides of the Cam, linked by the bizarre Mathematical Bridge, built in 1749 to hold together without the use of nuts and bolts – although they have had to be used in subsequent repairs.

Magdalene College
Pronounced "maudlin" – as is the Oxford college (see p230) – the college, on Bridge Street, was established in 1482. The diarist Samuel Pepys (1633–1703) was a student here and left his large library to the college on his death. The 12 red-oak book-cases have over 3,000 books. Magdalene was the last all-male Cambridge college and it started admitting women students only in 1988.

St John's College
Sited on St John's Street, the imposing turreted brick and stone gatehouse of 1514, with its colourful heraldic symbols, provides a fitting entrance to the second largest Cambridge college and its rich store of 16th- and 17th-century buildings. Its hall, most of it Elizabethan, has portraits of the college's famous alumni, such as the poet William Wordsworth (see p370) and the statesman Lord Palmerston. St John's spans the Cam and boasts two bridges, one built in 1712 and the other, the Bridge of Sighs, in 1831, based on its Venetian namesake.

Peterhouse
The first Cambridge college, on Trumping-ton Street, is also one of the smallest. The hall still has original features from 1286 but its best details are later – a Tudor fireplace which is backed with 19th-century tiles by William Morris (see pp224–5). A gallery connects the college to the 12th-century church of St Mary the Less, which used to be called St Peter's Church – hence the college's name.

William Morris tiles, Peterhouse

VISITORS' CHECKLIST
Practical Information
Cambridge Colleges can usually be visited from 2–5pm daily, but there are no set opening hours. See noticeboards at each college for daily opening times. Some colleges charge admission.

Trinity College
The largest college, situated on Trinity Street, was founded by Henry VIII in 1546 and has a massive court and hall. The entrance gate, with statues of Henry and James I (added later), was built in 1529 for King's Hall, an earlier college incorporated into Trinity. The Great Court features a late Elizabethan fountain – at one time the main water supply. The chapel, built in 1567, has life-size statues of college members, notably Roubiliac's statue of the scientist Isaac Newton (1755).

University Botanic Garden
A delightful place for a leisurely stroll, just off Trumpington Street, as well as an important academic resource, the garden has been on this site since 1846. It has a superb collection of trees and a sensational water garden. The winter garden is one of the finest in the country.

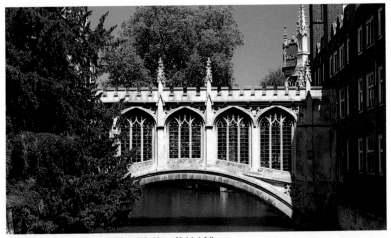

The Bridge of Sighs over the River Cam, linking the buildings of St John's College

THAMES VALLEY

Buckinghamshire · Oxfordshire · Berkshire · Bedfordshire · Hertfordshire

The mighty tidal river on which Britain's capital city was founded has modest origins, meandering from its source in the hills of Gloucestershire through the lush countryside towards London. Almost entirely agricultural land in the 19th century, the Thames Valley maintains its pastoral beauty despite the incursion of modern industry.

There are ancient royal connections with the area. Windsor Castle has been a residence of kings and queens for more than 900 years, and played a critical role in history in 1215, when King John set out from here to sign the *Magna Carta* at Runnymede on the River Thames. Further north, Queen Anne had Blenheim Palace built for her military commander, the 1st Duke of Marlborough. Elizabeth I spent part of her childhood at Hatfield House, and part of the Tudor palace still stands.

Several towns in this region, most notably Burford in Oxfordshire, developed as coach staging posts on the important trunk routes between London and the West Country. With the introduction of commuter transportation in the early 20th century, much of the area became an extension of suburbia and saw some imaginative experiments in Utopian town planning such as the garden city of Welwyn and the Quaker settlement at Jordons.

Oxford, the Thames Valley's principal city, owes its importance to the foundation of Britain's first university there in 1167; many of its colleges are gems of medieval architecture. In the 17th century, a number of battles during the Civil War *(see p56)* were fought around Oxford, which for a time was the headquarters of King Charles I, who was supported by the students. When the royalists were forced to flee Oxford, Cromwell made himself chancellor of the university.

The River Thames at Marlow, Buckinghamshire

◀ Autumn view of the Long Walk, Windsor Castle, Berkshire

Exploring the Thames Valley

The pleasant countryside of the Chiltern Hills and of the Thames Valley itself appealed to aristocrats who built stately homes close to London. Many of these are among the grandest in the country, including Hatfield House and Blenheim. Around these great houses grew picturesque villages, with half-timbered buildings and, as you move towards the Cotswolds, houses built in attractive buff-coloured stone. That the area has been inhabited for thousands of years is shown by the number of prehistoric remains, including the most remarkable chalk hillside figure, the White Horse of Uffington.

Sights at a Glance

1 Great Tew
2 Burford
3 Kelmscott
4 Vale of the White Horse
5 *Oxford pp226–31*
6 *Blenheim Palace pp232–3*
7 Stowe
8 Woburn Abbey
9 Waddesdon Manor
10 Roald Dahl Museum
11 ZSL Whipsnade Zoo
12 Knebworth House
13 Hatfield House
14 St Albans
15 Gardens of the Rose
16 Warner Bros. Studio Tour – The Making of Harry Potter
18 *Windsor pp239–41*

Walks and Tours

17 Touring the Thames

A thatched cottage, Upper Swarford, Banbury

For additional map symbols *see back flap*

Getting Around

As an important commuter belt, the Thames Valley is well served by public transport, as well as a good network of motorways and major roads into London. Mainline trains travel to all the major towns and there are many coach services that run from London to the major sights and attractions.

0 kilometres 10
0 miles 10

Leicester
Rushden
A6
Peterborough
Wollaston
A1
Milton
Ernest
Olney
Bedford
Sandy
A509
Kempston
M1
Biggleswade
Cambridge
Stony
Stratford
Newport Pagnell
Ouse
Clophill
A1
Henlow
Royston
Milton Keynes
A505
Bletchley
WOBURN
ABBEY
8
Flitwick
Letchworth
Baldock
A10
Winslow
Barton-le-Clay
Toddington
A6
Hitchin
Buntingford
A1(M)
Leighton
Buzzard
Dunstable
Stevenage
Whitchurch
Luton
M1
KNEBWORTH
HOUSE
WADDESDON
MANOR
11
A5
12
Much
Hadham
Harpenden
A602
WHIPSNADE
Welwyn Garden City
Hertford
esbury
A41
Tring
Hatfield
HATFIELD
HOUSE
A414
Hemel Hempstead
13
Hoddesdon
A4010
ALD DAHL
MUSEUM
10
Great
Missenden
GARDENS OF
THE ROSE
14
ST ALBANS
15
A10
himnor
Cheshunt
ills
A413
WARNER BROS.
STUDIO TOUR – THE
MAKING OF HARRY POTTER
16
Potter's Bar
M25
Watford
M1
High
Wycombe
Beaconsfield
Rickmansworth
Dartford
London
M40
THAMES
Cookham
Marlow
Maidenhead
M25
Uxbridge
Henley-
on-Thames
M4
Slough
WINDSOR
18
Bracknell
Wokingham
Sandhurst

Marlow Bridge, spanning the Thames

Key
— Motorway
— Major road
— Secondary road
⋯ Minor road
— Scenic route
⊢⊣ Main railway
— Minor railway

Radcliffe Camera, surrounded by Oxford's spires

❶ Great Tew

Oxfordshire. 🗺 250. 🚃 Oxford or Banbury then taxi. 🛈 Castle Quay Shopping Centre, Banbury (01295 753752).

🌐 visitnorthoxfordshire.com

This secluded village of ironstone was founded in the 1630s by Lord Falkland for estate workers. It was heavily restored between 1809 and 1811 in the Gothic style. Thatched cottages stand in gardens with clipped box hedges, and in the village centre is the 16th-century pub, the **Falkland Arms**, with its original period atmosphere.

Environs

Five miles (8 km) west are the **Rollright Stones**, three Bronze Age monuments. They comprise a stone circle of 77 stones, about 30 m (100 ft) in diameter, known as the King's Men; the remains of a burial chamber called the Whispering Knights; and the solitary King Stone.

Further north is **Banbury**, well known for its spicy flat cakes and its market cross, immortalized in the nursery rhyme, *Ride a Cock-horse to Banbury Cross*. The original medieval cross was destroyed but it was replaced in 1859.

🍺 **Falkland Arms Pub**
Great Tew. **Tel** 01608 683653. **Open** daily. **Closed** 25 Dec. 🖼

❷ Burford

Oxfordshire. 🗺 1,000. 🛈 High St (01993 823558).

A charming small town, Burford has hardly changed from Georgian times, when it was an important coach stop between Oxford and the West Country. Cotswold stone houses, inns and shops, many built in the 16th century, line its main street. **Tolsey Hall** is a Tudor house with an open ground floor where stalls are still set up. The house is located on the corner of Sheep Street, itself a reminder of the importance of the medieval wool trade (*see p211*).

Environs

Just east of Burford is **Swinbrook**, whose church contains the Fettiplace Monuments, six carved figures from the Tudor and Stuart periods. Two miles (3 km) beyond are the ruins of **Minster Lovell Hall**, a 15th-century manor house whose unusual dovecote survives intact.

A few miles south of Burford is **Cotswold Wildlife Park**, home to a diverse collection of mammals, reptiles and birds. **Witney**, to the west, has a town hall dating from 1730.

🏛 **Minster Lovell Hall**
Minster Lovell. **Open** daily. EH

🦓 **Cotswold Wildlife Park**
Burford. **Tel** 01993 823006. **Open** daily. **Closed** 25 Dec. ♿ 🖼
🌐 cotswoldwildlifepark.co.uk

❸ Kelmscott

Oxfordshire. 🗺 100. 🛈 The Corn Exchange, Faringdon (01367 242191).
🌐 faringdon.org

The imaginative designer and writer William Morris lived in this pretty Thameside village from 1871 until his death in 1896. He shared his house, the classic Elizabethan **Kelmscott Manor**, with fellow painter Dante Gabriel Rossetti (1828–82), who left after an affair with Morris's wife Jane – the model for many Pre-Raphaelite paintings.

The 19th-century
Banbury Cross

Cotswold stone houses, Burford, Oxfordshire

The formal entrance of the Elizabethan Kelmscott Manor

Morris and his followers in the Arts and Crafts movement were attracted by the medieval feel of the village and several cottages were later built in Morris's memory.

Today Kelmscott Manor has works of art by members of the movement – including some William de Morgan tiles. Morris is buried in the village churchyard, with a tomb designed by Philip Webb.

Two miles (3 km) to the east is **Radcot Bridge**, thought to be the oldest bridge still standing over the Thames. Built in the 13th century from the local Taynton stone, it was a strategic river crossing, and in 1387 was damaged in a battle between Richard II and his barons.

🏠 **Kelmscott Manor**
Kelmscott. **Tel** 01367 252486.
Open Apr–Oct: Wed & Sat (house & garden). 🅿 ♿ limited. 📷 ✏
Ⓦ kelmscottmanor.co.uk

❹ Vale of the White Horse

Oxfordshire. 🚉 Didcot. ℹ Old Abbey House, Abbey Close, Abingdon (01235 522711); 19 Church St, Wantage (01235 760176). Ⓦ abingdon.gov.uk

This lovely valley gets its name from the huge chalk horse, 100 m (350 ft) from nose to tail, carved into the hillside above Uffington. It is believed to be Britain's oldest hillside carving and has sparked many legends: some say it was cut by the Saxon leader Hengist (whose name means stallion in German), while others believe it is to do with Alfred the Great, thought to

have been born nearby. It is, however, a great deal older than either of these stories suggest, having been dated at around 1000 BC.

Nearby is the Celtic earth ramparts of the Iron Age hill fort, **Uffington Castle**. A mile (1.5 km) west along the Ridgeway, an ancient trade route, *(see p41)*, is an even older

monument, a large Stone Age burial mound which is known as **Wayland's Smithy**. This is immersed in legends that Sir Walter Scott *(see p516)* used in his novel *Kenilworth*.

The best view of the horse is to be had from Uffington village, which is also worth visiting for the **Tom Brown's School Museum**. This 17th-century school house contains exhibits devoted to the author Thomas Hughes (1822–96). Hughes set the early chapters of his Victorian novel, *Tom Brown's Schooldays*, here. The museum also contains material about excavations on White Horse Hill.

🏛 **Tom Brown's School**
Broad St, Uffington. ℹ 01367 820259. **Open** Easter–Oct: Sat, Sun & public hols (pm). ♿ limited. 📷
Ⓦ **museum.uffington.net**

Hillside Chalk Figures

It was the Celts who first saw the potential for creating large-scale artworks on the chalk hills of southern England. Horses – held in high regard by both the Celts and later the Saxons, and the objects of cult worship – were often a favourite subject, but people were also depicted, notably Cerne Abbas, Dorset *(see p273)* and the Long Man of Wilmington *(see p184)*. The figures may have served as religious symbols or as landmarks by which tribes identified their territory. Many chalk figures have been obliterated, because without any attention they are quickly overrun by grass. Uffington is "scoured", to prevent encroachment by grass, a tradition once accompanied by a fair and other festivities. There was a second flush of hillside carving in the 18th century, especially in Wiltshire. In some cases – for instance at Bratton Castle near Westbury – an 18th-century carving has been superimposed on an ancient one.

Britain's oldest hillside carving, the White Horse of Uffington

➎ Street-by-Street: Oxford

Oxford has long been a strategic point on the western routes into London – its name describes its position as a convenient spot for crossing the river (a ford for oxen). The city's first scholars, who founded the university, came from France in 1167. The development of England's first university created the spectacular skyline of tall towers and "dreaming spires".

Old Ashmolean
Now the Museum of the History of Science, this resplendent building was designed in 1683 to show Elias Ashmole's collection of curiosities. The displays were moved in 1845.

The Ashmolean Museum
displays one of Britain's foremost collections of fine art and antiquities.

St John's College

Balliol College

ST GILES

BEAUMONT STREET

MAGDALEN STREET

BROAD STREET

TURL STREET

BRASEN

Martyrs' Memorial
This commemorates the three Protestant martyrs, Latimer, Ridley and Cranmer, who were burned at the stake for heresy.

Coach station & Oxford Castle Quarter

CORNMARKET STREET

MARKET STREET

Trinity College

Oxford Story

| 0 metres | 100 |
| 0 yards | 100 |

Key

— Suggested route

Jesus College

Lincoln College

Railway station

ST ALDA

Covered market

Museum of Oxford

Percy Bysshe Shelley

Shelley (1792–1822), one of the Romantic poets (see p370), attended University College, Oxford, but was expelled after writing the revolutionary pamphlet The Necessity of Atheism. Despite that disgrace, the college has put up a memorial to him from his daughter-in-law.

Sheldonian Theatre
The first building designed by Wren (see p118) is the scene of Oxford University's traditional graduation ceremonies.

★ Radcliffe Camera
This Classical rotunda is Oxford's most distinctive building and is now a reading room of the Bodleian. It was one of the library's original buildings (*see p231*).

Bridge of Sighs
Resembling the steeply arched bridge in Venice of the same name, this picturesque landmark was built in 1914 and joins the old and new buildings of Hertford College.

New College

St Mary the Virgin Church

Queen's College

All Souls College

London

University College

Lincoln College Library

Botanic Garden and Magdalen College

Oriel College

Merton College

Corpus Christi College

★ Christ Church
Students still eat at long tables in all the college halls. Senior academics sit at the high table and grace is almost always said in Latin.

Exploring Oxford

Oxford is more than just a university city; it has one of Britain's most important car factories in the suburb of Cowley. Despite this, Oxford is dominated by institutions related to its huge academic community: like Blackwell's bookshop which has over 20,000 titles in stock. The two rivers, the Cherwell and the Isis (the name given to the Thames as it flows through the city), provide lovely riverside walks, or you can hire a punt and spend an afternoon on the Cherwell.

⛁ Ashmolean Museum

Beaumont St. **Tel** 01865 278002. **Open** Tue–Sun & public hols. **Closed** 24–26 Dec. ♿ 📷 Tue, Fri, Sat. 📱 📷
W ashmolean.org

One of the best museums in Britain outside London, the Ashmolean – the first purpose-built museum in England – opened in 1683, based on a display known as "The Ark" collected by the two John Tradescants, father and son.

On their many voyages to the Orient and the Americas they collected stuffed animals and tribal artifacts. On their death, the collection was acquired by the antiquarian Elias Ashmole, who donated it to the university and had a building made for the exhibits on Broad Street – the Old Ashmolean, now the Museum of the History of Science. In the 1800s, part of the Tradescant collection was moved to the University Galleries, a Neo-Classical building of 1845. This greatly expanded museum is now known as the Ashmolean.

What is left of the original curio collection is overshadowed by the other exhibits in the museum, in particular the paintings. These include Bellini's *St Jerome Reading in a Landscape* (late 15th century); Raphael's *Heads of Two Apostles* (1519); Turner's *Venice: The Grand Canal* (1840), Picasso's *Blue Roofs* (1901) and a large group of Pre-Raphaelites, including Rossetti and Millais. There are also fine Greek and Roman carvings and a collection of stringed musical instruments. Items of more local interest include a Rowlandson watercolour of Radcliffe Square in about 1790 and the Oxford Crown. This silver coin was minted here during the Civil War in 1644 *(see p56)* and forms part of the second-largest coin collection in Britain. Perhaps the single most important item is the gold enamelled ornament known as the Alfred Jewel *(see p51)*, which is more than 1,000 years old.

A building designed by Rick Mather provides the museum with twice as much space as it previously had, as well as a spectacular roof-top restaurant.

The entrance to the Ashmolean Museum

⛁ The University of Oxford Botanic Garden

Rose Lane. **Tel** 01865 286690. **Open** daily. **Closed** Good Fri, 25 Dec. ♿
Mar–Oct. Donation Nov–Feb. ♿ 📷
W botanic-garden.ox.ac.uk

Britain's oldest botanic garden was founded in 1621 – one ancient yew tree survives from that period. The entrance gates were designed by Nicholas Stone in 1633 and paid for, like the garden itself, by the Earl of Danby. His statue adorns the gate, along with those of Charles I and II. This delightful garden has an original walled garden, a more recent herbaceous border and rock garden, and an insectivorous house.

The 17th-century Botanic Gardens

⛁ Carfax Tower

Carfax Sq. **Tel** 01865 790522.
Open daily. **Closed** 1 Jan, 25 & 26 Dec. ♿ 📷

The tower is all that remains of the 14th-century Church of St Martin, demolished in 1896 so that the adjoining road could be widened. Watch the clock strike the quarter hours, and climb the 99 steps to the top for panoramic views of the city. Carfax was the crossing point of the original north-to-south and east-to-west routes through Oxford, and the word comes from the Latin *quadrifurcus* (four-forked).

⛁ Holywell Music Room

Holywell St. **Open** concerts only. ♿ ♿

This was the first building in Europe designed, in 1752, specifically for public musical performances. Previously, concerts had been held in private houses for invited guests only. Its two splendid chandeliers originally adorned Westminster Hall at the coronation of George IV in 1820, and were given by the king to Wadham College, of which the music room technically forms a part. The room is regularly used for contemporary and classical concerts.

� Museum of Oxford

St Aldates. **Tel** 01865 252351. **Open** 10am–5pm Mon–Sat, 11am–3pm Sun. **Closed** 1 Jan, 24–26 Dec, 31 Dec.

A well-organized display in the Victorian town hall illustrates the long history of Oxford and its university. Exhibits include a Roman pottery kiln. The main features are a series of well-reconstructed rooms, including one from an Elizabethan inn and an 18th-century student's room.

Martyrs' Memorial

Magdalen St.

This commemorates the three Protestants burned at the stake on Broad Street – Bishops Latimer and Ridley in 1555, and Archbishop Cranmer in 1556. On the accession of Queen Mary in 1553 *(see p55)*, they were committed to the Tower of London, then sent to Oxford to defend their views before the doctors of divinity who, after the hearing, condemned them as heretics.

The memorial was designed in 1843 by George Gilbert Scott and based on the Eleanor crosses erected in 12 English towns by Edward I (1239–1307) to honour his queen.

Oxford Castle

44–46 Oxford Castle. **Tel** 01865 260666. **Open** daily.

Following a £40-million development, this 1,000-year-old castle forms part of the Oxford Castle Quarter, an urban space that also includes shops, restaurants and a hotel.

Oxford Castle Unlocked

44–46 Oxford Castle. **Tel** 01865 260666. **Open** daily. **Closed** 24–26 Dec.

The secrets of the castle are revealed in this exhibition that looks at the site's turbulent past. Climb St George's Tower for panoramic views over the city.

Sheldonian Theatre

Broad St. **Tel** 01865 277299. **Open** call for details. **Closed** Christmas period, Easter & public hols.

w sheldon.ox.ac.uk

Completed in 1669, this was designed by Christopher Wren *(see p118)*, and paid for by Gilbert Sheldon, the Archbishop of Canterbury, as a location for university degree ceremonies. The Classical design of the D-shaped building is based on the Theatre of Marcellus in Rome. The octagonal cupola built in 1838 boasts a famous view from its huge Lantern. The theatre's painted ceiling shows the triumph of religion, art and science over envy, hatred and malice.

St Mary the Virgin Church

High St. **Tel** 01865 279111. **Open** daily. **Closed** Good Fri, 25, 26 Dec.

w university-church.ox.ac.uk

This, the official university church, is said to be the most visited parish church in England. The oldest parts date from the early 13th century and include the tower, from which there are fine views. Its Convocation House served as the university's first library

Thomas Cranmer statue, St Mary the Virgin Church

until the Bodleian was founded in 1488 *(see p231)*. The church is where the three Oxford Martyrs were pronounced heretics in 1555. An architectural highlight is the Baroque south porch.

Oxford University Museum of Natural History

Parks Rd. **Tel** 01865 272950. **Open** daily. **Closed** Easter, 24–26 Dec.

w oum.ox.ac.uk

Pitt Rivers Museum

Parks Rd. **Tel** 01865 270927. **Open** daily. **Closed** Easter, 24–26 Dec.

w prm.ox.ac.uk

Two of Oxford's most interesting museums adjoin each other. The first is a museum of natural history containing relics of dinosaurs as well as a stuffed dodo. This flightless bird has been extinct since the 17th century, but was immortalized by Lewis Carroll (an Oxford mathematics lecturer) in his book *Alice in Wonderland*. The Pitt Rivers Museum has an extensive ethnographic collection – masks and totems from Africa and the Far East – and archaeological displays, including exhibits collected by the explorer Captain Cook.

The impressive frontage of the Oxford University Museum of Natural History

Exploring Oxford University

Many of the 36 colleges which go to make up the university were founded between the 13th and 16th centuries and cluster around the city centre. As scholarship was then the exclusive preserve of the church, the colleges were designed along the lines of monastic buildings but were often surrounded by beautiful gardens. Although most colleges have been altered over the years, many still incorporate a lot of their original features.

The spectacular view of All Souls College from St Mary's Church

All Souls College
Founded in 1438 on the High Street by Henry VI, the chapel on the college's north side has a classic hammerbeam roof, unusual misericords (see p345) on the choir stalls and 15th-century stained glass.

Christ Church
The best way to view this, the largest of the Oxford colleges, is to approach through the meadows from St Aldate's. Christ Church dates from 1525 when Cardinal Wolsey founded it as an ecclesiastical college to train cardinals. The upper part of the tower in Tom Quad – a rectangular courtyard – was built by Wren (see p118) in 1682 and is the largest in the city. When its

bell, Great Tom, was hung in 1648, the college had 101 students, which is why the bell is rung 101 times at 9:05pm, to mark the curfew for students (which has not been enforced since 1963). The odd timing is because noon falls here five minutes later than at Greenwich (see p129). Christ Church has produced 13 British prime ministers in the last 200 years. Beside the main quad is the 12th-century Christ Church Cathedral, one of the smallest in England.

Lincoln College
One of the best-preserved of the medieval colleges, it was founded in 1427 on Turl Street, and the front quad and façade

are 15th century. The hall still has its original roof, including the gap where smoke used to escape. The Jacobean chapel is notable for its stained glass. John Wesley (see p283) was at college here and his rooms, now a chapel, can be visited.

Magdalen College
At the end of the High Street is perhaps the most typical and beautiful Oxford college. Its 15th-century quads in contrasting styles are set in a park by the Cherwell, crossed by Magdalen Bridge. Every May Day at 6am, the college choir sings from the top of Magdalen's bell tower (1508) – a 16th-century custom to mark the start of summer.

New College
One of the grandest colleges, it was founded by William of Wykeham in 1379 to educate clergy to replace those killed by the Black Death of 1348 (see p53).

Magdalen Bridge spanning the River Cherwell

Its magnificent chapel on New College Lane, restored in the 19th century, has vigorous 14th-century misericords and El Greco's (1541–1614) famous painting of St James.

Queen's College
Most of the college buildings date from the 18th century and represent some of the finest work from that period in Oxford. Its superb library was built in 1695 by Henry Aldrich (1647–1710) The front screen with its bell-topped gatehouse is a feature of the High Street.

Student Life

Students belong to individual colleges and usually live in them for the duration of their course. The university gives lectures, sets exams and awards degrees but much of the students' tuition and social life is based around their college. Many university traditions date back hundreds of years, like the graduation ceremonies at the Sheldonian, which are still held in Latin.

Graduation at the Sheldonian (see p228)

Merton College seen from Christ Church Meadows

St John's College

The impressive frontage on St Giles dates from 1437, when it was founded for Cistercian scholars. The library has lovely 17th-century bookcases and stained glass, and the college owns a magnificent collection of early embroidered vestments.

Trinity College

The oldest part of the college on Broad Street, Durham Quad, is named after the earlier college of 1296, which was incorporated into Trinity in 1555. The late 17th-century chapel has a magnificent reredos and wooden screen.

Corpus Christi College

The whole of the charming front quad on Merton Street dates from 1517, when the college was founded. The quad's sundial, topped by a pelican – the college symbol – bears an early 17th-century calendar. The chapel has a rare 16th-century eagle lectern.

Merton College

Off Merton Street, this is the oldest college (1264) in Oxford. Much of its hall dates from then, including a sturdy decorated door. The chapel choir contains allegorical reliefs representing music, arithmetic, rhetoric and grammar. Merton's Mob Quad served as a model for the later colleges.

Bodleian Library

Founded in 1320, the library was expanded in 1426 by Humphrey, Duke of Gloucester (1391–1447) and brother of Henry V, when his collection of manuscripts would not fit into the old library. It was refounded in 1602 by Thomas Bodley, a wealthy scholar, who insisted on strict rules: the keeper was forbidden to marry. The library is one of the six copyright deposit libraries in the country – it is entitled to receive a copy of every book published in Britain.

The Radcliffe Camera (1748), a domed Baroque rotunda, was built by James Gibbs as a library funded by a bequest from the Yorkshire physician Dr John Radcliffe (1650–1714).

Main entrance

This extension was built in 1630.

Duke Humphrey's Library has ceiling panels that carry the university crest and Latin motto *Dominus Illuminatio Mea* – the Lord is my Light.

The Divinity School (1488) has a unique vaulted ceiling with 455 carved bosses representing biblical scenes and both mythical and real beasts – one of the country's finest Gothic interiors.

❻ Blenheim Palace

After John Churchill, the 1st Duke of Marlborough, defeated the French at the Battle of Blenheim in 1704, Queen Anne gave him the Manor of Woodstock and had this palatial house built for him in gratitude. Designed by both Nicholas Hawksmoor and Sir John Vanbrugh *(see p402)*, it is a Baroque masterpiece. It was also the birthplace of Britain's World War II leader, Winston Churchill, in 1874.

Water Terraces
These magnificent gardens were laid out in the 1920s by French architect Achille Duchêne in 17th-century style, with detailed patterned beds and fountains.

Chapel
The marble monument to the 1st Duke of Marlborough and his family was sculpted by Michael Rysbrack in 1733.

KEY

① **The Grand Bridge** was begun in 1708. It has a 31 m (101 ft) main span and contains rooms within its structure.

② **Great Court**

③ **Grinling Gibbons lions (1709)**.

④ **Clock tower**

⑤ **East gate**

⑥ **The Italian Garden** contains the Mermaid Fountain (early 1900s) by US sculptor Waldo Story.

⑦ **The Green Drawing Room** has a full-length portrait of the 4th Duke by George Romney (1734–1802).

⑧ **Red Drawing Room**

⑨ **Green Writing Room**

⑩ **First State Room**

⑪ **Second State Room**.

⑫ **Third State Room**

⑬ **Great Hall** has a splendid ceiling by Thornhill in 1716, showing the 1st Duke of Marlborough presenting his plan for the Battle of Blenheim to Britannia.

⑭ **Blenheim Palace:** The Untold Story

Winston Churchill and his wife, Clementine

★ **Long Library**
This 55 m (183 ft) room was designed by Vanbrugh as a picture gallery. The portraits include one of Queen Anne by Sir Godfrey Kneller (1646–1723). The stucco on the ceiling is by Isaac Mansfield (1725).

VISITORS' CHECKLIST

Practical Information
Woodstock, Oxfordshire. **Tel** 0800 849 6500. **w** blenheimpalace. com Palace & Gardens: **Open** Feb–Oct: 10:30am–5:30pm daily; Nov–Dec: Wed–Sun. Park: **Open** 9am–5pm daily. 🐾 🎫 The Untold Story. 🖼 📷 ♿

Transport
🚌 S3 from Oxford train station.
🚂 Oxford.

Entrance

★ **Park and gardens**

Column of Victory
Grand Bridge
Triumphal Arch
Palace
Woodstock
Water Terraces
Car park
Italian Garden
Temple of Diana
Narrow-gauge railway
Rose Garden
Secret garden
Arboretum
Car park
Adventure playground
Butterfly House
Marlborough Maze

A house fit for a victorious general had to be surrounded by a park with suitably heroic monuments. They were kept when "Capability" Brown (see p30) re-landscaped the park (1764–74) and created the lake.

★ **Saloon**
French artist Louis Laguerre (1663–1721) painted the detailed scenes on the walls and ceiling.

Canaletto's *Entrance to the Arsenal* (1730) hangs at Woburn Abbey

❼ Stowe

Buckingham, Buckinghamshire.
Tel 01280 817156. 🚆 Milton Keynes then bus. **Open** daily. Stowe House:
Open school term time for guided tours only; for other times of year, see website for full details. 🅿 ♿ 🖥 📷
🅽🆃 🌐 stowe.co.uk/house

This is the most ambitious and important landscaped garden in Britain, as well as being one of the finest examples of the 18th-century passion for improving on nature to make it conform to fashionable notions of taste.

In the space of nearly 100 years the original garden, first laid out around 1680, was enlarged and transformed by the addition of monuments, Greek and Gothic temples, grottoes, statues, ornamental bridges, artificial lakes and "natural" tree plantings. Most of the leading designers and architects of the period contributed to the design, including Sir John Vanbrugh, James Gibbs and "Capability" Brown *(see p30)*. Brown was also married here and lived in one of the Boycott Pavilions.

From 1593 to 1921 the property was owned by the Temple and Grenville families – later the Dukes of Buckingham – until the large Palladian house at its centre was converted into an elite boys' school.

The family were soldiers and politicians in the liberal tradition, and many of the buildings and sculptures in the garden symbolize Utopian ideals of democracy and freedom. Some features deteriorated in the 19th century but a major restoration programme has returned much of the statuary to its former glory.

❽ Woburn Abbey

Woburn, Bedfordshire. **Tel** 01525 290333. 🚆 Flitwick then taxi. **Open** end Mar–Oct: daily. **Closed** Nov–mid-Mar. Grounds: **Open** daily (Fri–Sun in winter). 📷 🅿 ♿ ring first. 📷 by arrangement. 🅿
🌐 woburnabbey.co.uk

The Dukes of Bedford have lived here for over 350 years and were among the first owners of an English stately home to open their house to the public some 40 years ago. The abbey was built in the mid-18th century on the foundations of a large 12th-century Cistercian monastery. Its mix of styles range from Henry Flitcroft and Henry Holland *(see p32)*. The abbey's grounds are also popular for their 142-ha (350-acre) safari park and attractive deer park, home to nine species including the Manchurian Sika deer from China. The home's magnificent state apartments house an important private art collection which includes works by Reynolds (1723–92) and Canaletto (1697–1768).

❾ Waddesdon Manor

Nr Aylesbury, Buckinghamshire. **Tel** 01296 653226. 🚆 Aylesbury then taxi. House: **Open** Mar–Dec: Wed–Sun; Jan–Feb: Sat & Sun. Grounds: **Open** Mar–23 Dec: 10am–5pm Wed–Sun (11am Sat & Sun), bank hol Mon. 🅿 ♿ 🅿
🖥 📷 🌐 waddesdon.org.uk

Waddesdon Manor was built between 1874–89 by Baron Ferdinand de Rothschild and designed by French architect Gabriel-Hippolyte Destailleur. Built in the style of a French 16th-century chateau, the manor houses one of the world's finest collections of French 18th-century decorative art as well as Savonnerie carpets and Sèvres porcelain. The garden, originally laid out by French landscape gardener Elie Lainé, is renowned for its seasonal displays.

❿ Roald Dahl Museum

81–83 High St, Great Missenden, Buckinghamshire. **Tel** 01494 892192. 🚆 Great Missenden. **Open** 10am–5pm Tue–Fri, 11am–5pm Sat & Sun. 📷
🅿 ♿ 🌐 roalddahlmuseum.org

The magical world of Roald Dahl's stories comes to life in this award-winning museum. A series of biographical galleries explore the life and work of the children's writer, while the Story Centre's interactive exhibits allow children to make their own animation film, record dreams in a "dream bottle" or try their hand at creative writing.

The 17th-century Palladian bridge over the Octagon Lake in Stowe Park

Hatfield House, one of the largest Jacobean mansions in the country

⓫ ZSL Whipsnade Zoo

Nr Dunstable, Bedfordshire. **Tel** 01582 872171. �‍ Hemel Hempsted or Luton then bus. **Open** daily. **Closed** 25 Dec. 🅿 ♿ 🖵 🇼 zsl.org

The rural branch of London Zoo, this was one of the first zoos to minimize the use of cages, confining animals safely but without constriction.

At 240 ha (600 acres), it is Europe's largest conservation park, with more than 2,500 species. You can drive through some areas or go by steam train. Also popular are the adventure playground, the Cheetah Rock exhibit and the sea lions' underwater display.

⓬ Knebworth House

Knebworth, Hertfordshire. **Tel** 01438 812661. 🚅 Stevenage then taxi. **Open** Sat, Sun; two weeks at Easter: daily; Jul–Aug: daily. 🅿 🚻 ♿ limited. 🗺 🖵
🇼 knebworthhouse.com

A notable Tudor mansion, with a beautiful Jacobean banqueting hall, Knebworth was overlain with a 19th-century Victorian Gothic exterior by Lord Lytton, the head of the family. His eldest son, the 1st Earl of Lytton, was Viceroy of India, and exhibits illustrate the Delhi Durbar of 1877, when Queen Victoria became Empress of India.

A visit includes the house, gardens, park, and a dinosaur trail for children.

⓭ Hatfield House

Hatfield, Hertfordshire. **Tel** 01707 287010. 🚅 Hatfield. **Open** Easter–Sep: Wed–Sun & public hols. 🅿 🗺 ♿ ⊘ 🇼 hatfield-house.co.uk

One of England's finest Jacobean houses, Hatfield House was built between 1607 and 1611 for the powerful statesman Robert Cecil.

Its chief historical interest, though, lies in the surviving wing of the original Tudor Hatfield Palace, where Queen Elizabeth I (see pp54–5) spent much of her childhood. She held her first Council of State here when she was crowned in 1558. The palace was partly demolished in 1607 to make way for the new house, which contains mementoes of her life, including the *Rainbow* portrait painted around 1600 by Isaac Oliver. Visitors can attend medieval banquets in the old palace's Great Hall.

Originally laid out by Robert Cecil with help from John Tradescant, the gardens have been restored to reflect these Jacobean origins.

Famous Puritans

Three major figures connected with the 17th-century Puritan movement are celebrated in the Thames area. John Bunyan (1628–88), who wrote the allegorical tale *The Pilgrim's Progress*, was born at Elstow, near Bedford. A passionate Puritan orator, he was jailed for his beliefs for 17 years. The Bunyan Museum in Bedford is a former site of Puritan worship. William Penn (1644–1718), founder of Pennsylvania in the USA, lived, worshipped and is buried at Jordans, near Beaconsfield. A bit further north at

18th-century engraving of John Bunyan

Chalfont St Giles is the cottage where the poet John Milton (1608–74) stayed to escape London's plague. There he completed his greatest work, *Paradise Lost*. The house is now a museum based on his life and works.

William Penn, founder of Pennsylvania

John Milton painted by Pieter van der Plas

⑭ St Albans

Today a thriving market town and a base for London commuters, St Albans was for centuries at the heart of some of the most stirring events in English history. A regional capital of ancient Britain, it became a major Roman settlement and then a key ecclesiastical centre – so important that during the Wars of the Roses (see p53), two battles were fought for it. In 1455 the Yorkists drove King Henry VI from the town and six years later the Lancastrians retook it.

One of the oldest surviving pubs in England

Exploring St Albans

Part of the appeal of this ancient and fascinating town, little more than an hour's drive from London, is that its 2,000-year history can be traced vividly by visiting a few sites within easy walking distance of one another. There is a large car park within the walls of the Roman city of Verulamium, between the museum and St Michael's Church and across the road from the excavated theatre. From there it is a pleasant lakeside walk across the park, passing more Roman sites, Ye Olde Fighting Cocks inn, the massive cathedral and the historic High Street. Marking the centre of the town, the High Street is lined with several Tudor buildings and a clock tower dating from 1412, from which the curfew bell used to ring at 4am in the morning and 8:30pm at night.

🏛 Verulamium

Just outside the city centre are the walls of Verulamium, one of the first British cities the Romans established after their invasion of Britain in AD 43. Boudica (see p199) razed it to the ground during her unsuccessful rebellion against the Romans in AD 62, but its position on Watling Street, an important trading route, meant that it was quickly rebuilt on an even larger scale and the city flourished until 410.

🏛 Verulamium Museum

St Michael's St. **Tel** 01727 751810. **Open** daily. **Closed** 1 Jan, 25 & 26 Dec. 🎟 🚻 📷 🌐 stalbansmuseums.org.uk

This excellent museum tells the story of the city, but its main attraction is its splendid collection of well-preserved Roman artefacts, notably some breathtaking mosaic floors, including one depicting the head of a sea god, and another of a scallop shell. Other finds included burial urns and lead coffins.

On the basis of excavated plaster fragments, a Roman room has been painstakingly recreated, its walls painted in startlingly bright colours and geometric patterns.

Between here and St Albans Cathedral are a bath house with a mosaic, remnants of the ancient city wall and one of the original gates.

🍺 Ye Olde Fighting Cocks

Abbey Mill Lane. **Tel** 01727 869152. **Open** daily. 🚻

Believed to be England's oldest surviving pub, Ye Olde Fighting Cocks is certainly, with its octagonal shape, one of the most unusual. It originated as the medieval dovecote of the old abbey and moved here after the Dissolution (see p54).

🏛 Roman Theatre

Bluehouse Hill. **Tel** 01727 835035. **Open** daily. **Closed** 1 Jan, 25, 26 Dec. 🎟 📷 🌐 romantheatre.co.uk

Just across the road from the museum are the foundations of the open-air theatre, first built around AD 140 but enlarged several times. It is one of only six known to have been built in Roman Britain. Alongside it are traces of a row of Roman shops and a house, from which many of the museum's treasures – such as a bronze statuette of Venus – were excavated in the 1930s.

🏛 St Michael's Church

St Michael's. **Tel** 01727 835037. **Open** Apr–Sep: phone for details. 🚻

This church was first founded during the Saxon reign and is built partly with bricks taken from Verulamium, which by then was in decline. Numerous additions have been made since then, including a truly splendid Jacobean pulpit.

The church contains an early 17th-century monument to the statesman and writer Sir Francis Bacon; his father owned nearby Gorhambury, a large Tudor house, now in ruins.

A scallop shell, one of the mosaic floors at the Verulamium Museum

The imposing west side of St Albans Cathedral

The splendour of the Gardens of the Rose in June

St Albans Cathedral

Sumpter Yard. **Tel** 01727 860780.
Open daily. 11:30am & 2:30pm.
w stalbanscathedral.org

This outstanding example of medieval architecture has some classic features such as the 13th- and 14th-century wall paintings on the Norman piers.

It was begun in 793, when King Offa of Mercia founded the abbey in honour of St Alban, Britain's first Christian martyr, put to death by the Romans in the third century for sheltering a priest. The oldest parts, which still stand, were first built in 1077 and are easily recognizable as Norman by the round-headed arches and windows. They form part of the 84 m (276 ft) nave – the longest in England.

The pointed arches further east are Early English (13th century), while the decorated work of the 14th century was added when some of the Norman arches collapsed.

East of the crossing is what remains of St Alban's shrine – a marble pedestal made up of more than 2,000 tiny fragments. Next to it is the tomb of Humphrey, Duke of Gloucester *(see p231)*.

It was here at the cathedral that the English barons drafted the *Magna Carta* document *(see p52)*, which King John was then forced to sign.

⓯ Gardens of the Rose

Chiswell Green, Hertfordshire.
Tel 08458 334 344. St Albans then bus. **Open** summer: daily, but always call ahead.
w rnrs.org

The 5 ha (12 acre) garden of the Royal National Rose Society, with over 30,000 plants and 1,700 varieties, is at its peak in late June. The gardens trace the history of the flower as far back as the white rose of York, the red rose of Lancaster *(see p53)* and the Rosa Mundi – named by Henry II for his mistress Fair Rosamond after she was poisoned by Queen Eleanor in 1177. Highlights include roses in a garden setting, demonstrating different styles of planting.

⓰ Warner Bros. Studio Tour – The Making of Harry Potter

Leavesden, Hertfordshire.
Tel 08450 840900. Watford Junction then shuttle bus. **Open** daily.
Closed 25 & 26 Dec.

Visitors to the Warner Bros. studio can see original scenery, costumes and props from all eight Harry Potter movies. Among the sets are the iconic Great Hall and Diagon Alley. The largely self-guided tour offers glimpses into the off-camera world of the film-makers, including how animatronics and green-screen effects brought to life the monsters and marvels of Harry's world. Children can even ride broomsticks here. Tickets must be booked in advance.

George Bernard Shaw

Although a controversial playwright and known as a mischievous character, the Irish-born George Bernard Shaw (1856–1950) was a man of settled habits. He lived near St Albans in a house at Ayot St Lawrence, now called Shaw's Corner, for the last 44 years of his life, working until his last weeks in a summerhouse at the bottom of his large garden. His plays, combining wit with a powerful political and social message, still seem fresh today. One of the most enduring is *Pygmalion* (1913), on which the musical *My Fair Lady* is based. The house and garden are now a museum of his life and works.

⑰ Touring the Thames

The Thames between Pangbourne and Eton is leafy and romantic and best seen by boat. But if time is short, the road keeps close to its bank for much of the way. Swans glide gracefully below ancient bridges, voles dive into the water for cover, and elegant herons stand impassive at the river's edge. Huge beech trees overhang the banks which are lined with fine houses, their gardens sloping to the water. The tranquil scene has inspired painters and writers through the ages as well as previously operating as an important transport link.

⑥ Hambledon Mill
The white weather-boarded mill, which was operational until 1955, is one of the largest on the Thames as well as one of the oldest in origin. There are traces of the original 16th-century mill.

① Beale Park
The philanthropist Gilbert Beale (1868–1967) created a 10 ha (25 acre) park to preserve this beautiful stretch of river intact and breed endangered birds like owls, ornamental water fowl, pheasants and peacocks.

⑤ Henley
This lovely old river town boasts houses and churches dating from the 15th and 16th centuries and an important regatta, first held in 1829 (see p70).

④ Sonning Bridge
The 18th-century bridge is made up of 11 brick arches of varying width.

② Pangbourne
Kenneth Grahame (1859–1932), author of *The Wind in the Willows*, lived here. Pangbourne was used as the setting by artists Ernest Shepard in 1908 and Arthur Rackham in 1951 to illustrate the book.

Tips for Drivers

Tour length: 50 miles (75 km).
Stopping-off points: The picturesque town of Henley has a large number of riverside pubs which will make good stops for lunch. If you are boating you can often moor your boat alongside the river bank. (See also pp636–7.)

③ Whitchurch Mill
This charming village, linked to Pangbourne by a Victorian toll bridge, has a picturesque church and one of the many disused watermills that once harnessed the power of this stretch of river.

⑦ Cookham

This is famous as the home of Stanley Spencer (1891–1959), one of Britain's leading 20th-century artists. The former Methodist chapel, where Spencer worshipped as a child, has been converted into a gallery that contains some of his paintings and equipment. This work, entitled *Swan Upping* (1914–19), recalls a Thames custom.

⑧ Cliveden Reach
The beech trees lining this attractive stretch of river are in the grounds of Cliveden House (*see p166*).

Key

━━━ Tour route

━━━ Other roads

```
0 kilometres        10
0 miles        5
```

⑨ Eton College
Founded by Henry VI in 1440, Eton is Britain's most famous public school. It has a superb Perpendicular chapel (1441) with a series of English wall paintings (1479–88).

Boating Tours

In summer, scheduled river services run between Henley, Windsor, Runnymede and Marlow. Several companies operate from towns along the route. You can hire boats by the hour or the day or, for a longer tour, you can rent cabin cruisers and sleep on board (*see also p641*). Ring Salter Bros on 01865 243 421 for more information.

Salter Bros hire boats, moored at Henley

⑱ Windsor

Berkshire. 🚆 30,000 ➡ ℹ️ Thames St (01753 743900). 🌐 **windsor.gov.uk**

The town of Windsor is dwarfed by the enormous **castle** (*see pp240–41*) on the hill above – in fact its original purpose was to serve the castle's needs. The town is full of quaint Georgian shops, houses and inns. The most prominent building on the High Street is the **Guildhall** completed by Wren (*see p118*) in 1689, where Prince Charles and Camilla Parker-Bowles were married in 2005. **Eton College**, the most prestigious school in Britain, lies just a short walk away.

The huge 1,940-ha (4,800-acre) **Windsor Great Park** stretches from the castle three miles (5 km) to Snow Hill, where there is a statue of George III.

Environs
Four miles (7 km) to the southeast is the level grassy meadow, **Runnymede**. This is one of England's most historic sites, where in 1215 King John was forced by his rebellious barons to sign the *Magna Carta* (*see p52*), thereby limiting his royal powers. The dainty memorial pavilion at the top of the meadow was erected in 1957.

🎓 Eton College
Tel 01753 671177. **Open** mid-Mar–Oct: by guided tour only. Always call ahead. 🌐 **etoncollege.com**

King John signing the *Magna Carta*, Runnymede

Windsor Castle

The oldest continuously inhabited royal residence in Britain, the castle, originally made of wood, was built by William the Conqueror in around 1080 to guard the western approaches to London. He chose the site as it was on high ground and just a day's journey from his base in the Tower of London. Successive monarchs have made alterations that render it a remarkable monument to royalty's changing tastes. King George V's affection for it was shown when he chose Windsor for his family surname in 1917. The castle is an official residence of the Queen and her family who stay here many weekends.

King Henry VIII Gate and main exit

KEY

① **The Round Tower** was first built in wood by William the Conqueror. In 1170 it was rebuilt in stone by Henry II (see p52). It now houses the Royal Archives and Photographic Collection.

② **Statue of Charles II**

③ **The Audience Chamber** is where the Queen greets her guests.

④ **The Queen's Ballroom**

⑤ **Drawings Gallery** contains various pieces, including works by Holbein, Michelangelo and Leonardo da Vinci among others, though the art works and artists on display change from time to time.

⑥ **Queen Mary's Dolls' House,** designed by Sir Edwin Lutyens, was given to Queen Mary in 1924. The wine cellar contains genuine vintage wine.

⑦ **The fire of 1992** destroyed St George's Hall, which has since been rebuilt.

⑧ **Brunswick Tower**

⑨ **The East Terrace Garden** was created by Sir Jeffry Wyatville for King George IV in the 1820s.

★ **St George's Chapel**
The architectural highlight of the castle, it was built between 1475 and 1528 and is one of England's outstanding Perpendicular Gothic churches. Ten monarchs are buried here.

Albert Memorial Chapel
First built in 1240, it was rebuilt in 1485 and finally converted into a memorial for Prince Albert in 1863.

★ State Apartments
These rooms contain many
treasures, such as this
18th-century bed in the King's
State Bedchamber, hung in its
present splendour for the visit in
1855 of Napoleon III.

VISITORS' CHECKLIST

Practical Information
Castle Hill. **Tel** 020 7766 7304.
Open 9:45am–5:15pm (Nov–Feb:
to 4:15pm). (Last adm: 1 hr 15
mins before close.) **Closed** Good
Fri, 25 & 26 Dec. ✞ St Georges
Chapel (closed for services). ♿ ⬛ Ⓦ **royalcollection.org.uk**

Waterloo Chamber
This banqueting hall was created as part of
Charles Long's brief for the remodelling
of the castle in 1823.

Key

- 11th–13th centuries
- 14th century
- 15th–18th centuries
- 19th–20th centuries

Albert Memorial
Chapel (1485)

The Round
Tower (1080)

Middle
Ward

St George's Hall
(1357–68)

Lower Ward

St George's Chapel (1475–1528)

Upper Ward

Waterloo
Chamber (1820s)

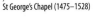

Windsor Castle's History
*Founded in 1080 as a motte and bailey (see p490), Henry
II and Edward III were responsible for the bulk of the work
until the castle was remodelled by George IV in 1823.*

THE WEST COUNTRY

The West Country at a Glance

The West Country forms a long peninsula bounded by the Atlantic to the north and the English Channel to the south, tapering down to Land's End, mainland Britain's westernmost point. Whether exploring the great cities and cathedrals, experiencing the awesome solitude of the moors and their prehistoric monuments, or simply enjoying the miles of coastline and mild climate, this region has an enduring appeal for holiday-makers.

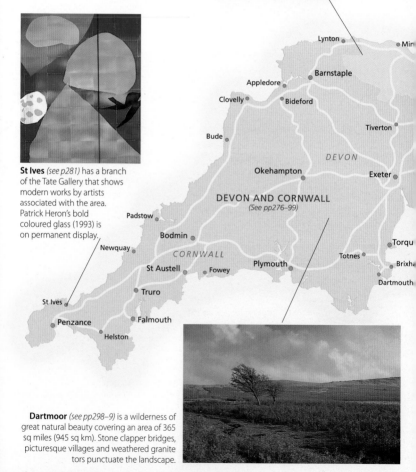

Exmoor's *(see pp254–5)* heather-clad moors and wooded valleys, grazed by wild ponies and red deer, lead down to some of Devon and Somerset's most dramatic cliffs and coves.

St Ives *(see p281)* has a branch of the Tate Gallery that shows modern works by artists associated with the area. Patrick Heron's bold coloured glass (1993) is on permanent display.

Lynton

Min

Barnstaple

Appledore

Clovelly

Bideford

Tiverton

Bude

DEVON

Okehampton

Exeter

DEVON AND CORNWALL
(See pp276–99)

Padstow

Bodmin

Newquay

Torqu

CORNWALL

Totnes

St Austell

Fowey

Plymouth

Brixh

Truro

Dartmouth

St Ives

Penzance

Falmouth

Helston

Dartmoor *(see pp298–9)* is a wilderness of great natural beauty covering an area of 365 sq miles (945 sq km). Stone clapper bridges, picturesque villages and weathered granite tors punctuate the landscape.

◄ Summer rainstorm over Exmoor National Park, viewed from Selworthy Beacon

Bath *(see pp262–3)* is named after the Roman baths that stand at the heart of the old city next to the splendid medieval abbey. It is one of Britain's liveliest and most rewarding cities, full of elegant Georgian terraces, built in local honey-coloured limestone by the two John Woods (Elder and Younger).

0 kilometres 25
0 miles 25

Stonehenge *(see pp266–7)*, the world-famous prehistoric monument, was built in several stages from 3000 BC. Moving and erecting its massive stones was an extraordinary feat for its time. It is likely that this magical stone circle was a place of worship to the sun.

Bristol
Chippenham
Veston-er-Mare
Bath
WILTSHIRE
Trowbridge
Wells
WESSEX
(See pp250–75)
Amesbury
ridgwater
Glastonbury
SOMERSET
Salisbury
Taunton
Shaftesbury
Yeovil
Blandford Forum
oniton
DORSET
Dorchester
Bournemouth
Poole
nouth
Weymouth
Swanage

Stourhead garden *(see pp270–71)* was inspired by the paintings of Claude and Poussin. Created in the 18th century, the garden is itself a work of art. Contrived vistas, light and shade and a mixture of landscape and gracious buildings, such as the Neo-Classical Pantheon at its centre, are vital to the overall effect.

Wells *(see pp256–7)* is a charming town nestling at the foot of the Mendip Hills. It is famous for its exquisite three-towered cathedral with an ornate west façade, featuring an array of statues. Alongside stand the moated Bishop's Palace and the 15th-century Vicar's Close.

Salisbury's *(see pp268–9)* cathedral with its soaring spire was the inspiration for one of John Constable's best-loved paintings. The picturesque Cathedral Close has a number of fine medieval buildings.

Coastal Wildlife

The long and varied West Country coastline, ranging from the stark, granite cliffs of Land's End to the pebble-strewn stretch of Chesil Bank, is matched with an equally diverse range of wildlife. Beaches are scattered with colourful shells, while rock pools form miniature marine habitats teeming with life. Caves are used by larger creatures, such as grey seals, and cliffs provide nest sites for birds. In the spring and early summer, an astonishing range of plants grow on the foreshore and cliffs which can be seen at their best from the Southwest Coastal Path *(see p40)*. The plants in turn attract numerous moths and butterflies.

Cliff-tops of Land's End with safe ledges for nesting birds

Chesil Bank is an unusual ridge of pebbles *(see p260)* stretching 18 miles (29 km) along the Dorset coast. The bank was created by storms and the pebbles increase in size from northwest to south-east due to varying strengths of coastal currents. The bank encloses a lagoon called the Fleet, habitat of the Abbotsbury swans, as well as a large number of wildfowl.

The Painted Lady, often seen on cliff-top coastal plants, migrates to Britain in the spring.

High tides wash up driftwood and shells.

Cliff-top turf contains many species of wild flowers.

Thrift, in hummocks of honey-scented flowers, is a familiar sight on cliff ledges in spring.

Yellowhammers are to be seen perched on cliff-top bushes.

Marram grass roots help hold back sand against wind erosion.

Grey seals come on land to give birth to their young. They can be spotted on remote beaches.

A Beachcomber's Guide

The best time to observe the natural life of the sea-shore is when the tide begins to roll back, before the scavenging seagulls pick up the stranded crabs, fish and sandhoppers, and the seaweed dries up. Much plant and marine life can be found in the secure habitat provided by rock pools.

Durdle Door was formed by waves continually eroding the weaker chalk layers of this cliff *(see p274)* in Dorset, leaving the stronger oolite to create a striking arch, known in geology as an eyelet.

Collecting shells

Most of the edible molluscs, such as scallops and cockles, are known as bivalves; others, such as whelks and limpets, are known as gastropods.

Great scallop

Common cockle

Common whelk

Common limpet

Seaweed, such as bladder wrack, can resemble coral or lichen when in water.

Rocks are colonized by clusters of barnacles, mussels and limpets.

Oystercatchers have a distinctive orange beak. They hunt along the shore, feeding on all kinds of shellfish.

Starfish can be aggressive predators on shellfish. The light-sensitive tips of their tentacles help them to "see" the way.

Mussels are widespread and can be harvested for food.

Rock pools teem with crabs, mussels, shrimps and plant life.

The Velvet Crab, often found hiding in seaweed, is covered with fine downy hair all over its shell.

Grey mullet, when newly hatched, can often be seen in rock pools.

West Country Gardens

Gardeners have long been attracted to the West Country. Its mild climate is perfect for growing tender and exotic plants, many of which were brought from Asia in the 19th century. As a result, the region has some of England's finest and most varied gardens, covering the whole sweep of garden styles and history *(see pp30–31)*, from the clipped formality of Elizabethan Montacute, to the colourful and crowded cottage-garden style of East Lambrook Manor.

Lanhydrock's *(p288)* clipped yews and low box hedges frame a blaze of colourful annuals.

Trewithen *(p285)* is renowned for its rare camellias, rhododendrons and magnolias, grown from seed collected in Asia. The huge garden is at its most impressive in March and June.

Cotehele *(p297)* has a lovely lush valley garden.

Lost Gardens of Heligan

Trelissick *(p285)* has memorable views over the Fal Estuary through shrub-filled woodland.

Glendurgan *(p285)* is a plant-lover's paradise set in a steep, sheltered valley.

DEVON AND CORNWALL (See pp276–99)

Lynton

Barnstap

Bideford

Bude

Bodmin

St Austell

Truro

Falmouth

Penzance

Helston

Plymouth

Totn

Trengwainton *(p280)* has a fine stream garden, whose banks are crowded with moisture-loving plants, beneath a lush canopy of New Zealand tree ferns.

Mount Edgcumbe *(p296)* preserves its 18th-century French, Italian and English gardens.

Overbecks (near Salcombe) enjoys a spectacular site over-looking the Salcombe Estuary. There are secret gardens, terraces and rocky dells.

Creative Gardening

Gardens are not simply collections of plants; they rely for much of their appeal on man-made features. Whimsical topiary, ornate architecture, fanciful statuary and mazes help to create an atmosphere of adventure or pure escapism. The many gardens dotted around the West Country offer engaging examples of the vivid imagination of designers.

Mazes were created in medieval monasteries to teach patience and persistence. This laurel maze at Glendurgan was planted in 1833.

Fountains and flamboyant statuary have adorned gardens since Roman times. Such eye-catching embellishments add poetic and Classical touches to the design of formal gardens, such as Mount Edgcumbe.

Knightshayes Court *(p293)* is designed as a series of formal garden "rooms", planted for scent, colour or seasonal effect.

East Lambrook Manor (near South Petherton) is a riot of colours, as old-fashioned cottage plants grow without restraint.

WESSEX
(See pp250–75)

Bristol
Marlborough
Weston-Super-Mare
Bath
Glastonbury
Bridgwater
Salisbury
Taunton
Shaftesbury
Yeovil
Honiton
Exeter
Bournemouth
Poole
Weymouth
Swanage
orquay

Stourhead *(see pp270–71)* is a magnificent example of 18th-century landscape gardening.

Athelhampton's *(p273)* gardens make use of fountains, statues, pavilions and columnar yews.

Montacute House *(p272)* has pavilions and a centuries-old yew hedge, and is renowned for its collection of old roses.

0 kilometres   25

0 miles   25

Parnham (near Beaminster), like many West Country gardens, has several parts devoted to different themes. Here conical yews complement the formality of the stone balustrade; elsewhere there are woodland, kitchen, shade and Mediterranean gardens.

Many garden buildings are linked by an element of fantasy; while country houses had to conform to everyday practicalities, the design of many smaller buildings gave more scope for imagination. This fanciful Elizabethan pavilion on the forecourt at Montacute House was first and foremost decorative, but sometimes served as a lodging house.

Topiary can be traced back to the Greeks. Since that time the sculpting of trees into unusual, often eccentric shapes has been developed over the centuries. The yew topiary of 1920s Knightshayes features a fox being chased by a pack of hounds. The figures form a delightful conceit and come into their own in winter when little else is in leaf.

WESSEX

Wiltshire · Somerset · Dorset

The natural and diverse beauty of this predominantly rural region is characterized by rolling hills and charming villages. The area is enriched by a wealth of historical and architectural attractions, ranging from the prehistoric stone circle of Stonehenge to the Roman baths and magnificent Georgian townscape of Bath.

Vast swathes of bare windswept downland give way to lush river valleys, and the contrast between the two may explain the origin in medieval times of the saying, "as different as chalk and cheese". The chalk and limestone hills provided pasture for sheep whose wool was exported to Europe or turned to cloth in mill towns such as Bradford-on-Avon. Meanwhile the rich cow-grazed pastures of the valleys produced the Cheddar cheese for which the region has become famous.

The area's potential for wealth was first exploited by prehistoric chieftains whose large, mysterious monuments, such as Stonehenge and Maiden Castle, are striking features of the landscape. From this same soil sprang King Arthur *(see p289)* and King Alfred the Great, about whom there are numerous fascinating legends. It was King Arthur who is thought to have led British resistance to the Saxon invasion in the 6th century. The Saxons finally emerged the victors and one of them, King Alfred, first united the West Country into one political unit, called the Kingdom of Wessex *(see p51)*.

Wilton House and Lacock Abbey, both former monasteries, were turned into splendid stately homes during the 16th century, due to the Dissolution of the Monasteries *(see pp54–5)*. Today, their previous wealth can be gauged by the size and grandeur of their storage barns.

Matching the many man-made splendours of the region, Wessex is rich in rare wildlife and plants.

Two visitors enjoying the Elizabethan gardens of Montacute House, Somerset

◀ View down to a winding road through the Cheddar Gorge

Exploring Wessex

From the rolling chalk plains around Stonehenge to the rocky cliffs of Cheddar Gorge and the heather-covered uplands of Exmoor, Wessex is a scenically varied microcosm of England. Reflecting the underlying geology, each part of Wessex contributes its own distinctive architecture, with the Neo-Classically inspired buildings of Bath giving way to the mellow brick and timber of Salisbury and the thatched flint-and-chalk cottages of the Dorset landscape.

0 kilometres 20
0 miles 10

Gloucester
Stone
Thornbury
Cardiff
A48
M5
Chipp
Sod
Avonmouth
Portishead
Mangotsfield
Clevedon
BRISTOL 6
Nailsea
Kingston Seymour
Chew Magna
BAT
Weston-Super-Mare
A37
A38
Marksbury
Bristol Channel
Axe
M5
Cheddar
CHEDDAR GORGE 5
Mendip Hills
Burnham-on-Sea
Wookey
Lynton
Lynmouth
Minehead
Brue
WELLS 3
Porlock
Dunster
Watchet
Huntspill
GLASTONBURY
Pilton
Dunkery Beacon 520m
Exford
Brendon Hills
Bridgwater
Street 4
Simonsbath
Quantock Hills
A39
Castle Cary
Brayford
EXMOOR 1
Exton
Somerton
Winc
Molland
Dulverton
Milverton
Hestercombe Garden
Langport
A303
Templec
Bampton
Wellington
TAUNTON 2
Ilchester
A361
M5
Corfe
A358
Montacute House
SHERBORNE 17
Exeter
A303
Ilminster
Yeovil
Yarcombe
Chard
Crewkerne
A37
Beaminster
Cerne Abbas
Charmouth
Frampton
A35
Hardy's C
Lyme Regis
Bridport
DORCHESTER 20
ABBOTSBURY 18
Lyme Bay
WEYMOUTH 19
Chesil Beach
Fortuneswell
Isle of Port

Exmoor National Park

Getting Around

Bath and Bristol are served by fast mainline trains, other major towns and seaside resorts by regional railways and long-distance bus services. Popular sights such as Stonehenge feature on many tour operators' bus excursions. The rural heart of Wessex, however, has little in the way of public transport and unless you have the time to walk the region's footpaths, you will need a car.

For additional map symbols see back flap

Sights at a Glance

Key

═══ Motorway
═══ Major road
── Secondary road
··· Minor road
── Scenic route
·•· Main railway
── Minor railway
△ Summit

Huge sarsen stones of Stonehenge, dating from around 3000 BC

❶ Exmoor National Park

The majestic cliffs plunging into the Bristol Channel along Exmoor's northern coast are interrupted by lush, wooded valleys carrying rivers from the high moorland down to sheltered fishing coves. Inland, wild rolling hills are grazed by sturdy Exmoor ponies, horned sheep and the local wild red deer. Buzzards are also a common sight wheeling over the bracken-clad terrain looking for prey. For walkers, Exmoor offers 1,000 km (620 miles) of wonderful public paths and varied, dramatic scenery, while the tamer perimeters of the National Park offer less energetic attractions – everything from traditional seaside entertainments to picturesque villages and ancient churches.

Heddon's Mouth
The River Heddon passes through woodland and meadows down to this attractive point on the coast.

The Valley of Rocks
Sandstone outcrops, eroded into fantastical shapes, characterize this natural gorge.

Lynton
Lynmouth

Barnstaple

Tiverton

Lynmouth
Above the charming fishing village of Lynmouth stands hill-top Lynton. The two villages are connected by a cliff railway (see p292).

KEY

① **Combe Martin** is a pretty setting for the Pack of Cards Inn (see p292).

② **Parracombe Old Church** has a Georgian interior with a full set of wooden furnishings.

③ **Oare's church** commemorates the writer R D Blackmore, whose romantic novel *Lorna Doone* (1869) is set in the area.

④ **Culbone church,** a mere 10.6 m (35 ft) in length, claims to be Britain's smallest parish church.

⑤ **Selworthy** is a picturesque village of thatched cottages.

⑥ **Minehead** is a major resort built around a pretty quay. A steam railway runs all the way from here to Bishop's Lydeard.

⑦ **Dunster** has an ancient castle and an unusual octagonal Yarn Market (c.1609) where local cloth was once sold.

⑧ **Tarr Steps** is an ancient "clapper" bridge built of stone slabs.

⑨ **Simonsbath** is a good starting point for walkers. The Exmoor ponies found locally are thought to descend from prehistoric ancestors.

⑩ **Watersmeet** is the spot in a beautifully wooded valley where the East Lyn and Hoar Oak Water join together in a tumbling cascade. There is also a tearoom with a pretty garden.

View east along the South West Coast Path

0 kilometres 5
0 miles 3

VISITORS' CHECKLIST

Practical Information
Somerset/Devon.
W exmoor-nationalpark.gov.uk
Dunster Castle, Dunster:
Tel 01643 821314. Open Mar–
Nov: daily. 🅿 ♿ 📷 NT
W nationaltrust.org.uk
National Park Centre Dulverton:
Open all year. Tel 01398 323841.

Transport
🚆 🚌 Tiverton Parkway then bus.
i Lee Rd, Lynton (01598 752225).

Porlock
The flower-filled village of Porlock has retained its charm, with winding streets, thatched houses and a fascinating old church.

Dunkery Beacon
▲ 520 m 1,704 ft

Dunkery Beacon
Rising to a height of 520 m (1,700 ft), this is the highest point on Exmoor.

Key
═══ A road
═══ B road
═══ Minor road
---- Coast path

For map symbols see back flap

❷ Taunton

Somerset. 🅰 66,000. 🚆 🚌 ℹ️ Paul St (01823 336344). 🛒 Thu (farmers'). 🌐 heartofsomerset.com

Taunton lies at the heart of a fertile region famous for its apples and cider, but it was the prosperous wool industry that financed the massive church of **St Mary Magdalene** (1488– 1514) with its glorious tower. Taunton's castle was the setting for the notorious Bloody Assizes of 1685 when "Hanging" Judge Jeffreys dispensed harsh retribution on the Duke of Monmouth and his followers for an uprising against King James II. The 12th-century building now houses the **Museum of Somerset**. A star exhibit is the Roman mosaic from a villa at Low Ham, Somerset, showing the story of Dido and Aeneas.

Environs
Hestercombe Garden is one of Sir Edwin Lutyens and Gertrude Jekyll's great masterpieces.

🏛️ **Museum of Somerset**
Castle Green. **Tel** 01823 255088. **Open** Tue–Sat. 🚻 ground floor. 📷 🌐 somerset.gov.uk/museums

🌷 **Hestercombe Garden**
Cheddon Fitzpaine. **Tel** 01823 413923. **Open** daily. 🚻 📷 📷 🚻 🌐 hestercombe.com

Somerset Cider

Somerset is one of the few English counties where real farmhouse cider, known as "scrumpy", is still made using the traditional methods. Cider once formed part of the farm labourer's wages and local folklore has it that various

Scrumpy cider

unsavoury additives, such as iron nails, were added to give strength. Cidermaking can be seen at **Sheppy's** farm, on the A38 near Taunton.

---

❸ Wells

Somerset. 🅰 10,000. 🚌 ℹ️ Cathedral Green (01749 671770). 🛒 Wed, Sat. 🌐 wellssomerset.com

Wells is named after St Andrew's Well, the sacred spring that bubbles up from the ground near the 13th-century **Bishop's Palace**, residence of the Bishop of Bath and Wells. A tranquil city, Wells is famous for its magnificent cathedral which was begun in the late 1100s. Penniless Porch, where beggars once received alms, leads from the bustling market place to the calm of the cathedral close. **Wells & Mendip Museum** has prehistoric finds from nearby Wookey Hole and other caves.

Environs
To the northeast of Wells lies the impressive cave complex of **Wookey Hole**, which has an extensive range of popular amusements.

🏛️ **Wells & Mendip Museum**
8 Cathedral Green. **Tel** 01749 673477. **Open** Mon–Sat. 🚻 🚻 limited. 📷 🌐 wellsmuseum.org.uk

🏰 **Wookey Hole**
Off A371. **Tel** 01749 672243. **Open** daily. 🚻 📷 📷 🌐 wookey.co.uk

The Vicars' Close, built in the 14th century for the Vicars' Choir, is one of the oldest complete streets in Europe.

The Chain Gate (1460)

The West Front features 300 fine medieval statues of kings, knights and saints – many of them life-size.

Cloisters

This graceful flight of steps curves up to the octagonal Chapter House which has delicate vaulting dating from 1306. The 32 ribs springing from the central column create a beautiful palm-tree effect.

Bishops' tombs circle the chancel. This sumptuous marble tomb, in the south aisle, is that of Bishop Lord Arthur Hervey, who was Bishop of Bath and Wells (1869–94).

Glastonbury Abbey, left in ruins in 1539 after the Dissolution

Wells Cathedral and the Bishop's Palace

The Close. **Tel** 01749 988111. **Open** daily. ♿ limited. Bishop's Palace: **Open** mid-Feb–mid-Dec: daily.

Wells has maintained much of its medieval character with its cathedral, Bishop's Palace and other buildings around the close forming a harmonious group. The most striking features of the cathedral are the west front and the "scissor arches" installed in 1338 to support the tower.

13th-century ruins of the Great Hall

The Bishop's Palace (1230–40)

Path leading round the moat

The palace moat is home to swans which ring a bell by the gatehouse when they want to be fed. Feeding times are at 11am and 4pm.

❹ Glastonbury

Somerset. 🚍 9,000. 🚌 ℹ Tribunal, High St (01458 832954). 🅿 Tue.
🌐 glastonburytic.co.uk

Shrouded in Arthurian myth and rich in mystical association, the town of Glastonbury was once one of the most important destinations for pilgrims in England. Now thousands flock here for the annual rock festival *(see p67)* and for the summer solstice on Midsummer's Day (21 June).

Over the years history and legend have become intertwined, and the monks who founded **Glastonbury Abbey**, around 700, found it profitable to encourage the association between Glastonbury and the mythical "Blessed Isle" known as Avalon – alleged to be the last resting place of King Arthur and the Holy Grail *(see p289)*.

The great abbey was left in ruins after the Dissolution of the Monasteries *(see p54)*. Even so, some magnificent relics survive, including parts of the vast Norman abbey church, the unusual Abbot's Kitchen, with its octagonal roof, and the Victorian farmhouse, now the **Somerset Rural Life Museum**.

Growing in the abbey grounds is a cutting from the famous Glastonbury thorn which is said to have miraculously grown from the staff of St Joseph of Arimathea. According to myth, he was sent around AD 60 to convert England to Christianity. The English hawthorn flowers at Christmas as well as in May.

The **Lake Village Museum** has some interesting finds from the Iron Age settlements that once fringed the marshlands around **Glastonbury Tor**. Seen for miles around, the Tor is a hill crowned by the remains of a 14th-century church.

🏛 **Somerset Rural Life Museum**
Chilkwell St. **Tel** 01458 831197. **Open** 10am–5pm Tue–Sat. **Closed** 1 Jan, Good Fri, 24–26 Dec. ♿ limited. 📷 closed winter.

🏛 **Lake Village Museum**
Tribunal, High St. **Tel** 01458 832954. **Open** Mon–Sat. **Closed** 25, 26 Dec.

❺ Cheddar Gorge

Described as a "deep frightful chasm" by novelist Daniel Defoe in 1724, Cheddar Gorge is a spectacular ravine cut through the Mendip plateau by fast-flowing streams during the interglacial phases of the last Ice Age. Cheddar has given its name to a rich cheese that originates from here and is now produced worldwide. The caves in the gorge provide the perfect environment of constant temperature and high humidity for storing and maturing the cheese.

The Cheddar Gorge Cheese Company is the only working Cheddar dairy in Cheddar. Visitors can see Cheddar being made, and taste and buy cheese in the store.

The B3135 road winds round the base of the 3 mile (5 km) gorge.

"Cheddar Man", a 9,000-year-old skeleton, is on display at Cheddar Caves and Gorge. The museum here looks at the prehistoric world of our cannibal ancestors.

A footpath follows the top of the gorge on its southern edge.

Gough's Cave is noted for its cathedral-like proportions.

The gorge is a narrow, winding ravine with limestone rocks rising almost vertically on either side to a height of 140 m (460 ft).

Cox's Cave contains unusually shaped stalactites and stalagmites.

A flight of 274 steps leads to the top of the gorge.

The rare Cheddar Pink is among the astonishing range of plant and animal life harboured in the rocks.

Lookout Tower has far-reaching views over the area to the south and west.

❻ Bristol

See pp260–61.

❼ Bath

See pp262–3.

Typical Cotswold-stone architecture
in Bradford-on-Avon

❽ Bradford-on-Avon

Wiltshire. 👥 11,000. 🚆 ℹ️ St
Margaret St (01225 865797). 🅿️ Thu.
🌐 bradfordonavon.co.uk

This lovely Cotswold-stone
town is full of flamboyant
houses built by wealthy wool
and cloth merchants in the 17th
and 18th centuries. One fine
Georgian example is **Abbey
House**, on Church Street.
Further along, **St Laurence
Church** is a remarkably
complete Saxon building
founded in 705 *(see p51)*.
Converted to a school and
cottage in the 12th century, it
was rediscovered in the 19th
century when a vicar
recognized the characteristic
cross-shaped roof.
   At one end of the medieval
Town Bridge is a small stone
cell, built as a chapel in the 13th
century but later used as a lock-
up for 17th-century vagrants. A
short walk away, near converted
mill buildings and a stretch of
the Kennet and Avon Canal, is
the 14th-century **Tithe Barn**
(see p36). There are several
teashops in the town and
canoe trips down the canal
are popular.

🏠 **Tithe Barn**
Pound Lane. **Open** daily. **Closed** 25,
26 Dec. 🅿️ EH

❾ Corsham

Wiltshire. 👥 12,000. ℹ️ 31 High St
(01249 714660).
🌐 corshamheritage.org.uk

The streets of Corsham are
lined with stately Georgian
houses in Cotswold stone.
St Bartholomew's Church has
an elegant spire and a lovely
carved alabaster tomb (1960) to
the late Lady Methuen, whose
family founded Methuen
publishers. The family acquired
Corsham Court in
1745 with its
picture gallery
and a
remarkable
collection of
Flemish, Italian
and English
paintings, including
works by Van Dyck,
Lippi and Reynolds.
Peacocks wander
through the grounds, adding
their colour and elegance to
the façade of the Elizabethan
mansion.

Peacock in grounds,
Corsham Court

🏠 **Corsham Court**
off A4. **Tel** 01249 701610.
Open mid-Mar–Sep: Tue–Thu, Sat,
Sun; Oct–mid-Mar: Sat, Sun (pm).
Closed Dec. 🅿️ ♿

❿ Lacock

Wiltshire. 👥 1,000.

Maintained in its pristine state
by the National Trust, the
picturesque village of Lacock
has provided the backdrop to
numerous BBC costume dramas,
including *Larkrise to Candleford*.
The meandering River Avon
forms the boundary to the
north side of the churchyard,
while humorous stone figures
look down from **St Cyriac
Church**. Inside the 15th-
century church is the
splendid Renaissance-
style tomb of Sir William
Sharington (1495–1553).
He acquired **Lacock
Abbey** after the
Dissolution of the
Monasteries *(see p54)*, but
it was a later owner, John
Ivory Talbot, who had the
buildings remodelled in the

Gothic revival style, in vogue in
the early 18th century. The
abbey is famous for the window
(in the south gallery) from
which his descendant William
Henry Fox Talbot, an early
pioneer of photography, took
his first picture in 1835. A
16th-century barn at the abbey
gates has been converted to
the **Fox Talbot Museum**, which
has displays on his experiments.

Environs
Designed by Robert
Adam *(see pp36–7)*
in 1769, **Bowood
House** includes
the laboratory
where Joseph
Priestley
discovered oxygen
in 1774, and a rich
collection of sculpture,
costumes and
paintings. Italianate
gardens surround the house
while the lake-filled grounds,
landscaped by "Capability"
Brown *(see p34)*, contain a Doric
temple, grotto, cascade and an
adventure playground.

🏠 **Lacock Abbey**
Lacock. **Tel** 01249 730459. **Open** Feb–
Oct: Wed–Mon (pm). **Closed** Good Fri.
🅿️ ♿ limited in house. NT
🌐 nationaltrust.org.uk

🏛 **Fox Talbot Museum**
Lacock. **Tel** 01249 730459. **Open** daily.
Closed 1 Jan, 25 Dec. 🅿️ ♿ NT

🏠 **Bowood House**
Derry Hill, nr Calne. **Tel** 01249 812102.
Open Apr–Oct: daily. 🅿️ ♿ 🚻
⛽ 🅿️

William Henry Fox
Talbot (1800–77)

❻ Bristol

It was in 1497 that John Cabot sailed from Bristol on his historic voyage to North America. The city, at the mouth of the Avon, became the main British port for transatlantic trade, pioneering the era of the ocean-going steam liner with the construction of Brunel's ss *Great Britain*. The city flourished as a major trading centre, growing rich on the distribution of wine, tobacco and, in the 17th century, slaves.

Because of its docks and aero-engine factories, Bristol was heavily bombed during World War II. In 2008, a multimillion-pound development programme was completed with the opening of Cabot Circus, a vast shopping centre. The old dock area has been brought back to life with bars, cafés, restaurants and art galleries lining the waterside.

Memorial to William Canynge the Younger (1400–74)

⌂ St Mary Redcliffe
Redcliffe Way. **Tel** 0117 9291487.
Open daily. ♿ 📷 by arrangement.
💻 🌐 stmaryredcliffe.co.uk

This magnificent 14th-century church was claimed by Queen Elizabeth I to be "the fairest in England". The church owes much to the generosity of William Canynge the Elder and Younger, both famous mayors of Bristol. Inscriptions on the tombs of merchants and sailors tell of lives devoted to trade in Asia and the West Indies. Look out for the Bristol maze in the north aisle.

Exploring Bristol

The oldest part of the city lies around Broad, King and Corn streets, known as the Old Quarter. The lively St Nicholas covered market, part of which occupies the **Corn Exchange**, was built by John Wood the Elder *(see p262)* in 1743. Outside are the famous Bristol Nails, four bronze 16th–17th-century pedestals which Bristol merchants used as tables when paying for goods – hence the expression "to pay on the nail". **St John's Gate**, at the head of Broad Street, has medieval statues of Bristol's two mythical founders, King Brennus and King Benilus. Between Lewins Mead and Colston Street, **Christmas Steps** is a steep lane lined with specialist shops and cafés. The **Chapel of the Three Kings** at the top was founded in 1504.

A group of buildings around the cobbled King Street include the 17th-century timber-framed **Llandoger Trow** inn. It is here that Daniel Defoe is said to have

The Two Sisters (c.1889) by Renoir, City Museum and Art Gallery

met Alexander Selkirk, whose true-life island exile served as the inspiration for Defoe's novel *Robinson Crusoe* (1719). Just up from here is the **Theatre Royal**, built in 1766, and home to the famous Bristol Old Vic.

Not far away, the renowned gallery the **Arnolfini**, on Narrow Quay, is a showcase for contemporary art, drama, dance and cinema.

On the Harbourside, **At-Bristol** (www.at-bristol.org.uk) combines an exciting, interactive science centre with a planetarium.

Not far from the Harbourside, elegant **Clifton** revels in ornate Regency crescents. The impressive **Clifton Suspension Bridge** by Brunel, completed in 1864, perfectly complements the drama of the steep Avon gorge. **Bristol Zoo Gardens** houses over 400 exotic and endangered species set in stunning gardens.

🏛 Brunel's ss Great Britain
Gas Ferry Rd. **Tel** 0117 9260680.
Open daily. **Closed** 24, 25 Dec. 🎫 ticket valid for one year. ♿ 📷 by appt. 💻 🍴 🌐 ssgreatbritain.org

Designed by Isambard Kingdom Brunel, this is the world's first large iron passenger ship. Launched in 1843, she travelled 32 times round the world before being abandoned in the Falkland Islands in 1886. The ship has been fully restored.

🏠 Georgian House
7 Great George St. **Tel** 0117 9211362.
Open Apr–Oct: Wed, Thu, Sat, Sun (Jul & Aug: Tue–Sun).
🌐 bristol.gov.uk/museums

Life in a wealthy Bristol merchant's house of the 1790s is illustrated by furnishings in the elegant drawing room and the servants' area.

🏛 M-Shed
Princes Wharf, Harbourside.
Tel 0117 3526600. **Open** Tue–Sun.
🎫 temp exhibits only. 💻 📷 ♿
🌐 mshed.org

This museum in a 1950s' harbourside transit shed focuses on the city's history. The story is told through objects and accounts of its people, transport, art and the slave trade. Temporary exhibitions take place regularly. There are also several historic vessels moored in the Wharf.

Bow of Brunel's SS *Great Britain*

Warehouses overlooking the Floating Harbour

VISITORS' CHECKLIST

Practical Information
Bristol. 430,000. *i*
Harbourside (09067 112 191 –
premium rate). daily.
Harbour Festival: late Jul; Balloon
Fiesta: Aug. **w** visitbristol.co.uk

Transport
7 miles (11 km) SW Bristol.
Temple Meads. Marlborough St.

Bristol Blue Glass Factory and Shop

Brislington. **Tel** 0117 972 0818.
Open Mon–Sat.
w bristol-glass.co.uk

The Bristol Blue Glass name
is over 350 years old and
represents the best tools,
techniques and traditions from
the past. Every piece of glass is
free blown and hand-made,
making each one unique and
collectable. Glass blowing
demonstrations take place at
the visitor centre, where there
is also a gallery shop.

Bristol Museum and Art Gallery

Queen's Rd. **Tel** 0117 922 3571.
Open daily. **Closed** 24, 25 Dec.
limited.
w bristol.gov.uk/museums

Varied collections include
Egyptology, dinosaur fossils,
Roman tableware, Chinese
glass and a fine collection
of European paintings with
works by Renoir and Bellini.
Bristol artists include Sir
Thomas Lawrence, Francis
Danby and the notorious
graffiti artist Banksy.

Bristol Cathedral

College Green. **Tel** 0117 9264879.
Open daily. Donation. limited.
w bristol-cathedral.co.uk

Bristol's cathedral, begun in 1140,
took an unusually long time to
build. Rapid progress was made
between 1298 and 1330, when
the inventive choir was rebuilt;
the transepts and tower were
finished in 1515, and another 350
years passed before the Victorian
architect, G E Street, built the
nave. Humorous medieval
carving abounds – a snail
crawling across the stone foliage
in the Berkeley Chapel, musical
monkeys in the Elder Lady
Chapel, and a fine set of wooden
misericords in the choir.

Bristol City Centre

① Bristol Museum and
   Art Gallery
② Georgian House
③ Bristol Cathedral
④ Brunel's SS *Great
   Britain*
⑤ M-Shed
⑥ St Mary Redcliffe

For map symbols *see back flap*

❼ Street-by-Street: Bath

Bath owes its magnificent Georgian town-scape to the bubbling pool of water at the heart of the Roman Baths. The Romans transformed Bath into England's first spa resort and it regained fame as a spa town in the 18th century. At this time the two John Woods (Elder and Younger), both architects, designed the city's Palladian-style buildings. Many houses bear plaques recording the numerous famous people who have resided here.

Assembly Rooms and Museum of Costume

No. 1 Royal Crescent

No. 17 is where the 18th-century painter Thomas Gainsborough lived *(see p167).*

The Circus
This is a daring departure from the typical Georgian square, by John Wood the Elder (1705–54).

0 metres	100
0 yards	100

Jane Austen Centre
(see p264), a permanent exhibition of film, costumes and books, tells the story of the author's time in Bath.

Key

— Suggested route

Milsom Street and New Bond Street contain some of Bath's most elegant shops.

★ Royal Crescent
Hailed the most majestic street in Britain, this graceful arc of 30 houses (1767–74) is the masterpiece of John Wood the Younger. West of the Royal Crescent, Royal Victoria Park (1830) is the city's largest open space.

Theatre Royal (1805)

Pulteney Bridge
This charming bridge (1769–74), designed by Robert Adam, is lined with shops and links the centre with the magnificent Great Pulteney Street. Look out for a rare Victorian pillar box on the east bank.

VISITORS' CHECKLIST

Practical Information
Bath. 🏠 85,000.
🅦 **visitbath.co.uk**
ℹ️ Abbey Chambers, Abbey Church Yard (0906 7112000 – premium rate). 📅 daily. 🎭 International Music Festival: May–Jun.

Transport
✈️ Bristol, 20 miles (32 km) W Bath. 🚆 🚌 Dorchester St.

The Building of Bath Museum

★ Roman Baths
Built in the 1st century, this bathing complex is one of Britain's greatest memorials to the Roman era.

★ Bath Abbey
The splendid abbey stands at the heart of the old city in the Abbey Church Yard, a paved courtyard enlivened by buskers. Its unique façade features stone angels climbing Jacob's Ladder to heaven.

Holburne Museum

Parade Gardens
Courting couples came to this pretty riverside park for secret liaisons in the 18th century.

Pump Rooms These tearooms once formed the social hub of the 18th-century spa community. They contain this decorative drinking fountain.

Sally Lunn's House (1482) is one of Bath's oldest houses.

Rail & coach stations

Exploring Bath

The beautiful and compact city of Bath is set among the rolling green hills of the Avon valley, and wherever you walk you will enjoy splendid views of the surrounding countryside. The traffic-free heart of this lively city is full of street musicians, museums, cafés and enticing shops, while the elegant honey-coloured Georgian houses, so characteristic of Bath, form an elegant backdrop to city life.

Bath Abbey, at the heart of the old city, begun in 1499

🏛 Bath Abbey

13 Kingston Bldgs, Abbey Churchyard. **Tel** 01225 422462. **Open** daily. **Closed** during services. Donation. 🚻 🌐 **bathabbey.org**

This splendid abbey was supposedly designed by divine agency. According to legend, God dictated the form of the church to Bishop Oliver King in a dream; this story has been immortalized in the wonderfully eccentric carvings on the west front. The bishop began work in 1499, rebuilding a church that had been founded in the 8th century. Memorials cover the walls and the varied Georgian inscriptions make fascinating reading. The spacious interior is remarkable for the fan vaulting of the nave, an addition made by Sir George Gilbert Scott in 1874.

🏛 National Trust Assembly Rooms and Fashion Museum

Bennett St. **Tel** 01225 477789. **Open** daily. **Closed** 25, 26 Dec. 🚻 for Fashion Museum. 🚻 📷 🌐 **fashionmuseum.co.uk**

The Assembly Rooms were built by Wood the Younger in 1769, as a meeting place for the elite and as a backdrop for glittering balls. Jane Austen's novel *Northanger Abbey* (1818) describes the gossip and flirtation here. In the basements is a collection of costumes from the 1500s to the present day.

🏛 Jane Austen Centre

40 Gay St. **Tel** 01225 443000. **Open** daily. **Closed** 1 Jan, 24–26 Dec. 🚻 limited. 📷 🏛 🌐 **janeausten.co.uk**

This site houses an exhibition about the author's life and how living in Bath affected her work.

🏛 No. 1 Royal Crescent

Royal Crescent. **Tel** 01225 428 126. **Open** daily. **Closed** 25 & 26 Dec. 🏛 🚻 🌐 **bath-preservation-trust.org.uk**

This museum lets you inside the first house of this beautiful Georgian crescent, giving a glimpse of what life was like for 18th-century aristocrats, such as the Duke of York, who probably lived here. It is furnished down to such details as the dog-powered spit used to roast meat in front of the fire.

🏛 Holburne Museum of Art

Great Pulteney St. **Tel** 01225 388569. **Open** daily. **Closed** Good Friday, 24–26 Dec. 🚻 🚻 limited. 📷 🏛 🌐 **bath.ac.uk/holburne**

This historic building is named after William Holburne of Menstrie (1793–1874), whose collections form the nucleus of the display of fine and decorative arts, including superb silver and porcelain. Paintings can be seen by British artists such as Gainsborough and Stubbs.

Roman Baths

Entrance in Abbey Churchyard. **Tel** 01225 477785. **Open** daily. **Closed** 25, 26 Dec. 🚻 🚻 limited. 🌐 **romanbaths.co.uk**

According to legend, Bath owes its origin to the Celtic King Bladud who discovered the curative properties of its natural hot springs in 860 BC. Cast out from his kingdom as a leper, Bladud cured himself by imitating his swine and rolling in the hot mud at Bath.

In the first century, the Romans built baths around the spring, as well as a temple dedicated to the goddess Sulis Minerva, who combined the attributes of the Celt water goddess Sulis and the Roman goddess Minerva. Among the Roman relics is a bronze head of the goddess.

Medieval monks of Bath Abbey also exploited the springs' properties, but it was when Queen Anne visited in 1702–3 that Bath reached its zenith as a fashionable watering place.

🛁 Thermae Bath Spa

Hot Bath St. **Tel** 01225 331234. **Open** 9am–10pm daily (last adm: 7:30pm). **Closed** 1 Jan, 25 & 26 Dec. 👤 under 16s not permitted. ♿ 🖥 📷
w thermaebathspa.com

Tourists have bathed in the warm, mineral-rich waters of the spa town of Bath since Roman times and the opening of the Thermae Bath Spa, in 2006, has once again made Bath a popular day-spa destination. There are three pools fed by natural thermal waters: the New Royal Bath has two baths including an open-air rooftop pool with superb views over the city; across the road, the oval Cross Bath is a more intimate open-air bath, ideal for shorter sessions. The spa also offers scented steam rooms, footbaths and an array of treatments, bookable in advance. The signature therapy is watsu, a water-based version of the shiatsu massage.

🏛 American Museum

Claverton Manor, Claverton Down. **Tel** 01225 460503. **Open** mid-Mar–Oct: Tue–Sun (daily in Aug). 🚫 ♿ limited. 🖥 📷
w american museum.org

Founded in 1961, this was the first American museum to be established in this country. The rooms in the 1820 manor house are decorated in many styles, from the rudimentary dwellings of the first settlers to the opulent style of 19th-century homes. The museum has special sections on Shaker furniture, quilts and Native American art, and a replica of George Washington's Mount Vernon garden of 1785.

A 19th-century American Indian weathervane

Richard "Beau" Nash (1674–1762)

Elected in 1704 as Master of Ceremonies, "Beau" Nash played a crucial role in transforming Bath into the fashionable centre of Georgian society. During his long career, he devised a never-ending round of games, balls and entertainment (including gambling) that kept the idle rich amused and ensured a constant flow of visitors.

The Great Bath

The open-air Great Bath, which stands at the heart of the Roman spa complex, was not discovered until the 1870s. Leading off this magnificent pool were various bathing chambers which became increasingly sophisticated over the four centuries the Romans were here. The baths fell into ruin, but extensive excavations have revealed the remarkable skill of Roman engineering.

The dome (1897) is based on St Stephen Walbrook church in London (see p116).

Around the edges of the bath are the bases of piers that once supported a barrel-vaulted roof.

York Street

A late 19th-century terrace bears statues of famous Romans such as Julius Caesar.

The sacred spring is enclosed by a reservoir now named the King's Bath.

The water flows from the spring into the corner of the bath at a constant temperature of 46° C (115° F).

The lead-lined bath, steps, column bases and paving stones around the edge all date from Roman times.

⑪ Stonehenge

Built in several stages from about 3000 BC, Stonehenge is Europe's most famous prehistoric monument. We can only guess at the rituals that took place here, but the alignment of the stones leaves little doubt that the circle is connected with the sun and the passing of the seasons, and that its builders possessed a sophisticated understanding of both arithmetic and astronomy. Despite popular belief, the circle was not built by the Druids, an Iron Age priestly cult that flourished in Britain from around 250 BC – more than 1,000 years after Stonehenge was abandoned.

Stonehenge as it is today

The Heel Stone casts a long shadow straight to the heart of the circle on Midsummer's day.

The Avenue forms a ceremonial approach to the site.

The Slaughter Stone, named by 17th-century antiquarians who believed Stonehenge to be a place of human sacrifice, was in fact one of a pair marking the entrance to the interiors.

The Outer Bank, dug around 3000 BC, is the oldest known phase of Stonehenge.

Building of Stonehenge

Stonehenge's monumental scale is more impressive given that the only tools available were made of stone, wood and bone. The labour involved in quarrying, transporting and erecting the huge stones was such that its builders must have been able to command immense resources and vast numbers of people. One method is explained below.

Reconstruction of Stonehenge

This illustration shows what Stonehenge probably looked like about 4,000 years ago.

A sarsen stone was moved on rollers and levered into a pit.

With levers supported by timber packing, it was gradually raised.

The stone was then pulled upright by about 200 men hauling on ropes.

The pit round the base was packed tightly with stones and chalk.

Wiltshire's Other Prehistoric Sites

The open countryside of the Salisbury Plain made this area an important centre of prehistoric settlement, and today it is covered in many ancient remains. Ringing the horizon around Stonehenge are scores of circular barrows, or burial mounds, where members of the ruling class were honoured with burial close to the temple site. Ceremonial bronze weapons and other finds excavated around Stonehenge and the other local prehistoric sites can be seen in the museum at Salisbury *(see pp268–9)* and the main museum at Devizes.

Silbury Hill

Silbury Hill is Europe's largest prehistoric earthwork, but despite extensive excavations its purpose remains a mystery. Built out of chalk blocks around 2750 BC, the hill covers 2 ha (5 acres) and rises to a height of 40 m (131 ft). Nearby **West Kennet Long Barrow** is the biggest chambered tomb in England,

The Sarsen Circle was erected around 2500 BC and is capped by lintel stones held in place by mortise and tenon joints.

The Bluestone Circle was built around 2500 BC out of some 80 slabs quarried in the Preseli Hills in south Wales.

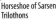

Horseshoe of Bluestones

Horseshoe of Sarsen Trilothons

Alternate ends of the lintel were levered up.

The weight of the lintel was supported by a timber platform.

The lintel was then levered sideways on to the uprights.

VISITORS' CHECKLIST

Practical Information
Off A303, Wilts. **Tel** 0870 333 1181. **Open** daily. mid-Mar–May: 9:30am–6pm; Jun–Aug: 9am–7pm; Sep–mid-Oct: 9:30am–6pm; mid-Oct–mid-Mar: 9:30am–4pm. **Closed** 20–22 Jun, 24–25 Dec. 🅿 🅖 🅒 🖵 🅔🅗
🅦 **english-heritage.org.uk**

Transport
🚌 Salisbury then Stonehenge tour bus.

Sarsen stone forming part of the Avebury Stone Circle

⑫ Avebury

Wiltshire. 🚐 500. 🚌 Swindon then bus. ℹ️ Green St (01672 539250). **Open** daily. 🖵 🅔🅗 🅝🅣
🅦 **nationaltrust.org.uk**

Built around 2500 BC, the **Avebury Stone Circle** surrounds the village of Avebury and was probably once some form of religious centre. Although the stones used are smaller than those at Stonehenge, the circle itself is larger. Superstitious villagers smashed many of the stones in the 18th century, believing the circle to have been a place of pagan sacrifice.

The original form of the circle is best appreciated by a visit to the excellent **Alexander Keiller Museum** to the west of the site, which illustrates in detail the construction of the circle. There is also a fascinating exhibition called "6,000 Years of Mystery", which explains the changing landscape of Avebury.

St James's Church has a Norman font carved with sea monsters, and a rare 15th-century choir screen.

Environs

A few minutes' drive east, **Marlborough** is an attractive town with a long and broad High Street lined with colonnaded Georgian shops.

🏛 **Alexander Keiller Museum**
Off High St. **Tel** 01672 538016. **Open** daily. **Closed** 24, 25 Dec. 🅿 🅖 🅿 🅒 🅒 🅝🅣
🅦 **nationaltrust.org.uk**

with numerous stone-lined "rooms" and a monumental entrance. Built as a communal cemetery around 3250 BC, it was in use for several centuries – old bodies were taken away to make room for newcomers.

Old Sarum is set within the massive ramparts of a 1st-century Romano-British hill fort. The Norman founders of Old Sarum built their own motte and bailey castle inside this ready-made fortification, and the remains of this survive along with the foundations of the huge cathedral of 1075. Above ground nothing remains of the town that once sat within the ramparts. The town's occupants

moved to the fertile river valley site that became Salisbury during the early 12th century (*see pp268–9*).

🏰 **Old Sarum**
Castle Rd. **Tel** 01722 335398. **Open** daily. **Closed** 1 Jan, 24–26 Dec. 🅿 🅒 🅔🅗

The chambered tomb of West Kennet Long Barrow (c.3250 BC)

⑬ Salisbury

The "new" city of Salisbury was founded in 1220, when the old hill-top settlement of Old Sarum *(see p267)* was abandoned, being too arid and windswept, in favour of a new site among the lush water meadows where the rivers Avon, Nadder and Bourne meet. Locally sourced Purbeck marble and Chilmark stone were used for the construction of a new cathedral which was built mostly in the early 13th-century, over the remarkably short space of 38 years. Its magnificent landmark spire – the tallest in England – was an inspired afterthought added in 1280–1310.

The early 14th-century house of John A'Port, Queen's Street

Street leading to the 13th-century **Church of St Thomas**, which has a lovely carved timber roof (1450), and a late 15th-century Doom painting, showing Christ seated in judgement and demons seizing the damned. Nearby in Silver Street, **Poultry Cross** was built in the 14th century as a covered poultry market. An intricate network of alleys fans out from this point with a number of fine timber-framed houses. In the large bustling **Market Place** the

Bishop's Walk and a sculpture by Elisabeth Frink (1930–93), Cathedral Close

Exploring Salisbury

The spacious and tranquil **Close**, with its schools, alms-houses and clergy housing, makes a fine setting for Salisbury's cathedral. Among the numerous elegant buildings here are the **Matrons' College**, built in 1682 as a home for widows and unmarried daughters of the clergy, and 13th-century **Malmesbury House** with its splendid early Georgian façade (1719), fronted by lovely wrought-iron gates. Other buildings of interest include the 13th-century **Medieval Hall**, the 13th-century **Wardrobe**, now a regimental museum, and the **Cathedral School**, housed in the 13th-century Bishop's Palace and famous for the quality of its choristers.

Beyond the walls of the Cathedral Close, Salisbury developed its chessboard layout, with areas devoted to different trades, perpetuated in street names such as Fish Row and Butcher Row. Leaving the Close through **High Street Gate**, you reach the busy High

KEY

① **Choir stalls**

② **Bishop Audley's Chantry**, a magnificent 16th-century monument to the bishop, is one of several small chapels clustered round the altar.

③ **The Trinity Chapel** contains the grave of St Osmund who was bishop of Old Sarum from 1078–1099.

④ **The Chapter House** has an original of the Magna Carta. Its walls have stone friezes of the Old Testament.

⑤ **The Cloisters** are the largest in England. They were added between 1263 and 1284 in the Decorated style.

⑥ **The graceful spire** soars to a height of 123 m (404 ft).

⑦ **A roof tour** takes you up to an external gallery at the base of the spire with views of the town and Old Sarum.

⑧ **The nave** is divided into ten bays by columns of polished Purbeck marble.

⑨ **The clock** dating from 1386 is the oldest working clock in Europe.

⑩ **Numerous windows** add to the airy and spacious atmosphere of the interior.

⑪ **North transept**

Guildhall is an unusual cream stone building from 1787–95, used for civic functions. More attractive are the brick and tile-hung houses on the north side of the square, many with Georgian façades concealing medieval houses.

🏠 Mompesson House

The Close. **Tel** 01722 335659. **Open** mid-Mar–Oct: Sat–Wed. 🅿️ ♿ limited. 📱 **NT** **W** **national trust.org.uk**

Built by a wealthy Wiltshire family in 1701, the handsomely furnished rooms of this house give an indication of life for the Close's inhabitants in the 18th century. The delightful garden, bounded by the north wall of the Close, has fine herbaceous borders.

🏛 Salisbury and South Wiltshire Museum

The Close. **Tel** 01722 332151. **Open** Mon–Sat (Jun–Sep: Sun pm). 🅿️ 📱 📷 **W** **salisburymuseum.org.uk**

In the medieval King's House, this museum has displays on early man, Stonehenge and nearby Old Sarum (*see p267*).

Environs

The town of Wilton is renowned for its carpet industry, founded by the 8th Earl of Pembroke

using French Huguenot refugee weavers. The town's ornate **church** (1844) is a brilliant example of Neo-Romanesque architecture, incorporating genuine Roman columns, Flemish Renaissance woodwork, German and Dutch stained glass and Italian mosaics.

Wilton House has been home to the Earls of Pembroke since it was converted from a nunnery after the Dissolution (*see p54*). The house, largely rebuilt by Inigo Jones in the 17th century, includes one of the original Tudor towers, a fine collection of art and a landscaped park with a Palladian bridge (1737). The Single and Double Cube State Rooms have magnificently frescoed ceilings and gilded stucco work, and were designed to hang a series of family portraits by Van Dyck.

🏠 Wilton House

Wilton. **Tel** 01722 746700. **Open** Easter weekend, May–Aug: Sun–Thu, bank hol Sat. 🅿️ ♿ ✏️ 📷

Double Cube room, designed by Inigo Jones in 1653

Salisbury Cathedral

The Close. **Tel** 01722 555120. **Open** daily. Donation. ♿ 📱 📷
W **salisburycathedral.org.uk**

The cathedral was mostly built between 1220 and 1258. It is a fine example of Early English Gothic architecture, typified by tall, sharply pointed lancet windows.

The West Front is decorated by rows of lavish symbolic figures and saints in niches.

The Longleat Tree tapestry (1980) depicting a 400-year history

⓮ Longleat House

Warminster, Wiltshire. **Tel** 01985 844400. 🚆 Warminster then taxi. House & Safari Park: **Open** mid-Feb–mid-Mar: Fri–Mon; mid-Mar–Oct: daily. 🅿️ ♿ 📷 🖥️ 📷
W longleat.co.uk

The architectural historian John Summerson coined the term "prodigy house" to describe the exuberance and grandeur of Elizabethan architecture that is so well represented at Longleat. The house was started in 1540, when John Thynne bought the ruins of a priory on the site for £53. Over the centuries subsequent owners have added their own touches. These include the Breakfast Room and Lower Dining Room (dating from the 1870s), modelled on the Venetian Ducal Palace, and erotic murals painted by the present owner, the 7th Marquess of Bath. Today, the Great Hall is the only remaining room which belongs to Thynne's time.

In 1949, the 6th Marquess was the first landowner in Britain to open his stately home to the public, in order to fund the maintenance and preservation of the house and its estate. Parts of the grounds, landscaped by "Capability" Brown *(see p30)*, were turned into an expansive safari park in 1966, where lions, tigers and other wild animals roam freely. This, along with other additions such as England's longest hedge maze, the Adventure Castle and Blue Peter Maze, and special events, now draw even more visitors than the house.

⓯ Stourhead

Stourhead is among the finest examples of 18th-century landscape gardening in Britain *(see pp30–31)*. The garden was begun in the 1740s by Henry Hoare (1705–85), who inherited the estate and transformed it into a breath-taking work of art. Hoare created the lake, surrounding it with rare trees and plants, and Neo-Classical Italianate temples, grottoes and bridges. The Palladian-style house, built by Colen Campbell *(see p32)*, dates from 1724.

Pantheon
Hercules is among the statues of Roman gods housed in the elegant Pantheon (1753).

★ Temple of Apollo
The Classical temples that dot the garden were all designed by influential architect Henry Flitcroft (1679–1769).

KEY

① **Turf Bridge**

② **The lake** was created from a group of medieval fishponds. Hoare dammed the valley to form a single expanse of water.

③ **A walk of** 2 miles (3 km) round the lake provides artistically contrived vistas.

④ **Iron Bridge**

⑤ **Gothic Cottage (1806)**

⑥ **Grotto** tunnels lead to an artificial cave with a pool and a life-size statue of the guardian of the River Stour, sculpted by John Cheere in 1748.

⑦ **Temple of Flora (1744)**

⑧ **Colourful shrubs** around the house include fragrant rhododendrons in spring.

⑨ **Stourton village** was incorporated into Hoare's overall design.

⑩ **Pelargonium House** is a historical collection of over 100 species and cultivars.

⑪ **The reception** offers information for your visit.

St Peter's Church
The parish church contains monuments to the Hoare family. The medieval Bristol Cross, nearby, was brought from Bristol in 1765.

Entrance and car park

★ Stourhead House
Reconstructed after a fire in 1902, the house contains fine Chippendale furniture. The art collection reflects Henry Hoare's Classical tastes and includes *The Choice of Hercules* (1637) by Nicolas Poussin.

⑯ Shaftesbury

Dorset. ⚙ 8,000. ▦ ℹ️ 8 Bell St (01747 853514). ⊖ Thu.
🌐 shaftesburydorset.com

Hilltop Shaftesbury, with its cobbled streets and 18th-century cottages is often used as a setting for films to give a flavour of Old England. Picturesque **Gold Hill** is lined on one side by a wall of the demolished **abbey**, founded by King Alfred in 888. Only the excavated remains of the abbey church survive, and many masonry fragments are found in the local museum.

The Almshouse (1437) adjoining the Abbey Church, Sherborne

⑰ Sherborne

Dorset. ⚙ 9,500. 🚆 ▦ 🚌 ℹ️ Digby Rd (01935 815411). ⊖ Thu, Sat.
🌐 visit-dorset.com

Few other towns in Britain have such a wealth of unspoilt medieval buildings. Edward VI *(see p45)* founded the famous Sherborne School in 1550, saving intact the splendid **Abbey Church** and other monastic buildings that might otherwise have been demolished in the Dissolution *(see p54)*. Remains of the Saxon church can be seen in the abbey's façade, but the most striking feature is the 15th-century fan-vaulted ceiling. **Sherborne Castle**, built by Sir Walter Raleigh *(see p55)* in 1594, is a wonderfully varied building that anticipates the flamboyant Jacobean style. Raleigh also lived briefly in the early 12th-century **Old Castle**, which now stands in ruins, demolished during the Civil War *(see p56)*.

Environs
West of Sherborne, past Yeovil, is the magnificent Elizabethan **Montacute House** *(see p249)*, set in 120 ha (300 acres) of grounds. It is noted for tapestries, and for the Tudor and Jacobean portraits in the vast Long Gallery.

🏰 **Sherborne Castle**
Off A30. **Tel** 01935 813182. Castle and grounds: **Open** Apr–Oct: Tue–Thu, Sat, Sun & bank hols (pm). 🐾 ▣ 🎁
🌐 sherbornecastle.com

🏰 **Old Castle**
Off A30. **Tel** 01935 812730. **Open** Easter–Oct: daily. 🐾 ♿ 🎁 EH

▦ **Montacute House**
Montacute. **Tel** 01935 823289. House: **Open** mid-Mar–Oct: Wed–Mon; Nov–mid-Mar: Sat & Sun. Grounds: **Open** mid-Mar–Oct: daily; Nov–mid-Mar: Wed–Sun. 🐾 ▨ 🎁 NT

⑱ Abbotsbury

Dorset. ⚙ 500. ℹ️ Bakehouse Market St (01305 871990).
🌐 abbotsbury-tourism.co.uk

The name Abbotsbury recalls the town's 11th-century Benedictine abbey of which little but the huge tithe barn, built around 1400, remains.
Nobody knows when the **Swannery** here was founded, but the earliest record dates to 1393. Mute swans come to nest in the breeding season, attracted by the reed beds along the Fleet, a brackish lagoon protected from the sea by a high ridge of pebbles called **Chesil Bank** *(see p246)*.

The Swannery at Abbotsbury

Its wild atmosphere makes an appealing contrast to the south coast resorts, although strong currents make swimming too dangerous. **Abbotsbury Sub-Tropical Gardens** are the frost-free home to many new plants, discovered by botanists travelling in South America and Asia.

🦢 **Swannery**
New Barn Rd. **Tel** 01305 871858. **Open** mid-Mar–Oct: daily. 🐾 ♿ ▣ 🎁

🌿 **Abbotsbury Sub-Tropical Gardens**
Off B3157. **Tel** 01305 871387. **Open** daily. **Closed** 25 Dec. 🐾 ♿ ▣ 🎁

⑲ Weymouth

Dorset. ⚙ 53,000. 🚆 ▦ 🚌 ℹ️ Pavilion Theatre, The Esplanade (01305 785747). ⊖ Thu.

Weymouth's popularity as a seaside resort began in 1789, when George III paid the first of many summer visits here. His statue is a prominent feature on the seafront. Here gracious Georgian terraces look across to the beautiful expanse of Weymouth Bay. Different in

Weymouth Quay, Dorset's south coast

For hotels and restaurants in this area see pp560–73 and pp582–603

character is the old town around Custom House Quay with its fishing boats and old seamen's inns. In 1944 the town played host to over 500,000 troops in advance of the D-Day Landings, and **Nothe Fort** has displays of World War II memorabilia.

🏛 **Nothe Fort**
Barrack Rd. **Tel** 01305 766626. **Open** Mar–Sep: daily; Oct, Nov, Feb: Sun.

⑳ Dorchester

Dorset. 🏔 19,000. 🚌 ℹ Antelope Walk (01305 267992). 🛍 Wed.
ⓦ visit-dorset.com

A 55 m (180 ft) giant carved on the chalk hillside, Cerne Abbas (National Trust)

Dorchester, the county town of Dorset, is still recognizably the town in which Thomas Hardy based his novel *The Mayor of Casterbridge* (1886). Here, among the many 17th- and 18th-century houses lining the High Street, is the **Dorset County Museum**, where the original manuscript of the novel is displayed. Dorchester has the only example of a **Roman town house** in Britain. The remains reveal architectural details including a fine mosaic. There are also finds from Iron Age and Roman sites on the outskirts of the town. **Maumbury Rings** (Weymouth Avenue), is a Roman amphitheatre, originally a Neolithic henge. To the west, many Roman graves have been found below the Iron Age hill fort, **Poundbury Camp**.

Environs
Just southwest of Dorchester, **Maiden Castle** (see p47) is a massive monument dating from around 100 BC. In AD 43 it was the scene of a battle when the Romans fought the Iron Age people of southern England.

To the north lies the charming village of **Cerne Abbas** with its magnificent medieval tithe barn and monastic buildings. The huge chalk figure of a giant on the hillside here is a fertility figure thought to represent either the Roman god Hercules or an Iron Age warrior.

East of Dorchester are the churches, thatched villages and rolling hills immortalized in Hardy's novels. Picturesque **Bere Regis** is the Kingsbere of *Tess of the D'Urbervilles*, where the tombs of the family whose name inspired the novel may be seen in the Saxon **church**. **Hardy's Cottage** is where the writer was born and **Max Gate** is the house he designed and lived in from 1885 until his death. His heart is buried with his family at **Stinsford** church – his body was given a public funeral at Westminster Abbey (pp96–7).

There are beautiful gardens (see p249) and a magnificent medieval hall at 15th-century **Athelhampton House**.

Hardy's statue, Dorchester

🏛 **Dorset County Museum**
High West St. **Tel** 01305 262735. **Open** Mon–Sat. **Closed** 25, 26 Dec. 📷 valid for one year. ♿ ltd. 📷
ⓦ dorsetcountymuseum.org

🏠 **Hardy's Cottage**
Higher Bockhampton. **Tel** 01305 262366. **Open** mid-Mar–Oct: Wed–Sun. 📷 🏠 ♿
🆖 garden only.

🏠 **Max Gate**
Alington Ave, Dorchester. **Tel** 01305 262538. **Open** mid-Mar–Oct: Wed–Sun. 📷 ♿ 📷

🏠 **Athelhampton House**
Athelhampton. **Tel** 01305 848363. **Open** Sun–Thu (Nov–Feb: Sun). 📷 ♿ gardens only. 📷 📷 📷
ⓦ athelhamptonhouse.co.uk

Thomas Hardy (1840–1928)

The vibrant, descriptive novels and poems of Thomas Hardy, one of England's best-loved writers, are set against the background of his native Dorset. The Wessex countryside provides a constant and familiar stage against which his characters enact their fate. Vivid accounts of rural life record a key moment in history, when mechanization was about to destroy ancient farming methods, just as the Industrial Revolution had done in the towns a century before (see pp58–9). Hardy's powerfully visual style has made novels such as *Tess of the D'Urbervilles* (1891) popular with modern film-makers, and drawn literary pilgrims to the villages and landscapes that inspired his fiction.

Nastassja Kinski in Roman Polanski's film *Tess* (1979)

㉑ Corfe Castle

Dorset. **Tel** 01929 481294. 🚋
Wareham then bus. **Open** daily.
Closed 25 & 26 Dec. 🅿 🚫 limited.
🗓 Mar–Oct; Nov–Feb by
arrangement. 💻 🏠 NT
w nationaltrust.org.uk

The spectacular ruins of Corfe
Castle romantically crown a
jagged pinnacle of rock above
the charming unspoilt village
that shares its name. The castle
has dominated the landscape
since the 11th century, first as a
royal fortification, then as the
dramatic ruins seen today. In
1635 the castle was purchased
by Sir John Bankes, whose wife
and her retainers – mostly
women – courageously held
out against 600 Parliamentary
troops, in a six-week siege
during the Civil War *(see pp56–
7)*. The castle was eventually
taken through treachery and in
1646 Parliament voted to
have it "slighted" – deliberately
blown up to prevent it
being used again. From the
ruins there are farreaching
views over the Isle of Purbeck
and its coastline.

The ruins of Corfe Castle, dating mainly from Norman times

㉒ Isle of Purbeck

Dorset. 🚋 Wareham. ⛴ Shell Bay,
Studland. 🛈 Swanage (01929
422885). **w** swanage.gov.uk

The Isle of Purbeck, which is in
fact a peninsula, is the source
of the grey shelly limestone,
known as Purbeck marble,
from which the castle and
surrounding houses were built.
The geology changes to the
southwest at **Kimmeridge**,
where the muddy shale is rich
in fossils and oil reserves. The
Isle, a World Heritage site, is
fringed with unspoilt beaches.
Studland Bay (National Trust) –
with its white sand and its sand-
dune nature reserve, rich in
birdlife – has been rated one of
Britain's best beaches. Sheltered
Lulworth Cove is almost
encircled by white cliffs, and
there is a fine cliff-top walk
to Durdle Door *(see p247)*, a
natural chalk arch.

The main resort in the area is
Swanage, the port where
Purbeck stone was transported
by ship to London, to be used
for everything from street
paving to church building.
Unwanted masonry from
demolished buildings was
shipped back and this is how
Swanage got its wonderfully
ornate **Town Hall** façade,
designed by Wren around 1668.

㉓ Poole

Dorset. 🗺 142,000. 🚋 🚌 ⛴ 🛈
Poole Quay (0845 2345560).
w pooletourism.com

Situated on one of the
largest natural harbours in
the world, Poole is an ancient,
still thriving, seaport. The
quay is lined with old warehouses, modern apartments
and a marina, overlooking a
safe sheltered bay. The **Poole
Museum**, partly housed in
15th-century cellars alongside
the quay, has four floors
of galleries.

Nearby **Brownsea Island**
(reached by boat from the quay)
is given over to a woodland
nature reserve with a waterfowl
and heron sanctuary. The fine

Beach adjoining Lulworth Cove, Isle of Purbeck

views of the Dorset coast add to the appeal of the island.

🏛 Poole Museum
High St. **Tel** 01202 262600. **Open** Apr–Oct: daily; Nov–Mar: Tue–Sun. **Closed** 1 Jan, 25, 26 Dec. ♿

✦ Brownsea Island
Poole. **Tel** 01202 707744. **Open** mid-Mar–Nov: daily (boat trips leave the quayside every 30 mins during the season). 🅿 ♿ 🛍 ▯ 📷 🅽🆃

Boats in Poole harbour

24 Wimborne Minster
Dorset. 🖼 6,500. 🚌 ℹ 29 High St (01202 886116). 🛍 Fri–Sun.
🆆 wimborneminster.net

The fine collegiate church of Wimborne's **Minster** was founded in 705 by Cuthburga, sister of King Ina of Wessex. It fell prey to marauding Danish raiders in the 10th century, and the imposing grey church we see today dates from the refounding by Edward the Confessor (see p51) in 1043. Stonemasons made use of the local Purbeck marble, carving beasts, biblical scenes, and a mass of zig-zag decoration.

The 16th-century **Priest's House Museum** has rooms furnished in the style of different periods and an enchanting hidden garden.

Environs
Designed for the Bankes family after the destruction of Corfe Castle, **Kingston Lacy** was acquired by the National Trust in 1981. The estate has always been farmed by traditional methods and is astonishingly rich in wildlife, rare flowers and butterflies. This quiet, forgotten corner of Dorset is grazed by rare Red Devon cattle and can be explored using paths and "green lanes" that date back to Roman and Saxon times. The fine 17th-century house on the estate contains an outstanding collection of paintings, including works by Rubens, Velázquez and Titian.

🏛 Priest's House Museum
High St. **Tel** 01202 882533. **Open** Apr–Oct: Mon–Sat. 🅿 ♿ limited. ▯ 📷

🏠 Kingston Lacy
On B3082. **Tel** 01202 883402. House: **Open** Mar–Oct: Wed–Sun. Gardens: **Open** daily. 🅿 ♿ gardens only. 🛍 📷 🅽🆃

25 Bournemouth
Dorset. 🖼 165,000. 🛫 🚆 🚌. ℹ Westover Road (0845 0511700).
🆆 bournemouth.co.uk

Bournemouth's popularity as a seaside resort is due to an almost unbroken sweep of sandy beach, extending from the mouth of Poole Harbour to Hengistbury Head. Most of the seafront is built up, with large seaside villas and exclusive hotels. To the west there are numerous clifftop parks and gardens, interrupted by beautiful wooded river ravines, known as "chines". The varied and colourful garden of **Compton Acres** was conceived as a museum of many different garden styles.

In central Bournemouth the amusement arcades, casinos, nightclubs and shops cater for the city's many visitors. In the summer, pop groups, TV comedians and the highly regarded Bournemouth

A road train on the popular seafront at Bournemouth

Marchesa Maria Grimaldi by Sir Peter Paul Rubens (1577–1640), Kingston Lacy

Symphony Orchestra perform at various venues in the city. The **Russell-Cotes Art Gallery and Museum**, housed in a late Victorian villa, has an extensive collection, with many fine Oriental and Victorian artefacts.

Environs
The magnificent **Christchurch Priory**, east of Bournemouth, is 95 m (310 ft) in length – the longest church in England. It was rebuilt between the 13th and 16th centuries and presents a sequence of different styles. The original nave, built around 1093, is an impressive example of Norman architecture, but the highlight is the intricate stone reredos, which features a Tree of Jesse, tracing the lineage of Christ. Next to the Priory are the ruins of a Norman **castle**.

Between Bournemouth and Christchurch, **Hengistbury Head** is well worth climbing for grassland flowers, butterflies and sea views, while **Stanpit Marsh**, to the west of Bournemouth, is an excellent spot for viewing herons and other wading birds.

🗺 Compton Acres
Canford Cliffs Rd. **Tel** 01202 700778. **Open** daily. 📷 🛍 ♿ 🛍
🆆 comptonacres.co.uk

🏛 Russell-Cotes Art Gallery and Museum
Eastcliff. **Tel** 01202 451858. **Open** Tue–Sun. ♿ 🛍 📷 🆆 russell-cotes. bournemouth.gov.uk

DEVON AND CORNWALL

Devon · Cornwall

Miles of magnificently varied coastline dominate this magical corner of Britain. Popular seaside resorts alternate with secluded coves and unspoilt fishing villages rich in maritime history. In contrast there are lush, exotic gardens and the wild terrain of the moorland interior, dotted with tors and historic remains.

Geographical neighbours, the counties of Devon and Cornwall are very different in character. Celtic Cornwall, with its numerous villages named after early Christian missionaries, is mostly stark and treeless at its centre. In many places it is still scarred by the remains of tin and copper mining that has played an important part in the economy for some 4,000 years. Yet this does not detract from the beauty and variety of the coastline dotted with lighthouses and tiny coves, and penetrated by deep tidal rivers.

Devon, by contrast, is a land of lush pasture divided into a patchwork of tiny fields and threaded with narrow lanes, whose banks support a mass of flowers from the first spring primroses to summer's colourful mixture of campion, foxglove, oxeye daisies and blue cornflowers. The leisurely pace of rural life here, and in Cornwall, contrasts with life in the bustling cities. Exeter with its magnificent cathedral, historic Plymouth, elegant Truro and Elizabethan Totnes are urban centres brimming with life and character.

The spectacular coastline and the mild climate of the region attract families, boating enthusiasts and surfers. For those in search of solitude, the Southwest Coastal Path provides access to the more tranquil areas. There are fishing villages and harbours whose heyday was in the buccaneering age of Drake and Raleigh *(see p55)*, and inland the wild moorland of Bodmin and Dartmoor, which provided inspiration for many romantic tales. Many of these are associated with King Arthur *(see p289)* who, according to legend, was born at Tintagel on Cornwall's dramatically contorted north coast.

Beach huts on the seafront at Paignton, near Torquay

◀ The picturesque seaside town of St Ives, Cornwall

Exploring Devon and Cornwall

Romantic Moorland dominates the inland parts of Devon and Cornwall, ideal walking country with few roads and magnificent views stretching for miles. By contrast the extensive coastline is indented by hundreds of sheltered river valleys, each one seemingly isolated from the rest of the world – one reason why Devon and Cornwall can absorb so many visitors and yet still seem uncrowded. Wise tourists get to know one small part of Devon or Cornwall intimately, soaking up the atmosphere of the region, rather than rushing to see everything in the space of a week.

Key

🟰 Motorway
🟰 Major road
🟰 Secondary road
⋯ Minor road
🟰 Scenic route
🟰 Main railway
— Minor railway
△ Summit

Sights at a Glance

❷ St Ives
❸ Penzance
❹ *St Michael's Mount pp282–3*
❺ Helston and the Lizard Peninsula
❻ Falmouth
❼ Truro
❽ St Austell
❾ *Eden Project pp286–7*
❿ Fowey
⓫ Bodmin
⓬ Tintagel
⓭ Bude
⓮ Clovelly
⓯ Bideford
⓰ Appledore
⓱ Barnstaple
⓲ Lynton and Lynmouth
⓳ Exeter
⓴ Torbay
㉑ Dartmouth
㉒ Totnes
㉓ Buckfastleigh
㉔ Burgh Island
㉕ Plymouth
㉖ Buckland Abbey
㉗ Cotehele
㉘ Morwellham Quay
㉙ *Dartmoor pp298–9*

Walks and Tours

❶ Penwith Tour

The dramatic cliffs of Land's End, England's most westerly point

Sub-tropical gardens at Torquay, the popular seaside resort

Getting Around

Large numbers of drivers, many towing caravans (trailers), travel along the M5 motorway and A30 trunk road from mid-July to early September and travel can be slow, especially on Saturdays. Once in Devon and Cornwall, allow ample time if you are travelling by car along the region's narrow and high-banked lanes. The regular train services, running from Paddington to Penzance, along Brunel's historic Great Western Railway, stop at most major towns. Aside from this, you are dependent on taxis or infrequent local buses.

Typical thatched, stone cottages, Buckland-in-the-Moor, Dartmoor

❶ Penwith Tour

This tour passes through a spectacular, remote Cornish landscape, dotted with relics of the tin mining industry, picturesque fishing villages and many prehistoric remains. The magnificent coastline varies between the gentle rolling moorland in the north and the rugged, windswept cliffs that characterize the dramatic south coast. The beauty of the area, combined with the clarity of light, has attracted artists since the late 19th century. Their work can be seen in Newlyn, St Ives and Penzance.

Tips for Drivers

Tour length: 31 miles (50 km)
Stopping-off points: There are pubs and cafés in most villages. Sennen Cove makes a pleasant mid-way stop. (*See also pp636–7.*)

① **Zennor**
The carved mermaid in the church recalls the legend of the mermaid who lured the local squire's son to her ocean lair.

② **Lanyon Quoit**
One of many prehistoric monuments, this chambered tomb is visible on the left from the road to Madron.

⑧ **Botallack Mine**
Derelict engine-houses clinging to the cliffside are a vivid reminder of the region's former industry of tin-mining.

③ **Trengwainton**
These gardens are noted for their luxuriance (*p248*).

⑦ **Land's End**
England's most westerly point is noted for its dramatic and wild landscape. A local exhibition reveals its history, geology and wildlife.

④ **Newlyn**
Cornwall's largest fishing port gave its name to a school of artists founded in the 1880s (*p282*). Examples of their work can be seen in the art gallery here.

⑤ **Merry Maidens**
This Bronze Age stone circle is said to be 19 girls turned to stone for dancing on Sunday.

⑥ **Minack Theatre**
This Ancient Greek-style theatre (1923) overlooks a magical bay of Porthcurno. It forms a magnificent backdrop for productions in summer.

Morvah • B3306 B3306 B3318 St Just • Madron • A3071 Penzance A30 B3306 B3283 B3315 A30 Sennen Cove A30 B3315 B3283 B3315 Mousehole Lamorna Porthcurno St Ives

Key

▬▬▬ Tour route
┈┈┈ Other roads

0 kilometres   3
0 miles   2

② St Ives

Cornwall. 🏛 11,000. 🚤 🚌 ℹ️
Street-an-Pol (01736 796297).
🌐 **stives.co.uk**

St Ives's **Barbara Hepworth Museum and Sculpture Garden** and **Tate St Ives** celebrate the work of a group of artists who set up a seaside art colony here from the 1920s. The former presents the sculptor's work in the house and garden where she lived and worked for many years. Tate St Ives, designed to frame a panoramic view of Porthmeor Beach, reminds visitors of the natural surroundings that inspired the art on display within. A museum at the Leach Pottery (www.leachpottery.com) celebrates the life and work of potter Bernard Leach,

The Lower Terrace, Tate St Ives

another luminary of the St Ives Society of Artists.

The town of St Ives remains a typical English seaside resort, surrounded by a crescent of golden sands. Popular taste rules in the many other art galleries tucked down winding alleys with names such as Teetotal Street, a legacy of the town's Methodist heritage. Many galleries are converted cellars and lofts where fish were once salted and packed. In between are whitewashed cottages with tiny gardens brimming with flowers, their vibrant colours made intense by the unusually clear light that first attracted artists to St Ives.

🏛 **Barbara Hepworth Museum and Sculpture Garden**
Barnoon Hill. **Tel** 01736 796226. **Open** daily (Nov–Feb: Tue–Sun). **Closed** 24–26 Dec. 🚫 📷 by appt. 🏛

🏛 **Tate St Ives**
Porthmeor Beach. **Tel** 01736 796226. **Open** daily (Nov–Feb: Tue–Sun). **Closed** 24–26 Dec; occasional rehanging – phone to check. 🚫 ♿ ✏️ 🏛
🌐 **tate.org.uk/visit/tate-st-ives**

Twentieth-Century Artists of St Ives

Ben Nicholson and Barbara Hepworth formed the nucleus of a group of artists that made a major contribution to the development of abstract art in Europe. In the 1920s, St Ives together with Newlyn *(see p280)* became a place for aspiring artists. Among the prolific artists associated with the town are the potter Bernard Leach (1887–1979) and the painter Patrick Heron (1920–99), whose *Coloured Glass Window (see p244)* dominates the Tate St Ives entrance. Much of the art on display at Tate St Ives is abstract and illustrates new responses to the rugged Cornish landscape, the human figure and the ever-changing patterns of sunlight on sea.

Barbara Hepworth (1903– 75) was one of the foremost abstract sculptors of her time. *Madonna and Child* (1953) can be seen in the church of St Ia.

John Wells' (1907–2000) key interests are in light, curved forms and birds in flight, as revealed in *Aspiring Forms* (1950).

Ben Nicholson's (1894–1982) work shows a change in style from simple scenes, such as the view from his window, to a preoccupation with shapes – as seen in this painting *St Ives, Cornwall* (1943–5). Later, his interest moved towards pure geometric blocks of colour.

❸ Penzance

Cornwall. 🚗 38,000. 🚉 🚌 🚢 *i*
Station Approach (01736 335530).
🌐 penzance.co.uk

Penzance is a bustling resort with a climate so mild that palm trees and sub-tropical plants grow happily in the lush **Morrab Gardens**. The town commands fine views of St Michael's Mount and a great sweep of clean sandy beach.

The main road through the town is Market Jew Street, at the top of which stands the magnificent domed Market House (1837), fronted by a statue of Sir Humphrey Davy (1778–1829). Davy, who came from Penzance, invented the miner's safety lamp which detected lethal gases.

Chapel Street is lined with curious buildings, none more striking than the flamboyant **Egyptian House** (1835), with its richly painted façade and lotus bud decoration. Just as curious is **Admiral Benbow Inn** (1696) on the same street, which has a pirate perched on the roof looking out to sea. The **Penlee House Gallery and Museum** has pictures by the Newlyn School of artists.

Environs

A short distance south of Penzance, **Newlyn** *(see p280)* is Cornwall's largest fishing port, which has given its name to the local school of artists founded by Stanhope Forbes (1857–1947). They painted outdoors, aiming to capture the fleeting impressions of wind, sun and sea. Continuing south, the coastal road ends at **Mousehole** (pronounced Mowzall), a pretty,

The Egyptian House (1835)

popular village with a tiny harbour, tiers of cottages and a maze of narrow alleys.

North of Penzance, overlooking the magical Cornish coast, **Chysauster** is a fine example of a Romano-British village. The site has

❹ St Michael's Mount

Marazion, Cornwall. **Tel** 01736 710507; tide and ferry information 01736 710265. 🚢 from Marazion (Mar–Oct) or on foot at low tide. Castle: **Open** mid-Mar–Oct: Sun–Fri. Garden: **Open** mid-Apr–Jun: Mon–Fri; Jul–Sep: Thu & Fri. 🚻 🎒 📷 🏠 NT of castle by appt.

St Michael's Mount emerges dramatically from the waters of Mounts Bay. According to ancient Roman historians, the mount was the island of Ictis, an important centre for the Cornish tin trade during the Iron Age. It is dedicated to the archangel St Michael who, according to legend, appeared here in 495.

When the Normans conquered England in 1066 *(see pp50–51)*, they were struck by the island's resemblance to their own Mont-St-Michel, whose Benedictine monks were invited to build a small abbey here. The abbey was absorbed into a fortress at the Dissolution *(see p355)*, when Henry VIII set up a chain of coastal defences to counter an expected attack from France. In 1659 St Michael's Mount was purchased by Colonel John St Aubyn, whose descendants subsequently turned the fortress into a magnificent house.

View of St Michael's Mount from Marazion

Harbourside village

Access to the island is by boat from Marazion or on foot by a cobbled causeway at low tide.

The rocky slopes were planted with sub-tropical trees and shrubs by the St Aubyn family.

Plan of Main Floor

Exit
Entrance
Sir John's Room
Ante Room
Library
Staircase to Armoury and Exit
Chevy Chase Room
North Terrace
Priory Church
Choir
South Terrace
Blue Drawing Room
Hall
Map Room
Long Passage
Smoking Room

remained almost undisturbed since it was abandoned during the 3rd century.

From Penzance, regular boat services depart for the **Isles of Scilly**, a beautiful archipelago forming part of the same granite mass as Land's End, Bodmin Moor and Dartmoor. Along with tourism, flower-growing forms the main source of income here.

🏛 Penlee House Gallery and Museum

Morrab Rd. **Tel** 01736 363625. **Open** May–Sep: 10am–5pm Mon–Sat; Oct–Apr: 10:30am–4:30pm Mon–Sat. **Closed** 1 Jan, 25–26 Dec. 🅿 ♿ but free admission on Sat. ♿ 📷
w penleehouse.org.uk

🏛 Chysauster

Off B3311. **Tel** 07831 757934. **Open** Apr–Oct: daily. 🅿 📷 EH

The Growth of Methodism

John Wesley (1703–91)

The hard-working and independent mining and fishing communities of the West Country had little time for the established church, but they were won over by the new Methodist religion, with its emphasis on hymn singing, open-air preaching and regular or "methodical" Bible reading. When John Wesley, the founder of Methodism, made the first of many visits to the area in 1743, sceptical Cornishmen pelted him with stones. His persistence, however, led to many conversions and by 1762 he was preaching to congregations of up to 30,000 people. Simple places of worship were built throughout the county; one favoured spot was the amphitheatre **Gwennap Pit**, at Busveal, south of Redruth. Methodist memorabilia can be seen in the Royal Cornwall Museum in Truro *(see p285)*.

Castle entrance

The South Terrace forms the roof of the large Victorian wing. Beneath it there are five floors of private quarters.

The Blue Drawing Room was formed from the Lady Chapel in the mid-18th century and is decorated in charming Rococo Gothic style. It contains fine plaster work, furniture and paintings by Gainsborough and Thomas Hudson.

The Armoury displays sporting weapons and military trophies brought back by the St Aubyn family from various wars.

The Priory Church, rebuilt in the late 14th century, forms the summit of the island. Beautiful rose windows are found at both ends.

The Chevy Chase Room takes its name from a plaster frieze (1641) representing hunting scenes.

Pinnacles of serpentine rock at Kynance Cove (National Trust), Lizard Peninsula

❺ Helston and the Lizard Peninsula

Cornwall. 🚌 from Penzance.
🌐 visitcornwall.com

The attractive town of Helston makes a good base for exploring the windswept coastline of the Lizard Peninsula. The town is famous for its Furry Dance, which welcomes spring with dancing through the streets *(see p66)*; the **Folk Museum** explains the history of this ancient custom. The Georgian houses and inns of Coinagehall Street are a reminder that Helston was once a thriving stannary town where tin ingots were brought for weighing and stamping before being sold. Locally mined tin was brought down river to a harbour at the bottom of this street until access to the sea was blocked in the 13th century by a shingle bar that formed across the estuary. The bar created the freshwater lake, Loe Pool, and an attractive walk skirts its wooded shores. In 1880, Helston's trade was taken over by a new harbour created to the east on the River Helford, at Gweek. Today, Gweek is the home of the **Cornish Seal Sanctuary**, where sick seals are nursed before being returned to the sea.

Cornwall's tin mining industry, from Roman to recent times, is covered at **Poldark Mine** where underground tours show the working conditions of 18th-century miners. Another attraction is **Flambards**

Experience, with its recreations of a Victorian village and of Britain during the Blitz.

Further south is Britain's most southerly tourist attraction, the Lizard Lighthouse Heritage Centre. Built in 1619, the tower was automated in 1998. Interactive displays describe the workings of a lighthouse.

Local shops sell souvenirs carved from serpentine, a soft greenish stone which forms the unusual-shaped rocks that rise from the sandy beach at picturesque **Kynance Cove**.

🏛 **Folk Museum**
Market Place, Helston. **Tel** 01326 564027. **Open** Mon–Sat (am only). **Closed** Christmas week. ♿ ♿ 🏠
🌐 cornwall.gov.uk

🦭 **Cornish Seal Sanctuary**
Gweek. **Tel** 01326 221361. **Open** daily. **Closed** 25 Dec. ♿ ♿ ▢ 🏠
🌐 sealsanctuary.com

🏛 **Poldark Mine**
Wendron. **Tel** 01326 573173. **Open** Apr–mid-Jul, Sep, Oct: Sun–Fri; mid-Jul–Aug: daily. 📷 compulsory, by appt. ▢ 🏠 🌐 poldark-mine.co.uk

🏛 **Flambards Experience**
Culdrose Manor, Helston. **Tel** 01326 573404. **Open** Easter–mid-Nov: daily (last adm: 2:30pm). ♿ ♿ 🚗 🏠
🌐 flambards.co.uk

🏛 **Lizard Lighthouse Heritage Centre**
Helston. **Tel** 01326 290202. **Open** Jun–Oct: Tue–Fri & Sun (Aug: Tue–Sun).

❻ Falmouth

Cornwall. 🏠 22,000. 🚂 🚌 ⛴ ℹ 11 Market Strand (01326 313394).
🛥 Tue. 🌐 falmouth.co.uk

Falmouth stands at the point where seven rivers flow into a long stretch of water called the **Carrick Roads**. The drowned river valley is so deep that huge ocean-going ships can sail up almost as far as Truro. Numerous creeks are ideal for boating excursions to view the varied scenery and birdlife.

Falmouth has the third largest naturally deep harbour after Sydney and Rio de Janeiro, and it forms the most interesting part of this seaside resort. On the harbour

Cornish Smugglers

In the days before income tax was invented, the main form of government income came from tax on imported luxury goods, such as brandy and perfume. Huge profits were to be made by evading these taxes, which were at their height during the Napoleonic Wars (1780–1815). Remote Cornwall, with its coves and rivers penetrating deep into the mainland, was prime smuggling territory; estimates put the number of people involved, including women and children, at 100,000. Some notorious families resorted to deliberate wrecking, setting up deceptive lights to lure vessels onto the sharp rocks, in the hope of plundering the wreckage.

waterfront stands the **National Maritime Museum Cornwall**, part of a large waterside complex, which includes cafés, shops and restaurants. The museum is dedicated to the great maritime tradition of Cornwall and contains Britain's finest public collection of historic and contemporary small craft. Exhibits look at maritime themes and the story of those whose lives depended on the sea.

The many old houses on the harbour include the **Customs House** and the chimney alongside, known as the "King's Pipe" because it was used for burning contraband tobacco seized from smugglers in the 19th century. **Pendennis Castle** and St Mawes Castle opposite, were built by King Henry VIII. Towards the town centre is the **Falmouth Art Gallery**, with one of Cornwall's most important art collections.

Environs

To the south, **Glendurgan** (see p248) and **Trebah** gardens are both set in sheltered valleys leading down to delightful sandy coves on the Helford River.

🏛 **National Maritime Museum Cornwall**
Discovery Quay, Falmouth. **Tel** 01326 313388. **Open** daily. **Closed** 25 & 26 Dec. 🅿 ♿ 💻 📷 🌐 nmmc.co.uk

🏰 **Pendennis Castle**
The Headland. **Tel** 01326 316594. **Open** Apr–Oct: daily; Nov–Mar: Sat & Sun. **Closed** 1 Jan, 24–26 Dec. 🅿 ♿ limited. 🎫 💻 📷 EH

Truro Cathedral, designed by J L Pearson and completed in 1910

🏛 **Falmouth Art Gallery**
The Moor. **Tel** 01326 313863. **Open** Mon–Sat. 🌐 **falmouthartgallery.com**

🌳 **Glendurgan**
Mawnan Smith. **Tel** 01326 252020. **Open** mid-Feb–Oct: Tue–Sun & pub hols (Aug: daily). **Closed** Good Fri. 🅿 📷 ♿ NT

🌳 **Trebah**
Mawnan Smith. **Tel** 01326 252200. **Open** daily. 🅿 📷 ♿ 💻 🌐 **trebah-garden.co.uk**

❼ Truro

Cornwall. 🚶 19,000. 🚌 🚍 ℹ Boscawen St (01872 274555). 🛒 Wed & Sat (farmers' market). 🌐 **tourism.truro.gov.uk**

Once a market town and port, Truro is now the administrative capital of Cornwall. Truro's many gracious Georgian buildings reflect its prosperity during the tin mining boom of the 1800s. In 1876 the 16th-century parish church was rebuilt to create the first new **cathedral** to be built in England since Wren built St Paul's (see pp118–19) in the 17th century. With its central tower, lancet windows and spires, the cathedral is an exuberant building that looks more French than English.

Truro's cobbled streets and alleys lined with craft shops are also a delight to explore. The **Royal Cornwall Museum** provides an excellent introduction to the history of the county with displays on tin mining, Methodism (see p283) and smuggling.

🏛 **Royal Cornwall Museum**
River St. **Tel** 01872 272205. **Open** Mon–Sat. **Closed** public hols. ♿ 💻 📷 🌐 **royalcornwallmuseum.org.uk**

🌳 **Trewithen**
Grampound Rd. **Tel** 01726 883647. **Open** Mar–May: daily; Jun–Sep: Mon–Sat. 🅿 ♿ by arrangement. 💻 📷 🌐 **trewithengardens.co.uk**

🌳 **Trelissick**
Feock. **Tel** 01872 862090. **Open** daily. **Closed** 25 Dec. 🅿 ♿ 🚻 📷 NT

The "Cornish Alps": china-clay spoil tips north of St Austell

❽ St Austell

Cornwall. 🚶 20,000. 🚌 🚍 ℹ Texaco Service Station, Southbourne Rd (01726 879500). 🛒 Sat–Sun. 🌐 **visitthecornishriviera.co.uk**

The busy industrial town of St Austell is the capital of the local china-clay industry which rose to importance in the 18th century. Clay is still a vital factor here; China was the only other place where such quality and quantity of clay could be found. Spoil tips are a prominent feature; on a sunny day they look like snow-covered peaks, meriting the local name the "Cornish Alps".

Environs

The famous **Lost Gardens of Heligan** are an amazing restoration project to recreate the extraordinary gardens created by the Tremayne family from the 16th century to World War I. At the **Wheal Martyn China Clay Museum**, nature trails weave through clay works that operated from 1878 until the 1920s.

🌳 **Lost Gardens of Heligan**
Pentewan. **Tel** 01726 845100. **Open** daily. **Closed** 24 & 25 Dec. 🅿 ♿ 🚻 💻 📷 🌐 **heligan.com**

🏛 **Wheal Martyn China Clay Museum**
Carthew. **Tel** 01726 850362. **Open** daily. **Closed** 22 Dec–1 Jan. 🅿 ♿ limited. 💻 📷 🌐 **wheal-martyn.com**

� Eden Project

The Eden Project is a global garden for the 21st century, and a dramatic setting in which to tell the fascinating story of mankind's dependence on plants. Two futuristic conservatories called Biomes have been designed to mimic the environments of warmer climes: one hot and humid, the other warm and dry. The outer Biome is planted with species that thrive in the Cornish climate. The Eden Project seeks to educate by telling the story of plants, people and places. The relationship between humans and nature is interpreted by artists throughout the site. The Core education centre is used for exhibitions, films and workshops. For an aerial view of the Biomes, visitors can ride over them on the longest zip wire in England (660 m/2,165 ft).

④ **Tropical South America**
Some plants in this area reach enormous proportions. The leaves of the giant waterlily can be up to 2 m (6 ft) across.

③ **West Africa**
Iboga is central to the African religion Bwiti. Highly hallucinogenic, it is an integral part of initiation ceremonies.

② **Malaysia**
The Titan arum grows within this rainforest display. The flower will grow to 3 m (8 ft) and smell of rotting flesh.

① **Tropical Islands**
Set apart from the rest of the world, these islands have many fascinating plants. The rare Madagascar Periwinkle (*Catharanthus roseus*) is thought to help cure leukemia.

The site

Access to the site, with its outdoor and covered Biomes, is via the Visitor Centre.

Rainforest Biome
① Tropical Islands
② Malaysia
③ West Africa
④ Tropical South America
⑤ Crops & cultivation

Mediterranean Biome
⑥ The Mediterranean
⑦ South Africa
⑧ California

Building Eden
Cornwall's declining china clay industry has left behind many disused pits. The Eden Project makes ingenious use of this industrial landscape. After partly infilling a pit, the massive Biomes were nestled into its base and walls.

Transparent hexagons made of ultra-light hi-tech plastic

⑤ Crops and cultivation
The coffee plant (*Coffea arabica*) is one of the many plants on display that are used in our everyday lives.

Rainforest biome
This vast conservatory houses a lush jungle of trees and plants. The dome includes a treetop-level viewing platform and aerial walkway.

The entrance to both the Rainforest and Mediterranean Biomes is via the Link, where the Eden Bakery is located.

⑨ Crops & cultivation

Outdoor Biome
⑩ Pollination
⑪ Cornish crops
⑫ Plants for taste
⑬ Global gardeners
⑭ Beer & brewing
⑮ Rope & fibre
⑯ Hemp
⑰ Steppe & Prairie
⑱ Eco-engineering
⑲ Tea
⑳ Lavender
㉑ Fuel
㉒ Myth & folklore

㉓ Biodiversity & Cornwall
㉔ Play
㉕ Flowers in the making
㉖ Health
㉗ Flowerless garden
㉘ Sense of Memory Garden

Key
==== Land Train

The Stage
Eden Arena
The Core
Visitor Centre

0 metres   150
0 yards   150

View of Polruan across the estuary from Fowey

⑩ Fowey

Cornwall. 🅿 2,000. 🚌 🚻 5 South St (01726 833616). 🆆 fowey.co.uk

Fowey (pronounced Foy), has been immortalized under the name of Troy Town in the humorous novels of Sir Arthur Quiller-Couch (1863–1944), who lived here in a house called **The Haven**. A resort favoured by many wealthy Londoners with a taste for yachting and expensive seafood restaurants, Fowey is the most gentrified of the Cornish seaside towns.

Daphne du Maurier

The period romances of Daphne du Maurier (1907–89) are inextricably linked with the wild Cornish landscape where she grew up. *Jamaica Inn* established her reputation in 1936, and with the publication of *Rebecca* two years later she found herself one of the most popular authors of her day. *Rebecca* was made into a film directed by Alfred Hitchcock, starring Joan Fontaine and Lord Laurence Olivier.

The picturesque charm of the flower-filled village is undeniable, with its tangle of tiny steep streets and its views across the estuary to Polruan. The church of **St Fimbarrus** marks the end of the ancient Saint's Way footpath from Padstow – a reminder of the Celtic missionaries who arrived on the shores of Cornwall to convert people to Christianity. Its flower-lined path leads to a majestic porch and carved tower. Inside there are some fine 17th-century memorials to the Rashleigh family whose seat, Menabilly, became Daphne du Maurier's home and featured as Manderley in *Rebecca* (1938).

Jamaica Inn, Bodmin Moor

Environs

For a closer look at the town of **Polruan** and the ceaseless activity of the harbour there is a number of river trips up the little creeks. At the estuary mouth are the twin towers from which chains were once hung to demast invading ships – an effective form of defence.

A fine stretch of coast leads further east to the picturesque fishing villages of **Polperro**, nestling in a narrow green ravine, and neighbouring **Looe**.

Upriver from Fowey is the tranquil town of **Lostwithiel**. Perched on a hill just to the north are the remains of the Norman **Restormel Castle**.

🏰 Restormel Castle

Lostwithiel. **Tel** 01208 872687. **Open** Apr–Oct: daily. 🅿 📷 EH

⑪ Bodmin

Cornwall. 🅿 14,000. 🚄 Bodmin Parkway. 🚌 Bodmin. 🆇 Mount Folly Sq, Bodmin (01208 76616). 🆆 bodminlive.com

Bodmin, Cornwall's ancient county town, lies on the sheltered western edge of the great expanse of moorland that shares its name. The history and archaeology of the town and moor is covered by **Bodmin Town Museum**, while **Bodmin Jail**, where public executions took place until 1909, is a gruesome tourist attraction. The churchyard is watered by the ever-gushing waters of a holy spring, and it was here that St Guron established a Christian cell in the 6th century. The **church** is dedicated to St Petroc, a Welsh missionary who founded a monastery here. The monastery has disappeared, but the bones of St Petroc remain, housed in a splendid 12th-century ivory casket in the church.

For a pleasant day out, ride the **Bodmin & Wenford Railway**, a steam train which departs from Bodmin Station, or take part in a Victorian murder trial at **The Courtroom Experience**, run by the tourist office.

South of Bodmin is the **Lanhydrock** estate. Amid its extensive wooded acres and formal gardens *(see p248)* lies the massive Victorian manor house, rebuilt after a fire in 1881, but retaining some Jacobean features. The fine 17th-century plaster ceiling in the Long Gallery depicts scenes from the Bible.

The desolate wilderness of Bodmin Moor is noted for its network of prehistoric field boundaries. The main attraction, however, is the 18th-century **Jamaica Inn**, made famous by Daphne du Maurier's tale of smuggling and romance. Today there is a restaurant and bar based on du Maurier's novel, and a small museum. A

The ruins of Tintagel Castle on the north coast of Cornwall

30-minute walk from the Inn is **Dozmary Pool**, reputed to be bottomless until it dried up in 1976. According to legend, the dying King Arthur's sword Excalibur was thrown into the pool.

To the east is **Altarnun**. Its spacious 15th-century church of **St Nonna** is known as the "Cathedral of the Moor".

Bodmin Town Museum
Mt Folly Sq, Bodmin. **Tel** 01208 77067. **Open** Easter–Oct: Mon–Sat, Good Fri. **Closed** pub hols.

Bodmin Jail
Berrycombe Rd, Bodmin. **Tel** 01208 76292. **Open** daily. **Closed** 25 Dec.
bodminjail.org

Lanhydrock
Bodmin. **Tel** 01208 265950. House: **Open** Mar–Oct: Tue–Sun & public hols. Gardens: **Open** mid-Feb–Oct: daily.

⓬ Tintagel

Cornwall. 1,700. Bossiney Rd (01840 779084). Thu (summer).
visitboscastleandtintagel.com

The romantic and mysterious ruins of **Tintagel Castle**, built around 1240 by Earl Richard of Cornwall, sit high on a hill-top surrounded by slate cliffs. Access to the castle is via two steep staircases clinging to the cliffside where pink thrift and purple sea lavender abound.

The earl was persuaded to build in this isolated, wind-swept spot by the popular belief, derived from Geoffrey of Monmouth's fictitious *History of the Kings of Britain*, that this was the birthplace of the legendary King Arthur.

Large quantities of fine eastern Mediterranean pottery dating from around the 5th century have been discovered, indicating that the site was an important trading centre, long before the medieval castle was built. Whoever lived here, perhaps the ancient Kings of Cornwall, could evidently afford a luxurious lifestyle.

A clifftop path leads from the castle to Tintagel's **church**, which has Norman and Saxon masonry. In Tintagel village the **Old Post Office** is a rare example of a 14th-century restored and furnished Cornish manor house.

Environs
A short distance to the east, **Boscastle** is a pretty National Trust village. The River Valency runs down the middle of the main street to the fishing harbour, which is sheltered from the sea by high slate cliffs. Access from the harbour to the sea is via a channel cut through the rocks.

Tintagel Castle
Tintagel Head. **Tel** 01840 770328. **Open** Apr–Oct: daily; Nov–Mar: Sat & Sun. **Closed** 1 Jan, 24–26 Dec. EH
english-heritage.org.uk/tintagel

Old Post Office
Fore St. **Tel** 01840 770024. **Open** Mar–Oct: daily.

⓭ Bude

Cornwall. 9,000. Crescent car park (01288 354240). Easter–Oct: Fri. **visitbude.info**

Wonderful beaches around this area make Bude a popular resort for families. The expanse of clean golden sand that attracts visitors today once made Bude a bustling port. Shelly, lime-rich sand was transported along a canal to inland farms where it was used to neutralize the acidic soil. The canal was abandoned in 1880 but a short stretch survives, providing a haven for birds such as kingfishers and herons.

Kingfisher

King Arthur

Historians think the legendary figure of King Arthur has some basis in historical fact. He was probably a Romano-British chieftain or warrior who led British resistance to the Saxon invasion of the 6th century *(see pp50–51)*. Geoffrey of Monmouth's *History of the Kings of Britain* (1139) introduced Arthur to literature with an account of the many legends connected with him – how he became king by removing the sword Excalibur from a stone, his final battle with the treacherous Mordred, and the story of the Knights of the Round Table *(see p174)*. Other writers, such as Alfred, Lord Tennyson, took up these stories and elaborated on them.

King Arthur, from a 14th-century chronicle by Peter of Langtoft

⑭ Clovelly

Devon. 🚉 350. **Tel** 01237 431781.
Town & Visitors' Centre **Open** daily.
Closed 25 & 26 Dec. 🅿 ♿ Visitors'
Centre. 🆆 clovelly.co.uk

Clovelly has been a noted beauty spot since the novelist Charles Kingsley (1819–75) wrote about it in his stirring story of the Spanish Armada, *Westward Ho!* (1855). The whole village is privately owned and has been turned into a tourist attraction, with little sign of the flourishing fishing industry to which it owed its birth. It is a charming village with steep, traffic-free cobbled streets rising up the cliff from the harbourside, white-washed houses and gardens brimming with brightly coloured flowers. There are superb views from the lookout points and fine coastal paths to explore from the tiny quay.

Hobby Drive is a scenic 3-mile (5-km) approach on foot to the village which runs through woodland along the coast. The road was constructed in 1811–29 to give employment to local men who had been

Bideford's medieval bridge, 203 m (666 ft) long with 24 arches

made redundant at the end of the Napoleonic Wars (*see pp58–9*).

⑮ Bideford

Devon. 🚉 14,000. 🚌 🏮 Burton Art Gallery, Kingsley Rd (01237 471455). 🚻 Tue, Sat.

Strung out along the estuary of the River Torridge, Bideford grew and thrived on importing tobacco from the New World. Some 17th-century merchants' houses survive in Bridgeland Street, including the splendid bay-windowed house at No. 28 (1693). Beyond is Mill Street, leading to the parish church

and the fine medieval bridge. The quay stretches from here to a pleasant park and a statue that commemorates Charles Kingsley, whose novels helped bring visitors to the area in the 19th century.

Environs
To the west of Bideford, the village **Westward Ho!** was built in the late 19th century and named after Kingsley's popular novel. It is notable for its surfing seas and the oldest golf club in England, the Royal North Devon. Rudyard Kipling (*see p167*) was at school here and the hill to the south, known as **Kipling Tors**, was the background for *Stalky & Co* (1899). Also to the west is **Hartland Abbey**, built as a monastery c.1157, now a family home. The BBC filmed parts of *Sense and Sensibility* here. Visitors can enjoy a museum, art and antiques, as well as gardens.

Henry Williamson's *Tarka the Otter* (1927) describes the otters of the **Torridge Valley**. Part of a Tarka Trail has been laid out along a disused railway line beside the Torridge for walkers and cyclists. Bicycles can be hired from the old railway station. The trail passes close to the magnificent **Rosemoor Garden**. Day trips run from either Bideford or Ilfracombe (depending on the tide) to **Lundy** island, which is abundant in birds and wildlife.

🌸 **RHS Rosemoor Garden**
Great Torrington. **Tel** 01805 624067.
Open daily. **Closed** 25 Dec. 🅿 ♿
✏ 🏠 🆆 rhs.org.uk/gardens/
rosemoor

🏛 **Hartland Abbey**
nr. Bideford. **Tel** 01237 441264. **Open**
Apr–Sep: Sun–Thu. 🅿 🚌 🏠 ♿
limited. 🆆 hartlandabbey.com

Fishing boats in Clovelly's harbour

Fishermen's cottages, Appledore

⑯ Appledore

Devon. 🚉 2,500. 🛈 Bideford (01237 477676).

Appledore's remote position at the tip of the Torridge Estuary has helped to preserve its charms intact. Busy boatyards line the long riverside quay, which is also the departure point for fishing trips and ferries to the sandy beaches of Braunton Burrows on the opposite shore. Timeworn Regency houses line the main street which runs parallel to the quay, and behind is a network of narrow cobbled lanes with 18th-century fishermen's cottages. Several shops retain their original bow-windows and sell an assortment of crafts, antiques and souvenirs.

Uphill from the quay is the **North Devon Maritime Museum**, with an exhibition on the experiences of Devon emigrants in Australia and displays explaining the work of local shipyards. The tiny **Victorian Schoolroom** which is affiliated to the museum, shows various documentary

videos on local trades such as fishing and shipbuilding.

🏛 **North Devon Maritime Museum**
Odun Rd. **Tel** 01237 422064.
Open May–Sep: daily; Apr, Oct: Mon–Fri. 🅿 ♿ ltd. 📷
🌐 **northdevonmaritimemuseum.co.uk**

⑰ Barnstaple

Devon. 🚉 33,000. 🚆 🚌 🛈 The Square (01271 375000). 🛒 Mon–Sat (Apr–Nov only).

Although Barnstaple is an important distribution centre for the whole region, its town centre remains calm due to the exclusion of traffic. The massive glass-roofed **Pannier Market** (1855) has stalls of organic food, much of it produced by farmers' wives to supplement their income. Nearby is **St Peter's Church** with its twisted broach spire, said to have been caused by a lightning strike which warped the timbers in 1810.

On the Strand is a wonderful arcade topped with a statue of Queen Anne, now the **Heritage Centre**. This was built as an exchange where merchants traded the contents of their cargo boats moored on the River Taw alongside. Nearby is the 15th-century bridge and the **Museum of Barnstaple and North Devon**, where displays cover local history and the 700-year-old pottery industry, as well as local wildlife, such as the otters. The 180-mile (290 km) Tarka Trail circuits around Barnstaple; 35 miles (56 km) of it can be cycled.

Environs
Just west of Barnstaple, **Braunton "Great Field"** covers over 120 ha (300 acres) and is a well-preserved relic of medieval open-field cultivation. Beyond lies

Statue of Queen Anne (1708)

Barnstaple's Pannier Market

Braunton Burrows, one of the most extensive wild-dune reserves in Britain. It is a must for plant enthusiasts who would like to spot sea kale, sea holly, sea lavender and horned poppies growing in their natural habitat. The sandy beaches and pounding waves at nearby Croyde and Woolacombe, are favourites among surfing enthusiasts, but there are also calmer areas of warm shallow water and rock pools.

Arlington Court and National Trust Carriage Museum, north of Barnstaple, has a collection of horse-drawn vehicles, model ships, magnificent perennial borders and a lake.

🏛 **Museum of Barnstaple and North Devon**
The Square. **Tel** 01271 346747.
Open Mon–Sat. **Closed** 24 Dec–1 Jan.
♿ ltd. 📷 🌐 **devonmuseums.net**

🏠 **Arlington Court and National Trust Carriage Museum**
Arlington. **Tel** 01271 850296.
Open Easter–Oct: daily. 🅿 ♿ limited. 💻 📷 **NT**

The village of Lynmouth

⑱ Lynton and Lynmouth

Devon. 🅰 2,000. 🚌 ℹ️ Town Hall, Lee Rd, Lynton (01598 752225).
🌐 lynton-lynmouth-tourism.co.uk

Situated at the point where the East and West Lyn rivers meet the sea, Lynmouth is a picturesque, though rather commercialized, fishing village. The pedestrianized main street, lined with shops selling seaside souvenirs, runs parallel to the Lyn, now a canal with high embankments to protect against flash floods. One flood devastated the town at the height of the holiday season in 1952. The scars caused by the flood, which was fuelled by heavy rain on Exmoor, are now overgrown by trees in the pretty **Glen Lyn Gorge**, which leads north out of the village. Lynmouth's sister town, Lynton, is a mainly Victorian village perched on the clifftop 130 m (427 ft) above, giving lovely views across the Bristol Channel to the Welsh coast. It can be reached from the harbour front by a cliff railway (open March to October), by road or by a steep path.

Environs
Lynmouth makes an excellent starting point for walks on Exmoor. There is a 2 mile (3 km) trail that leads south-east to tranquil **Watersmeet** *(see p255)*. On the western edge of Exmoor, **Combe Martin** *(see p254)* lies in a sheltered valley. On the main street, lined with Victorian villas, is the 18th-century Pack of Cards Inn, built by a gambler with 52 windows, for each card in the pack.

⑲ Exeter

Exeter is Devon's capital, a bustling and lively city with a great deal of character, despite the World War II bombing that destroyed much of its city centre. Built high on a plateau above the River Exe, the city is encircled by substantial sections of Roman and medieval wall, and the street plan has not changed much since the Romans first laid out what is now the High Street. Elsewhere the Cathedral Close forms a pleasant green, and there are cobbled streets and narrow alleys which invite leisurely exploration. For shoppers there is a wide selection of big stores and smaller speciality shops.

Exploring Exeter
The intimate green and the close surrounding Exeter's distinctive cathedral were the setting for Anthony Trollope's novel *He Knew He Was Right* (1869). Full of festive crowds listening to buskers in the summer, the close presents an array of architectural styles. One of the finest buildings here is the Elizabethan **Mol's Coffee House**. Among the other historic buildings that survived World War II are the magnificent **Guildhall** (1330) on the High Street (one of Britain's oldest civic buildings), the opulent **Custom House** (1681) by the quay, and the elegant 18th-century **Rougemont House** which stands near the remains of a Norman **castle** built by William the Conqueror *(see pp50–51)*.

The port area has been transformed into a tourist attraction with its early 19th-century warehouses converted into craft shops, antique galleries and cafés. Boats can be hired for cruising down the short stretch of canal. The **Quay House Visitor Centre**

The timber-framed Mol's Coffee House (1596), Cathedral Close

West front and south tower, Cathedral Church of St Peter

(www.exeter.gov.uk; open daily April–October; weekends November–March) has audio-visual and other displays on the history of Exeter.

🏛 Cathedral Church of St Peter
Cathedral Close. **Tel** 01392 255573. **Open** daily. 🏠 ♿ 🚫

Exeter's cathedral is one of the most gloriously ornamented in Britain. Except for the two Norman towers, the cathedral is mainly 14th century and built in the style aptly known as Decorated because of the swirling geometric patterns of the stone work. The West Front, the largest single collection (66) of medieval figure sculptures in England, includes kings, apostles and prophets. Started in the 14th century, it was completed by 1450. Inside, the splendid Gothic vaulting sweeps from one end of the church to the other, impressive in its uniformity and punctuated by gaily painted ceiling bosses.

Among the tombs around the choir is that of Edward II's treasurer, Walter de Stapledon (1261–1326), who was murdered by a mob in London. Stapledon raised much of the

Collection of shells and other objects in the library of A La Ronde

money needed to fund the building of this cathedral.

⬆ Underground Passages

Paris St. **Tel** 01392 665 887.
Open Jun–Sep: daily; Oct–May: Tue–Sun.

Under the city centre lie the remains of Exeter's medieval water-supply system. An excellent video and guided tour explain how the stone-lined tunnels were built in the 14th and 15th centuries on a slight gradient in order to bring in fresh water for townspeople from springs outside the town. Includes a heritage centre, which explains its history.

⬆ St Nicholas Priory

The Mint. **Tel** 01392 665858.
Open phone for details. limited.

Built in the 12th century, this building has retained many of its original features and rooms. These help visitors to trace its fascinating history from austere monastic beginnings, through its secular use as a Tudor residence for wealthy merchants, to its 20th-century incarnation as five separate business premises for various tradesmen including a bootmaker and an upholsterer.

🏛 Royal Albert Memorial Museum and Art Gallery

Queen St. **Tel** 01392 265858.
Open Tue–Sun.

This museum has a wonderfully varied collection, including Roman remains, a zoo of stuffed animals, West Country art and a particularly good ethnographic display. Highlights include displays on silverware, watches and clocks.

19th-century head of an Oba, Royal Albert Museum

Environs

South of Exeter on the A376, the eccentric **A La Ronde** is a 16-sided house built in 1796 by two spinster cousins, who decorated the interior with shells, feathers and souvenirs gathered while on tours of Europe.

Further east, the unspoilt Regency town of **Sidmouth** lies in a sheltered bay. There is an eclectic array of architecture, the earliest buildings dating from the 1820s when Sidmouth became a popular summer resort. Thatched cottages stand opposite huge Edwardian villas, and elegant terraces line the seafront. In summer the town hosts the famous International Festival of Folk Arts (see p67).

North of Sidmouth lies the magnificent church at **Ottery St**

Mary. Built in 1338–42 by Bishop Grandisson, the church is clearly a scaled-down version of Exeter Cathedral, which he also helped build. In the churchyard wall is a memorial to the poet Coleridge who was born in the town in 1772.

Nearby **Honiton** is famous for its extraordinarily intricate and delicate lace, made here since Elizabethan times.

To the north of Exeter, **Killerton** is home to the National Trust's costume collection. Here, displays of bustles and corsets and vivid tableaux illustrate aristocratic fashions from the 18th century to the present day.

Further north near Tiverton, is **Knightshayes Court**, a Victorian Gothic mansion with fine gardens (see p249).

🏠 A La Ronde

Summer Lane, Exmouth. **Tel** 01395 265514. **Open** Feb–Oct: daily; Nov–Jan: Sat & Sun. **Closed** 16 Dec–4 Jan.

🏠 Killerton

Broadclyst. **Tel** 01392 881345. House:
Open mid-Feb–Dec: daily. Garden:
Open daily.

🏠 Knightshayes Court

Bolham. **Tel** 01884 254665. **Open** mid-Feb–Oct: daily; Nov–22 Dec: Wed–Sun; 23–31 Dec: Thu–Tue. **Closed** 25 Dec. limited.

Mexican dancer at Sidmouth's International Festival of Folk Arts

⑳ Torbay

Torbay. 🚉 🚌 Torquay, Paignton. 𝒊 Vaughan Parade, Torquay (01803 211211). 🅦 englishriviera.co.uk

The seaside towns of Torquay, Paignton and Brixham form an almost continuous resort around the great sweep of sandy beach and blue waters of Torbay. Because of its mild climate, semi-tropical gardens and exuberant Victorian hotel architecture, this popular coastline has been dubbed the English Riviera. In the Victorian era Torbay was patronized by the wealthy. Today, the theme is mass entertainment, and there are plenty of attractions, mostly in and around Torquay.

Torre Abbey includes the remains of a monastery founded in 1196. The mansion dates back to the 17th century, and houses an art gallery and museum, though other rooms have been preserved as they were in the 1920s, when it was still a private residence.. **Torquay Museum** nearby covers natural history and archaeology, including finds from **Kents Cavern**, on the outskirts of the town. This is one of England's most important prehistoric sites, and the spectacular caves include displays on people and animals who lived here up to 350,000 years ago.

The charming miniature town of **Babbacombe Model Village** is north of Torquay, while a mile (1.5 km) inland is the lovely village of **Cockington**. Visitors travel by horse-drawn carriage to the preserved Tudor manor house, church and thatched cottages.

In Paignton, the celebrated **Paignton Zoo** teaches children about the planet's wildlife, and from here you can take the steam railway – an ideal way to visit Dartmouth.

Continuing south from Paignton, the pretty town of Brixham was once England's most prosperous fishing port.

🏛 **Torre Abbey**
King's Drive, Torquay. **Tel** 01803 293593. **Open** Mar–Dec: Wed–Sun. **Closed** 25 Dec. 🐾 🖼 🛗 🛒 📷

Bayards Cove, Dartmouth

🏛 **Torquay Museum**
Babbacombe Rd, Torquay. **Tel** 01803 293975. **Open** daily (Nov–Easter: Mon–Sat). **Closed** Christmas wk. 🐾 🛗 🖥 📷 🅦 torquaymuseum.org

🕳 **Kents Cavern**
Ilsham Rd, Torquay. **Tel** 01803 215 136. **Open** daily. **Closed** 25 & 26 Dec. 🐾 📷 🚫 🖥 🅦 kents-cavern.co.uk

🏛 **Babbacombe Model Village**
Hampton Ave, Torquay. **Tel** 01803 315 315. **Open** daily. **Closed** 25 Dec. 🐾 🛗 🖥

🐾 **Paignton Zoo**
Totnes Rd, Paignton. **Tel** 0844 474 2222. **Open** daily. **Closed** 25 Dec. 🐾 🛗 🚫 📷 🅦 paingtonzoo.org.uk

㉑ Dartmouth

Devon. 👥 5,500. 🚌 𝒊 Mayors Ave (01803 834224). 🛍 Tue & Fri am. 🅦 discoverdartmouth.com

Sitting high on the hill above the River Dart is the **Royal Naval College**, where British naval officers have trained since 1905. Dartmouth has always been an important port and it was from here that English fleets set sail to join the Second and Third Crusades. Some 18th-century houses adorn the cobbled quay of Bayards Cove, while carved timber buildings line the 17th-century Butterwalk, home to **Dartmouth Museum**. To the south is **Dartmouth Castle** (1388).

🏛 **Dartmouth Museum**
Butterwalk. **Tel** 01803 832923. **Open** daily. **Closed** 1 Jan, 25 & 26 Dec. 🐾 📷 🅦 devonmuseums.net

🕳 **Dartmouth Castle**
Castle Rd. **Tel** 01803 833588. **Open** daily (Nov–Easter: Sat & Sun). **Closed** 1 Jan, 24–26 Dec. 🐾 📷 🇪🇭

Torquay, on the "English Riviera"

Stained-glass window in Blessed Sacrament Chapel, Buckfast Abbey

㉒ Totnes

Devon. 🏔 7,500. 🚌🚲🚃🚉 ℹ
Town Mill (01803 863168). 🛍 Tue am
(May–Sep), Fri, Sat.
W totnesinformation.co.uk

Totnes sits at the highest
navigable point on the River
Dart with a Norman **castle**
perched high on the hill above.
Linking the two is the steep
High Street, lined with bow-
windowed Elizabethan houses.
Bridging the street is the
Eastgate, part of the medieval
town wall. Life in the town's
heyday is explored in the
Totnes Elizabethan Museum,
which also has a room devoted
to the mathematician Charles
Babbage (1791–1871), who is
regarded as the pioneer
of modern computers. There
is a **Guildhall**, and a
church with a delicately
carved and gilded
rood screen. On
Tuesdays in the
summer, market
stallholders dress in
Elizabethan costume.

Environs
A few miles north of
Totnes, **Dartington
Hall** has 10 ha (25 acres)
of lovely gardens and
hosts a music school
every August, when concerts
are held in the timbered
14th-century Great Hall.

Stallholders in
Totnes market

🏰 **Totnes Castle**
Castle St. **Tel** 01803 864406.
Open Apr–Oct: daily; Nov–Mar: Sat &
Sun. 🅿 EH

🏛 **Totnes Elizabethan
Museum**
Fore St. **Tel** 01803 863821.
Open Easter–Oct: Mon–Fri. 🅿
👤 limited.

🏛 **Guildhall**
Rampart Walk. **Tel** 01803 862147.
Open Apr–Oct: Mon–Fri. 🅿

🌳 **Dartington Hall Gardens**
Tel 01803 862367. **Open** daily.
W dartington.org

㉓ Buckfastleigh

Devon. 🏔 3,300. 🚌 ℹ Fore St
(01364 644522).

This market town, situated on
the edge of Dartmoor (see
pp298–9), is dominated by
Buckfast Abbey. The
original abbey, founded
in Norman times, fell
into ruin after the
Dissolution of the
Monasteries and it
was not until 1882
that a small group of
French Benedictine
monks set up a new
abbey here. Work on
the present building
was financed by
donations and carried
out by the monks. The abbey
was completed in 1938 and lies
at the heart of a thriving
community. The fine mosaics
and modern stained-glass
window are also the work of
the monks.

Nearby is the **Buckfast
Butterfly Farm and Otter
Sanctuary**, and the **South Devon
Steam Railway** terminus where
steam trains leave for Totnes.

🏰 **Buckfast Abbey**
Buckfastleigh. **Tel** 01364 645500.
Open daily. **Closed** Good Fri, 25–27
Dec. 👤 🅿 📷 W buckfast.org.uk

🦋 **Buckfast Butterfly Farm and
Otter Sanctuary**
Buckfastleigh. **Tel** 01364 642916.
Open Easter–Nov: daily. 🅿 👤
W ottersandbutterflies.co.uk

㉔ Burgh Island

Devon. 🚉 Plymouth, then taxi. ℹ
The Quay, Kingsbridge (01548 853
195). W kingsbridgeinfo.co.uk

The short walk across the sands
at low tide from Bigbury-on-
Sea to Burgh Island takes you
back to the era of the 1920s
and 1930s. It was here that the
millionaire Archibald Nettlefold
built the luxury **Burgh Island**
hotel (see p566) in 1929.
Created in Art Deco style with a
natural rock sea-bathing pool,
this was the exclusive retreat of
figures such as the Duke of
Windsor and Noel Coward. The
restored hotel is worth a visit
for the photographs of its
heyday and the Art Deco
fittings. You can also explore
the island and **Pilchard Inn**
(1336), reputed to be haunted
by the ghost of a smuggler.

The Art Deco style bar in Burgh
Island Hotel

㉕ Plymouth

Plymouth. ☒ 250,000. ✈ ⛴ 🚌 🚆
ℹ The Mayflower, The Barbican
(01752 306330). 🅿 Mon–Sat.
🌐 visitplymouth.co.uk

The tiny port from which Drake,
Raleigh, the Pilgrim Fathers,
Cook and Darwin all set sail on
pioneering voyages has now
grown to a substantial city,
much of it boldly rebuilt after
wartime bombing.
Old Plymouth clusters
around the **Hoe**, the
famous patch of turf
on which Sir Francis
Drake is said to have
calmly finished his
game of bowls as the
Spanish Armada
approached the port
in 1588 (see pp54–5).

Drake's coat of arms

Today the Hoe is a pleasant park
and parade ground surrounded
by memorials to naval men,
including Drake himself.
Alongside Charles II's **Royal
Citadel**, built to guard the
harbour in the 1660s. On the
harbour is the **National Marine
Aquarium**. Nearby is the
Mayflower Stone and Steps,
the spot where the Pilgrim
Fathers set sail for the New
World in England's third and
successful attempt at
colonization in 1620. The
popular **Plymouth Mayflower
Exhibition** explores the story of
the Mayflower and the creation
of the harbour. Interactive
graphics are used to tell the
tales of merchant families and
emigration to the
New World.

Environs: A boat
tour of the harbour
is the best way to
see the dockyards
where warships
have been built
since the
Napoleonic Wars.
There are also
splendid views of various fine
gardens, such as **Mount
Edgcumbe Park** (see p248),
scattered around the coastline.
East of the city, the 18th-century
Saltram House has two rooms
by Adam (see pp32–3) and
portraits by Reynolds, who was
born in nearby Plympton.

Mid-18th-century carved wood
chimneypiece, Saltram House

🏛 **Royal Citadel**
The Hoe. **Open** May–Sep: Tue & Thu.
🕐 only. 👥 EH
🌐 english heritage.org.uk

🐟 **National Marine Aquarium**
Rope Walk, Coxside. **Tel** 08448 937938.
Open daily. **Closed** 25 Dec. 👥 ♿ ☐
🌐 national-aquarium.co.uk

🏛 **Plymouth Mayflower
Exhibition**
3–5 The Barbican. **Tel** 01752 306 331.
Open daily (Nov–Apr: Mon–Sat).

🏠 **Mount Edgcumbe Park**
Cremyll, Torpoint. 🚌 from
Torpoint car park. **Tel** 01752 822236.
House: **Open** Apr–Sep: Sun–Thu.
Grounds: **Open** all year. 👥 🕐 ♿
☐ 🏠 ⁄⁄
🌐 mountedgcumbe.gov.uk

🏛 **Saltram House**
Plympton. **Tel** 01752 333500. Gallery:
Open mid-Mar–Oct: Sat–Thu; mid-
Feb–mid-Mar: Sat & Sun. Gardens:
Open all year. 👥 ♿ ⁄⁄ ☐ 🏠 NT

㉖ Buckland Abbey

Yelverton, Devon. **Tel** 01822 853607.
🚌 from Yelverton. **Open** mid-Feb–
Oct & 6–22 Dec: daily; Nov: Fri–Sun.
Closed 25 Dec–mid-Feb. 👥 ♿ ⁄⁄
🏠 NT 🌐 nationaltrust.org.uk

Founded by the Cistercian
monks in 1278, Buckland
Abbey was converted to a
house after the Dissolution
of the Monasteries and
became the home of Drake
from 1581–96. Many of the
monastic buildings survive
in a garden setting, notably
the 14th-century tithe barn
(see p32). Drake's life is explained
through paintings and
memorabilia in the house.

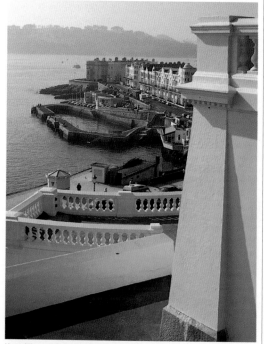

View of Plymouth Harbour from the Hoe

㉗ Cotehele

St Dominick, Cornwall. **Tel** 01579
351346. �" Calstock. House
Open mid-Mar–Oct: Sat–Thu & Good
Fri. Grounds: **Open** daily. 🔲 🚻
♿ limited. 🅽🆃 ⬚ ▭

Magnificent woodland and
lush river scenery make
Cotehele (pronounced Coteal)
one of the most delightful
spots on the River Tamar and a
rewarding day can be spent
exploring the estate. Far from
civilization, tucked into its
wooded fold in the Cornish
countryside, Cotehele has
slumbered for 500 years. The
main attraction is the house
and valley garden at its centre.
Built mainly between 1489 and
1520, it is a rare example of a
medieval house, set around
three courtyards with a
magnificent open hall, kitchen,
chapel and a warren of private
parlours and chambers. The
romance of the house is enhanced by colourful terraced
gardens to the east, leading via
a tunnel into a richly planted
valley garden. The path
through this garden passes a
large domed medieval
dovecote and descends to a
quay, to which lime and coal
were once shipped. There are
fine views up and down the
winding reed-fringed Tamar
from Prospect Tower, and a
gallery on the quayside
specializes in local arts and
crafts. The estate includes a
village, a quay with a small
maritime museum, working
mill buildings, ancient lime
kilns and workshops with
19th-century equipment.

Medieval dovecote in the gardens
of Cotehele estate

Spanish Armada and British fleets in the English Channel, 1588

Sir Francis Drake

Sir Francis Drake (c.1540–1596) was the first Englishman to
circumnavigate the globe and he was knighted by Elizabeth I in 1580.
Four years later he introduced tobacco and potatoes to England, after
bringing home 190 colonists who had tried to establish a settlement
in Virginia. To many, however, Drake was no more than an
opportunistic rogue, renowned for his exploits as a "privateer", the
polite name for a pirate. Catholic Spain was the bitter enemy and
Drake further endeared himself to queen and people by his part in
the victory over Philip II's Armada (see pp54–5), defeated by bad
weather and the buccaneering spirit of the English.

㉘ Morwellham Quay

Near Tavistock, Devon. **Tel** 01822
832766. �" Gunnislake. **Open** daily.
Closed 1 Jan, 24–26 Dec. 🔲 🚻 ♿
limited. ⬚ ▭
🆆 morwellham-quay.co.uk

Morwellham Quay was a
neglected and overgrown
industrial site until 1970, when
members of a local trust began
restoring the abandoned
cottages, schoolhouse, farmyards,
quay and copper mines to their
original condition.

Today, Morwellham Quay is a
thriving and rewarding
industrial museum, where you
can easily spend a whole day
partaking in the typical activities
of a Victorian village, from
preparing the shire horses for a
day's work, to riding a tramway
deep into a copper mine in the
hillside behind the village. The
museum is brought to life by
characters in costumes, some of
whom give demonstrations
throughout the day. You can
watch, or lend a hand to the
cooper while he builds a barrel,

Industrial relics at Morwellham Quay
in the Tamar Valley

attend a lesson in the
schoolroom, take part in
Victorian playground games
or dress up in 19th-century
hooped skirts, bonnets, top
hats or jackets. The staff, who
convincingly play the part of
villagers, lead you through
their lives and impart a huge
amount of information about
the history of this small coppermining community.

㉘ Dartmoor National Park

The high, open moorland of central Dartmoor provides the eerie background for Conan Doyle's thriller, *The Hound of the Baskervilles* (1902). Here at Princetown, surrounded by weathered outcrops of granite tors is one of Britain's most famous prisons. Also dotting the landscape are scores of prehistoric remains which have survived because of the durability of granite. Elsewhere the mood is very different. Streams tumble through wooded and boulder-strewn ravines forming cascades and waterfalls, and thatched cottages nestle in the sheltered valleys around the margins of the moor. Many establishments offer cream teas and warming fires to weary walkers.

Brentor
This volcanic hill crowned by a tiny church (first built in 1130) is visible for miles.

Postbridge
Dartmoor's northern moor can be explored from the village of Postbridge. The gently rolling moorland is crossed by many dry-stone walls.

KEY

① **High Moorland Visitor Centre**

② **The Ministry of Defence** uses much of this area for training but access is available on non-firing days (0800 458 4868 to check).

③ **Lydford Gorge** (open Apr–Oct) is a dramatic ravine; leading to a waterfall.

④ **Okehampton** has the Museum of Dartmoor Life and a ruined 14th-century castle.

⑤ **Castle Drogo** is a magnificent mock-castle built by the architect Sir Edwin Lutyens (see p33) in 1910–30.

⑥ **Grimspound** is the impressive remains of a Bronze Age settlement.

⑦ **Dartmeet** marks the lovely confluence point of the East and West Dart rivers.

⑧ **Becky Falls** is a 22-m (72-ft) waterfall set in delightful woodlands.

⑨ **Haytor Rocks** is one of the most popular of the many tors.

⑩ **Bovey Tracey** has an extensive woodland reserve.

⑪ **Buckfast Abbey** was founded by King Canute (see p163) in 1018.

⑫ **Dartmoor Butterfly and Otter Sanctuary**

⑬ **South Devon Steam Railway**

Dartmoor Ponies
These small, tough ponies have lived on the moor since at least the 10th century.

VISITORS' CHECKLIST

Practical Information
Devon.
i Dartmoor National Park Authority's Centre (01822 890 414). **w** dartmoor-npa.gov.uk
Okehampton Castle, Castle Lane, Okehampton: **Tel** 01837 52844. **Open** Apr–Oct daily.
⚑ EH
Museum of Dartmoor Life, West St, Okehampton: **Tel** 01837 52295. **Open** Apr–mid-Dec: Mon–Sat. **Closed** 24 Dec–1 Jan
⚑ *♿* limited.
Castle Drogo, Drewsteignton: **Tel** 01647 433 306. **Open** mid-Feb–Oct: daily. Gardens: **Open** daily. *⚑* *♿* gardens only. *⚑*
▯ *📷* NT

Transport
≷ *🚌* Exeter, Plymouth, Totnes then bus.

Hound Tor
Nearby lie the remains of a Medieval settlement abandoned in the 14th century.

Buckland-in-the-Moor
One of the many picturesque villages on Dartmoor.

0 kilometres 5
0 miles 5

Key

━━━ A road
══ B road
═══ Minor road

For map symbols see back flap

THE MIDLANDS

The Midlands at a Glance

The Midlands is an area that embraces wonderful landscapes and massive industrial cities. Visitors come to discover the wild beauty of the rugged Peaks, cruise slowly along the Midlands canals on gaily painted narrowboats and explore varied and enchanting gardens. The area encompasses the full range of English architecture from mighty cathedrals and humble churches to charming spa towns, stately homes and country cottages. There are fascinating industrial museums, many in picturesque settings.

Locator Map

Tissington Trail *(see p341)* combines a walk through scenic Peak District countryside with an entertaining insight into the ancient custom of well dressing.

Ironbridge Gorge *(see pp318–19)* was the birthplace of the Industrial Revolution *(see pp352–3)*. Now a World Heritage Site, it is a reminder of the lovely countryside in which the original factories were located.

The Cotswolds *(see pp308–9)* are full of delightful houses built from local limestone, on the profits of the medieval wool trade. Snowshill Manor (above) is situated near the unspoilt village of Broadway.

Warrington

Chester

CHESHIRE

Crewe

Stoke-on-Trent

STAFFORD-SHIRE

SHROPSHIRE

Shrewsbury

Telford

Wolverhampt

THE HEART
OF ENGLAND
(See pp310–333)

Birmingham

Ludlow

WORCESTER-SHIRE

Leominster

Stratforc
Upon-Avo

HEREFORD-SHIRE

Worcester

Hereford

Tewkesbury

Ross-on-Wye

Cheltenham

Gloucester

GLOUCESTER-SHIRE

Cirencester

Stratford-upon-Avon *(see pp328–31)* has many picturesque houses connected with William Shakespeare's life, some of which are open to visitors. These black-and-white timber-framed buildings, such as Anne Hathaway's house (left), are typical examples of Tudor architecture *(see pp306–7)*.

◀ Panoramic view of Edale in the Peak District National Park

Chatsworth House *(see pp338–9)*, a magnificent Baroque edifice, is famous for its gorgeous garden. The "Conservative Wall", a greenhouse for exotic plants, is pictured right.

Worksop

Chesterfield

NOTTINGHAM-SHIRE

Mansfield

Lincoln

LINCOLNSHIRE

Newark-on-Trent

Boston

RBY-HIRE

Derby

Nottingham

EAST MIDLANDS
(See pp334–347)

Loughborough

LEICESTERSHIRE

Stamford

Leicester

Corby

Coventry

NORTHAMPTON-SHIRE

RWICK-HIRE

Warwick

Northampton

Lincoln Cathedral *(see p345)*, a vast, imposing building, dominates the ancient town. Inside are splendid misericords and the superb 13th-century Angel Choir, which has 30 carved angels.

Burghley House *(see pp346–7)* is a dazzling landmark for miles around in the flat East Midlands landscape, with architectural motifs from the European Renaissance.

0 kilometres   25

0 miles   25

Warwick Castle *(see pp326–7)* is an intriguing mixture of medieval power base and country house, complete with massive towers, battlements, a dungeon and state rooms, such as the Queen Anne Bedroom (left).

Canals of the Midlands

One of England's first canals opened in 1761, built in the northwest by the 3rd Duke of Bridgewater to link the coal mine on his Worsley estate with Manchester's textile factories. This heralded the start of a canal-building boom and by 1805, a 3,000 mile (4,800 km) network of waterways had been dug across the country, linking into the natural river system. Canals provided the cheapest, fastest way of transporting goods, until competition began to arrive from the railways in the 1840s. Cargo transport ended in 1963 but today nearly 2,000 miles (3,200 km) of canals are still navigable, for travellers who wish to take a leisurely cruise on a narrowboat.

The Grand Union Canal (pictured in 1931) is 300 miles (485 km) long and was dug in the 1790s to link London with the Midlands.

Lock-keepers were provided with canalside houses.

Lockside inns cater for narrowboats.

The Farmer's Bridge is a flight of 13 locks in Birmingham. Locks are used to raise or lower boats from one level of the canal to another. The steeper the gradient, the more locks are needed.

Heavy V-shaped timber gates close off the lock.

Water pressing against the gate keeps it shut.

The towpath is where horses pulled the canal boats before engines were invented. They were changed periodically for fresh animals.

Narrowboats have straight sides and flat bottoms and are pointed at both ends. Cargo space took up most of the boat, with a small cabin for the crew. Exteriors were brightly painted.

Midlands Canal Network

The industrial Midlands was the birthplace of the English canal system and still has the biggest concentration of navigable waterways.

0 kilometres 50

0 miles 50

Chester

Trent & Mersey

Macclesfield

Shropshire Union

Severn

Lincoln

Trent

Witham

Nottingham

The Wash

Wolverhampton

Staffordshire & Worcester

Birmingham

Welland

Stamford

Nene

Worcester

Grand Union

Worcester & Birmingham

London

Key

■ Canal
■ River

VISITORS' CHECKLIST

Practical Information
Canal boat holidays: Blake's Holidays/Hoseasons **Tel** 0844 847 1356; Canal Cruising Co **Tel** 01785 813982 (office hours only); Black Prince Holidays **Tel** 01527 575115; ABC Leisure Group Ltd **Tel** 0330 333 0595. Canal museums (phone to check opening times): Gloucester Waterways Museum (01452 318200; see p333); The Canal Museum, Stoke Bruerne **Tel** 01604 862229; National Waterways Museum, Ellesmere Port. **Tel** 0151 3555017.
w canalrivertrust.org.uk

Canal

Footbridge

A windlass fills or lowers water levels.

A balance beam swings the gates open.

Canal Locks

Canals used tunnels, embankments and locks for the speedy transportation of goods across country. Locks were used to convey boats up or down hills.

The Edstone Aqueduct, just north of Stratford-upon-Avon, carries the canal in a cast iron trough. This is supported on brick piers for 180 m (495 ft), over roads and a busy railway line.

Canal Art

Canal boat cabins are very small and every inch of space is utilized to make a comfortable home for the occupants. Interiors were enlivened with colourful paintings and attractive decorations.

Furniture was designed to be functional and to brighten up the cramped cabin.

Narrowboats are often decorated with ornamental brass.

Water cans were also painted. The most common designs were roses and castles, with local variations in style.

Tudor Manor Houses

Many striking manor houses were built in central England during the Tudor Age *(see pp54–5)*, a time of relative peace and prosperity. The abolition of the monasteries meant that vast estates were broken up and sold to secular landowners, who built houses to reflect their new status *(see p32)*. In the Midlands, wood was the main building material, and the gentry flaunted their wealth by using timber panelling for flamboyant decorative effect.

The decorative moulding on the south wing dates from the late 16th century. Ancient motifs, such as vines and trefoils, are combined with the latest imported Italian Renaissance styles.

The rectangular moat was for decoration rather than defence. It surrounds a recreated knot garden *(see p30)* that was laid out in 1972 using plants known to have been available in Tudor times.

The Long Gallery was one of the last parts to be built (c.1560–62). It has original plasterwork portraying *Destiny* (left) and *Fortune*.

Jetties (overhanging upper stories)

Brickwork chimney

Tudor Mansions and Tudor Revival

There are many sumptuously decorated Tudor mansions in the Midlands. In the 19th century Tudor Revival architecture became a very popular "Old English" style, intended to invoke family pride and values rooted in the past.

Hardwick Hall in Derbyshire, whose huge kitchen is pictured, is one of the finest Tudor mansions in the country. These buildings are known as "prodigy" houses *(see p346)* due to their gigantic size.

Charlecote Park, Warwickshire, is a brick mansion built by Sir Thomas Lucy in 1551–59. It was heavily restored in Tudor style in the 19th century, but has a fine original gatehouse. According to legend, the young William Shakespeare *(see pp328–31)* was caught poaching deer in the park.

Entrance

The Little Parlour was an informal reception room. The biblical scene of *Susannah and the Elders (right)* expressed religious faith and learning.

The Great Hall (c.1504–08) is the oldest part of the house, and in Tudor times was the most important. The open-plan hall was the main communal area for dining and entertainment.

Wood panelling

Courtyard

Little Moreton Hall

The Moreton family home *(see p315)* was built between 1504 and 1610, from a number of box-shapes, fitted together. Wood panelling and jetties displayed the family's wealth.

The patterned glazing in the great bay window is typically 16th century: small pieces of locally made glass were cut into various shapes and held in place by lead glazing bars.

Packwood House in Warwickshire is a timber-framed mid-Tudor house with extensive 17th-century additions. The unusual garden of clipped yew trees dates from the 17th century and is supposed to represent the Sermon on the Mount.

Wightwick Manor, West Midlands, was built in 1887–93. It is a fine example of Tudor Revival architecture and has superb late 19th-century furniture and decorations.

Moseley Old Hall, Staffordshire, has a red brick exterior concealing its early 17th-century timber frame. The King's Room is where Charles II hid after the Battle of Worcester *(see pp56–7)*.

Building with Cotswold Stone

The Cotswolds are a range of limestone hills running over 50 miles (80 km) in a north-easterly direction from Bath *(see pp262–65)*. The thin soils are difficult to plough but ideal for grazing sheep, and the wealth engendered by the medieval wool trade was poured into building majestic churches and opulent town houses. Stone quarried from these hills was used to build London's St Paul's Cathedral *(see pp118–19)*, as well as the villages, barns and manor houses that make the landscape so picturesque.

Arlington Row Cottages in Bibury, a typical Cotswold village, were built in the 17th century for weavers whose looms were set up in the attics.

Windows were taxed and glass expensive. Workers' cottages had only a few, not very large windows made of small panes of glass.

A drip mould keeps rain off the chimney.

The roof is steeply pitched to carry the weight of the tiles. These were made by master craftsmen who could split blocks of stone into sheets by using natural fault lines.

Cotswold Stone Cottage

The two-storey Arlington Row Cottages are asymmetrical and built of odd-shaped stones. Small windows and doorways make them quite dark inside.

Timber lintels and doors

Timber framing was cheaper than stone, and was used for the upper rooms in the roof.

Variations in Stone

Cotswold stone is warmer-toned in the north, pearly in central areas and light grey in the south. The stone seems to glow with absorbed sunlight. It is a soft stone that is easily carved and can be used for many purposes, from buildings to bridges, headstones and gargoyles.

"Tiddles" is a cat's gravestone in Fairford churchyard.

Lower Slaughter gets its name from the Anglo-Saxon word *slough*, or muddy place. It has a low stone bridge, over the River Eye.

Cotswold Stone Towns and Villages

The villages and towns on this map are prime examples of places built almost entirely from stone. By the 12th century almost all of the villages in the area were established. Huge deposits of limestone resulted in a wealth of stone buildings. Masons worked from distinctive local designs that were handed down from generation to generation.

① Winchcombe
② Broadway
③ Stow-on-the-Wold
④ Upper and Lower Slaughter
⑤ Bourton-on-the-Water
⑥ Sherborne
⑦ Northleach
⑧ Painswick
⑨ Bibury
⑩ Fairford

Wool merchants' houses were built of fine ashlar (dressed stone) with ornamental cornerstones, doorframes and windows.

The eaves here have a dentil frieze, so-called because it resembles a row of teeth.

The door frame has a rounded pediment on simple pilasters.

Stone Gargoyles

In Winchcombe's church, 15th-century gargoyles reflect a combination of pagan and Christian beliefs.

Pagan gods warded off pre-Christian evil spirits.

Fertility figures, always important in rural areas, were incorporated into Christian festivals.

Human faces often caricatured local church dignitaries.

Animal gods represented qualities such as strength in pagan times.

Cotswold Stone House

This early Georgian merchant's house in Painswick shows the fully developed Cotswold style, which borrows decorative elements from Classical architecture.

Dry-stone walling is an ancient technique used in the Cotswolds. The stones are held in place without mortar.

A stone cross (16th century) in Stanton village, near Broadway, is one of many found in the Cotswolds.

Table-top and "tea caddy", fine 18th-century tombs, can be found in Painswick churchyard.

THE HEART OF ENGLAND

Cheshire · Gloucestershire · Herefordshire · Shropshire · Staffordshire · Warwickshire · Worcestershire

Britain's great attraction is its variety, and nowhere is this more true than at the heart of the country, where the Cotswold hills, enfolding stone cottages and churches, give way to the flat, fertile plains of Warwickshire. Shakespeare Country borders on the industrial heart of England, once known as the workshop of the world.

Coventry, Birmingham, the Potteries and their hinterlands have been manufacturing iron, textiles and ceramics since the 18th century. In the 20th century these industries have declined, and a new type of museum has developed to commemorate the towns' industrial heyday and explain the manufacturing processes which were once taken for granted. Ironbridge Gorge and Quarry Bank Mill, Styal, where the factories are now living museums, are fascinating industrial sites and enjoy beautiful surroundings.

These landscapes may be appreciated from the deck of a narrowboat, making gentle progress along the Midlands canals, to the region on the border with Wales known as the Marches. Here the massive walls of Chester and the castles at Shrewsbury and Ludlow recall the Welsh locked in fierce battle with Norman barons and the Marcher Lords. The Marches are now full of rural communities served by the peaceful market towns of Leominster, Malvern, Ross-on-Wye and Hereford. The cities of Worcester and Gloucester both have modern shopping centres, yet their majestic cathedrals retain the tranquillity of an earlier age.

Cheltenham has Regency terraces, Cirencester a rich legacy of Roman art and Tewkesbury a solid Norman abbey. Finally, there is Stratford-upon-Avon, where William Shakespeare, the Elizabethan dramatist, lived and died.

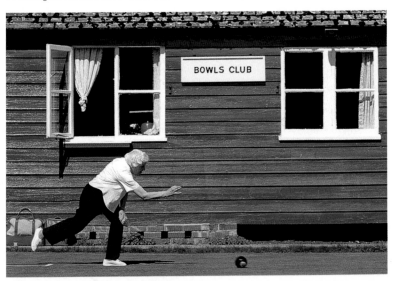

Leisurely village pastimes, reminiscent of a more tranquil age

◄ Gardens behind the house of Mary Arden, Shakespeare's mother

Exploring the Heart of England

The heart of England, more than any other region, takes its character from the landscape. Picturesque houses, pubs and churches, made from timber and Cotswold stone, create an idyllic and peaceful setting that visitors love to explore. The area around Birmingham and Stoke-on-Trent, however – once the industrial hub of England – contrasts sharply. The bleak concrete skyline may not appeal, but the area has a fascinating history that is reflected in the self-confident Victorian art and architecture, and a series of award-winning industrial heritage museums.

Arlington Row: stone cottages in the Cotswold village of Bibury

Sights at a Glance

1. Quarry Bank Mill, Styal
2. Chester
3. Stoke-on-Trent
4. Shrewsbury
5. *Ironbridge pp318–19*
6. Ludlow
7. Leominster
8. Hereford
9. Ross-on-Wye
10. Ledbury
11. Great Malvern
12. Worcester
13. Birmingham
14. Coventry
16. *Warwick pp325–7*
17. *Stratford-upon-Avon pp328–31*
18. Chipping Campden
19. Tewkesbury
20. Cheltenham
21. Gloucester
22. Cirencester

Walks and Tours

15. Midlands Garden Tour

For additional map symbols *see back flap*

Getting Around

The Heart of England is easily reached by train, with mainline rail services to Cheltenham, Worcester, Birmingham, and Coventry. The M5 and M6 motorways are the major road routes but are frequently congested. Long-distance buses provide regular shuttle services to Cheltenham and Birmingham. Travelling within the region is best done by car. Rural roads are delightfully empty, although major attractions, such as Stratford-upon-Avon, may be very crowded during the summer.

0 kilometres 10

0 miles 10

View of the Wye Valley, at Symonds Yat

1 QUARRY BANK MILL
Wilmslow
Macclesfield
Congleton
Hartington
*Little
Moreton Hall*
Leek
Crewe
Tunstall
Newcastle-
under-Lyme
3 STOKE-ON-TRENT
Upper Tean
Stone
Uttoxeter
Weston
Tutbury
Derby
Woodseaves
Stafford
Burton upon
Trent
Rugeley
Nottingham
Penkridge
Cannock
Lichfield
Telford
RONBRIDGE
Brownhills
Tamworth
Wolverhampton
Walsall
Leicester
Bridgnorth
West
Bromwich
Sutton Coldfield
Nuneaton
Dudley
Wolvey
Stourbridge
13 BIRMINGHAM
Northampton
Longbridge
Bournville
14 COVENTRY
Rugby
Knowle
Alvechurch
Redditch
Droitwich
Studley
16 WARWICK
Royal
Leamington Spa
Alcester
12 WORCESTER
17 STRATFORD-UPON-AVON
GREAT
ALVERN
Evesham
15
Halford
Oxford
11
Upton
upon Severn
18 CHIPPING CAMPDEN
LEDBURY
Broadway
TEWKESBURY **19**
Winchcombe
Stow-on-
the-Wold
Huntley
20 CHELTENHAM
21 GLOUCESTER
Oxford
Northleach
Stroud
Bibury
Horsley
22 CIRENCESTER
Tetbury
Swindon
Bristol
Bath

Key

▬ Motorway

▬ Major road

▬ Secondary road

▪▪▪ Minor road

▬ Scenic route

➤ Main railway

— Minor railway

Reader's House, Ludlow, opposite
St Laurence's Church

Quarry Bank Mill, a working reminder of the Industrial Revolution

❶ Quarry Bank Mill, Styal

Cheshire. **Tel** 01625 527468. 🚋 Manchester Airport or Wilmslow, then bus. **Open** Mar–Oct: daily; Nov–Feb: Wed–Sun (gardens closed in winter). **Closed** 24 & 25 Dec. 🅿️ 👌 limited. 🔗 📷 NT 🌐 **nationaltrust.org.uk**

The history of the Industrial Revolution (see pp58–9) is brought vividly to life at Quarry Bank Mill, an early factory now transformed into a museum and private garden. Here, mill master Samuel Greg first used the waters of the Bollin Valley in 1784 to power the water frame, a machine for spinning raw cotton fibres into thread. By the 1840s, the Greg cotton empire was one of the biggest in Britain, and the mill produced bolts of material to be exported all over the world.

Today the massive old mill buildings have been restored to house a living museum of the cotton industry. This dominated the Manchester area for nearly 200 years, but was finally destroyed by foreign competition. The entire process, from the spinning and weaving to the bleaching, printing and dyeing, is shown through a series of reconstructions, demonstrations and hands-on displays. The weaving shed is full of clattering looms producing textiles. There are fascinating contraptions that demonstrate how water can be used to drive machinery, including an enormous wheel, 50 tons in weight and 7 m (24 ft) high, that is still used to power the looms.

The Greg family realized the importance of having a healthy, loyal and stable work-force. A social history exhibition explains how the mill workers were housed in the purpose-built village of Styal, in spacious cottages which had vegetable gardens and toilets. Details of their wages, working conditions and medical facilities are displayed on information boards.

There are costumed guided tours of the nearby **Apprentice House**. Local orphans lived here, and were sent to work up to 12 hours a day at the mill when they were just six or seven years old. Visitors can try the beds in the house and even sample the medicine they were given. Quarry Bank Mill is surrounded by over 115 ha (284 acres) of woodland.

❷ Chester

Cheshire. 🗺 120,000. 🚋 🚌 ℹ️
Town Hall, Northgate St (0845 6477868). 🚪 Mon–Sat.
🌐 **visitchester.com**

First settled by the Romans (see pp48–9), who established a camp in AD 79 to defend fertile land near the River Dee, the main streets of Chester are now lined with timber buildings. These are the **Chester Rows**, which, with their two tiers of shops and continuous upper gallery, anticipate today's multistorey shops by several centuries.

Although their oriel windows and decorative timber-work are mostly 19th century, the Rows were first built in the 13th and 14th centuries, and some of the original buildings are still standing. The façade of the 16th-century **Bishop Lloyd's House** in Watergate Street is the most richly carved in Chester. The Rows are at their most varied and attractive where Eastgate Street meets Bridge Street. Here, views of the cathedral and the town walls give the impression of a perfectly preserved medieval city. This illusion is helped by the Town Crier, who calls the hour and announces news in summer from the Cross, a reconstruction of the 15th-century stone crucifix that was destroyed in the Civil War (see pp56–7).

Chester's 1897 clocktower

The **Grosvenor Museum,** south of the Cross, explains the town's history. To the north is the **cathedral**. The choir stalls have splendid misericords

Examples of the intricate carving on Bishop Lloyd's House, a Tudor building in Watergate Street, Chester

The Chester Rows, where shops line the first-floor galleries

(see p345), with scenes including a quarrelling couple. In sharp contrast are the delicate spire-lets on the stall canopies. The cathedral is surrounded on two sides by the **city walls**, originally Roman but rebuilt at intervals. The best stretch is from the cathedral to Eastgate, where a wrought-iron **clock** was erected in 1899. The route to Newgate leads to a **Roman amphitheatre** built in AD 100.

🏛 **Grosvenor Museum**
Grosvenor St. **Tel** 01244 972197. **Open** Mon–Sat, Sun pm. **Closed** 1 Jan, Good Fri, 25 & 26 Dec. 🏛 🖧 limited.
W visitchester.com

🏛 **Roman Amphitheatre**
Little St John St. **Tel** 01244 402009. **Open** daily.

❸ **Stoke-on-Trent**

Stoke-on-Trent. 🏔 240,000. 🚆 🚌
ℹ Tourist office, Victoria Hall, Cultural Quarter, Hanley (01782 236000). 🛍 Mon–Sat. W visitstoke.co.uk

From the mid-18th century, Staffordshire became a leading centre for mass-produced ceramics. Its fame arose from the fine bone china and porcelain products of Wedgwood, Minton, Doulton and Spode, but the Staffordshire potteries also make a wide range of utilitarian products such as baths, toilets and wall tiles.

In 1910 a group of six towns – Longton, Fenton, Hanley, Burslem, Tunstall and Stoke – merged to form the conurbation of Stoke-on-Trent, also known as the Potteries. Writer Arnold Bennett (1867–1931) depicted this area as the "Five Towns" in his novels.

The **Gladstone Pottery Museum** is a Victorian complex of workshops, kilns, galleries and an engine house. There are demonstrations of traditional pottery techniques. The **Potteries Museum and Art Gallery** in Hanley has historic and modern ceramics, and items from the Anglo-Saxon "Staffordshire Horde".

Josiah Wedgwood founded his pottery in 1769 and built a workers' village, Etruria. The last surviving steam-powered pottery mill is on display at the **Etruria Industrial Museum**.

Environs
About 10 miles (16 km) north of Stoke-on-Trent is **Little Moreton Hall** (see p307), a Tudor manor house.

🏛 **Gladstone Pottery Museum**
Uttoxeter Rd, Longton. **Tel** 01782 237777. **Open** daily. **Closed** 24 Dec–2 Jan. 🏛 🖧 🖥 🛍 📷
W stokemuseums.org.uk/gpm

🏛 **Potteries Museum and Art Gallery**
Bethesda St, Hanley. **Tel** 01782 232323. **Open** daily. **Closed** 25 Dec–1 Jan. 🖧 🖥 🛍
W stokemuseums.org.uk/pmag

🏛 **Etruria Industrial Museum**
Lower Bedford St, Etruria. **Tel** 01782 233144. **Open** Apr–Nov: Wed–Sun; Dec–Mar: tour only, book ahead. 📷
🖧 🖥 🛍
W stokemuseums.org.uk/eim

🏛 **Little Moreton Hall**
Congleton, off A34. **Tel** 01260 272018. **Open** hours vary; check website. 📷 NT W nationaltrust.org.uk/little-moreton-hall

Staffordshire Pottery

An abundance of water, marl, clay and easily mined coal to fire the kilns enabled Staffordshire to develop as a ceramics centre; and local supplies of iron, copper and lead were used for glazing. In the 18th century, pottery became widely accessible and affordable. English bone china, which used powdered animals' bones for strength and translucence, was shipped all over the world, and Josiah Wedgwood (1730–95) introduced simple, durable crockery – though his best known design is the blue jasperware decorated with white Classical themes. Coal-powered bottle kilns fired the clay until the 1950s Clean Air Acts put them out of business. They have been replaced by electric or gas-fired kilns.

Wedgwood candlesticks, 1785

Timber-framed, gabled mansions in Fish Street, Shrewsbury

❹ Shrewsbury

Shropshire. 🚇 70,000. 🚉 🚌 **ℹ**
01743 258888. 🏛 Tue, Wed, Fri, Sat.
🎭 Shrewsbury Flower Show (mid-Aug). **W** visitshrewsbury.com

Shrewsbury is almost an island, enclosed by a great loop of the River Severn. A gaunt **castle** of red sand-stone, built 1066–74, guards the entrance to the town, standing on the only section of land not surrounded by the river. Such defences were necessary on the frontier between England and the wilder Marches of Wales, whose inhabitants fiercely defied Saxon and Norman invaders (see pp50–51). The castle, rebuilt over the centuries, now houses the Shropshire Regimental Museum.

Roman silver mirror in Rowley's House Museum

In AD 60 the Romans (see pp48–9) built the garrison town of Viroconium, modern Wroxeter, 5 miles (8 km) east of Shrewsbury. Finds from the excavations are displayed at **Shrewsbury Museum and Art Gallery**, including a decorated silver mirror from the 2nd century and other luxury goods imported by the Roman army.

The town's medieval wealth as a centre of the wool trade is evident in the many timber-framed buildings found along the High Street, Butcher Row,

and Wyle Cop. Two of the grandest High Street houses, **Ireland's Mansions** and **Owen's Mansions**, are named after Robert Ireland and Richard Owen, the wealthy wool merchants who built them in 1575 and 1592 respectively. Similarly attractive buildings in Fish Street frame a view of the **Prince Rupert Hotel**, which was briefly the headquarters of Charles I's nephew, Rupert, in the English Civil War (see pp56–7).

Outside the loop of the river, the **Abbey Church** survives from the medieval monastery. It has a number of interesting memorials, including one to Lieutenant WES Owen MC, better known as the war poet Wilfred Owen (1893–1918), who taught at the local Wyle Cop school and was killed in the last days of World War I.

Environs
To the south of Shrewsbury, the road to Ludlow passes through the landscapes celebrated in the 1896 poem by AE Housman (1859–1936), *A Shropshire Lad*. Highlights include the bleak moors of **Long Mynd**, with 15 prehistoric barrows, and **Wenlock Edge**, wonderful walking country with glorious, far-reaching views.

🏰 **Shrewsbury Castle**
Castle St. **Tel** 01743 358516. **Open** hours vary; call for details. **Closed** late Dec–mid-Feb. 🔲 🔶 🔲

🏛 **Shrewsbury Museum and Art Gallery**
The Music Hall, Market Sq. **Tel** 01743 258885. **Open** May–Sep: daily; Apr, Oct: Mon–Sat. 🔶 limited. 🔲
W shrewsburymuseums.com

❺ Ironbridge Gorge

See pp318–19.

❻ Ludlow

Shropshire. 🚇 10,000. 🚉 **ℹ** Castle St (01584 875053). 🏛 Mon, Wed, Fri, Sat. 🎭 music & drama (end Jun).
W ludlow.org.uk

Ludlow attracts large numbers of visitors to its splendid castle, but there is much else to see in this town, with its small shops and its lovely Georgian and half-timbered Tudor buildings. Ludlow is an important area of geological research and the **museum**, just off the town centre, has fossils of the oldest known animals and plants.

The ruined **castle** is sited on cliffs high above the River Teme. Built in 1086, it was damaged in the Civil War (see pp56–7) and abandoned in 1689. *Comus*, a court masque using music and drama, by John Milton (1608–74) was first performed here in 1634 in the Great Hall. Prince Arthur (1486–1502), elder brother of Henry VIII

The 13th-century south tower and hall of Stokesay Castle, near Ludlow

(see pp54–5), died at Ludlow Castle. His heart is buried in **St Laurence Church** at the other end of Castle Square, as are the ashes of the poet A E Housman. The east end of the church backs onto the **Bull Ring**, with its timber buildings. Two inns vie for attention across the street: **The Bull**, with its Tudor back yard, and **The Feathers**, with its flamboyant façade, whose name recalls the feathers used in arrowmaking, once a local industry.

Environs

About 5 miles (8 km) north of Ludlow, in a lovely setting, is **Stokesay Castle**, a fortified manor house with a colourful moated garden.

🏰 **Ludlow Castle**
Castle Square. **Tel** 01584 873355.
Open daily (Dec & Jan: Sat & Sun only). 🅿 🛆 🖥 🖋 🅿

🏛 **Ludlow Museum**
Castle St. **Tel** 0845 678 9024. **Open** Apr–Oct: Mon–Sat (Jun–Aug: daily). 🛆

🏰 **Stokesay Castle**
Craven Arms, A49. **Tel** 01588 672544. **Open** times vary; call for details. 🅿 🖥 🅿 EH

❼ Leominster

Herefordshire. 🚶 11,000. 🚆
ℹ Corn Sq (01568 616460). 🏠 Fri.
🌐 leominstertourism.co.uk

Farmers come to Leominster (pronounced "Lemster") from all over this rural region to buy supplies. There are two buildings of note in the town, which has been a wool-manufacturing centre for 700 years. In the town centre stands the magnificent Grade II-listed **Grange Court**, carved with bold and bizarre figures in 1633. Nearby is the **priory**, whose imposing Norman portal is carved with an equally strange mixture of mythical birds and beasts. The lions, at least, can be explained: medieval monks believed the name of Leominster was derived from *monasterium leonis*, "the monastery of the lions". In fact, *leonis* probably comes from medieval, rather than Classical Latin, and it means

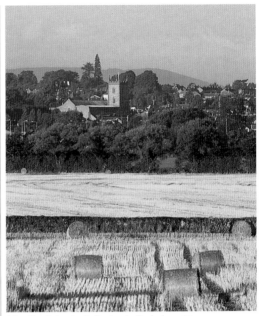

A view of Leominster, set on the River Lugg in rolling border country

"of the marshes". The aptness of this description can readily be seen in the green lanes around the town, following the lush river valleys.

Environs

South of the town, the magnificent gardens and parkland at **Hampton Court** have been restored and include island pavilions and a maze. To the west of the town, along the River Arrow, are the villages of **Eardisland** and **Pembridge**, with their well-kept gardens and timber-framed houses. **Berrington Hall**, 3 miles (5 km) north of Leominster, is a Neo-Classical house set in grounds by "Capability" Brown.

Gatehouse of Stokesay Castle, near Ludlow

Inside are beautifully preserved ceiling decorations and period furniture.

To the northeast of Leominster is **Tenbury Wells**, which enjoyed brief popularity as a spa in the 19th century. The River Teme flows through it, full of minnows, trout and other fish and beloved of the composer Sir Edward Elgar *(see p321)*, who came to seek inspiration on its banks. The river also feeds **Burford House Gardens**, on the western outskirts of Tenbury Wells, where the water is used to create streams, fountains and pools that are rich in unusual moisture-loving plants.

🌷 **Hampton Court Gardens**
nr Hope Under Dinmore. **Tel** 01568 797 777. **Open** Apr–Oct: 10:30am–5pm (call for winter opening times). 🅿 🛆 🖋 🅿 🅿
🌐 hamptoncourt.org.uk

🏛 **Berrington Hall**
Berrington. **Tel** 01568 615721. **Open** Mar–Oct, mid-late Dec: daily; Nov–mid-Dec: Sat & Sun. 🅿 🖋 🅿 NT

🌷 **Burford House Gardens**
Tenbury Wells. **Tel** 01584 810777. **Open** daily. **Closed** 1 Jan, 25 & 26 Dec. 🛆 🖋 🅿 🌐 burford.co.uk

⑤ Ironbridge Gorge

Ironbridge Gorge was one of the most important centres of the Industrial Revolution *(see pp58–9)*. It was here, in 1709, Abraham Darby I (1678–1717) pioneered the use of inexpensive coke, rather than charcoal, to smelt iron ore. The use of iron in bridges, ships and buildings transformed Ironbridge Gorge into one of the world's great iron-making centres. Industrial decline in the 20th century led to the Gorge's decay, although today it has been restored as an exciting complex of industrial archaeology, with several museums strung along the wooded banks of the River Severn.

VISITORS' CHECKLIST

Practical Information
Shropshire. 🚐 2,900.
🌐 ironbridge.org.uk
ℹ️ Museum of the Gorge (01952 433424). **Open** daily. **Closed** 1 Jan, 24, 25 Dec. Some sites closed Nov–Apr, call for details.
🚻 most sites. 📷 📹 by arrangement. 🖥️ 🚻 🏠

Transport
🚆 Telford then bus (0871 2002233).

The Museum of Iron, topped by a cast-and wrought-iron clock

Coalbrookdale Museum of Iron

The history of iron and the men who made it is traced in this remarkable museum. Abraham Darby I's discovery of how to smelt iron ore with coke allowed the mass production of iron, paving the way for the rise of large-scale industry. His original blast furnace forms the museum's centrepiece.

One of the museum's themes is the history of the Darby dynasty, a Quaker family who had a great impact on the Coalbrookdale community.

Ironbridge led the world in industrial innovation, producing the first iron wheels and cylinders for the first steam engine. Cast-iron statues, many of them commissioned for the 1851 Great Exhibition *(see pp60–61)*, are among the many Coalbrookdale Company products on display. They include a bronze figure of Andromeda and many sculptures of stags and hounds.

One of the Darby family's homes in the nearby village of Coalbrookdale, **Rosehill House** (open during the summer), has been furnished in mid-Victorian style.

Museum of the Gorge

This partly castellated, Victorian building was a warehouse for storing products from the ironworks before they were shipped down the River Severn. The warehouse is now home to the Museum of the Gorge, and has displays illustrating the history of the Severn and the development of the water industry. Until the arrival of the railways in the mid-19th century, the Severn was the main form of transport and communication to and from the Gorge. Sometimes too shallow, at other times in flood, the river was not a particularly reliable means of transportation; by the 1890s river trading had stopped completely.

The highlight of the museum is a wonderful 12 m (40 ft) model of the Gorge as it would have appeared in 1796, complete with foundries, cargo boats and growing villages.

Europe (1860), statue in the Museum of Iron

Jackfield Tile Museum

There have been potteries in this area since the 17th century, but it was not until the Victorian passion for decorative tiles that Jackfield became famous. There were two tilemaking factories here – Maw and Craven Dunnill – that produced a tremendous variety of tiles from clay mined nearby. Talented designers created an astonishing range of images. The Jackfield Tile Museum,

Peacock Panel (1928), one of the tile museum's star attractions

in the old Craven Dunnill works, has a collection of the decorative floor and wall tiles that were produced here from the 1850s to the 1960s. On certain days, visitors can watch small-scale demonstrations of traditional methods of tile-making in the old factory buildings, including the kilns and the decoration workshops.

Ironbridge Gorge Sights

① Coalbrookdale
   Museum of Iron
② Museum of the Gorge
③ Iron Bridge
④ Jackfield Tile Museum
⑤ Coalport China Museum
⑥ Blists Hill Victorian Town

Coalport China Museum

In the mid-19th century the Coalport Works was one of the largest porcelain manufacturers in Britain, and its name was synonymous with fine china. Today the china workshops have been converted into a museum, where visitors can watch demonstrations of the various stages of making porcelain, including the skills of pot-throwing, painting and gilding. There is a superb collection of 19th-century china housed in one of the museum's distinctive bottle-shaped kilns. Nearby is the **Tar Tunnel**, an important source of natural bitumen discovered 110 m (360 ft) underground in the 1700s.

Coalport China Museum with its bottle-shaped kiln

It once yielded 20,500 litres (4,500 gal) of tar every week. Visitors can still explore part of the tunnel (Apr–Oct). There is also a programme of drop-in creative workshops and events.

The Iron Bridge

Abraham Darby III (grandson of the first man to smelt iron with coke) cast the world's first iron bridge in 1779, revolutionizing building methods in the process. Spanning the Severn, the bridge is a monument to the ironmasters' skills. The toll-house on the south bank charts its construction.

Blists Hill Victorian Town

This enormous open-air museum recreates Victorian life in an East Shropshire coalfield town. A group of 19th-century buildings has been recon-structed on the 20 ha (50 acre) site of Blists Hill, an old coal mine that used to supply the ironworks in the Gorge. Here, people in period costume enact roles and perform tasks such as iron forging.

The site has period housing, a church and even a Victorian school. Visitors can change money into old coinage to buy items from the baker or even pay for a drink in the local pub.

The centrepiece of Blists Hill is a complete foundry that still produces wrought iron. One of the most spectacular sights is the Hay Inclined Plane, which was used to transport canal boats up and down a steep slope. Other attractions include steam engines, a saddlers, a doctors, a chemist, a candle-makers and a sweetshop.

8 Hereford

Herefordshire. 🗺 55,700. 🚉 🚌 ℹ️
King St (01432 268430). 🚗 Wed
(cattle, general), Sat (general).
🌐 **visitherefordshire.co.uk**

Once the capital of the Saxon
kingdom of West Mercia,
Hereford is today an attractive
town which serves the needs of
a primarily rural community. A
cattle market is held here every
Wednesday, and local produce
is sold at the covered market in
the town centre. Almost
opposite, the Jacobean timber-
framed **Old House** of 1621 is
now a museum of local history.

In the **cathedral**, only a short
stroll away, interesting features
include the Lady Chapel, in
richly ornamented Early English
style, the *Mappa Mundi* (see
below) and the Chained Library,
whose 1,500 books are tethered
by iron chains to bookcases as
a precaution against theft. The
story of these national treasures
is told through models, original
artifacts and interactive
computer technology.
The best place for an
overall view of the
cathedral is at the
Bishop's Meadow,
south of the centre,
leading down to the
banks of the Wye.

Hereford's many
rewarding museums
include the **City
Museum and Art
Gallery**, noted for its Roman
mosaic and for watercolours by
local artists, and the **Cider
Museum**. In the museum,
visitors can discover the history

Hereford's 17th-century Old House, furnished in period style, in the centre of high town

of traditional cider making.
This includes exploring the
champagne cellars and learning
how the barrels are made.
There are still over 30 traditional
cider-makers operating in
Herefordshire.

Detail of figures on
Kilpeck Church

Environs

During the 12th
century, Oliver de
Merlemond made a
pilgrimage from
Hereford to Spain.
Impressed by several
churches he saw on
the way, he brought
French masons over to
England and
introduced their techniques to
this area. One result was **Kilpeck
Church**, 6 miles (10 km)
southwest, full of splendid
carvings including lustful figures

showing their genitals, tail-biting
dragons and snakes. At **Abbey
Dore**, 4 miles (6 km) west, the
Cistercian abbey church is
complemented by the serene
riverside gardens and tranquil
arboretum of **Abbey Dore Court**.

🏛 **Old House**
High Town. **Tel** 01432 260694. **Open**
Apr–Sep: Tue–Sun; Oct–Mar: Tue–Sat;
public hols. **Closed** 25 & 26 Dec, 1 Jan,
Good Fri. ♿ limited. 📷
🌐 **herefordshire.gov.uk**

🏛 **City Museum and Art Gallery**
Broad St. **Tel** 01432 260692.
Open Tue–Sat. **Closed** 1 Jan,
Good Fri, 25 & 26 Dec. ♿ 📷
🌐 **herefordshire.gov.uk**

🏛 **Cider Museum**
Ryelands St. **Tel** 01432 354207. **Open**
Tue–Sat. **Closed** 1 Jan , 25 & 26 Dec,
Good Fri. 🅿 ♿ limited. 📷 by
arrangement. 🖥 📷
🌐 **cidermuseum.co.uk**

9 Ross-on-Wye

Herefordshire. 🗺 10,000. 🚌 ℹ️
Market House (01989 562768). 🚗
Thu, Sat; farmers' market 1st Fri of
month.
🌐 **visitherefordshire.co.uk**

The fine town of Ross sits on a
cliff of red sandstone above the
water meadows of the River
Wye. There are wonderful views
over the river from the cliff-top
gardens, given to the town by a
local benefactor, John Kyrle

Medieval View

Hereford Cathedral's most
celebrated treasure is the
Mappa Mundi, the Map of the
World, drawn in 1290 by a
clergyman, Richard of
Haldingham. The world is
depicted here on Biblical
principles: Jerusalem is at the
centre, the Garden of Eden
figures prominently and
monsters inhabit the margins
of the world.

Central detail, *Mappa Mundi*

The Wye Valley at Symonds Yat

(1637–1724). Kyrle was lauded by the poet Alexander Pope (1688–1744) in his *Moral Essays on the Uses of Riches* (1732) for using his wealth in a practical way, and he came to be known as "The Man of Ross". There is a memorial to Kyrle in **St Mary's Church**.

Environs

Downstream from Ross, the river Wye negotiates a huge, incised meander at **Symonds Yat**. Viewing points and forest walks offer dramatic views across wooded gorges.

Goodrich Castle, 5 miles (8 km) south of Ross, is a 12th-century red sandstone fort on a rock above the river.

Goodrich Castle
Goodrich. **Tel** 01600 890538. **Open** mid-Feb, Apr–Oct: daily; Nov–Mar: Sat & Sun). 🅿 EH 🖥 (Apr–Sep).

⓾ Ledbury

Herefordshire. 🅰 9,900. 🚲 🚐 *i*
Ice Bytes, 38 The Homend (0844 567 8650). 🆆 **visitledbury.info**

Ledbury's main street is lined with timbered houses, including the **Market Hall** which dates from 1655. Church Lane, a cobbled lane running up from the High Street, has lovely 16th-century buildings: the **Heritage Centre** and **Butcher Row House** are both now museums. **St Michael and All Angels Church** has a massive detached bell tower, ornate Early English decoration and interesting monuments.

Medieval tile from the Priory at Great Malvern

Heritage Centre
Church Lane. **Open** Easter–Oct: daily. ♿

Butcher Row House
Church Lane. **Open** Easter–Oct: daily.

⓫ Great Malvern and the Malverns

Worcestershire. 🅰 35,000. 🚲 🚐 *i*
21 Church St (01684 892289). 🖐 Fri; farmers' market 3rd Sat of month.
🆆 **visitthemalverns.org**

The ancient granite rock of the Malvern Hills rises from the plain of the River Severn, its 9 miles (15 km) of glorious scenery

visible from afar. Composer Sir Edward Elgar (1857–1934) wrote many of his greatest works here, including the oratorio *The Dream of Gerontius* (1900), inspired by what the diarist John Evelyn (1620–1706) described as "one of the goodliest views in England". Elgar's home was in **Little Malvern**, whose truncated Church of St Giles, set on a steep, wooded hill, lost its nave when the stone was stolen during the Dissolution *(see p343)*. **Great Malvern**, capital of the hills, is graced with 19th-century buildings which look like Swiss sanitoria: patients would stay at institutions such as Doctor Gulley's Water Cure Establishment. The water gushing from the hillside at St Ann's Well, above the town, is bottled and sold throughout Britain. The town is home to the famous Morgan cars (contact 01684 584580 to arrange a factory visit).

Malvern's highlight is the **Priory**, with its 15th-century stained-glass windows and medieval misericords. The old monastic fishponds below the church form the lake of the **Priory Park**. Here the theatre hosts performances of Elgar's music and plays by George Bernard Shaw.

A view of the Malverns range, formed of hard Pre-Cambrian rock

⓬ Worcester

Worcestershire. 🚗 95,000. 🚆 🚌 ℹ️
High St (01905 726311). 🏪 Mon–Sat.
🌐 visitworcester.com

Worcester is one of many English cities whose character has been transformed by modern development. The architectural highlight is still the **cathedral**, off College Yard, which suffered a collapsed tower in 1175 and a disastrous fire in 1203, before the present structure was started in the 13th century.

The nave and central tower were completed in the 1370s, after building was severely interrupted by the Black Death, which decimated the labour force (see p52). The most recent and ornate addition was made in 1874, when Sir George Gilbert Scott (see p469) designed the High Gothic choir, incorporating 14th-century carved misericords.

There are many interesting tombs, including King John's, a

Charles I holding a symbol of the Church on Worcester's Guildhall

masterpiece of medieval carving, in front of the altar. Prince Arthur, Henry VIII's brother (see p317), who died at the age of 15, is buried in the chantry chapel south of the altar. Underneath, the huge Norman crypt survives from the first cathedral (1084). From the cathedral cloister, a gate leads to College Green

and out into Edgar Street and its Georgian houses. Here the **Worcester Porcelain Museum** displays Royal Worcester porcelain dating back to 1751. On the High Street, north of the cathedral, the **Guildhall** of 1721 is adorned with statues of Stuart monarchs, reflecting the city's Royalist allegiances. In Cornmarket is **Ye Olde King Charles House**, in which Prince Charles, later Charles II, hid after the Battle of Worcester in 1651 (see pp56–7).

Some of Worcester's finest timber buildings are found in Friar Street: **The Greyfriars**, built around 1480, has been restored in period style. The **Commandery** was originally an 11th-century hospital. It was rebuilt in the 15th century and used by Prince Charles as a base during the Civil War. Now a museum, it has a fine hammerbeam roof.

Elgar's Birthplace was the home of composer Sir Edward Elgar (see p322) and contains memorabilia of his life.

🏛 Worcester Porcelain Museum
Severn St. **Tel** 01905 21247. **Open** Easter–Oct: Mon–Sat; Nov–Easter: Tue–Sat. **Closed** public hols. 🚫 ♿
📷 ♻️ 🏪
🌐 worcester porcelainmuseum.org

🏠 The Greyfriars
Friar St. **Tel** 01905 23571. **Open** hours vary; call for details. 🚫 NT

🏛 Commandery
Sidbury. **Tel** 01905 361821. **Open** daily. **Closed** 1 Jan, 25–26 Dec. 🏪 🚫

🏛 Elgar's Birthplace
Lower Broadheath. **Tel** 01905 333224. **Open** daily. **Closed** 24 Dec–mid-Jan. 🚫 ♿ limited. 🏪
🌐 elgarmuseum.org

⓭ Birmingham

Birmingham. 🚗 1,037,000. ✈️ 🚆 🚌
ℹ️ New St (0844 888 3883). 🏪 Mon–Sat. 🌐 visitbirmingham.com

Brum, as it is affectionately known to its inhabitants, grew up as a major centre of the Industrial Revolution in the 19th century. A vast range of manufacturing trades was based in Birmingham and was responsible for the rapid development of grim factories

Worcester Cathedral, overlooking the River Severn

The Last of England, Ford Madox Brown, Birmingham Art Gallery

and cramped housing. Since the clearance of several of these areas after World War II, Birmingham has raised its cultural profile. The city succeeded in enticing Sir Simon Rattle to conduct the City of Birmingham Symphony Orchestra (1980–98), and persuaded the former Royal Sadler's Wells Ballet (now the Birmingham Royal Ballet) to leave London for the more up-to-date facilities of Birmingham. The **National Exhibition Centre**, 8 miles (13 km) east of the centre, draws thousands of people to its conference, lecture and exhibition halls.

Set away from the massive Bullring shopping centre, Birmingham's 19th-century civic buildings are excellent examples of Neo-Classical architecture. Among them are the **Birmingham Museum and Art Gallery**, where the collection includes outstanding works by Pre-Raphaelite artists such as Sir Edward Burne-Jones (1833–98), who was born in Birmingham, and Ford Madox Brown (1821–93). The museum also

organizes some interesting temporary exhibitions of art, such as works by J M W Turner (1775–1851). Birmingham's extensive canal system is now used mainly for leisure boating *(see pp304–5)*, and several former warehouses have been converted into museums and galleries.

Thinktank, Birmingham Science Museum celebrates the city's contributions to the world of railway engines, aircraft, and the motor trade. The old jewellery quarter has practised its traditional crafts here since the 16th century.

Suburban Birmingham has many attractions, including the **Botanical Gardens** at Edgbaston, and **Cadbury World** at Bournville, where there is a visitor centre dedicated to chocolate (booking ahead is advisable). Bournville village was built in 1890 by the Cadbury brothers for their workers and is a pioneering example of a garden suburb.

🏛 **Birmingham Museum and Art Gallery**
Chamberlain Sq. **Tel** 0121 303 2834. **Open** daily. **Closed** 25 & 26 Dec. 🚻 🖥 📷

🏛 **Thinktank**
Millennium Point. **Tel** 0121 202 2222. **Open** daily. **Closed** 24–26 Dec.

🌿 **Botanical Gardens**
Westbourne Rd, Edgbaston. **Tel** 0121 454 1860. **Open** daily. **Closed** 25 Dec. 🚻 🖥 🐾 📷 by appt. 🖊

🏛 **Cadbury World**
Linden Rd, Bournville. **Tel** 0845 450 3599. **Open** daily (Nov–Jan: call for details). **Closed** first two weeks Jan. 🐾 🚻

Epstein's *St Michael Subduing the Devil*, on Coventry Cathedral

⑭ Coventry

Coventry. 🗺 316,000. 🚂 🚌 ℹ Cathedral Tower (024 7622 5616). 🖂 Mon–Sat. 🌐 **visitcoventryand warwickshire.co.uk**

As an armaments centre, Coventry was a prime target for German bombing raids in World War II, and in 1940 the **cathedral** in the city centre was hit. After the war the first totally modern cathedral by Sir Basil Spence (1907–76) was built alongside the ruins. It includes sculptures by Sir Jacob Epstein and a tapestry by Graham Sutherland.

The **Herbert Gallery and Museum** has displays on the 11th-century legend of Lady Godiva, who rode naked through the streets. The **Coventry Transport Museum** has the largest collection of Britain's road transport in the world, including cars, cycles and models, and features the fastest car in the world as well as interactive displays.

🏛 **Herbert Gallery and Museum**
Jordan Well. **Tel** 024 7683 2386. **Open** daily (Sun: pm) 1 Jan. 📷 📷

🏛 **Coventry Transport Museum**
Hales St. **Tel** 024 7623 4270. **Open** daily. **Closed** 24–26 Dec. 🚻 📷 📷
🌐 **transport-museum.com**

Stately civic office buildings in Victoria Square, Birmingham

⑮ Midlands Garden Tour

The charming Cotswold stone buildings perfectly complement the lush gardens for which the region is famous. This picturesque route from Warwick to Cheltenham is designed to show every type of garden, from tiny cottage plots, brimming with bell-shaped flowers and hollyhocks, to the deer-filled, landscaped parks of stately homes. The route follows the escarpment of the Cotswold Hills, taking in spectacular scenery and some of the prettiest Midlands villages on the way.

Tips for Drivers

Tour length: 35 miles (50 km).
Stopping-off points: Hidcote Manor has excellent lunches and teas; there are refreshments at Kiftsgate Court and Sudeley Castle. Travellers will find a good choice in Broadway, from traditional pubs and tea shops to the deluxe Lygon Arms. (See also pp636–7.)

⑨ **Cheltenham Imperial Gardens**
These colourful public gardens on the Promenade were laid out in 1817–18 to encourage people to walk from the town to the spa (see p332).

⑧ **Sudeley Castle**
The restored castle is complemented by box hedges, topiary and an Elizabethan knot garden (see p30). Catherine Parr, Henry VIII's widow, died here in 1548.

Oxford

Winchcombe

Evesham

M5

Gloucester
M5

CHELTENHAM

Stroud

Cirencester ↓

Oxford

⑤ **Broadway**
In this village, wisteria and cordoned fruit trees cover 17th-century cottages that have immaculate gardens.

⑦ **Stanway House**
This Jacobean manor has many lovely trees in its grounds and a pyramid above a cascade of water.

⑥ **Snowshill Manor**
This Cotswold stone manor contains an extraordinary collection, from bicycles to Japanese armour. There are walled gardens and terraces full of *objets d'art* such as the clock (left). The colour blue is a recurrent theme.

① **Warwick Castle**
The castle's gardens
(see pp326–7) include the
Mound, planted in medieval
style, with grass, oaks, yew
trees and box hedges.

② **Anne Hathaway's Cottage**
This has a pretty,
informal 19th-century-
style garden (see p331).

③ **Hidcote Manor Gardens**
Started in the early years of
the 20th century, these
beautiful gardens pioneered
the idea of a garden as a series
of outdoor "rooms", enclosed
by high yew hedges and
planted according to themes.

④**Kiftsgate Court Garden**
This charmingly naturalistic garden
lies opposite Hidcote Manor. It has
many rare and unusual plants on a
series of hillside terraces, including the
enormous "Kiftsgate" Rose, nearly
30 m (100 ft) high.

Key

═══ Motorway

─── Tour route

─── Other roads

0 kilometres   5

0 miles   5

⑯ **Warwick**

Warwickshire. 🅰 30,000. 🚋 🚌 ℹ
The Courthouse, Jury St (01926
492212). 🏠 Sat.
🅦 visitwarwick.co.uk

Warwick suffered a major fire in
1694, but some medieval
buildings survived. **St John's
House Museum** in St John's is a
charming Jacobean mansion
housing reconstructions of a
Victorian parlour, kitchen and
classroom. At the west end of
the High Street, a row of
medieval guild buildings were
transformed in 1571 by the Earl
of Leicester, who founded the
Lord Leycester Hospital as a
refuge for his old soldiers.

The arcaded **Market Hall
Museum** (1670) is part of the
Warwickshire Museum, renowned
for its unusual tapestry map of
the county, woven in 1558.

In Church Street, to the south
of St Mary's Church, is the
Beauchamp Chapel (1443–64).
It is a superb example of
Perpendicular architecture and
has tombs of the Earls of
Warwick. There is a view of
Warwick Castle (see pp326–7)
from St Mary's tower.

🏛 **St John's House Museum**
St John's. **Tel** 01926 412132. **Open**
Tue–Sat. ♿ limited.

🏨 **Lord Leycester Hospital**
High St. **Tel** 01926 491422. **Open** Tue–
Sun & public hols. **Closed** Good Fri, 25
Dec. Gardens: **Open** same as house but
Easter–Sep only. 🎫 💻 ♿ ltd. 📷

🏛 **Market Hall Museum**
Market Place. **Tel** 01926 412500.
Open Tue–Sat. ♿ limited. 📷

The Lord Leycester Hospital, now a
home for ex-servicemen

Warwick Castle

Warwick's magnificent castle is the finest medieval fortress in the country. The original Norman castle was rebuilt in the 13th and 14th centuries, when huge outer walls and towers were added, mainly to display the power of the great feudal magnates, the Beauchamps and, in the 1400s, the Nevilles, the Earls of Warwick. The castle passed in 1604 to the Greville family who, in the 17th and 18th centuries, transformed it into a great country house. In 1978 the owners of Madame Tussaud's *(see p108)* bought the castle and set up tableaux of wax portraits to illustrate its history.

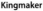

Kingmaker
Dramatic displays recreate medieval life as "Warwick the Kingmaker", Richard Neville, prepared for battle in the Wars of the Roses.

Royal Weekend Party
The portrait of the valet is part of the award-winning exhibition of the Prince of Wales's visit in 1898.

KEY

① **Princess Tower**

② **Merlin: The Dragon Tower** houses characters from the BBC TV series *Merlin*, including the great dragon itself.

③ **The Mound** has remains of the motte and bailey castle (see p490) and the 13th-century keep.

④ **Ramparts and towers**, of local grey sandstone, were added in the 14th and 15th centuries.

⑤ **The Gatehouse** is defended by portcullises and "murder holes" through which boiling pitch was dropped onto attackers beneath.

⑥ **The Castle Dungeon** is a chilling, live dramatisation of plague-ridden medieval Warwick.

⑦ **Caesar's Tower**

⑧ **The Mill and Engine House**

★ **Great Hall and State Rooms**
Medieval apartments were transformed into the Great Hall and State Rooms. A mark of conspicuous wealth, they display a collection of family treasures from around the world.

View of Warwick Castle, south front, by Antonio Canaletto (1697–1768)

★ **Guy's Tower**
Completed around 1393, the tower had lodgings for guests and members of the Earl of Warwick's retinue.

Entrance

Shield (1745)

	1000	1200	1400	1600	1800

1068 Norman motte and bailey castle built

1264 Simon de Montfort, champion of Parliament against Henry III, attacks Warwick Castle

1478 Castle reverts to Crown after murder of Richard Neville's son-in-law

1890s–1910 Visits from future Edward VII

1268–1445 Much of the present castle built by the Beauchamp family, Earls of Warwick

1449–1471 Richard Neville, Earl of Warwick, plays leading role in Wars of the Roses

1604 James I gives castle to Sir Fulke Greville

1600–1800 Interiors remodelled and gardens landscaped

1871 Fire damages the Great Hall

1642 Siege of the Castle of Royalist Troops

⑰ Street-by-Street: Stratford-upon-Avon

Situated on the west bank of the River Avon, in the heart of the Midlands, is one of the most famous towns in England. Stratford-upon-Avon dates back to at least Roman times but its appearance today is that of a small Tudor market town, with mellow, half-timbered architecture and tranquil walks beside the tree-fringed Avon. This image belies its popularity as the most visited tourist attraction outside London, with eager hordes flocking to see buildings connected to William Shakespeare or his descendants.

Bancroft Gardens
There is an attractive boat-filled canal basin here and a 15th-century causeway.

★ Shakespeare's Birthplace
This building was almost entirely reconstructed in the 19th century, but in the style of the Tudor original.

0 metres 100
0 yards 100

Shakespeare Centre

Tourist information

WATERS

BRIDGE STREET

SHEEP STREET

UNION STREET

HIGH STREET

CHA

HENLEY STREET

MEER STREET

WOOD STREET

ELY STREET

To train station

Harvard House
The novelist Marie Corelli (1855–1924) had this house restored. Next door is the 16th-century Garrick Inn.

Town Hall
Built in 1767, there are traces of 18th-century graffiti on the front of the building saying *God Save the King*.

Royal Shakespeare Theatre and Swan Theatre
Home of the Royal Shakespeare Company (RSC), the Swan Theatre is located on the western bank of the River Avon.

VISITORS' CHECKLIST

Practical Information
Warwickshire. 🅟 25,000.
🅦 shakespeare-country.co.uk
ℹ️ Bridgefoot **Tel** 0871 978 0841.
🚌 Fri. 🎭 Shakespeare's Birthday: Apr; Stratford Festival: Jul.

Transport
✈️ Birmingham, 20 miles (32 km) NW of Stratford-upon-Avon.
🚉 Alcester Rd. 🚌 Bridge St.

Nash's House
The foundations of New Place, where Shakespeare died, form the garden beside this house.

★ Holy Trinity Church
Shakespeare's grave and copies of the parish register entries recording his birth and death are here.

Edward VI Grammar School

Guild Chapel

★ Hall's Croft
John Hall, Shakespeare's son-in-law, was a doctor. This delightful house includes an exhibition of medicine in Shakespeare's time.

ne Hathaway's ttage

Key
— Suggested route

Exploring Stratford-upon-Avon

William Shakespeare was born in Stratford-upon-Avon on St George's Day, 23 April 1564. Admirers of his work have been coming to the town since his death in 1616. In 1847 a public appeal successfully raised the money to buy the house in which he was born. As a result Stratford has become a literary shrine to Britain's greatest dramatist. It also has a thriving cultural reputation as the provincial home of the prestigious Royal Shakespeare Company, whose dramas are usually performed in Stratford before playing a second season in London *(see pp156–7)*.

Anne Hathaway's Cottage, home of Shakespeare's wife

Around Stratford

The centre of Stratford-upon-Avon has many buildings that are connected with William Shakespeare and his descendants. On the High Street corner is the **Cage**, a 15th-century prison. It was converted into a house where Shakespeare's daughter Judith lived, and is now a shop. At the end of the High Street, the **Town Hall** has a statue of Shakespeare on the façade given by David Garrick (1717–79), the actor who in 1769 organized the first Shakespeare festival.

The High Street leads into Chapel Street where the half-timbered **Nash's House** is a museum of local history. It is also the site of **New Place**, where Shakespeare died in 1616, and which is now a herb and knot garden *(see p30)*. In Church Street opposite, the **Guild Chapel** (1496) has a *Last Judgement* painting (c.1500) on the chancel wall. Shakespeare is thought to have attended the **Edward VI Grammar School** (above the former Guildhall) next door.

A left turn into Old Town leads to **Hall's Croft**, home of Shakespeare's daughter Susanna, which displays 16th- and 17th-century medical artefacts. An avenue of lime trees leads to **Holy Trinity Church**, where Shakespeare is buried. A walk along the river follows the Avon to **Bancroft Gardens**, which lies at the junction of the River Avon and the Stratford Canal.

🏠 Shakespeare's Birthplace

Henley St. **Tel** 01789 204016. **Open** daily. **Closed** 25 Dec. ♿ ♿ limited. 📷 🌐 shakespeare.org.uk
Bought for the nation in 1847, when it was a public house, Shakespeare's Birthplace was converted back to Elizabethan style. Objects associated with Shakespeare's father, John, a glovemaker and wool merchant, are on display. There is a birth room, in which Shakespeare was supposedly born, and another room has a window etched with visitors' autographs, including that of Sir Walter Scott *(see p516)*.

Holy Trinity Church, seen across the River Avon

⊞ Harvard House

High St. **Closed** not open to the public.

Built in 1596, this ornate house was the home of Katherine Rogers, whose son, John Harvard, emigrated to America in 1637. He died the following year, leaving money and a small library to the New College in Cambridge, Massachusetts. They expressed their gratitude by renaming the college in his honour. Harvard never actually lived in this house, however.

Environs

At Shottery, 1 mile (1.5 km) west of Stratford, is **Anne Hathaway's Cottage**, home of Shakespeare's wife before their marriage *(see p325)*. Also worth a visit is **Mary Arden's Farm** in Wilmcote, home of Shakespeare's grandparents and childhood home of his mother, Mary Arden. There are farm animals, archery and falconry displays.

⊞ Anne Hathaway's Cottage

Cottage Lane. **Tel** 01789 292100. **Open** daily. **Closed** 25 & 26 Dec. 🅿 🖼

⊞ Mary Arden's Farm

Station Rd. **Tel** 01789 293455. **Open** Apr–Oct: daily. 🅿 🖼 🖼 🖼
w shakespeare.org.uk

Kenneth Branagh in *Hamlet*

The Royal Shakespeare Company

The Royal Shakespeare Company is renowned for its new interpretations of Shakespeare's work. It was established in the 1960s as a resident company for the 1932 Shakespeare Memorial Theatre, now the Royal Shakespeare Theatre. It has seen the brightest and best theatrical talent tread its boards, from Laurence Olivier and Vivien Leigh to Helen Mirren and Kenneth Branagh. The RSC also tours, with regular seasons in London, Newcastle and even New York.

Grevel House, the oldest house in Chipping Campden

⑱ Chipping Campden

Gloucestershire. 🚍 2,500. 🛈 High St (01386 841206).
w visitchippingcampden.com

This perfect Cotswold town is kept in pristine condition by the Campden Society. Set up in the 1920s, the Society has kept alive the traditional skills of stonecarving and repair that make Chipping Campden such a unified picture of golden-coloured and lichen-patched stone. Visitors travelling from the northwest along the B4035 first see a group of ruins: the remains of **Campden Manor**, begun around 1613 by Sir Baptist Hicks, 1st Viscount Campden. The manor was burned by Royalist troops to stop it being sequestered by Parliament at the end of the Civil War *(see pp56–7)*, but the almshouses opposite the gateway were spared. They were designed in the form of the letter "I" (which is Latin for "J"), a symbol of the owner's loyalty to King James I.

The town's **Church of St James**, one of the finest in the Cotswolds, was built in the 15th century, financed by merchants who bought wool from Cotswold farmers and exported it at a high profit. Inside the church there are many elaborate tombs, and a magnificent brass dedicated to William Grevel, describing him as "the flower of the wool merchants of England". He built **Grevel House** (c.1380) in the High Street, the oldest in a fine row of buildings, which is distinguished by a double-storey bay window.

Viscount Campden donated the **Market Hall** in 1627. His contemporary, Robert Dover, founded in 1612 the "Cotswold Olimpicks", long before the modern Olympic Games had been established. The 1612 version included such painful events as the shin-kicking contest. It still takes place on the first Friday after each Spring Bank Holiday, followed by a torchlit procession into town ready for the Scuttlebrook Wake Fair on the next day. The setting for the games is a spectacular natural hollow on **Dover's Hill** above the town, worth climbing on a clear day for the marvellous views over the Vale of Evesham.

The 17th-century Market Hall in Chipping Campden

Tewkesbury's abbey church overlooks the town, crowded onto the bank of the River Severn

⑲ Tewkesbury

Gloucestershire. 🚉 11,000.
ℹ Church St (01684 855040).
🛒 Wed, Sat.
🌐 visittewkesbury.info

This lovely town sits on the confluence of the rivers Severn and Avon. It has one of England's finest Norman abbey churches, **St Mary the Virgin**, which locals saved during the Dissolution of the Monasteries (see p54) by paying Henry VIII £453. Around the church, with its bulky tower and Norman façade, timbered buildings are crammed within the bend of the river. Warehouses are a reminder of past wealth, and Borough Mill on Quay Street, the only mill left harnessed to the river's energy, still grinds corn.

Pump Room detail, Cheltenham

Environs

Boat trips run from the river to **Twyning**'s riverside pub, 6 miles (10 km) north.

⑳ Cheltenham

Gloucestershire. 🚉 110,000. 🚆 🚌
ℹ 77 Promenade (01242 522878).
🛒 Sun; farmers' market 2nd & last Fri
of month. 🌐 visitcheltenham.com

Cheltenham's reputation for elegance was first gained in the late 18th century, when high society flocked to the spa

town to "take the waters", following the example set by George III (see pp58–9). Many gracious terraced houses were built, in a Neo-Classical style, along broad avenues. These survive around the Queen's Hotel, near **Montpellier**, a lovely Regency arcade lined with craft and antique shops, and in the **Promenade**, with its smart department stores and couturiers. A more modern atmosphere prevails in the Regency Arcade, where the star attraction is the 1987 **clock** by Kit Williams: visit on the hour to see fish blowing bubbles over the onlookers' heads.

Cheltenham Art Gallery & Museum is worth a visit to see its unusual collection of furniture and other crafts made by members of the influential Arts and Crafts Movement (see p33), whose strict principles of utilitarian design were laid down by William Morris (see p224).

The **Pittville Pump Room** (1825–30), modelled on the Greek Temple of Ilissos in Athens, is frequently used for performances during the town's renowned annual festivals of music (July) and literature (October).

The event that really attracts the crowds is the Cheltenham

Gold Cup – the premier event of the National Hunt season – held in March (see p70).

🏛 **Art Gallery & Museum**
Clarence St. **Tel** 01242 237431.
Open Mon–Sat. **Closed** 1 Jan,
25 Dec & public hols. ♿
📷 by arrangement. 🖥 📷
🌐 cheltenhammuseum.org.uk

🏛 **Pittville Pump Room**
Pittville Park. **Tel** 0844 5762210.
Open Wed–Mon. **Closed** 1 Jan, 25 &
26 Dec, public hols & frequently for
functions: call to check. ♿
🌐 pittvillepumproom.org.uk

Fantasy clock, by Kit Williams, in Cheltenham's Regency Arcade

Gloucester Cathedral's nave

❷❶ Gloucester

Gloucestershire. 🏛 110,000.
🚉 🚌 ℹ 28 Southgate St
(01452 396572). 🅿 Wed, Sat.
🌐 thecityofgloucester.co.uk

Gloucester has played a prominent role in the history of England. It was here that William the Conqueror ordered a vast survey of all the land in his kingdom, that was to be recorded in the *Domesday Book* of 1086 *(see p52)*.

The city was popular with the Norman monarchs and in 1216 Henry III was crowned in its magnificent **cathedral**. The solid, dignified nave was begun in 1089. Edward II *(see p443)*, who was murdered in 1327 at Berkeley Castle, 14 miles (22 km) to the southwest, is buried in a tomb near the high altar. Many pilgrims came to honour Edward's tomb, leaving behind generous donations, and Abbot Thoky was able to begin rebuilding in 1331. The result was the wonderful east window and the cloisters, where the fan vault was developed and then copied in other churches all over the country.

The impressive buildings around the cathedral include College Court, with its **House of the Tailor of Gloucester** museum, in the house that the children's author Beatrix Potter used as the setting *(see p371)* for her illustrations of that story. A museum complex has been created in the **Gloucester Docks**, part of which is still a port, linked to the Bristol Channel by the Gloucester and

Sharpness Canal (opened in 1827). In the old port, and housed in a Victorian warehouse, the **Gloucester Waterways Museum** relates the history of canals. A gallery called Move It looks at how canals were built.

🏛 **House of the Tailor of Gloucester**
College Court. **Tel** 01452 422856.
Open Mon–Sat (Sun: pm only).
Closed public hols. 🅰

🏛 **Gloucester Waterways Museum**
Llanthony Warehouse, Gloucester Docks. **Tel** 01452 318200. **Open** daily.
Closed 25 Dec. 🅰 ♿ 🅿 📷
🌐 gloucesterwaterwaysmuseum.org.uk

❷❷ Cirencester

Gloucestershire. 🏛 20,000. 🚌
ℹ Market Place (0845 260 8452).
🅿 Mon, Tue (cattle) & Fri.
🌐 cirencester.com

Known as the capital of the Cotswolds, Cirencester has as its focus a market place, where there is a market every Monday and Friday. Overlooking the market is the **Church of St John Baptist**, whose "wineglass" pulpit (1515) is one of the few pre-Reformation pulpits to survive in England. To the west, **Cirencester Park** was laid out by the 1st Earl of Bathurst from 1714, with help from the poet Alexander Pope *(see p321)*. The mansion is surrounded by a

massive yew hedge. Clustering round the park entrance are the 17th- and 18th-century wool merchants' houses of Cecily Hill, built in grand Italianate style. Much humbler Cotswold houses are to be found in Coxwell Street, and underlying this is a Roman town, evidence of which emerges when the ground is dug.

The **Corinium Museum** is an impressive modern museum. It features excavated objects in a series of tableaux illustrating life in a Roman household.

🏛 **Cirencester Park**
Cirencester Park. **Tel** 01285 653135.
Open daily. ♿
🌐 cirencesterpark.co.uk

🏛 **Corinium Museum**
Park St. **Tel** 01285 655611. **Open** daily (Sun: pm only). **Closed** 1 Jan, 25 & 26 Dec. ♿ 🅿 📷
🌐 cotswold.gov.uk

Cirencester's fine parish church, one of the largest in England

Art and Nature in the Roman World

Cirencester was an important centre of mosaic production in Roman days. Fine examples of the local style are shown in the Corinium Museum and mosaics range from Classical subjects, such as Orpheus taming lions and tigers with the music of his lyre,

to the naturalistic depiction of a hare. At Chedworth Roman Villa, 8 miles (13 km) north, mosaics are inspired by real life. In the *Four Seasons* mosaic, *Winter* shows a peasant, dressed in a woollen hood and a wind-blown cloak, clutching a recently caught hare in one hand and a branch for fuel in the other.

Hare mosaic, Corinium Museum

EAST MIDLANDS

Derbyshire · Leicestershire · Lincolnshire
·Northamptonshire · Nottinghamshire

Three very different kinds of landscape greet visitors to the East Midlands. In the west, wild moors rise to the craggy heights of the Peak District. These give way to the low-lying plain and the massive industrial towns at the region's heart. In the east, hills and limestone villages stretch to a long, flat seaboard.

The East Midlands owes much of its character to a conjunction of the pastoral with the urban. The spa resorts, historical villages and stately homes coexist within a landscape shaped by industrialization. Throughout the region there are swathes of scenic countryside – and grimy industrial cities.

The area has been settled since prehistoric times. The Romans mined lead and salt, and they built a large network of roads and fortresses. Anglo-Saxon and Viking influence is found in many of the place names. During the Middle Ages profits from the wool industry enabled the development of towns such as Lincoln, which still has many fine old buildings. The East Midlands was the scene of ferocious battles during the Wars of the Roses and

the Civil War, and insurgents in the Jacobite Rebellion reached as far as Derby.

In the west of the region is the Peak District, Britain's first national park. Created in 1951, it draws crowds in search of the wild beauty of the heather-covered moors, or the wooded dales of the River Dove. The peaks are very popular with rock climbers and hikers.

The eastern edge of the Peaks descends through stone-walled meadows to sheltered valleys. The Roman spa of Buxton adds a final note of elegance before the flatlands of south Derbyshire, Leicestershire and Nottinghamshire are reached. An area of coal mines and factories since the late 18th century, the landscape was improved greatly by a 10-year planting scheme of the National Forest.

Well dressing dance, a tradition at Stoney Middleton in the Peak District

◀ Night-time view of the cathedral and Cathedral Square, Lincoln

Exploring the East Midlands

The East Midlands is a popular tourist destination, easily
accessible by road, but best explored on foot. Numerous
well-marked trails pass through the Peak District National
Park. There are superb country houses at Chatsworth and
Burghley and the impressive historic towns of Lincoln
and Stamford to discover.

Sights at a Glance

1. Buxton
2. Chatsworth *pp338–9*
3. Matlock Bath
6. Nottingham
7. Lincoln *pp344–5*
8. Burghley *pp346–7*
9. Stamford
10. Northampton

Walks and Tours

4. Tissington Trail
5. Peak District Tour

View of Burghley House from the
north courtyard

Getting Around

The M6, M1 and A1 are the principal road routes to the East
Midlands, but they are subject to frequent delays because
of the volume of traffic they carry. It can be faster and more
interesting to find cross-country routes to the region, for
example through the attractive countryside and villages
around Stamford and Northampton. Some roads in the
Peak District become very congested during the summer
and an early start to the day is advisable. Lincoln and
Stamford are well served by fast mainline trains from
London. Rail services in the Peak District are far more
limited, but local lines run as far as Matlock and Buxton.

Key

═══ Motorway

═══ Major road

─── Secondary road

∷∷∷ Minor road

─── Scenic route

─▪─ Main railway

─── Minor railway

△ Summit

Peak District countryside seen from the Tissington Trail

For additional map symbols *see back flap*

Lincoln Cathedral towering over half-timbered buildings

A180
Kingston upon Hull
Humberston
A159
A15
Caistor
A16
Saltfleet
Doncaster
Blyton
Waddingham
Bawtry
Gainsborough
Market Rasen
Louth
Mablethorpe
A1(M)
Blyth
A1
Retford
A156
Marton
Dunholme
A16
Alford
Worksop
A614
A46
A158
Baumber
Ingoldmells
Tuxford
A57
LINCOLN
Bardney
Horncastle
Mansfield
A46
Waddington
A158
Spilsby
Skegness
ton in Ashfield
Coningsby
Stickford
kby in Ashfield
Newark-on-Trent
A15
Leadenham
A52
Hucknall
A17
Ruskington
Sibsey
Benington
Arnold
A46
Claypole
A1
Honington
Sleaford
A16
A60
Bingham
A17
Boston
The
NOTTINGHAM
A52
Grantham
A52
Donington
Sutterton
Wash
Denton
Great Ponton
ng Eaton
Upper Broughton
A607
Pinchbeck
Holbeach
Sutton Bridge
A46
Melton Mowbray
A1
Bourne
The Fens
oughborough
Stretton
A15
Baston
King's Lynn
Mountsorrel
A606
A16
Bedford Level
Oakham
STAMFORD
field
Rutland Water
Ketton
BURGHLEY HOUSE
Leicester
Billesdon
A47
A47
Oadby
Uppingham
A43
A6
Elton
Market Harborough
Corby
Oundle
A4304
A605
Swinford
A14
Kettering
Thrapston
gby
A14
Crick
A508
A43
A6
Cambridge
Wellingborough
Rushden
A45
Wollaston
aventry
NORTHAMPTON
Roade
Grand Union Canal
M1
Milton Keynes

0 kilometres   15

0 miles   15

Buxton Opera House, a late 19th-century building restored in 1979

❶ Buxton

Derbyshire. 🚇 21,300. 🚈 🚌 ℹ️
Pavilion Gardens (01298 23114). 🛒
Tue, Sat. 🌐 visitbuxton.co.uk

Buxton was developed as a spa town by the 5th Duke of Devonshire during the late 18th century. It has many fine Neo-Classical buildings, including the **Devonshire Royal Hospital** (1790), originally stables, at the entrance to the town. The **Crescent** was built (1780–90) to rival Bath's Royal Crescent (see p262) and is being restored.

The town baths were at the southwest end. Here, a spring where water surges from the ground at a rate of 7,000 litres (1,540 gallons) an hour can be seen. Buxton water is bottled and sold but there is a public fountain at **St Ann's Well**, opposite.

Steep gardens known as the Slopes lead from the Crescent to the small but worthwhile **Museum and Art Gallery**, with geological and archaeological displays. Behind the Crescent, overlooking the **Pavilion Gardens**, is the striking 19th-century iron and glass Pavilion, and the splendidly restored **Opera House**, where a music and arts festival is held in summer.

🏛️ **Buxton Museum and Art Gallery**
Terrace Rd. **Tel** 01629 533540. **Open** Easter–Sep: Tue–Sun & pub hols; Oct–Easter: Tue–Sat. **Closed** 1 Jan, 24–26 Dec. 🛒 🖼️ 🌐 derbyshire.gov.uk

🎡 **Pavilion Gardens**
St John's Rd. **Tel** 01298 23114. **Open** daily. **Closed** 25 Dec. 🛒 🔗 🖼️ 📷

❷ Chatsworth House and Gardens

Chatsworth is one of Britain's most impressive stately homes. Between 1687 and 1707, the 1st Duke of Devonshire replaced the old Tudor mansion with this Baroque palace. The house has a 42-hectare (105-acre) garden, landscaped in the 1760s by "Capability" Brown (see p30) and developed by head gardener Joseph Paxton (see pp60–61) in the mid-1800s.

First house built in 1552 by Bess of Hardwick

★ **Cascade**
Water tumbles down the steps of the Cascade, built in 1696 to a French design.

KEY

① Paxton's "Conservative Wall" is a wood-and-glass conservatory wall designed in 1848 by Joseph Paxton, the creator of Chatsworth's Great Conservatory (now demolished).

② **Summerhouse**

③ **Round ponds, known as the Spectacles**

④ **Grotto**

⑤ **Paxton's rock garden**

⑥ **Maze: site of Paxton's Great Conservatory**

⑦ **Canal pond**

⑧ **Seahorse fountain**

Garden entrance

House entrance

South front and canal pond with Emperor fountain

VISITORS' CHECKLIST

Practical Information
Derbyshire.
Tel 01246 565300.
Open mid-Mar–Dec:
11am–4:30pm (gardens:
11am–5pm) daily.
w chatsworth.org

Transport
Chesterfield, then bus.

★ **Chapel**
The chapel (1693) is resplendent with art and marble.

State Rooms
The rooms have fine interiors and superb art, such as this *trompe l'oeil* by Jan van der Vaart (1651–1727).

❸ Matlock Bath

Derbyshire. 🚗 9,500. 🚄 ℹ️ Matlock
Station (01335 343666).
🅦 matlock.org.uk

Matlock was developed as a spa
from the 1780s. Interesting
buildings include a former
hydrotherapy centre (1853) on
the hill above the town, which is
now used for council offices. On
the hill opposite is the mock-
Gothic Riber Castle.

From Matlock, the A6 winds
through the beautiful Derwent
Gorge to Matlock Bath. Here,
cable cars ascend to the **Heights
of Abraham** pleasure park, with
caves, nature trail and extensive
views. Lead-mining is the subject
of the **Peak District Mining
Museum**, and visitors can
inspect the old **Temple Mine**
nearby. Sir Richard Arkwright's
Cromford Mill (1771), a World
Heritage Site and the first ever
water-powered cotton spinning
mill, lies at the southern end of
the gorge *(see p343)*.

Cable cars taking visitors to the Heights of Abraham

🎪 **Heights of Abraham**
On A6. **Tel** 01629 582365. **Open**
Feb–Oct: daily. 🅿️ 🚻 limited. 📷 🖥️
🅦 heightsofabraham.com

🏛️ **Peak District Mining Museum**
The Pavilion, off A6. **Tel** 01629 583834.
Open Apr–Oct: daily; Nov–Mar:
Wed–Sun. 🚗 🚻 🖥️ 📷
🅦 peakmines.co.uk

⛏️ **Temple Mine**
Temple Rd, off A6. **Tel** 01629 583834.
Open call for details. 🚗

⛏️ **Cromford Mill**
Mill Lane, Cromford. **Tel** 01629
824297. **Open** daily. **Closed** 25 Dec.
🚗 🚻 📷
🅦 arkwrightsociety.org.uk

❹ Tissington Trail

See p341.

❺ Peak District Tour

See pp342–3.

❻ Nottingham

Nottinghamshire. 🚗 269,000. 🚄 🚌
ℹ️ Smithy Row (0844 477 5678). 🖥️
daily. 🅦 nottinghamcity.gov.uk

The name of Nottingham often
conjures up the image of the
evil Sheriff, adversary of Robin
Hood. **Nottingham Castle**
stands on a rock riddled with
underground passages. The
castle houses a museum, with
displays on the city's history,
and what was Britain's first
municipal art gallery, featuring
works by Sir Stanley Spencer
(1891–1959) and Dante Gabriel
Rossetti (1828–82). At the foot
of the castle, Britain's oldest
tavern, **Ye Olde Trip to
Jerusalem** (1189), is still in
business. Its name may refer to
the 12th- and 13th-century

crusades, but much of it
is 17th-century.

There are several museums
nearby, including the **Museum
of Nottingham Life**, which
looks at life in Nottingham over
the last 300 years, and **Wollaton
Hall and Deer Park**, an
Elizabethan mansion housing a
natural history museum.

Nottingham's redeveloped
city centre includes an award-
winning Old Market Square.

Environs
Stately homes within a few
miles of Nottingham include
the Neo-Classical **Kedleston
Hall** *(see pp32–3)*. "Bess of
Hardwick", Countess of
Shrewbury *(see p338)*, built
the spectacular **Hardwick
Hall** *(see p306)*.

🏰 **Nottingham Castle
and Museum**
Friar Lane. **Tel** 0115 9153700.
Open Tue–Sun. **Closed** 1 Jan, 24–27
Dec. 🚗 🚻 🖥️ of the caves. 🖥️ 📷

🏛️ **Wollaton Hall and Deer Park**
Wollaton. **Tel** 0115 9153900. **Open**
daily. **Closed** 25 & 26 Dec. 🚻 🖥️ 📷
🖥️ fee.

🏛️ **Museum of Nottingham Life**
Castle Boulevard. **Tel** 0115 915 3700.
Open daily. **Closed** 1 Jan, 24–26 Dec.
🚻 📷
🅦 nottinghamcity.gov.uk

🏛️ **Kedleston Hall**
Off A38. **Tel** 01332 842191.
Open mid-Feb–Oct: Sat–Wed (pm).
🚗 🚻 🖥️ 📷 NTS

🏛️ **Hardwick Hall**
Off A617. **Tel** 01246 850430.
Open mid-Feb–Oct: Wed–Sun.
🚗 🚻 limited. 🖥️ 📷 NTS

Robin Hood of Sherwood Forest

England's most colourful folk hero was a
legendary bowman, whose adventures are
depicted in numerous films and stories. He
lived in Sherwood Forest, near Nottingham,
with a band of "merry men", robbing the
rich to give to the poor. As part of an
ancient oral tradition, Robin Hood figured
mainly in ballads; the first written records
of his exploits date from the 15th
century. Today historians think that he
was not one person, but a composite of
many outlaws who refused to conform to
medieval feudal constraints.

Victorian depiction of Friar Tuck
and Robin Hood

❹ Tissington Trail

The full-length Tissington Trail runs for 13 miles (22 km), from the town of Ashbourne to Parsley Hay, where it meets the High Peak Trail. This is a short version, taking an easy route along a dismantled railway line around Tissington village and providing good views of the beautiful White Peak countryside. The Derbyshire custom of well dressing is thought to have originated in pre-Christian times. It was revived in the early 17th century, when the Tissington village wells were decorated in thanksgiving for deliverance from the plague, in the belief that the fresh water had had a medicinal effect. Well dressing is still an important event in the Peakland calendar, and can be seen in other villages where the water supplies were prone to dry up.

③ **Crakelow Cutting**
The view to the north is of open farmland, dotted with small stands of trees.

Crakelow Farm

② **Railway Cutting**
The old railway's lime-stone cuttings are now home to wild flowers, lizards and butterflies.

④ **Downhill Track**
The track runs along an 18th-century dry-stone wall, built as a result of land enclosure.

Key

--- Route

==== Minor road

A515

Town Head Farm

0 metres 500
0 yards 500

A515

Tissington

P

B5056

① **Old Station**
Tissington's old railway station has a refreshment hatch.

⑤ **Tissington Hall Well**
This and the other four wells in Tissington are decorated on Ascension Day (the 40th day after Easter). Framed boards have a layer of clay into which rice, seeds and flower petals are pressed.

Tips for Walkers

Starting point: Old Station. 🛈 Ashbourne Tourist Information (01335 343666). **Getting there:** Car from Buxton, Matlock or Ashbourne. **Length:** 3 miles (5 km). **Difficulty:** Mostly flat trail along unused railway trackbed and path. 🆆 visitpeakdistrict.com

❺ Peak District Tour

The Peak District's natural beauty and sheep-grazed crags contrast with the factories of nearby valley towns. Designated Britain's first National Park in 1951, the area has two distinct types of landscape. In the south are the gently rolling hills of the limestone White Peak. To the north, west and east are the wild, heather-clad moorlands of the Dark Peak peat bogs, superimposed on millstone grit.

⑤ Edale
The high plateau above scenic Edale marks the starting point of the 256 mile (412 km) Pennine Way footpath *(see p40)*.

Tips for Drivers

Tour length: 40 miles (60 km).
Stopping-off points: There are refreshments at Crich Tramway Village and Arkwright's Mill in Cromford. Eyam has good old-fashioned tea shops. The Nag's Head in Edale is a charming Tudor inn. Buxton has many pubs and cafés. *(See also pp636–7.)*

⑥ Buxton
This lovely spa town's opera house *(see p338)* is known as the "theatre in the hills" because of its magnificent setting.

⑦ Arbor Low
This stone circle, known as the "Stonehenge of the North", dates from around 2000 BC and consists of 46 recumbent stones enclosed by a ditch.

Key

 Tour route
═══ Other roads

⑧ Dovedale
Popular Dovedale is one of the prettiest of the Peak District's river valleys, with its stepping stones, thickly wooded slopes and wind-sculpted rocks. Izaak Walton (1593–1683), author of *The Compleat Angler,* used to fish here.

Map labels: ⑤ HOLLINS CR◯, 410 m 1,345 ft, A625, Stockport, Manchester, A6, A623, DA, A5004, A53, ⑥, Wye, A515, A5270, A6, Dove

④ Hathersage
There are spectacular panoramic views over the moors above Hathersage, which is thought to be "Morton" in Charlotte Brontë's *(see p416) Jane Eyre.*

③ Eyam
This is famous for the villagers' self-imposed quarantine to contain the plague of 1665–6. There is a fine Saxon cross in the churchyard.

② Crich Tramway Village
This unique museum is in a disused quarry. Visitors can take rides on old trams from all over the world, along reconstructed Victorian streets.

① Cromford
Arkwright's Mill *(see p340)* was the world's first water-powered cotton mill. It stands next to the Cromford Canal, part of which can be toured by horse-drawn narrowboats in the summer.

HIGH RAKE 391 m
1,283 ft

Chesterfield

Bakewell

Matlock

Cromford

Crich

Mansfield

Derby

White Peak

Harboro Rocks
379 m
1,243 ft

Carsington Water

Ashbourne

Derby

0 kilometres   3
0 miles   2

❼ Street-by-Street: Lincoln

Surrounded by the flat landscape of the Fens, Lincoln rises dramatically on a stone ridge above the River Witham, the three towers of its massive cathedral visible from afar. The Romans *(see pp48–9)* founded the first fortress here in AD 50. By the time of the Norman Conquest *(see p51)*, Lincoln was one of the most important cities in England (after London, Winchester and York). The city's wealth was due to its strategic importance for the export of wool from the Lincolnshire Wolds to Europe. Lincoln has managed to retain much of its historic character. Many remarkable medieval buildings have survived, most of which are along the aptly named Steep Hill, leading to the cathedral.

3rd-century
Newport Arch

Museum of
Lincolnshire Life

WESTGATE

BAILGATE

CASTLE HILL

STEEP HILL

DRURY LANE

MICHAELGATE

★ Lincoln Castle
The early Norman castle, rebuilt at intervals, acted as the city prison from 1787 to 1878. The chapel's coffin-like pews served to remind felons of their fate.

Norman House
(1180)

Key

— Suggested route

0 metres   100
0 yards   100

15th-century
Stonebow Gate and
bus and railway stations

Jew's House
Lincoln had a large medieval Jewish community. This mid-12th-century stone house, one of the oldest of its kind, was owned by a Jewish merchant.

For hotels and restaurants in this area see pp560–73 and pp582–603

VISITORS' CHECKLIST

Practical Information
Lincoln. 🚹 90,000.
w visitlincolnshire.com
ℹ️ Castle Hill (01522 545458).

Transport
✈ Humberside, 30 miles (48 km);
E Midlands, 51 miles (82 km). 🚆
St Mary St. 🚌 Melville St.

★ Lincoln Cathedral
Built in 1068, the cathedral is a
harmonious mix of Norman and Gothic
styles. Inside, highlights include the Angel
Choir and the Lincoln Imp.

Alfred, Lord Tennyson
A statue of the Lincolnshire-
born poet (1809–92) stands
in the grounds.

Exchequergate
Arch

The 14th-century
Pottergate Arch

Victorian
Arboretum

Ruins of Medieval
Bishop's Palace

Greestone Stairs

Misericords

Misericords are ledges that
project from the underside
of the hinged seat of a choir
stall, which provide support
while standing.

St Francis of Assisi

Lincoln Cathedral's misericords
in the early Perpendicular-style
canopied choir stalls are some
of the best in England. The
wide variety of subjects includes
parables, fables, myths, biblical
scenes and irreverent
images from daily life.

One of a pair of lions

**The Collection –
Usher Gallery**
This is packed with
clocks, ceramics, and
silver. There are
paintings by Peter de
Wint (1784–1849) and
JMW Turner (see p95).

8 Burghley House

William Cecil, 1st Lord Burghley (1520–98) was Queen Elizabeth I's adviser and confidant for 40 years and built the wonderfully dramatic Burghley House in 1555–87. The roof line bristles with stone pyramids, chimneys disguised as Classical columns and towers shaped like pepper pots. The busy skyline resolves itself into a symmetrical pattern when viewed from the west, where a lime tree stands, one of many planted by "Capability" Brown (see p30) when the surrounding deer park was landscaped in 1760. The interior walls are lavishly decorated with Italian paintings of Greek gods enacting their dramas. Historical learning activities are available all year in the education centre, and the Elizabethan "garden of surprises" features a moss house, swivelling Caesar bust and water jets.

★ **Old Kitchen**
Gleaming copper pans hang from the walls of the fan-vaulted kitchen, little altered since the Tudor period.

North Gate
Intricate examples of 19th-century wrought-iron work adorn the principal entrances.

KEY

① **The Gatehouse**, with its side turrets, is a typical feature of the "prodigy" houses of the Tudor era (see p306).

② **Mullioned windows** were added in 1683 when glass became less expensive.

③ **A chimney** has been disguised as a Classical column.

④ **Cupolas** were very fashionable details, inspired by European Renaissance architecture.

⑤ **The Billiard Room** has many fine portraits inset in oak panelling.

⑥ **Obelisk and clock** (1585)

⑦ **The Great Hall** has a double hammer-beam roof and was a banqueting hall in Elizabethan days.

⑧ **The wine cooler** (1710) is thought to be the largest in existence.

⑨ **The Fourth George Room**, one of a suite, is panelled in oak stained with ale.

West Front
Featuring the Burghley crest, the West Front was finished in 1577 and formed the original main entrance.

★ Heaven Room
Gods tumble from the sky, and satyrs and nymphs play on the walls and ceiling in this masterpiece by Antonio Verrio (1639–1707).

★ Hell Staircase
Verrio painted the ceiling to show Hell as the mouth of a cat crammed with tormented sinners. The staircase, of local stone, was installed in 1786.

❾ Stamford

Lincolnshire. 🚹 20,000. 🚆 🚌 *i* 27 St Mary's St (01780 755611). 🏪 Fri. W southwestlincs.com

Stamford is a showpiece town, famous for its churches and Georgian townhouses. The town retains a medieval street plan, with a warren of winding streets and cobbled alleys.

The spires of the medieval churches (five survive of the original eleven) give Stamford the air of a miniature Oxford.

Barn Hill, leading up from All Saints Church, is the best place for a view of Stamford's Georgian architecture in all its variety. Below it is Broad Street and High Street, where the Public Library is fronted by Tuscan columns. Inside is the **Discovering Stamford** exhibition, which tells the town's development through the ages, as well as the 6-m (20-ft) Stamford Tapestry, a depiction of the town's history in wool.

🏛 **Discovering Stamford**
Stamford Library, High St. **Tel** 01522 782010. **Open** Mon–Sat. ♿
W lincolnshire.gov.uk

❿ Northampton

Northamptonshire. 🚹 212,000. 🚆 🚌 *i* Sessions House, George Row (01604 838800). 🏪 Mon–Sat (Thu: antiques). W northamptonshire. gov.uk

This market town was once a centre for shoe-making, and the **Museum and Art Gallery** holds the world's largest collection of footwear. One of many fine old buildings is the Victorian Gothic **Guildhall**. Six miles west of the town is **Althorp**, family home of Diana Princess of Wales. Visitors can tour the house, grounds, see an exhibition on Diana and her island resting place.

🏛 **Northampton Museum and Art Gallery**
Guildhall Rd. **Tel** 01604 838111. **Open** daily (Sun: pm). **Closed** 25, 26 Dec. ♿ 📷

🏛 **Althorp**
Great Brington (off A428). **Tel** 01604 770107. **Open** Jul & Aug. **Closed** 31 Aug. 🎨 📷 ♿ 📷 W althorp.com

THE NORTH COUNTRY

The North Country at a Glance

Rugged coastlines, spectacular walks and climbs, magnificent stately homes and breathtaking cathedrals all have their place in the north of England, with its dramatic history of Roman rule, Saxon invasion, Viking attacks and border skirmishes. Reminders of the industrial revolution are found in towns such as Halifax, Liverpool and Manchester, and peace and inspiration in the dramatic scenery of the Lake District, with its awe-inspiring mountains and waters.

Locator Map

Hadrian's Wall *(see pp426–7)*, built around AD 120 to protect Roman Britain from the tribes to the north, cuts through rugged Northumberland National Park scenery.

The Lake District *(see pp358–73)* is a combination of superb peaks, tumbling rivers and falls and shimmering lakes such as Wastwater.

Yorkshire Dales National Park *(see pp388–90)* creates a delightful environment for walking and touring the farming landscape, scattered with attractive villages such as Thwaite, in Swaledale.

The Walker Art Gallery *(see pp382–3)* in Liverpool is one of the jewels in the artistic crown of the north, with an internationally renowned collection ranging from Old Masters to modern art. Sculpture includes John Gibson's *Tinted Venus* (c.1851–6).

◀ Sunrise at St Mary's Lighthouse, near Whitley Bay

NORTHUMBERL.

Hexham

Carlisle

NORTHUMB
(See pp418–33

Cockermouth

Penrith

Whitehaven · Keswick

CUMBRIA

Windermere

Kendal

Barrow-in-Furness

Lancaster

LANCASHIRE AND THE LAKES
(See pp358–83)

Skipton

Blackpool

Blackburn

Burnley

Preston

LANCASHIRE

Southport

Rochdale

Bolton

Wigan

Manchester

Liverpool

Stockport

Durham Cathedral *(see pp432–3),* a striking Norman structure with an innovative southern choir aisle and fine stained glass, has towered over the city of Durham since 1093.

Fountains Abbey *(see pp394–5),* one of the finest religious buildings in the north, was founded in the 12th century by monks who desired simplicity and austerity. Later the abbey became extremely wealthy.

0 kilometres 25

0 miles 25

• Alnwick

• Morpeth

ewcastle
oon Tyne •

• Sunderland

• Durham

JRHAM

• Hartlepool

rnard
stle •

Middlesbrough •

• Darlington

Richmond •

• Whitby

• Helmsley

ORTH / YORKSHIRE

Scarborough •

• Ripon

YORKSHIRE AND
THE HUMBER REGION
(See pp384–417)

Bridlington •

• Harrogate

WEST
ORKSHIRE

• York

EAST RIDING
OF YORKSHIRE

• Leeds

• Bradford

• Kingston
upon Hull

• Wakefield

uddersfield •

• Scunthorpe

• Grimsby

• Barnsley

• Doncaster

SOUTH
YORKSHIRE

• Sheffield

Castle Howard *(see pp402–3),* a triumph of Baroque architecture, offers many magnificent settings, including this long gallery (1805–10), designed by CH Tatham.

York *(see pp408–413)* is a city of historical treasures, ranging from the medieval to Georgian. Its magnificent minster has a large collection of stained glass and the medieval city walls are well preserved. Other sights include churches, narrow alleyways and notable museums.

The Industrial Revolution in the North

The face of Northern England in the 19th century was dramatically altered by the development of the coal mining, textile and shipbuilding industries. Lancashire, Northumberland and the West Riding (see p385) of Yorkshire all experienced population growth and migration to cities. The hardships of urban life were partly relieved by the actions of several wealthy industrial philanthropists, but many people lived in extremely deprived conditions. Although most traditional industries have now declined sharply or disappeared as demand has moved elsewhere, a growing tourist industry has developed in many of the former industrial centres.

Back-to-backs or colliers' rows, such as these houses at Easington, were provided by colliery owners from the 1800s onwards. They comprised two small rooms for cooking and sleeping, and an outside toilet.

1842 Coal Mines Act prevented women and children from working in harsh conditions in the mines.

1815 Sir Humphrey Davy invented a safety oil lamp for miners. Light shone through a cylindrical gauze sheet which prevented the heat of the flame igniting methane gas in the mine. Thousands of miners benefited from this device.

Coal mining was a family industry in the North of England with women and children working alongside the men.

1750	1800
Pre-Steam	Steam Age
1750	1800

1781 Leeds-Liverpool Canal opened. The building of canals facilitated the movement of raw materials and finished products, and aided the process of mechanization immeasurably.

1830 Liverpool and Manchester railway opened, connecting two of the biggest cities outside London. Within a month the railway carried 1,200 passengers.

Hebden Bridge (see p416), a typical West Riding textile mill town jammed into the narrow Calder Valley, typifies a pattern of workers' houses surrounding a central mill. The town benefited from its position when the Rochdale Canal (1804) and then the railway (1841) took advantage of this relatively low-level route over the Pennines.

Halifax's Piece Hall (see p417) is the most impressive surviving example of industrial architecture in northern England. It is the only complete 18th-century cloth market building in Yorkshire. Merchants sold measures of cloth known as "pieces" from rooms lining the cloisters inside. The hall is undergoing renovation until 2015, but parts of it are still accessible.

Saltaire *(see p415)* was a model village built by the wealthy cloth merchant and mill-owner Sir Titus Salt (1803–76), for the benefit of his workers. Seen here in the 1870s, it included houses and facilities such as shops, gardens and sportsfields, with almshouses, a hospital, school and chapel. A disciplinarian, Salt banned alcohol and pubs from Saltaire.

George Hudson (1800–71) built the first railway station in York *(see p412)* in 1840–42. In the 1840s he owned more than a quarter of the railways in Britain and was known as the "railway king".

Strikes to improve working conditions were common. Violence flared in July 1893 when colliery owners locked miners out of their pits and stopped their pay after the Miners' Federation resisted a 25 per cent wage cut. Over 300,000 men struggled without pay until November, when work resumed at the old rate.

Port Sunlight *(see p383)* was founded by William Hesketh Lever (1851–1925) to provide housing for workers at his Sunlight soap factory. Between 1889 and 1914 he built 800 cottages. Amenities included a pool.

1850	1900
Full Mechanization	
1850	1900

Power loom weaving transformed the textile industry while creating unemployment among skilled hand loom weavers. By the 1850s, the West Riding had 30,000 power looms, used in cotton and woollen mills. Of 79,000 workers, over half were to be found in Bradford alone.

Joseph Rowntree (1836–1925) founded his chocolate factory in York in 1892, having formerly worked with George Cadbury. As Quakers, the Rowntrees believed in the social welfare of their workers (establishing a model village in 1904), and, with Terry's confectionary (1767), they made a vast contribution to York's prosperity. Today, Nestlé Rowntree makes one of the most popular chocolate bars, the Kit Kat, and York is Britain's chocolate capital.

Furness dry dock was built in the 1890s when the shipbuilding industry moved north, in search of cheap labour and materials. Barrow-in-Furness, Glasgow *(see pp520–23)* and Tyne and Wear *(see p428)* were the new centres.

North Country Abbeys

Northern England has some of the finest and best preserved religious houses in Europe. Centres of prayer, learning and power in the Middle Ages, the larger of these were designated abbeys and were governed by an abbot. Most were located in rural areas, considered appropriate for a spiritual and contemplative life. Viking raiders had destroyed many Anglo-Saxon religious houses in the 8th and 9th centuries *(see pp50–51)* and it was not until William the Conqueror founded the Benedictine Selby Abbey in 1069 that monastic life revived in the north. New orders, Augustinians in particular, arrived from the Continent and by 1500 Yorkshire had 83 monasteries.

Ruins of St Mary's Abbey today

The Liberty of St Mary was the name given to the land around the abbey, almost a city within a city. Here, the abbot had his own market, fair, prison and gallows – all exempt from the city authorities.

St Mary's Abbey

Founded in York in 1086, this Benedictine abbey was one of the wealthiest in Britain. Its involvement in the wool trade in York and the granting of royal and papal privileges and land led to a relaxing of standards by the early 12th century. The abbot was even allowed to dress in the same style as a bishop, and was raised by the pope to the status of a "mitred abbot". As a result, 13 monks left in 1132, to found Fountains Abbey *(see pp394–5)*.

Gatehouse and St Olave's church

Interval tower

Water tower

Hospitium or guest house

Monasteries and Local Life

As one of the wealthiest landowning sections of society, the monasteries played a vital role in the local economy. They provided employment, particularly in agriculture, and dominated the wool trade, England's largest export during the Middle Ages. By 1387 two thirds of all wool exported from England passed through St Mary's Abbey, the largest wool trader in York.

Cistercian monks tilling their land

Where to See Abbeys Today

Fountains Abbey *(see pp394–5)*, founded by Benedictine monks and later taken over by Cistercians, is the most famous of the numerous abbeys in the region. Rievaulx *(see p397)*, Byland *(see p396)* and Furness *(see p372)* were all founded by the Cistercians, and Furness became the second wealthiest Cistercian house in England after Fountains. Whitby Abbey *(see p400)*, sacked by the Vikings, was later rebuilt by the Benedictine order. The northeast is famous for its early Anglo-Saxon monasteries, such as Hexham, Lindisfarne and Jarrow *(see pp422–3)*.

Mount Grace Priory *(see p398)* founded in 1398, is the best-preserved Carthusian house in England. The former individual gardens and cells of each monk are still clearly visible.

The Dissolution of the Monasteries (1536–40)

By the early 16th century, the monasteries owned one-sixth of all English land and their annual income was four times that of the Crown. Henry VIII ordered the closure of all religious houses in 1536, acquiring their wealth in the process. His attempt at dissolution provoked a large uprising of Catholic northerners led by Robert Aske later that year. The rebellion failed and Aske and others were executed for conspiracy. The dissolution continued under Thomas Cromwell, who became known as "the hammer of the monks".

Thomas Cromwell (c.1485–1549)

The large Abbot's House testified to the grand lifestyle that late medieval abbots adopted.

The Chapter House, an assembly room, was the most important building after the church.

Lavatory

Kitchen

The Abbey Wall had battlements added in 1318 to protect it against raids by Scottish armies.

The Warming House was the only room in the monastery, apart from the kitchen, which had a fire.

Refectory

Common parlour

Cloister

Kirkham Priory, an Augustinian foundation of the 1120s, enjoys a tranquil setting on the banks of the River Derwent, near Malton. The finest feature of the ruined site is the 13th-century gatehouse which leads into the priory complex.

Kirkstall Abbey was founded in 1152 by monks from Fountains Abbey. The well-preserved ruins of this Cistercian house near Leeds include the church, the late Norman chapter house and the abbot's lodging. This evening view was painted by Thomas Girtin (1775–1802).

Easby Abbey lies beside the River Swale, outside the pretty market town of Richmond. Among the remains of this Premonstratensian house, founded in 1155, are the 13th-century refectory and sleeping quarters and 14th-century gatehouse.

The Geology of the Lake District

The Lake District contains some of England's most spectacular scenery. Concentrated in just 900 sq miles (231 sq km) are the highest peaks, deepest valleys and longest lakes in the country. Today's landscape has changed little since the end of the Ice Age 10,000 years ago, the last major event in Britain's geological history. But the glaciated hills which were revealed by the retreating ice were once part of a vast mountain-chain whose remains can also be found in North America. The mountains were first raised by the gradual fusion of two ancient landmasses which, for millions of years, formed a single continent. Eventually the continent broke into two, forming Europe and America, separated by the widening Atlantic Ocean.

Honister Pass, with its distinctive U-shape, is an example of a glaciated valley, once completely filled with ice.

Geological History

The oldest rock formed as sediment under an ocean called Iapetus. Some 450 million years ago, Earth's internal movements made two continents collide, and the ocean disappear.

1 The collision buckled the former sea bed into a mountain range. Magma rose from Earth's mantle, altered the sediments and cooled into volcanic rock.

2 In the Ice Age, glaciers slowly excavated huge rock basins in the mountainsides, dragging debris to the valley floor. Frost sculpted the summits.

3 The glaciers retreated 10,000 years ago, their meltwaters forming lakes in valleys dammed by debris. As the climate improved, plants colonized the fells.

Radiating Lakes

The diversity of lakeland scenery owes much to its geology: hard volcanic rocks in the central lakes give rise to rugged hills, while soft slates to the north produce a more rounded topography. The lakes form a radial pattern, spreading out from a central volcanic rock zone.

Scafell Pike is the highest peak in England. One of the three Scafell Pikes, its two neighbours are Broad Crag and Ill Crag.

Great Gable

Old Man of Coniston

Coniston Water

Wastwater is the deepest of the lakes. Its south-eastern cliffs are streaked with granite scree – the debris formed each year as rock shattered by the winter frost tumbles down during the spring thaw.

Man on the Mountain

The sheltered valley floors with their benign climate and fertile soils are ideal for settlement. Farmhouses, dry-stone walls, pasture and sheep pens are an integral part of the landscape. Higher up, the absence of trees and bracken are the result of wind and a cooler climate. Old mine workings and tracks are the relics of once-flourishing industries.

Plantations of coniferous trees are a 20th-century feature of the landscape. Much has been done in recent years to soften their impact.

Summer grazing

Dry-stone walls *(see p309)*

Tracks

Copper and graphite mines

400–500m (130–170ft)

300–400m (100–130 ft)

Sheep pens for winter grazing

Slate and other local stone has long been incorporated into buildings: slate roofs, stone walls, lintels and bridges.

Hedges

Bassenthwaite Lake

▲ Blencathra

Derwent Water

▲ Helvellyn

Ullswater

▲ Place Fell

High Street

Windermere

Skiddaw is composed of slate, formed when the muddy sediment of the ancient ocean floor was altered by extreme pressure.

Striding Edge is a long, twisting ridge which leads to the summit of Helvellyn. It was sharpened by the widening of the valleys on either side caused by the build up of glaciers.

The Langdale Pikes are remnants of the volcanic activity which once erupted in the area. They are made of hard igneous rocks, known as Borrowdale Volcanics. Unlike the Skiddaw Slates, they have not eroded smoothly, so they leave a craggy skyline.

LANCASHIRE AND THE LAKES

Cumbria · Lancashire

The landscape painter John Constable (1776–1837) declared that the Lake District, now visited by 18 million people annually, had "the finest scenery that ever was". The Normans built many religious houses here, and William II created estates for English barons. Today, the National Trust is its most important landowner.

Within the 30 mile (45 km) radius of the Lake District lies an astonishing number of fells and lakes. Today, all looks peaceful, but from the Roman occupation to the Middle Ages, the northwest was a turbulent area, as successive kings and rulers fought over the territory. Historians can revel in the various Celtic monuments, Roman remains, stately homes and monastic ruins. Although the scenery is paramount, there are many outdoor activities as well as spectator sports, such as Cumbrian wrestling, and wildlife to observe.

Lancashire's portfolio of tourist attractions includes the fine county town of Lancaster, bright Blackpool with its autumn illuminations and fairground attractions, and the peaceful seaside beaches to the south. Inland, the most appealing regions are the Forest of Bowland, a sparse expanse of heathery grouse moor, and the picturesque Ribble Valley. Further south still are the industrial conurbations of Manchester and Merseyside, where the attractions are more urban. There are many fine Victorian buildings in Manchester, where the industrial quarter of Castlefield has been revitalized. Liverpool, with its restored Albert Dock, is best known as the seaport city of the Beatles. It has a lively club scene and is increasingly used as a film location. Both cities have good art galleries and museums.

Jetty at Grasmere, one of the most popular lakes in the Lake District

◄ Aerial view over Keswick to a mist-covered Derwent Water, Lake District National Park

Exploring Lancashire and the Lakes

The Lake District's natural scenery outweighs any of its man-made attractions. Its natural features are the result of geological upheavals over millennia (*see pp356–7*), and at 978 m (3,210 ft), Scafell Pike is its highest peak. Human influences have left their mark too: the main activities are quarrying, mining, farming and tourism.

The Lakes are most crowded in summer when activities include lake trips and hillwalking. The best bases are Keswick and Ambleside, while there are also good hotels on the shores of Windermere and Ullswater and in the Cartmel area.

Lancashire's Bowland Forest is an attractive place to explore on foot, with picturesque villages. Further south, the historic town of Lancaster has excellent museums and a castle.

Watersports on Derwentwater in the Northern Fells and Lakes area

Getting Around

For many, the first glimpse of the Lake District is from the M6 near Shap, but the A6 is a more dramatic route. You can reach Windermere by train, but you need to change at Oxenholme, on the mainline route from Euston to Glasgow. Penrith also has rail services and bus links into the Lakes. La'al Ratty, the miniature railway up Eskdale, and the Lakeside & Haverthwaite railway, which connects with the steamers on Windermere, make for enjoyable outings. Regular buses link all the main centres where excursions are organized. Seasonal minibus services connect some of the more remote passes and valleys.

Lancaster, Liverpool and Manchester are on the main rail and bus routes and also have airports. For Blackpool, you may need to change trains in Preston. Wherever you go in the area, one of the best means of getting around is on foot.

For additional map symbols see back flap

Sights at a Glance

1. Carlisle
2. Penrith
3. Dalemain
4. Ullswater
5. Keswick
6. *Northern Fells and Lakes pp364–5*
7. Cockermouth
8. Newlands Valley
9. Buttermere
10. Borrowdale
11. Wastwater
12. Eskdale
13. Duddon Valley
14. Langdale
15. Grasmere and Rydal
16. Ambleside
17. Windermere
18. Coniston Water
19. Kendal
20. Furness Peninsula
21. Cartmel
22. Levens Hall
23. Morecambe Bay
24. Leighton Hall
25. Lancaster
26. Ribble Valley
27. Blackpool
28. Salford Quays
29. *Manchester pp376–9*
30. *Liverpool pp380–83*

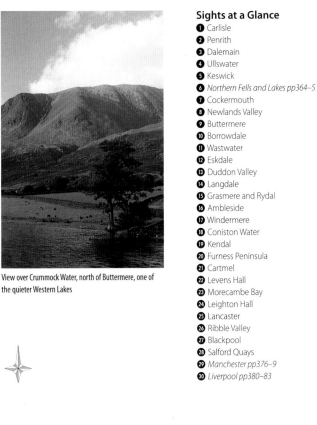

View over Crummock Water, north of Buttermere, one of the quieter Western Lakes

| 0 kilometres | 20 |
| 0 miles | 10 |

Key

━━ Motorway

━━ Major road

━━ Secondary road

┄┄ Minor road

── Scenic route

╍╍ Main railway

── Minor railway

△ Summit

Imposing façade of the Museum of Liverpool

❶ Carlisle

Cumbria. 🚶 72,000. 🚆 🚌 **i** The
Old Town Hall, Green Market (01228
625600). **w discover carlisle.co.uk**

Due to its proximity to the
Scottish border, this city has
long been a defensive site.
Known as Luguvalium by the
Romans, it was an outpost
of Hadrian's Wall *(see
pp426–7)*. Carlisle was
sacked and pillaged
repeatedly by the Danes,
the Normans and
border raiders, and
suffered damage as a
Royalist stronghold under
Cromwell *(see p56)*.
Today, Carlisle is the
capital of Cumbria. In its
centre are the timber-
framed Guildhall and
market cross, and forti-
fications still exist around
its West Walls, drum-
towered gates and its
Norman **castle**. The castle
tower has a small museum
devoted to the King's Own
Border Regiment. The
cathedral dates from 1122
and features a decorative
east window. Carlisle's
Tullie House Museum
recreates the city's past
with sections on Roman
history and Cumbrian
wildlife. Nearby lie the
evocative ruins of

Saxon iron sword in the Tullie
House Museum

Façade of Hutton-in-the-Forest with medieval tower on the right

Lanercost Priory (c.1166) and
Birdoswald Roman Fort.

🏰 Carlisle Castle
Castle Way. **Tel** 01228 591922.
Open Apr–Oct: daily; Nov–Mar: Sat &
Sun. **Closed** 1 Jan, 24–26 Dec. 🅿 ♿
ltd. ⬛ 📷 EH

🏛 Tullie House Museum
Castle St. **Tel** 01228 618718.
Open daily (Sun: pm). **Closed** 1 Jan,
25 & 26 Dec 🅿 ♿ 📷 ⬛ EH

🏯 Lanercost Priory
Nr Brampton. **Tel** 016977 3030.
Open Apr–Sep: daily, Oct: Thu–
Mon; Nov–Mar: Sat & Sun. 📷 🅿
EH ♿ ltd.

🏰 Birdoswald Roman Fort
Gilsland, Brampton. **Tel** 016977 47602.
Open Apr–Oct: daily; Nov–Mar: Sat &
Sun. **Closed** 1 Jan, 24–26, 31 Dec. 🅿
⬛ 📷 EH

❷ Penrith

Cumbria. 🚶 15,000. **i** Robinson's
School, Middlegate (017688 67466).
📅 Tue, Sat, Sun. **w visiteden.gov.uk**

Timewarp shopfronts on
the market square and a
14th-century **castle** of
sandstone are Penrith's main
attractions. There are some
strange hogback stones in St
Andrew's churchyard, allegedly
a giant's grave, but more likely
Anglo-Viking headstones.

Environs
Just northeast of Penrith at Little
Salkeld is a famous Bronze Age
circle (with 66 tall stones) known
as **Long Meg and her Daughters**.
Six miles (9 km) northwest of
Penrith lies **Hutton-in-the-
Forest**. The oldest part of this
house is the 13th-century tower.
Inside is a magnificent Italianate
staircase, a sumptuously panelled
17th-century Long Gallery, a
delicately stuccoed Cupid Room
dating from the 1740s, and
several Victorian rooms. Outside,
you can walk around the walled
garden and topiary terraces, or
explore the woods.

🏰 Penrith Castle
Ullswater Rd. **Tel** 0870 333 1181.
House: Open daily. ♿ grounds. EH

🏠 Hutton-in-the-Forest
Off B5305. **Tel** 017684 84449. House:
Open Easter–Sep: Wed, Thu, Sun &
pub hols (pm). Grounds: **Open** Apr–
Oct: Sun–Fri. 🅿 ♿ ltd. ⬛ 📷

❸ Dalemain

Penrith, Cumbria. **Tel** 017684 86450.
🚆 🚌 Penrith then taxi. **Open** Apr–
Oct: Sun–Thu. 🅿 ♿ limited. ⬛ 📷
📷 **w dalemain.com**

A seemly Georgian façade gives
this fine house near Ullswater
the impression of architectural
unity, but hides a much-altered
medieval and Elizabethan

Traditional Cumbrian Sports

Cumberland wrestling is one of the most interesting sports
to watch in the summer months. The combatants, often clad
in longjohns and embroidered velvet pants, clasp one another
in an armlock and attempt to topple each other over. Technique
and good balance outweigh physical force. Other traditional
Lakeland sports include fell-racing, a gruelling test of speed and
stamina up and down local peaks at ankle-breaking speed. Hound-
trailing is also a popular sport in which specially bred hounds
follow an aniseed trail over
the hills. Sheep-dog trials,
steam fairs and flower
shows take place in
summer. The Egremont
Crab Fair in September is
famous for its face-pulling,
or "gurning", competition.

Cumberland wrestlers

Sheep resting at Glenridding, on the southwest shore of Ullswater

structure with a maze of rambling passages. Public rooms include a superb Chinese drawing room with hand-painted wallpaper, and a panelled 18th-century drawing room. Several small museums occupy various outbuildings, and the gardens contain a fine collection of fragrant shrub roses and a huge silver fir.

Sumptuous Chinese drawing room at Dalemain

➍ Ullswater

Cumbria. ➔ Penrith. **ℹ** Main car park, Glenridding, Penrith (017684 82414). **W** ullswater.com

Often considered the most beautiful of all Cumbria's lakes, Ullswater stretches from gentle farmland near Penrith to dramatic hills and crags at its southern end. The main western shore road can be very busy.

In summer, two restored Victorian steamers ply regularly from Pooley Bridge to Glen-ridding. One of the best walks crosses the eastern shore from Glenridding to Hallin Fell and the moorland of Martindale. The western side passes Gowbarrow, where Wordsworth's imm-ortalized "host of golden daffodils" bloom in spring *(see p370)*.

➎ Keswick

Cumbria. 🔼 5,000. **ℹ** Moot Hall, Market Sq (017687 72645). **W** golakes.co.uk

Popular as a tourist venue since the end of the 18th century, Keswick has guest houses, a summer repertory theatre, outdoor equipment shops and a popular street market. Its most striking central building is the **Moot Hall**, dating from 1813, now used as the tourist office. The town prospered on wool and leather until, in Tudor times, deposits of graphite and copper were discovered. Mining then took over as the main industry and Keswick became an important centre for pencil manufacture. In World War II, hollow pencils were made to hide espionage maps on thin paper. The factory includes the **Pencil Museum** with interesting audiovisual shows. Among the

many fine exhibits at the **Keswick Museum and Art Gallery** are the original manuscripts of Lakeland writers, musical stones and many other curiosities.

To the east of the town lies the ancient stone circle of Castlerigg, thought to be older than Stonehenge.

🏛 **Pencil Museum**
Carding Mill Lane. **Tel** 017687 73626. **Open** 9:30am–5pm daily. **Closed** 1 Jan, 25, 26 Dec. 🅿 &️ 🖥 📷
W pencilmuseum.co.uk

🏛 **Keswick Museum and Art Gallery**
Fitz Park, Station Rd. **Tel** 017687 73263. **Open** 10am–4pm Tue–Sat & public hols. &️ 📷

Outdoor equipment shop in Keswick

❻ Northern Fells and Lakes

Many visitors praise this northern area of the Lake District National Park for its scenery and geological interest *(see pp356–7)*. It is ideal walking country, and nearby Derwentwater, Thirlmere and Bassenthwaite provide endless scenic views, rambles and opportunities for watersports. Large areas surrounding the regional centre of Keswick *(see p363)* are accessible only on foot, particularly the huge mass of hills known as Back of Skiddaw – located between Skiddaw and Caldbeck – or the Helvellyn range, east of Thirlmere.

Lorton Vale
The lush, green farmland south of Cockermouth creates a marked contrast with the more rugged mountain landscapes of the central Lake District. In the village of Low Lorton is the private manor house of Lorton Hall, dating from the 15th century.

KEY

① **The Whinlatter Pass** is an easy route from Keswick to the farmland of Lorton Vale. It gives a good view of Bassenthwaite Lake and a glimpse of Grisedale Pike.

② **Bassenthwaite** is best viewed from the east shore; however, accessibility is limited. Parking is easier from the west side.

③ **Blencathra**, also known as Saddleback because of its twin peaks (868 m; 2,847 ft), is a challenging climb, especially in winter.

④ **Thirlmere** was created as a reservoir to serve Manchester in 1879.

Derwentwater
Surrounded by woodland slopes and fells, this attractive oval lake is dotted with tiny islands. One of these was inhabited by St Herbert, a disciple of St Cuthbert *(see p423)*, who lived there as a hermit until 687. Boats from Keswick provide lake excursions.

Map labels: Carlisle, B5291, Workington, A66, Bassenthwaite Lake, High Lorton, LORTON VALE, Whinlatter Pass, B5292, A591, River Derwent, Braithwaite, B5289, Loweswater, Newlands Beck, Grange, Derwent Water, Buttermere

The Major Peaks

The Lake District hills are the highest in England. Although they seem small by Alpine or world standards, the scale of the surrounding terrain makes them look extremely grand. Some of the most important peaks are shown on the following pages. Each peak is regarded as having its own personality. This section shows the Skiddaw fells, which are north of Keswick.

Map labels: Blencathra, Skiddaw, Grisedale Pike, Grasmoor, Knott Rigg, Helvellyn, Great Gable, High Street, Wastwater Screes, Scafell, Hard Knott, The Old Man of Coniston

Key

▬ From ① Blencathra to ② Cockermouth *(see opposite)*

▬ From ③ Grisedale Pike to ④ the Old Man of Coniston *(see pp366–7)*

▬ From ⑤ the Old Man of Coniston to ⑥ Windermere and Tarn Crag *(see pp368–9)*

— National Park boundary

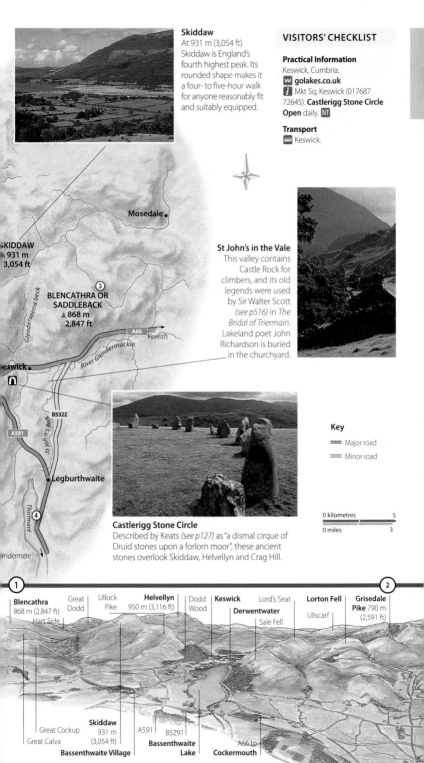

Skiddaw

At 931 m (3,054 ft) Skiddaw is England's fourth highest peak. Its rounded shape makes it a four- to five-hour walk for anyone reasonably fit and suitably equipped.

VISITORS' CHECKLIST

Practical Information
Keswick, Cumbria.
w golakes.co.uk
i Mkt Sq, Keswick (017687 72645). **Castlerigg Stone Circle Open** daily. NT

Transport
Keswick.

Mosedale

SKIDDAW
931 m
3,054 ft

BLENCATHRA OR SADDLEBACK
868 m
2,847 ft

Glenderaterra beck

A66   Penrith

River Glendermackin

Keswick

B5322

A591

St John's Beck

Legburthwaite

Thirlmere

Windermere

St John's in the Vale

This valley contains Castle Rock for climbers, and its old legends were used by Sir Walter Scott (see p516) in The Bridal of Triermain. Lakeland poet John Richardson is buried in the churchyard.

Key

━━ Major road
━━ Minor road

0 kilometres   5
0 miles   3

Castlerigg Stone Circle

Described by Keats (see p127) as "a dismal cirque of Druid stones upon a forlorn moor", these ancient stones overlook Skiddaw, Helvellyn and Crag Hill.

1 — 2

Blencathra
868 m (2,847 ft)
Hart Side

Great Dodd

Ullock Pike

Helvellyn
950 m (3,116 ft)

Dodd Wood

Keswick

Derwentwater

Lord's Seat

Sale Fell

Ullscarf

Lorton Fell

Grisedale Pike
790 m (2,591 ft)

Great Cockup
Great Calva

Skiddaw
931 m
(3,054 ft)

A591

B5291

Bassenthwaite Village

Bassenthwaite Lake

A66 to
Cockermouth

For additional map symbols see back flap

Crummock Water, one of the quieter "western lakes"

❼ Cockermouth

Cumbria. 🗺 8,000. 🚅 Workington.
🚌 ℹ 4 Kings Arms Lane, off Main
St (01900 822634).
Ⓦ **western-lakedistrict.co.uk**

Colourwashed terraces and
restored workers' cottages
beside the river are especially
attractive in the busy market
town of Cockermouth, which
dates from the 12th century.
The place not to miss is the
handsome **Wordsworth House**,
in the Main Street, where the
poet was born (see p370). This
fine Georgian building still
contains a few of the family's
possessions, and is furnished
in the style of the late 18th
century. Wordsworth mentions
the attractive terraced garden,
which overlooks the River
Derwent, in his *Prelude*. The
local parish church contains a
Wordsworth memorial window.

Cockermouth **castle** is partly
ruined but still inhabited; it is
open to the public occasionally,
most often during the
Cockermouth Festival, which
is held in July. The **Jennings
Brewery** invites visitors for
tours and tastings.

🏛 **Wordsworth House**
Main St. **Tel** 01900 824805.
Open Mar–Oct: Sat–Wed.
🐾 non-members. 📷 NT
Ⓦ **wordsworthhouse.org.uk**

🏭 **Jennings Brewery**
Castle Brewery. **Tel** 0845 1297190.
Open Mon–Sat (Jan: Sat only; Jul, Aug:
daily). 🎫 📷
Ⓦ **jennings brewery.co.uk**

❽ Newlands Valley

Cumbria. 🚅 Penrith then bus. 🚌
Cockermouth. ℹ Market Sq,
Keswick (017687 72645).
Ⓦ **lake-district.gov.uk**

From the gently wooded shores
of Derwentwater, the Newlands
Valley runs through a scattering
of farms towards rugged
heights of 335 m (1,100 ft) at
the top of a pass, where steps
lead to a waterfall, Moss Force.
Grisedale Pike, Cat Bells and
Robinson all provide excellent
fell walks. Local mineral
deposits of copper, graphite,
lead and even small amounts of
gold and silver were extensively
mined here from Elizabethan
times onwards. **Little Town** was
used as a setting by Beatrix
Potter (see p371) in The Tale of
Mrs Tiggywinkle.

Kitchen, with an old range and tiled floor, at Wordsworth House

Blencathra
868 m (2,847 ft)

Grisedale
Pike
790 m (2,591 ft)

Grasmoor
850 m (2788 ft)
Wandope

White
Pike

Robinson
Great Dodd
Dalehead

Fleetwith Pike

Raise

Looking
Stead

Helvellyn
950 m (3,118 ft)

Knott Rigg

Crummock Water

Ennerdale

Buttermere

Buttermere village

Pillar

Mosedale
Innominate Tarn
and Haystacks

Great Gab
899 m (2,94

Kirk Fell

Black Sail Pass

❾ Buttermere

Cumbria. 🚂 Penrith. 🚌 Keswick. 🚌 Penrith to Keswick; Keswick to Buttermere. 🅸 Town Hall, Market St, Cockermouth (01900 822634).

Interlinking with Crummock Water and Loweswater, Buttermere and its surroundings contain some of the most appealing countryside in the region. Often known as the "western lakes", the three are remote enough not to become too crowded. Buttermere is a jewel amid grand fells: High Stile, Red Pike and Haystacks. Here the ashes of the celebrated hill-walker and author of fell-walking books, A W Wainwright, were scattered.

The village of Buttermere, with its handful of houses and inns, is a popular starting point for walks round all three lakes. Loweswater is the furthest and therefore the quietest, surrounded by woods and hills. Nearby Scale Force is the highest waterfall in the Lake District, plunging 52 m (170 ft).

Verdant valley of Borrowdale, a favourite with artists

❿ Borrowdale

Cumbria. 🚂 Penrith. 🚌 Keswick. 🅸 Moot Hall, Keswick (01768 774649).

This romantic valley, subject of a myriad sketches and watercolours before photography stole the scene, lies beside the densely wooded shores of Derwentwater under towering crags. It is a popular trip from Keswick and a great variety of walks are possible along the valley.

The tiny hamlet of **Grange** is one of the prettiest spots, where the valley narrows dramatically to form the "Jaws of Borrowdale". Nearby Castle Crag has superb views.

From Grange you can complete the circuit of Derwentwater along the western shore, or move southwards to the more open farmland around Seatoller. As you head south by road, look out for a National Trust sign (*see p33*) to the **Bowder Stone**, a delicately poised block weighing nearly 2,000 tonnes, which may have fallen from the crags above or been deposited by a glacier millions of years ago.

Two attractive hamlets in Borrowdale are **Rosthwaite** and **Stonethwaite**. Also worth a detour, preferably on foot, is Watendlath village, off a side road near the famous beauty spot of **Ashness Bridge**.

Walking in the Lake District

Typical Lake District stile over dry-stone wall

Two long-distance footpaths pass through the Lake District's most spectacular scenery. The 70 mile (112 km) Cumbria Way runs from Carlisle to Ulverston via Keswick and Coniston. The western section of the Coast-to-Coast Walk (*see pp40–41*) passes through this area. There are hundreds of shorter walks along lake shores, nature trails or following more challenging uphill routes. Walkers should stick to paths to avoid erosion, and check weather conditions at www.lakedistrictweatherline.co.uk.

④

Scafell Pike 978 m (3,210 ft)
Langdale Pikes
Hard Knott 550 m (1,803 ft)
Hardknott Pass
Carrs
Grey Friar
Swirl How
Dow Crag
Old Man of Coniston 803 m (2,633 ft)
Caw

Harter Fell
Seathwaite Tarn

water
Wastwater Screes
Crinkle Crags 815 m (2,674 ft)
Blea Tarn
Eskdale
Ravenglass and Eskdale Railway
Seathwaite
River Duddon

Convivial Wasdale Head Inn at Wasdale Head

⓫ Wastwater

Wasdale, Cumbria. �+ Whitehaven.
ℹ Lowes Court Gallery, Egremont (01946 820693).

A silent reflection of truly awesome surroundings, black, brooding Wastwater is a mysterious, evocative lake. The road from Nether Wasdale continues along its northwest side. Along its eastern flank loom walls of sheer scree over 600 m (2,000 ft) high. Beneath them the water looks inky black, whatever the weather, plunging an icy 80 m (260 ft) from the waterline to the bottom to form England's deepest lake. You can walk along the screes, but it is an uncomfortable and dangerous scramble. Sailing and power boats are banned, but fishing permits are available from the nearby National Trust camp site.

At Wasdale Head lies one of Britain's grandest views: the austere pyramid of Great Gable, centrepiece of a fine mountain composition, with the huge forms of Scafell and Scafell Pike. The scenery is utterly unspoilt, and the only buildings lie at the far end of the lake: an inn and a tiny church commemorating fallen climbers. Here the road ends, and you must turn back or take to your feet, following signs for Black Sail Pass and Ennerdale, or walk up the grand fells ahead. Wasdale's irresistible backdrop was the inspiration of the first serious British mountaineers, who flocked here during the 19th century, insouciantly clad in tweed jackets, carrying little more than a length of rope slung over their shoulders.

⓬ Eskdale

Cumbria. �+ Ravenglass then narrow-gauge railway to Eskdale (Easter–Oct: daily; Dec–Feb: phone to check).
🅦 **ravenglass-railway.co.uk**
ℹ Lowes Court Gallery, Egremont (01946 820693). 🅦 **eskdale.info**

The pastoral delights of Eskdale are best encountered over the gruelling Hardknott Pass, which is the most taxing drive in the Lake District, with steep gradients. You can pause below the 393-m (1,291-ft) summit to explore the Roman Hardknott Fort or enjoy the lovely view. As you descend into Eskdale, rhododendrons and pines flourish in a landscape of small hamlets, narrow lanes and gentle farmland. The main settlements are the villages of Boot and Eskdale Green, and Ravenglass, the only coastal village in the Lake District National Park.

Just south of Ravenglass is the impressive **Muncaster Castle**, the richly furnished home of the Pennington family. Another way to enjoy the scenery is to take the miniature railway (known as La'al Ratty) from Ravenglass to Dalegarth.

🏠 **Muncaster Castle**
Ravenglass. **Tel** 01229 717614. Castle: **Open** mid-Mar–Oct: Sun–Fri (pm) & public hols. Garden: **Open** Feb–Dec: daily. 📷 📖 ♿ ground floor and garden. 🖥 🅦 **muncaster.co.uk**

Remains of the Roman Hardknott Fort, Eskdale

5

Walna Scar

Old Man of Coniston
803 m (2,633 ft)
Dow Crag

Buck Pike

Levers Water

Swirl How

Wetherlam

Lord's Rake

Scafell Pike
978 m (3,210 ft)

Bow Fell

Langdale Pikes: Pike o'Stickle,
Harrison Stickle and Sergeant Man

Great End

Skiddaw
931 m
(3,054 ft)

Yewdale

Coniston Water

Coniston Village

Tarn Hows

Crinkle Crags
815 m (2,674 ft)

Pike o'Blisco

Wrynose Fell

Little Langdale

Little Langdale Tarn

Elterwater
Elterwater Village

Grasmere (lake and village)

Thirlmere

6

5

Autumnal view of Seathwaite, in the Duddon Valley, a popular centre for walkers and climbers

⓭ Duddon Valley

Cumbria. 🚋 Foxfield, Ulverston. 🛈
The Square, Broughton-in-Furness
(01229 716115; Easter–Oct only).
🆆 duddonvalley.co.uk

Also known as Dunnerdale, this
picturesque tract of countryside
inspired 35 of Wordsworth's
sonnets *(see p370)*. The prettiest
stretch lies between Ulpha and
Cockley Beck. In autumn the
colours of heather moors and a
light sprinkling of birch trees are
particularly beautiful. Stepping
stones and bridges span the
river at intervals, the most
charming being Birk's Bridge,
near Seathwaite. At the
southern end of the valley,
where the River Duddon meets
the sea at Duddon Sands, is the
pretty village of Broughton-in-
Furness. Note the stone slabs
once used for fish on market
day in the square.

⓮ Langdale

Cumbria. 🚋 Windermere. 🛈 Market
Cross, Ambleside (0844 2250544).
🆆 golakes.co.uk

Stretching from Skelwith Bridge,
where the Brathay surges
powerfully over waterfalls, to
the summits of Great Langdale
is the two-pronged Langdale
Valley. Walkers and climbers
throng here to take on Pavey
Ark, Pike o'Stickle, Crinkle Crags
and Bow Fell. The local
mountain rescue teams are the
busiest in Britain.

Great Langdale is the more
spectacular valley and it is often
crowded, but quieter Little
Langdale has many attractions
too. It is worth completing the
circuit back to Ambleside via
the southern route, stopping at
Blea Tarn. Reedy Elterwater is a
picturesque spot, once a site of
the gunpowder industry.
Wrynose Pass, west of Little
Langdale, climbs to 390 m
(1,281 ft), a warm-up for
Hardknott Pass further on. At its
top is Three Shires Stone,
marking the former boundary
of the old counties of
Cumberland, Westmorland
and Lancashire.

⑥

Heron Pike
Fairfield
Helvellyn
Striding Edge
Ambleside
Snarker Pike
Red Screes
Kirkstone Pass
Ullswater
High Street
Troutbeck
Stony Cove
Pike
High Rise
Harter Fell
Skeggles Water
Branstree
Sadgill
Tarn Crag
Green Quarter Fell
ydal Water
wks-
ad
**Troutbeck
Bridge**
Windermere
A592
A591
Kentmere
**Windermere
Town**
River Sprint

Rydal Water, one of the major attractions of the Lake District

⑮ Grasmere and Rydal

Cumbria. Grasmere 🏔 700. Rydal 🏔 100. 🚌 Grasmere. ℹ️ Central Bldgs, Market Cross, Ambleside (08442 250 544). 🆆 grasmereandrydal.org.uk

The poet William Wordsworth lived in both these villages on the shores of two lakes. Fairfield, Nab Scar and Loughrigg Fell rise steeply above their reedy shores and offer good opportunities for walking. Grasmere is now a sizable settlement, and the famous Grasmere sports *(see p362)* attract large crowds every August.

The Wordsworth family is buried in St Oswald's Church, and crowds flock to the annual ceremony of strewing the church's earth floor with fresh rushes. Most visitors head for **Dove Cottage**, where the poet spent his most creative years. The museum in the barn behind includes such artefacts as the great man's socks. The Wordsworths moved to **Rydal Mount**, in Rydal in 1813 and lived here until 1850. The grounds have waterfalls

and a summerhouse. Dora's Field nearby is a blaze of daffodils in spring and the Fairfield Horseshoe offers an energetic walk.

🏛 Dove Cottage and the Wordsworth Museum
Off A591 nr Grasmere.
Tel 015394 35544. **Open** daily (Nov–Feb: Wed–Mon). **Closed** 24–26 Dec, mid-Jan–mid-Feb. 🐾 📷 💻 📷
🆆 wordsworth.org.uk

🏛 Rydal Mount
Rydal. **Tel** 015394 33002.
Open Mar–Oct: daily; Nov–Feb: Wed–Sun. **Closed** Jan, 25 & 26 Dec. 🐾 ♿ limited. 📷

⑯ Ambleside

Cumbria. 🏔 3,400. 🚌 ℹ️ Central Buildings, Market Cross (0844 2250544). 🍴 Wed. 🆆 golakes.co.uk

Ambleside has good road connections to all parts of the Lakes and is an attractive base, especially for walkers and climbers. Mainly Victorian in character, it has a range of outdoor clothing, crafts and specialist food shops. An enterprising little cinema and a summer classical music festival add life in the evenings. Sights in town are small-scale: the remnants of the Roman fort of Galava, AD 79, Stock Ghyll Force waterfall and **Bridge House**, now a National Trust information centre.

Environs
Within easy reach of Ambleside is the scenic Loughrigg Fell. At nearby Troutbeck is the restored farmhouse of **Townend**, dating from 1626, whose interior gives an insight into Lakeland domestic life.

The tiny Bridge House over Stock Beck in Ambleside

William Wordsworth (1770–1850)

Best known of the Romantic poets, Wordsworth was born in the Lake District and spent most of his life there. After school in Hawkshead and a period at Cambridge, a legacy enabled him to pursue his literary career. He settled at Dove Cottage with his sister Dorothy and in 1802 married an old school friend, Mary Hutchinson. They lived simply, walking, bringing up their children and receiving visits from poets such as Coleridge and de Quincey. Wordsworth's prose works include one of the earliest guidebooks to the Lake District.

Beatrix Potter and the Lake District

Although best known for her children's stories with characters such as Peter Rabbit and Jemima Puddleduck, which she also illustrated, Beatrix Potter (1866–1943) became a champion of conservation in the Lake District after moving there in 1906. She married William Heelis, devoted herself to farming, and was an expert on Herdwick sheep. To conserve her beloved countryside, she donated land to the National Trust.

Cover illustration of *Jemima Puddleduck* (1908)

mills in Cumbria that once served the textiles industry. The **World of Beatrix Potter** recreates her characters in an exhibition, and a film tells her life story.

Beatrix Potter wrote many of her books at **Hill Top**, the 17th-century farmhouse at Near Sawrey, northwest of Windermere. The house is furnished with many of Potter's possessions and left as it was in her lifetime. The **Beatrix Potter Gallery** in Hawkshead holds annual exhibitions of her manuscripts and illustrations.

🏛 Townend
Troutbeck, Windermere.
Tel 015394 32628. **Open** Apr–Oct: Wed–Sun; Sun & bank hol Mon: pm. 🅿 **NT**

⓱ Windermere

Cumbria. 🚉 Windermere. 🚌 Victoria St. ℹ Victoria St (015394 46499) or Glebe Rd, Bowness-on-Windermere (015394 42895).

At over 10 miles (16 km) long, this dramatic watery expanse is England's largest lake. Industrial magnates built mansions around its shores long before the railway arrived. Stately **Brockhole**, now a national park visitor centre, was one such grand estate. When the railway reached Windermere in 1847, it enabled crowds of workers to visit the area on day trips.

Today, a year-round car ferry service connects the lake's east and west shores (it runs between Ferry Nab and Ferry

House), and summer steamers link Lakeside, Bowness and Ambleside on the north-south axis. Belle Isle, a wooded island on which a unique round house stands, is one of the lake's most attractive features, but landing is not permitted. **Fell Foot Park** is at the south end of the lake, and there are good walks on the northwest shore. A quite stunning viewpoint is Orrest Head 238 m (784 ft), northeast of Windermere town.

Environs
Bowness-on-Windermere, on the east shore, is a popular centre. Many of its buildings display Victorian details, and St Martin's Church dates back to the 15th century. The **Blackwell Arts and Crafts House** is one of Britain's most beautiful houses from the early 20th century. It still boasts all of its original features. The **Stott Park Bobbin Mill** is the last working example of over 70 such

🅸 Brockhole Visitor Centre
On A591. **Tel** 015394 46601.
Open daily. 🅱 🖵 🏠

🍃 Fell Foot Park
Newby Bridge. **Tel** 015395 31273.
Open daily. 🅱 🖵 **NT**

🏛 Blackwell Arts and Crafts House
Bowness-on-Windermere. **Tel** 015394 46139. **Open** daily. 🅿 🖵

🏛 Stott Park Bobbin Mill
Finsthwaite. **Tel** 01539 531087.
Open Apr–Oct: Mon–Fri & public hols.
🅿 🚫 🏠 **EH**

🏛 World of Beatrix Potter
The Old Laundry, Crag Brow. **Tel** 015394 88444. **Open** daily. **Closed** 25 Dec, mid-Jan–mid-Feb. 🅿 🖵 🅱 🏠

🚌 Hill Top
Near Sawrey, Ambleside. **Tel** 015394 36269. House: **Open** Feb–Oct: Sat–Thu; Garden: **Open** Feb–Dec: daily. 🅿 **NT**

🏛 Beatrix Potter Gallery
The Square, Hawkshead. **Tel** 015394 36355. **Open** Feb–Oct: Sat–Thu. 🅿 🏠 **NT**

Boats moored along the shore at Waterhead, near Ambleside, the north end of Windermere

Peaceful Coniston Water, the setting of Arthur Ransome's novel, *Swallows and Amazons* (1930)

⑱ Coniston Water

Cumbria. 🚆 Windermere then bus. 🚌 Ambleside then bus. ℹ️ Coniston car park, Ruskin Ave (015394 41533); Coniston Boating Centre. **Tel** 015394 41366. **W** conistontic.org

For the finest view of this lovely lake, you need to climb a little. The 19th-century art critic, writer and philosopher John Ruskin had a fine view from his house, **Brantwood**, where his paintings can be seen today. Contemporary art exhibitions and events take place throughout the year.

An enjoyable excursion is the summer lake trip from Coniston Pier on the National Trust steam yacht, *Gondola*, calling at Brantwood. Alternatively, boats can be hired at the Coniston Boating Centre. The lake was also the scene of Donald Campbell's fatal attempt on the world water speed record in 1967. The green slate village of Coniston, once a centre for coppermining, now caters for walkers.

To the northwest is **Hawkshead**, a quaint, traffic-free village with timber-framed houses. To the south is the vast Grizedale Forest, dotted with woodland sculptures and popular with mountain bikers.

Just north of Coniston Water is the man-made **Tarn Hows**, a landscaped tarn surrounded by woods. There is a pleasant climb up the 803 m (2,635 ft) Old Man of Coniston.

🏛 Brantwood

Off B5285, nr Coniston. **Tel** 015394 41396. **Open** mid-Mar–mid-Nov: 11am–5pm daily; mid-Nov–mid-Mar: 11am–4:30pm Wed–Sun. 🅿️ 🚻 🖥 📷 ♿ limited.

⑲ Kendal

Cumbria. 🚹 28,000. 🚆 ℹ️ 25 Stramongate (01539 735891). 🛒 Wed, Sat. **W** southlakeland.gov.uk

A busy market town, Kendal is the administrative centre of the region and the southern gateway to the Lake District. Built in grey limestone, it has an arts centre, the **Brewery**, and a central area which is best enjoyed on foot. **Abbot Hall**, built in 1759, has paintings by Turner and Romney, as well as Gillows furniture. In addition, the hall's stable block contains the **Museum of Lakeland Life**, with occasional workshops demonstrating local crafts and trades. There are dioramas of geology and wildlife in the **Kendal Museum**.

About 3 miles (5 km) south of the town is 14th-century **Sizergh Castle**, with a fortified tower, carved fireplaces and a lovely garden.

Kendal mint cake, the famous lakeland energy-booster for walkers

🏛 Abbot Hall Art Gallery & Museum of Lakeland Life

Kendal. **Tel** 01539 722464. **Open** Gallery: mid-Jan–mid-Dec: Mon–Sat; Museum: Mon–Sat all year (mid-Jul–mid-Sep: both daily). 🅿️ ♿ gallery. 📷 by arrangement. 🖥 📷 **W** abbothall.org.uk

🏛 Kendal Museum

Station Rd. **Tel** 01539 815597. **Open** Wed–Sat. **Closed** Christmas week. 📷 **W** kendalmuseum.org.uk

🏰 Sizergh Castle

Off A591 & A590. **Tel** 01539 60951. **Open** Mar–Oct: Sun–Thu. 🅿️ ♿ ground floor & grounds. 🖥 NT 📷

⑳ Furness Peninsula

Cumbria. 🚆 🚌 Barrow-in-Furness. ℹ️ Forum 28, Duke St, Barrow-in-Furness (01229 876505). **W** barrowbc.gov.uk

Barrow-in-Furness (*see p353*) is the peninsula's main town. Its **Dock Museum**, built over a Victorian dock where ships were repaired, traces the history of Barrow using interactive computer displays.

Ruins of the red sandstone walls of **Furness Abbey** remain in the wooded Vale of Deadly Nightshade, with a small exhibition of monastic life. The historic town of Ulverston received its charter in 1280. Stan Laurel, of Laurel and Hardy fame, was born here in 1890. His memorabilia **museum** has a cinema. In the nearby village of Gleaston is the **Gleaston Water Mill**, a 400-year-old, working corn mill.

Dock Museum
North Rd, Barrow-in-Furness. **Tel** 01229 876400. **Open** Easter–Oct: Wed–Sun; Nov–Easter: Wed–Sun; public hols. 🚻 ♿ 📷
🌐 dockmuseum.org.uk

Furness Abbey
Vale of Deadly Nightshade. **Tel** 01229 823420. **Open** Apr–Sep: Thu–Mon; Oct–Mar: Sat & Sun. **Closed** 1 Jan, 24–26 Dec. 📷 🎧 ♿ limited. EH

Gleaston Water Mill
Gleaston. **Tel** 01229 869244. **Open** Tue–Sun. 🌐 watermill.co.uk

Laurel and Hardy Museum
Upper Brook St, Ulverston. **Tel** 01229 582292. **Open** Feb–Dec: daily; Jan: Thu, Sat & Sun. **Closed** 25–26 Dec. 📷 ♿ 🌐 laurel-and-hardy.co.uk

Staircase at Holker Hall

㉑ Cartmel
Cumbria. 🚗 700. ℹ️ Main St, Grange-over-Sands (015395 34026). 🌐 grangeoversands.net

The highlight of this pretty village is its 12th-century **priory**, one of the finest Cumbrian churches. Little remains of the original priory except the gatehouse in the village centre.

The restored church has an attractive east window, a stone-carved 14th-century tomb, and beautiful misericords.

Cartmel also boasts a small racecourse. The village has given its name to its surroundings, a hilly district of green farmland with mixed woodland and limestone scars.

A major local attraction is **Holker Hall**, former residence of the Dukes of Devonshire. Inside are lavishly furnished rooms, with fine marble fireplaces, and a superb oak staircase. Outside are stunning gardens and a deer park.

Holker Hall
Cark-in-Cartmel. **Tel** 015395 58328. **Open** Apr–Nov: daily. 🎧 ♿ limited. 📷 by arrangement. 🚻 📷
🌐 holker-hall.co.uk

㉒ Levens Hall
Nr Kendal, Cumbria. **Tel** 015395 60321. 🚌 from Kendal or Lancaster. **Open** Easter–mid-Oct: Sun–Thu. 📷 🎧 ♿ gardens only. 🚻
🌐 levenshall.co.uk

The outstanding attraction of this Elizabethan mansion is its topiary, but the house itself has much to offer. Built around a 13th-century tower, it contains a fine collection of Jacobean furniture and water-colours by Peter de Wint (1784–1849). Also

of note are the ornate ceilings, Charles II dining chairs, the earliest example of English patchwork and the gilded hearts on the drainpipes.

The 18th-century Turret Clock has a single hand, a common design of the period.

Main entrance

Box hedges were a common component of geometrically designed gardens of this period.

The yew and box topiary was designed in 1694 by French horticulturist Guillaume Beaumont.

The complex topiary, shaped into cones, spirals and pyramids, is kept in shape by gardeners. Some specimens are 6 m (20 ft) high.

Over 300 years old, the garden's box-edged beds are filled with colourful herbaceous displays.

Morecambe Bay, looking northwest towards Barrow-in-Furness

㉓ Morecambe Bay

Lancs. 🚆 Morecambe. ⛴ Heysham
(to Isle of Man). 🛈 Marine Rd.
(01524 582808).
🌐 citycoastcountryside.co.uk

The best way to explore
Morecambe Bay is by train
from Ulverston to Arnside. The
track follows a series of low
viaducts across a huge
expanse of glistening tidal flats
where thousands of wading
birds feed and breed. The bay
is one of the most important
bird reservations in the
country. On the Cumbrian side
of the bay, retirement homes
have expanded the sedate
Victorian resort of Grange-
over-Sands. Nearby, **Hampsfell**
and **Humphrey Head Point**
give fine views.

㉔ Leighton Hall

Carnforth, Lancashire. **Tel** 01524 734
474. 🚌 to Yealand Conyers (from
Lancaster). **Open** May–Sep: 2–5pm
Tue–Fri & bank hols (also Sun in Aug).
📷 ♿ ground floor only. 🛍 📷 📷
🌐 leightonhall.co.uk

Leighton Hall's estate dates back
to the 13th century, but most of
the building is 19th-century,
including its Neo-Gothic façade.
It is owned by the Gillow family,
of the Lancastrian furniture
business, whose products are
prized antiques. Excellent pieces
can be seen here, including a
ladies' work-box inlaid with
biblical scenes. In the
afternoons the hall's large
collection of birds of prey
display their aerial prowess.

㉕ Lancaster

Lancashire. 🚗 46,000. 🚆 🚌 🛈
Meeting House Lane (01524 582394).
🛒 Mon–Sat.
🌐 citycoastcountryside.co.uk

Despite its size, the small
county town of Lancaster
has a long history. The
Romans named it after their
camp over the River Lune.
Originally a defensive site,
it developed into a
prosperous port. Today, its
university and cultural
life thrive. The
Norman **Lancaster
Castle** was expanded
in the 14th and 16th
centuries. From the 13th
century right up to 2011, it
was a crown court and a prison.
The Shire Hall is decorated with
600 heraldic shields. Some

Tawny eagle at
Leighton Hall

fragments from Hadrian's Tower
are 2,000 years old.

The nearby priory church of
St Mary is on Castle Hill. Its
main features include a Saxon
doorway and carved
14th-century choir stalls. There
is an outstanding museum of
furniture in the 17th-century
Judge's Lodgings, while the
Maritime Museum contains
displays on the port's history.
The **City Museum**, based in the
old town hall, concentrates on
the history of Lancaster.

The splendid **Lune Aqueduct**
carries the canal over the River
Lune on five wide arches. Other
attractions are found in
Williamson Park, site of the 1907
Ashton Memorial. This folly was
built by the linoleum magnate
and politician, Lord Ashton.
There are fine views from the
top of this 67 m (220 ft)
domed structure. Opposite is
a tropical butterfly house.

Environs
North of Lancaster, the small
town of **Carnforth** has
some interesting
sights. **Leighton Moss
Nature Reserve** is the
largest reedbed in the
northwest and home to
birds such as Breeding
Bitterns and Bearded Tits. The
restored **Carnforth Station** is
the setting for David Lean's
classic film *Brief Encounter*, shot

Crossing the Sands

Morecambe Bay sands are very dangerous. Travellers used to cut
across the bay at low tide to shorten the long trail around the Kent
estuary. Many perished as they were caught by rising tides or
quicksand, and sea fogs hid the paths. Locals who knew the bay
became guides, and today you can travel with a guide from Kents
Bank to Hest Bank near Arnside.

The High Sheriff of Lancaster Crossing Morecambe Sands (anon)

here in 1945. Information on Carnforth sights is available at **W** citycoastcountryside.co.uk

🏰 Lancaster Castle
Castle Parade. **Tel** 01524 64998. **Open** daily. **Closed** 1 Jan, 25 & 26 Dec. only (limited when court is in session). lancastercastle.com

🏛 Judge's Lodgings
Church St. **Tel** 01524 32808. **Open** Apr–Jun, Oct: daily (Sat & Sun: pm only); Jul–Sep: daily. **Closed** Nov–Good Fri. limited.

🏛 Maritime Museum
Custom House, St George's Quay. **Tel** 01524 64637. **Open** daily (Nov–Easter: pm). **Closed** 24–26, 31 Dec, 1 Jan. lancashire.gov.uk

🏛 City Museum
Market Sq. **Tel** 01524 64637. **Open** Mon–Sat. **Closed** 24 Dec–2 Jan.

🌳 Williamson Park
Wyresdale Rd. **Tel** 01524 33318. **Open** daily. **Closed** 1 Jan, 25 & 26 Dec. limited.

26 Ribble Valley
Lancashire. 🚃 Clitheroe. 🛈 Market Pl., Clitheroe (01200 425566). 🛍 Tue, Thu, Sat. **W** visitribblevalley.co.uk

Clitheroe, a small market town with a hilltop castle, is a good centre for exploring the Ribble Valley's rivers and old villages, such as Slaidburn. Ribchester has a **Roman Museum**, and there is a ruined **Cistercian abbey** at Whalley. To the east is 560 m (1,830 ft) Pendle Hill, with a Bronze Age burial mound at its peak.

🏛 Roman Museum
Ribchester. **Tel** 01254 878261. **Open** daily. by arrangement.

🏰 Whalley Abbey
Whalley. **Tel** 01254 828400. **Open** daily. **Closed** 24 Dec–2 Jan. whalleyabbey.co.uk

27 Blackpool
Lancashire. 🚗 150,000. 🛈 Festival House, Promenade (01253 478222). **W** visitblackpool.com

Blackpool remains a unique experience despite, rather than because of, a major regeneration project on the promenade. A wall of amusement arcades,

Coming from the Mill (1930) by L S Lowry *(see p379)*

piers, bingo halls and fast-food stalls stretch behind the sands. At night, entertainers strut their stuff under the bright lights. The town attracts thousands of visitors in September and October when the Illuminations trace the skeleton of the 158 m (518 ft) Blackpool Tower. Blackpool's resort life dates back to the 18th century, but it burst into prominence when the railway first arrived in 1840, bringing Lancastrian workers to their holiday resort.

Blackpool Tower, painted gold for its centenary in 1994

28 Salford Quays
Salford. 🚊 Harbour City (from Manchester). 🛈 The Lowry, Pier 8 (0161 848 8601). **W** thequays.org.uk

The Quays, to the west of Manchester city centre (15 minutes by tram), were once the terminal docks for the **Manchester Ship Canal**. After the docks closed in 1982, the area became sadly run down but since the 1990s a massive redevelopment plan has changed the area dramatically. In 2011, major national media outlets such as the BBC and ITV made Salford Quays their home when Media City was opened. A host of shops, restaurants and cafés sprang up around the centre.

There is a wealth of entertainment, leisure and cultural facilities on offer, including **The Lowry** *(see p379)*, the **Manchester United Museum** *(see p379)*, the **Imperial War Museum North** *(see p379)*, the **Salford Museum and Art Gallery** and The Lowry Outlet Mall, as well as a multiplex cinema.

There are various water-based activities and ship-canal cruises. Media City, opposite the Lowry, is an important centre for radio and television production.

🏛 Salford Museum and Art Gallery
Peel Park, The Crescent. **Tel** 0161 778 0800. **Open** Mon–Fri, Sat & Sun pm. **Closed** 25 & 26 Dec.

㉙ Manchester

Manchester dates back to Roman times, when in AD 79, Agricola set up a base called Mamucium. It rose to prominence in the late 18th century, when Richard Arkwright introduced cotton processing. By 1830, the first railway linked Manchester and Liverpool, and in 1894 the Manchester Ship Canal *(see p375)* opened, allowing cargovessels inland. Civic buildings sprang up from the proceeds of cotton wealth, but these were in stark contrast to the slums of the mill-workers. Social discontent led writers, politicians and reformers to espouse liberal or radical causes.

The achievements of football team Manchester United and the international success of bands such as The Smiths, The Stone Roses and Oasis gave Manchester a cachet of cool during the 1980s and 1990s. Devastation caused by an IRA car-bombing of the city centre in 1996 was seized as an opportunity to redevelop the main shopping areas. This regeneration has since spread to other areas of the city, notably the old dockside area of Salford Quays.

Exploring Manchester

Manchester is a fine, compact city with much to see in its central areas. The Victorian era of cotton wealth has gifted the city an imposing heritage of industrial architecture, much of which is providing sites for development. The former central railway station, for example, is now **Manchester Central**, a huge exhibition and conference complex. Among other fine 19th-century buildings are the dramatic **John Rylands Library** on Deansgate, founded over 100 years ago by the widow of a local cotton millionaire, and the 1856 Renaissance-style **Free Trade Hall**, now the Radisson Edwardian hotel, which stands on the site of the Peterloo Massacre.

The National Football Museum (formerly Urbis)

Manchester City Centre

① Free Trade Hall
② Manchester Central
③ John Rylands Library
④ Manchester Town Hall
⑤ Royal Exchange
⑥ National Football Museum
⑦ Manchester Art Gallery
⑧ Museum of Science and Industry in Manchester

The Neo-Gothic Town Hall by Alfred Waterhouse

🏛 Manchester Town Hall

Albert Square. **Tel** 0161 234 5000.
Open Mon–Fri. 🚻 🅿 once a month
on Wed & Sat – call 0161 440 0277.

Manchester's majestic town hall was designed by Liverpool-born Alfred Waterhouse (1830–1905), an architect who would later find fame with his Natural History Museum in London. Waterhouse won the commission for the building in an architectural competition, his design finding favour for making best use of the awkward triangular site.

The building was completed in 1877 in an English Gothic style with its roots in the 13th century. Tours are available, but visitors can also explore the building on their own. Sign in inside the main entrance, where a statue of General Agricola, the Roman who founded Manchester in AD 79, looks down on passersby. The highlight is the Great Hall adorned by 12 murals painted by celebrated Pre-Raphaelite painter Ford Madox Brown.

Throughout the building the decoration includes numerous examples of cotton flowers and bees, the latter a symbol of Manchester's industriousness, as well as a brand mark for the city's famous bitter Boddingtons. In the square in front of the town hall is Manchester's **Albert Memorial**, dedicated to the consort of Queen Victoria, which is similar in style but predates the one in London's Hyde Park.

🏛 Royal Exchange Theatre

St Ann's Square. **Tel** 0161 833 9833. **Open** Mon–Sat. 🚻 💻 📷
🌐 royalexchange.co.uk

Built in 1729, the Manchester Royal Exchange, as it was then known, was once claimed to be the "biggest room in the world". It was built as the main trading hall of the cotton industry and at the end of the 19th century it was reckoned that over 80 per cent of world trade in cloth was controlled from these premises. During the Second World War the building was severely damaged by bombs. This coincided with the decline of the cotton trade in the United Kingdom and when the Exchange was rebuilt it was reduced to half its original size. The doors were finally closed to trading in 1968. A daring scheme saw the main hall converted into a theatre in the mid-1970s with the auditorium enclosed in a high-tech structure supported by the old building's pillars; it nestles like a lunar module beneath the great dome. The rest of the Exchange building contains an arcade, shops and cafés.

VISITORS' CHECKLIST

Practical Information
Manchester. 🚉 500,000. ℹ️
0161 237 1010. 📧 daily.
🌐 visitmanchester.com

Transport
✈️ Off M56 11 miles (18 km)
S Manchester. 🚆 Piccadilly,
Victoria, Oxford Rd. 🚌 Coach
station: Chorlton St Bus station:
Piccadilly Gdns, Shude Hill 🚏
Market St, Piccadilly Gdns.

🏛 National Football Museum

Cathedral Gdns. **Tel** 0161 605 8200.
Open 10am–5pm Mon–Sat,
11am–5pm Sun. 🚻 🚫 💻 📷

The National Football Museum has relocated from its original location in Preston to Manchester. It is housed in a striking, ski slope-shaped glass building, originally the Urbis museum. The visit begins with a glass-elevator ride up the incline, then proceeds down through three staggered floors of exhibits.

The museum has a huge collection of football memorabilia. Especially worth admiring is the ball from the 1966 World Cup Final.

Across the plaza from the museum is **Manchester Cathedral**, which largely dates from the 19th century but stands on a site that has been occupied by a church for over a millennium.

The Peterloo Massacre

In 1819, the working conditions of Manchester's factory workers were so bad that social tensions reached breaking point. On 16 August, 50,000 people assembled in St Peter's Field to protest at the oppressive Corn Laws. Initially peaceful, the mood darkened and the poorly trained mounted troops panicked, charging the crowd with their sabres.

Eleven were killed and many wounded. The incident was called Peterloo (the Battle of Waterloo had taken place in 1815). Reforms such as the Factory Act came in that year.

G Cruikshank's Peterloo Massacre cartoon

For map symbols see back flap

Museum of Science and Industry, set in old passenger railway buildings

Museum of Science and Industry

Liverpool Rd. **Tel** 0161 832 2244.
Open daily. **Closed** 1 Jan, 24–26 Dec.
mosi.org.uk

One of the largest science museums in the world, the spirit of scientific enterprise and industrial might of Manchester's heyday is conveyed here. Among the best sections are the Power Hall, a collection of working steam engines, the Electricity Gallery, tracing the history of domestic power, and an exhibition on the Liverpool and Manchester Railway. A collection of planes that made flying history are displayed in the Air and Space Gallery.

Manchester Museum

Oxford Road. **Tel** 0161 275 2648.
Open daily. **Closed** 1 Jan, 24–26 Dec.
museum.manchester.ac.uk

Part of Manchester University, this venerable museum (opened 1885) houses around six million items from all ages and all over the world, but it specializes in Egyptology and zoology. The collection of ancient Egyptian artefacts is one of the largest in the United Kingdom and numbers about 20,000 objects including monumental stone sculpture and mummies, displayed with their coffins and funerary goods. There are also various sections that deal with funerary masks, tomb models and mummified animals. The zoological collections number over 600,000 objects, ranging from stuffed animals to a cast of one of the most complete skeletons of a Tyrannosaurus Rex dinosaur.

The original museum building was designed by Alfred Waterhouse, the same architect responsible for the city's magnificent Town Hall (*see p377*).

Whitworth Art Gallery

University of Manchester, Oxford Rd.
Tel 0161 275 7450. **Open** daily (Sun: pm). **Closed** 24 Dec–2 Jan, Good Fri.
whitworth.manchester.ac.uk

Jacob Epstein's *Genesis*, Whitworth Art Gallery

The Stockport-born machine tool manufacturer and engineer Sir Joseph Whitworth bequeathed money for this gallery, originally intended to be a museum of industrial art and design that would inspire the city's textile trade. Founded in 1889, it has been a part of the University of Manchester since 1958. The fine red-brick building is from the Edwardian period, while the modern interior dates from the 1960s.

The gallery houses a superb collection of drawings, sculpture, contemporary art, textiles and prints. Jacob Epstein's *Genesis* nude occupies the entrance, and there is an important collection of British watercolours by Turner (*see p95*), Girtin and others. Look out for the Japanese woodcuts and the Collection of historic and modern wallpapers, built up from donations from wallpaper manufacturers, as well as through the gallery's active Collecting Policy.

There is a well-developed Education Department that organizes a full programme of activities for groups and individuals of all ages and abilities, for both formal and informal learning.

Manchester Art Gallery

Mosley St & Princess St. **Tel** 0161 235 8888. **Open** Tue–Sun. **Closed** Mon (except Bank Holidays), 24–26, 31 Dec, 1 Jan, Good Fri.
manchestergalleries.org

The original gallery building was designed by Sir Charles Barry (1795–1860) in 1824 and contains an excellent collection of British art, notably Pre-Raphaelites such as William Holman Hunt and Dante Gabriel Rossetti. Early Italian, Flemish and French Schools are also represented.

The gallery has a fine collection of decorative arts, from the Greeks to Picasso to contemporary craftworkers, in the Gallery of Craft & Design. There is also a changing programme of special exhibitions in two fantastic galleries on the top floor. Most exhibitions are free, and there is a programme of accompanying events for adults and families.

A lively space called the Clore Interactive Gallery offers a combination of real art works and hands-on activities for children.

The gallery also runs an education programme that includes learning activities with artists, writers and performers.

Lawrence Alma-Tadema, *Etruscan Vase Painters*, Manchester Art Gallery

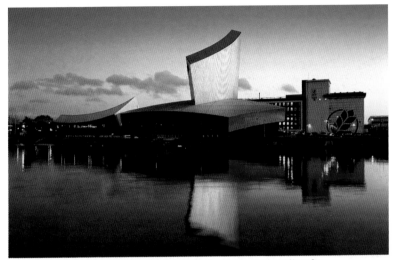
Exterior of the Imperial War Museum North, designed by Daniel Libeskind to represent a globe shattered by conflict

⛭ Lowry Centre
Pier 8, Salford Quays. **Tel** 0843 208 6000. **Open** daily. Admission free, but donations requested. ♿ 🚻 🖥 📷 🖼 **thelowry.com.**

On a prominent site beside the Manchester Ship Canal, the Lowry is a shimmering, silvery arts and entertainment complex that combines two theatres, a restaurant, terrace bars and cafes, art galleries and a shop.

The centre is named after celebrated reclusive artist Laurence Stephen Lowry (1887– 1976), who was born locally and lived all his life in the Manchester area. A rent collector by day, in his leisure hours he painted cityscapes dominated by the smoking chimneys of industry beneath heavy soot filled skies.

However, he is most famous as a painter of "matchstick men", the term frequently applied to the crowds of slight and ghostly figures peopling his canvases. Some of Lowry's work is displayed in one of the galleries here; another hosts regularly changing temporary exhibitions. There is also a room where a 20-minute documentary "Meet Mr Lowry" is screened throughout the day.

The centre provides many facilities and activities for children, and is perfect for a family day out.

⛭ Imperial War Museum North
Trafford Wharf Road, Salford Quays. **Tel** 0161 836 4000. **Open** daily. **Closed** 24–26 Dec. 🖼 ♿ 🚻 🖥 📷 **iwm.org.uk.**

This most striking piece of modern architecture comes courtesy of Daniel Libeskind, the architect nominated to design a replacement for New York's World Trade Center. His Manchester building is a waterfront collision of three great aluminium shards, representing a globe shattered by conflict. Inside, a vast, irregular space is used to display a small but well presented collection of military hardware and ephemera, with nine "silos" devoted to exhibits on people's experiences of war.

On the hour the lights are extinguished for an audiovisual display using the angled walls of the main hall.

As visitors leave they are invited to take the elevator up the 55-metre (180-ft) "Air Shard" for views over the city.

⛭ Manchester United Museum
Salford Quays. **Tel** 0161 868 8000. **Open** daily (except match days). Tours must be booked in advance. 🖼 🖥 📷 🚌 **manutd.com**

Premier League football (soccer) team Manchester United's ground Old Trafford also includes a purpose-built museum. In addition to the historic displays there is much interactive fun such as a chance to test your own penalty-taking skills.

The museum tour takes in the dressing rooms, the trophy room and the players' lounge and culminates in a walk down the tunnel tracing the route taken by players at every home game.

Manchester United Museum on the grounds of Old Traffford football stadium

③⓪ Liverpool

Traces of settlement on Merseyside date back to the 1st century. In 1207 "Livpul", a fishing village, was granted a charter by King John. The population was only 1,000 in Stuart times, but during the 17th and 18th centuries Liverpool's westerly seaboard gave it a leading edge in the lucrative Caribbean slave trade. The first docks opened in 1715 and eventually stretched 7 miles (11 km) along the Mersey. Liverpool's first ocean steamer set out from here in 1840, and would-be emigrants to

the New World poured into the city from Europe, including a flood of Irish refugees from the potato famine. Many settled permanently in Liverpool, and a large, mixed community developed. Today, the port handles even greater volumes of cargoes than in the 1950s and 1960s, but container ships use Bootle docks. Despite economic and social problems, the irrepressible "Scouse" or Liverpudlian spirit re-emerged in the Swinging Sixties, when four local lads stormed the pop scene. Many people still visit Liverpool to pay homage to the Beatles, but the city is also known for its orchestra, the Liverpool Philharmonic, its sport and its universities. Liverpool was the Capital of Culture in 2008.

Liver Bird on the Royal Liver Building

Victorian ironwork, restored and polished, at Albert Dock

Exploring Liverpool

Liverpool's waterfront by the Pier Head, guarded by the mythical Liver Birds (a pair of cormorants with seaweed in their beaks) on the **Royal Liver Building**, is one of the most easily recognized in Britain. Nearby are the famous ferry terminal across the River Mersey and the revitalized docklands. Other attractions

Liverpool City Centre

① Cavern Quarter
② World Museum Liverpool
③ The Walker pp382–3
④ St George's Hall
⑤ Metropolitan Cathedral
⑥ Beatles Story
⑦ Tate Liverpool
⑧ Merseyside Maritime Museum
⑨ Museum of Liverpool
⑩ Royal Liver Building
⑪ Town Hall

For additional map symbols see back flap

include top-class museums and fine galleries, such as the **Walker** *(see pp382–3)*. Its wealth of interesting architecture includes some fine Neo-Classical buildings in the city centre, such as the gargantuan **St George's Hall**, and two cathedrals.

Albert Dock

i 0151 708 7334. **Open** daily. **Closed** 1 Jan, 25 Dec. some attractions.

w albertdock.com

Ship's bell in the Maritime Museum

There are five ware-houses surrounding Albert Dock, all designed by Jesse Hartley in 1846. The docks were closed by 1972. After a decade of dereliction, these Grade I listed buildings were restored in a development that includes museums, galleries, shops, restaurants, bars and businesses.

🏛 Merseyside Maritime Museum

Albert Dock. **Tel** 0151 478 4499. **Open** 10am–5pm daily. **Closed** 1 Jan, 24–26 Dec. limited.

w liverpoolmuseums.org.uk

Devoted to the history of the Port of Liverpool, this large complex has good sections on ship-building and the Cunard and White Star liners. The area on the Battle of the Atlantic in World War II includes models and charts. Another gallery deals with emigration to the New World. The **UK Border Agency National Museum** is also located here, and examines the history of the subject, including smuggling, as well as customs and excise today. Next door is the **International Slavery Museum**. Across the quayside is the rebuilt Piermaster's House and the Cooperage.

🏛 Museum of Liverpool

Pier Head, Albert Dock. **Tel** 0151 478 4545. **Open** 10am–5pm daily. **Closed** 1 Jan, 24–26 Dec.

w liverpoolmuseums.org.uk/mol

The Museum of Liverpool is housed in a stunning building on the waterfront. Inside, visitors learn the story of this famous city, including its contributions to the fields of music, popular culture, sport and industry, as well as its role in the wider world.

🏛 Beatles Story

Britannia Vaults. **Tel** 0151 709 1963. **Open** 10am–6pm daily. **Closed** 25, 26 Dec. **w beatlesstory.com**

In a walk-through exhibition, this museum records the history

VISITORS' CHECKLIST

Practical Information
Liverpool. 445,000.
i Albert Dock (0151 233 2008).
Sun (heritage market).
0906 680 6886; Liverpool Show: May; Clipper Round the World Yacht Race: Jun; Beatles Week: Aug.
w visitliverpool.com

Transport
7 miles (11 km) SE Liverpool.
Lime St. Norton St. from Pier Head to the Wirral, also sightseeing trips; to Isle of Man & N Ireland.

of The Beatles' meteoric rise to fame, from their first record, *Love Me Do*, through Beatlemania to their last live appearance together in 1969, and their eventual break-up. The hits that mesmerized a generation can be heard.

🏛 Tate Liverpool

Albert Dock. **Tel** 0151 702 7400. **Open** 10am–5pm Tue–Sun (Jun–Aug: daily). **Closed** Good Fri, 24–26 Dec. some exhibitions.

w tate.org.uk/liverpool

Tate Liverpool has one of the best contemporary art collections outside London. Marked by bright blue and orange panels and arranged over three floors, the gallery was converted from an old warehouse by architect James Stirling. It opened in 1988 as Tate Britain's *(see p95)* first out-station.

Albert Dock quay beside the River Mersey

The Beatles

Liverpool has produced many good bands and a host of singers, comedians and entertainers before and since the 1960s. But the Beatles – John Lennon, Paul McCartney, George Harrison and Ringo Starr – were the most sensational, and locations associated with the band, however tenuous, are revered as shrines in Liverpool. Bus and walking tours trace the hallowed ground of the Salvation Army home at Strawberry Fields and Penny Lane (both outside the city centre), as well as the boys' old homes. The most visited site is Mathew Street, near Moorfields Station, where the Cavern Club first throbbed to the Mersey Beat. The original site is now a shopping arcade, but the bricks have been used to create a replica. Nearby are statues of the Beatles and Eleanor Rigby.

Liverpool: The Walker Art Gallery

Founded in 1877 by Sir Andrew Barclay Walker, a local brewer and Mayor of Liverpool, this gallery houses one of the finest art collections in Britain. Paintings range from early Italian and Flemish works to Rubens, Rembrandt, and French Impressionists such as Degas's *Woman Ironing* (c.1892–5). Among the strong collection of British artists from the 18th century onward are works by Millais and Turner and Gainsborough's *Countess of Sefton* (1769). There is 20th-century art by Hockney and Sickert, and the sculpture collection includes works by Henry Moore and the contemporary artist Banksy.

Shells (1878) Albert Joseph Moore painted female figures based on antique statues. Influenced by Whistler *(see p523)*, he adopted subtle shading.

Interior at Paddington (1951) Lucian Freud's friend Harry Diamond posed for six months for this picture, intended by the artist to "make the human being uncomfortable".

15

14

13

12

4

5

8

7

9

10

11

Big Art for Little Artists Gallery

Ground floor

First floor

Façade was designed by H H Vale and Cornelius Sherlock.

Main entrance

The Sleeping Shepherd Boy (c.1835) The great Neo-Classical sculptor of the mid-19th century, John Gibson (1790–1866), used traditional colours to give his statuary a smooth appearance.

Gallery Guide

All the picture galleries are on the first floor.
Rooms 1–2 house medieval and Renaissance paintings; Rooms 3 and 4 have 17th-century Dutch, French, Italian and Spanish art. British 18th- and 19th-century works are in Rooms 5–9. Rooms 11–15 have 20th-century and contemporary British art, and Room 10 has Impressionists and Post-Impressionists.

VISITORS' CHECKLIST

Practical Information
William Brown St. **Tel** 0151 478
4199. **Open** 10am–5pm daily.
Closed 1 Jan, 25–26 Dec. 🅰️ 🖥️
📷 🅦 **liverpoolmuseums.org.
uk/walker**

Transport
🚆 Lime St. 🚌 Empire Theatre,
Lime St, Queen Sq, Paradise St.

The 7th-century Kingston Brooch in
World Museum Liverpool

🏛️ World Museum Liverpool
William Brown St. **Tel** 0151 478 4393.
Open 10am–5pm daily. **Closed** 25 &
26 Dec. 🅰️ 🖥️ 📷
🅦 **liverpoolmuseums.org.uk/wml**

Six floors of exhibits in this
excellent museum include
collections of Egyptian, Greek
and Roman pieces, natural
history, archaeology, space and
time. Highlights include the
hands-on Weston Discovery
Centre, a planetarium, the Clore
Natural History Centre, an
aquarium and a Bug House.

🏛️ Anglican Cathedral
St James' Mount. **Tel** 0151 709 6271.
Open 7:30am–6pm daily. 🅰️ 🅱️ 🖥️
📷 🅦 **liverpoolcathedral.org.uk**

Although Gothic in style, this
building was only completed in
1978. The largest Anglican
cathedral in the world is a fine
red sandstone edifice designed
by Sir Giles Gilbert Scott. The
foundation stone was laid in
1904 by Edward VII but, dogged
by two world wars, building work
dragged on to modified designs.

🏛️ Metropolitan Cathedral of Christ the King
Mount Pleasant. **Tel** 0151 709 9222.
Open 7:30am–6pm daily. Donation.
🖥️ 🅱️ 📷 🅦 **liverpoolmetro
cathedral.org.uk**

Liverpool's Roman Catholic
cathedral rejected traditional
forms in favour of a striking
modern design. Early plans,
drawn up by Pugin and later by
Lutyens *(see p33)* in the 1930s,
proved too expensive. The final
version, brainchild of Sir
Frederick Gibberd and built
from 1962–7, is a circular
building surmounted by a
stylized crown of thorns 88 m
(290 ft) high. It is irreverently
known as "Paddy's Wigwam" by
non-Catholics (a reference to
Liverpool's large Irish
population). Inside, the stained-

**Christ Discovered in the
Temple** *(1342)* Simone
Martini's Holy Family
conveys emotional tension
through highly expressive
body language.

Key to Floor Plan
- ☐ 13th–17th-century European
- ☐ 18th–19th-century British, Pre-Raphaelites and Victorian
- ☐ Impressionist/Post-Impressionist
- ☐ 20th-century and contemporary British
- ☐ Sculpture gallery
- ☐ Craft and design gallery
- ☐ Merseyside people and places
- ☐ Special exhibitions
- ☐ Non-exhibition space

glass lantern, designed by John
Piper and Patrick Reyntiens,
floods the circular nave with
diffused blueish light. There is a
fine bronze of Christ by
Elisabeth Frink (1930–94).

Environs
A spectacular, richly timbered
building dating from 1490, **Speke
Hall** lies 6 miles (10 km) east of
Liverpool's centre, on the banks
of the River Mersey. The oldest
parts of the hall enclose a
cobbled courtyard dominated by
two yew trees, Adam and Eve.

Birkenhead on the Wirral
peninsula has been linked to
Liverpool by ferry for over 800
years. Now, road and rail tunnels
supplement access. The Norman
Priory is still in use on Sundays,
and stately Hamilton Square
was designed from 1825–44
by J Gillespie Graham, one of
the architects of Edinburgh's
New Town.

On the Wirral side is **Port
Sunlight Village** *(see p353)*, a
Victorian garden village built by
enlightened soap manufacturer
William Hesketh Lever for his
factory workers. He also
founded the **Lady Lever Art
Gallery** here for his collection of
works of art, including Pre-
Raphaelite paintings.

🏠 Speke Hall
The Walk, Speke. **Tel** 0151 427 7231.
Open mid-Feb–mid-Mar, Nov–early
Dec: Sat & Sun; mid-Mar–mid-Jul,
Sep–Oct: Wed–Sun; mid-Jul–Aug:
Tue–Sun. 🅰️ 🅱️ limited. 🖥️ 📷 NT

🏠 Port Sunlight Museum and Garden Village
23 King George's Drive, Port Sunlight,
Wirral. **Tel** 0151 644 6466.
Open 10am–5pm daily. **Closed** 1 Jan,
25 & 26 Dec. 📷 🅰️ 🅱️ 🖥️ 📷
🅦 **portsunlightvillage.com**

Entrance to the half-timbered manor house
of Speke Hall

YORKSHIRE AND THE HUMBER REGION

North Yorkshire · East Riding of Yorkshire

With the historic city of York at its heart, this is an area of picturesque moorland and valleys. To the north lie the Yorkshire Dales and the North York Moors; eastwards, a coastline of beaches; and southwards, a landscape of lush meadows.

Yorkshire was originally made up of three separate counties, formerly known as "Ridings". Today it covers over 5,000 sq miles (12,950 sq km). The northeast section has dramatic scenery that was carved by glaciers in the Ice Age. Farming was the original livelihood, and the dry-stone walls weaving up precipitous scars and fells were used to divide the land. Imposed on this were the industries of the 19th century; crumbling viaducts are as much a part of the scenery as the grand houses of those who profited from them.

Close to the Humber, the landscape is very different, dominated historically by the now flagging fishing industry, and geographically by lush, sprawling meadows. Its coastline is exceptional, and further north are the attractions of wide, sandy beaches and bustling harbour towns. Yet it is the contrasting landscapes that make the area so appealing, ranging from the grandeur of the Humber Bridge to the ragged cliff coast around Whitby, and the flat expanse of Sunk Island.

The city of York, where Roman and Viking relics exist side by side, is second only to London in the number of visitors that tread its streets. Indeed the historical centre of York is the region's foremost attraction. Those in search of a real taste of Yorkshire, however, should head for the countryside. In addition to excellent touring routes, a network of rewarding walking paths range from mellow ambles along the Cleveland Way to rocky scrambles over the Pennine Way at Pen-y-Ghent.

Lobster pots on the quayside at the picturesque fishing port of Whitby

◄ Ribblehead Viaduct on the Settle-to-Carlisle railway line, North Yorkshire

Exploring Yorkshire and the Humber Region

Yorkshire covers a wide area, once made up of three counties or "Ridings". Until the arrival of railways, mining and the wool industry in the 19th century, the county was a farming area. Dry-stone walls dividing fields still pepper the northern part of the county, alongside 19th-century mill chimneys and country houses. Among the many abbeys are Rievaulx and the magnificent Fountains. The medieval city of York is a major attraction, as are Yorkshire's beaches. The Humber region is characterized by the softer, rolling countryside of the Wolds, and its nature reserves attract enormous quantities of birds.

Rosedale Abbey village in the North York Moors

Sights at a Glance

1. Yorkshire Dales
3. Harrogate
4. Knaresborough
5. Ripley
6. Newby Hall
7. *Fountains Abbey pp394–5*
8. Ripon
9. Sutton Bank
10. Byland Abbey
11. Coxwold
12. Nunnington Hall
13. Helmsley
14. Rievaulx Abbey
15. Mount Grace Priory
16. Hutton-le-Hole
17. North York Moors
18. North York Moors Railway
19. Whitby
20. Robin Hood's Bay
21. Scarborough
22. *Castle Howard pp402–3*
23. Eden Camp
24. Wharram Percy
25. Burton Agnes
26. Bempton and Flamborough Head
27. Beverley
28. Burton Constable
29. Kingston upon Hull
30. Holderness and Spurn Head
31. Grimsby
32. *York pp408–13*
33. Harewood House
34. Leeds
35. Bradford
36. Haworth
37. Hebden Bridge
38. Halifax
39. National Coal Mining Museum for England
40. Yorkshire Sculpture Park
41. Magna

Walks

2. Malham Walk

Section of Lendal Bridge (1863)
crossing the Ouse in York

Guisborough
Hinderwell
Stokesley
Great Ayton
A171
A19
WHITBY **19**
A172
ROBIN **20**
HOOD'S
BAY
MOUNT GRACE **15**
PRIORY
NORTH YORK MOORS
Goathland
orthallerton
Cleveland Hills
17
Rosedale Abbey
NORTH YORKSHIRE **18**
MOORS RAILWAY
HUTTON-LE-HOLE **16**
Scalby
SCARBOROUGH **21**
AULX ABBEY **14**
HELMSLEY **13**
Pickering
A170
Brompton
Filey
9
A170
NUNNINGTON HALL **12**
Derwent
Staxton
SUTTON **10**
BANK
BYLAND
ABBEY
Hovingham
A64
A165
shforth
COXWOLD **11**
EDEN CAMP **23**
Malton
Rudston
BEMPTON **26**
Flamborough Head
WBY HALL
CASTLE **22**
HOWARD
Boroughbridge
WHARRAM PERCY **24**
Sledmere
A614
Bridlington
BURTON AGNES **25**
A19
Haxby
A64
Fridaythorpe
A166
Driffield
Skipsea
ARESBOROUGH
Ouse
A59
Stamford Bridge
The Wolds
forth
YORK **32**
Derwent
A1079
Pocklington
Hutton Cranswick
Wetherby
Leven
Hornsea
Tadcaster
A1(M)
Escrick
A165
A64
Aberford
Riccall
A19
Holme on
Spalding Moor
Market
Weighton
BEVERLEY **27**
BURTON **28**
CONSTABLE
Garforth
Selby
A614
Cottingham
Roos
A63
M62
A63
Castleford
Snaith
Howden
Goole
Whitton
Welton
KINGSTON **29**
UPON HULL
Withernsea
HOLDERNESS & **30**
SPURN HEAD
field
Humber
Kaye
Ouse
Barton-upon-
Humber
A1
A19
M18
Trent
A15
Easington
Hemsworth
Askern
Thorne
Appleby
Ulceby
Immingham
Spurn
Head
South Kirkby
Crowle
A18
Scunthorpe
A180
sley
A635
M180
Broughton
GRIMSBY **31**
Cleethorpes
Wombwell
Doncaster
Belton
Brigg
Waltham
nisbrough
Scotter
A15
Caistor
A16
M18
A1(M)
Misterton
NA
Rotherham
Bawtry
field
Anston
M1
Nottingham

0 kilometres   15
0 miles   10

Getting Around

The area is served by the A1, the M1, the
M62 and the A59. Trains run to major cities
such as York and Leeds, and there are train
or coach (bus) links between many towns
and hamlets. The Yorkshire Dales and
North York Moors national parks are good
for walkers, and cyclists can enjoy rides
around York and the River Humber.

Key

Motorway
Major road
Secondary road
Minor road
Scenic route
Main railway
Minor railway

❶ Yorkshire Dales

The Yorkshire Dales is a farming landscape, formed from three principal dales, Swaledale, Wharfedale and Wensleydale, and a number of smaller ones, such as Deepdale. Glaciation in the Ice Age helped carve out these steep-sided valleys, and this scenery contrasts with the high moorlands. However, 12 centuries of settlement have altered the landscape in the form of cottages, castles and villages which create a delightful environment for walking. A national park since 1954, the area provides recreation while serving local community needs.

Monk's Wynd – one of Richmond's narrow, winding streets

Exploring Swaledale

Swaledale's prosperity was founded largely on wool, and it is famous for its herds of sheep that graze on the wild higher slopes in the harshest weather. The fast-moving river Swale that gives the northernmost dale its name travels from bleak moorland down magnificent waterfalls into the richly wooded lower slopes, passing through the village of Reeth and the town of Richmond.

🏰 Richmond Castle

Tower Street. **Tel** 0870 333 1181.
Open Apr–Sep: daily; Oct: Thu–Mon; Nov–Mar: Sat & Sun. **Closed** 1 Jan, 24–26 Dec. 🅿 🅰 limited. 🄿 EH

Swaledale's main point of entry is the medieval market town of Richmond. Alan Rufus, the Norman 1st Earl of Richmond, began building the castle in 1071, and some of the masonry on the curtain walls probably dates from that time. It has a fine Norman keep, 30 m (100 ft) high with walls 3.3 m (11 ft) thick. An 11th-century arch leads into a courtyard containing Scolland's Hall (1080), one of England's oldest buildings.

Richmond's marketplace was once the castle's outer bailey. Its quaint, narrow streets gave rise to the song, *The Lass of Richmond Hill* (1787), written by Leonard McNally for his wife, Frances I'Anson, who was brought up in Hill House, on Richmond Hill. Turner *(see p95)* depicted the town many times. The Georgian

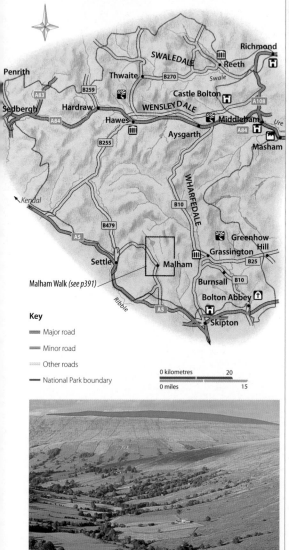

Key

━━ Major road
━━ Minor road
┅┅ Other roads
── National Park boundary

0 kilometres   20
0 miles   15

Malham Walk *(see p391)*

The green, rolling landscape of Deepdale, near Dent

Theatre (1788) is the only one of its age still surviving.

🏛 Swaledale Folk Museum
Reeth Green. **Tel** 01748 884118.
Open Easter–Oct: daily; Nov–Mar: call to check. 🚻 ▣ 🏛

Reeth, a town that became known as the centre of the lead-mining industry, houses this museum in a former Methodist Sunday school (1830). Included in it are mining and wool-making artifacts (wool from the hardy Swaledale sheep was another mainstay of the economy) and brass band memorabilia.

🌿 Buttertubs
Near Thwaite, on the B6270 Hawes road, are a series of fluted limestone potholes that streams fall into. These became known as the Buttertubs when farmers going to market lowered their butter into the holes to keep it cool.

Buttertubs, near Thwaite

Exploring Wensleydale
The largest of the Yorkshire dales, Wensleydale is famous for its cheese and also for James Herriot's books and the television series, *All Creatures Great and Small*. It is easy walking country for anyone seeking an alternative to major moorland hikes.

🏛 Dales Countryside Museum
Station Yard, Hawes. **Tel** 01969 666210.
Open 10am–5pm daily. **Closed** 24–26 Dec, 1 Jan. 🚻 ♿ 🏛

In a former railway goods warehouse in Hawes, capital of Upper Wensleydale, is a fascinating museum, filled with

Barrels at the Theakston Brewery

items from life and industry in the 18th- and 19th-century Upper Dales. This includes cheese-and butter-making equipment. Wensleydale cheese was created by monks at nearby Jervaulx Abbey. There is also a rope-making works a short walk away.

Hawes is one of the highest market towns in England, at 259 m (850 ft) above sea level. It is a thriving centre where thousands of sheep and cattle are auctioned each summer.

🌿 Hardraw Force
🚻 at Green Dragon Inn, Hardraw.

At the tiny village of Hardraw, nearby, is England's tallest single-drop waterfall, with no outcrops to interrupt its 29 m (96 ft) fall. It became famous in Victorian times when the daredevil Blondin walked across it on a tightrope. Today, you can walk right under it and look through the stream without getting wet.

🌿 Aysgarth Falls
ℹ National Pk Centre (01969 662910). **Open** Apr–Oct: daily; Nov–Dec & Feb–Mar: Fri–Mon. ▣

An old packhorse bridge gives a clear view of the point at which the previously placid River Ure suddenly begins to plunge in foaming torrents over wide limestone shelves. Turner painted the impressive lower falls in 1817.

🏛 Theakston Brewery
Masham. **Tel** 01765 680000. **Open** daily. **Closed** 23 Dec–early Jan. 🚻 🍴 🏛 🅆 theakstons.co.uk

The pretty town of Masham is the home of Theakston's brewery, creator of the potent ale Old Peculier. The history of this local family brewery from its origin in 1827 is on display in the visitors'

centre. Masham village itself has an attractive square once used for sheep fairs, surrounded by 17th- and 18th-century houses.

🏰 Bolton Castle
Castle Bolton, nr Leyburn. **Tel** 01969 623981. **Open** daily. **Closed** Nov–weekend before Easter. 🚻 ▣ 🏛
🅆 **boltoncastle.co.uk**

Situated in the village of Castle Bolton, this spectacular medieval fortress was built in 1379 by the 1st Lord Scrope, Chancellor of England. Its most notorious period was from 1568 to 1569 when Mary, Queen of Scots *(see p515)* was held prisoner here by Elizabeth I *(see pp54–5)*.

🏰 Middleham Castle
Middleham, nr Leyburn. **Tel** 0870 333 1181. **Open** Apr–Sep: daily; Oct: Sat–Wed; Nov–Mar: Sat & Sun. **Closed** 1 Jan, 24–26 Dec. 🚻 ♿ ltd. 🆔

Owned by Richard Neville, Earl of Warwick, it was built in 1170. The castle is better known as home to Richard III *(see p53)* when he was made Lord of the North. It was once one of the strongest fortresses in the north but became uninhabited during the 15th century, when many of its stones were used for nearby buildings. The keep provides a fine view of the landscape.

Remains of Middleham Castle, once residence of Richard III

Extensive ruins of Bolton Priory, dating from 1154

Exploring Wharfedale

This dale is characterized by gritstone moorland, contrasting with quiet market towns along meandering sections of river. Many consider Grassington a central point for exploring Wharfedale, but the showpiece villages of Burnsall, overlooked by a 506 m (1,661 ft) fell, and Buckden, near Buckden Pike (701 m/2,302 ft), also make excellent bases.

Nearby are the Three Peaks of Whernside, 736 m (2,416 ft), Ingleborough, 724 m (2,376 ft) and Pen-y-Ghent 694 m (2,278 ft). They are known for their potholes and tough terrain, but this does not deter keen walkers from attempting to climb them all in one day. If you sign in at the Pen-y-Ghent café at Horton-in-Ribblesdale, at the centre of the Three Peaks, and complete the 20 mile (32 km) course, reaching the summit of all three peaks in less than 12 hours, you can qualify for membership of the Three Peaks of Yorkshire Club.

Burnsall

St Wilfrid's, Burnsall. **Tel** 01756 720331. **Open** Apr–Oct: daily to dusk.
Preserved in St Wilfrid's church graveyard are the original village stocks, gravestones from Viking times and a headstone carved in memory of the Dawson family by sculptor Eric Gill (1882–1940). The village has a five-arched bridge and hosts Britain's oldest fell race every August.

Grassington Folk Museum

The Square, Grassington. **Tel** 01756 753287. **Open** 2–4pm Tue–Sun. limited.
This museum is set in two 18th-century lead miners' cottages. Its exhibits illustrate the domestic and working history of the area, including farming and lead mining.

Bolton Priory

Bolton Abbey, Skipton. **Tel** 01756 718000. **Open** daily.
One of the most beautiful areas of Wharfedale is around the village of Bolton Abbey, set in an estate owned by the Duke of Devonshire. While preserving its astounding beauty, its managers have incorporated over 30 miles (46 km) of footpaths, many suitable for the disabled and young families.

The ruins of Bolton Priory, established by Augustinian canons in 1154 on the site of a Saxon manor, are extensive. They include a church, chapter house, cloister and prior's lodging. These all demonstrate the wealth accumulated by the canons from the sale of wool from their flocks of sheep. The priory nave is still used as a parish church. Another attraction of the estate is the "Strid", a point where the River Wharfe surges spectacularly through a gorge, foaming yellow and gouging holes out of the rocks.

Stump Cross Caverns

Greenhow Hill, Pateley Bridge. **Tel** 01756 752780. **Open** Mar–Nov: daily; Dec–Feb: Sat, Sun & pub hols. stumpcrosscaverns.co.uk
These caves were formed over a period of half a million years: trickles of underground water formed intertwining passages and carved them into fantastic shapes and sizes. Sealed off in the last Ice Age, the caves were only discovered in the 1850s, when lead miners sank a mine shaft into the caverns.

Skipton Castle

High St. **Tel** 01756 792442. **Open** daily (Sun: pm). **Closed** 25 Dec. skiptoncastle.co.uk
The market town of Skipton is still one of the largest auctioning and stockraising centres in the north. Its 11th-century castle was almost entirely rebuilt by Robert de Clifford in the 14th century. Beautiful Conduit Court was added by Henry, Lord Clifford, in Henry VIII's reign. The central yew tree was planted by Lady Anne Clifford in 1659 to mark restoration work to the castle after Civil War damage.

Conduit Court (1495) and yew tree at Skipton Castle

❷ Malham Walk

The Malham area, shaped by glacial erosion 10,000 years ago, has one of Great Britain's most dramatic limestone landscapes. The walk from Malham village can take over four hours if you pause to enjoy the view-points and take a detour to Gordale Scar. Those who are short of time tend to go only as far as Malham Cove. This vast natural amphitheatre, formed by a huge geological tear, is like a giant boot-heel mark in the landscape. Above lie the deep crevices of Malham Lings, where rare flora such as hart's-tongue flourishes. Unusual plants grow in the lime-rich Malham Tarn, said to have provided inspiration for Charles Kingsley's *The Water Babies* (1863). Coot and mallard visit the tarn in summer and tufted duck in winter.

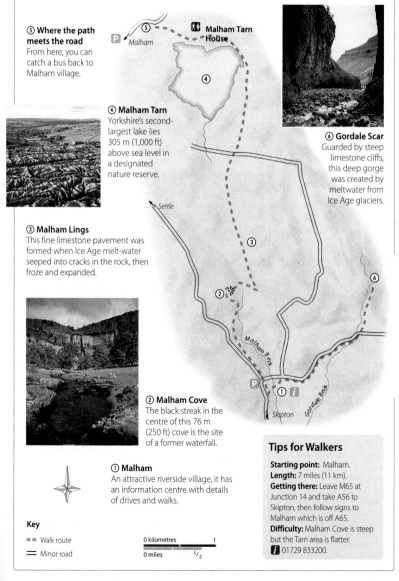

⑤ Where the path meets the road
From here, you can catch a bus back to Malham village.

④ Malham Tarn
Yorkshire's second-largest lake lies 305 m (1,000 ft) above sea level in a designated nature reserve.

⑥ Gordale Scar
Guarded by steep limestone cliffs, this deep gorge was created by meltwater from Ice Age glaciers.

③ Malham Lings
This fine limestone pavement was formed when Ice Age melt-water seeped into cracks in the rock, then froze and expanded.

② Malham Cove
The black streak in the centre of this 76 m (250 ft) cove is the site of a former waterfall.

① Malham
An attractive riverside village, it has an information centre with details of drives and walks.

Key

▪▪ Walk route

━ Minor road

0 kilometres   1

0 miles   ½

Tips for Walkers

Starting point: Malham.
Length: 7 miles (11 km).
Getting there: Leave M65 at Junction 14 and take A56 to Skipton, then follow signs to Malham which is off A65.
Difficulty: Malham Cove is steep but the Tarn area is flatter.
i 01729 833200.

A 1920s poster advertising the spa town of Harrogate

❸ Harrogate

North Yorkshire. 🗺 72,000. 🚇 🚌 ℹ The Royal Baths, Crescent Rd (0845 389 3223). 🅆 **harrogate.co.uk**

Between 1880 and World War I, Harrogate was the north's leading spa town, with nearly 90 medicinal springs. It was ideal for aristocrats who, after a tiring London season, were able to stop for a health cure before journeying on to grouse-shooting in Scotland.

Today, Harrogate's main attractions are its spa town atmosphere, fine architecture, public gardens and its conven-ience as a centre for visiting North Yorkshire and the Dales.

The naturally welling spa waters may not currently be in use, but you can still go for a Turkish bath in one of the country's most attractive steam rooms. The entrance at the side of the Royal Bath Assembly Rooms (1897) is unassuming, but once inside, the century-old **Harrogate Turkish Baths** are a visual feast of tiled Victoriana.

The town's spa history is recorded in the **Royal Pump Room Museum**. At the turn of the century, the waters were thought to be rich in iron early in the day. So, between 7am and 9am the 1842 octagonal building would have been filled with rich and fashionable people drinking glasses of water. Poorer people could take water from the pump outside. Today you can sample the waters and enjoy the museum's exhibits, including a Penny Farthing bicycle.

Harrogate is also known for the rainbow-coloured flowerbeds in **The Stray**, a common space to the south of the town centre, and for the ornamental **RHS Harlow Carr Gardens**, owned by the Royal Horticultural Society. Visitors can enjoy the delicious cakes at **Bettys Café Tea Rooms**.

🚇 Harrogate Turkish Baths
The Royal Baths, Crescent Rd. **Tel** 01423 556746. **Open** Women: Mon, Tue & Thu (pm); Fri (am); Sun. Mixed (in bathing suits): Mon (eve), Wed, Thu (eve), Sat & Sun. 🚾

🏛 Royal Pump Room Museum
Crown Pl. **Tel** 01423 556188. **Open** daily (Sun: pm only). **Closed** 1 Jan, 24–26 Dec. 🚾 🦽 🎁

🚇 Bettys Café Tea Rooms
1 Parliament St. **Tel** 01423 814070. **Open** daily. **Closed** 1 Jan, 25 & 26 Dec. 🅆 **bettys.co.uk**

🌷 RHS Harlow Carr Gardens
Crag Lane. **Tel** 01423 565418. **Open** daily. **Closed** 25 Dec. 🚾 🦽 🍴 🖥 🅆 **rhs.org.uk**

❹ Knaresborough

North Yorkshire. 🗺 15,000. 🚇 🚌 from Harrogate. ℹ 9 Castle Courtyard, Market Place (08453 890177). 🍴 Wed.

Perched precipitously above the River Nidd is one of England's oldest towns, mentioned in the Domesday Book of 1086 (see p52). Its historic streets – which link the church, John of Gaunt's ruined castle, and the market place with the river – are now lined with fine 18th-century houses.

Nearby is **Mother Shipton's Cave**, reputedly England's oldest tourist attraction. It first went on show in 1630 as the birthplace of Ursula Sontheil, a famous local prophetess. Today, people

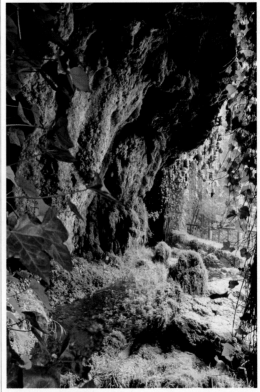

Mother Shipton's Cave, Knaresborough, with objects encased in limestone

For hotels and restaurants in this area see pp560–73 and pp582–603

The south front of Newby Hall

can view the effect the well near her cave has on objects hung below the dripping surface. Almost any item, from umbrellas to soft toys, will become encased in limestone within a few weeks.

Mother Shipton's Cave
Prophesy House, High Bridge. **Tel** 01423 864600. **Open** Easter– Oct: daily; Feb–Easter: Sat, Sun. **Closed** Nov–Jan.

❺ Ripley

North Yorkshire. 250. from Harrogate or Ripon. Harrogate (0845 893223). **harrogate.gov.uk**

Since the 1320s, when the first generation of the Ingilby family lived in an early incarnation of **Ripley Castle**, the village has been made up almost exclusively of castle employees. The influence of one 19th-century Ingilby had the most visual impact. In the 1820s, Sir William Amcotts Ingilby was so entranced by a village in Alsace Lorraine that he created a similar one in French Gothic style, complete with an *Hôtel de Ville*. Present-day Ripley has a cobbled market square, and quaint cottages line the streets.

Ripley Castle, with its 15th-century gatehouse, was where Oliver Cromwell *(see p56)* stayed following the Battle of Marston Moor. The 28th generation of Ingilbys live here, and it is open for tours. The attractive grounds contain two lakes and a deer park, as well as more formal gardens.

Ripley Castle
Ripley. **Tel** 01423 770152. **Open** Apr– Oct: daily; Mar, Nov: Tue, Thu, Sat & Sun; Dec–Feb: Sat & Sun. Gardens: **Open** daily all year. **Closed** 1 Jan, 25 & 26 Dec.

❻ Newby Hall

Nr Ripon, North Yorkshire. **Tel** 0845 4504068. **Open** Apr–Jun & Sep: Tue– Sun; Jul & Aug: daily. **newbyhallandgardens.com**

Newby Hall stands on land once occupied by the de Nubie family in the 13th century and has been in the hands of the current family since 1748. The central part of the present house was built in the late 17th century, in the style of Sir Christopher Wren.

Visitors will find 25 acres of gardens to explore. Laid out in a series of compartmentalized areas off a main axis, each garden is planted to come into flower during a different season. There is also a Woodland Discovery Walk, with contemporary sculpture.

For children, there is an adventure garden with activities and a miniature railway that runs through the gardens alongside the river Ure. River boat rides are also available. Each year a number of special events are staged, including Plant Fairs, a Historic Vehicle Rally and two Craft fairs.

❼ Fountains Abbey

See pp394–5.

❽ Ripon

North Yorkshire. 16,000. from Harrogate. Minster Rd (0845 389 0178). Thu. **visitripon.org**

Ripon, a charming small city, is best known for the cathedral and "the watch", which has been announced since the Middle Ages by the Wakeman. In return for protecting Ripon citizens, he would charge an annual toll of two pence per household. Today, a man still blows a horn in the Market Square each evening at 9pm, and every Thursday a handbell is rung to open the market.

The **Cathedral of St Peter and St Wilfrid** is built above a 7th-century Saxon crypt. At less than 3 m (10 ft) high and just over 2 m (7 ft) wide, it is held to be the oldest complete crypt in England. The cathedral is known for its collection of misericords *(see p345)*, which include both pagan and Old Testament examples. The architectural historian Sir Nikolaus Pevsner (1902–83) considered the cathedral's West Front the finest in England.

Ripon's **Prison and Police Museum**, housed in the 1686 "House of Correction", looks at police history and the conditions in Victorian prisons.

Prison and Police Museum
St Marygate. **Tel** 01765 690799. **Open** Apr–Oct: daily (pm only). **Closed** Nov–Mar. **riponmuseums.co.uk**

Ripon's Wakeman, blowing his horn in the Market Square

❼ Fountains Abbey

Nestling in the wooded valley of the River Skell are the extensive sandstone ruins of Fountains Abbey and the outstanding water garden of Studley Royal. Fountains Abbey was founded by Benedictine monks in 1132 and joined the Cistercian order three years later. By the mid-12th century it had become the wealthiest abbey in Britain, though it fell into ruin during the Dissolution *(see p54)*. In 1720, John Aislabie, the MP for Ripon and Chancellor of the Exchequer, developed the land and forest of the abbey ruins. He began work, continued by his son William, on the famous water garden, statuary and Classical temples in the grounds. Studley Royal and the Abbey became a World Heritage Site in 1986.

The Abbey

The abbey buildings were designed to reflect the Cistercians' desire for simplicity and austerity. The abbey frequently dispensed charity to the poor and the sick, as well as travellers.

The Chapel of Nine Altars at the east end of the church was built from 1203 to 1247. It is ornate, compared to the rest of the abbey, with an 18-m (60-ft) high window complemented by another at the western end of the nave.

Abbot's house

Chapter house

Cloister

Kitchen

Monks' infirmary hall

Refectory

Lay brothers' infirmary

Lay brothers' refectory

Cellarium and dormitory undercroft, with vaulting 90 m (300 ft) long, was used for storing fleeces which the abbey monks sold to Venetian and Florentine merchants.

Fountains Hall
Built by Sir Stephen Proctor around 1604, with stones from the abbey ruins, its design is attributed to architect Robert Smythson. It included a great hall with a minstrels' gallery and an entrance flanked by Classical columns.

KEY

① **Fountains Mill** is one of the finest monastic watermills in Britain.
② **River Skell**
③ **Visitor centre and car park**
④ **Paths leading to the estate park**
⑤ **Canal**
⑥ **Banqueting House**
⑦ **Cascade**
⑧ **Lake**
⑨ **Footpath to St Mary's Church**
⑩ **Octagon Tower**
⑪ **Moon Pond**
⑫ **Anne Boleyn's Seat** is a Gothic alcove with a fine view of the abbey. It was built in the late 18th century to replace her statue.

★ **Abbey**
This was built by using stones taken from the Skell valley.

St Mary's Church
This sumptuous Victorian Gothic church was built by architect William Burges in 1871–8. Inside, the choir stalls are decorated with multi-coloured carved parrots.

VISITORS' CHECKLIST

Practical Information
Studley Royal Estate, Ripon. **Tel** 01765 608888. **w** nationaltrust. org.uk/fountainsabbey **Open** 10am–5pm daily (Oct–Mar: to 4pm, or dusk if earlier). **Closed** every Fri in Jan, Nov, Dec; 24 & 25 Dec.

Transport
from Ripon (May–Sep) or Harrogate.

Temple of Fame
The columns of this domed building are made of hollow timber but look like sandstone.

★ Temple of Piety
This garden house was originally dedicated to Hercules. It was renamed as a symbol of filial piety by William Aislabie after his father's death in 1742.

The 19th-century white horse above Kilburn, seen on one of the walks around Sutton Bank

❾ Sutton Bank

North Yorkshire. 🚆 Thirsk. ℹ️ Sutton Bank (01845 597426). 🌐 **northyork moors.org.uk/suttonbank**

Notorious among motorists for its 1 in 4 gradient, which climbs for about 107 m (350 ft), Sutton Bank itself is known for its panoramic views. On a clear day you can see across the Vale of York to the Dales *(see pp388–9)*. William and his sister Dorothy Wordsworth stopped here to admire the vista in 1802, on their way to visit his future wife, Mary Hutchinson, at Brompton. There is a visitor centre at the top of the Bank, from which it is a pleasant walk to the white horse above Kilburn.

❿ Byland Abbey

Coxwold, York. **Tel** 01347 868 614. 🚌 from York or Helmsley. 🚆 Thirsk. **Open** Apr–Jun, Sep: Thu–Mon; Jul–Aug: daily; Oct–Mar: Sat & Sun. 🅿️ ♿ limited. 🇪🇭

This Cistercian monastery was founded in 1177 by monks from Furness Abbey in Cumbria. It featured what was then the largest Cistercian church in Britain, 100 m (328 ft) long and 41 m (135 ft) wide across the transepts. The layout of the monastery, including cloisters and the west front of the church, is still visible, as is the green and yellow glazed tile floor. Fine workmanship is shown in carved stone details and in the capitals, kept in the small museum.

In 1322 the Battle of Byland was fought nearby, and King Edward II *(see p44)* narrowly escaped capture when the invading Scottish army learned that he was dining with the Abbot. In his hurry to escape, the king had to leave many treasures behind, which were looted by the invading soldiers.

⓫ Coxwold

North Yorkshire. 🗺️ 185. ℹ️ 49 Market Place, Thirsk (01845 522755). 🌐 **coxwoldvillage.co.uk**

Situated just inside the bounds of the North York Moors National Park *(see p399)*, this charming village nestles at the foot of the Howardian Hills. Its pretty houses are built from local stone, and the 15th-century church has some fine Georgian box pews and an impressive octagonal tower. But Coxwold is best known as the home of the author Laurence Sterne (1713–68), whose

Shandy Hall, home of author Laurence Sterne, now a museum

writings include *Tristram Shandy* and *A Sentimental Journey.*

Sterne moved here in 1760 as the church curate. He rented a rambling house that he named **Shandy Hall** after a Yorkshire expression meaning eccentric. Originally built as a timber-framed, open-halled house in the 15th century, it was modernized in the 17th century and Sterne later added a façade. His grave lies beside the porch at Coxwold's church.

🚪 Shandy Hall
Coxwold. **Tel** 01347 868465.
Open May–Sep: Wed & Sun (pm). 🅿
♿ limited. Gardens: **Open** May–Sep: Sun–Fri. 📷

⑫ Nunnington Hall

Nunnington, York. **Tel** 01439 748283.
🚃 Malton, then bus or taxi. **Open**
Feb–Oct: Tue–Sun; Nov–mid-Dec: Sat & Sun. **Closed** mid-Dec–Jan. 📷 🚫
♿ ground floor. 🖥 NT

Set in alluring surroundings, this 17th-century manor house is a combination of architectural styles, including features from the Elizabethan and Stuart periods. Both inside and outside, a notable architectural feature is the use of the broken pediment (the upper arch is left unjoined).

Nunnington Hall was a family home until 1952, when Mrs Ronald Fife donated it to the National Trust. A striking feature is the panelling in the Oak Hall. Formerly painted, it extends

The miniature Queen Anne drawing room at Nunnington Hall

over the three-arched screen to the Great Staircase. Nunnington's collection of 22 miniature furnished period rooms is popular with visitors.

A mid-16th-century tenant Dr Robert Huickes, physician to Henry VIII *(see pp54–5),* is best known for advising Elizabeth I that she should not, at the age of 32, consider having any children.

⑬ Helmsley

North Yorkshire. 🚶 1,600. 🚌 from Malton or Scarborough. 🛈 Helmsley Castle (01439 770173). 📅 Fri.
🌐 **northyorkmoors.org.uk/ helmsley**

This pretty market town is noted for its castle, now an imposing ruin. Built from 1186 to 1227, its main function and strength as a fortress is illustrated by the remaining keep, tower and curtain walls. The original D-shaped keep had one part blasted away in the Civil War *(see p56),* but remains the dominant feature.

The castle was so impregnable that there were few attempts to force entry. However, in 1644, after holding out for a three-month seige against Sir Thomas Fairfax, the Parliamentary general, the castle was finally taken.

Helmsley church tower

⑭ Rievaulx Abbey

Nr Helmsley, North Yorkshire. **Tel** 01439 798228. 🚃 Thirsk or Scarborough, then bus or taxi. **Open** Apr–Sep: daily; Oct: Thu–Mon; Nov–Mar: Sat & Sun. **Closed** 1 Jan, 2 weeks late Feb, 24–26 Dec. 🚫 ♿ limited. 📷 EH

Rievaulx is perhaps the finest abbey in the area, due to both its dramatic setting in the steep wooded valley of the River Rye and its extensive remains. It is surrounded by steep banks that form natural barriers from the outside world. Monks of the French Cistercian order from Clairvaux founded this, their first major monastery in Britain, in 1132. The main buildings were finished before 1200. The layout of the chapel, kitchens and infirmary give an idea of monastic life.

Rievaulx Abbey, painted by Thomas Girtin (1775–1802)

Mount Grace Priory ruins, with farm and mansion in foreground

⑮ Mount Grace Priory

On A19, NE of Northallerton, North Yorks. **Tel** 01609 883494. ⟥ Northallerton then bus 89. **Open** Apr–Sep: Thu–Mon; Oct: Thu–Sun; Nov: Sat & Sun. 🏠 🚹 ground floor, shop & grounds. 📷 EH

Founded by Thomas Holland, Duke of Surrey, and in use from 1398 until 1539, this is the best-preserved Carthusian or charterhouse monastery *(see pp354–5)* in England. The monks took a vow of silence and lived in solitary cells, each with his own garden and an angled hatch so that he would not even see the person serving his food. They only met at matins, vespers and feast-day services. Attempts at escape by those who could not endure the rigour of the rules were punished by imprisonment.

The ruins of the priory include the former prison, gatehouse and outer court, barns, guesthouses, cells and the church. The 14th- century church, the best-preserved section of the site, is particularly small, as it was only rarely used by the community. A cell has been reconstructed to give an impression of monastic life.

⑯ Hutton-le-Hole

North Yorkshire. 🚠 400. ⟥ Pickering then bus (seasonal service). 🛈 Ryedale Folk Museum (01751 417367). 🌐 **northyorkmoors.org.uk**

This picturesque village is characterized by a spacious green, grazed by roaming sheep, and surrounded by houses, an inn and shops. Characteristic white wooden fencing lines the village green and grass verges. Its cottages, some with date panels over

Wheelwright's workshop at Ryedale Folk Museum

the doors, are made from limestone, with red pantiled roofs. In the village centre is the excellent **Ryedale Folk Museum**, which records the lifestyle of an agricultural community using ancient artifacts and reconstructed buildings.

🏛 **Ryedale Folk Museum**
Hutton-le-Hole. **Tel** 01751 417367. **Open** late Jan–mid-Dec: daily. 🏠 🚹 📷 🌐 **ryedalefolkmuseum.co.uk**

⑰ North York Moors

See p399.

⑱ North Yorkshire Moors Railway

Pickering & Grosmont, North Yorkshire. **Tel** 01751 472508. **Open** Apr–Oct: daily; Nov–Mar: some weekends (call for details). 🏠 🚹 📷 🌐 **nymr.co.uk**

Designed in 1831 by George Stephenson as a route through the North York Moors and linking with the Esk Valley, Pickering and Whitby *(see p386)*, this railway was considered an engineering miracle. Due to budget constraints, Stephenson had to lay the route down the mile-long (1.5 km) incline between Goathland and Beck Hole. The area around Fen Bog had to be stabilized using timber, heather, brushwood and fleeces so that a causeway could be built over it. A horse was used to pull a coach along the track at 10 miles (16 km) per hour. After horsepower came steam, and for almost 130 years the railway linked Whitby to the rest of the country. In the early 1960s the line to Pickering was closed, but in 1967 a group of locals began a campaign to relaunch it, and in 1973 it reopened. Today, steam engines run the 24-mile (38-km) line from Pickering via Levisham, Newtondale Halt and Goathland before terminating at Whitby, through the scenic heart of the North York Moors.

⓱ North York Moors

The area between Thirsk, Teesside and Scarborough is known as the North York Moors National Park. The landscape consists of beautiful moors interspersed with lush green valleys. Until the advent of coal, the communities' local source of fuel was turf. In the 19th century, the Industrial Revolution demands for ironstone, lime and alum were met by the extractive industries. Tourism is significant here, with 6 million annual visitors, despite a local population of just 24,000.

Mallyan Spout
A footpath leads to this waterfall from Goathland.

Farndale
During springtime, this area is famous for the beauty and profusion of its daffodils.

"Fat Betty" White Cross
Crosses and standing stones are a feature of the Moors.

Goathland A centre for forest and moorland walks, it is a stopping point for the North Yorkshire Moors Railway.

The Moors National Park Centre, Danby

Egton Bridge

Whitby

Lealholm

Beck
West

Wheeldale
Gill

Thorgill

Seven

Hartoft
Beck

Rutmoor Beck

Bloworth Beck

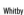

Dove

Rosedale Abbey Named after the priory that has long since gone, this beautiful village still has some remains of the kilns from its 19th-century ironstone mining industry.

Hutton-le-Hole
This lovely village has the excellent Ryedale Folk Museum.

Spaunton

Wade's Causeway
Often called the Roman Road, its origins and destination are unknown. Long considered Roman in date, this is now less certain, although it may date from towards the end of the Roman occupation.

VISITORS' CHECKLIST

Practical Information
North Yorkshire.
ℹ Sutton Bank (01845 597426); Moors Centre (01439 772737)
ⓦ northyorkmoors.org.uk

Transport
🚉 Danby. 🚌 Pickering (Easter–Oct)

Lastingham
Lastingham's church, dating from 1078, has a Norman crypt with stone carving.

| 0 kilometres | 2 |
| 0 miles | 2 |

For map symbols see back flap

⑲ Whitby

Whitby's known history dates back to the 7th century, when a Saxon monastery was founded on the site of today's famous 13th-century abbey ruins. In the 18th and early 19th centuries it became an industrial port and shipbuilding town, as well as a whaling centre. In the Victorian era, the red-roofed cottages at the foot of the east cliff were filled with workshops crafting jet into jewellery and ornaments. Today, the tourist shops that have replaced them sell antique-crafted examples of the distinctive black gem.

VISITORS' CHECKLIST

Practical Information
North Yorkshire. 🚇 13,500. 🛈 Langborne Rd (01723 383637). 🚆 Tue, Sat. 🎣 Angling Festival: Apr, Jun, Sep; Lifeboat Day: Jun; Folk Week: Aug; Whitby Regatta: Aug. 🌐 discover yorkshirecoast. com

Transport
✈ Teeside, 44 miles (70 km) ÑW Whitby. 🚋 Station Sq.

Exploring Whitby

Whitby is divided into two by the estuary of the River Esk. The Old Town, with its pretty cobbled streets and pastel-hued houses, huddles round the harbour. High above it is St Mary's Church with a wood interior reputedly fitted by ships' carpenters. The ruins of the 13th-century Whitby Abbey, nearby, are still used as a landmark by mariners. From them you get a fine view over the still-busy harbour, strewn with colourful nets. A pleasant place for a stroll, the harbour is overlooked by an imposing bronze clifftop statue of the explorer Captain James Cook (1728–79), who was apprenticed as a teenager to a Whitby shipping firm.

Lobster pots lining the quayside of Whitby's quaint harbour

Medieval arches above the nave of Whitby Abbey

🏛 Whitby Abbey

Abbey Lane. **Tel** 01947 603568. **Open** times vary; call for details. **Closed** 1 Jan, 24–26 Dec. 🚫 🛗 📷 EH

The monastery founded in 657 was sacked by Vikings in 870. In the 11th century it was rebuilt as a Benedictine Abbey. The ruins date mainly from the 13th century.

🏛 St Mary's Parish Church

East Cliff. **Tel** 01947 606578. **Open** daily.
Stuart and Georgian alterations to this Norman church have left a mixture of twisted wood columns and maze-like 18th-century box pews. The 1778 triple-decker pulpit has rather avant-garde decor – ear-trumpets used by a Victorian rector's deaf wife.

🏛 Captain Cook Memorial Museum

Grape Lane. **Tel** 01947 601900. **Open** Feb–Nov: daily. 🚫 📷 🛗 limited. 🌐 cookmuseum whitby.co.uk

The young James Cook slept in the attic of this 17th-century harbourside house when he was apprenticed nearby. The museum has displays of period furniture and watercolours by artists who travelled on his voyages.

🏛 Whitby Museum and Pannett Art Gallery

Pannett Park. **Tel** 01947 602908 (museum), 01947 602051 (gallery). **Open** Tue–Sun & public hols. **Closed** 24 Dec– 2 Jan. 🚫 museum only. 🛗 limited. 📷 🌐 whitbymuseum.org.uk

The Pannett Park grounds, museum and gallery were a gift of Whitby solicitor, Robert Pannett (1834–1920), to house his art collection. Among the museum's treasures are objects illustrating local history, such as jet jewellery, and Captain Cook artifacts.

The three-storey extension at the museum houses a costume gallery and photography and map collections.

🏛 Caedmon's Cross

East Cliff.
On the path side of the abbey's clifftop graveyard is the cross of Caedmon, an illiterate labourer who worked at the abbey in the 7th century. He experienced a vision that inspired him to compose cantos of Anglo-Saxon religious verse, which are still sung today.

Cross of Caedmon (1898)

⑳ Robin Hood's Bay

North Yorkshire. 🚶 1,400. 🚌 🚆 Whitby. ℹ Langbourne Rd, Whitby (01723 383637). 🌐 **yorkshire.com/ places/yorkshire-coast**

Legend has it that Robin Hood (see p340) kept his boats here in case he needed to make a quick getaway. The village has a history as a smugglers' haven, and many houses have ingenious hiding places for contraband. The cobbled main street is so steep that visitors need to leave their vehicles in the car park at the top. In the village centre, narrow streets full of colour-washed stone cottages huddle around a quaint quay. There is a rocky beach with rock pools for children to play in. At low tide, the pleasant walk south to Boggle Hole takes 15 minutes, but you need to keep an eye on the tides.

The fishing port and town of Scarborough nestling round the harbour

Cobbled alley in the Bay Town area of Robin Hood's Bay

㉑ Scarborough

North Yorkshire. 🚶 51,000. 🚆 🚌 ℹ Brunswick Shopping Centre (01723 383636). 🛒 Mon–Sat. 🌐 **discoveryorkshirecoast.com**

The history of Scarborough as a resort can be traced back to 1626, when it became known as a spa. In the Industrial Revolution (see pp352–3) it was nicknamed "the Queen of the Watering Places", but the post-World War II trend for holidays abroad has meant fewer visitors. The town has two beaches; the South Bay amusement arcades contrast with the quieter North Bay. Playwright Alan Ayckbourn premiers his work at the Stephen Joseph theatre, and Anne Brontë (see p416) is buried in St Mary's Church.

Bronze and Iron Age relics have been found on the site of **Scarborough Castle**. The **Rotunda** (1828–9), which underwent a major refurbishment during 2007, was one of Britain's first purpose-built museums. Works by the local artist Atkinson Grimshaw (1836–93) hang in **Scarborough Art Gallery**. The **Sea Life and Marine Sanctuary**'s baby seals are its main attraction.

🏰 **Scarborough Castle**
Castle Rd. **Tel** 01723 372451. **Open** Apr–Sep: daily; Oct: Thu–Mon; Nov– Mar: Sat & Sun. **Closed** 1 Jan, 24–26 Dec. 🚫 ♿ 🖥 📷 EH

🏛 **Rotunda Museum**
Vernon Rd. **Tel** 01723 353665. **Open** Tue–Sun. **Closed** 1 Jan, 25 & 26 Dec. 🚫 📷

🏛 **Scarborough Art Gallery**
The Crescent. **Tel** 01723 374753. **Open** Tue–Sun. **Closed** 1 Jan, 25 & 26 Dec. 📷 🚫 🖥 🌐 scarborough museumstrust.co.uk

🐟 **Sea Life and Marine Sanctuary**
Scalby Mills Rd. **Tel** 01723 373414. **Open** daily. **Closed** 25 Dec. 🚫 ♿ 🖥 📷 🌐 visitsealife.com

The Growing Popularity of Swimming

During the 18th century, sea-bathing came to be regarded as a healthy pastime, and from 1735 onwards men and women, on separate stretches of the coast, could be taken out into the sea in bathing huts, or "machines". In the 18th century, bathing was segregated although nudity was permitted. The Victorians brought in fully clothed bathing, and 19th-century workers from Britain's industrial heartlands used the new steam trains to visit the coast for their holidays. At this time, British seaside resorts such as Blackpool (see p375) and Scarborough expanded to meet the new demand.

A Victorian bathing hut on wheels

㉒ Castle Howard

Still owned and lived in by the Howard family, Castle Howard was created by Charles, 3rd Earl of Carlisle. In 1699, he commissioned Sir John Vanbrugh, a man of dramatic ideas but with no previous architectural experience, to design a palace for him. Vanbrugh's grand designs of 1699 were put into practice by architect Nicholas Hawksmoor *(see p32)*, and the main body of the house was completed by 1712. The West Wing was built in 1753–9, using a design by Thomas Robinson, son-in-law of the 3rd Earl. In the 1980s, Castle Howard was used as the location for the television version of Evelyn Waugh's novel *Brideshead Revisited* (1945) and again for the film version in 2008.

Temple of the Four Winds
Vanbrugh's last work, designed in 1724, has a dome and four Ionic porticoes. Situated in the grounds at the end of the terrace, it is typical of an 18th-century "landscape building".

Bust of the 7th Earl
J H Foley sculpted this portrait bust, which stands at the top of the Grand Staircase in the West Wing, in 1870.

KEY

① **East Wing**

② **The front façade** boldly faces north, which is unusual for the 17th century, while all the state rooms have a southerly aspect, with superb views over the gardens.

③ **North Front**

④ **Antique Passage** is where antiquities collected in the 18th and 19th centuries by the various Earls of Carlisle are displayed. The plethora of mythical figures and gods reflects contemporary interest in Classical civilizations.

⑤ **West Wing**

★ **Great Hall**
Rising 20 m (66 ft), from its 515 sq m (5,500 sq ft) floor to the dome, the Great Hall has columns by Samuel Carpenter (1660–1713), wall paintings by Pellegrini and a circular gallery.

Chapel Stained Glass
Admiral Edward Howard altered the chapel in 1870–75. The windows were designed by Edward Burne-Jones and made by William Morris & Co.

VISITORS' CHECKLIST

Practical Information
A64 from York. **Tel** 01653 648 333.
🆆 castlehoward.co.uk
House: **Open** hours vary; call or see website for details. Grounds: **Open** 10am–5:30pm daily (to 4pm Dec–Feb). 🚻 ♿ 🏪 🎁

Transport
🚆 York then bus, or Malton then taxi.

★ Long Gallery
Displayed here are paintings and sculptures commissioned by the Howard family, including works by Reynolds and Pannini.

Tourist entrance

Sir John Vanbrugh

Vanbrugh (1664–1726) trained as a soldier, but became better known as a playwright, architect and member of the Whig nobility. He collaborated with Hawksmoor over the design of Blenheim Palace, but his bold architectural vision, later greatly admired, was mocked by the establishment. He died while working on the garden buildings and grounds of Castle Howard.

Museum Room
Furniture here includes Regency chairs, a bronze collection and this 17th-century cabinet.

㉓ Eden Camp

Malton, North Yorkshire. **Tel** 01653
697777. ⟷ Malton then taxi.
Open daily. 🏠 📷 ♿ 🛒
🅦 edencamp.co.uk

This is an unusual, award-
winning theme museum which
pays tribute to the British
people during World War II.
Italian and German prisoners of
war were kept at Eden Camp
between 1939 and 1948. Today,
some original huts built by
Italian prisoners in 1942 are used
as a museum, with period
tableaux and a soundtrack. Each
hut adopts a theme to take the
visitor through civilian life in
war-time, from Chamberlain's
radio announcement of the
outbreak of hostilities to the
coming of peace. Visitors,
including schoolchildren and
nostalgic veterans, can see the
Doodlebug V-1 bomb which
crashed outside the Officers'
Mess, take tea in the canteen or
experience a night in the Blitz.
A tour can last for several hours.

British and American flags by the
sign for Eden Camp

㉔ Wharram Percy

North Yorkshire. **Tel** 0870 333 1181.
🅘 01653 600 048. ⟷ Malton, then
taxi. **Open** daily. EH
🅦 english-heritage.org.uk

This is one of England's
most important deserted
medieval village sites. Excavations
have unearthed evidence of a
30-household community, with
two manors, and the remains of a
medieval church. There is also a
millpond which has beautiful
wild flowers in late spring.
Wharram Percy is set in a pretty
valley, sign-posted off the B1248
from Burdale, in the heart of the
Wolds. It is about 20 minutes'
walk from the car park and makes
an ideal picnic stop.

Alabaster carving on the chimney-piece at Burton Agnes

㉕ Burton Agnes

On A614, nr Driffield, East Riding. **Tel**
01262 490324. ⟷ Driffield, then bus.
Open Apr–Oct: daily. 🏠 ♿ limited.
🛒 📷 🅦 burtonagnes.com

Of all the grand houses in this
area, Burton Agnes Hall is a firm
favourite. This is partly because
the attractive, redbrick Elizabethan mansion has such a
homely atmosphere. One of the
first portraits you see in the
Small Hall is of Anne Griffith,
whose father, Sir Henry, built the
house. There is a monument to
him in the local church.

Burton Agnes has remained
in the hands of the original
family and has changed little
since it was built, between 1598
and 1610. You enter it by the
turreted gatehouse, and the
entrance hall has a fine Elizabethan alabaster chimney
piece. The massive oak staircase
is an impressive example of
Elizabethan woodcarving.

In the library is a collection of
Impressionist and Post-
Impressionist art,
pleasantly out of
character with the rest
of the house,
including works by André
Derain, Renoir and Augustus
John. The extensive grounds
include a purpose-built play
area for children.

㉖ Bempton Cliffs and Flamborough Head

East Riding. ⟷ Bempton. 🚌
Bridlington. 🅘 Bempton Cliffs Visitor
Centre (01262 851179).
🅦 rspb.org.uk

Bempton, which consists of
5 miles (8 km) of steep chalk
cliffs between Speeton and
Flamborough Head, is the
largest seabird-breeding colony
in England, and is famous for its
puffins. The ledges and fissures
provide ideal nest-sites for more
than 100,000 pairs of birds.
Today, eight

Nesting gannet on the chalk cliffs at Bempton

different species, including skinny black shags and kittiwakes, thrive on the Grade 1 listed (see p623) Bempton cliffs. Bempton is the only mainland site for goose-sized gannets, well known for their dramatic fishing techniques. May, June and July are the best bird-watching months.

The spectacular cliffs are best seen from the north side of the Flamborough Head peninsula.

㉗ Beverley

East Riding of Yorkshire. 🚍 30,000. 🅸 34 Butcher Row (01482 391672). 🔄 Sat. 🆆 **visithullandeastyorkshire.com**

The history of Beverley dates back to the 8th century, when Old Beverley served as a retreat for John, later Bishop of York, who was canonized for his healing powers. Over the centuries Beverley grew as a medieval sanctuary town. Like York, it is an attractive combination of both medieval and Georgian buildings.

The best way to enter Beverley is through the last of five medieval town gates, the castellated North Bar (rebuilt 1409–10). The bars were

Minstrel Pillar in St Mary's Church

constructed so that market goods had to pass through them and a toll (levy) paid.

The skyline is dominated by the twin towers of the magnificent **Beverley Minster**. This was co-founded in 937 by Athelstan, King of Wessex, in place of the church that John of Beverley had chosen as his final resting place in 721. The decorated nave is the earliest surviving building work which dates back to the early 1300s. It is particularly famous for its 16th-century choir stalls and 68 misericords (see p345).

The minster contains many early detailed stone carvings, including a set of four from about 1308 that illustrate figures with ailments such as toothache and lumbago. On the north side of the altar is the richly carved 14th-century Gothic Percy tomb, thought to be that of Lady Idoine Percy. Also on the north side is the Fridstol, or Peace Chair, said to date from 924–39, the time of Athelstan.

Anyone who sat on it would be granted 30 days' sanctuary. Within the North Bar, **St Mary's Church** has a 13th-century chancel and houses Britain's largest number

The inspiration for Lewis Carroll's White Rabbit, St Mary's Church

of medieval stone carvings of musical instruments. The brightly painted 16th-century Minstrel Pillar is particularly notable. Painted on the panelled chancel ceiling are portraits of monarchs after 1445. On the richly sculpted doorway of St Michael's Chapel is the grinning pilgrim rabbit said to have inspired Lewis Carroll's White Rabbit in *Alice in Wonderland*.

There is a great day out to be had at **Beverley Races**, with various theme days throughout the season and excellent food and drink.

🏛 **Beverley Minster**
Minster Yard. **Tel** 01482 868 540.
Open daily. ♿ 📷 🖥 📅
🆆 **beverleyminster.org.uk**

Beverley Minster, one of Europe's finest examples of Gothic architecture

28 Burton Constable

Nr Hull, East Yorkshire. **Tel** 01964 562400. 🚆 Hull then taxi. **Open** Easter–Oct: Sat–Thu. 🅿️ ♿ 📷 🖥️ 🏠 W burtonconstable.com

The Constable family have been leading landowners since the 13th century, and have lived at Burton Constable Hall since work began on it in 1570. It is an Elizabethan house, altered in the 18th century by Thomas Lightholer, Thomas Atkinson and James Wyatt. Today, its 30 rooms include Georgian and Victorian interiors. It has a fine collection of Chippendale furniture and family portraits dating from the 16th century. Most of the collections of prints, textiles and drawings belong to Leeds City Art Galleries. The family still lives in the south wing.

Painting of Burton Constable (c.1690) by an anonymous artist

The Princes' Dock in Kingston upon Hull's restored docks area

29 Kingston upon Hull

Kingston upon Hull. 🔢 263,000. 🚆 🚌 🚢 ℹ️ Paragon St. (01482 223559). 🛒 Mon–Sat. W visithullandeastyorkshire.com

There is a lot more to Hull than the heritage of a thriving fishing industry. The restored town centre docks are attractive, and Hull's Old Town, laid out in medieval times, is all cobbled, winding streets and quaintly askew red-brick houses. You can follow the "Seven Seas" Fish Trail, a path of inlaid metal fishes on the city's pavements that illustrates the many different varieties that have been landed in Hull, from anchovy to shark. In Victoria Square is the **Maritime Museum**. Built in 1871

as the offices of the Hull Dock Company, it traces the city's maritime history. Among its exhibits are an ornate whalebone and vertebrae bench and a display of complicated rope knots such as the Eye Splice and the Midshipman's Hitch.

An imposing Elizabethan building, **Hands on History**, explores Hull's story through a collection of some of its families' artifacts.

In the heart of the Old Town, the **William Wilberforce House** is one of the surviving examples of the High Street's brick merchants' dwellings. Its first-floor oak-panelled rooms date from the 17th century. As well as examining the transatlantic slave trade, and contemporary forms of slavery,

there are exhibitions on West African culture and the Wilberforce family.

Nearby is the **Streetlife Museum of Transport**, Hull's most popular and noisiest museum, loved by children. It features Britain's oldest tramcar. At the mouth of the River Hull, **The Deep** is the world's only "submarium", in a stunning building and dramatic setting. With lots of exciting sea life and state-of-the-art technology, it is ideal for families.

🏛️ **Maritime Museum**
Queen Victoria Sq. **Tel** 01482 300300. **Open** daily (Sun: pm). ♿ 🏠 W hullcc.gov.uk/museums

🏛️ **Hands on History**
South Churchside. **Tel** 01482 300300. **Open** daily (Sun: pm). **Closed** 1 Jan, Good Fri, 24–28 Dec. 🏠 ♿

William Wilberforce (1758–1833)

William Wilberforce, born in Hull to a merchant family, was a natural orator. After studying Classics at Cambridge, he entered politics and in 1784 gave one of his first public addresses in York. The audience was captivated, and Wilberforce realized the potential of his powers of persuasion. From 1785 onwards, adopted by the Pitt government as spokesman for the abolition of slavery, he conducted a determined and conscientious campaign. But his speeches won him enemies, and in 1792, threats from a slave-importer meant that he needed a constant armed guard. In 1807 his bill to abolish the lucrative slave trade became law.

A 19th-century engraving of Wilberforce by J Jenkins

🏛 **William Wilberforce House**
High St, Hull. **Tel** 01482 300300.
Open daily (Sun: pm). 🏠 🚻 limited.

🏛 **Streetlife Museum of Transport**
High St, Hull. **Tel** 01482 300300.
Open Mon–Sat, Sun pm. 🚻 🏠

🐟 **The Deep**
Hull (via Citadel Way). **Tel** 01482 381 000.
Open daily. **Closed** 24, 25 Dec. 🚻 🏠
🖥 🏠 P W thedeep.co.uk

③⓪ Holderness and Spurn Head

East Riding of Yorkshire. 🚆 Hull
(Paragon St) then bus. ℹ 120
Newbegin, Hornsea (01964 536404).

This curious flat area east of Hull, with straight roads and delicately waving fields of oats and barley, in many ways resembles Holland, except that its windmills are mostly disused. Beaches stretch for 30 miles (46 km) along the coastline. The main resort towns are **Withernsea** and **Hornsea**.

The Holderness landscape only exists because of erosion higher up the coast. The sea continues to wash down tiny bits of rock which accumulate. Around 1560, this began to form a sandbank, and by 1669 it had became large enough to be colonized as Sonke Sand. The last bits of silting mud and debris joined the island to the mainland as recently as the 1830s. Today, you can drive through the eerie, lush wilderness of Sunk Island on the way east to Spurn Head. This is located at the tip of the Spurn Peninsula, a 3.5 mile (6 km) spit of land that has also built up as the result of coastal erosion elsewhere. Flora, fauna and birdlife have been protected here by the Yorkshire Wildlife Trust since 1960. Walking here gives the eerie feeling that the land could be eroded from under your feet at any time. A surprise discovery at the end of Spurn Head is a tiny community of pilots and lifeboat crew, constantly on call to guide ships into the Humber estuary, or help cope with disasters.

Fishing boat at Grimsby's National Fishing Heritage Centre

③① Grimsby

NE Lincs. 🚗 92,000. 🚆 🚌 ℹ
Cleethorpes Library, Alexandra Road,
Cleethorpes (01472 323111).
W nelincs.gov.uk

Perched at the mouth of the River Humber, legend claims Grimsby was founded in the 9th century by a Danish fisherman by the name of Grim. It rose to prominence in the 19th century as one of the world's largest fishing ports. Its first dock was opened in 1800 and, with the arrival of the railways, the town secured the means of transporting its catch all over the country. Even though the traditional fishing industry had declined by the 1970s, dock area redevelopment has ensured that Grimsby's unique heritage is retained.

This is best demonstrated by the award-winning **National Fishing Heritage Centre**, a museum that recreates the industry in its 1950s heyday, capturing the atmosphere of the period. Visitors sign on as crew members on a trawler and, by means of vivid interactive displays, travel from the back streets of Grimsby to the Arctic fishing grounds. On the way, they can experience the roll of the ship, the smell of the fish and the heat of the engine. The tour ends with a look at the restored 1950s trawler, the *Ross Tiger*.

Other attractions in Grimsby include a restored Victorian shopping street called Abbeygate, a market and a wide selection of restaurants. Nearby seaside resorts of Cleethorpes, Mablethorpe and Skegness offer miles of golden sands.

🏛 **National Fishing Heritage Centre**
Heritage Sq, Alexandra Dock.
Tel 01472 323345. **Open** Tue–Sun.
Closed 1 Jan, 25–26 Dec. 🚻 🚻 🏠
🖥 🏠

Isolated lighthouse at Spurn Head, at the tip of Spurn Peninsula

⊕ Street-by-Street: York

The city of York has retained so much of its medieval structure that walking into its centre is like entering a living museum. Many of the ancient timbered houses, perched on narrow, winding streets, such as the Shambles, are protected by a conservation order. Much of the centre is pedestrianized and there are always student bikes bouncing over cobbled streets. Its strategic position led to its development as a railway centre in the 19th century.

★ York Minster
England's largest medieval church was begun in 1220 (see pp410–11).

Stonegate
The medieval red devil is a feature of this street, built over a Roman road.

Thirsk ←   Helmsley ↑

York Art Gallery

St Mary's Abbey

Yorkshire Museum is home to some of the most fascinating archeology in the country.

Lendal Bridge

↓ Railway station, coach station, National Railway Museum, and Leeds

DEANGATE

HIGH PETERGATE   LOW PETERG

ST LEONARDS PLACE

DUNCOMBE PLACE

MINSTER YARD

STONEGATE

BLAKE STREET

DAVYGATE

MUSEUM STREET

LENDAL STREET

CONEY STREET

OUSE

Ye Old Starre Inne is one of the oldest pubs in ork.

Guildhall
This two-headed medieval roof boss is on the 15th-century Guildhall, situated beside the River Ouse and restored after bomb damage during World War II.

St Olave's Church
The 11th-century church, next to the gatehouse of St Mary's Abbey (see p354), was founded by the Earl of Northumbria in memory of St Olaf, King of Norway. To the left is the Chapel of St Mary on the Walls.

Monk Bar

↑ Scarborough

★ Jorvik
The many artifacts on show here illustrate the time when York was a strategic Viking town. The street names ending in "gate" come from the Danish word *gata*, meaning "street" or "way".

Holy Trinity Church

King's Square

VISITORS' CHECKLIST

Practical Information
York. 202,500.
1 Museum St (01904 550099).
daily. Jorvik Festival: Feb; Early Music Festival: Jul. (Association of Voluntary Guides, from Exhibition Sq): Apr–Oct: 10:15am & 2:15pm daily (Jun–Aug: also 6:45pm); Nov–Mar: 10:15am daily, 1:15pm Fri–Sun.
W visityork.org

Transport
Leeds Bradford, 32 miles (50 km) NW. Station Rd. Station Rd.

COLLIERGATE

ST SAVIOURGATE

THE SHAMBLES

THE STONEBOW

FOSSGATE

WHIP · MA · WHOP · MA · GATE

Whip-ma-whop-ma-gate
York's tiniest street has the city's longest name, which dates from Saxon times and means "neither one thing nor the other".

Merchant Adventurer's Hall, built for a guild of merchant adventurers in the 14th century, is now a visitor attraction.

PARLIAMENT STREET

PAVEMENT

PICCADILLY

FOSS

★ York Castle Museum
Converted from two prisons, this museum *(see p412)* features print and blacksmith workshops, and the cell formerly used by highwayman Dick Turpin (1706–39).

FRIERGATE

OUSEGATE

CASTLE GATE

CLIFFORD STREET

TOWER STREET

P

→ Hull

Clifford's Tower

Fairfax House

St Mary's Church

| 0 metres | 100 |
| 0 yards | 100 |

Key

— Suggested route

York Minster

The largest medieval Gothic cathedral north of the Alps, and seat of the Archbishop of York, York Minster is 158 m (519 ft) long and 76 m (249 ft) wide across the transepts. It is also home to the largest collection of medieval stained glass in Britain (see p413). The word "minster" refers to a missionary teaching church in Anglo-Saxon times. The first minster began as a wooden chapel used to baptize King Edwin of Northumbria in 627. There have been several cathedrals on or near the site, including an 11th-century Norman structure. The present minster was begun in 1220 and completed 250 years later. In 1984, fire damage led to a £2.25 million restoration programme.

Central Tower
This lantern tower was reconstructed in 1420–65 (after partial collapse in 1405) from a design by the master stonemason William Colchester.

South transept entrance

KEY

① **Great East Window (p409)**

② **The Quire** has a vaulted entrance with a 15th-century boss of the Assumption of the Virgin.

③ **The 16th-century rose window**

④ **The western towers,** with their 15th-century decorative panelling and elaborate pinnacles, contrast with the simpler design of the north transept. The southwest tower is the minster belfry.

⑤ **West Window**

⑥ **Great West Door**

⑦ **The Nave,** begun in 1291, was severely damaged by fire in 1840. Rebuilding costs were heavy, but it was re-opened with a new peal of bells in 1844.

★ Chapter House
A Latin inscription near the entrance of the wooden-vaulted Chapter House (1260–85) reads: "As the rose is the flower of flowers, so this is the house of houses".

★ Choir Screen
Sited between the choir and the nave, this 15th-century stone screen depicts kings of England from William I to Henry VI, and has a canopy of angels.

VISITORS' CHECKLIST

Practical Information
Deangate, York. **Tel** 0844
939 0011. **Open** Mon–Sat:
9am–5pm (from 9:30am
Nov–Mar); Sun: noon–5pm.
Opening times may change
subject to major services.
Closed Good Fri, Easter Sun,
24 & 25 Dec. 🔊 to Minster,
Undercroft & the Orb.
🔔 Mon–Sat: 7:30am,
7:45am, 12:30pm (also at
noon Sat), 5:15pm (evensong);
Sun: 8am, 10am, 11:30am,
4pm. ♿ main floors. 📷
📷 📷 **w** **yorkminster.org**

The impressive façade of York Minster
in the city centre

Timbered interior of the Merchant Adventurers' Hall

🏛 Monk Bar

This is one of York's finest
original medieval gates, situated
at the end of Goodramgate.
It is vaulted on three floors,
and the portcullis still works. In
the Middle Ages, the rooms
above it were rented out, and it
was a prison in the 16th century.
Its decorative details include
men holding stones ready to
drop on intruders.

Preparing for a Fancy Dress Ball (1833) by
William Etty, York Art Gallery

🏛 York Art Gallery

Exhibition Sq. **Tel** 01904 687687.
Closed for redevelopment; due to
re-open Easter 2015. 📷 ♿ 📷 📷
w **yorkartgallery.org.uk**

This Italianate building of 1879
holds a wide-ranging collection
of paintings from western Europe
dating from the early 1500s. There
is also a large, internationally
significant collection of British
and foreign studio ceramics.
Work by Bernard Leach, William
Staite Murray and Shoji Hamada
is on display alongside details of
the potters themselves and
those who collected their work.

On re-opening in 2015, the
gallery will have expanded to
host major international shows.

🏛 Clifford's Tower

Clifford's St. **Tel** 01904 646940. **Open**
Apr–Oct: daily; Nov–Mar: Sat & Sun.
Closed 1 Jan, 24–26 & 31 Dec. 📷 **EH**
📷 **w** **english-heritage.org.uk**

Sited on top of a mound that
William the Conqueror built for
his original wooden castle,
destroyed by fire during anti-Jewish
riots in 1190, Clifford's Tower
dates from the 13th century. Built
by Henry III, it was named after the
de Clifford family, who were
constables of the castle.

🏛 DIG – An Archaeological Adventure

St Saviourgate. **Tel** 01904 615505.
Open daily (best to book in advance).
Closed 24 & 25 Dec. 📷 ♿ 📷 📷

Housed in a restored
medieval church, this centre
invites visitors to become
archaeological detectives and
discover how archaeologists
have pieced together clues
from the past to unravel the
history of the Viking age
in York.

🏛 Merchant Adventurers' Hall

Fossgate. **Tel** 01904 654818. **Open**
Mar–Oct: daily; Nov–Feb: Mon–Sat.
Closed 24 Dec–3 Jan. 📷 ♿ 📷
w **theyorkcompany.co.uk**

Built by a guild of Yorkshire
merchants in 1357, this is one of
the largest timber-framed
medieval buildings in Britain. The
Great Hall is probably the best
example of its kind in Europe.
Among its paintings is an un-
attributed 17th-century copy of
Van Dyck's portrait of Charles I's
queen, Henrietta Maria. Below
the Great Hall is the hospital,
which was used by the guild until
1900, and a private chapel.

Exploring York

The appeal of York is its many layers of history. A medieval city constructed on top of a Roman one, it was first built in AD 71, when it became capital of the northern province and was known as Eboracum. It was here that Constantine the Great was made emperor in 306, and reorganized Britain into four provinces. A hundred years later, the Roman army had withdrawn. Eboracum was renamed Eoforwic, under the Saxons, and then became a Christian stronghold. The Danish street names are the reminder that it was a Viking centre from 867, and one of Europe's chief trading bases. Between 1100 and 1500 it was England's second city. The glory of York is the minster (see pp410–11). The city also boasts 18 medieval churches, 3 mile long (4.8 km) medieval city walls, elegant Jacobean and Georgian architecture and fine museums.

Grand staircase and fine plaster ceiling at Fairfax House

York Castle Museum
The Eye of York. **Tel** 01904 687687.
Open daily. **Closed** 1 Jan, 25 & 26 Dec.
ground floor only. **w** yorkcastlemuseum.org.uk

Housed in two 18th-century prisons, the museum has a fine folk collection, started by Dr John Kirk of the market town of Pickering. Opened in 1938, its period displays include a Jacobean dining room, a moorland cottage, and a 1950s front room. It also contains an exhibition on the traditions of birth, marriages and death in Britain from 1700 to 2000.

The most famous exhibits include the reconstructed Victorian street of Kirkgate, complete with shopfronts, and the Anglo Saxon York Helmet, discovered in 1982.

York Minster
See pp410–11.

Jorvik
Coppergate. **Tel** 01904 615505.
Open daily (pre-booking advised).
Closed 24–26 Dec. ring first.
w jorvik-viking-centre.co.uk

This centre is built on the site of the original Viking settlement which archaeologists uncovered at Coppergate. Using new technology, a dynamic vision of 10th-century York is recreated, with smells bringing the Viking world to life. At the centre's sister attraction, DIG, visitors can take part in an archaeological excavation.

Yorkshire Museum and St Mary's Abbey
Museum Gardens. **Tel** 01904 687687.
Open daily.
Yorkshire Museum made the news when it purchased the 15th-century Middleham Jewel for £2.5 million, one of the finest pieces of English Gothic jewellery found this century. Other exhibits include 2nd-century Roman mosaics and an Anglo-Saxon silver gilt bowl.

St Mary's Abbey (see p354) hosts the medieval York Mystery Plays occasionally.

Fairfax House
Castlegate. **Tel** 01904 655543.
Open mid-Feb–Dec: daily (Sun: pm only; Mon: tours only). **Closed** 24–26 Dec, Jan, early Feb. limited.
w fairfaxhouse.co.uk

From 1755 to 1762 Viscount Fairfax built this fine Georgian town house for his daughter, Anne. The house was designed by John Carr (see p32), and restored in the 1980s. Between 1920 and 1965 it was a cinema and dancehall. Today, visitors can see the bedroom of Anne Fairfax (1725–93), and a fine collection of 18th-century furniture, porcelain and clocks.

National Railway Museum
Leeman Rd. **Tel** 0844 815 3139.
Open daily. **Closed** 24–26 Dec.
w nrm.org.uk

In what is the world's largest railway museum, nearly 200 years of history are explored using a variety of visual aids. Visitors can try wheel-tapping and shunting in the interactive gallery, or find out what made Stephenson's Rocket so successful. Exhibits include uniforms, rolling stock from 1797 onward and Queen Victoria's Royal Train carriage, as well as the very latest rail innovations.

Reproduction of Stephenson's Rocket (right) and 1830s first-class carriage in York's National Railway Museum

The Stained Glass of York Minster

York Minster houses the largest collection of medieval stained glass in Britain, some of it dating from the late 12th century. The glass was generally coloured during production, using metal oxides to produce the desired colour, then worked on by craftsmen on site. When a design had been produced, the glass was first cut, then trimmed to shape. Details were painted on, using iron oxide-based paint which was fused to the glass by firing in a kiln. Individual pieces were then leaded together to form the finished window. Part of the fascination of the minster glass is its variety of subject matter. Some windows were paid for by lay donors who specified a particular subject, others reflect ecclesiastical patronage.

Miracle of St Nicholas (late 12th century) was put in the nave over 100 years after it was made. It shows a Jew's conversion to Christianity.

The Five Sisters in the north transept are the largest examples of *grisaille* glass in Britain. This popular 13th-century technique involved creating fine patterning on clear glass and decorating it with black enamel.

St John the Evangelist, in part of the Great West Window (c.1338), is holding an eagle, itself an example of stickwork, where paint is scraped off to reveal clear glass.

St John Glimpses God in Majesty depicts St John gazing through a trapdoor into heaven. God is set in a mandorla, illuminated by lamps.

St John Sailing to Patmos illustrates the saint's exile to the Greek island where he had several visions. Much original glass is preserved in this piece.

The Orb gives visitors the chance to see five East Window panels up close, with one of the five changing on a monthly basis.

㉝ Harewood House

Leeds. **Tel** 0113 2181010. 🚌 Leeds then bus. **Open** Apr–31 Oct: daily. 📷 ♿ by arrangement. 🅿 📷
w harewood.org

Designed by John Carr in 1759, Harewood House is the Yorkshire home of the Earl and Countess of Harewood.

The grand Palladian exterior is impressive, with interiors created by Robert Adam and an unrivalled collection of 18th-century furniture made specifically for Harewood by Yorkshire-born Thomas Chippendale (1711–79). There are paintings by Italian and English artists, including Reynolds and Gainsborough, and two watercolour rooms. The grounds by "Capability" Brown (see p30) include the **Harewood Bird Garden**, which has exotic species and a breeding programme of certain endangered varieties.

Bali starling, one of Harewood's rare birds

㉞ Leeds

Leeds. 🗺 750,000. ✈ 🚃 🚌 *i* Leeds City Station (0113 2425242). 🛒 Mon–Sat. **w** leedsliveitloveit.com

The third-largest of Britain's provincial cities, Leeds was at its most prosperous during the Victorian period. The most impressive legacy from this era is a series of ornate, covered shopping arcades. Also of note is the **Town Hall**, designed by Cuthbert Brodrick and opened by Queen Victoria in 1858.

Today, although Leeds is primarily an industrial city, it also offers a thriving cultural scene. Productions at **The Grand** by Opera North, one of Britain's top operatic companies, are of a high quality.

The **Leeds Art Gallery** has impressive collections of British 20th-century art and of Victorian paintings, including works by local artist Atkinson Grimshaw (1836–93). Among the late 19th-century French art are works by Signac, Courbet and

Sisley. The Henry Moore Institute, added in 1993, is devoted to the research and display of sculpture of all periods. It comprises a study centre, library, galleries and an archive of material on Moore and other sculptural pioneers.

The **Armley Mills Museum**, in a 19th-century woollen mill, explores the industrial heritage of Leeds. Filled with original equipment, recorded sounds and models in 19th-century workers' clothes, it traces the history of the ready-to-wear industry. The **Leeds City Museum** charts the history of Leeds with ethnographical and archaeological exhibits.

A striking waterfront development by the River Aire has attracted two museums. The **Royal Armouries Museum** is the UK's national museum of arms and armour, home to a vast array of weaponry from around the world. The **Thackray Medical Museum** is an inter-active display of medical advances, from a re-created Victorian slum to modern-day medical challenges.

For children, **Tropical World** features crystal pools, a rainforest house, butterflies and tropical fish. There is also a farm and a Rare Breeds centre in the grounds of the Tudor-Jacobean **Temple**

The County Arcade, one of Leeds' restored shopping arcades

Newsam House, which has major art and furniture collections.

🏛 **Leeds Art Gallery**
The Headrow. **Tel** 0113 2478256.
Open daily (Sun: pm). **Closed** pub hols. 📷 ♿ 🛒

🏛 **Armley Mills Museum**
Canal Rd, Armley. **Tel** 0113 2637 861.
Open Tue–Sun (Sun: pm), pub hols.
Closed 1 Jan, 25, 26 Dec. 📷 ♿ 📷

🏛 **Leeds City Museum**
Millennium Sq. **Tel** 0113 2243732.
Open Tue–Sun. **Closed** pub hols. ♿
📷 📷

🏛 **Royal Armouries**
Armouries Drive. **Tel** 0113 2201999.
Open daily. **Closed** 24–26 Dec. ♿
🛒 📷

🏛 **Thackray Medical Museum**
Beckett St. **Tel** 0113 2444343. **Open** daily. **Closed** 1 Jan, 24–26, 31 Dec. 📷
♿ 🛒 **w** thackraymuseum.org

🌿 **Tropical World Canal Gdns, Princes Ave.**
Tel 0113 3957400. **Open** daily. **Closed** 25, 26 Dec. 📷 ♿ 🛒 📷

🏯 **Temple Newsam House**
Off A63. **Tel** 0113 2645535. **Open** Tue–Sun. **Closed** Jan, 25 & 26 Dec. 📷 🛒 📷

Working loom at the Armley Mills Museum in Leeds

The Other Side (1990–93) by David Hockney at Bradford's 1853 Gallery in Saltaire

㉟ Bradford

Bradford. 🅰 294,000. ✈ 🚢 🚌 🅸
City Hall, Centenary Square (01274
433678). 🛍 Mon–Sat.
🅦 visitbradford.com

In the 16th century, Bradford was a thriving market town, and the opening of its canal in 1774 boosted trade. By 1850, it was the world's capital for worsted (fabric made from closely twisted wool). Many of the city's well-preserved civic and industrial buildings date from this period, such as the Wool Exchange on Market Street. In the 1800s a number of German textile manufacturers settled in what is now called Little Germany. Their houses are characterized by decorative stone carvings that illustrated the wealth and standing of the occupants.

Daguerreotype camera by Giroux (1839)

The **National Media Museum**, founded in 1983, explores the technology and art of these media. There is a television section called TV Heaven, where visitors can ask to watch their favourite programme. They are also encouraged to see themselves read the news on TV. The giant IMAX screen uses the world's largest film format. Film subjects include journeys into space, the ocean and the natural world.

The **Cartwright Hall Art Gallery** displays 19th- and 20th-century British art and collections of contemporary art from South Asia. **Bradford Industrial Museum** is housed in an original spinning mill. As well as seeing and hearing all the mill machinery, you can ride on a horse-drawn tram. Saltaire, a Victorian industrial village (*see p353*), is on the outskirts of the city. Built by Sir Titus Salt for his Salts Mill workers, it was completed in 1873. The **1853 Gallery** has the world's largest collection of works by David Hockney, born in Bradford.

🏛 **National Media Museum**
Pictureville. **Tel** 0870 7010200.
Open daily (school hols); Tue–Sun (school terms); public holidays.
Closed 24–26 Dec. 🅿 🅿 ⃠
🅦 nationalmediamuseum.org.uk

🏛 **Cartwright Hall Art Gallery**
Lister Park. **Tel** 01274 431212.
Open Tue–Sat. **Closed** Good Fri, 25–26 Dec. 🅿 ⃠ 🅿

🏛 **Bradford Industrial Museum**
Moorside Mills, Moorside Rd.
Tel 01274 435900. **Open** Tue–Sat, Sun (pm), public hols.
Closed Good Fri, 25–26 Dec. 🅿 🅿
🅦 bradfordmuseums.org

🏛 **1853 Gallery**
Salts Mill, Victoria Rd. **Tel** 01274 531 163.
Open daily. **Closed** 1 Jan, 25–26 Dec.
🅿 ⃠ 🖥 🅿 🅦 saltsmill.org.uk

Bradford's Asian Community

Immigrants from the Indian subcontinent originally came to Bradford in the 1950s to work in the mills, but with the decline of the textile industry many began small businesses. By the mid-1970s there were 1,400 such enterprises in the area. Almost one fifth were in the food sector, born out of simple cafés catering for millworkers whose families were far away. As Indian food became more popular, these restaurants thrived, and today there are over 200 serving the highly spiced dishes of the Indian subcontinent.

Curry in a Bradford restaurant

Haworth Parsonage, home to the Brontë family, now a museum

🟠 Haworth

Bradford. 🔢 5,000. 🚇 Keighley. ℹ️
2–4 West Lane (01535 642329).
🟦 haworth-village.org.uk

The setting of Haworth, in bleak Pennine moorland dotted with farmsteads, has changed little since it was home to the Brontë family. The village boomed in the 1840s, when there were more than 1,200 hand-looms in operation, but it is more famous today for the Brontë connection.

You can visit the **Brontë Parsonage Museum**, home from 1820–61 to novelists Charlotte, Emily and Anne, their brother Branwell and their father, the Revd Patrick Brontë. Built in 1778–9, the house remains decorated as it was during the 1850s. Eleven rooms, including the children's study and Charlotte's room, display letters, manuscripts, furniture and personal objects.

The nostalgic Victorian **Keighley and Worth Valley Railway** runs through Haworth. It stops at Oakworth station, where parts of *The Railway Children* were filmed. At the end of the line is the Railway Museum at Oxenhope.

🏛️ **Brontë Parsonage Museum**
Church St. **Tel** 01535 642323.
Open daily. **Closed** 24–27 Dec; Jan.
📷 🚫 ♿ limited.
🟦 bronte.org.uk

Charlotte Brontë's childhood story book, for her sister, Anne

The Brontë Sisters

Charlotte Brontë (1816–55)

During a harsh, motherless childhood, Charlotte, Emily and Anne retreated into fictional worlds of their own, writing poems and stories. As adults, they had to work as governesses, but still published a poetry collection in 1846. Only two copies were sold, but in the following year Charlotte's *Jane Eyre*, became a bestseller, arousing interest in Emily's *Wuthering Heights* and Anne's *Agnes Grey*. After her siblings' deaths in 1848–9, Charlotte published her last novel, *Villette*, in 1852. She married the Revd Nicholls, her father's curate, in 1854, but died shortly afterwards.

🟠 Hebden Bridge

Calderdale. 🔢 12,500. 🚇 ℹ️ Butlers Wharf (01422 843831). 🟤 Thu.
🟦 visitcalderdale.com

Hebden Bridge is a delightful South Pennines former mill town, surrounded by steep hills and former 19th-century mills. The houses seem to defy gravity as they cling to the valley sides. Due to the gradient, one house is made from two bottom floors, and the top two floors form another unit. To separate ownership of these "flying freeholds", an Act of Parliament was devised.

There is a superb view of Hebden Bridge from nearby **Heptonstall**, where the poet Sylvia Plath (1932–63) is buried. The village contains a Wesleyan chapel (1764).

🟠 Halifax

Calderdale. 🔢 88,000. 🚇 🚌 ℹ️
Piece Hall (01422 368725). 🟤 Thu–Sat. 🟦 yorkshire.com/places/halifax

Halifax's history has been influenced by textiles since the Middle Ages, but today's visual reminders date mainly from the 19th century, with stone-built terraced housing and several fine buildings. The wool trade helped to make the Pennines into Britain's industrial backbone.

Until the mid-15th century cloth production was modest, but vital enough to contribute towards the creation of the 13th-century Gibbet Law, which stated that anyone caught stealing cloth could be executed. There is a replica of the gibbet, a forerunner of the guillotine, used for decapitation at the bottom of Gibbet Street. Many of Halifax's 18th- and 19th-century buildings owe their existence to wealthy cloth traders. Sir Charles Barry (1795–1860), architect of the Houses of Parliament, was commissioned by the Crossley family to design the Town Hall. They also paid for the landscaping of the People's Park by the creator of the Crystal Palace, Sir Joseph Paxton

Large Two Forms (1966–9) by Henry Moore at Yorkshire Sculpture Park

(1801–65). Thomas Bradley's 18th-century **Piece Hall** was where wool merchants once sold their cloth, trading in one of the 315 "Merchants' Rooms". It has a beautifully restored Italianate courtyard where Halifax's market takes place.

Eureka! is the hands-on National Children's Museum with exhibits such as the Giant Mouth Machine. **Shibden Hall Museum** is a fine period house, parts of which date to the 15th century.

Environs

The nearby village of **Sowerby Bridge** was an important textile centre from the Middle Ages to the 1960s. Today visitors come to enjoy the scenic canals.

🏛 **Eureka!**
Discovery Rd. **Tel** 01422 330069. **Open** Tue–Sun (daily in school hols). **Closed** 24–26 Dec. 🅿 ♿ ▯
w eureka.org.uk

🏛 **Shibden Hall Museum**
Listers Rd. **Tel** 01422 352246. **Open** daily (Sun: pm). **Closed** 24 Dec–2 Jan. 📷 🅿 ▯

❸ National Coal Mining Museum

Wakefield. **Tel** 01924 848806. 🚆 Wakefield then bus. **Open** daily (last tour 3:15pm – booking advised). Children under 5 not allowed underground. **Closed** 24–26 Dec, 1 Jan. ♿ 🅿 ▯ 📷 w ncm.org.uk

Housed in the old Caphouse Colliery, this museum offers the chance to go into a real mine shaft: warm clothing is advised.

An underground tour takes you 137 m (450 ft) down, equipped with a hat and a miner's lamp. Enter narrow seams and see exhibits such as life-size working models. Other displays depict mining from 1820 to the present day.

❹ Yorkshire Sculpture Park

Wakefield. **Tel** 01924 832631. 🚆 Wakefield then bus. **Open** daily. **Closed** 24, 25, 29–31 Dec. ♿ ▯ 📷 w ysp.co.uk

This is one of Europe's leading open-air galleries, situated in 200 ha (500 acres) of 18th-century parkland dotted with changing exhibitions of the work of Henry Moore, Anthony Caro, Eduardo Chillida, Barbara Hepworth, Antony Gormley and others. The indoor display spaces include the ambitious visitor centre, which leads on to the stunning Underground Gallery exhibition space.

❹ Magna

Rotherham. **Tel** 01709 720002. 🚆 Rotherham Central or Sheffield then bus (No. 69). **Open** daily. **Closed** 1 Jan, 24–26 & 31 Dec. 🅿 ♿ ▯ 📷 w visitmagna.co.uk

A former steel works has been imaginatively converted into a huge science adventure centre, with an emphasis on interactive exhibits, noise and spectacle designed to appeal to 4–15-year-olds. In the Air, Fire, Water and Earth Pavilions visitors can get close to a tornado, operate real diggers or discover what it's like to detonate a rock face. There are also multi-media displays on the lives of steelworkers and on how a giant furnace operated, as well as a show that features robots with artificial intelligence that evolve and learn as they hunt each other down.

The Face of Steel display at Magna

NORTHUMBRIA

Northumberland · County Durham

England's northeast extremity is a tapestry of moorland, ruins, castles, cathedrals and huddled villages. With Northumberland National Park and Kielder Water reservoir to the north, a rugged eastern coastline, and the cities of Newcastle and Durham to the south, the area combines a dramatic history with abundant natural beauty.

The empty peaceful hills, rich wildlife and panoramic vistas of Northumberland National Park belie the area's turbulent past. Warring Scots and English, skirmishing tribes, cattle drovers and whisky smugglers have all left traces on ancient routes through the Cheviot Hills. Slicing through the southern edge of the National Park is the famous reminder of the Romans' 400-year occupation of Britain, Hadrian's Wall, the northern boundary of their empire.

Conflict between Scots and English continued for 1,000 years after the Romans departed, and even after the 1603 union between the two crowns, which left the border much further north. A chain of massive crenellated medieval castles punctuates the coastline, while other forts that once defended the northern flank of England along the River Tweed lie mostly in ruins. Seventh-century Northumbria was the cradle of Christianity under St Aidan, but this was sharply countered by Viking violence from 793 onward, as the Scandinavian invaders raided the monasteries. But a reverence for Northumbrian saints is in the local psyche, and St Cuthbert and the Venerable Bede are both buried in Durham Cathedral. The influence of the Industrial Revolution, concentrated around the mouths of the rivers Tyne, Wear and Tees, made Newcastle upon Tyne the north's main centre for coal mining and ship-building. Today, the city is famous for its "industrial heritage" attractions and urban regeneration schemes.

Section of Hadrian's Wall, built by the Romans in about 120, looking east from Cawfields

◀ Antony Gormley's sculpture *Angel of the North*, Gateshead

Exploring Northumbria

Historic sites are plentiful along Northumbria's coast. South of Berwick-upon-Tweed, a causeway leads to the ruined priory and castle on Lindisfarne, and there are major castles at Bamburgh, Alnwick and Warkworth. The hinterland is a region of wide open spaces, with wilderness in the Northumberland National Park, and fascinating Roman remains of Hadrian's Wall at Housesteads and elsewhere. The glorious city of Durham is dominated by its castle and cathedral, and Newcastle upon Tyne has a lively nightlife.

Sights at a Glance

1. Berwick-upon-Tweed
2. Lindisfarne
3. Farne Islands
4. Bamburgh
5. Alnwick Castle
6. Warkworth Castle
7. Kielder Water
8. Cheviot Hills
9. Hexham
10. Corbridge
11. *Hadrian's Wall pp426–7*
12. Newcastle upon Tyne
13. Beamish Open Air Museum
14. *Durham pp432–3*
16. Middleton-in-Teesdale
17. Barnard Castle

Walks and Tour

15. North Pennines Tour

The wilderness of Upper Coquetdale in the sparsely populated Cheviot Hills

For additional map symbols *see back flap*

DISFARNE
🏛🏠 ❷
ARNE ISLANDS ❸
lford ❹BAMBURGH
🏠🏛 Seahouses
B1340
A1
ooperton Embleton
ngham
Aln
WICK CASTLE ❺🏛🏛 Alnmouth
Shilbottle
WARKWORTH ❻
thbury CASTLE 🏠 Amble
tramlington Broomhill
Felton
nghorsley Widdrington
A1
A697 A1068
Ashington
Morpeth
B6343
Whalton Bedlington Blyth
Belsay A189
Cramlington
Ponteland A1
A19 Whitley Bay
Pont ✈
Newburn Gosforth Tynemouth
9 ❶❷NEWCASTLE UPON TYNE South Shields
ne 🏛🏛🏛❶
Prudhoe Gateshead Boldon
A692
Washington
BEAMISH OPEN Sunderland
AIR MUSEUM ❶❸🏛 A1(M)
Stanley Chester-le-Street
Consett Houghton-le-Spring
Lanchester A691 A690 Hetton-le-Hole
❶❹ DURHAM
w Law Brandon 🏠🏠🏛 Peterlee
ingham Willington Wheatley Hill
Coxhoe A19
Spennymoor Hartlepool
Ferryhill
Bishop Auckland Sedgefield Seaton Carew
Shildon A689
Newton Aycliffe Redcar
A688 Billingham Saltburn-by-the-Sea
🏠🏛 Staindrop A68 Loftus
BARNARD Stockton-on-Tees Middlesbrough
CASTLE A1(M) A66 A171 Whitby
Tees Darlington
York ↓ ↓Northallerton

The rugged coastline of Northumberland, with Bamburgh Castle in the distance

Getting Around

North of Newcastle, the A1068 meets the A1 linking the sights of the Northumbrian coast, and continuing on to Scotland. Two spectacular inland routes, the A696 and the A68, merge near Otterburn to skirt the Northumberland National Park. A mainline railway links Durham, Newcastle and Berwick, but a car is necessary to explore Northumbria comprehensively.

Key

▬ Motorway
▬ Major road
— Secondary road
⋯ Minor road
▬ Scenic route
╍ Main railway
— Minor railway
△ Summit

Quayside, Newcastle upon Tyne

View over Berwick-upon-Tweed's three bridges

● Berwick-upon-Tweed

Northumberland. ⚑ 13,000. ⚞ 🛈 106 Mary Gate (01289 301780). ⊖ Wed, Sat. ⊡ **visitnorthumberland.com**

Between the 12th and 15th centuries Berwick-upon-Tweed changed hands 14 times in the wars between the Scots and English. Its position, at the mouth of the river which divides the two nations, made the town strategically vital.

The English finally gained permanent control in 1482 and maintained Berwick as a fortified garrison. Ramparts dating from 1555, 1.5 miles (2.5 km) long and 23 ft (7 m) thick, offer superb views over the Tweed. Within the 18th-century barracks are the **King's Own Scottish Borderers Regimental Museum**, an **art gallery**, and **By Beat of Drum**, charting the history of British infantrymen.

🏛 King's Own Scottish Borderers Regimental Museum
The Barracks. **Tel** 01289 307426. **Open** Easter–Sep: Mon–Fri. **Closed** public hols. 🅿 📷 ⊡ **kosb.co.uk/museum**

❷ Lindisfarne

Northumberland. ⚞ Berwick-upon-Tweed then bus. 🛈 106 Mary Gate, Berwick-upon-Tweed (01289 389004). ⊡ **lindisfarne.org.uk**

Twice daily a long, narrow neck of land sinks under the North Sea tide for five hours, separating Lindisfarne, or Holy Island, from the coast. At low tide, visitors stream over the causeway to the island made famous by St Aidan, St Cuthbert and the Lindisfarne gospels. Nothing remains of the Celtic monks' monastery, finally abandoned in 875 after successive Viking attacks, but the magnificent arches of the 11th-century **Lindisfarne Priory** are still visible.

After 1540, stones from the priory were used to build **Lindisfarne Castle**, which was restored and made into a private home by Sir Edwin Lutyens (see p33) in 1903. It includes a walled garden by Gertrude Jekyll (see p31).

🏰 Lindisfarne Castle
Holy Island. **Tel** 01289 389244. Castle: **Open** Mar–Oct & Feb half-term: Tue–Sun. Gardens: **Open** Tue–Sun all year. Opening times depend on tide – phone to check. 🅿 NT

❸ Farne Islands

Northumberland. ⚞ from Sea-houses (Apr–Oct). 🛈 106 Mary Gate, Berwick-upon-Tweed (01289 301780); Seahouses (01655 301777). NT

There are between 15 and 28 Farne Islands off the coast from Bamburgh, some of them periodically covered by sea. Nature wardens and lighthouse keepers share them with seals, puffins and other seabirds. Boat tours depart from **Seahouses** harbour and can land on Staple and Inner Farne, site of St Cuthbert's 14th-century chapel, or Longstone, where Grace Darling's lighthouse is located.

Lindisfarne Castle (1540), the main landmark on the island of Lindisfarne

Celtic Christianity

The Irish monk St Aidan arrived in Northumbria in 635 from the island of Iona, off western Scotland, to evangelize the north of England. He founded the monastery on the island of Lindisfarne, and it became one of the most important centres for Christianity in England. This and other monastic communities thrived in Northumbria, becoming rich in scholarship, although the monks lived simply. It also emerged as a place of pilgrimage after miracles were reported at the shrine of St Cuthbert, Lindisfarne's most famous bishop. But the monks' pacifism made them defenceless against 9th-century Viking raids.

St Aidan's Monastery was added to over the centuries to become Lindisfarne Priory. This 8th-century relic with interlaced animal decorations is from a cross at the site.

The Venerable Bede (673–735), the most brilliant early medieval scholar, was a monk at the monastery of St Paul in Jarrow. He wrote *The Ecclesiastical History of the English People* in 731.

St Aidan (600–651), an Irish missionary, founded a monastery at Lindisfarne and became Bishop of Northumbria in 635. This 1960 sculpture of him, by Kathleen Parbury, is in Lindisfarne Priory grounds.

St Cuthbert (635–87) was the monk and miracle worker most revered of all. He lived as a hermit on Inner Farne (a chapel was built there in his memory) and later became Bishop of Lindisfarne.

Lindisfarne Priory was built by Benedictines in the 11th century, on the site of St Aidan's earlier monastery.

The Lindisfarne Gospels

Held in the British Library, this book of richly illustrated portrayals of Gospel stories is one of the masterpieces of the "Northumbrian Renaissance" which left a permanent mark on Christian art and history-writing. The work was carried out by monks at Lindisfarne under the direction of Bishop Eadfrith, around 700. Monks managed to save the book and took it with them when they fled from Lindisfarne in 875 after suffering Viking raids. Other treasures were plundered.

Elaborately decorated initial to the *Gospel of St Matthew* (c.725)

Illustration of Grace Darling from the 1881 edition of *Sunday at Home*

❹ Bamburgh

Northumberland. 🏔 1,100. 🚄
Berwick. 🛈 Seahouses (01665
301777; Apr–Oct); 106 Mary Gate,
Berwick-upon-Tweed (01289 301780).

Due to Northumbria's history
of hostility against the Scots,
there are more strongholds
and castles here than in any
other part of England. Most
were built from the 11th to
the 15th centuries by local
warlords, as was Bamburgh's
red sandstone **castle**. Its
coastal position had been
fortified since prehistoric times,
but the first major stronghold
was built in 550 by a Saxon
chieftain, Ida the Flamebearer.

In its heyday between 1095
and 1464, Bamburgh was
the royal castle that
was used by the
Northumbrian kings for
coronations. By the end
of the Middle Ages it had
fallen into obscurity, then in
1894 it was bought by
Newcastle arms tycoon Lord
Armstrong, who restored it.
Works of art are exhibited in
the cavernous Great Hall,
and there are suits of armour
and medieval artifacts in
the basement.

Bamburgh's other
main attraction is the
tiny **Grace Darling
Museum** which
celebrates the bravery
of the 23-year-old, who, in 1838,
rowed through tempestuous
seas with her father, the keeper
of the Longstone lighthouse, to
rescue nine people from the
wrecked *Forfarshire* steamboat.

🏠 **Bamburgh Castle**
Bamburgh. **Tel** 01668 214515. **Open**
mid-Feb–Oct: daily; Nov–mid-Feb: Sat
& Sun. 🗐 🛗 🛒 🗐
🌐 **bamburghcastle.com**

🏛 **Grace Darling Museum**
Radcliffe Rd. **Tel** 01668 214910. **Open**
daily (closed Mon in winter). ♿

❺ Alnwick Castle

Alnwick, Northumberland. **Tel** 01665
510777. 🚄 🚌 Alnmouth. **Open**
April–Oct: daily. 🗐 ♿ limited. 🖥
🗐 🌐 **alnwickcastle.com**

Dominating the pretty market
town of Alnwick on the River
Aln, this castle doubled as
Hogwarts in the first two Harry
Potter movies. It is the main
seat of the Duke of Northumberland, whose family, the
Percys, have lived here since
1309. This border
stronghold has
survived many battles,
but now sits peacefully
amongst landscape
designed by "Capability"
Brown. The stern
medieval exterior belies
the treasure house
within, furnished in
palatial Renaissance
style with a collection of
Meissen china and
paintings by Titian, Van
Dyck and Canaletto.
The Postern Tower
contains early British
and Roman relics.

Carrara marble fireplace
(1840) at Alnwick Castle

The **Regimental Museum of
Royal Northumberland
Fusiliers** is in the Abbot's
Tower. Other attractions
are the Percy State coach
and the dungeon.

❻ Warkworth Castle

Warkworth, nr Amble. **Tel** 01665
711423. 🚄 🚌 518 from Newcastle.
Open Apr–Oct: daily; Nov–mid-Feb:
Sat & Sun. **Closed** 1 Jan, 24–26 Dec.
🗐 🗐 EH ♿ limited.

Warkworth Castle sits on a
green hill overlooking the River
Coquet. It was one of the Percy
family homes. Shakespeare's
Henry IV features the castle in
the scenes between the Earl of
Northumberland and his son,
Harry Hotspur. Much of the
present-day castle remains date
from the 14th century. The
unusual turreted, cross-shaped
keep is a central feature of the
castle tour.

Warkworth Castle reflected in
the River Coquet

❼ Kielder Water

Northumberland. 🛈 Bellingham
Tourist Information Centre (01434
220616). **Open** daily. ♿
🌐 **visitkielder.com**

One of the top attractions
of Northumberland, Kielder
Water lies close to the
Scottish border, surrounded
by spectacular scenery.
With a perimeter of
27 miles (44 km), it is Britain's
largest man-made lake, and
offers facilities for sailing,
windsurfing, canoeing,
water-skiing and fishing.
In summer, the cruiser
Osprey departs from Leaplish
on trips around the lake. The
Kielder Water Exhibition, at the
Visitor Centre, depicts the
history of the valley from the
Ice Age to the present day.

❾ Cheviot Hills

These bare, beautiful moors, smoothed into rounded humps by Ice Age glaciers, form a natural border with Scotland. Walkers and outdoor enthusiasts find a near-wilderness unmatched anywhere else in England. This remotest extremity of the Northumberland National Park nevertheless has a long and vivid history. Roman legions, warring Scots and English border raiders, cattle drovers and whisky smugglers have all left traces along the ancient routes and tracks they carved out here.

VISITORS' CHECKLIST

Practical Information
Northumberland. 🛈 Wooler.
Tel 01668 282123.
🌐 northumberlandnational park.org.uk

Transport
🚆 Berwick-upon-Tweed.

The Cheviots' isolated burns and streams are a stronghold in England for the shy, elusive otter.

Chew Green Camp, which to the Romans was *ad fines*, or, "towards the last place", has fine views from the remaining fortified earthworks.

Uswayford Farm track

Byrness

Uswayford Farm, is perhaps the most remote farm in England, and one of the hardest to reach. It is set in deserted moorland.

Labels on map:
Berwick-upon-Tweed
B6351
A697
Kirk Yetholm
College Burn
Wooler
Harthope Burn
A697
Kidland Forest
Breamish
Cheviot Hills
Usway Burn
Clennell Street track
Uswayford
Alwin
Alwinton
Harbottle
Holystone
A68
Rede
B6341
Grasslees Burn
Otterburn
Elsdon
A696
Newcastle-upon-Tyne

0 kilometres 5
0 miles 5

The Pennine Way, starts in Derbyshire and ends at Kirk Yetholm in Scotland. The final stage (shown here) goes past Byrness, crosses the Cheviots and traces the Scottish border.

Alwinton, a tiny village built mainly from grey stone, is situated beside the River Coquet. It is an access point for many fine walks in the area, and the wild landscape is deserted except for sheep.

Key

▬▬▬ A roads
▬▬▬ B roads
═══ Minor roads
- - - Pennine Way

For additional map symbols *see back flap*

9 Hexham

Northumberland. 🗺 11,500. 🚉 🚌
ℹ Wentworth Car Park (01434
652220). 🕐 Tue.
🌐 **visitnorthumberland.com**

The busy market town of
Hexham was established in
the 7th century, growing up
around the church and
monastery built by St Wilfrid,
but the Vikings sacked and
looted it in 876. In 1114,
Augustinians began work
on a priory and abbey on the
original church ruins to create

Hexham Abbey, which still
towers over the market square.
The Saxon crypt, built partly
with stones from the former
Roman fort at Corbridge, is all

Ancient stone carvings at Hexham Abbey

that remains of St Wilfrid's
Church. The south transept
has a 12th-century night
stair: stone steps leading from
the dormitory. In the chancel
is the Frith Stool, a Saxon
throne in the centre of a
circle which protected
fugitives.
   Medieval streets, many with
Georgian and Victorian
shopfronts, spread out from
the market square, The
15th-century Moot Hall was
once a council chamber and
the old gaol (jail) contains a
museum of border history.

⑪ Hadrian's Wall

On the orders of Emperor Hadrian, a 73-mile (117-km) wall was erected
across northern England to mark and defend the northern limits of the
British province and the northwest border of the Roman Empire. The work
took two years and was completed in AD 122. Troops were stationed at
milecastles along the wall, and large turrets, later forts, were built at 5-mile
(8-km) intervals. The wall was abandoned in 383 as the Empire crumbled,
but much of it remains. In 1987 it was declared a World Heritage Site.

Location of Hadrian's Wall

KEY

① **Carvoran Fort** is probably pre-
Hadrianic. Little of the fort survives,
but the Roman Army museum
nearby covers the wall's history.

② **Great Chesters Fort** was built
facing east to guard Caw Gap, but
there are few remains today. To the
south and east of the fort are traces
of a civil settlement and a bathhouse.

③ **Vindolanda** is the site of
several forts. The first timber fort
dated from AD 90 and a stone fort
was not built until the 2nd century.
The museum has a collection of
Roman writing tablets providing
details of food, clothes and work.

④ **Housesteads Settlement**
includes the remains of terraced
shops or taverns.

⑤ **Carrawburgh Fort**, a 500-man
garrison, guarded the Newbrough
Burn and North Tynedale
approaches.

⑥ **Limestone Corner Milecastle**
is sited at the northernmost part of
the wall and has magnificent views
of the Cheviot Hills (see p425).

⑦ **Chesters Fort** was a
bridgehead over the North Tyne. In
the museum are altars, sculptures
and inscriptions.

⑧ **Chesters Bridge** crossed the
Tyne. The original Hadrianic bridge
was rebuilt in 207. The remains of
this second bridge abutment can
still be seen.

Cawfields, 2 miles (3 km) north
of Haltwhistle, is the access
point to one of the highest and
most rugged sections of the
wall. To the east, the wall and a
series of milecastles sit on
volcanic crags.

Hexham Abbey
Market Place. **Tel** 01434 602031.
Open 9:30am–5pm daily.

Border History Museum
Old Gaol, nr Hallgate. **Tel** 01434
652349. **Open** Feb–Oct: daily;
Nov: Mon, Tue, Sat.

⑩ Corbridge

Northumberland. 🚶 3,500. 🚆 ℹ️
Hill St (01434 632815).

This quiet town conceals a few
historic buildings constructed
with stones from the Roman
garrison town of nearby
Corstopitum. Among these are

the thickset Saxon tower of
St Andrew's Church and the
14th-century fortified tower
house built to protect the
local clergyman. Excavations
of Corstopitum, now known
as **Corbridge Roman
Town–Hadrian's Wall**, have
exposed earlier forts, a well-
preserved granary, temples,
fountains and an aqueduct.

**Corbridge Roman Town–
Hadrian's Wall**

Tel 01434 632349. **Open** Apr–Oct: daily;
Nov–Mar: Sat & Sun. **Closed** 1 Jan,
24–26 Dec. limited.

The parson's 14th-century fortified tower
house at Corbridge

Housesteads Fort is the best-
preserved site on the wall, with
fine views over the countryside.
The excavated remains include
the commanding officer's house
and a Roman hospital.

0 metres	500
0 yards	500

⑤ ⑥ ⑦ ⑧

**Sewingshields
Milecastle,** with
magnificent views
west to Housesteads,
is one of the best
places for walking. This
reconstruction shows
the layout of a Roman
milecastle on the wall.

Emperor Hadrian (76–138) came to Britain
in 120 to order a stronger defence system.
Coins were often cast to record emperors'
visits, such as this bronze *sestertius*. Until
1971, the penny was abbreviated to *d,* short
for *denarius,* a Roman coin.

The Wall Coast-to-Coast

see above

B6318 · A689 · A69 · A689 · A686 · A69 · A68 · A1 · **Newcastle** · A19 · A1(M)
B5307 · **Carlisle** · B6413 · A595 · M6

Key

〜〜〜 Route of the wall

The wall runs eastward from Bowness on the Solway Firth
to the mouth of the Tyne at Wallsend. The B6318 and A69
provide access to major sites.

0 kilometres	20
0 miles	20

⑫ Newcastle upon Tyne

🏔 273,000. ✈ 🚄 🚌 🚢 ℹ️ Quayside (0191 277 8000). 🏺 Sun.
🌐 newcastlegateshead.com

Newcastle owes its name to its Norman **castle** which was founded in 1080 by Robert Curthose, the eldest son of William the Conqueror *(see p51)*. The Romans had bridged the Tyne and built a fort on the site 1,000 years earlier. During the Middle Ages it was used as a base for English campaigns against the Scots. From the Middle Ages, the city flourished as a coal mining and exporting centre. It was known in the 19th century for engineering, steel production and later as the world's foremost shipyard. The city's industrial base has declined, but "Geordies", as inhabitants of the city are known, have refocused their civic pride on the Metro Centre shopping mall in the nearby town of Gateshead, southwest of the city, and Newcastle United soccer team.

The city's lively night scene includes clubs, pubs and ethnic restaurants. The visible trappings of its past are reflected in the magnificent **Tyne Bridge** and in **Earl Grey's Monument**,

Bridges crossing the Tyne at Newcastle

as well as the grand façades in the city centre thoroughfares, such as Grey Street.

Notable dramatic features in Gateshead include **Baltic Centre for Contemporary Art**, Sage Gateshead, the international centre for music, and the tilting Gateshead Millennium Bridge.

🏰 The Castle Keep
St Nicholas St. **Tel** 0191 232 7938. **Open** daily. **Closed** 1 Jan, Good Fri, 24–26 Dec. 🎫 🔲
🌐 castlekeep-newcastle.org.uk

Curthose's original wooden "new castle" was rebuilt in stone in the 12th century. Only the thickset, crenellated keep remains intact with two suites of royal apartments. A series of staircases spiral up to the renovated battlements, from which there are fine views over the city and the Tyne.

---

⑬ Beamish, The North of England Open Air Museum

This giant open air museum, spread over 120 ha (300 acres) of County Durham, re-creates an authentic picture of family, working and community life in the northeast in the 19th and early 20th centuries. It includes an Edwardian town and pit village, a working Victorian farm and a Georgian steam railway. A tramway serves the different parts of the museum, which carefully avoids romanticizing the past.

The station, which dates back to 1913, has a platform, a signal box, a wrought-iron footbridge and a goods yard.

🚻 🔲

Home Farm recreates the atmosphere of an old-fashioned farm. Rare breeds of cattle and sheep, more common before the advent of mass breeding, can be seen.

School

Miners' houses were tiny, oil-lit dwellings, backing onto vegetable gardens and owned by the colliery.

Chapel

St Nicholas Cathedral

St Nicholas Sq. **Tel** 0191 232 1939.
Open daily.

This is one of Britain's tiniest cathedrals. There are remnants inside of the original 11th-century Norman church on which the present 14th- and 15th-century structure was founded. Its most striking feature is its ornate "lantern tower" – half tower, half spire – of which there are only three others in Britain.

Bessie Surtees' House

41–44 Sandhill. **Tel** 0191 2691200.
Open Mon–Fri. **Closed** 24 Dec–7 Jan, public hols. limited.

The story of beautiful, wealthy Bessie, who lived here before eloping with penniless John Scott, later Lord Chancellor of England, is the romantic tale behind these half-timbered 16th- and 17th-century houses.

Reredos of the Northumbrian saints in St Nicholas Cathedral

The window through which Bessie escaped now has a blue glass pane.

Tyne Bridge

Newcastle–Gateshead. **Open** daily.
Opened in 1928, this steel arch was the longest of its type in Britain with a span of 162 m (531 ft). Designed by Mott, Hay and Anderson, it soon became the city's most potent symbol.

Earl Grey's Monument

Grey St.

Benjamin Green created this memorial to the 2nd Earl Grey, Liberal Prime Minister from 1830 to 1834.

Baltic Centre for Contemporary Art

Gateshead. **Tel** 0191 478 1810.
Open daily.
balticmill.com

This former grain ware-house has been converted by architect Dominic Williams into a major international centre for contemporary art, one of the biggest in Europe, with amazing views of Tyneside from its rooftop restaurant.

The Town has a sweet factory, newspaper office, solicitor, dentist and music teacher. There is also a pub.

VISITORS' CHECKLIST

Practical Information
Beamish, Co. Durham.
Tel 0191 3704000.
beamish.org.uk
Open Apr–Oct: 10am–5pm daily (last adm: 3pm); Nov–Mar: Town and Colliery Village only 10am–4pm Tue–Thu, Sat & Sun.

Transport
Newcastle, then bus.

The Co-op stocked everything a family needed at the turn of the century. A full range of foods available in 1913 is displayed.

Pockerley Old Hall

The 1825 Railway

Steam Winding Engine

Mahogany Drift mine, a tunnel driven into coal seams near the surface, was here long before the museum and was worked from the 1850s to 1958. Visitors are given guided tours underground.

P Entrance

Houses built by the London Lead Company in Middleton-in-Teesdale

⓮ Durham

See pp432–3.

⓯ North Pennines Tour

See p431.

Cotherstone cheese, a speciality of the Middleton-in-Teesdale area

⓰ Middleton-in-Teesdale

Co. Durham. 🅰 1,100. 🚆 Darlington. 🅸 10 Market Place (01833 641001).

Clinging to a hillside amid wild Pennine scenery on the River Tees is this old lead mining town. Many of its rows of grey stone cottages were built by the London Lead Company, a paternalistic, Quaker-run organization who influenced every corner of its employees' daily lives.

The company began mining in 1753, and soon it virtually owned the town. Workers were expected to observe strict temperance, send their children to Sunday school and conform to the many company maxims. Today, mining has ceased in Teesdale, with Middleton standing as a monument to the 18th-century idea of the "company town". The offices of the London Lead Company can still be seen, as well as Nonconformist chapels from the era and a memorial fountain made of iron.

The crumbly Cotherstone cow's milk cheese, a speciality of the surrounding dales, is available in local shops.

⓱ Barnard Castle

County Durham. 🅰 5,000. 🚆 Darlington. 🅸 Woodleigh, Flatts Rd (03000 262626). 🛒 Wed. 🅦 thisisdurham.com

Barnard Castle, known in the area as "Barney", is a little town full of character, with old shopfronts and a cobbled market overlooked by the ruins of the Norman castle from which it takes its name. The original Barnard Castle was built around 1125–40 by Bernard Balliol, ancestor of the founder of Balliol College, Oxford *(see p226)*. Later, the market town grew up around the fortification.

Today, Barnard Castle is known for the extraordinary French-style château to the east of the town, surrounded by acres of formal gardens. Started in 1860 by the local aristocrat John Bowes and his French wife Josephine, an artist and actress, it was never a private residence, but always intended as a museum and public monument. The château finally opened in 1892, by which time the couple were both dead. Nevertheless, the **Bowes Museum** stands as a monument to his wealth and her extravagance.

The museum houses a strong collection of Spanish art which includes El Greco's *The Tears of St Peter,* dating from the 1580s, and Goya's *Don Juan Meléndez Váldez,* painted in 1797. Clocks, porcelain, furniture, musical instruments, toys and tapestries are among its treasures.

🏛 **Bowes Museum**
Barnard Castle. **Tel** 01833 690606. **Open** 10am–5pm daily. **Closed** 1 Jan, 25 & 26 Dec. 🅿 ♿ 📷 (summer). 🛒 📷 🅦 thebowesmuseum.org.uk

The Bowes Museum, a French-style château in Barnard Castle

⓯ North Pennines Tour

Starting just to the south of Hadrian's Wall, this tour explores the South Tyne Valley, and Upper Weardale. It crosses one of England's wildest and most remote tracts of moorland, then heads north again. The high ground is mainly blanketed with heather, dotted with sheep or criss-crossed with dry-stone walls, a feature of this region. Harriers and other birds hover above, and streams tumble into valleys of tightly huddled villages.

Celts, Romans and other settlers have left imprints on the North Pennines, now named an Area of Outstanding Natural Beauty. Lead mining and stone quarrying have long co-existed with farming.

Sheep grazing on the moors

① Haltwhistle
In the Church of the Holy Cross is the tombstone of John Ridley, brother of Protestant martyr, Nicholas Ridley, burnt at the stake in 1555 *(see p226)*.

② Bardon Mill
To the north is the Roman fort and civilian settlement of Vindolanda *(see p426)*.

③ Haydon Bridge
There are some delightful walks near this spa town where the painter John Martin was born in 1789. Nearby Langley Castle is worth a visit.

④ Hexham
A pretty old town *(see p426)*, Hexham has a fine abbey.

⑧ Allendale
With its capital at Allendale Town, this is an area of spectacular scenery, with many walking and trout fishing opportunities.

⑦ Killhope Lead Mine
This fully restored 19th-century lead mine boasts an enormous waterwheel.

⑤ Blanchland
Some houses in this lead-mining village are built on the site of a 12th-century abbey, using the original stone.

Tips for Drivers

Tour length: 50 miles (80 km)
Stopping-off points: Several pubs in Stanhope serve bar meals, and the Durham Dales Centre provides teas all year round. Horsley Hall Hotel at Eastgate serves meals all day. (See also pp636–7.)

0 kilometres 5
0 miles 5

⑥ Stanhope
An 18th-century castle overlooks the market square. The giant stump of a fossilized tree, said to be 250 million years old, guards the graveyard.

Key

⎯ Tour route
= Other roads

⑭ Durham

The city of Durham was built on Island Hill or "Dunholm" in 995. This rocky peninsula, which defies the course of the River Wear's route to the sea, was chosen as the last resting place for the remains of St Cuthbert. The relics of the Venerable Bede were brought to the site 27 years later, adding to its attraction for pilgrims. Durham Cathedral was treated by architects as an experiment for geometric patterning, while the Castle served as the Episcopal Palace until 1832, when Bishop William van Mildert gave it up and surrendered part of his income to found Britain's third university. The 23 ha (57 acre) peninsula has many footpaths, views and fine buildings.

★ **Cathedral**
Built from 1093 to 1274, this is a striking Norman structure.

KEY

① **Prebend's footbridge** was built in 1777. A sculpture by Colin Wilbourn is situated at the "island" end.

② **Old Fulling Mill** is a largely 18th-century building, housing a museum of archaeology.

③ **Town Hall** (1851)

④ **St Nicholas' Church** (1857)

⑤ **University buildings** were built by Bishop John Cosin in the 17th century.

⑥ **Palace Green**

⑦ **Church of St Mary le Bow**

⑧ **Kingsgate Footbridge** was built 1962–3 and leads to North Bailey.

⑨ **St Cuthbert's Tomb**

⑩ **South Bailey**

⑪ **College gatehouse**

⑫ **Church of St Mary the Less**

⑬ **College Green**

⑭ **Monastic kitchen**

"Our Daily Bread" Window
This modern stained-glass window in the north nave aisle was donated in 1984 by a local department store.

Galilee Chapel
Architects began work on the exotic Galilee Chapel in 1170, drawing inspiration from the Great Mosque of Cordoba in Andalusia. It was altered by Bishop Langley (d.1437) whose tomb is by the west door.

★ Castle
Begun in 1072, the castle is a fine Norman fortress. The keep, sited on a mound, is now part of the university.

Tunstal's Chapel
Situated at the end of the Tunstal's Gallery, the castle chapel was built c.1542. Its fine woodwork includes this unicorn misericord *(see p345)*.

Castle Gatehouse
Traces of Norman stonework can be seen in the outer arch, while the sturdy walls and upper floors are 18th century, rebuilt in a style dubbed "gothick" by detractors.

Cathedral Architecture

The vast dimensions of the 900-year-old columns, piers and vaults, and the inventive giant lozenge and chevron, trellis and dogtooth patterns carved into the stone columns, are the main innovative features of Durham Cathedral. It is believed that 11th- and 12th-century architects such as Bishop Ranulph Flambard tried to unify all parts of the structure. This can be seen in the south aisle of the nave below.

Ribbed vaults, criss-crossing above the nave, are now common in church ceilings. One of the major achievements of Gothic architecture, they were first built at Durham.

The lozenge shape is a pattern from prehistoric carving, but never before seen in a cathedral.

Chevron patterns on some of the piers in the nave are evidence of Moorish influence.

WALES

Wales at a Glance

Wales is a country of outstanding natural beauty with varied landscapes. Visitors come to climb dramatic mountain peaks, go walking in the forests, fish in the broad rivers and enjoy the miles of unspoilt coastline. The country's many seaside resorts have long been popular with English holidaymakers. As well as outdoor pursuits there is the vibrancy of Welsh culture, with its strong Celtic roots, to be experienced. Finally there are many fine castles, ruined abbeys, mansions and cities full of magnificent architecture.

Beaumaris Castle was intended to be a key part of Edward I's "iron ring" to contain the rebellious Welsh *(see p440)*. Begun in 1295 but never completed, the castle *(see p442)* has a sophisticated defence structure that is unparalleled in Wales.

Llanberis and Snowdon *(see p455)* is an area famous for dramatic, high peaks, long popular with climbers. Snowdon's summit is most easily reached from Llanberis. Its Welsh name, *Yr Wyddfa*, means "great tomb" and it is the legendary burial place of a giant slain by King Arthur *(see p289)*.

Portmeirion *(see pp458–9)* is a private village whose astonishing buildings seem rather incongruous in the Welsh landscape. The village was created by the architect Sir Clough Williams-Ellis to fulfill a personal ambition. Some of the buildings are assembled from pieces of architecture taken from sites around the country.

St David's is the smallest city in Britain. The cathedral *(see pp468–9)* is the largest in Wales, and its nave is noted for its carved oak roof and beautiful rood screen. Next to the cathedral is the medieval Bishop's Palace, now a ruin.

Holyhead

Bangor

Caernarfon

GWYNED

Porthmadog

Aberystwyth

Aberaeron

CEREDIGION

Fishguard

St. David's

*PEMBROKE-
SHIRE*

*CARMARTHE
SHIRE*

Carmarthen

Pembroke   Tenby

Swanse

◄ Sunrise over Cribyn, as seen from Pen y Fan, in the Brecon Beacons National Park

Conwy Castle guards one of the best-preserved medieval fortified towns in Britain *(see pp450–51)*. Built by Edward I, the castle was besieged and came close to surrender in 1294. It was taken by Owain Glyndŵr's supporters in 1401.

Locator Map

0 kilometres 25

0 miles 25

Conwy

Queensferry

NWY

FLINTSHIRE

Betws-y-Coed

Ruthin

DENBIGH-SHIRE

Wrexham

NORTH WALES

(See pp444–59)

Llangollen

ellau

Welshpool

chynlleth

POWYS

Llandrindod Wells

SOUTH AND MID-WALES

(See pp460–79)

Hay on Wye

landovery

Brecon

Monmouth

Merthyr Tydfil

MONMOUTH-SHIRE

GLAMORGAN

Newport

gend

Cardiff

Barry

The Brecon Beacons *(see pp472–3)* is a national park, a lovely area of mountains, forest and moorland in South Wales, which is a favourite with walkers and naturalists. Pen-y-Fan is one of the principal summits.

Cardiff Castle's *(see pp476–7)* Clock Tower is just one of many 19th-century additions by the eccentric but gifted architect William Burges. His flamboyant style still delights and amazes visitors.

A PORTRAIT OF WALES

Long popular with British holidaymakers, the many charms of Wales are now becoming better known internationally. They include spectacular scenery and a vibrant culture specializing in male-voice choirs, poetry and a passionate love of team sports. Governed from Westminster since 1536, Wales retains its own distinct Celtic identity, and in 1999 it finally gained partial devolution.

Much of the Welsh landmass is covered by the Cambrian Mountain range, which effectively acts as a barrier from England. Wales is warmed by the Gulf Stream and has a mild climate, with more rain than most of Britain. The land is unsuitable for arable farming, but sheep and cattle thrive; the drove roads, along which sheep used to be driven across the hills to England, are now popular walking trails. It is partly because of the rugged terrain that the Welsh have managed to maintain their separate identity and their ancient language.

Welsh is an expansive, musical language, spoken by only 19 per cent of the 3 million inhabitants, but in parts of North Wales it is still the main language of conversation. There is an official bilingual policy: road signs are in Welsh and English, even in areas where Welsh is little spoken. Welsh place names intrigue visitors, being made up of native words that describe features of the landscape or ancient buildings. Examples include *Aber* (river mouth), *Afon* (river), *Fach* (little), *Llan* (church), *Llyn* (lake) and *Nant* (valley).

Wales was conquered by the Romans, but not by the Saxons. The land and the people therefore retained Celtic patterns of settlement and husbandry for six centuries before the Norman Conquest in 1066. This allowed time for the development of a distinctive Welsh nation whose homogeneity continues to this day.

The early Norman kings subjugated the Welsh by appointing "Marcher Lords" to control areas bordering England. A string of massive castles provides evidence of the turbulent years when Welsh insurrection was a constant threat. It was not until 1535 that Wales formally became part of Britain, and it would take nearly 500 years before the people of Wales regained partial autonomy.

Religious non-conformism and radical politics are deeply rooted in Welsh consciousness. Saint David converted the country to Christianity in the 6th century. Methodism, chapel and tee-totalism became firmly entrenched in the Welsh psyche during the 19th century. Even today some pubs stay closed on Sundays. A long-standing oral tradition in Wales has produced many outstanding public speakers, politicians and actors. Welsh labour leaders have played important roles in the British trade union movement and the development of socialism.

Mountain sheep: a familiar sight in rural Wales

A *gorsedd* (assembly) of bards at the eisteddfod

figures and magic were part of the oral tradition of the Dark Ages. They were first written down in the 14th century as the *Mabinogion,* which has inspired Welsh poets up to the 20th century's Dylan Thomas. The male-voice choirs found in many towns, villages and factories, particularly in the industrial south, express the Welsh musical heritage. Choirs compete in eisteddfods: festivals that celebrate Welsh culture.

In the 19th century, the opening of the South Wales coalfield in Mid-Glamorgan – for a time the biggest in the world – led to an industrial boom, with mass migration from the countryside to the iron and steelworks. This prosperity was not to last: apart from a brief respite in World War II, the coal industry has been in terminal decline for decades, causing severe economic hardship. Today tourism is being promoted in the hope that the wealth generated, by outdoor activities in particular, will be able to take "King Coal's" place.

Welsh heritage is steeped in song, music, poetry and legend rather than handicrafts, although one notable exception is the carved Welsh lovespoon – a craft recently revived. The well-known Welsh love of music derives from the ancient bards: minstrels and poets, who may have been associated with the Druids. Bardic tales of quasi-historical

Welsh lovespoon

Conwy's picturesque, medieval walled town, fronted by a colourful harbour

The History of Wales

Wales has been settled since prehistoric times, its history shaped by many factors, from invasion to industrialization. The Romans set up bases in the mountainous terrain, but it was effectively a separate Celtic entity when Offa's Dyke was built as the border with England in 770. Centuries of cross-border raids and military campaigns followed before England and Wales were formally united by the Act of Union in 1535. The rugged northwest, the former stronghold of the Welsh princes, remains the heartland of Welsh language and culture.

Owain Glyndwr, heroic leader of Welsh opposition to English rule

Ornamental Iron Age bronze plaque from Anglesey

The Celtic Nation

Wales was settled by waves of migrants in prehistoric times. By the Iron Age (see pp46–7), Celtic farmers had established hillforts and their religion, Druidism. From the 1st century AD until the legions withdrew around 400, the Romans built fortresses and roads, and mined lead, silver and gold. During the next 200 years, Wales was converted to Christianity by missionaries from Europe. St David (see pp468–9), the Welsh patron saint, is said to have turned the leek into a national symbol. He persuaded soldiers to wear leeks in their hats to distinguish themselves from Saxons during a 6th-century skirmish.

The Saxons (see pp50–51) failed to conquer Wales, and in 770 the Saxon King Offa built a defensive earthwork along the unconquered territory (see p465). Beyond Offa's Dyke the people called themselves Y Cymry (fellow countrymen) and the land Cymru. The Saxons called the land "Wales" from the Old English wealas, meaning foreigners. It was divided into kingdoms of which the main ones were Gwynedd in the north, Powys in the centre and Dyfed in the south. There were strong trade, cultural and linguistic links between each.

Marcher Lords

The Norman invasion of 1066 (see p51) did not reach Wales, but the border territory ("the Marches") was given by William the Conqueror to three powerful barons based at Shrewsbury, Hereford and Chester. These Marcher Lords made many incursions into Wales and controlled most of the lowlands. But Welsh princes held the mountainous northwest and exploited English weaknesses. Under Llywelyn the Great (d.1240), North Wales was almost completely

Edward I designating his son Prince of Wales in 1301

independent; in 1267 his grandson, Llywelyn the Last, was acknowledged as Prince of Wales by Henry III.

In 1272 Edward I came to the English throne. He built fortresses and embarked on a military campaign to conquer Wales. In 1283 Llywelyn was killed in a skirmish, a shattering blow f or the Welsh. Edward introduced English law and proclaimed his son Prince of Wales (see p448).

Owain Glyndwr's Rebellion

Welsh resentment against the Marcher Lords continued to grow until it led to rebellion. In 1400 Owain Glyndŵr (c.1350–1416), a descendant of the Welsh princes, laid waste to English-dominated towns and castles. Declaring himself Prince of Wales, he managed to find Celtic allies in Scotland, Ireland, Northumbria and even France. In 1404 Glyndŵr captured Harlech and Cardiff, and formed his first Cynulliad, or parliament, in Machynlleth (see p466). In 1408, however, the French made a truce with the English king, Henry IV. The rebellion then failed and Glyndŵr went into hiding until his death.

Union with England

Wales suffered greatly during the Wars of the Roses *(see p53)* as Yorkists and Lancastrians tried to gain control of the strategically important Welsh castles. The wars ended in 1485, and the Welshman Henry Tudor, born in Pembroke, became Henry VII. The Act of Union in 1535 and other laws abolished the Marcher Lordships, giving Wales parliamentary representation in London instead. English practices replaced inheritance customs and English became the language of the courts and administration. The Welsh language survived, partly helped by the church and by Dr William Morgan's translation of the Bible in 1588.

Miners from South Wales pictured in 1910

Vernacular Bible, which helped to keep the Welsh language alive

Industry and Radical Politics

The industrialization of south and east Wales began with the development of open-cast coal mining near Wrexham and Merthyr Tydfil in the 1760s. Convenient ports and the arrival of the railways helped the process. By the second half of the 19th century open-cast mines had been superseded by deep pits in the Rhondda Valley.

Living and working conditions were poor for industrial and agricultural workers. A series of "Rebecca Riots" in South Wales between 1839 and 1843, involving tenant farmers (dressed as women) protesting about tithes and rents, was forcibly suppressed. The Chartists, trade unions and the Liberal Party had much Welsh support.

The rise of Methodism *(see p283)* roughly paralleled the growth of industry: 80 per cent of the population was Methodist by 1851. The Welsh language persisted, despite attempts by the British government to discourage its use, which included punishing children caught speaking it.

Wales Today

In the 20th century the Welsh became a power in British politics. David Lloyd George, although not born in Wales, grew up there and was the first British Prime Minister to come from a Welsh family. Aneurin Bevan, a miner's son who became a Labour Cabinet Minister, helped create the National Health Service *(see p63)*.

In 1926 the Welsh Nationalist Party Plaid Cymru was formed. In 1955 Cardiff was recognized as the capital of Wales *(see p474)* and four years later the red dragon became the emblem on Wales' new flag. Plaid Cymru won two parliamentary seats at Westminster in 1974, and in a 1998 referendum the Welsh espoused limited home rule. The National Assembly for Wales is housed in the stunning Y Senedd, on the waterfront in Cardiff Bay.

The 1967 Welsh Language Act made Welsh compulsory in schools; the TV channel S4C (Sianel 4 Cymru) now broadcasts many programmes in Welsh.

From the 1960s the steel and coal industries declined, creating mass unemployment. This has been partly alleviated by the emergence of high-tech industries, and by growth in tourism: Cardiff is home to many major tourist attractions including the Millennium Stadium and Cardiff Bay, Europe's largest waterfront development *(see pp474–5)*. Wales also has a strong sporting presence, especially in rugby. In 2010 the Ryder Cup golf tournament was held in Wales for the first time in its history.

Girl in traditional Welsh costume

Castles of Wales

Wales is rich in romantic medieval castles. Soon after the Battle of Hastings, in 1066 *(see p51)*, the Normans turned their attentions to Wales. They built earth and timber fortifications, later replaced by stone castles, initiating a building programme that was pursued by the Welsh princes and invading forces. Construction reached its peak during the reign of Edward I *(see p440)*. As the need for security lessened in the later Middle Ages, some castles became stately homes.

The north gatehouse was planned to be 18 m (60 ft) high, providing lavish royal accommodation, but its top storey was never built.

The inner ward was lined with a hall, granary, kitchens and stables.

The inner wall, with an inner passage, was higher than the curtain wall to permit simultaneous firing.

Rounded towers, with fewer blind spots than square ones, gave better protection.

Arrow slit

Beaumaris Castle

The last of Edward I's Welsh castles *(see p448)*, this perfectly symmetrical, concentric design was intended to combine impregnable defence with comfort. Invaders would face many obstacles before reaching the inner ward.

Moat

Curtain wall

Where to See Welsh Castles

In addition to Beaumaris, in North Wales there are medieval forts at Caernarfon *(see p448)*, Conwy *(see p450)* and Harlech *(see p458)*. Edward I also built Denbigh, Flint (near Chester) and Rhuddlan (near Rhyll). In South and mid-Wales, Caerphilly (near Cardiff), Kidwelly (near Carmarthen) and Pembroke were built between the 11th and 13th centuries. Spectacular sites are occupied by Cilgerran (near Cardigan), Criccieth (near Porthmadog) and Carreg Cennen *(see p472)*. Chirk Castle, near Llangollen, is a good example of a fortress that has since become a stately home.

Caerphilly, 6 miles (10 km) north of Cardiff, is a huge castle with concentric stone and water defences that cover 12 ha (30 acres).

Harlech Castle *(see p458)* is noted for its massive gatehouse, twin towers and the fortified stairway to the sea. It was the headquarters of the Welsh resistance leader Owain Glyndŵr *(see p440)* from 1404–8.

Castell-Y-Bere

This native Welsh castle at the foot of Cader Idris *(see p444)* was founded by Llywelyn the Great in 1221 *(see p426)*, to secure internal borders rather than to resist the English.

Entrance

The D-shaped, elongated tower is a typical feature of Welsh castles.

The castle's construction follows the shape of the rock. The curtain walls are too low and insubstantial to be of much practical use.

Drawbridge

The Chapel Tower has a beautiful medieval chapel.

Twin-towered gatehouse

The protected dock, on a channel that originally led to the sea, received supplies during sieges.

Edward I *(see p440)* was the warrior king whose castles played a key role in the subjugation of the Welsh people.

Edward I and Master James of St George

In 1278 Edward I brought over from Savoy a master stonemason who became a great military architect, James of St George. Responsible for planning and building at least 12 of Edward's fine Welsh castles, James was paid well and liberally pensioned off, indicating the esteem in which he was held by the king.

A plan of Caernarfon Castle illustrates how its position, on a promontory surrounded by water, has determined the building's shape and defence.

Caernarfon Castle *(see p448)*, birthplace of the ill-fated Edward II *(see p331)*, was intended to be the official royal residence in North Wales, and has palatial private apartments.

Castell Coch was restored in Neo-Gothic style by Lord Bute and William Burges *(see p476)*. Mock-castles were built by many Victorian industrialists.

Conwy Castle *(see p451)*, like many other castles, required forced labour on a massive scale for its construction.

NORTH WALES

Conwy · Isle of Anglesey · Gywnedd · Denbighshire · Flintshire · Wrexham

The North Wales landscape has a dramatic quality reflected in its history. In prehistoric times, Anglesey was a stronghold of the religious elite known as the Druids. Roman and Norman invasions concentrated on the coast, leaving the mountains to the Welsh. These wild areas are the centre of Welsh language and culture.

Defence and conquest have been constant themes in Welsh history. North Wales was the scene of ferocious battles between the Welsh princes and Anglo-Norman monarchs determined to establish English rule. The string of formidable castles which still stand in North Wales are as much a testament to Welsh resistance as to the wealth and strength of the invaders. Several massive fortresses, including Beaumaris, Caernarfon and Harlech, almost surround the rugged high country of Snowdonia, an area that even today maintains an untamed quality.

Sheep and cattle farming are the basis of the rural economy here, though there are also large areas of forestry. Along the coast, tourism is a major activity. Llandudno, a purpose-built Victorian resort, popularized the sandy northern coastline in the 19th century. The area continues to attract large numbers of visitors, though major development is confined to the narrow coastal strip that lies between Prestatyn and Llandudno, leaving the island of Anglesey and the remote Lleyn Peninsula largely untouched. The Lleyn Peninsula remains one of the strongholds of the Welsh language, along with rather isolated inland communities, such as Dolgellau and Bala.

No part of North Wales can truly be called industrial, though there are still remnants of the once-prosperous slate industry in Snowdonia, where the stark, grey quarries provide a striking contrast to the natural beauty of the surrounding mountains. At the foot of Snowdon (the highest mountain in Wales), the villages of Beddgelert, Betws-y-Coed and Llanberis are popular bases for walkers who come to enjoy the spectacular views and striking beauty of this remote region.

Caernarfon Castle, one of the forbidding fortresses built by Edward I

◄ Fiery sunset over Conwy Harbour

Exploring North Wales

The dominant feature of North Wales is Snowdon, the highest mountain in Wales. Snowdonia National Park extends dramatically from the Snowdon massif south beyond Dolgellau, with thickly wooded valleys, mountain lakes, moors and estuaries. To the east are the softer Clwydian Hills, and unspoilt coastlines can be enjoyed on Anglesey and the beautiful Lleyn Peninsula.

A lighthouse perched on the sea cliffs of Anglesey

Key

- Major road
- Minor road
- Secondary road
- Scenic route
- Main railway
- Minor railway
- △ Summit

The peaks and moorland of Snowdonia

For additional map symbols *see back flap*

Getting Around

The main route into North Wales from the northwest of England is the A55, a good dual carriageway which bypasses several places that used to be traffic bottlenecks, including Conwy. The other main route through the region is the A5 Shrewsbury to Holyhead road, which follows a trail through the mountains pioneered by the 19th-century engineer Thomas Telford *(see p451)*. Rail services run along the coast to Holyhead, connecting with ferries across the Irish Sea to Dublin and Dun Laoghaire. Scenic branch lines travel from Llandudno Junction to Blaenau Ffestiniog (via Betws-y-Coed) and along the southern Lleyn Peninsula.

Sights at a Glance

1. Caernarfon
2. Beaumaris
3. *Conwy pp450–51*
4. Llandudno
5. Ruthin
6. Llangollen
7. Bala
8. Betws-y-Coed
9. Blaenau Ffestiniog
10. Llanberis and Snowdon
11. Beddgelert
12. Lleyn Peninsula
13. *Portmeirion pp458–9*
14. Harlech
15. Dolgellau
16. Aberdyfi

The imposing castle built at Conwy by Edward I in the 13th century

Caernarfon Castle, built by Edward I as a symbol of his power over the conquered Welsh

❶ Caernarfon

Gwynedd. 🏛 10,000. 🚌 ℹ Castle Ditch (01286 672232). 🏪 Sat. 🌐 visitsnowdonia.info

One of the most famous castles in Wales, Caernarfon Castle, looms over this busy town set at the mouth of the Seiont River. Both town and castle were created after Edward I's defeat of the last native Welsh prince, Llywelyn ap Gruffydd (Llywelyn the Last) in 1283 *(see p440)*. The town walls merge with modern streets that spread beyond the medieval centre to a market square. Overlooking the town and its harbour, **Caernarfon Castle**

The Investiture

In 1301 the future Edward II became the first English Prince of Wales *(see p440)*, a title since held by the British monarch's eldest son. In 1969 the investiture in Caernarfon Castle of Prince Charles *(above)* as Prince of Wales drew 500 million TV viewers.

(see p443), with its polygonal towers, was built as a seat of government for North Wales. Caernarfon was a thriving port in the 19th century, and during this period the castle ruins were restored by the architect Anthony Salvin. Displays in the castle include the Royal Welch Fusiliers Museum, and exhibitions tracing the history of the Princes of Wales and exploring the importance of the castle in Welsh history.

Situated on the hill above the town are the ruins of **Segontium**, a Roman fort built in about AD 78. Local legend claims that the first Christian Emperor of Rome, Constantine the Great, was born here in 280.

🏰 **Caernarfon Castle**
Y Maes. **Tel** 01286 677617. **Open** daily. 🚻 📷 call for details. 📷 🌐 cadw.wales.gov.uk

🏰 **Segontium**
Beddgelert Rd. **Open** daily. **Closed** 1 Jan, 24, 25 & 26 Dec. ♿ limited. 📷 🌐 cadw.wales.gov.uk

❷ Beaumaris

Isle of Anglesey. 🏛 2,000. 🚌 ℹ Llanfair PG, Station Site, Holyhead Rd, Anglesey (01248 713177). 🌐 visitanglesey.co.uk

Handsome Georgian and Victorian architecture gives Beaumaris the air of a resort on England's southern coast. The buildings reflect this sailing centre's past role as Anglesey's

chief port, before the island was linked to the mainland by the road and railway bridges built across the Menai Strait in the 19th century. This was the site of Edward I's last, and possibly greatest, **castle** *(see p442)*, which was built to command this important ferrying point to the mainland of Wales.

Ye Olde Bull's Head inn, on Castle Street, was built in 1617. Its celebrated literary patrons have included Dr Samuel Johnson (1709–84) and Victorian novelist Charles Dickens *(see p193)*.

The town's **Courthouse**, was built in 1614, and the restored 1829 **Gaol** preserves its soundproofed punishment room and a huge treadmill for prisoners. Two public hangings took place here. Richard Rowlands, the last victim, protested his innocence and cursed the church clock as he was led to the gallows, declaring that its four faces would never show the same times again. It failed to show consistent times until it had an overhaul in 1980.

🏰 **Beaumaris Castle**
Castle St. **Tel** 01248 810361. **Open** daily. 📷 ♿ 📷 🌐 cadw.wales.gov.uk

🏛 **Courthouse**
Castle St. **Tel** 01248 811691. **Open** Apr–Sep: Sat–Thu. ♿ limited. 🌐 visitanglesey.co.uk

🏛 **Gaol**
Bunkers Hill. **Tel** 01248 810921. **Open** Apr–Sep: Sat–Thu. 📷 ♿ limited. 📷 🌐 visitanglesey.co.uk

Alice in Wonderland

Penmorfa, Llandudno, was the summer home of the Liddells. Their friend, Charles Dodgson (1832–98), would entertain young Alice Liddell with stories of characters such as the White Rabbit and the Mad Hatter. As Lewis Carroll, Dodgson wrote his magical tales in *Alice's Adventures in Wonderland* (1865) and *Through the Looking-Glass* (1871).

Arthur Rackham's illustration (1907) of *Alice in Wonderland*

❸ Conwy

See pp450–51.

Llandudno's crescent-shaped bay

❹ Llandudno

Conwy. 🏔 20,000. 🚌🚆 ℹ️ Library Building, Mostyn St (01492 577577). 🌐 visitllandudno.org.uk

Llandudno retains much of the holiday spirit of the 19th century, when the new railways brought crowds to the coast. Its **pier**, the longest in Wales at more than 700 m (2,295 ft), and its canopied walkways recall the heyday of seaside holidays. The town is also proud of its association with the author Lewis Carroll *(see above)*. Sculptures relating to *Alice in Wonderland* are all over town, including a Mad Hatter on the promenade. The exhibits at the **Llandudno Museum** explore Llandudno's history from Roman times onwards.

Llandudno's cheerful seaside atmosphere owes much to a strong sense of its Victorian roots – unlike many British seaside towns, which embraced the flashing lights and funfairs of the 20th century. To take full advantage of its sweeping

beach, Llandudno was laid out between its two headlands, Great Orme and Little Orme.

Great Orme, a designated Area of Conservation, and nature reserve, rises to 207 m (670 ft) and has a ski slope and the longest toboggan run in Europe. In the Bronze Age copper was mined here; the **copper mines** and their excavations are open to the public. The **church** on the headland was built from timber in the 6th century by St Tudno, rebuilt in stone in the 13th century, restored in 1855 and is still in use. Local history and wildlife can be traced in an information centre on the summit.

There are two effortless ways to reach the summit: on the **Great Orme Tramway**, one of only three cable-hauled street tramways in the world (the others are in San

Francisco and Lisbon), or by the **Llandudno Cable Car**. Both run from April to October.

🏛 **Llandudno Museum**
Gloddaeth St. **Tel** 01492 876517.
Open 10:30am–1pm, 2–5pm Tue–Sat (from 2:15pm Sun) (Nov–Easter: 1:30–4:30pm Tue–Sat). 🅿 ♿ limited.

⛏ **Great Orme Copper Mines**
Great Orme. **Tel** 01492 870447.
Open mid-Mar–Oct: 10am–4:30pm daily. 🅿 ♿ limited. 📷 📱
🌐 **greatormemines.info**

❺ Ruthin

Denbighshire. 🏔 5,200. 🚌 🚆 1st Tue of every month; Thu (indoor).
🌐 **visitruthin.com**

Ruthin's long-standing prosperity as a market town is reflected in its fine half-timbered medieval buildings. These include the NatWest and Barclays banks in St Peter's Square. The former was a 15th-century courthouse and prison, the latter the home of Thomas Exmewe, Lord Mayor of London in 1517–18. **Maen Huail** ("Huail's stone"), a boulder outside Barclays, is said to be where King Arthur *(see p289)* beheaded Huail, a love rival.

St Peter's Church, on the edge of St Peter's Square, was founded in 1310 and has a Tudor oak roof in the north aisle. Next to the Castle Hotel is the 17th-century pub **The Myddleton Arms**, whose unusual, Dutch-style, dormer windows are known locally as the "eyes of Ruthin".

The "eyes of Ruthin", an unusual feature in Welsh architecture

❸ Street-by-Street: Conwy

Conwy is one of Britain's most underrated historic towns. Until the early 1990s it was famous as a traffic bottleneck, but thanks to a town bypass, its concentration of architectural riches – unparalleled in Wales – can now be appreciated. The castle dominates: a brooding, intimidating monument built by Edward I *(see p442).* But Conwy is set apart from other medieval towns by its amazingly well-preserved town walls. Fortified with 21 towers and three gateways, the walls form an almost unbroken shield around the old town.

Smallest House
This fisherman's cottage on the quayside, just over 3 m (10 ft) high, is said to be the smallest house in Britain.

Plas Mawr, the "Great Mansion", was built by a nobleman, Robert Wynne, in 1576.

St Mary's Church
This medieval church is where William Wordsworth was inspired to write his poem "We Are Seven".

Bangor

BERRY STREET

CHAPEL STREET

HIGH STREET

LANCASTER SQUARE

CHURCH STREET

UPPER GATE STREET

ROSEMARY LANE

Upper Gate

Llywelyn's Statue
Llywelyn the Great *(see p440)* was arguably Wales's most successful medieval leader.

Aberconwy House
This restored 14th-century town house was once the home of a wealthy merchant.

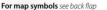

For map symbols *see back flap*

Thomas Telford

Thomas Telford (1757–1834) was the gifted Scottish engineer responsible for many of Britain's roads, bridges and canals. The Menai Bridge *(see p448)*, the Pontcysyllte Aqueduct *(see p454)* and Conwy Bridge are his outstanding works in Wales. Telford's graceful bridge at Conwy has aesthetic as well as practical qualities. Completed in 1826 across the mouth of the Conwy estuary, it was designed in a castellated style to blend with the castle. Before the bridge's construction the estuary could only be crossed by ferry.

VISITORS' CHECKLIST

Practical Information
Conwy. 🔼 8,000.
🅦 conwy.com 🛈 01492
577566. Aberconwy House
Tel 01492 592246. **Open** mid-Mar–Oct: Wed–Mon (Jul & Aug: daily), Nov & Dec: Sat & Sun.
Closed Jan–mid-Mar. 🎨 📷 NT
Conwy Castle **Tel** 01492 592358.
Open daily. 🎨 📷 Smallest
House **Tel** 01492 593484.
Open Apr–Oct: daily. 🎨

Transport
🚆 Conwy.

Entrance to castle

Railway bridge

Telford's Suspension Bridge

Chester

CASTLE STREET

CASTLE STREET

EHILL STREET

NEW BRIDGE

Key
— Suggested route

0 metres 50
0 yards 50

★ **Town Walls**
These remarkably well-preserved medieval walls are 1,280 m (4,200 ft) long and over 9 m (30 ft) high.

★ **Conwy Castle**
This atmospheric watercolour, *Conway Castle (c.1770)*, is by the Nottingham artist Paul Sandby.

For hotels and restaurants in this area see pp560–73 and pp582–603

Pontcysyllte Aqueduct, built in 1795–1805, carrying the Llangollen Canal

❻ Llangollen

Denbighshire. 🅼 3,500. 🚌
🛈 y Capel, Castle St (01978 860828).
🚲 Tue. 🆆 llangollen.org.uk

Best known for its annual Eisteddfod (festival), this pretty town sits on the River Dee, which is spanned by a 14th-century bridge. The town became notorious in the 1700s, when two Irishwomen, Sarah Ponsonby and Lady Eleanor Butler, the "Ladies of Llangollen", set up house together in the half-timbered **Plas Newydd**. Their unconventional dress and literary enthusiasms attracted such celebrities as the Duke of Wellington *(see p166)* and William Wordsworth *(see p370)*. The ruins of a 13th-century castle, **Castell Dinas Brân**, occupy the summit of a hill overlooking the house.

Environs
Boats on the **Llangollen Canal** sail from Wharf Hill in summer and cross the spectacular 300 m (1,000 ft) long Pontcysyllte Aqueduct, built by Thomas Telford *(see p451)* and now a UNESCO World Heritage Site.

🏛 **Plas Newydd**
Hill St. **Tel** 01978 862834.
Open Apr–Oct: Wed–Sun. 🚗 🛗
limited. 🅿 📷 NT

❼ Bala

Gwynedd. 🅼 2,000. 🚌 from
Wrexham. 🛈 Penllyn, Pensarn Rd
(01678 521021). 🆆 visitbala.org

Bala Lake, Wales's largest natural lake, lies between the Aran and Arenig mountains at the fringes of Snowdonia National Park. It is popular for water-sports and boasts a unique fish called a *gwyniad*, which is related to the salmon.

The little grey-stone town of Bala is a Welsh-speaking community, its houses strung out along a single street at the eastern end of the lake. Thomas Charles (1755–1814), a Methodist church leader, once lived here. A plaque on his former home recalls Mary Jones who walked 28 miles (42 km) barefoot from Abergynolwyn to buy a Bible. This led to Charles establishing the Bible Society, providing cheap bibles to the working classes.

The narrow-gauge **Bala Lake Railway** follows the lake shore from Llanuwchllyn, 4 miles (6 km) southwest.

❽ Betws-y-Coed

Conwy. 🅼 600. 🚆 🛈 Royal Oak
Stables (01690 710426).
🆆 betws-y-coed.co.uk

This village near the peaks of Snowdonia has been a hill-walking centre since the

19th century. To the west are the **Swallow Falls**, where the River Llugwy flows through a wooded glen. The bizarre **Ty Hyll** ("Ugly House"), is a *tŷ unnos* ("one-night house"); traditionally, houses erected between dusk and dawn on common land were entitled to freehold rights, and the owner could enclose land as far as he could throw an axe from the door. To the east is **Waterloo Bridge**, built by Thomas Telford to celebrate the victory against Napoleon.

🏛 **Ty Hyll**
Capel Curig. **Tel** 01286 685498.
House: **Open** Easter–Sep: daily.
Grounds: **Open** daily. 🅿 🛗 limited.

The ornate Waterloo Bridge, built in 1815 after the famous battle

A view of the Snowdonia countryside from Llanberis Pass, the most popular route to Snowdon's peak

❾ Blaenau Ffestiniog

Gwynedd. 🚶 4,800. 🚌 ℹ️ Betws-y-Coed (01690 710426). 🛒 Tue (Jun–Sep).

Blaenau Ffestiniog, once the slate capital of North Wales, sits among mountains riddled with quarries. The **Llechwedd Slate Caverns**, overlooking Blaenau, opened to visitors in the early 1970s, marking a new role for the declining industrial town. The electric Miners' Tramway takes passengers on a tour into the original caverns; there are also mountain-bike trails.

On the Deep Mine tour, visitors descend on Britain's steepest passenger incline railway to the underground chambers, while sound effects recreate the atmosphere of a working quarry. The dangers included landfalls and floods, as well as the more gradual threat of slate dust breathed into the lungs.

There are slate-splitting demonstrations on the surface, a quarryman's cottage and a re-creation of a Victorian village to illustrate the cramped and basic living conditions endured by workers between the 1880s and 1945.

The narrow-gauge **Ffestiniog Railway** (*see pp456–7*) runs from Blaenau to Porthmadog.

🏛 **Llechwedd Slate Caverns**
Off A470. **Tel** 01766 830306. **Open** daily (Jan–mid-Mar: Wed–Sun).
🚻 ♿ except Deep Mine. 🎦 🎁
🌐 **llechwedd-slate-caverns.co.uk**

❿ Llanberis and Snowdon

Gwynedd. 🚶 2,100. ℹ️ Electric Mountain Visitor Centre (01286 870765). 🌐 **visitsnowdonia.info**

Snowdon, which at 1,085 m (3,560 ft) is the highest peak in Wales, is the main focus of the vast Snowdonia National Park, whose scenery ranges from this rugged mountain country to moors and sandy beaches.

The easiest route to Snowdon's summit begins in Llanberis: the 5 mile (8 km) **Llanberis Track**. From Llanberis Pass, the Miners' Track (once used by copper miners) and the Pyg Track are alternative paths. Walkers should beware of sudden weather changes and dress accordingly. The narrow-gauge **Snowdon Mountain Railway**, which opened in 1896, is an easier option.

Llanberis was a major 19th-century slate town, with grey terraces hewn into the hills. Other attractions are the 13th-century shell of **Dolbadarn Castle**, and, above Llyn (Lake) Peris, the **Electric Mountain**, which has tours of Europe's biggest hydro-electric pumped storage station.

🏰 **Dolbadarn Castle**
Off A4086 nr Llanberis.
Tel 01286 870765. **Open** daily.

ℹ️ **Electric Mountain**
Llanberis. **Tel** 01286 870636.
Open daily. 🚻 ♿ 🎦 🎁
🌐 **electricmountain.co.uk**

Britain's Centre of Slate

Welsh slates provided roofing material for Britain's new towns in the 19th century. In 1898, the slate industry employed nearly 17,000 men, a quarter of whom worked at Blaenau Ffestiniog. Foreign competition and new materials later took their toll. Quarries such as Dinorwig in Llanberis and Llechwedd in Blaenau Ffestiniog now survive on the tourist trade.

The dying art of slate-splitting

The village of Beddgelert, set among the mountains of Snowdonia

⓫ Beddgelert

Gwynedd. 🗺 500. 🛈 Canolfan-
Hebog (01766 890615).
🌐 beddgelerttourism.com

Beddgelert enjoys a spectacular
location in Snowdonia. The village
sits on the confluence of the
Glaslyn and Colwyn rivers at the
approach to two mountain passes:
the beautiful Nant Gwynant Pass,
which leads to Snowdonia's highest reaches, and the Aberglaslyn
Pass, a narrow wooded gorge
which acts as a gateway to the sea.

Business was given a boost by
Dafydd Pritchard, the landlord
of the Royal Goat Hotel, who in
the early 19th century adapted
an old Welsh legend to
associate it with Beddgelert.
Llywelyn the Great *(see p440)*
is said to have left his faithful
hound Gelert to guard his infant
son while he went hunting. He
returned to find the cradle
overturned and Gelert covered
in blood. Thinking the dog had
savaged his son, Llywelyn
slaughtered Gelert, but then

discovered the boy, unharmed,
under the cradle. Nearby was
the corpse of a wolf, which
Gelert had killed to protect
the child. To support the tale,
Pritchard created **Gelert's Grave**
(*bedd Gelert* in Welsh) by the
River Glaslyn, a mound of stones
a short walk south of the village.

Environs
There are many fine walks in the
area: one leads south to the
Aberglaslyn Pass and along a
section of the Welsh Highland
Railway (www.festrail.co.uk), with
its steam trains. The **Sygun Copper
Mine**, 1 mile (1.5 km) northeast
of Beddgelert, offers self-guided
tours of caverns recreating the
life of Victorian miners.

🏛 Sygun Copper Mine
On A498. **Tel** 01766 890595.
Open Mar–Nov: daily; Feb half term.
🅿 ⓰ limited. 🖥 📷
🌐 syguncoppermine.co.uk

Ffestiniog Railway

The Ffestiniog narrow-gauge railway takes
a scenic 14 mile (22 km) route from
Porthmadog Harbour to the mountains
and the slate town of Blaenau Ffestiniog
(see p455). Designed to carry slate from the
quarries to the quay, the railway replaced
a horse-drawn tramway constructed in
1836, operating on a 60 cm (2 ft) gauge.
After closure in 1946, it was reconstructed
by volunteers and re-opened in sections
from 1955–82.

Steam-traction trains were first used on
the Ffestiniog Railway in 1863. There are
some diesel engines, but most trains on
the route are still steam-hauled.

⑫ Lleyn Peninsula

Gwynedd. 🚆 🚌 Pwllheli. 🚌 Aberdaron to Bardsey Island. ℹ️ Min-y-don, Station Sq, Pwllheli (01758 613000). 🌐 **visitsnowdonia.info**

This 24-mile (38-km) finger of land points southwest from Snowdonia into the Irish Sea. Although it has popular beaches, notably at Pwllheli, Criccieth, Abersoch and Nefyn, the coast's overriding feature is its untamed beauty. Views are at their most dramatic in the far west and along the mountain-backed northern shores.

The windy headland of **Braich-y-Pwll**, to the west of Aberdaron, looks out towards Bardsey Island, the "Isle of 20,000 Saints". This became a place of pilgrimage in the 6th century, when a monastery was founded here. Some of the saints are said to be buried in the churchyard of the ruined 13th-century **St Mary's Abbey**. Close by is **Porth Oer**, a small bay also known as "Whistling Sands" (the sand is meant to squeak, or whistle, underfoot).

East of Aberdaron is the 4 mile (6.5 km) bay of **Porth Neigwl**, known in English as Hell's Mouth, the scene of many shipwrecks due to the bay's treacherous currents. Hidden in sheltered grounds above Porth Neigwl bay, 1 mile (1.5 km) northeast of Aberdaron, is **Plas-yn-Rhiw**, a small, medieval manor house with Tudor and Georgian additions and lovely gardens.

The former quarrying village and "ghost town" of **Llithfaen**, tucked away below the sheer cliffs of the mountainous north coast, is now a centre for Welsh language studies.

🏛️ Plas-yn-Rhiw
Off B4413. **Tel** 01758 780219. **Open** Apr & Oct: Thu–Sun; May–Aug: Wed–Mon; Sep: Thu–Mon. ♿ limited. **NT**

Llithfaen village, now a language centre, on the Lleyn Peninsula

Tan-y-Bwlch is in the heart of Snowdonia National Park. Nature trails lead through woods to the lovely Llyn Mair.

Betwys-y-coed

Blaenau Ffestiniog

Tanygrisiau

Moelwyn Tunnel

Campbell's Platform

Tan-y-Bwlch ℹ️ P

Dduallt

Plas Halt

A496

A487

A496

Dolgellau, Bala

Tanygrisiau is a request stop for a power station visitor centre, and is near a waterfall and a lake.

VISITORS' CHECKLIST

Practical Information
ℹ️ 01766 516000. **Tel** bookings 01766 516024. **Open** daily. **Closed** 25 Dec. 🌐 festrail.co.uk

Transport
🚆 Porthmadog.

Key

━━ Ffestiniog Railway

○ Station

── British Rail

═══ Major roads

For additional map symbols *see back flap*

⑬ Portmeirion

Gwynedd. **Tel** 01766 770000. 🚆
Minffordd. **Open** daily **Closed** 25 Dec.
🅿 ♿ limited. 🎫 📷 🍴 🛍
W portmeirion-village.com

This bizarre Italianate village on a private peninsula at the top of Cardigan Bay was created by Welsh architect Sir Clough Williams-Ellis (1883–1978). He fulfilled a childhood dream by building a village "to my own fancy on my own chosen site". About 50 buildings surround a central piazza, in styles from Oriental to Gothic. Visitors can stay at the luxurious hotel or in one of the charming village cottages. Portmeirion has been an atmospheric location for many films and television programmes, including the popular 1960s television series *The Prisoner*.

Sir Clough Williams-Ellis at Portmeirion

Hercules is a life-size 19th-century copper statue near the Town Hall, where a 17th-century ceiling, rescued from a demolished mansion, depicts his legend.

Fountain Cottage is where Noel Coward (1899–1973) wrote *Blithe Spirit*.

Swimming pool

The Amis Reunis is a stone replica of a boat that sank in the bay.

The Portmeirion Hotel overlooks the bay. It has a dining room designed by Sir Terence Conran.

---

⑭ Harlech

Gwynedd. 🏔 2,000. 🚆 ℹ High St (01766 780658). **W** eryri-npa.gov.uk

This small town with fine beaches is dominated by **Harlech Castle**, a medieval fortress *(see p442)* built by Edward I between 1283 and 1289. The castle sits on a precipitous crag, with superb views of Tremadog Bay and the Lleyn Peninsula to the west, and Snowdonia to the north. When the castle was built, the sea reached a fortified stairway cut into the cliff, so that supplies could arrive by ship, but now the sea has receded. A towering gatehouse protects the inner ward, enclosed by walls and four round towers.

Despite its defences, Harlech Castle fell to Owain Glyndŵr *(see p440)* in 1404, and served as his court until its recapture four years later. The song *Men of Harlech* is thought to have been inspired by the castle's heroic resistance during an eight-year siege in the Wars of the Roses *(see p53)*.

🏰 **Harlech Castle**
Castle Sq. **Tel** 01766 780552. **Open** daily. **Closed** 1 Jan, 24–26 Dec. ♿
📷 **W** cadw.wales.gov.uk

⑮ Dolgellau

Gwynedd. 🏔 2,700. ℹ Eldon Sq (01341 422888). 🛒 Fri (livestock).

The dark local stone gives a stern, solid look to this market town, where the Welsh language and customs are still very strong. It lies in the long shadow of the 892 m (2,927 ft) mountain of Cader Idris where, according to legend, anyone who spends a night on its summit will awake a poet or a madman – or not at all.

Dolgellau was gripped by gold fever in the 19th century, when high-quality gold was discovered in the Mawddach

Harlech Castle's strategic site overlooking mountains and sea

For hotels and restaurants in this area see pp560–73 and pp582–603

Triumphal Arch

Central Piazza

Lodge

Campanile

Royal Dolphin Cottage

Bristol Colonnade

Viewing platform

The Lady's Lodge, next door to the intriguing Prisoner Shop.

The Pantheon was built in 1960–61, but lack of funds meant that the dome was originally made from plywood instead of copper and painted green. The Pantheon's unusual façade is formed by the upper half of a music room fireplace by Norman Shaw (see p33).

Dolgellau's grey-stone buildings, dwarfed by the mountain scenery

Valley nearby. The deposits were not large enough to sustain an intensive mining industry for long. Nevertheless, up until 1999, small amounts were mined and crafted locally into fine jewellery.

Dolgellau is a good centre for walking, whether you wish to take gentle strolls through beautiful leafy countryside or strenuous hikes across extreme terrain with dramatic mountain views. The lovely **Cregennen lakes** are set high in the hills above the thickly wooded

Mawddach Estuary to the northwest; north are the harsh, bleak **Rhinog moors**, one of Wales's last true wildernesses.

⑯ Aberdyfi

Gwynedd. 780. Wharf Gardens (01654 767321).
aberdyfi.org

Perched on the mouth of the Dyfi Estuary, this little harbour resort and sailing centre makes the most of its splendid but rather confined location, its

houses occupying every yard of a narrow strip of land between mountain and sea. In the 19th century, local slate was exported from here, and between the 1830s and the 1860s about 100 ships were built in the port. *The Bells of Aberdovey*, a song by Charles Dibdin for his opera *Liberty Hall* (1785), tells the legend of Cantref-y-Gwaelod, thought to have been located here, which was protected from the sea by dykes. One stormy night, the sluice gates were left open by Prince Seithenyn, when he was drunk, and the land was lost beneath the waves. The submerged church bells are said to peal under the water to this day.

Neat Georgian houses by the sea, Aberdyfi

SOUTH AND MID-WALES

Cardiff, Swansea & Environs · Ceredigion Carmarthenshire · Monmouthshire · Powys · Pembrokeshire

South and mid-Wales are less homogeneous regions than North Wales. Most of the population lives in the southeast corner. To the west is Pembrokeshire, the loveliest stretch of Welsh coastline. To the north the industrial valleys give way to the wide hills of the Brecon Beacons and the rural heartlands of central Wales.

South Wales's coastal strip has been settled for many centuries. There are prehistoric sites in the Vale of Glamorgan and Pembrokeshire. The Romans established a major base at Caerleon, and the Normans built castles all the way from Chepstow to Pembroke. In the 18th and 19th centuries, coal mines and ironworks opened in the valleys of South Wales, attracting immigrants from all over Europe. Close communities developed here, focused on the coal trade, which turned Cardiff from a sleepy coastal town into the world's busiest coal-exporting port.

The declining coal industry has again changed the face of this area: spoil heaps have become green hills, and the valley towns struggle to find alternative forms of employment. Coal mines such as Blaenafon's Big Pit are now tourist attractions; today, many of the tour guides taking visitors underground are ex-miners, who can offer a first-hand glimpse of the hard life found in mining communities before the pits closed.

The southern boundary of the Brecon Beacons National Park marks the beginning of rural Wales. With a population sparser than anywhere in England, this is an area of small country towns, hill-sheep farms, forestry plantations and spectacular man-made lakes.

The number of Welsh-speakers increases and the sense of Welsh culture becomes stronger as you travel further from the border with England, with the exception of an English enclave in south Pembrokeshire.

Walkers admiring the view at Llyn y Fan Fach, in the Brecon Beacons National Park

◀ The imposing entrance to the Wales Millennium Centre in Cardiff

Exploring South and Mid-Wales

Magnificent coastal scenery marks the Pembrokeshire Coast National Park and cliff-backed Gower Peninsula, while Cardigan Bay and Carmarthen Bay offer quieter beaches. Walkers can enjoy grassy uplands in the Brecon Beacons and gentler country in the leafy Wye Valley. Urban life is concentrated in the southeast of Wales, where old mining towns line the valleys north of Cardiff, the capital.

Cliffs of the Pembrokeshire Coast National Park

Getting Around

The M4 motorway is the major route into Wales from the south of England, and there are good road links west of Swansea running to the coast. The A483 and A488 give access to mid-Wales from the Midlands. Frequent rail services connect London with Swansea, Cardiff and the ferry port of Fishguard.

Sights at a Glance

1. Powis Castle
2. Knighton
3. Hay-on-Wye
4. Llandrindod Wells
5. Elan Valley
6. Machynlleth
7. Aberystwyth
8. Aberaeron
9. St Davids pp468–9
10. Tenby
11. Swansea and the Gower Peninsula
13. Brecon Beacons pp472–3
14. Cardiff pp474–5
15. Caerleon
16. Blaenavon
17. Monmouth
18. Tintern Abbey

Walks and Tours

12. Wild Wales Tour

Llanrhaeadr-
ym-Mochnant
Tanat
↗ Wrexham
Llanfyllin A483
Dolgellau
Shrewsbury
Mallwyd A458 Llangadfan Middletown
A470 Llanfair Welshpool
Caereinion 1 POWIS CASTLE
Llanbrynmair A483
Moelfre Carno Montgomery
468m Severn
A470
Caersws Newtown
Llyn A489 Ludlow
Clywedog
Wye
Llanidloes A483
Llangurig Beacon Hill
547m
ELAN Llanbister
VALLEY A470 KNIGHTON 2 Teme
5 Rhayader
Elan Village Penybont Presteigne
erwen Caban Coch LLANDRINDOD
Res. Reservoir 4 WELLS
WILD A44
Newbridge Llanfihangel-
WALES on Wye nant-Melan
Builth Wells
iynne Beulah
rion A483
Llanwrtyd Clyro
Wells 3 HAY-ON-WYE
A483 Upper Llyswen
ndovery Chapel Hay Bluff
677m
A40 Sennybridge Usk Talgarth Hereford
sk Libanus A479 Llanthony
oit Brecon Priory
13 Pen y Fan Black
A470 886m Tretower Mountains
RECON BEACONS Crickhowell A465
Dan-yr-Ogof Abergavenny Ross-on-Wye
Caves Brynmawr A465 A40
Abercraf Ebbw Vale Raglan 17 MONMOUTH
n-Neath Merthyr BLAENAVON A449
Tydfil Abertillery 16 Gloucester
Resolven A4042 TINTERN
465 Aberdare Pontypool ABBEY 18
eath Treorchy Bargoed Chepstow
ort Talbot Pontypridd A470 Cwmbran
Abercarn 15 CAERLEON
Risca M4
Caerphilly Newport Caldicot
Llantrisant Taff
Bridgend M4 St. Mellons Bristol
Museum of Mouth of
thcawl Welsh Life 14 the Severn
CARDIFF
Cowbridge Penarth
Llantwit Major Barry
Rhoose
Bristol Channel

Key

══ Motorway
══ Major road
══ Secondary road
┈┈ Minor road
── Scenic route
╍╍ Main railway
── Minor railway
△ Summit

The rolling hills near Knighton, on the borderlands
between Wales and England

0 kilometres 15
0 miles 10

A detail of Cardiff Castle's clocktower, part of the ornate
embellishments added in the 19th century

Italianate terraces and formal gardens at Powis Castle, adding a Mediterranean air to the Welsh borderlands

❶ Powis Castle

Welshpool, Powys. **Tel** 01938 551944. 🚆 Welshpool then bus. **Open** daily. **Closed** 25 Dec. 🐾 🅱️ limited. 📷 🅝🆃 🆆 nationaltrust.org.uk/powis-castle

Powis Castle – the spelling is an archaic version of "Powys" – has outgrown its military roots. Despite its sham battlements and dominant site, 1 mile (1.6 km) to the southwest of the town of Welshpool, this red-stone building has served as a country mansion for centuries. It began life in the 13th century as a fortress, built by the princes of Powys to control the border with England.

The castle is entered through one of few surviving medieval features: a gateway, built in 1283 by Owain de la Pole. The gate is flanked by two towers.

The castle's lavish interiors soon banish all thoughts of war. A **Dining Room**, decorated with fine 17th-century panelling and family portraits, was originally designed as the castle's Great Hall. The **Great Staircase**, added in the late 17th century and

elaborately decorated with carved fruit and flowers, leads to the main apartments: an early 19th-century library, the panelled **Oak Drawing Room** and the Elizabethan **Long Gallery**, where ornate plasterwork on the fireplace and ceiling date from the 1590s. In the **Blue Drawing Room** there are three 18th-century Brussels tapestries.

The Herbert family bought the property in 1587 and were proud of their Royalist connections; the panelling in the **State Bedroom** bears the

The richly carved 17th-century Great Staircase

royal monogram. Powis Castle was defended for Charles I in the Civil War (see pp56–7), but fell to Parliament in 1644. The 3rd Baron Powis, a supporter of James II, had to flee the country when William and Mary took the throne in 1688 (see pp56–7).

The castle's **Clive Museum** has an exhibition concerning "Clive of India" (1725–74), the general and statesman who helped strengthen British control in India in the mid-18th century. The family's link with Powis Castle was established by the 2nd Lord Clive, who married into the Herbert family and became the Earl of Powis in 1804. The **gardens** at Powis are among the best-known in Britain, with their series of elegant Italianate terraces, adorned with statues, niches, balustrades, hanging gardens and sinuous mounded yew trees, all stepped into the steep hillside beneath the castle walls. Created between 1688 and 1722, these are the only formal gardens of this period in Britain that are still kept in their original form (see pp30–31).

❷ Knighton

Powys. 🏘 3,500. 🚆 ℹ️ Offa's Dyke Centre, West St (01547 528753). 📅 Thu. 🌐 visitknighton.co.uk

Knighton's Welsh name, Tref y Clawdd ("The Town on the Dyke"), reflects its status as the only original settlement on **Offa's Dyke**. In the 8th century, King Offa of Mercia (central and southern England) constructed a ditch and bank to mark out his territory, and to enable the enforcement of a Saxon law: "Neither shall a Welshman cross into English land without the appointed man from the other side, who should meet him at the bank and bring him back again without any offence being committed." Some of the best-preserved sections of the 6-m-(20-ft-) high earth-work lie in the hills around Knighton. The Offa's Dyke Footpath runs for 177 miles (285 km) along the border between England and Wales.

Knighton is set on a steep hill, sloping upwards from **St Edward's Church** (1877) with its medieval tower, to the summit, where a castle once stood. The main street leads via the market square, marked by a 19th-century clock tower, along **The Narrows**, a Tudor street with little shops. **The Old House** on Broad Street is a medieval "cruck" house (curved timbers form a frame to support the roof), with a hole in the ceiling instead of a chimney.

Knighton's clock

❸ Hay-on-Wye

Powys. 🏘 1,500. ℹ️ Oxford Rd (01497 820144). 📅 Thu. 🌐 hay-on-wye.co.uk

Book-lovers from all over the world come to this quiet border town in the Black Mountains. Hay-on-Wye has more than 30 second-hand bookshops stocking millions of titles, and in early summer hosts a prestigious Festival of Literature and the Arts. The town's love affair with books began when a bookshop was opened in the 1960s by Richard Booth, who claims the (fictitious) title of King of Independent Hay and lived in **Hay Castle**, a 17th-century mansion in the grounds of the original 13th-century castle (now owned by a charitable trust). Hay's oldest inn, the 16th-century **Three Tuns** on Bridge Street, is still functioning and has an attractive half-timbered façade.

Environs: Hay-on-Wye sits on the approach to the Black Mountains and is surrounded by rolling hills. To the south are the heights of Hay Bluff and the Vale of Ewyas, where the 12th-century ruins of **Llanthony Priory** (*see p473*) retain fine pointed arches.

🏰 **Hay Castle**
Closed until further notice.
🌐 haycastletrust.com

❹ Llandrindod Wells

Powys. 🏘 5,000. 🚆 ℹ️ Town Hall, Temple Street (01597 822600). 📅 Fri.

Llandrindod is a perfect example of a Victorian town, with canopied streets, delicate

One of Hay-on-Wye's bookshops

wrought ironwork, gabled villas and ornamental parklands. This purpose-built spa town became Wales's premier inland resort of the 19th century. Its sulphur and magnesium spring waters were taken to treat skin complaints and a range of other ailments.

The town now makes every effort to preserve its Victorian character, with a lake and the well-tended **Rock Park Gardens**. The restored 19th-century **Pump Room** in Temple Gardens is where, during the last full week of August, residents don period costume and cars are banned from the town centre.

The **Radnorshire Museum** traces the town's past as one of a string of 19th-century Welsh spas which included Builth, Llangammarch and **Llanwrtyd** (now a pony trekking centre).

🏛 **Radnorshire Museum**
Temple Street. **Tel** 01597 824513.
Open Tue–Sat. **Closed** 1 Jan, 25 & 26 Dec. 🖼 ♿

Victorian architecture on Spa Road, Llandrindod Wells

Craig Goch, one of the original chain of Elan Valley reservoirs

❺ Elan Valley

Powys. 🚉 Llandrindod. 🛈 Rhayader (01597 810898). 🌐 elanvalley.org.uk

A string of spectacular reservoirs, the first of the country's man-made lakes, has made this one of Wales's most famous valleys. **Caban Coch, Garreg Ddu, Pen-y-Garreg** and **Craig Goch**, were created between 1892 and 1903 to supply water to Birmingham, 73 miles (117 km) away. They form a chain of lakes about 9 miles (14 km) long, holding 50 billion litres (13 billion gallons) of water. Victorian engineers selected these high moorlands on the Cambrian Mountains, for their high annual rainfall of 1,780 mm (70 in). The choice created bitter controversy and resentment: more than 100 people had to move from the valley that was flooded in order to create Caban Coch.

Unlike their more utilitarian modern counterparts, these dams were built during an era when decoration was seen as an integral part of any design. Finished in dressed stone, they have an air of grandeur which is lacking in the huge **Claerwen** reservoir, a stark addition built during the early 1950s to double the lakes' capacity. Contained by a 355 m (1,165 ft) dam, it lies 4 miles (6 km) along the B4518 that runs through Elan Valley and offers magnificent views.

The remote moorlands and woodlands surrounding the lakes are an important habitat for wildlife; the red kite can often be seen here. The **Elan Valley Visitors' Centre**, beside the Caban Coch dam, describes the construction of the lakes, as well as the valley's own natural history. **Elan Village**, set beside the centre, is an unusual example of a model workers' village, built during the 1900s to house the waterworks staff. Outside the centre is a statue inspired by the poem "Prometheus Unbound" by Percy Bysshe Shelley (see p226), who stayed in the valley at the mansion of Nantgwyllt in 1810 with his wife, Harriet. The house now lies underneath the waters of Caban Coch, along with the rest of the old village. Among the buildings submerged were the village school and a church.

The trail from Machynlleth to Devil's Bridge, near Aberystwyth

❻ Machynlleth

Powys. 🏘 2,200. 🚉 🛈 Welshpool (01938 552043). 🛒 Wed. 🌐 exploremidwales.com

Half-timbered buildings and Georgian façades appear among the grey-stone houses in Machynlleth. It was here that Owain Glyndŵr, Wales's last native leader (see p440), held a parliament in 1404. The restored Parliament House now houses the **Owain Glyndŵr Centre**.

The ornate **Clock Tower**, in the middle of Maengwyn Street, was erected in 1874 by the Marquess of Londonderry to mark the coming of age of his heir, Lord Castlereagh. The Marquess lived in **Plas Machynlleth**, a 17th-century house in parkland off the main street, which now houses a restaurant and offices.

Senedd-dy
Owain Glyndŵr
Tywysog Cymru

Arddangosfa

Parliament House sign, Machynlleth

Environs
In an old slate quarry 2.5 miles (4 km) to the north, a "village of the future" is run by the **Centre for Alternative Technology**. A water-balanced cliff railway takes summer visitors to view low-energy houses and organic gardens, to see how to make the best of Earth's resources.

🏛 **Owain Glyndŵr Centre** Maengwyn St. **Tel** 01654 702932. **Open** Mar–Dec: Tue–Sat. ♿ 📷

🏛 **Centre for Alternative Technology** On A487. **Tel** 01654 705950. **Open** daily. **Closed** early Jan. 🅿 🍴 ♿ 🚻 📷 🌐 cat.org.uk

❼ Aberystwyth

Ceredigion. 🏘 14,000. 🚉 🚌 🛈 Terrace Rd (01970 612125). 🌐 discoverceredigion.co.uk

This seaside and university town claims to be the cultural capital of mid-Wales. By the standards of this rural area, "Aber" is a big place, its population increased for much of the year by students.

To Victorian travellers, Aberystwyth was the "Biarritz of Wales". There have been no great

Buskers on Aberystwyth's seafront

Savin's Hotel

When the Cambrian Railway opened in 1864, businessman Thomas Savin put £80,000 into building a new hotel in Aberystwyth for package tourists. The scheme made him bankrupt, but the seafront building, complete with mock-Gothic tower, was bought by campaigners attempting to establish a Welsh university. The "college by the sea" opened in 1872, and is now the University of Aberystwyth.

Mosaics on the college tower

changes along the promenade, with its gabled hotels, since the 19th century. **Constitution Hill,** a steep outcrop at the northern end, can be scaled in summer on the electric **Cliff Railway,** built in 1896. At the top, in a *camera obscura*, a lens projects views of the town. The ruined **Aberystwyth Castle** (1277) is located south of the promenade. In the town centre, the **Ceredigion Museum,** set in a former music hall, traces the history of the town.

To the northeast of the town centre, **The National Library of Wales,** next to the university, has a valuable collection of ancient Welsh manuscripts, as well as copies of every book published in England and Ireland.

Environs

During the summer the narrow-gauge Vale of Rheidol Railway runs 12 miles (19 km) to **Devil's Bridge,** where a dramatic series of waterfalls plunges through a wooded ravine and a steep trail leads to the valley floor.

🏛 **Ceredigion Museum**
Terrace Rd. **Tel** 01970 633088.
Open Mon–Sat. **Closed** Good Fri, 25 Dec–2 Jan. 📷 🚻
w discoverceredigion.co.uk

❽ Aberaeron

Ceredigion. 🚶 1,500. 🚉 Aberystwyth, then bus. 🛈 Pen Cei (01545 570602).
w discoverceredigion.co.uk

Aberaeron's harbour, lined with Georgian houses, became a trading port and shipbuilding centre in the early 19th century. Its orderly streets were laid out in pre-railway days, when the ports along Cardigan Bay enjoyed considerable wealth. The last boat was built here in 1994 and its harbour is now full of holiday sailors. The harbour can be crossed via a wooden footbridge.

The town is filled with delis, fishmongers and butchers selling local produce. On the quayside, the Hive honey ice-cream parlour serves world-renowned ice creams to a loyal clientele.

Rows of brightly painted Georgian houses lining the purpose-built harbour at Aberaeron

❾ St Davids

St David, the patron saint of Wales, founded a monastic settlement in this remote corner of southwest Wales in about 550, which became one of the most important Christian shrines. The present cathedral, built in the 12th century, and the Bishop's Palace, added a century later, are set in a grassy hollow below St Davids town, officially Britain's smallest city. The date of St David's death, 1 March, is commemorated throughout Wales.

St Davids' Cathedral, the largest in Wales

Bishop's Palace

The bishop's residence, built between 1280 and 1350 and now in ruins, had lavish private apartments.

Entrance

★ Great Hall

The open arcade and decorated parapet were added by Bishop Gower (1328–47) to unify different sections of the palace.

KEY

① **Palace latrines**

② **Rose window**

③ **The Bishop's Hall,** smaller than the Great Hall, may have been reserved for private use.

④ **The Private Chapel** was a late 14th-century addition, built, like the rest of the palace, over a series of vaults.

⑤ **St Mary's College Chapel**

⑥ **Bishop Vaughan's Chapel** has a fine fan-vaulted early Tudor roof.

Typical medieval window   Wooden screen

Great Hall

This reconstruction shows the hall before the lead was stripped from the roof. Bishop Barlow, St Davids' first Protestant bishop (1536–48), is thought to have been responsible for the lead's removal.

Vault

★ Nave Ceiling
The roof of the nave is lowered and hidden by an early 16th-century oak ceiling. A beautiful 14th-century rood screen divides the nave from the choir.

VISITORS' CHECKLIST

Practical Information
Cathedral Close, St Davids.
Tel 01437 720202.
W stdavidscathedral.org.uk
Open 9am–5pm daily (Sun: pm). ⓖ ⓒ ▣

Transport
⮞ Haverfordwest then bus.

Stained-Glass Window
In the nave's west end, eight panels, produced in the 1950s, radiate from a central window showing the dove of peace.

Cathedral

St David was one of the founders of the 6th-century monastic movement, so this was an important site of pilgrimage. Three visits here equalled one to Jerusalem.

Entrance

Tower Lantern Ceiling
The medieval roof was decorated with episcopal insignia when restored in the 1870s by Sir George Gilbert Scott.

★ St David's Shrine
A statue of the saint is placed near the shrine. Thought to symbolize the Holy Spirit, a dove is said to have landed on David's shoulder as he spoke to a gathering of bishops.

Sixteenth-Century Choir Stalls
The royal coat of arms on one of the carved choir stalls shows that the sovereign is a member of St Davids' Chapter. There are some interesting misericords *(see p345)* in these stalls.

❿ Tenby

Pembrokeshire. 👥 5,000. 🚌 🚆 🚤
ℹ️ Upper Park Road (01834 842 402).
🌐 **visitpembrokeshire.com**

Tenby has successfully trodden the fine line between over-commercialization and popularity, refusing to submit its historic character to the garish excesses of some seaside towns. Georgian houses overlook its handsome harbour, which is backed by a well-preserved medieval clifftop town of narrow streets and passages. The old town was defended by a headland fortress, now ruined, flanked by two wide beaches and a ring of 13th-century walls. These survive to their full height in places, along with a fortified gateway, the **Five Arches**.

The three-storeyed **Tudor Merchant's House** is a 15th-century relic of Tenby's highly prosperous seafaring days, with original fireplaces and chimneys. There are regular boat trips from the harbour to **Caldey Island**, 3 miles (5 km) offshore, home of a perfume- and chocolate-making monastic community.

🏛️ **Tudor Merchant's House**
Quay Hill. **Tel** 01834 842279. **Open** Apr–Oct: Wed–Mon (Aug: daily); Nov–Feb: Sat & Sun (Feb half-term: daily). 🐾 **NT** 📷 for pre-booked parties.

The Plantagenet House Restaurant, next to the Tudor Merchant's House

⓫ Swansea and the Gower Peninsula

Swansea. 👥 239,000. 🚌 🚆 🚤
ℹ️ Plymouth St (01792 468321). 🛍️ Mon–Sat. 🌐 **visitswanseabay.com**

Swansea, Wales's second city, is set along a wide, curving bay. The city centre was rebuilt after heavy bombing in World War II but, despite the modern buildings, a traditional Welsh atmosphere prevails. This is particularly noticeable in the excellent food market, full of Welsh delicacies such as laverbread *(see p580)* and locally caught cockles.

The award-winning **Maritime Quarter** redevelopment has transformed the old docklands, and is worth a visit. A statue of copper magnate John Henry Vivian (1779–1855) overlooks the marina. The Vivians, a leading Swansea family, founded the **Glynn Vivian Art Gallery**, which has exquisite Swansea pottery and porcelain. Archaeology and Welsh history feature at the **Swansea Museum**, the oldest museum in Wales.

The life and work of local poet Dylan Thomas (1914–53) is celebrated in the **Dylan Thomas Centre**. A permanent exhibition, Man and Myth, includes the original drafts of his poems, letters and memorabilia. His statue overlooks the Maritime Quarter. Thomas spent his childhood in the city's suburbs. **Cwmdonkin Park** was the scene of an early poem, *The Hunchback in the Park,* and its water garden has a memorial stone quoting from his *Fern Hill.*

The **National Waterfront Museum** tells the story of industry and innovation in Wales over the past 300 years. The ultra-modern slate and glass building incorporates historic warehouses.

Swansea's most celebrated son, the poet Dylan Thomas

Picturesque fishermen's cottages at the Mumbles seaside resort

Swansea Bay leads to the **Mumbles**, a popular watersports centre at the gateway to the 19-mile-long (30 km) Gower Peninsula, which in 1956 was the first part of Britain to be declared an Area of Outstanding Natural Beauty. A string of sheltered, south-facing bays leads to Oxwich and Port-Eynon beaches.

Rhossili's enormous beach leads to north Gower and a coastline of low-lying burrows, salt marshlands and cockle beds. The peninsula is littered with ancient sites such as **Parc Le Breose**, a prehistoric burial chamber.

Near Camarthen is the **National Botanic Garden of Wales**, with formal gardens centred on The Great Glasshouse which contains a Mediterranean ecosystem.

🏛️ **Glynn Vivian Art Gallery**
Alexandra Rd. **Open** call for details.
📷 🌐 **glynnviviangallery.org**

🏛️ **Swansea Museum**
Victoria Rd. **Tel** 01792 653763.
Open Tue–Sun & public hols.
♿ limited. 📷
🌐 **swansea.gov.uk**

🏛️ **Dylan Thomas Centre**
Somerset Pl. **Tel** 01792 463980. **Open** daily. ♿ 🌐 **dylanthomas.com**

🏛️ **National Waterfront Museum**
Oystermouth Rd. **Tel** 02920 573600.
Open daily. ♿ 📷
🌐 **museumwales.ac.uk**

🌿 **National Botanic Garden of Wales**
Middleton Hall, Llanarthne.
Tel 01558 668768. **Open** daily.
Closed 25 Dec. 📷 ♿ 📷 📷 📷
🌐 **gardenofwales.org.uk**

⑫ Wild Wales Tour

This tour weaves across the Cambrian Mountains' windswept moors, green hills and high, deserted plateaux. New roads have been laid to the massive Llyn Brianne Reservoir, north of Llandovery, and the old drover's road across to Tregaron has a tarmac surface. But the area is still essentially a "wild Wales" of hidden hamlets, isolated farmsteads, brooding highlands and traditional, quiet market towns.

⑥ Llanidloes
The town was a centre of religious and social unrest in the 17th and 18th centuries *(see p441)*. There is a rare example of a free-standing Tudor market hall. The medieval church was restored in the late 19th century.

⑤ Elan Valley
This is an area of lakes and important wildlife habitats *(see p466)*.

④ Devil's Bridge
This is a popular, romantic beauty spot with waterfalls, rocks, wooded glades and an ancient stone bridge – built by the Devil, according to legend.

③ Strata Florida
This famous ruined abbey was an important political, religious and educational centre during the Middle Ages.

Tips for drivers

Length: 87 miles (140 km), including the scenic Claerwen Reservoir detour.
Stopping-off points: There are many good tea shops and restaurants in the market towns of Llandovery and Llanidloes. *(See also pp636–7.)*

② Twm Siôn Cati's Cave
This illustration shows the retreat of a 16th-century poet, Tom John, a Welsh outlaw who subsequently achieved respectability by marrying an heiress.

① Llandovery
At the confluence of two rivers, this pretty town has a ruined castle, a cobbled market square and charming Georgian façades.

Key

▬▬▬ Tour route
═══ Other roads

0 kilometres   5
0 miles   5

Map labels: Llangurig, Aberystwyth, Ystwyth, Craig Goch Reservoir, Rhayader, Garreg Ddu Reservoir, Claerwen Reservoir, Elan Village, Caban Coch Reservoir, Teifi, Tregaron, Llyn Brianne Reservoir, Carmarthen, Wye

Road numbers: B4518, A470, B4518, A470, A44, B4518, A44, A470, B4518, A4120, B4343, B4574, B4343, B4340, B4343, A485, B4343, A485, B4343, A483, A40, A40, A409

⑬ Brecon Beacons

The Brecon Beacons National Park covers 520 sq miles (1,345 sq km) from the Wales–England border almost all the way to Swansea. There are four mountain ranges within the park: the Black Mountain (to the west), Fforest Fawr, the Brecon Beacons and the Black Mountains (to the east). Much of the area consists of high, open country with smooth, grassy slopes on a bedrock of red sandstone. The park's southern rim has limestone crags, wooded gorges, waterfalls and caves. Visitors can enjoy many outdoor pursuits, from fishing in the numerous reservoirs to pony trekking, caving and walking.

Llyn y Fan Fach
This remote, myth-laden glacial lake is a 4 mile (6.5 km) walk from Llanddeusant.

Key

— A road

═ B road

═ Minor road

- - Footpath

KEY

① **The Black Mountain**, a largely overlooked wilderness of knife-edged ridges and high, empty moorland, fills the western corner of the National Park.

② **Fforest Fawr** ("Great Forest") is named after an area that was a medieval royal hunting ground.

③ **Brecon** is an old market town with handsome Georgian buildings.

④ **Tretower Castle and Court**, comprise a ruined Norman keep and a late-medieval manor house.

⑤ **The Black Mountains** form part of the border with England.

Carreg Cennen Castle
Spectacularly sited, the ruined medieval fortress of Carreg Cennen (see p442) stands on a sheer limestone cliff near the village of Trapp.

Dan-yr-Ogof Caves
A labyrinth of caves runs through the Brecon Beacons. Guided tours of two large caves are offered here.

Hay Bluff
At 677 m (2,221 ft), Hay Bluff looks out across border country. A narrow mountain road climbs from Hay-on-Wye to the Gospel Pass before dropping to Llanthony.

VISITORS' CHECKLIST

Practical Information
Powys. 🛈 National Park Visitor Centre, nr. Libanus, Powys. **Tel** 01874 623366. Carreg Cennen Castle, Trapp. **Tel** 01558 822291. **Open** daily. 🚗 Dan-yr-Ogof Caves, Abercraf. **Tel** 01639 730284. **Open** Apr–Oct. Llanthony Priory, Llanthony. **Tel** 01443 336 106. **Open** daily. Tretower Castle, Crickhowell. **Tel** 01874 730279. **Open** daily. **Closed** Nov–Mar. ♿ 🎁 📷

Transport
🚆 Abergavenny.

Llanthony Priory
This 12th-century ruin has simply carved but elegant stonework. In the 19th century a small hotel (still open) was built in part of the priory.

Monmouthshire and Brecon Canal
This peaceful waterway, completed in 1812, was once used to transport raw materials between Brecon and Newport. It is now popular with leisure boats.

Pen y Fan
At 886 m (2,907 ft), Pen y Fan is the highest point in South Wales. Its distinctive, flat-topped summit, once a Bronze Age burial ground (see pp46–7), can be reached by footpaths from Storey Arms on the A470.

For map symbols see back flap

⑭ Cardiff

Cardiff was first occupied by the Romans, who built a fort here in AD 55 *(see pp48–9)*. Little is known of its subsequent history until Robert FitzHamon *(see p476)*, a knight in the service of William the Conqueror, was given land here in 1093. By the 13th century, the settlement was substantial enough to be granted a royal charter, but it remained a quiet country town until the 1830s when the Bute family, who inherited land in the area, began to develop it as a port. By 1913 this was the world's busiest coal-exporting port, profiting from rail links with the South Wales mines. Its wealth paid for grandiose architecture, while the docklands became a raucous boom-town. Cardiff was confirmed as the first Welsh capital in 1955, by which time demand for coal was falling and the docks were in decline. The city is now being transformed by urban renewal programmes.

Fireplace detail in the Banqueting Hall, Cardiff Castle

City Hall's dome, adorned with a dragon, the emblem of Wales

Exploring Cardiff

Cardiff is a city with two focal points. The centre, laid out with Victorian and Edwardian streets and gardens, is the first of these. There is a Neo-Gothic castle and Neo-Classical civic buildings, as well as indoor shopping malls and a 19th-century **covered market**. Canopied arcades, lined with shops, lead off the main streets, the oldest being the **Royal Arcade** of 1858. The **Millennium Stadium** (on the site of Cardiff Arms Park, the first home of Welsh rugby) opened in 1999 with the Rugby World Cup, and is open for tours most days.

To the south of the centre, the docklands have been transformed into the second focal point by the creation of the freshwater lake and waterfront of Cardiff Bay. **Y Senedd**, which opened in 2006, houses the National Assembly for Wales. Free guided tours are available but booking is essential. Other attractions in the area are **Techniquest**, a hands-on science museum, and the impressive **Wales Millennium Centre**. A leading cultural venue, it stages a range of arts performances including musicals, ballet and stand-up comedy. It is also home to the Welsh National Opera.

The wooden **Norwegian Church** was first erected in 1868 for Norwegian sailors bringing wooden props for use in the coal pits of the South Wales valleys. Once surrounded by warehouses, it was taken apart and rebuilt during the dockland development.

Also in Cardiff Bay, the Red Dragon Centre houses a range of entertainment and food outlets, while the **Doctor Who Experience**, featuring memorabilia and props from the show, is also based on the waterfront. The classic BBC television series has been made in Cardiff since 2004, and many of the city's landmarks appear on screen.

🏰 Cardiff Castle
See pp476–7.

🏛 City Hall and Civic Centre
Cathays Park. **Tel** 029 2087 1727. **Open** Mon–Fri. **Closed** public hols. 🚻 📷 🔲 cardiffcityhall.com

Cardiff's civic centre of Neo-Classical buildings in white Portland stone is set among parks and avenues around Alexandra Gardens. The City Hall (1905), one of its first buildings, is dominated by its 60 m (200 ft) dome and clock tower.

The entrance to the Wales Millennium Centre

Members of the public can visit the first-floor Marble Hall, which is furnished with Siena marble columns and statues of Welsh heroes, among them St David, Wales's patron saint *(see pp468–9)*. Cardiff University is based in the Civic Centre, Cathays Park.

🏛 National Museum Cardiff

Cathays Park. **Tel** 029 2039 7951. **Open** Tue–Sun, public hols. **Closed** 1, 2 Jan & 24, 25 Dec. 🚻 🛗 📷 **w museumwales.ac.uk**

Opened in 1927, the museum occupies an impressive civic building with a colonnaded portico, guarded by a statue of David Lloyd George *(see p441)*. The art collection is among the finest in Europe, with works on display by Renoir, Monet and Van Gogh.

Statue of Welsh politician David Lloyd George

🏛 Craft in the Bay

The Flourish, Lloyd George Ave, Cardiff Bay. **Tel** 029 2048 4611. **Open** 10:30am–5:30pm daily. 🚻 📷

There is also an extensive craft gallery, where exhibitions are organized by the Makers' Guild in Wales. The gallery offers a wide variety of craft displays and demonstrations, including textile weaving and ceramic making.

Environs

Established during the 1940s at St Fagans, on the western edge of the city, the open-air **St Fagans National History Museum** was one of the first of its kind. Buildings from all over Wales, including workers' terraced cottages, farmhouses, a tollhouse, row of shops, chapel and old school-house have been carefully reconstructed within the 40-ha (100-acre) parklands, along with a recreated Celtic village. There is also a Tudor mansion which can be visited, boasting its own beautiful gardens in the grounds.

Llandaff Cathedral lies in a deep, grassy hollow beside the River Taf at Llandaff, 2 miles (3 km) northwest of the city centre. The cathedral was first a medieval building, occupying the site of a 6th-century monastic community.

Restored after suffering severe bomb damage during World War II, it was eventually reopened in 1957 with the addition of Sir Jacob Epstein's huge, stark statue, *Christus,* which is mounted on a concrete arch.

🏛 St Fagans National History Museum

St Fagans. **Tel** 029 2057 3500. **Open** daily. 🚻 🚼 **w museumwales.ac.uk**

Cardiff City Centre

① National Museum Cardiff
② City Hall & Civic Centre
③ *Cardiff Castle pp476–7*
④ Millennium Stadium
⑤ Cardiff Market
⑥ Craft in the Bay
⑦ Techniquest
⑧ Y Senedd
⑨ Norwegian Church

0 metres 500
0 yards 500

Key to Symbols *see back flap*

Cardiff Castle

Cardiff Castle began life as a Roman fort, whose remains are separated from later work by a band of red stone. A keep was built within the Roman ruins in the 12th century. Over the following 700 years, the castle passed to several powerful families and eventually to John Stuart, son of the Earl of Bute, in 1776. His great-grandson, the 3rd Marquess of Bute, employed the "eccentric genius", architect William Burges, who created an ornate mansion between 1869 and 1881, rich in medieval images and romantic detail.

Arab Room
The gilded ceiling, with Islamic marble and lapis lazuli decorations, was built in 1881.

★ Summer Smoking Room
This was part of a complete bachelor suite in the Clock Tower, that also included a Winter Smoking Room.

KEY

① **Clock Tower**

② **Herbert Tower**

③ **The Octagon Tower,** also called the Beauchamp Tower, is the setting for Burges's Chaucer Room, decorated with themes from the *Canterbury Tales (see p190).*

④ **The Bute Tower** had a suite of private rooms added in 1873, including a dining room, bedroom and sitting room.

Main entrance to apartments

1107 Castle inherited by Mabel FitzHamon, whose husband is made Lord of Glamorgan

AD 55 Roman fort constructed

1183 Castle damaged during Welsh uprising

1423–49 Beauchamp family adds the Octagon Tower and Great Hall ceiling

1445–1776 Castle passes in turn to Nevilles, Tudors and Herberts

1869 3rd Marquess of Bute begins reconstruction

| 1000 | 1200 | 1400 | 1600 | 1800 |

1093 First Norman fort built by Robert FitzHamon of Gloucester

1308–1414 Despenser family holds castle

1776 Bute family acquires the castle

1947 The castle is giv in trust to city of Care

Chaucer Room wall detail

★ **Banqueting Hall**
The design and decoration of this room
depicts the castle's history, making
impressively ingenious use of the murals
and castellated fireplace.

★ **Roof Garden**
Using tiles, shrubs and a
central fountain, Burges
aimed to create a
Mediterranean feel in this
indoor garden, turning it
into the crowning glory of
the castle's apartments.

★ **Library**
Carved figures representing ancient
characters of Greek, Assyrian, Hebrew
and Egyptian alphabets decorate the
library's chimneypiece.

Remains of Caerleon's amphitheatre, built in the 2nd century

❶ Caerleon

Newport. 👥 8,700. 🅘 5 High St (01633 422656). 🆆 newport.gov.uk

Together with York *(see pp408–9)* and Chester *(see pp314–15)*, Caerleon was one of only three fortress settlements in Britain built for the Romans' elite legionary troops. From AD 74 Caerleon *(Isca* to the Romans, after the River Usk, which flows beside the town) was home to the 2nd Augustan Legion, which had been sent to Wales to crush the native Silures tribe. The remains of their base now lie between the modern town and the river.

An altar at Caerleon's Legion Museum

The excavations at Caerleon are of great social and military significance. The Romans built not just a fortress for their crack 5,500-strong infantry division but a complete town to service their needs, including a stone amphitheatre. Judging by the results of the excavation work carried out since the archaeologist Sir Mortimer Wheeler unearthed the amphitheatre in 1926, Caerleon is one of the largest and most important Roman military sites in Europe. The defences enclosed an area of 20 ha (50 acres), with 64 rows of barracks, arranged in pairs, a hospital, and a bath-house complex.

Outside the settlement, the amphitheatre's large stone foundations have survived in an excellent state of preservation. Six thousand spectators could enjoy the blood sports and gladiators' combat.

More impressive still is the fortress baths complex, which opened to the public in the mid-1980s. The baths were designed to bring all the home comforts to an army posted to barbaric Britain. The Roman troops could take a dip in the open-air swimming pool, play sports in the exercise yard or covered hall, or enjoy a series of hot and cold baths.

Nearby are the foundations of the only Roman legionary barracks on view in Europe. The many excavated artifacts, including a collection of engraved gemstones, are displayed at the **National Roman Legion Museum**.

🏛 **National Roman Legion Museum**
High St. **Tel** 02920 573550. **Open** Mon– Sat, Sun (pm). **Closed** 1 Jan, 24–26 Dec. ♿ 🏠
🆆 museumwales.ac.uk

Big Pit Mining Museum, reminder of a vanished industrial society

❶ Blaenavon

Torfaen. 👥 6,350. 🅘 Church Rd (01495 742333). 🆆 visitblaenavon. co.uk

Commercial coal-mining has now all but ceased in the South Wales valleys – an area which only 100 years ago was gripped by the search for its "black gold". Though coal is no longer produced at **Big Pit** in Blaenavon, the **National Coal Museum** provides a vivid reminder of this tough industry. The Big Pit closed as a working mine in 1980, and opened three years later as a museum. Visitors follow a marked-out route around the mine's surface workings to the miners' baths, the blacksmith's forge, the workshops and the engine house. There is also a replica of an underground gallery, where mining methods are explained. But the climax of any visit to Big Pit is beneath the ground. Kitted out with helmets, lamps and safety batteries, visitors descend by cage 90 m (300 ft) down the mineshaft and then are guided by ex-miners on a tour of the underground workings and pit ponies' stables.

Across the valley from Big Pit stand the 18th-century smelting furnaces and workers' cottages that were once part of the **Blaenavon Ironworks**, and which are now a museum.

🏛 **Big Pit National Coal Museum**
Blaenavon. **Tel** 01495 790311. **Open** mid-Feb–Nov: daily; Dec & Jan: phone for details. ♿ phone first. 🎫 📷 🏠

🏛 **Blaenavon Ironworks**
North St. **Tel** 01495 792615. **Open** daily (Nov–Mar: Fri–Sun). 🎫 📷 🏠

❶ Monmouth

Monmouthshire. 👥 9,000. 🚌 🅘 Shire Hall (01600 775257). 🏠 Fri, Sat. 🆆 wyedeantourism.co.uk

This market town, which sits at the confluence of the Wye and Monnow rivers, has many historical associations. The 11th-century castle, behind Agincourt Square, is in ruins but the **Regimental Museum**, beside it, remains open to the public. The castle was the birthplace of

Monnow Bridge in Monmouth, once a watchtower and jail

Henry V *(see p53)* in 1387. Statues of Henry V (on the façade of Shire Hall) and Charles Stewart Rolls stand in the Square. Rolls, born at nearby Hendre, was the co-founder of Rolls-Royce cars.

Lord Horatio Nelson *(see p58)*, the famous admiral, visited Monmouth in 1802. An excellent collection of Nelson memorabilia, gathered by Lady Llangattock, mother of Charles Rolls, is displayed at the **Nelson Museum**.

Monmouth was the county town of the old Monmouthshire. The wealth of elegant Georgian buildings, including the elaborate **Shire Hall**, which dominates Agincourt Square, reflect its former status. The most famous architectural feature in Monmouth is **Monnow Bridge**, a narrow

13th-century gateway on its western approach, thought to be the only surviving fortified bridge gate in Britain.

For a lovely view over the town, climb the Kymin, a 256 m (840 ft) hill crowned by a **Naval Temple** built in 1801.

Monmouth is the world's first Wikipedia town. QR barcodes placed in strategic places offer visitors with smart phones up-to-date information.

🏰 Monmouth Castle and Regimental Museum
The Castle. **Tel** 01600 772175. **Open** Apr–Oct: daily; Nov–Mar: on request. **Closed** 25 Dec. 🔥 📷 🆆 monmouth castlemuseum.org.uk

🏛 Nelson Museum
Priory St. **Tel** 01600 710630. **Open** daily (Sun: pm). 🔥 📷

⓲ Tintern Abbey

Monmouthshire. **Tel** 01291 689251. 🚌 Chepstow then bus. **Open** daily **Closed** 1 Jan, 24–26 Dec. 📷 🎫 🔥 🆆 cadw.wales.gov.uk

Ever since the 18th century, travellers have been enchanted by Tintern's setting in the steep and wooded Wye Valley and by the majestic ruins of its abbey. Poets were often inspired by the scene. Wordsworth's sonnet, *Lines composed a few miles above Tintern Abbey*, embodied his romantic view of landscape:

once again
Do I behold these steep and lofty cliffs,
That on a wild, secluded scene impress
Thoughts of more deep seclusion

The abbey was founded in 1131 by Cistercian monks, who cultivated the surrounding lands (now forest), and developed it as an influential religious centre. By the 14th century this was the richest abbey in Wales, but along with other monasteries it was dissolved in 1536. Its skeletal ruins are now left roofless and exposed, the soaring arches and windows giving them a poignant grace and beauty.

Tintern Abbey in the Wye Valley, in the past a thriving centre of religion and learning, now a romantic ruin

SCOTLAND

Scotland at a Glance

Stretching from the rich farmlands of the Borders to a chain of
isles only a few degrees south of the Arctic Circle, the Scottish
landscape has a diversity without parallel in Britain. As you
travel northwest from Edinburgh, the land becomes more
mountainous and its archaeological treasures more
numerous. In the far northwest, Scotland's earliest
relics stand upon the oldest rock on Earth.

Stornoway

Skye *(see pp538–9)*
renowned for its
dramatic scenery,
has one of
Scotland's most
striking coastlines.
On the east coast, a
stream plunges over
Kilt Rock, a cliff of
hexagonal basalt
columns named
after its likeness to
an item of Scottish
national dress.

Tarbert

Ullapool

Lochmaddy

Uig

HIGHLAND

Kyle of
Lochalsh

Mallaig

Fort Will

Tobermory

Oban

Inverary

ARGYLL
AND BUTE

Greenock

Pa

AYRS

The Trossachs *(see pp498–9)* are a beautiful range of hills
straddling the border between the Highlands and the
Lowlands. At their heart, the forested slopes of Ben Venue rise
above the still waters of Loch Achray.

Campbeltown

Ayr

DUMF
ANL
GALLO

Stranraer

Culzean Castle *(see pp526–7)*
stands on a cliff's edge on the
Firth of Clyde, amid an extensive
country park. One of the jewels
of the Lowlands, Culzean is a
magnificent showcase of work
by the Scottish-born architect,
Robert Adam *(see p32)*.

◀ Tower of the Balmoral Hotel in Edinburgh

SHETLAND

Lerwick

0 kilometres 50

0 miles 50

Locator Map

ORKNEY

Kirkwall

Thurso

Wick

Dornoch

The Cairngorms *(see pp548–9)* cover an area prized for its beauty and diversity of wildlife, though there are also many historical relics to be found, such as this early 18th-century arch at Carrbridge.

Elgin

Fraserburgh

MORAY

verness

Peterhead

HIGHLANDS
ND ISLANDS
(See pp528–53)

ABERDEEN-
SHIRE

Aberdeen

Braemar

Royal Deeside *(see pp544–5)* in the Grampians has been associated with British royalty since Queen Victoria bought Balmoral Castle in 1852.

ANGUS

Montrose

Forfar

Arbroath

ERTH AND
KINROSS

Dundee

Perth

St Andrews

LING

FIFE

Stirling

Kirkcaldy

Dunfermline

Dunbar

sgow

Edinburgh

Motherwell

Edinburgh
(see pp508–15) is the capital of Scotland. Between its medieval castle and the Palace of Holyroodhouse stretches the Royal Mile – a concentration of historic sights, ranging from the old Scottish Parliament buildings to the house of John Knox. Georgian terraces predominate in the New Town.

Peebles

Galashiels

SCOTTISH
BORDERS

HE LOWLANDS
(See pp494–527)

Hawick

umfries

Castle
Douglas

The Burrell Collection *(see pp524–5)*, on the southern outskirts of Glasgow, is a museum of some of the city's greatest art treasures. It is housed in a spacious, glass building opened in 1983.

A PORTRAIT OF SCOTLAND

From the grassy hills of the Borders to the desolate Cuillin Ridge of Skye, the landscape of Scotland is breathtaking in its variety. Lonely glens, sparkling lochs and ever-changing skies give the land a challenging character, which is reflected in the qualities of the Scottish people. Tough and self-reliant, they have made some of Britain's finest soldiers, its boldest explorers and most astute industrialists.

The Scots are proud of their separate identity and their own systems of law and education and, in 1998, voted over-whelmingly for their own parliament. Many Scots welcomed this as a long-awaited reversal of the Act of Union that united the English and Scottish parliaments in 1707. But despite their national pride, they are not a homogeneous people, the main division is between traditionally Gaelic-speaking Highlanders, and the Lowlanders who spoke Scots, a form of Middle English which is now extinct. Today, though Gaelic survives (chiefly in the Western Isles), most people speak regional dialects or richly accented English. Many Scottish surnames derive from Gaelic: the prefix "mac" means "son of". A Norse heritage can be found in the far north, where Shetlanders welcome the annual return of the sun during the Viking fire festival, Up Helly Aa.

In the 16th century, a suspicion of authority and dislike of excessive

A hammer-thrower at the Braemar Games

flamboyance attracted many Scots to the Presbyterian church with its absence of bishops and its stress on simple worship. The Presbyterian Church of Scotland was established in 1689, though a substantial Catholic minority remained which today predominates in the crofting (small-scale farming) communities of the Western Isles. Now sparsely populated, the Isles preserve a rural culture that once dominated the Highlands, a region that is the source of much that is distinctively Scottish. The clan system originated there, along with the tartans, the bagpipes and such unique sports as tossing the caber – a large tree trunk. Highland sports, along with traditional dances, are still performed at annual games (see p68).

Edinburgh bagpiper

Resourcefulness has always been a prominent Scottish virtue, and Scotland has produced a disproportionately high number of Britain's geniuses. James Watt designed the first effective steam engine to power the Industrial Revolution, while Adam Smith became the 18th century's most influential economist. In the 19th century, James Simpson discovered the anaesthetic qualities of chloroform, James Young developed the world's first

The Viking festival, Up Helly Aa, in Lerwick, Shetland

one of 19th century-America's biggest business empires.

With some of the harshest weather conditions in Europe it is perhaps less surprising that Scotland has bred numerous explorers, including polar explorer William Speirs Bruce and African missionary David Livingstone. There is also a strong intellectual and literary tradition, from the 18th-century philosopher David Hume, through novelists Sir Walter Scott and Robert Louis Stevenson, to the poetry of Robert Burns. Today Scotland hosts a variety of arts festivals, such as Edinburgh's.

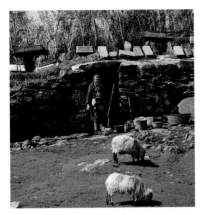

A traditional stone croft on the Isle of Lewis

oil refinery and Alexander Bell revolutionized communications by inventing the telephone. The 20th century saw one of the greatest advances in medicine with the discovery of penicillin by Alexander Fleming.

The Scots are also known for being shrewd businessmen, and have always been prominent in finance: both the Bank of England and the Royal Bank of France were founded by Scots, while Andrew Carnegie created

Detail of Edinburgh's Festival Fringe office

With a population density only one-fifth of England and Wales, Scotland has vast tracts of untenanted land which offer numerous outdoor pleasures. It is richly stocked with game, and the opening of the grouse season on 12 August is a highlight on the social calendar. Fishing and hill-walking are popular and in winter thousands flock to the Cairngorms and Glencoe for skiing. Though the weather may be harsher than elsewhere, the Scots will claim that the air is purer – and that enjoying rugged conditions is what distinguishes them from their soft southern neighbours.

The blue waters of Loch Achray in the heart of the Trossachs, north of Glasgow

The History of Scotland

Since the Roman invasion of Britain, Scotland's history has been characterized by its resistance to foreign domination. The Romans never conquered the area, and when the Scots extended their kingdom to its present boundary in 1018, a long era of conflict began with England. After many wars, the Scots finally accepted union with the "auld enemy": first with the union of crowns, and then with the Union of Parliament in 1707. In 1999 the inauguration of the Scottish Parliament was a dramatic change.

An elaborately carved Pictish stone at Aberlemno, Angus

Early History

There is much evidence in Scotland of important prehistoric population centres, particularly in the Western Isles, which were peopled mostly by Picts who originally came from the Continent. By the time Roman Governor Julius Agricola invaded in AD 81, there were at least 17 independent tribes, including the Britons in the southwest, for him to contend with.

The Romans reached north to the Forth and Clyde valleys, but the Highlands deterred them from going further. By 120, they had retreated to the line where the Emperor Hadrian had built his wall to keep the Picts at bay (not far from today's border). By 163 the Romans had retreated south for the last time. The Celtic influence began when "Scots" arrived from Ireland in the 6th century, bringing the Gaelic language with them. The Picts and Scots united under Kenneth McAlpin in 843, but the Britons remained separate until 1018, when they became part of the Scottish kingdom.

The English Claim

The Norman Kings regarded Scotland as part of their territory but seldom pursued the claim. William the Lion of Scotland recognized English sovereignty by the Treaty of Falaise (1174), though English control never spread to the northwest. In 1296 William Wallace, supported by the French (the start of the Auld Alliance, which lasted two centuries), began the long war of independence. During this bitter conflict, Edward I seized the sacred Stone of Destiny from Scone (see p502), and took it to Westminster Abbey. The war lasted for more than 100 years. Its great hero was Robert the Bruce, who defeated the English in 1314 at Bannockburn. The English held the upper hand after that, even though the Scots would not accept their rule.

John Knox statue in Edinburgh

The Road to Union

The seeds of union between the crowns were sown in 1503 when James IV of Scotland married Margaret Tudor, daughter of Henry VII. When her brother, Henry VIII, came to the throne, James sought to assert independence but was defeated and killed at Flodden Field in 1513. His granddaughter, Mary, Queen of Scots (see p515), married the French Dauphin in order to cement the Auld Alliance and gain assistance in her claim to the throne of her English cousin, Elizabeth I. She had support from the Catholics wanting to see an end to Protestantism in England and Scotland. However,

Bruce in Single Combat at Bannockburn (1906) by John Hassall fiery preacher John Knox won support for the Protestants and established the Presbyterian Church in 1560. Mary's Catholicism led to the loss of her Scottish throne in 1568, and her subsequent flight to England, following defeat at Langside. Finally, after nearly 20 years of imprisonment she was executed for treason by Elizabeth in 1587.

Union and Rebellion

On Elizabeth I's death in 1603, Mary's son, James VI of Scotland, succeeded to the English throne and became James I, king of both countries. Thus the crowns were united, though it was 100 years before the formal Union of Parliaments in 1707. During that time, religious differences within the country reached boiling point. There were riots when the Catholic-influenced Charles I restored bishops to the Church of Scotland and authorized the printing of a new prayer book. This culminated in the signing, in Edinburgh in 1638, of the National Covenant, a document that condemned all Catholic doctrines. Though the Covenanters were suppressed, the Protestant William of Orange took over the English throne in 1688 and the crown passed out of Scottish hands.

In 1745, Bonnie Prince Charlie *(see p539)*, descended from the Stuart kings, tried to seize the throne from the Hanoverian George II. He marched far into England, but was driven back and defeated at Culloden field *(see p541)* in 1746.

The factories on Clydeside, once creators of the world's greatest ships

Industrialization and Social Change

In the late 18th and 19th centuries, technological progress transformed Scotland from a nation of crofters to an industrial powerhouse. In the notorious Highland Clearances *(see p535)*, from the 1780s on, landowners ejected tenants from their smallholdings and gave the land over to sheep and other livestock. The first ironworks was established in 1760 and was soon followed by coal mining, steel production and shipbuilding on the Clyde. Canals were cut, railways and bridges built.

A strong socialist movement developed as workers sought to improve their conditions. Keir Hardie, an Ayrshire coal miner, in 1892 became the first socialist elected to parliament, and in 1893 founded the Independent Labour Party. The most enduring symbol of this time is the spectacular Forth rail bridge *(see p506)*.

Scotland Today

Although the status of the country appeared to have been settled in 1707, a strong nationalist sentiment remained and was heightened by the Depression, which had severe effects on the heavily industrialized Clydeside.

This was when the Scottish National Party formed, advocating self-rule. The Nationalists asserted themselves in 1950 by stealing the Stone of Scone from Westminster Abbey.

The discovery of North Sea oil in 1970 sparked a nationalist revival and, in 1979, the Government promised to establish a separate assembly if 40 per cent of the Scottish electorate endorsed the plan in a referendum. This figure was finally surpassed in 1998, and the Scottish Parliament was inaugurated in 1999. A referendum on full independence is scheduled for September 2014.

A North Sea oil rig, helping to provide prosperity in the 1970s

Articles of Union between England and Scotland, 1707

Clans and Tartans

The clan system, by which Highland society was divided into tribal groups led by autocratic chiefs, can be traced to the 12th century, when clans were already known to wear the chequered wool cloth later called tartan. All members of the clan bore the name of their chief, but not all were related by blood. Though they had noble codes of hospitality, the clansmen had to be warriors to protect their herds, as can be seen from their mottoes. After the Battle of Culloden *(see p541)*, all the clan lands were forfeited to the Crown, and the wearing of tartan was banned for nearly 100 years.

The Mackays, also known as the Clan Morgan, won lasting renown during the Thirty Years War.

The MacLeods are of Norse heritage. The clan chief still lives in Dunvegan Castle, Skye *(see p538)*.

The MacDonalds were the most powerful of all the clans, holding the title of Lords of the Isles.

Clan Chief

The chief was the clan's patriarch, judge and leader in war, commanding absolute loyalty from his clansmen who gave military service in return for his protection. The chief summoned his clan to do battle by sending a runner across his land bearing a burning cross.

Bonnet with eagle feathers, clan crest and plant badge.

Basket-hilted sword

Dirk

Sporran, or pouch, made of badger's skin.

Feileadhmor, or "great plaid" (the early kilt), wrapped around waist and shoulder.

The Mackenzies received much of the lands of Kintail *(see p534)* from David II in 1362.

The Campbells were a widely feared clan who fought the Jacobites in 1746 *(see p541)*.

The Black Watch, raised in 1729 to keep peace in the Highlands, was one of the Highland regiments in which the wearing of tartan survived. After 1746, civilians were punished by exile for up to seven years for wearing tartan.

The Sinclairs came from France in the 11th century and became Earls of Caithness in 1455.

The Frasers came to Britain from France with William the Conqueror *(see p51)* in 1066.

George IV, dressed as a Highlander, visited Edinburgh in 1822, the year of the tartan revival. Many tartan "setts" (patterns) date from this time, as the original ones were lost.

The Gordons were famously good soldiers; the clan motto is "by courage, not by craft".

The Stuarts were Scotland's royal dynasty. Their motto was "no one harms me with impunity".

The Douglas clan were prominent in Scottish history, though their origin is unknown.

Clan Territories

The territories of 10 prominent clans are marked here with their clan crests. Dress tartans tend to be colourful, while hunting tartans are darker.

Plant Badges

Each clan had a plant associated with its territory. It was worn on the bonnet, especially on the day of battle.

Scots pine was worn by the MacGregors of Argyll.

Rowan berries were worn by the Clan Malcolm.

Ivy was worn by the Clan Gordon of Aberdeenshire.

Spear thistle, now a national symbol, was a Stuart badge.

Cotton grass was worn by the Clan Henderson.

Highland Clans Today

Once the daily dress of the clansmen, the kilt is now largely reserved for formal occasions. The one-piece *feileadh-mor* has been replaced by the *feileadh-beag*, or "small plaid", made from approximately 7 m (23 ft) of material with a double apron fastened at the front with a silver pin. Though they exist now only in name, the clans are still a strong source of pride for Scots, and many still live in areas traditionally belonging to their clans. Many visitors to Britain can trace their Scots ancestry *(see p35)* to the Highlands.

Modern Highland formal dress

Evolution of the Scottish Castle

There are few more romantic sights in the British Isles than a Scottish castle on an island or at a lochside. These formidable retreats, often in remote settings, were essential all over the Highlands, where incursions and strife between the clans were common. From the earliest Pictish *brochs (see p47)* and Norman-influenced motte and bailey castles, the distinctively Scottish stone tower-house evolved, first appearing in the 14th century. By the mid-17th century fashion had become more important than defence, and there followed a period in which numerous huge Scottish palaces were built.

Detail of the Baroque façade, Drumlanrig

Motte and Bailey

These castles first appeared in the 12th century. They stood atop two adjacent mounds enclosed by a wall, or palisade, and defensive ditches. The higher mound, or motte, was the most strongly defended as it held the keep and chief's house. The lower bailey was where the people lived. Of these castles little more than earthworks remain today.

Keep, with chief's house, lookout and main defence

All that remains today of Duffus Castle, Morayshire

Duffus Castle, (c.1150), was atypically made of stone rather than wood. Its fine defensive position dominates the surrounding flatlands north of Elgin.

Bailey enclosing dwellings and storehouses

Motte of earth or rock, some-times partially man-made

Early Tower-House

Designed to deter local attacks rather than a major assault, the first tower-houses appeared in the 13th century, though their design lived on for 400 years. They were built initially on a rectangular plan, with a single tower divided into three or four floors. The walls were unadorned, with few windows. Defensive structures were on top, and extra space was made by building adjoining towers. Extensions were made as vertically as possible, to minimize the area open to attack.

Crenellated parapet for sentries

Featureless, straight walls with arrow slits for windows

Claypotts Castle (c.1570) with uniquely projecting garrets above its towers

Small, inconspicuous doorway

Braemar Castle (c.1630), a conglomeration of extended towers

Neidpath Castle, standing upon a steep rocky crag above the River Tweed, is an L-shaped towerhouse dating from the late 14th century. Once a stronghold for Charles II, its walls still bear damage from a siege conducted by Oliver Cromwell *(see p56)*.

Later Tower-House

Though the requirements of defence were being replaced by those of comfort, the style of the early tower-house remained popular. By the 17th century, wings for accommodation were being added around the original tower (often creating a courtyard). The battlements and turrets were kept more for decorative than defensive reasons.

Drum Castle *(see p545)*, a 13th-century keep with a mansion house extension from 1619

Priest's room with secret access   The original 15th-century tower-house

Round angle tower, containing stairway

A 16th-century horizontal extension

Traquair House *(see p517)*, by the Tweed, is reputedly the oldest continuously inhabited house in Scotland. The largely unadorned, roughcast exterior dates to the 16th century, when a series of extensions were built around the original 15th-century tower-house.

Decorative, corbelled turret

Blair Castle *(see p547)*, incorporating a medieval tower

Classical Palace

By the 18th century, the defensive imperative had passed and castles were built in the manner of country houses, rejecting the vertical tower-house in favour of a horizontal plan (though the building of imitation fortified buildings continued into the 19th century with the mock-Baronial trend). Outside influences came from all over Europe, including Renaissance and Gothic revivals, and echoes of French châteaux.

Dunrobin Castle (c.1840), Sutherland

Larger windows due to a lesser need for defence

Balustrades instead of battlements

Decorative cupola

Drumlanrig Castle *(see p518)* was built in the 17th century. There are many traditional Scots aspects as well as such Renaissance features as the decorated stairway and façade.

Renaissance-style colonnade

Baroque horseshoe stairway

The Flavours of Scotland

At its best, Scottish food is full of the natural flavour of the countryside. Served with few sauces or spices, its meat is lean and tasty. Beef doesn't get better than Aberdeen Angus, the lamb is full flavoured, and the venison superb. Scottish salmon and trout are renowned, but there are also excellent mussels, lobster and crabs. Wheat does not grow here, so oatcakes and bannocks (flat, round loaves) replace bread. The Scots have a sweet tooth, not just for cakes and shortbread but also for toffee and butterscotch.

Smoked Salmon

Pedigree Aberdeen Angus cattle grazing the Scottish moors

The Lowlands

The pasturelands of southern Scotland nourish dairy cattle and sheep, producing cheeses such as Bonnet, Bonchester and Galloway Cheddar. To accompany them are summer fruits such as loganberries, tayberries and strawberries that ripen in the Carse of Gowrie beside the River Tay. Oats, the principal cereal, appears in much Scottish cookery, from porridge to oatcakes. Pearl barley is also a staple, used in Scotch Broth (made with mutton and vegetables) or in a milk pudding. Oats are also used in the making of haggis, a round sausage of sheep or venison offal – the "chieftain o' the puddin' race", as the poet Robert Burns described it. It is often served with "neeps and tatties" (mashed swede and potato).

The Highlands

From the Highlands comes wonderful game, including grouse, partridge, capercaillie (a large type of grouse) and deer. Fish are smoked around the coast, the west coast producing kippers, the east coast Finnan haddock, notably Arbroath Smokies. Smoked white fish is the main ingredient of Cullen Skink, a soup served on Burns' Night.

Lobster Trout Oysters Salmon
Mussels
Selection of fresh Scottish fish and seafood

Traditional Scottish Food

Kippers (oak-smoked herrings) are one way to start the day in Scotland, and porridge – traditionally served with salt rather than sugar – is another, although oatcakes or some other kind of griddled scone are usually present. A bowl of porridge would once last all week, just as one-pot Scotch broths bubbled in iron cauldrons over peat fires for days. Sometimes broths were made with kale or lentils, or they might contain an old boiling fowl and leeks, in which case they were known as cock-a-leekie. Any leftover meat went into making stovies, a potato and onion hash. The evening meal in Scotland is traditionally "high tea" taken in the early evening which might start with smoked fish, cold meats and pies, followed by shortbread, fruit cake or drop scones, all washed down with cups of tea.

Oats

Haggis with neeps and tatties
This is the definitive Scottish dish, traditionally served on Burns' Night (25 January).

How Whisky is Made

Traditionally made from just barley, yeast and stream water, Scottish whisky (from the Gaelic *usquebaugh*, or the "water of life") takes a little over three weeks to produce, though it must be given at least three years to mature. Maturation usually takes place in oak casks, often in barrels previously used for sherry. The art of blending was pioneered in Edinburgh in the 1860s.

Barley grass

1 Malting is the first stage. Barley grain is soaked in water and spread on the malting floor. With regular turning the grain germinates, producing a "green malt". Germination stimulates the production of enzymes which turn the starches into fermentable sugars.

2 Drying of the barley halts germination after 12 days of malting. This is done over a peat fire in a pagoda-shaped malt-kiln. The peat-smoke gives flavour to the malt and eventually to the mature whisky. The malt is gleaned of germinated roots and then milled.

3 Mashing of the ground malt, or "grist", occurs in a large vat, or "mash tun", which holds a vast quantity of hot water. The malt is soaked and begins to dissolve, producing a sugary solution called "wort", which is then extracted for fermentation.

4 Fermentation occurs when yeast is added to the cooled wort in wooden vats, or "wash-backs". The mixture is stirred for hours as the yeast turns the sugar into alcohol, producing a clear liquid called "wash".

5 Distillation involves boiling the wash twice so that the alcohol vaporizes and condenses. In copper "pot stills", the wash is distilled – first in the "wash still", then in the "spirit still". Now purified, with an alcohol content of 57 per cent, the result is young whisky.

6 Maturation is the final process. The whisky mellows in oak casks for a legal minimum of three years. Premium brands give the whisky a 10- to 15-year maturation, though some are given up to 50 years.

Traditional drinking vessels, or *quaichs*, made of silver

Blended whiskies are made from a mixture of up to 50 different single malts.

Single malts vary according to regional differences in the peat and stream water used.

THE LOWLANDS

Clyde Valley · Central Scotland · Fife · The Lothians Ayrshire · Dumfries and Galloway · The Borders

Southeast of the Highland boundary fault line lies a part of Scotland very different in character from its northern neighbour. If the Highlands embody the romance of Scotland, the Lowlands have traditionally been her powerhouse. Lowlanders have always prospered in agriculture and in industry and commerce.

Being the region of Scotland closest to the English border, the Lowlands inevitably became the crucible of Scottish history. For centuries after the Romans built the Antonine Wall *(see p48)* across the Forth–Clyde isthmus, the area was engulfed in conflict. The Borders are scattered with the castles of a territory in uneasy proximity to rapacious neighbours, and the ramparts of Stirling Castle overlook no fewer than seven different battlefields fought over in the cause of independence.

The ruins of medieval abbeys, such as Melrose, also bear witness to the dangers of living on the invasion route from England, though the woollen trade founded by their monks still flourishes in Peebles and Hawick.

North of the Borders lies Edinburgh, the cultural and administrative capital of Scotland. With its Georgian squares dominated by a medieval castle, it is one of Europe's most elegant cities. While the 18th and 19th centuries saw a great flowering of the arts in Edinburgh, the city of Glasgow became a merchant city second only to London. Fuelled by James Watt's development of the steam engine in the 1840s, Glasgow became the cradle of Scotland's Industrial Revolution, which created a prosperous cotton industry and launched the world's greatest ships.

Both cities retain this dynamism today: Edinburgh annually hosts the world's largest open-access arts festival, and Glasgow is acclaimed as a model of post-industrial renaissance.

A juggler performing at the Edinburgh Festival, an annual arts extravaganza

◀ The Old Town quarter of Edinburgh, with the castle in the background

Exploring the Lowlands

The Lowlands are traditionally all the land south of the fault line stretching northeast from Loch Lomond to Stonehaven. Confusingly, they include plenty of wild upland country. The region illustrates the diversity of Scotland's scenery. The wooded valleys and winding rivers of the borders give way to the stern hills of the Cheviots and Lammermuirs. Fishing villages cling to the rocky east coast, while the Clyde coast and its islands are dotted with holiday towns. Inland lies the Trossachs, a romantic area of mountain, loch and woodland east of Loch Lomond that is a magnet for walkers (see pp40–41) and well within reach of Glasgow.

Loch Katrine seen from the Trossachs

Sights at a Glance

Walks and Tours

For additional map symbols see back flap

Key

- ━━━ Motorway
- ━━━ Major road
- ━━━ Secondary road
- ┄┄┄ Minor road
- ━━━ Scenic route
- ┈┈┈ Main railway
- ─── Minor railway
- △ Summit

Getting Around

Access to the Lowlands is made easy from the south by the M74 to Glasgow or A702 to Edinburgh which connect the region to the M6 in England. Other motorways lead to Edinburgh, Glasgow, Stirling and Perth, north of which A roads lead to the Highlands. Glasgow, Edinburgh and Glasgow Prestwick have international airports. Ferries from Ardrossan provide access to the Isle of Arran.

0 kilometres 20

0 miles 20

Edinburgh Castle viewed from Princes Street

❶ The Trossachs

Combining the ruggedness of the Grampians with the pastoral tranquillity of the Borders, this beautiful region of craggy hills and sparkling lochs is the colourful meeting place of the Lowlands and Highlands. Home to a wide variety of wildlife, including the golden eagle, peregrine falcon, red deer and the wildcat, the Trossachs have inspired numerous writers, including Sir Walter Scott *(see p516)* who made the area the setting for several of his novels. It was the home of Scotland's folk hero, Rob Roy, who was so well known that, in his own lifetime, he was fictionalized in *The Highland Rogue* (1723), a novel attributed to Daniel Defoe.

Loch Katrine
The setting of Sir Walter Scott's *Lady of the Lake* (1810), this freshwater loch can be explored on the Victorian steamer SS *Sir Walter Scott*, which cruises from the Trossachs Pier.

Loch Lomond
Britain's largest freshwater lake was immortalized in a ballad composed by a local Jacobite soldier, dying far from home. He laments that though he will return home before his companions who travel on the high road, he will be doing so on the low road (of death).

Key

- ▬▬ A road
- ▬▬ B road
- ═══ Minor road
- – – Footpath

0 metres 5
0 yards 5

Fort William ↑

Inveruglas •

Loch Arklet

B829

A82

Tarbet •

BEN LOMOND
▲ 974 m
3,196 ft

Kinlocha

BEN UIRD
▲ 596 m
1,955 ft

B837

B837

• Luss

①

Balma

A82

LOCH LOMOND

A82

• Balloch
i

↓ Glasgow

KEY

① **The West Highland Way**, provides a good footpath through the area.

② **The Duke's Pass**, between Callander and Aberfoyle, affords some of the finest views in the area.

③ **Rob Roy's grave**

Luss
With its exceptionally picturesque cottages, Luss is one of the prettiest villages in the Lowlands. Surrounded by grassy hills, it occupies one of the most scenic parts of Loch Lomond's western shore.

Inchmahome Priory
Mary, Queen of Scots (see p515) was hidden in this island priory to escape the armies of Henry VIII (see p516).

Callander
This is the most popular town from which to explore the Trossachs and films of the area are shown at the information centre.

Rob Roy (1671–1734)

Robert MacGregor, known as Rob Roy (Red Robert) from the colour of his hair, grew up as a herdsman near Loch Arklet. After a series of harsh winters, he took to raiding richer Lowland properties to feed his clan, and was declared an outlaw by the Duke of Montrose who then burned his house to the ground. After this, Rob's Jacobite (see p541) sympathies became inflamed by his desire to avenge the crime. Plundering the duke's lands and repeatedly escaping from prison earned him a reputation similar to England's Robin Hood (see p340). He was pardoned in 1725 and spent his last years freely in Balquhidder, where he is buried.

Queen Elizabeth Forest Park
There are woodland walks through this vast tract of countryside, home to black grouse and red deer, between Loch Lomond and Aberfoyle.

The 17th-century town house of the Dukes of Argyll, Stirling

❷ Stirling

Stirling. 🏙 34,000. 🚆 🚌
🛈 St John St (01786 475019).
🌐 visitstirling.org

Situated between the Ochil Hills and the Campsie Fells, Stirling grew up around its castle, historically one of Scotland's most important fortresses. Below the castle the Old Town is still protected by the original 16th-century walls, built to keep Mary Queen of Scots safe from Henry VIII. The medieval **Church of the Holy Rude**, on Castle Wynd, where the infant James VI was crowned in 1567, has one of Scotland's few surviving hammerbeam oak roofs. The ornate façade of **Mar's Wark** is all that remains of a grand palace which, though never completed, was commissioned in 1570 by the 1st Earl of Mar. It was destroyed by the Jacobites (*see p541*) in 1746. Opposite stands the beautiful 17th-century town house of the Dukes of Argyll.

Environs

Two miles (3 km) south, the **Bannockburn Heritage Centre** stands by the field where Robert the Bruce defeated the English (*see p486*). After the battle, he dismantled the castle so it would not fall back into English hands. A bronze equestrian statue commemorates the man who is an icon of Scottish independence.

🛈 **Bannockburn Heritage Centre**
Glasgow Rd. **Tel** 0844 493 2139.
Open Mar–Oct: 10am–5:30pm daily; other times by appointment.
Closed 24 Dec–Feb. ♿ ♿ NTS

Stirling Castle

Rising high on a rocky crag, this magnificent castle, which dominated Scottish history for centuries, now remains one of the finest examples of Renaissance architecture in Scotland. Legend says that King Arthur (*see p289*) wrested the original castle from the Saxons, but there is no evidence of a castle before 1124. The present building dates from the 15th and 16th centuries and was last defended, against the Jacobites (*see p541*), in 1746. From 1881 to 1964 the castle was a depot for recruits into the Argyll and Sutherland Highlanders, though now it serves no military function.

Entrance

KEY

① **Forework**

② **Prince's Tower**

③ **The King's Old Building** houses the Regimental Museum of the Argyll and Sutherland Highlanders.

④ **Nether Bailey**

⑤ **The Great Hall**, built in 1500, has been restored to its former splendour.

⑥ **The Elphinstone Tower** was made into a gun platform in 1714.

Robert the Bruce
In the esplanade, this modern statue shows Robert the Bruce sheathing his sword after the Battle of Bannockburn in 1314.

★ **Palace**
The restored interiors of the royal apartments contain the Stirling Heads. These Renaissance roundels depict 38 figures, thought to be contemporary members of the royal court.

VISITORS' CHECKLIST

Practical Information
Castle Esplanade, Stirling.
Tel 01786 450000. **Open** 9:30am–6pm (Oct–Mar: to 5pm) daily.
Closed 25 & 26 Dec. 🖼 except museum. ♿ limited. 📷 🔲 💻
📱 🆆 stirlingcastle.gov.uk

★ **Chapel Royal**
Seventeenth-century frescoes by Valentine Jenkins adorn the chapel, reconstructed in 1594.

Grand Battery
Seven guns stand on this parapet, built in 1708 during a strengthening of defences following the revolution of 1688 *(see p57)*.

Stirling Battles

At the highest navigable point of the Forth and holding the pass to the Highlands, Stirling occupied a key position in Scotland's struggles for independence. Seven battlefields can be seen from the castle; the 67-m (220-ft) Wallace Monument at Abbey Craig recalls William Wallace's defeat of the English at Stirling Bridge in 1297, foreshadowing Bruce's victory in 1314 *(see p486)*.

The Victorian Wallace Monument

Stirling Castle in the Time of the Stuarts, painted by Johannes Vorsterman (1643–99)

Perth seen from the east across the Tay

❸ Doune Castle

Doune, Stirling. **Tel** 01786 841742.
🚄 🚌 Stirling then bus.
Open Apr–Sep: 9:30am–5:30pm
daily; Oct: 9:30am–4:30pm daily;
Nov–Mar: 9:30am–4:30pm Mon–Wed,
Sat & Sun; last entry 30 mins before
close. **Closed** 21 Dec–8 Jan.
🎧 ♿ limited.
Ⓦ historic-scotland.gov.uk

Constructed as the residence
of Robert, Duke of Albany, in
the 14th century, **Doune Castle**
was a Stuart stronghold until
it fell into ruin in the 18th
century. Now fully restored,
it is one of the most complete
castles of its time and offers
a unique insight into the
royal household.

The Gatehouse, once a self-
sufficient residence, leads to
the central courtyard off which
is the Great Hall. Complete
with its reconstructed open-
timber roof, minstrels' gallery
and central fireplace, the Hall
adjoins the Lord's Hall and

Private Room. A number of
private stairs and narrow
passages reveal the ingenious
ways the royal family tried to
hide during times of danger.
The castle was the setting for
the 1975 film, *Monty Python
and the Holy Grail.*

❹ Perth

Perthshire. 🗺 45,000. 🚄 🚌
ℹ West Mill St (01738 450600).
Ⓦ perthshire.co.uk

Once the capital of medieval
Scotland, Perth's rich heritage is
reflected in many of its buildings. It was in the **Church of
Saint John**, founded in 1126,
that John Knox *(see p487)*
delivered many of his fiery
sermons. The Victorianized **Fair
Maid's House**, on North Port,
is one of the oldest houses in
town (c.1600) and was the
fictional home of the heroine
of Sir Walter Scott's *(see p516)
The Fair Maid of Perth* (1828).

In **Balhousie Castle**, the
Museum of the Black Watch
commemorates the first
Highland regiment, while
the **Perth Museum & Art
Gallery** has displays on local
industry and exhibitions of
Scottish art.

Environs
Two miles (3 km) north of
Perth, the Gothic mansion
of **Scone Palace** stands on
the site of an abbey destroyed
in 1559. Between the 9th
and 13th centuries, Scone
guarded the sacred Stone of
Destiny *(see pp486–7)*, now
kept in Edinburgh Castle
(see pp510–11). Some of Mary,
Queen of Scots' *(see p515)*
embroideries are on display.

🏰 **Balhousie Castle**
RHQ Black Watch, Hay St.
Tel 0173 863 8152.
Open 9:30am–5pm daily
(Nov–Apr: to 5pm Mon–Sat).

🏛 **Perth Museum & Art Gallery**
78 George St. **Tel** 01738 632488.
Open 10am–5pm Mon–Sat. ♿

🏰 **Scone Palace**
A93 to Braemar. **Tel** 01738 552300.
Open Apr–Oct: 9:30am–5pm daily
(to 4pm Sat). 🎧 ♿
Ⓦ scone-palace.co.uk

❺ Glamis Castle

Forfar, Angus. **Tel** 01307 840393. 🚄
🚌 Dundee then bus. **Open** Mar–Oct:
10am–6pm (last adm: 4:30pm) daily.
🎧 📷 Ⓦ glamis-castle.co.uk

Glamis Castle with statues of James VI (left) and Charles I (right)

With the pinnacled fairytale outline of a Loire chateau, the imposing medieval towerhouse of **Glamis Castle** began as a royal hunting lodge in the 11th century but underwent extensive reconstruction in the 17th century. It was the childhood home of Queen Elizabeth the Queen Mother, and her former bedroom can be seen with a youthful portrait by Henri de Laszlo (1878–956).

Many rooms are open to the public, including Duncan's Hall, the oldest in the castle and Shakespeare's setting for the king's murder in *Macbeth*.

❻ Dundee

Dundee City. 🚶 142,000. 🚉 ✈ 🚌 🚏
🛈 Discovery Point, Discovery Quay (01382 527527). 🚢 daily; farmers' market 3rd Sat of month.
🌐 **angusanddundee.co.uk**

Famed for its three Js of jam, jute mills and journalism – see the statues of publisher DC Thomson's *Beano* and *Dandy* comic characters near the grand venue of Caird Hall – **Dundee** is a hub of creative industries and science.

Due in 2015 is Kengo Kuma's stunning V&A design museum, set on the waterfront with dramatic views across the Tay, Britain's most powerful river.

Nearby is the royal research ship **Discovery**, built here in 1901 for Captain Scott's first voyage to the Antarctic. At Victoria Dock is **HMS Unicorn** (1824), Britain's oldest warship still afloat. The North Carr lightship (1932) sets sail from

View of St Andrews over the ruins of the cathedral

May to September for dolphin-watching trips from beachside Broughton Ferry. The **McManus Galleries**' collection of Dundee-related art and artefacts is housed in a splendid Victorian Gothic building. Walk along Riverside to the Tay Rail Bridge (1887) to learn about the famous disaster and spot seals on the sandbanks.

🏛 HMS *Unicorn*
Victoria Docks, City Quay.
Tel 01382 200900.
Open Apr–Oct: daily;
Nov–Mar: Wed–Sun.
♿ 🚻 limited.
🌐 **frigateunicorn.org**

🏛 *Discovery*
Discovery Point.
Tel 01382 309060. **Open** daily (Sun pm). ♿ 🚻
🌐 **rrsdiscovery.com**

🏛 McManus Galleries
Albert Sq. **Tel** 01382 307200. **Open** 10am–5pm Mon–Sat, 12:30–4:30pm Sun. 🚻 🌐 **mcmanus.co.uk**

❼ St Andrews

Fife. 🚶 17,000. 🚉 Leuchars. 🚌 Dundee. 🛈 70 Market St (01334 472021). 🌐 **standrews.co.uk**

Scotland's oldest university town and one-time ecclesiastical capital, **St Andrews** is now a shrine to golfers from all over the world *(see below)*. Its three main streets and numerous cobbled alleys, full of crooked housefronts, dignified university buildings and medieval churches, converge on the venerable ruins of the 12th-century **cathedral**. Once the largest in Scotland, the cathedral was later pillaged for stones to build the town. **St Andrew's Castle** was built for the bishops of the town in 1200. The dungeon can still be seen. The city's golf courses to the west are each open for a modest fee. The **British Golf Museum** tells how the city's Royal and Ancient Golf Club became the ruling arbiter of the game.

St Mary's College insignia, St Andrews University

🏰 St Andrew's Castle
The Scores. **Tel** 01334 477196. **Open** Apr–Sep: 9:30–5:30pm daily; Oct–Mar: 9:30–4:30pm daily. **Closed** 1 & 2 Jan, 25 & 26 Dec. 🚻 ♿

🏛 British Golf Museum
Bruce Embankment. **Tel** 01334 460 046. **Open** Jan–Mar: 10am–4pm daily; Apr–Oct: 9:30am–5pm daily; Nov–Dec: 10am–4pm daily. ♿ 🚻

The Ancient Game of Golf

Scotland's national game was pioneered on the sandy links around St Andrews. The earliest record dates from 1457, when golf was banned by James II on the grounds that it was interfering with his subjects' archery practice. Mary, Queen of Scots *(see p515)* enjoyed the game and was berated in 1568 for playing straight after the murder of her husband Darnley.

Mary, Queen of Scots at St Andrews in 1563

The central courtyard of Falkland Palace, bordered by rose bushes

❽ East Neuk

Fife. 🚊 Leuchars. 🚌 Glenrothes & Leuchars. 🛈 70 Market Street, St Andrews (01334 472021).

A string of pretty fishing villages scatters the shoreline of the **East Neuk** (the eastern "corner") of Fife, stretching from Earlsferry to Fife Ness. Much of Scotland's medieval trade with Europe passed through these ports, a connection reflected in the Flemish-inspired crow-stepped gables of many of the cottages. Although the herring industry has declined and the area is now a peaceful holiday centre, the sea still dominates village life. Until the 1980s, fishing boats were built at St Monans, a charming town of narrow twisting streets, while Pittenweem is the base for the East Neuk fishing fleet.

The town is also known for **St Fillan's Cave**, the retreat of a 9th-century hermit whose relic was used to bless the army of Robert the Bruce *(see p486)* before the Battle of Bannockburn. A church stands among the cobbled lanes and colourful cottages of Crail; the stone by the church gate is said to have been hurled to the mainland from the Isle of May by the Devil.

Several 16th- to 19th-century buildings in the village of Anstruther contain the **Scottish Fisheries Museum** which tells the area's history with the aid of interiors, boats and displays on whaling. From the village you can embark for the nature reserve on the **Isle of May** which teems with seabirds and grey seals. The statue of Alexander Selkirk in Lower Largo recalls the local boy whose adventures inspired Daniel Defoe's *Robinson Crusoe* (1719). Disagreeing with his captain, he was dumped on a desert island for four years.

🏛 Scottish Fisheries Museum
St Ayles, Harbourhead, Anstruther. **Tel** 01333 310628. **Open** Apr–Sep: 10am–5:30pm Mon–Sat (to 4:30pm Oct–Mar), 11am–5pm Sun (from noon Oct–Mar). **Closed** 25 & 26 Dec, 1 & 2 Jan. 🅿 🚻 🆆 scotfishmuseum.org

❾ Falkland Palace

Falkland, Fife. **Tel** 0844 4932186. 🚊 🚌 from Ladybank. **Open** Mar–Oct: 11am–5pm Mon–Sat, 1–5pm Sun. 🅿 🏛 🚻 🆆 nts.org.uk

This stunning Renaissance palace was designed as a hunting lodge of the Stuart kings. Although its construction was begun by James IV in 1500, most of the work was carried out by his son, James V *(see p514)*, in the 1530s. Under the influence of his two French wives he employed French workmen to redecorate the façade of the East Range with dormers, buttresses and medallions, and to build the beautifully proportioned South Range. The palace fell into ruin during the years of the Commonwealth *(see p56)* and was occupied briefly by Rob Roy *(see p499)* in 1715.

After buying the estates in 1887, the 3rd Marquess of Bute became the Palace Keeper and restored it. The richly panelled interiors are filled with superb furniture and portraits of the Stuart monarchs. The royal tennis court is the oldest in Britain.

❿ Dunfermline

Fife. 🅰 48,000. 🚊 🚌 🛈 1 High St (01383 720999). 🆆 visitdunfermline.com

Scotland's capital until 1603, Dunfermline is dominated by the ruins of the 12th-century abbey and palace which recall its royal past. In the 11th century, the town was the seat of King Malcolm III, who founded a priory on the present site of the **Abbey Church**. With its Norman nave and 19th-century choir, the church contains the tombs of 22 Scottish kings and queens, including Robert the Bruce *(see p486)*.

The ruins of King Malcolm's **palace** soar over the beautiful gardens of Pittencrieff Park. Dunfermline's most famous son, philanthropist Andrew Carnegie (1835–1919), had been forbidden entrance to the park as a boy. After making his fortune, he bought the entire

The Palace Keeper

Due to the size of the royal household and the necessity for the king to be itinerant, the office of Keeper was created by the medieval kings who required custodians to maintain and replenish the resources of their many palaces while they were away. Now redundant, it was a hereditary title and gave the custodian permanent and often luxurious lodgings.

James VI's bed in the Keeper's Bedroom, Falkland Palace

Pittencrieff estate and gave it to the people of Dunfermline. He was born in the town, though moved to Pennsylvania in his teens. There he made a vast fortune in the iron and steel industry. The **Carnegie Birthplace Museum** is still furnished as it was when he lived there, and tells the story of his meteoric career.

fiff Carnegie Birthplace Museum
Moodie St. **Tel** 01383 724302. **Open** Mar–Nov: 10am–5pm Mon–Sat; 2–5pm Sun. 🅿 ♿

The 12th-century Norman nave of Dunfermline Abbey Church

⓫ Culross

Fife. 🅰 400. 🚆 Dunfermline. 🚌 Dunfermline. 🅽🆃🆂 🛈 The Palace (0844 4932189). **Open** Apr–Aug: noon–5pm Mon–Thu (daily Jun–Aug); Sep–Oct: noon–4pm Thu–Mon. 🅽🆃🆂 Garden **Open** 10am–6pm (or dusk if earlier). 🅿 ♿ ltd. 🎫 🅿 🎁 Music & Arts: Jun.

An important religious centre in the 6th century, the town of Culross is said to have been the birthplace of St Mungo in 514.

Now a beautifully preserved 16th- and 17th-century village, Culross prospered in the 16th century with the growth of its coal and salt industries, most notably under Sir George Bruce. He took charge of the Culross colliery in 1575 and created a drainage system called the "Egyptian Wheel" which cleared a mile-long (1.5 km) mine beneath the River Forth.

During its subsequent decline Culross stood unchanged for over 150 years. The National Trust for Scotland began restoring the town in 1932 and now provides a guided tour, which starts at the **Visitors' Centre**.

Built in 1577, Bruce's **palace** has the crow-stepped gables, decorated windows and red pantiles typical of the period. The interior retains its original early 17th-century painted ceilings. Crossing the Square, past the **Oldest House**, dating from 1577, head for the **Town House** to the west. Behind it, a cobbled street known as the Back Causeway (with its raised section for nobility) leads to the turreted **Study**, built in 1610 as a house for the Bishop of Dunblane. The main room is open to visitors and should be seen for its original Norwegian ceiling. Continuing northwards to the ruined abbey, fine church and Abbey House, don't miss the Dutch-gabled **House with the Evil Eyes**.

The 16th-century palace of industrialist George Bruce, Culross

⓬ Linlithgow Palace

Linlithgow, West Lothian. **Tel** 01506 842896. 🚆 🚌 **Open** Apr–Sep: 9:30am–5:30pm daily; Oct–Mar: 9:30am–4:30pm daily. **Closed** 25, 26 Dec, 1, 2 Jan. 🅿 ♿ limited. 🅦 historic-scotland.gov.uk

On the edge of Linlithgow Loch stands the former royal palace of **Linlithgow**. Today's remains are mostly of the palace of James I in 1425. The scale of the building is demonstrated by the 28 m (94 ft) long Great Hall, with its huge fireplace and windows. Mary, Queen of Scots (see p515), was born here in 1542.

⓭ Falkirk Wheel

Lime Rd, Falkirk. **Tel** 08700 500208 (booking line). 🚆 Falkirk. **Open** Feb–Nov: Boat trips from 5 trips Wed–Sat in winter to 3 trips per hour daily in summer. Visitor Centre 10am–5:30pm daily. 🅿 boat trip. 🖥 🎁 🅦 thefalkirkwheel.co.uk

This impressive boat lift is the first ever to revolve, and the centrepiece of Scotland's canal regeneration scheme. Once important for commercial transport, the Union and the Forth and Clyde canals were blocked by several roads in the 1960s. Now the Falkirk Wheel gently swings boats between the two waterways creating an uninterrupted link between Glasgow and Edinburgh. Visitors can ride the wheel on boats that leave from the Visitor Centre.

The rotating Falkirk Wheel boat lift

⓮ Hopetoun House

West Lothian. **Tel** 0131 331 2451. 🚆
Dalmeny then taxi. **Open** Apr–Sep:
10:30am–5pm (last entry 4pm). 🅿
♿ 👶 limited. 📷 for groups – book
ahead. 🖥 ⓦ hopetounhouse.co.uk

An extensive parkland by the
Firth of Forth, designed in the
style of Versailles, is the setting
for one of Scotland's finest
stately homes. The original
house was built by 1707; it was
later absorbed into William
Adam's grand extension. The
dignified, horseshoe-shaped
plan and lavish interior
plasterwork represent
Neo-Classical 18th-century
architecture at its finest. The
drawing rooms, with their
Rococo plasterwork and highly
ornate mantelpieces, are
particularly impressive. The
Marquess of Linlithgow, whose
family still occupies part of the
house, is a descendant of the
1st Earl of Hopetoun, for whom
the house was built.

A wooden panel above the main stair,
depicting Hopetoun House

⓯ Forth Bridges

Edinburgh. 🚆 Dalmeny, North
Queensferry. 🚌 South Queensferry.

The small town of South
Queensferry is dominated by
the two great bridges that span
the mile (1.6 km) across the
River Forth to North Queensferry. The spectacular rail bridge,
the first major steel-built bridge
in the world, was opened in
1890 and remains one of
the greatest engineering
achievements of the late

The shattered crags and cliffs of St Abb's Head

Victorian era. Its massive
cantilevered sections are held
together by more than 6.5
million rivets, and the painted
area adds up to some 55 ha
(135 acres). The saying "like
painting the Forth Bridge" has
become a byword for non-stop,
repetitive endeavour. The
bridge also inspired *The Bridge*
(1986) by writer Iain Banks
(1954–2013).

The neighbouring road
bridge was the largest
suspension bridge outside the
USA when it opened in 1964.
There are plans to perch a
viewing platform atop the
101-m (330-ft) rail bridge,
and a new road bridge is
due to be completed in 2016.

South Queensferry got its
name from the 11th-century
Queen Margaret *(see p511)*,
who used the ferry here on her
journeys between Edinburgh
and the royal palace at
Dunfermline *(see p505)*.

⓰ Edinburgh

See pp508–15.

⓱ St Abb's Head

Scottish Borders. 🚆 Berwick-upon-
Tweed. 🚌 from Edinburgh. Ⓝ🆃🆂

The jagged cliffs of St Abb's Head,
rising 91 m (300 ft) from the
North Sea near the southeastern
tip of Scotland, offer a spectacular
view of thousands of seabirds
wheeling and diving below. This
80 ha (200 acre) nature reserve is
an important site for cliff-nesting
sea birds and becomes, during
the May to June breeding
season, the home of more than
50,000 birds, including fulmars,
guillemots, kittiwakes and
puffins that throng the headland
near the fishing village of St Abbs.
The village has one of the few
unspoiled working harbours
on Britain's east coast. A clifftop
trail begins at the **Visitors'
Centre**, where displays include
identification boards and a
touch table where young
visitors can get to grips with
wings and feathers.

ℹ Visitors' Centre
St Abb's Head. **Tel** 018907 71672.
Open Apr–Oct: 10am–5pm daily. 📷

The huge, cantilevered Forth Rail Bridge, seen from South Queensferry

⓲ A Tour of the Borders

Because of their proximity to England, the Scottish Borders are scattered with the ruins of many ancient buildings destroyed in the conflicts between the two nations. Most poignant of all are the Border abbeys, whose magnificent architecture bears witness to their former spiritual and political power. Founded during the 12th-century reign of David I, the abbeys were destroyed by Henry VIII *(see p516)*.

② Kelso Abbey
The largest of the Border Abbeys, Kelso was once the most powerful ecclesiastical establishment in Scotland.

⑥ Melrose Abbey
Once one of the richest abbeys in Scotland, it is here that Robert the Bruce's heart is buried *(see p516)*.

① Floors Castle
The largest inhabited castle in Scotland, it is the Duke of Roxburghe's ancestral home and was built in the 18th century by William Adam.

⑤ Scott's View
This was Sir Walter Scott's favourite view of the Borders. Out of habit his horse stopped here during Scott's funeral procession.

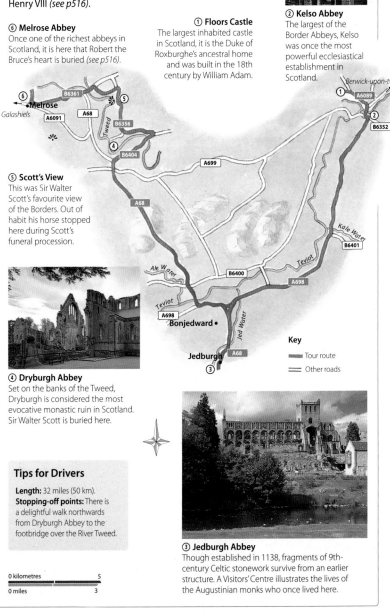

④ Dryburgh Abbey
Set on the banks of the Tweed, Dryburgh is considered the most evocative monastic ruin in Scotland. Sir Walter Scott is buried here.

Key

🔳🔳 Tour route
══ Other roads

Tips for Drivers

Length: 32 miles (50 km).
Stopping-off points: There is a delightful walk northwards from Dryburgh Abbey to the footbridge over the River Tweed.

③ Jedburgh Abbey
Though established in 1138, fragments of 9th-century Celtic stonework survive from an earlier structure. A Visitors' Centre illustrates the lives of the Augustinian monks who once lived here.

0 kilometres   5
0 miles   3

⑯ Edinburgh

With its striking medieval and Georgian districts, overlooked by the extinct volcano of Arthur's Seat and, to the northeast, Calton Hill, Edinburgh is widely regarded as one of Europe's most handsome capitals. The city is famous for the arts (it was once known as "the Athens of the North"), a pre-eminence reflected in its hosting every year of Britain's largest arts extravaganza, the Edinburgh Festival *(see p513)*. Its museums and galleries display the riches of many cultures.

The doorway of the Georgian House, 7 Charlotte Square

Exploring Edinburgh

Edinburgh falls into two main sightseeing areas, divided by Princes Street, the city's most famous thoroughfare and commercial centre. The Old Town straddles the ridge between the castle and the Palace of Holyroodhouse, with most of the city's medieval history clustered in the alleys of the Grassmarket and Royal Mile areas. The New Town, to the north, evolved after 1767 when wealthy merchants expanded the city beyond its medieval walls. This district contains Britain's finest concentration of Georgian architecture.

▥ National Gallery of Scotland

The Mound. **Tel** 0131 624 6200.
Open 10am–5pm Fri–Wed, 10am–7pm Thu (extended during the festival). 🏛 for special exhibitions. ♿ 💻 📷 by appt.
w nationalgalleries.org

One of Britain's finest art galleries, the National Gallery of Scotland is worth visiting for its 15th- to 19th-century British and European paintings alone,

though plenty more can be found to delight the art-lover. Highlights among the Scottish works include portraits by Allan Ramsay and Henry Raeburn, such as his *Reverend Robert Walker Skating on Duddingston Loch* (c.1800). The Early German collection includes Gerard David's almost comic-strip treatment of the *Three Legends of Saint Nicholas* (c.1500). Works by Raphael, Titian and Tintoretto accompany southern European paintings such as Velázquez's *An Old Woman Cooking Eggs* (1620) and the entire room devoted to *The Seven Sacraments* (c.1640) by Nicholas Poussin.

The Weston Link is an underground complex that connects the gallery with the Royal Scottish Academy. It contains a lecture theatre/cinema, shop, restaurant, café, and an IT and education room.

Raeburn's *Rev. Robert Walker Skating on Duddingston Loch*

▦ Georgian House

7 Charlotte Sq. **Tel** 0844 493 2118.
Open Mar: 11am–4pm daily; Apr–Jun & Sep–Oct: 10am–5pm daily; Jul–Aug: 10am–6pm daily; Nov: 11am–3pm daily. (Last adm: half an hour before closing.) 📷 ♿ limited. **NTS**
w nts.org.uk

In the heart of the New Town, Charlotte Square is a superb example of Georgian architecture, its north side, built in the 1790s, being a masterwork by the architect Robert Adam *(see pp32–3)*. The Georgian House at No. 7 has been furnished and repainted in its original 18th-century colours which provide a memorable introduction to the elegance of wealthy New Town life. In stark contrast, "below stairs" is the household staff's living quarters, demonstrating how Edinburgh's working class lived and worked.

The view from Dugald Stewart Monument on Calton Hill, looking west towards the castle

🏛 Scottish National Gallery of Modern Art One and Two

75 Belford Rd. **Tel** 0131 624 6200.
Open 10am–5pm daily (Aug: to 6pm).
🚻 🖥 **nationalgalleries.org**

Housed in a 19th-century school to the northwest of the city centre, the Modern One gallery features most European and American 20th-century greats, from Vuillard and Picasso, to Magritte and Lichtenstein. Work by John Bellany can be found among the Scottish painters. Sculpture by Henry Moore is on display in the grounds. The adjacent Modern Two gallery showcases Dada and Surrealist art.

Lichtenstein's *In the Car*, National Gallery of Modern Art

🏛 National Museum of Scotland

Chambers St. **Tel** 0300 123 6789.
Open 10am–5pm daily. **Closed** 25 Dec. 🎫 🚻 🖥 free. ✏
🖥 **nms.ac.uk**

This purpose-built museum houses the Scottish Collections of the National Museums of Scotland. Exhibitions tell the story of Scotland, the land and its people, dating from its geological beginnings right up to the constitutionally exciting events of today.

The museum's key exhibits include the famous medieval *Lewis Chessmen*; *Pictish Chains*, known as Scotland's earliest crown jewels, and the *Ellesmere* railway locomotive. There is also a special exhibition gallery which houses fascinating temporary displays.

🏛 Scottish National Portrait Gallery

1 Queen St. **Tel** 0131 624 6200.
Open 10am–5pm daily (to 7pm Thu).
🚻 ✏ by appointment.
🖥 **nationalgalleries.org**

The Scottish National Portrait Gallery provides a unique visual history of Scotland told through the portraits of those who shared it, from Robert the Bruce *(see p486)* to Queen Anne. Portraits of other famous Scots include Robert Burns *(see p519)* by Alexander Nasmyth. Since a major refurbishment, there is a greater emphasis on photography at the gallery, such as Alexander Hutchinson's moving record of the lost community of St Kilda, and Scottish art, alongside a dynamic exhibition programme.

Edinburgh City Centre

① Georgian House
② *Edinburgh Castle pp510–11*
③ Scottish National Portrait Gallery
④ National Gallery of Scotland
⑤ Gladstone's Land
⑥ Greyfriars Bobby
⑦ St Giles Cathedral
⑧ Parliament House
⑨ National Museum of Scotland
⑩ Museum of Childhood
⑪ Palace of Holyroodhouse

Key to Symbols *see back flap*

Edinburgh Castle

Standing upon the basalt core of an extinct volcano, Edinburgh Castle is an assemblage of buildings dating from the 12th to the 20th centuries, reflecting its changing role as fortress, royal palace, military garrison and state prison. Though there is evidence of Bronze Age occupation of the site, the original fortress was built by the 6th- century Northumbrian King Edwin, from whom the city takes its name. The castle was a favourite royal residence until the Union of Crowns *(see p487)* in 1603, after which the king resided in England. After the Union of Parliaments in 1707, the Scottish regalia were walled up in the Palace for over a hundred years. The castle is now the zealous possessor of the so-called Stone of Destiny, a relic of ancient Scottish kings which was seized by the English in 1296 from Scone Palace, Perthshire and not returned until 1996.

Scottish Crown
On display in the palace, the Crown was restyled by James V of Scotland in 1540.

Governor's House
Complete with Flemish-style crow-stepped gables, this building was constructed for the governor in 1742. It can only be viewed from the outside only as it is still reserved for ceremonial use.

Vaults
This French graffiti, dating from 1780, recalls the many prisoners who were held in the vaults during the wars with France in the 18th and 19th centuries.

KEY

① Old Back Parade

② Military Prison

③ **The Half Moon Battery** was built in the 1570s as a platform for the artillery defending the northeastern wing of the castle.

④ **The Esplanade** is the location of the Military Tattoo *(see p513)*.

Mons Meg

Positioned outside St Margaret's Chapel, the siege gun (or *bombard*) Mons Meg was made in Belgium in 1449 for the Duke of Burgundy, who gave it to his nephew, James II of Scotland. It was used by James against the Douglas family in their stronghold of Threave Castle *(see p519)* in 1455, and later by James IV against Norham Castle in England. After exploding during a salute to the Duke of York in 1682, it was kept in the Tower of London until it was returned to Edinburgh in 1829, at Sir Walter Scott's request.

Argyle Battery
This fortified wall commands a spectacular view to the north beyond the city's Georgian district of New Town.

★ Royal Palace
Mary, Queen of Scots *(see p515)* gave birth to James VI in this 15th-century palace, where the Scottish regalia are on display.

Entrance

→ Royal Mile

③

④

★ Great Hall
With its restored open-timber roof, the Hall dates from the 15th century and was the meeting place of the Scottish parliament until 1639.

St Margaret's Chapel
This stained-glass window depicts Malcolm III's saintly queen, to whom the chapel is dedicated. Probably built by her son, David I, in the early 12th century, the chapel is the castle's oldest existing building.

Exploring the Royal Mile: Castlehill to High Street

The Royal Mile is a stretch of four ancient streets (from Castlehill to Canongate) which formed the main thoroughfare of medieval Edinburgh, linking the castle to the Palace of Holyroodhouse. Confined by the city wall, the "Old Town" grew upwards, with some tenements climbing to 20 storeys. It is still possible, among the 66 alleys and closes off the main street, to sense the city's medieval past.

THE PALACE OF HOLYROODHOUSE

EDINBURGH CASTLE

Locator Map

Gladstone's Land is a preserved 17th-century merchant's house.

Scotch Whisky Heritage Centre introduces visitors to Scotland's national drink.

The Camera Obscura contains an observatory from which to view the city, plus optical illusions and giant kaleidoscopes.

LAWNMARKET

Edinburgh Castle ←

CASTLE HILL

Lady Stair's House
This 17th-century house is now a museum of the lives and works of Burns, Scott (see p516) and Stevenson.

The "Hub" (c.1840) has the city's highest spire.

🏛 Gladstone's Land
477B Lawnmarket. **Tel** 0844 493 2120. **Open** Easter–Oct: 10am–5pm daily (Jul & Aug: to 6:30pm). (Last adm: 30 mins before closing.) 🎧 ♿ ✂ NTS

This 17th-century merchant's house provides a window on life in a typical Old Town house before overcrowding drove

The bedroom of Gladstone's Land

the rich to the Georgian New Town. "Lands", as they were known, were tall, narrow buildings erected on small plots of land. The six-storey Gladstone's Land was named after Thomas Gledstanes, the merchant who built it in 1617. The house still has the original arcade booths on the street front and a painted ceiling with fine Scandinavian floral designs. Though extravagantly furnished, it also contains items which are a reminder of the less salubrious side of the old city, such as wooden overshoes which had to be worn in the dirty streets. A chest in the beautiful Painted Chamber is said to have been given by a

Dutch sea captain to a Scottish merchant who saved him from a shipwreck. A similar house, Morocco Land, can be found on Canongate (see p515).

🏛 Parliament House
Parliament Sq, High St. **Tel** 0131 348 5000. **Open** 9am–5pm Mon–Fri. **Closed** public hols. ♿ limited.

This majestic, Italianate building was constructed in the 1630s for the Scottish parliament. Parliament House has been home to the Court of Session and the Supreme Court since the Union of Parliaments (see p487) in 1707. It is worth seeing, as much for the spectacle of its gowned and wigged advocates as for the stained-glass window in its Great Hall, commemorating the inauguration of the Court of Session by James V, in 1532.

The Signet Library has a lavish interior; it was described by King George IV as the "finest drawing room in Europe".

St Giles Cathedral
A bagpiping angel can be found on the arched entrance to the Chapel of the Thistle.

B A N K   S T R E E T

H I G H   S T R E E T

G E O R G E   I V   B R I D G E

Rib-vaulting in the Thistle Chapel, St Giles Cathedral

The City Chambers were designed by John Adam in the 1750s.

Charles II Statue

The Heart of Midlothian is an arrangement of granite cobblestones on the former site of the city jail.

Parliament House was built in 1639. The Scottish parliament convened here from 1640 until 1707.

⬆ St Giles Cathedral
Royal Mile. **Tel** 0131 225 9442.
Open May–Sep: 9am–7pm Mon–Fri, 9am–5pm Sat, 1–5pm Sun; Oct–Apr: 9am–5pm Mon–Sat, 1–5pm Sun.
Closed 1 & 2 Jan, 25 & 26 Dec.
🔲 donation. 🔲
w stgilescathedral.org.uk

Properly known as the High Kirk (church) of Edinburgh, it is ironic that St Giles is popularly known as a cathedral. Though it was twice the seat of a bishop in the 17th century, it was from here that John Knox *(see p487)* directed the Scottish Reformation with its emphasis on individual worship freed from the authority of bishops. A tablet marks the place where Jenny Geddes, a stallholder from a local market, scored a victory for the Covenanters *(see p487)* by hurling her stool

at a preacher reading from an English prayer book in 1637.

The Gothic exterior is dominated by a 15th-century tower. Inside, the impressive Thistle Chapel can be seen, with its elaborate rib-vaulted roof

and carved heraldic canopies. The chapel honours the knights, past and present, of the Order of the Thistle. The carved royal pew in the Preston Aisle is used by the Queen when she stays in Edinburgh.

Edinburgh Festival

Every year, for three weeks in late summer *(see p67)*, Edinburgh hosts one of the world's most important arts festivals, with every available space (from theatres to street corners) overflowing with performers. It has been held in Edinburgh since 1947 and brings together the best in international contemporary theatre, music, dance and opera. The alternative Festival Fringe balances the classic productions with a host of innovative performances. The most popular event is the Edinburgh Military Tattoo, held on the Castle Esplanade – a spectacle of Scottish infantry battalions marching to pipe bands. Also popular are the Edinburgh Book Festival and Edinburgh Film Festival (held in June).

Street performer from the Edinburgh Festival Fringe

Exploring the Royal Mile: High Street to Canongate

The second section of the Royal Mile passes two monuments to the Reformation: John Knox House and the Tron Kirk. The latter is named after a medieval *tron* (weighing beam) that stood nearby. The Canongate was once an independent district, owned by the canons of the Abbey of Holyrood, and sections of its south side have been restored. Beyond Morocco's Land, the road stretches for the final half-mile (800 m) to the Palace of Holyroodhouse.

Locator Map

HIGH STREET

SOUTH BRIDGE STREET

The Mercat Cross marks the city centre. It was here that Bonnie Prince Charlie *(see p539)* was proclaimed king in 1745.

The Tron Kirk was built in 1630 for the Presbyterians who left St Giles Cathedral when it came under the Bishop of Edinburgh's control.

🏛 Museum of Childhood

42 High St. **Tel** 0131 529 4142. **Open** 10am–5:45pm daily. **Closed** 25–27 Dec. ♿ limited. 🔳 cac.org.uk

This lovely museum is not merely a toy collection but a magical insight into childhood. Founded in 1955 by a city councillor, Patrick Murray (who claimed to enjoy eating children for breakfast), it was the first museum in the world to be devoted to the history and theme of childhood. The collection includes medicines, school books and prams as well as galleries full of old-fashioned toys. With its nickel-odeon, antique slot machines and the general enthusiasm of visitors, this has been called the world's noisiest museum.

🏛 Palace of Holyroodhouse

East end of Royal Mile. **Tel** 0131 556 5100. **Open** Apr–Oct: 9:30am–6pm; Nov–Mar:

An 1880 automaton of the Man on the Moon, Museum of Childhood

The entrance to the Palace of Holyroodhouse, seen from the west

9:30am–4:30pm daily. **Closed** 25 & 26 Dec and during royal visits. 📷 ♿ limited. 🔳 royalcollection.org.uk

Now the Queen's official Scottish residence, the Palace of Holyroodhouse is named after the "rood", or cross, which King David I is said to have seen between the antlers of a stag he was hunting here in 1128. The present palace was built in 1529 to accommodate James V *(see p505)* and his French wife, Mary of Guise, though it was remodelled in the 1670s for Charles II. The Royal Apartments (including the Throne Room and Royal Dining Room) are used for investitures and banquets whenever the Queen visits the palace. A chamber in the James V tower is associated with the unhappy reign of Mary, Queen of Scots. It was here, in 1566, that she saw the murder of her trusted Italian secretary, David Rizzio, by her jealous husband, Lord Darnley. She had married Darnley a year earlier in Holyroodhouse chapel.

Bonnie Prince Charlie held court here in 1745 in the Jacobite *(see p541)* rising.

John Knox House
Dating from 1490, the oldest house in the city was the home of John Knox *(see p487)* in the 1560s. He is said to have died in an upstairs room.

Morocco Land is a
reproduction of a 17th-century tenement house. It takes its name from the statue of a Moor which adorns the entrance.

→ Morocco Land

CANONGATE

→ The Palace of Holyroodhouse

MUSEUM OF CHILDHOOD

Museum of Childhood
Though created as a museum for adults by a city councillor who was known to dislike children, this lively musem now attracts flocks of young visitors.

Moubray House was to be the signing place of the Treaty of Union in 1707 *(see p473)*, until a mob forced the authorities to retreat to another venue.

🏛 National Museum of Scotland
Chambers St. **Tel** 0300 123 6789. **Open** 10am–5pm daily. **Closed** 25 Dec. 🏠 ♿ 📷 ✏ ⬛ **W** nms.ac.uk

Two adjoining buildings, the Victorian former Royal Gallery and a modern sculptural edifice of Moray sandstone, house collections that tell the story of Scotland – its geology, natural history, scientific advancements, art and design. The exhibits include the Columbia Printing Press and a Stevenson lighthouse lens as well as Baird's first television and a model of the famous "Rocket" steam locomotive. The Scottish Galleries span the millennia with artifacts from prehistory to the present day.

The soaring Grand Gallery houses Window on the World, the single largest museum installation in the whole of the United Kingdom. It features a spectacular array of exhibits from around the world, covering everything from culture and creativity to the diversity of our planet.

🏛 Greyfriars Bobby
Near the gateway to Greyfriars Church stands the statue of a Skye terrier. It commemorates the dog who, for 14 years, is said to have guarded the grave of his master, John Gray. The people of Edinburgh cared for Bobby until his death in 1872.

Parvati, at the National Museum of Scotland

Mary, Queen of Scots (1542–87)
Born only days before the death of her father, James V, the young Queen Mary spent her childhood in France, after escaping Henry VIII's invasion of Scotland *(see p516)*. A devout Catholic, she married the French Dauphin, and made claims on the English throne. This alarmed Protestants throughout England and Scotland, and when she returned as a widow to Holyroodhouse, aged 18, she was harangued for her faith by John Knox *(see p487)*. In 1567 she was accused of murdering her second husband, Lord Darnley. Two months later, when she married the Earl of Bothwell (also implicated in the murder), rebellion ensued. She lost her crown and fled to England where she was held prisoner for 20 years, before being charged with treason and beheaded at Fotheringhay.

The ruins of Melrose Abbey, viewed from the southwest

⓲ Melrose Abbey

Abbey Street, Melrose, Scottish Borders. **Tel** 01896 822562. **Open** 9:30am–4:30pm daily (Apr–Sep: to 5:30pm). (Last adm: 30 mins before closing.) **Closed** 1, 2 Jan, 25, 26 Dec. ltd. **historic-scotland.gov.uk**

The rose-pink ruins of this beautiful Border abbey (see p507) bear testimony to the hazards of standing in the path of successive English invasions. Built by David I in 1136 for Cistercian monks from Yorkshire, and also to replace a 7th-century monastery, Melrose was repeatedly ransacked by English armies, notably in 1322 and 1385. The final blow, from which none of the abbeys recovered, came in 1545 during Henry VIII's destructive Scottish policy known as the "Rough Wooing". This resulted from the failure of the Scots to ratify a marriage treaty between Henry VIII's son and the infant Mary, Queen of Scots (see p515). What remains of the abbey are the outlines of cloisters, the kitchen and other monastic buildings and the shell of the abbey church with its soaring east window and profusion of medieval carvings. The rich decorations of the south exterior wall include a gargoyle shaped like a pig playing the bagpipes.

An embalmed heart, found here in 1920, is probably that of Robert the Bruce (see p486), who had decreed that his heart be taken on a crusade to the Holy Land. It was returned to Melrose after its bearer, Sir James Douglas (see p519), was killed in Spain.

⓳ Abbotsford House

Galashiels, Scottish Borders. **Tel** 01896 752043. from Galashiels. **Open** Apr–Sep: 9:30am–5pm daily; Oct–Mar: 10am–4pm daily. limited. **scottsabbotsford.co.uk**

Few houses bear the stamp of their creator so intimately as Abbotsford House, the home of Sir Walter Scott for the last 20 years of his life. He bought a farm here in 1811, known as Clarteyhole ("dirty hole" in Scots), though he soon renamed it Abbotsford, after the monks of Melrose Abbey who used to cross the River Tweed nearby. He later demolished the house to make way for the turreted building we see today, funded by the sales of his novels.

Scott's library contains more than 9,000 rare books and his collections of historic relics reflect his passion for the heroic past. An extensive collection of arms and armour includes Rob Roy's broadsword (see p499). Stuart mementos include a crucifix that belonged to Mary, Queen of Scots and a lock of Bonnie Prince Charlie's (see p539) hair. The small study in which he wrote his Waverley novels can be visited as can the room, overlooking the river, in which he died in 1832.

Sir Walter Scott

Sir Walter Scott (1771–1832) was born in Edinburgh and trained as a lawyer. He is best remembered as a major champion and literary figure of Scotland, whose poems and novels (most famously his Waverley series) created enduring images of a heroic wilderness filled with the romance of the clans. His orchestration, in 1822, of the state visit of George IV to Edinburgh (see p489) was an extravaganza of Highland culture that helped re-establish tartan as the national dress of Scotland. He served as Clerk of the Court in Edinburgh's Parliament House (see p512) and for 30 years was Sheriff of Selkirk in the Scottish Borders, which he loved. He put the Trossachs (see pp498–9) firmly on the map with the publication of the Lady of the Lake (1810). His final years were spent writing to pay off a £114,000 debt following the failure of his publisher in 1827. He died with his debts paid, and was buried at Dryburgh Abbey (see p507).

The Great Hall at Abbotsford, adorned with arms and armour

㉑ Traquair House

Peebles, Scottish Borders. **Tel** 01896 830 323. ☒ from Peebles. **Open** Apr–Sep: 11am–5pm daily; Oct: 11am–4pm daily; Nov: 11am–3pm Sat & Sun. ♿ 🅿 limited. **W** **traquair.co.uk**

As Scotland's oldest contin-uously inhabited house, Traquair has deep roots in Scottish religious and political history, stretching back over 900 years. Evolving from a fortified tower to a stout-walled 17th-century mansion (*see p491*), the house was a Catholic Stuart stronghold for 500 years. Mary, Queen of Scots (*see p515*) was among the many monarchs to have stayed here and her bed is covered by a counterpane which she made. Family letters and engraved Jacobite (*see p541*) drinking glasses are among relics recalling the period of the Highland rebellions.

After a vow made by the 5th Earl, Traquair's Bear Gates (the "Steekit Yetts"), which closed after Bonnie Prince Charlie's (*see p539*) visit in 1745, will not reopen until a Stuart reascends the throne. A secret stairway leads to the Priest's Room which attests to the problems faced by Catholic families until Catholicism was legalized in 1829. Traquair House Ale is still produced in the 18th-century brewhouse.

Mary, Queen of Scots' crucifix, Traquair House

㉒ Biggar

Clyde Valley. ▩ 2,300. 🛈 High St (01877 220069).

This typical Lowland market town has a number of museums worth visiting. The **Gladstone Court Museum** boasts a reconstructed Victorian street complete with a milliner's, printer's and a village library, while the grimy days of the town's industrial past are recalled at the **Gasworks Museum**, with its collection of engines, gaslights and appliances. Established in 1839 and preserved in the 1970s, the Biggar Gasworks is the only remaining rural gasworks in Scotland.

🏛 **Gladstone Court Museum**
Northback Rd. **Tel** 01899 221050. **Open** Easter–Sep: 11am–4:30pm Mon, Tue, Thu–Sat, 2–4:30pm Sun. ♿ 🅿

🏛 **Gasworks Museum**
Gasworks Rd. **Tel** 01899 221070. **Open** Jun–Sep: 2–5pm daily.

㉓ Pentland Hills

The Lothians. ☒ Edinburgh, then bus. 🛈 Regional Park Headquarters, Biggar Rd, Edinburgh (0131 529 2401).

The Pentland Hills, stretching for 16 miles (26 km) southwest of Edinburgh, offer some of the best hill-walking country in the Lowlands. Leisurely walkers can saunter along the many signposted footpaths, while the more adventurous can take the chairlift at the Hillend dry ski slope to reach the higher ground leading to the 493 m (1,617 ft) hill of Allermuir. Even more ambitious is the classic scenic route along the ridge from Caerketton to West Kip.

To the east of the A703, in the lee of the Pentlands, stands the exquisite and ornate 15th-century **Rosslyn Chapel**. It was originally intended as a church, but after the death of its founder, William Sinclair, it was also used as a burial ground for his descendants. The delicately wreathed Apprentice Pillar recalls the legend of the apprentice carver who was killed by the master stone-mason in a fit of jealousy at his pupil's superior skill.

🏠 **Rosslyn Chapel**
Roslin. **Tel** 0131 4402159. **Open** daily (Sun: pm only). ♿ 🅿

Details of the decorated vaulting in Rosslyn Chapel

The Classical 18th-century tenements of New Lanark on the banks of the Clyde

㉔ New Lanark

Clyde Valley. 🗺 185. 🚉 🚌 Lanark.
ℹ Horsemarket, Ladyacre Rd
(01555 661345). ♿ 🏪 daily.
🌐 **newlanark.org**

Situated by the falls of the River Clyde, the village of New Lanark was founded in 1785 by the industrial entrepreneur David Dale. Ideally located for the working of its water-driven mills,

David Livingstone

Scotland's great missionary doctor and explorer was born in Blantyre where he began working life as a mill boy at the age of ten. Livingstone (1813–73) made three epic journeys across Africa, from 1840, promoting "commerce and Christianity". He became the first European to see Victoria Falls and died in 1873 while searching for the source of the Nile. He is buried in Westminster Abbey *(see pp96–7)*.

the village was Britain's largest cotton producer by 1800. Dale and his successor, Robert Owen, were philanthropists whose reforms proved that commercial success need not undermine the wellbeing of the workforce. Now a museum, New Lanark is a window on to working life in the early 19th century. Audio-visual shows tell the story of New Lanark and Robert Owen's progressive ideals, and how they apply as much today and in the future as they did in the 1820s.

Environs
15 miles (24 km) north, Blantyre has a memorial to the famous Scottish explorer David Livingstone.

🏛 **New Lanark**
New Lanark Visitor Centre. **Tel** 01555 661345. **Open** 10am–5pm daily (Nov–Mar: to 4pm). 🅿 ♿ 🎦 groups only, by appt – book ahead.

㉕ Glasgow

See pp520–25.

㉖ Sanquhar

Dumfries & Galloway. 🗺 2,100.
🚉 🚌 ℹ 64 Whitesands, Dumfries (01387 253862).

Now of chiefly historic interest, the town of **Sanquhar** was famous in the history of the Covenanters *(see p487)*. In the

1680s, two declarations opposing the rule of bishops were pinned to the Mercat Cross, the site of which is now marked by a granite obelisk. The first protest was led by a local teacher, Richard Cameron, whose followers became the Cameronian regiment. The Georgian **Tolbooth** was designed by William Adam *(see p552)* in 1735 and houses a local interest museum and tourist centre. The Post Office, opened in 1763, is the oldest in Britain, predating the mail coach service.

㉗ Drumlanrig Castle

Thornhill, Dumfries & Galloway.
Tel 01848 331555. 🚉 🚌 Dumfries, then bus. **Open** Grounds: Easter–Sep: 10am–5pm daily; Nov–Mar: 11am–4pm Sat & Sun. Castle: Easter–Aug: 11am–4pm daily. 🅿 ♿ 🎦
🌐 **drumlanrig.com**

Rising squarely from a grassy platform, the massive fortress-palace of **Drumlanrig** *(see p491)*

The Baroque front steps and doorway of Drumlanrig Castle

was built from pink sandstone between 1679 and 1691 on the site of a 15th-century Douglas stronghold. A formidable multi-turreted exterior contains a priceless collection of art treasures such as paintings by Holbein and Rembrandt, as well as such Jacobite relics as Bonnie Prince Charlie's camp kettle and sash. The emblem of a crowned and winged heart, shown throughout the castle, recalls Sir James, the "Black Douglas", who bore Robert the Bruce's *(see p486)* heart while on crusade. After being mortally wounded he threw the heart at his enemies with the words "forward brave heart!"

The sturdy island fortress of Threave Castle on the Dee

㉘ Threave Castle

Castle Douglas, Dumfries & Galloway. **Tel** 07711 223101. 🚂 Dumfries. **Open** Apr–Oct: 9:30am–4:30pm last outward boat (Oct: 3:30pm) daily. 🅿 🌐 historic-scotland.gov.uk

This menacing giant of a tower, a 14th-century Black Douglas *(see above)* stronghold standing on an island in the Dee, commands the most complete medieval riverside harbour in Scotland. Douglas's struggles against the early Stewart kings culminated in his surrender here after a two-month siege in 1455 – but only after James II had brought the cannon Mons Meg *(see p510)* to batter the castle. Threave was dismantled after Protestant Covenanters *(see p487)* defeated its Catholic defenders in 1640. Inside the tower, only the shell of

the kitchen, great hall and domestic levels remains. Over the 15th-century doorway is the "gallows knob", a reminder of when the owners are said to have boasted that it never lacked its noose. Access to the castle is by small boat.

㉙ Whithorn

Dumfries & Galloway. 🚶 900. 🚂 Stranraer. 👬 Dashwood Sq, Newton Stewart (01671 402431). 🌐 visitdumfriesandgalloway.co.uk

The earliest site of continuous Christian worship in Scotland, Whithorn (meaning white house) takes its name from the white chapel built here by St Ninian in 397. Though nothing remains of his chapel, a guided tour of the archaeological dig reveals evidence of Northumbrian, Viking and Scottish settlements ranging from the 5th to the 19th centuries. A visitors' centre, **The Whithorn Story**, provides information on the excavations and contains a collection of carved stones. One, dedicated to Latinus, dates to 450, making it Scotland's earliest Christian monument.

🏛 The Whithorn Story

The Whithorn Trust, 45–47 George St. **Tel** 01988 500508. **Open** Easter–Oct: 10:30am–5pm daily. 🅿 🌐 whithorn.com

㉚ Culzean Castle

See pp526–7.

Scottish Textiles

Weaving in the Scottish Borders goes back to the Middle Ages, when monks from Flanders established a thriving woollen trade with the Continent. Cotton became an important source of wealth in the Clyde Valley during the 19th century, when handloom weaving was overtaken by powerdriven mills. The popular Paisley patterns were based on Indian designs.

A colourful pattern from Paisley

Robert Burns surrounded by his creations, by an unknown artist

㉛ Burns Cottage

Robert Burns Birthplace Museum, Alloway, South Ayrshire. **Tel** 0844 4932601. 🚂 Ayr, then bus. **Open** Oct–Mar: 10am–4pm; Apr–Sep. 10am–5:30pm; daily. **Closed** 25 & 26 Dec, 1 & 2 Jan. 🅿 🚻 🌐 burnsmuseum.org.uk

Robert Burns (1759–96), Scotland's favourite poet, was born and spent his first seven years in this small thatched cottage in Alloway. Built by his father, the restored cottage still contains much of its original furniture. A modern museum displays many of Burns's manuscripts along with early editions of his works. Much of his poem *Tam o' Shanter* (1790) is set in Alloway, which commemorates him with elegant monuments on the outskirts of the village.

Burns became a celebrity following the publication in 1786 of the Kilmarnock Edition of his poems. Scots everywhere gather to celebrate Burns Night *(see p69)* on his birthday, 25 January.

㉕ Glasgow

Though its Celtic name, *Glas cu*, means "dear green place", Glasgow is more often associated with its industrial past, and once enjoyed the title of Second City of the Empire (after London). Glasgow's architectural standing, as Scotland's finest Victorian city, reflects its era of prosperity, when ironworks, cotton mills and shipbuilding were fuelled by Lanarkshire coal. The Science Centre sits on the Clyde's revitalized south bank, and Glasgow rivals Edinburgh *(see pp508–15)* in the arts, with galleries such as the Kelvingrove and the Burrell Collection *(see pp524–5).*

Glasgow's medieval cathedral viewed from the southwest

Exploring Glasgow

With some relics of its grimy industrial past and glossy new image, modern Glasgow is a city of contrasts. The deprived East End, with its busy weekend market, "the Barras", stands by the restored 18th-century Merchant City and Victorian George Square. The more affluent West End prospered in the 19th century as a retreat for wealthy merchants escaping the industrialized Clydeside, and it is here that restaurants, bars, parks and Glasgow University can be found. South Side, next to affluent Pollokshields, is Pollok Country Park, site of the Burrell Collection. An underground network and good bus and rail links provide easy travel around the city.

Glasgow Cathedral

2 Castle St. **Tel** 0141 5528198. **Open** Apr–Sep: 9:30am–5:30pm Mon–Sat, 1–5pm Sun; Oct–Mar: 9:30am–4:30pm Mon–Sat, 1–4:30pm Sun.

As one of the only cathedrals to escape destruction during the Scottish Reformation *(see pp486–7)* – by adapting itself to Protestant worship – this is a rare example of an almost complete 13th-century church.

It was built on the site of a chapel founded by the city's patron saint, St Mungo, a 6th-century bishop of Strathclyde. According to legend, Mungo placed the body of a holy man named Fergus on a cart yoked to two wild bulls, telling them to take it to the place ordained by God. In the "dear green place" at which the bulls stopped he built his church. The cathedral is on two levels. The crypt contains the tomb of St Mungo, surrounded

Glasgow City Centre

① Hunterian Art Gallery
② Museum of Transport
③ Art Gallery and Museum
④ Tenement House
⑤ Glasgow School of Art
⑥ Willow Tea Room
⑦ Provand's Lordship
⑧ Glasgow Cathedral
⑨ St Mungo Museum of Religious Art
⑩ People's Palace

Dalí's *Christ of St John of the Cross* at the Kelvingrove Art Gallery *(see p523)*

illustrates religious themes with superb artifacts, including a 19th-century dancing Shiva and an Islamic painting entitled the *Attributes of Divine Perfection* (1986) by Ahmed Moustafa. Other religious paintings on display include *Crucifixion VII* (1988) by Scottish artist Craigie Aitchison. An exhibition on religion in Glasgow throws light on the life of the missionary David Livingstone *(see p518)*. Outside you can visit Britain's only permanent Zen Buddhist garden.

by an intricate forest of columns springing up to end in delicately carved rib-vaulting. The Blackadder Aisle, reputed to have been built over a cemetery blessed by St Ninian *(see p519)*, has a ceiling thick with decorative bosses.

🏛 St Mungo Museum of Religious Life and Art

2 Castle St. **Tel** 0141 2761625. **Open** 10am–5pm Tue–Thu & Sat, 11am–5pm Fri & Sun. ♿ ☐ by appt. ☐ ☐
Situated in the cathedral precinct, this museum is a world first. The main exhibition

🏠 Tenement House

145 Buccleuch St. **Tel** 0844 4932197. **Open** Mar–Oct: 1–5pm daily. ⬛ ☐ ☐ by appt. ⬛ **nts.org.uk**
Less a museum than a time capsule, the Tenement House is an almost undisturbed record of life in a modest Glasgow flat in a tenement estate during the early 20th century. Glasgow owed much of its vitality and neighbourliness to tenement life, though many of these Victorian and Edwardian apartments were to earn a bad name for poverty and overcrowding, and many have now been pulled down.

The preserved Edwardian kitchen of the Tenement House

The Tenement House was first owned by Miss Agnes Toward who lived here from 1911 until 1965. It remained largely unaltered and, since Agnes threw very little away, it is now a treasure trove of social history. The parlour, previously used only on formal occasions, has afternoon tea laid out on a white lace cloth. The kitchen, with its coal-fired range and box bed, is filled with the tools of a vanished era such as a goffering iron for crisping waffles, a washboard and a stone hot-water bottle.

Agnes's lavender water and medicines are still in the bathroom, as though she had stepped out for a minute 70 years ago, and forgotten to return home.

The Kelvingrove Art Gallery and the Glasgow University buildings, viewed from the south

Glasgow's medieval house, Provand's Lordship

Provand's Lordship

3 Castle St. **Tel** 0141 2761625.
Open 10am–5pm Tue–Thu & Sat,
11am–5pm Fri & Sun.
W glasgowmuseums.com

Now a museum, Provand's Lordship was built as a canon's house in 1471, and is the city's oldest surviving house. Its low ceilings and austere wooden furnishings create a vivid impression of life in a wealthy 15th-century household. It is thought that Mary, Queen of

Mackintosh's interior of the Willow Tea Room

Scots *(see p515)* may have stayed here in 1566 when she made a visit to see her cousin and husband, Lord Darnley.

Willow Tea Room

217 Sauchiehall St (also 97 Buchanan St). **Tel** 0141 332 0521. **Open** 9am–5pm Mon–Sat, 11am–5pm Sun.
W willowtearooms.co.uk

This is the sole survivor of a series of delightful tea rooms created by Charles Rennie Mackintosh in 1904 for the celebrated restaurateur Miss Kate Cranston. Everything from the high-backed chairs to the tables and cutlery was his design. In particular, the 1904 Room de Luxe sparkles with silver furniture and flamboyant leaded glass work. The No. 97 Buchanan Street branch opened in 1997, and re-creates Cranston's original Ingram Street Tea Rooms. It features painstaking replicas of Mackintosh's light and airy White Dining Room and atmospheric Chinese, or "Blue", Room.

Riverside Museum

Pointhouse Quay. **Tel** 0141 2872720.
Open 10am–5pm Mon–Thu & Sat,
11am–5pm Fri & Sun.
W glasgowmuseums.com

Model ships and ranks of gleaming Scottish-built steam engines, cars and motorcycles recall the 19th and early 20th centuries, when Glasgow's supremacy in shipbuilding, trade and manufacturing made her the "second city" of the British Empire. Old Glasgow's transition into a modern city can be seen through fascinating footage of the town in the cinema and through a series of three street reconstructions covering 1890–1930, 1930–60 and 1960–80. Don't miss the *Tall Ship Glenlee*, berthed just outside the museum on the River Clyde.

Striking Riverside Museum, housing Glasgow's transport collection

Glasgow Necropolis

Cathedral Sq. **Tel** 0141 2873961.
Open daily. limited.

Behind the cathedral, the reformer John Knox *(see p487)* surveys the city from his Doric pillar overlooking a Victorian cemetery. It is filled with crumbling monuments to the dead of Glasgow's wealthy merchant families.

A Mackintosh floral design

Charles Rennie Mackintosh

Glasgow's most celebrated designer, Charles Rennie Mackintosh (1868–1928), entered Glasgow School of Art at 16. After his first big break with the Willow Tea Room, he became a leading figure in the Art Nouveau movement, developing a unique style that borrowed from Gothic and Scottish Baronial designs. He believed a building should be a fully integrated work of art, creating furniture and fittings that complemented the overall construction. No-where is this total design better seen than in the Glasgow School of Art, which he designed in 1896. Unrecognized in his lifetime, Mackintosh's work is now widely imitated. Its characteristic straight lines and flowing detail are the hallmark of early 20th-century Glasgow style, in all fields of design from textiles to architecture.

🏛 People's Palace

Glasgow Green. **Tel** 0141 2760788.
Open 10am–5pm Tue–Thu & Sat,
11am–5pm Fri & Sun. **Closed** 1 & 2
Jan, 25 & 26 Dec. 🅰 🖥 🏛
w glasgowmuseums.com

This Victorian sandstone
structure was built in 1898
as a cultural museum for the
people of Glasgow's East End.
It houses everything from
temperance tracts to trade-
union banners, suffragette
posters to comedian Billy
Connolly's banana-shaped
boots, providing a social history
of the city from the 12th century.
A conservatory at the back
contains an exotic winter garden.

🏛 Glasgow School of Art

167 Renfrew St. **Tel** (tours) 0141 566
1472. **Open** tour only, reserve
ahead. 🏛 🅰 🅱 limited.
w gsa.ac.uk

Widely considered to be Charles
Rennie Mackintosh's greatest
architectural work, the Glasgow
School of Art was built between
1897 and 1909 to a design he
submitted in a competition. It
was built in two periods due to
financial constraints. The later,
western wing displays a softer
design than the more severe
eastern half, built only a few
years earlier and compared by a
contemporary critic to a prison.

A student guide takes you
through the building to the
Furniture Gallery, Board Room
and the Library, the latter a
masterpiece of spatial
composition. Each room is an
exercise in contrasts between
height, light and shade with
innovative details echoing the
architectural themes of the
structure. How much of the
school can be viewed depends
on curricular requirements at
the time of visiting.

🏛 Hunterian Art Gallery

82 Hillhead St. **Tel** 0141 3304221.
Open 10am–5pm Tue–Sat,
11am–4pm Sun. **Closed** 24 Dec–
5 Jan & public hols. 🏛 🅱 ltd.
w gla.ac.uk/hunterian

Built to house a number of
paintings bequeathed to
Glasgow University by ex-
student and physician Dr
William Hunter (1718–83), the

George Henry's *Japanese Lady with a Fan* (1894), Kelvingrove Art Gallery

Hunterian Art Gallery contains
Scotland's largest print
collection and works by major
European artists stretching back
to the 16th century. A collection
of work by Charles Mackintosh
is supplemented by a complete
reconstruction of No. 6
Florentine Terrace, where
he lived from 1906 to 1914.
A major collection of 19th-
and 20th-century Scottish art
includes work by William
McTaggart (1835–1910), but the
gallery's most famous collection
is of work by the painter James
McNeill Whistler (1834–1903).

Whistler's *Sketch for Annabel Lee* (c.1869),
Hunterian Art Gallery

🏛 Kelvingrove Art Gallery and Museum

Argyle St, Kelvingrove. **Tel** 0141 276
9599. **Open** 10am–5pm Mon–Thu
& Sat, 11am–5pm Fri & Sun.
Closed 1 & 2 Jan, 25 & 26 Dec.
w glasgowlife.org.uk/museums

The imposing red sandstone
building that is Kelvingrove is
a striking Glasgow landmark –
even though it was supposedly
built the wrong way round –
and the gallery and museum
is the most visited in Scotland.
Having undergone a major
(£27.9 million) refurbishment,
the gallery and museum
house an impressive array
of art and artifacts. The
outstanding collection has
paintings of inestimable
value, including works by
Botticelli, Giorgione (*The
Adulteress Brought Before Christ*),
Rembrandt and Dalí (*Christ of
St John of the Cross, see p521*).
Its impressive representation
of 17th-century Dutch and
19th-century French art is augmented by the home-grown
talent of the Glasgow Boys and
the Scottish Colourists.

The Georgian Pollok House, viewed from the south

🏠 Pollok House

2060 Pollokshaws Rd. **Tel** 0844 493 2202. **Open** 10am–5pm daily. **Closed** 1 & 2 Jan, 25 & 26 Dec. 🅿 NTS 🅦 nts.org.uk

Pollok House is Glasgow's finest 18th-century domestic building and contains one of Britain's best collections of Spanish paintings. The Neo-Classical central block was finished in 1750, the sobriety of its exterior contrasting with the exuberant plasterwork within. The Maxwells have lived at Pollok since the mid-13th century, but the male line ended with Sir John Maxwell, who added the grand entrance hall in the 1890s and designed most of the terraced gardens and parkland beyond.

Hanging above the family silver, porcelain, hand-painted Chinese wallpaper and Jacobean glass, the Stirling Maxwell collection is strong on British and Dutch schools, including William Blake's *Sir Geoffrey Chaucer and the Nine and Twenty Pilgrims* (1745) and William Hogarth's portrait of James Thomson, who wrote the words to *Rule Britannia*.

Spanish 16th- to 19th-century art predominates: El Greco's *Lady in a Fur Wrap* (1541) hangs in the library, while the drawing room contains works by Francisco de Goya and Esteban Murillo. In 1966 Anne Maxwell Macdonald gave the house and 146 ha (361 acres) of parkland to the City of Glasgow. The park provides the site for the city's fascinating Burrell Collection.

Glasgow: The Burrell Collection

Given to the city in 1944 by Sir William Burrell (1861–1958), a wealthy shipping owner, this internationally acclaimed collection is the jewel in Glasgow's crown, with objects of major importance in numerous fields of interest. The building was purpose-built in 1983. In the sun, the stained glass blazes with colour, while the shaded tapestries seem a part of the surrounding woodland.

Figure of a Lohan
This sculpture of Buddha's disciple dates from the Ming Dynasty (1484).

Bull's Head
Dating from the 7th century BC, this bronze head from Turkey was once part of a cauldron handle.

Hutton Castle Drawing Room
This is a reconstruction of the Drawing Room at Burrell's own home – the 16th-century Hutton Castle, near Berwick-upon-Tweed. The Hall and Dining Room can also be seen nearby.

Hornby Portal
This detail shows the arch's heraldic display. The 14th-century portal comes from Hornby Castle in Yorkshire.

Main entrance

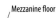

Rembrandt van Rijn
This self-portrait, signed and dated 1632, has pride of place among the paintings hanging in the 16th- and 17th-century room.

VISITORS' CHECKLIST

2060 Pollokshaws Rd, Glasgow.
Tel (0141) 287 2550. **Open**
10am–5pm Mon–Thu, Sat;
11am–5pm Fri, Sun. 🖼 📷 ♿
♿ 🅿 🚻 👶 🎥
w glasgowmuseums.com

Transport
🚆 Pollokshaws West. 45, 47, 48, 57 from Glasgow.

Mezzanine floor

Gallery Guide

Except for a mezzanine-floor display of paintings, the exhibitions are on the ground floor. Right of the entrance hall, rooms are devoted to tapestries, stained glass and sculpture, while ancient civilizations, Oriental art and the period galleries are ahead.

Matthijs Maris
This popular Dutch painter's ethereal style appealed to late 19th-century tastes. *The Sisters* (1875) is one of over 50 Maris works acquired by Burrell.

Key to Floorplan

- ☐ Ancient Civilizations
- ☐ Oriental Art
- ☐ Medieval and Post-Medieval European art, Stained Glass and Tapestries
- ☐ Period Galleries
- ☐ Hutton Castle Rooms
- ☐ Paintings and Drawings
- ☐ Temporary Exhibition Area

Ground floor

Lecture theatre

★ **Tapestries**
Scenes from the Life of the Virgin (c.1450), a Swiss work in wool and linen, is one of many tapestries on show.

★ **Stained Glass**
This 15th-century Norwich School panel, depicting a youth snaring birds, is one of many secular themes illustrated in the stained-glass display.

㉚ Culzean Castle

Standing on a cliff's edge in an extensive parkland estate, the 15th-century keep of Culzean (pronounced Cullayn), home of the Earls of Cassillis, was remodelled between 1777 and 1792 by the Neo-Classical architect Robert Adam (see p32). Restored in the 1970s, it is now a major showcase of his later work. The grounds became Scotland's first public country park in 1969 and, with farming flourishing alongside ornamental gardens, they reflect both the leisure and everyday activities of a great country estate.

View of Culzean Castle (c.1815), by Nasmyth

KEY

① **The clock tower,** fronted by the circular carriageway, was originally the coach house and stables. The clock was added in the 19th century, and today the buildings are used for residential and educational purposes and a shop.

② **Lord Cassillis' Rooms** contain typical mid-18th-century furnishings, including a gentleman's wardrobe of the 1740s.

③ **The Eisenhower Presentation** honours the general who was given the top floor of Culzean in gratitude for his role in World War II.

④ **Carriageway**

A Plan of Culzean Castle

First Floor

- Blue Drawing Room
- Long Drawing Room
- Lord Cassillis' Rooms
- State Bedroom
- Round Drawing Room
- Dressing Room
- Eisenhower Presentation
- Front Hall
- Entrance
- Library
- Kitchen
- Dining Room
- Scullery
- Armoury
- Ailsa Exhibition
- Oval Staircase
- **Ground Floor**

Armoury
Displayed on the walls is the world's most important collection of flintlock pistols, used by the British Army and Militia between the 1730s and 1830s.

Fountain Court
This sunken garden is a good place to begin a tour of the grounds to the east.

③

④

★ Round Drawing Room
With its authentically restored 18th-century colour scheme, this elegant saloon perches on the cliff's edge 46 m (150 ft) above the Firth of Clyde. The carpet is a copy of the one designed by Adam.

★ Oval Staircase
Illuminated by an overarching skylight, the staircase, with its Ionic and Corinthian pillars, is considered one of Adam's finest achievements.

THE HIGHLANDS AND ISLANDS

Aberdeenshire · Moray · Argyll & Bute · Perth & Kinross Shetland · Orkney · Western Isles · Highlands · Angus

Most of the stock images of Scottishness – clans and tartans, whisky and porridge, bagpipes and heather – originate in the Highlands and enrich the popular picture of Scotland as a whole. But for many centuries the Gaelic-speaking, cattle-raising Highlanders had little in common with their southern neighbours.

Clues to the non-Celtic ancestors of the Highlanders lie scattered across the Highlands and Islands in the form of stone circles, brochs and cairns some over 5,000 years old. By the end of the 6th century, the Gaelic-speaking Celts had arrived from Ireland, along with St Columba who taught Christianity. Its fusion with Viking culture in the 8th and 9th centuries produced St Magnus Cathedral in the Orkney Isles.

For over 1,000 years, Celtic Highland society was founded on a clan system, built on family ties to create loyal groups dependent on a feudal chief.

However, the clans were systematically broken up by England after 1746, following the defeat of the Jacobite attempt on the British crown, led by Bonnie Prince Charlie *(see p525)*. A more romantic vision of the Highlands started in the early 19th century. Its creation was largely due to Sir Walter Scott, whose novels and poetry depicted the majesty and grandeur of a country previously considered merely poverty-stricken and barbaric. Another great popularizer was Queen Victoria, whose passion for Balmoral helped to establish the trend for acquiring Highland sporting estates. But behind the sentimentality lay harsh economic realities that drove generations of Highlanders to seek a new life overseas.

Today, over half the inhabitants of the Highlands and Islands still live in communities of less than 1,000. Oil and tourism have supplemented fishing and whisky as the main businesses, and population figures are rising.

A wintry dawn over the Cairngorms, the home of Britain's only herd of reindeer

◄ The Ring of Brodgar, a stone circle on the Mainland, the largest island in Orkney

Exploring the Highlands and Islands

To the north and west of Stirling (the historic gateway to the Highlands) lie the magnificent mountains and glens, fretted coastlines and lonely isles that are the epitome of Scottish scenery. Inverness, the Highland capital, makes a good starting point for exploring Loch Ness and the Cairngorms, while Fort William holds the key to Ben Nevis. Inland from Aberdeen lie Royal Deeside and the Spey Valley whisky heartland. The romantic Hebrides can be reached by ferry from Oban or Ullapool.

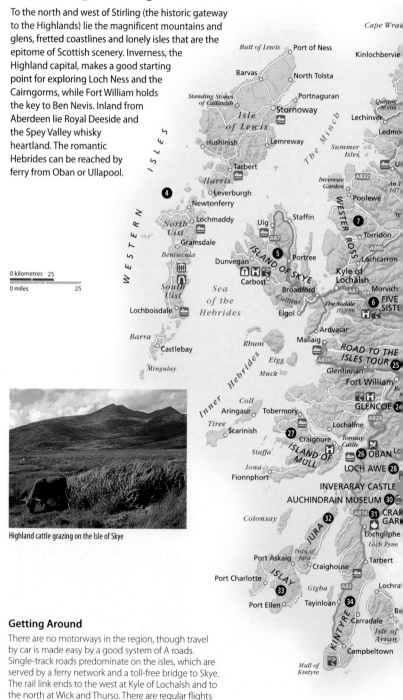

Highland cattle grazing on the Isle of Skye

Getting Around

There are no motorways in the region, though travel by car is made easy by a good system of A roads. Single-track roads predominate on the isles, which are served by a ferry network and a toll-free bridge to Skye. The rail link ends to the west at Kyle of Lochalsh and to the north at Wick and Thurso. There are regular flights from Edinburgh to Inverness, Aberdeen and Wick.

For additional map symbols *see back flap*

Colour-washed houses at the harbour
of Tobermory, Mull

Sights at a Glance

1. Shetland
2. Orkney
3. John o'Groats
4. Western Isles
5. *Skye pp538–9*
6. Five Sisters
7. Wester Ross
8. Dornoch
9. Strathpeffer
10. Black Isle
11. Loch Ness
12. Inverness
13. Culloden
14. Fort George
15. Cawdor Castle
16. Elgin
17. Aberdeen
19. Dunkeld
20. Pitlochry
22. Blair Castle

23. *Cairngorms pp548–9*
24. Glencoe
26. Oban
27. Mull
28. Loch Awe
29. Inveraray Castle
30. Auchindrain Museum
31. Crarae Gardens
32. Jura
33. Islay
34. Kintyre

Walks and Tours
18. Royal Deeside Tour
21. Killiecrankie Walk
25. Road to the Isles Tour

Key

━━━ Motorway

━━━ Major road

━━━ Secondary road

┈┈┈ Minor road

━━━ Scenic route

╍╍╍ Main railway

─── Minor railway

△ Summit

❶ Shetland

Shetland. 🚹 22,000. ✈️ ⛴ from Aberdeen and Stromness on mainland Orkney. 🚌 Lerwick (01595 693434). 🌐 **visit.shetland.org**

Lying six degrees south of the Arctic Circle, the rugged Shetland islands are Britain's most northerly region and were, with Orkney, part of the kingdom of Norway until 1469. In the main town of Lerwick, this Norse heritage is remembered during the ancient midwinter festival Up Helly Aa *(see p484)*, in which costumed revellers set fire to a replica Viking longship. Also in the town, the **Shetland Museum** tells the story of a people dependent on the sea, right up to modern times with the discovery of North Sea oil and gas in the 1970s.

The Iron Age tower, **Mousa Broch**, can be visited on its isle by boat from Sandwick. There is more ancient history at Jarlshof where a museum explains the sprawling sea-front ruins which span 3,000 years.

A boat from Lerwick sails to the isle of Noss where grey seals bask beneath sandstone cliffs crowded with Shetland's seabirds – a spectacle best seen between May and June. Other wildlife includes otters and killer whales.

🏛 **Shetland Museum**
Hay's Dock, Lerwick. **Tel** 01595 695057. **Open** daily (pm only Sun).
🌐 **shetland-museum.org.uk**

❷ Orkney

Orkney. 🚹 20,000. ✈️ ⛴ from Gills Bay, Caithness; John o'Groats (May–Sep); Scrabster, Aberdeen. 🛈 West Castle St, Kirkwall (01856 872856).
🌐 **visitorkney.com**

The fertile isles of Orkney are remarkable for the wealth of prehistoric monuments which place them among Europe's most trea-sured archaeological sites. In the town of Kirkwall, the sandstone **St Magnus Cathedral** stands amid a charming core of narrow streets. Its many interesting tombs include that of its 12th-century patron saint. Nearby, the early 17th-century **Earl's Palace** is widely held to be

The Shetland Seabird Isles

As seabirds spend most of their time away from land, nesting is a vulnerable period in their lives. The security provided by the inaccessible cliffs at such sites as Noss and Hermaness on Unst finds favour with thousands of migrant and local birds.

Puffin

Great Skua

Fulmar

Black Guillemot

Razorbills

Herring Gull

one of Scotland's finest Renaissance buildings. To the west of Kirkwall lies Britain's most impressive chambered tomb, the cairn of **Maes Howe**. Dating from 2000 BC, the tomb has runic graffiti on its walls believed to have been left by Norsemen returning from the crusades in 1150.

Nearby, the great **Standing Stones of Stenness** may have been associated with Maes Howe rituals, though these still remain a mystery. Further west, on a bleak heath, stands the Bronze Age **Ring of Brodgar**.

Another archaeological treasure can be found in the Bay of Skail – the complete Stone Age village of **Skara Brae**. It was unearthed by a storm in 1850, after lying buried for 4,500 years. Further south, the town of Stromness was a vital centre of

The Norman façade of the St Magnus Cathedral, Orkney

Scotland's herring industry in the 18th century. Its story is told in the local museum, while the **Pier Arts Centre** displays British and international art.

🏛 **Earl's Palace**
Palace Rd, Kirkwall. **Tel** 01856 871918. **Open** Apr–Oct: 9:30am–5:30pm daily. 🅿️ ♿ ltd.
🌐 **historic-scotland.gov.uk**

🏛 **Pier Arts Centre**
Victoria St, Stromness. **Tel** 01856 850209. **Open** 10:30am–5pm Tue–Sat.
🌐 **pierartscentre.com**

❸ John o'Groats

Highland. 🚹 300. ✈️ 🚆 🚌 Wick ⛴ John o'Groats to Burwick, Orkney (May–Sep). 🛈 John o'Groats (01955 611373).

Some 876 miles (1,409 km) north from Land's End, Britain's most northeasterly mainland village faces Orkney, 8 miles (13 km) across the turbulent Pentland Firth. The village takes its name from a 15th-century Dutchman John de Groot, who, to avoid accusations of favouritism, is said to have built an octagonal house here with one door for each of his eight heirs. The spectacular cliffs and rock stacks of Duncansby Head lie a few miles further east.

❹ Western Isles

Western Scotland ends with this remote chain of islands, made of some of the oldest rock on Earth. Almost treeless landscapes are divided by countless waterways, the western, windward coasts edged by miles of white sandy beaches. For centuries, the eastern shores, composed largely of peat bogs, have provided the islanders with fuel. Man has been here for 6,000 years, living off the sea and the thin turf, though such monuments as an abandoned Norwegian whaling station on Harris attest to the difficulties in commercializing the islanders' traditional skills. Gaelic, part of an enduring culture, is widely spoken.

The Black House Museum, a traditional croft on Lewis

The Uists, Benbecula and Barra

Western Isles. 🏛 3,600. ✈ Barra, Benbecula. ⛴ Uig (Skye), Ullapool, Oban. 🚌 ⛴ Oban, Mallaig, Kyle of Lochalsh. 🅸 Lochmaddy, North Uist (01876 500321); Lochboisdale, South Uist (01878 700286); Castlebay, Barra (01871 810336). 🅆 visitthebrides.com

After the dramatic scenery of Harris, the lower-lying, largely waterlogged southern isles may seem an anticlimax, though they nurture secrets well worth discovering. Long, white, sandy beaches fringe the Atlantic coast, edged with one of Scotland's natural treasures: the lime-rich soil known as *machair*. During the summer months, the soil is covered with wild flowers.

From **Lochmaddy**, North Uist's main village, the A867 crosses 3 miles (5 km) of causeway to Benbecula, the isle from which Flora MacDonald smuggled Bonnie Prince Charlie *(see p539)* to Skye. Another causeway leads to South Uist, with its golden beaches renowned as a National Scenic Area. From Lochboisdale, a ferry sails to the tiny isle of Barra. The ferry docks in Castlebay, affording an unforgettable view of **Kisimul Castle**, the ancestral stronghold of the MacNeils of Barra.

The monumental Standing Stones of Callanish in northern Lewis

Lewis and Harris

Western Isles. 🏛 20,000. ✈ Stornoway. ⛴ Uig (Skye), Ullapool, Kyle of Lochalsh. 🅸 Stornoway, Lewis (01851 703088).
🅆 visitthebrides.com
The Blackhouse. Tel 01851 710395.
Open 9:30am–4:30pm daily (Apr–Sep: to 5:30pm). 🅿 ♿ ✍ 🅿

Forming the largest landmass of the Western Isles, Lewis and Harris are a single island, though Gaelic dialects differ between the two areas. From **Stornoway**, with its bustling harbour and colourful house fronts, the ancient **Standing Stones of Callanish** are only 16 miles (26 km) to the west. Just off the road on the way to Callanish are the ruins of **Carloway Broch**, a Pictish *(see p486)* tower over 2,000 years old. The more recent past can be explored at Arnol's **Blackhouse** – a showcase of crofting life as it was until only 50 years ago.

South of the rolling peat moors of Lewis, a range of mountains marks the border with Harris, which one enters as one passes Aline Lodge at the head of Loch Seaforth. Only a little less spectacular than the "Munros" (peaks over 914 m; 3,000 ft) of

the mainland and the Isle of Skye *(see pp538–9)*, the mountains of Harris are a paradise for the hillwalker and, from their summits on a clear day, the distant Isle of St Kilda can be seen 50 miles (80 km) to the west.

The ferry port of Tarbert stands on a slim isthmus separating North and South Harris. Some local weavers of the famous Harris Tweed still follow the old tradition of using plants to make their dyes.

From the port of Leverburgh, close to the southern tip of Harris, a ferry can be taken to the isle of North Uist, where a causeway has been built to Berneray.

The remote and sandy shores of South Uist

The western side of the Five Sisters of Kintail, seen from above Loch Duich

❺ Skye

See pp538–9.

❻ The Five Sisters

Skye & Lochalsh. 🚆 Kyle of Loch-alsh. 🚌 Glenshiel. 🛈 Bayfield Road, Portree, Isle of Skye (01478 614906). 🆆 visithighlands.com

Dominating one of Scotland's most haunting regions, the awesome summits of the Five Sisters of Kintail rear into view at the northern end of Loch Cluanie as the A87 enters Glen Shiel. The **Visitor Centre** at Morvich offers ranger-led excursions in the summer. Further west, the road passes **Eilean Donan Castle**, con-nected by a bridge. A Jacobite *(see p541)* stronghold, it was destroyed in 1719 by English warships. In the 19th century it was restored and now contains Jacobite relics.

🏠 **Eilean Donan Castle**
Off A87, nr Dornie. **Tel** 01599 555 202. **Open** Feb–Dec: 10am–6pm (from 9am Jul–Aug) daily. 🚫
🆆 eileandonancastle.com

❼ Wester Ross

Ross & Cromarty. 🚆 Achnasheen, Strathcarron. 🛈 Gairloch (01445 712071). 🆆 visithighlands.com

Leaving Loch Carron to the south, the A890 enters the northern Highlands and the great wilderness of Wester Ross. The Torridon Estate includes some of the oldest mountains

on Earth (Torridonian rock is over 600 million years old), and is home to red deer, wild cats and wild goats. Peregrine falcons and golden eagles nest in the towering sandstone mass of Liathach, above the village of Torridon with its breathtaking views over Applecross to Skye. The **Torridon Countryside Centre** provides guided walks in season and information on the region's natural history. The estate is open all year.

To the north, the A832 cuts through the Beinn Eighe National Nature Reserve in which remnants of the ancient Caledonian pine forest still stand on the banks and isles of Loch Maree.

Along the coast, exotic gardens thrive in the warming currents of the Gulf Stream, most impressive being **Inver-ewe Garden** created in 1862 by Osgood Mackenzie (1842–1922). May and June are the months to see the display of

Typical Torridonian mountian scenery in the Wester Ross

rhododendrons and azaleas; July and August for the herbaceous borders.

🏛 **Torridon Countryside Centre**
Torridon. **Tel** 0844 493 2229. **Open** Apr–Sep: 10am–5pm Sun–Fri. Estate: **Open** daily all year. 🚫 ♿ NTS
🆆 nts.org.uk

🌿 **Inverewe Garden**
Off A832, nr Poolewe. **Tel** 0844 493 2225. **Open** daily. 🚫 ♿ NTS

❽ Dornoch

Sutherland. 🚹 1,200. 🚆 Golspie, Tain. 🛈 The Square, Dornoch (08452 255121). 🆆 visithighlands.com

With its first-class golf course and extensive sandy beaches, **Dornoch** is a popular holiday resort, though it has retained a peaceful atmosphere. Now the parish church, the medieval cathedral was all but destroyed in a clan dispute in 1570; it was finally restored in the 1920s for its 700th anniversary. A stone at the beach end of River Street marks the place where Janet Horne, the last woman to be tried in Scotland for witchcraft, was executed in 1722.

Environs
Twelve miles (19 km) northeast of Dornoch is the stately Victorianized pile of **Dunrobin Castle**, magnificently situated in a great park with formal gardens overlooking the sea. Since the 13th century, this has been the seat of the Earls of Sutherland.

Many of its rooms are open to visitors. A steam-powered fire engine is among the miscellany of objects on display.

South of Dornoch stands the town of **Tain**. A place of pilgrimage for medieval kings, it became an administrative centre of the Highland Clearances. All is explained in the heritage centre, **Tain Through Time**.

🏠 Dunrobin Castle
Nr Golspie. **Tel** 01408 633177. **Open** Apr, May, Sep & Oct: 10:30am–4:30pm daily (from noon Sun); Jun–Aug: 10:30am–5pm daily. Falconry displays: 11:30am & 2pm. 🅿

🏛 Tain Through Time
Tower St. **Tel** 01862 894089. **Open** Apr–Oct: 10am–5pm Mon–Fri (Jun–Aug: also Sat). 🅿 ♿ 📷
W tainmuseum.org.uk

The serene cathedral precinct in the town of Dornoch

❾ Strathpeffer

Ross & Cromarty. 🚶 1,500.
🚌 Dingwall, Inverness. 🚌 Inverness.
ℹ Real Sweets, The Pump Room, The Square (07801 759217).
W visitscotland.com

Standing 5 miles (8 km) from the Falls of Rogie and to the east of the Northwest Highlands, this popular town still has the refined charm for which it was well known in Victorian times, when it flourished as a spa and health resort. The grand hotels and gracious layout of Strathpeffer recall the days when royalty from all over Europe used to flock to the chalybeate- and sulphur-laden springs, which were believed to help in the cure of tuber-culosis, and in the treatment of rheumatism.

The shores of the Black Isle in the Moray Firth

❿ The Black Isle

Ross & Cromarty. 🚌 🚌 Inverness.
ℹ Visit Scotland (01463 252401).

Though the drilling platforms in the Cromarty Firth are reminders of how oil has changed the local economy, the peninsula of the Black Isle is still largely composed of farmland and fishing villages. The town of **Cromarty** was an important port in the 18th century, with thriving rope and lace industries. Many of its merchant houses still stand; the museum in the **Cromarty Courthouse** provides heritage tours of the town. The **Hugh Miller Museum** is a museum to the theologian and geologist Hugh Miller (1802–56), who was born here. **Fortrose** has a ruined 14th-century cathedral, while a stone on Chanonry Point commemorates the Brahan Seer, a 17th-century prophet burnt alive in a tar barrel by the Countess of Seaforth after he foresaw her husband's infidelity. Chanonry Point is also renowned as a great spot for bottlenose dolphin-watching. For local archaeology, visit **Groam House Museum** in Rosemarkie.

🏛 Cromarty Courthouse
Church St, Cromarty. **Tel** 01381 600 418. **Open** Apr–Sep: noon–4pm Sun–Thu. 🅿

📷 Hugh Miller Museum
Church St, Cromarty. **Tel** 0844 493 2158. **Open** late Mar–Sep: daily; Oct: Tue, Thu & Fri (pm). 🅿 NTS ♿ limited.

🏛 Groam House Museum
High St, Rosemarkie. **Tel** 01381 620961. **Open** Apr–Oct: 11am–4:30pm Mon–Fri, 2–4:30pm Sat; Nov: 2–4pm Sat.

The Highland Clearances

During the heyday of the clan system *(see p488)*, tenants paid their clan chiefs rent for their land in the form of military service. However, with the decline of the clan system after the Battle of Culloden *(see p541)* and the coming of sheep from the borders, landowners were able to command a financial rent their tenants were unable to afford and the land was bought up by Lowland and English farmers. In what became known as "the year of the sheep" (1792), thousands of tenants were evicted to make way for sheep. Many emigrated to Australia, America and Canada. Ruins of their crofts can still be seen in Sutherland and Wester Ross.

The Last of the Clan (1865) by Thomas Faed

❺ Isle of Skye

The largest of the Inner Hebrides, Skye can be reached by the bridge linking Kyle of Lochalsh and Kyleakin. A turbulent geological history has given the island some of Britain's most varied and dramatic scenery. From the rugged volcanic plateau of northern Skye to the ice-sculpted peaks of the Cuillins, the island is divided by numerous sea lochs, leaving the traveller never more than 8 km (5 miles) from the sea. North of the Dunvegan are small caves and white beaches, while Limestone grasslands predominate in the south, where the hillsides, home of sheep and cattle, are scattered with the ruins of crofts abandoned during the Clearances *(see p535)*. Historically, Skye is best known for its association with Bonnie Prince Charlie.

Kilmu

Western Isles

Uig

LOCH SNIZORT

• Lusta

B886

• Milovaig

B884

Dunvegan

Skeab

A850

A863

Dunvegan Castle
For over seven centuries, Dunvegan Castle has been the seat of the chiefs of the Clan MacLeod. It contains the Fairy Flag, a fabled piece of magic silk treasured for its protection in battle.

Portnalong •

B8009

• Talisker   • Carb

⑧

0 kilometres   10

0 miles   5

C

SGURR ALA

993 m
(3,258

S

Cuillins
Britain's finest mountain range is within walking distance of Sligachan, and in summer a boat sails from Elgol to the desolate inner sanctuary of Loch Coruisk. As he fled across the surrounding moorland, Bonnie Prince Charlie is said to have claimed: "Even the Devil shall not follow me here!"

KEY

① **Grave of Flora MacDonald**

② **Kilt Rock**

③ **Luib** has a beautiful thatched cottage, preserved as it was 100 years ago.

④ **Bridge to mainland**

⑤ **Otters** can be seen from the haven in Kylerhea.

⑥ **Armadale Castle Gardens and**

Museum of the Isles houses the Clan Donald visitor centre.

⑦ **Loch Coruisk**

⑧ **The Talisker Distillery** produces one of the best Highland malts, often described as "the lava of the Cuillins".

⑨ **Skeabost** has the ruins of a chapel which is associated with St Columba. Medieval tombstones can be found in the graveyard.

Key

▬▬ Major road

▭▭ Minor road

═══ Narrow lane

Quiraing

A series of landslides has exposed the roots of this volcanic plateau, revealing a fantastic terrain of spikes and towers. They are easily explored off the Uig to Staffin road.

The Storr

The erosion of this basalt plateau has created the Old Man of Storr, a monolith rising to 49 m (160 ft) by the Portree road.

Portree

With its colourful harbour, Portree (meaning "port of the king") is Skye's metropolis. It received its name after a visit by James V in 1540.

Bonnie Prince Charlie

The last of the Stuart claimants to the Crown, Charles Edward Stuart (1720–88), came to Scotland from France in 1745 to win the throne. After marching as far as Derby, his army was driven back to Culloden, where it was defeated. Hounded for five months through the Highlands, he escaped to Skye, disguised as the maidservant of a woman called Flora MacDonald, from Uist. From the mainland, he sailed to France in September 1746, and died in Rome. Flora was buried in 1790 at Kilmuir, on Skye, wrapped in a sheet taken from the bed of the "bonnie" (handsome) prince.

The prince, disguised as a maidservant

Kilchrist Church

This ruined pre-Reformation church's last service was held in 1843. It once served Skye's most populated areas, though the surrounding moors are now deserted.

The ruins of Urquhart Castle on the western shore of Loch Ness

⓫ Loch Ness

Inverness. 🚆 🚌 Inverness.
ℹ️ Castle Wynd, Inverness (01463 252401). 🌐 visitscotland.com

At 24 miles (39 km) long, one mile (1.5 km) at its widest and up to 305 m (1,000 ft) deep, **Loch Ness** fills the northern half of the Great Glen fault from Fort William to Inverness. It is joined to lochs Oich and Lochy by the 22-mile (35-km) Caledonian Canal, designed by Thomas Telford *(see p451)*.

The Loch Ness Monster

First sighted by St Columba in the 6th century, "Nessie" has attracted increasing attention since ambiguous photographs were taken in the 1930s. Though serious investigation is often undermined by hoaxers, sonar techniques continue to yield enigmatic results: plesiosaurs, giant eels and too much whisky are the most popular explanations. Nessie appears to have a close relative in the waters of Loch Morar *(see p550)*.

On the western shore, the A82 passes the ruins of the 16th-century **Urquhart Castle**, which was blown up by government supporters in 1692 to prevent it falling into Jacobite hands. A short distance west, **Loch Ness Centre and Exhibition** offers a wealth of audio-visual information.

🏰 **Urquhart Castle**
Nr Drumnadrochit.
Tel 01456 450551.
Open 9:30am–6pm daily (Oct–Feb: to 4:30pm). (Last adm: 45 mins before closing.)
🚫 ♿ 📷

🏛️ **Loch Ness Centre and Exhibition**
Drumnadrochit. **Tel** 01456 450573.
Open Nov–Easter: 10am–3:30pm daily; Easter–Oct: 9:30am–5pm daily.
🚫 ♿ 🖥️ 📷 🌐 lochness.com

⓬ Inverness

Highland. 🚌 60,000. 🚆 🚌 ℹ️
Castle Wynd (01463 234353).
🌐 visitscotland.com

As the Highland capital, Inverness makes an ideal base from which to explore the surrounding countryside. The Victorian castle dominates the town centre, the oldest buildings of which are found in nearby Church Street. Today the castle is used as law courts.

The **Inverness Museum and Art Gallery** provides a good introduction to the history of the Highlands with exhibits including a lock of Bonnie Prince Charlie's *(see p539)* hair and a fine collection of Inverness silver. The **Scottish Kiltmaker Visitor Centre** explores the history and tradition of Scottish kilts as well as workshops, while those in search of tartans and knitwear should visit **Ben Wyvis Kilts**. **Jacobite Cruises** run a variety of year-round cruises along the Caledonian Canal and on to Loch Ness. The unfolding scenery makes this a most pleasant and tranquil way to spend a sunny afternoon.

Kilt maker with royal Stuart tartan

🏛️ **Museum and Art Gallery**
Castle Wynd. **Tel** 01463 237114.
Open Apr–Oct: Mon–Sat; Nov–Mar: Thu–Sat. ♿ 🌐 inverness.highland.museum

🏰 **Ben Wyvis Kilts**
Highland Rail House, Station Square.
Tel 01463 715448. **Open** daily. ♿

🏛️ **Scottish Kiltmaker Visitor Centre**
Huntly St. **Tel** 01463 222781.
Open daily. **Closed** 1 Jan, 25 Dec. 📷

Jacobite Cruises
Glenurquhart Road. **Tel** 01463 233 999. **Open** daily. 📷 ♿
🌐 jacobite.co.uk

⓭ Culloden

Inverness. 🚆 🚌 Inverness. **NTS**
🌐 nts.org.uk/culloden

A desolate stretch of moorland, Culloden looks much as it did on 16 April 1746, the date of the last battle to be fought on British soil *(see p487)*. Here the Jacobite cause, with Bonnie Prince Charlie's *(see p539)* leadership, finally perished under the onslaught of Hanoverian troops led by the Duke of Cumberland. All is explained in the **NTS Visitor Centre**.

Environs

Signposted for a mile (1.5 km) or so east are the outstanding Neolithic burial sites, the **Clava Cairns**.

ℹ NTS Visitor Centre
On the B9006 east of Inverness. **Tel** 0844 4932159. **Open** Apr–Oct: 9am–5:30pm daily; Nov–Dec & Feb– Mar: 10am–4pm daily. **Closed** 24 Dec–1 Feb. 🅿 ♿ **NTS**

⓮ Fort George

Inverness. **Tel** 01667 460232. 🚆 🚌 Inverness, Nairn. **Open** Apr–Sep: 9:30am–5:30pm daily (to 4:30pm Oct– Mar). **Closed** 25 & 26 Dec. 🅿 ♿ 📷
🌐 historic-scotland.gov.uk

One of the finest works of European military architecture, Fort George stands on a wind-swept promontory jutting into the Moray Firth, ideally located to suppress the Highlanders. Completed in 1769, the fort was built after the Jacobite risings to discourage further rebellion in the Highlands and has remained

The Jacobite Movement

The first Jacobites (mainly Catholic Highlanders) were the supporters of James II of England (James VII of Scotland) who was deposed by the "Glorious Revolution" of 1688 *(see p57)*. With the Protestant William of Orange on the throne, the Jacobites' desire to restore the Stuart monarchy led to the uprisings of 1715 and 1745. The first, in support of James VIII, the "Old Pretender", ended at the Battle of Sheriffmuir (1715). The failure of the second uprising, with the defeat at Culloden, saw the end of Jacobite hopes and led to the end of the clan system and the suppression of Highland culture for over a century *(see p489)*.

James II, by Samuel Cooper (1609–72)

The drawbridge on the eastern side of Cawdor Castle

a military garrison ever since. The Fort houses the **Regimental Museum** of the Highlanders Regiment, and some of its barrack rooms reconstruct the conditions of the common soldiers stationed here more than 200 years ago. The **Grand Magazine** contains an outstanding collection of arms and military equipment. The battlements also make an excellent place from which to watch dolphins in the Moray Firth.

⓯ Cawdor Castle

On B9090 (off A96). **Tel** 01667 404401. 🚆 Nairn, then bus. 🚌 from Inverness. **Open** May–Sep: 10am–5:30pm daily. 🅿 ♿ gardens & ground floor only. 📷
🌐 cawdorcastle.com

With its turreted central tower, moat and drawbridge, Cawdor Castle is one of the most romantic stately homes in the Highlands. Though the castle is famed for being the 11th-century home of Shakespeare's *(see p326)* Macbeth and the scene of his murder of King Duncan, it is not historically proven that either came here.

An ancient holly tree preserved in the vaults is said to be the one under which, in 1372, Thane William's donkey, laden with gold, stopped for a rest during its master's search for a place to build a fortress. According to legend, this was how the site for the castle was chosen. Now, after 600 years of continuous occupation (it is still the home of the Thanes of Cawdor) the house is a treasury of family history, containing a number of rare tapestries and portraits by the 18th-century painters Joshua Reynolds (1723–92) and George Romney (1734–1802). Furniture in the Pink Bedroom and Woodcock Room includes work by Chippendale and Sheraton. In the Old Kitchen, the huge Victorian cooking range stands as a shrine to below-stairs drudgery. The grounds provide nature trails and a nine-hole golf course.

A contemporary picture, *The Battle of Culloden* (1746), by D Campbell

⑯ Elgin

Moray. 🗺 26,000. 🚆 🚌 ℹ️ 17 High St, Moray (01343 562608).

With its cobbled marketplace and crooked lanes, the popular holiday centre of Elgin still retains much of its medieval layout. The 13th-century **cathedral** ruins next to King Street are all that remain of one of Scotland's architectural triumphs, the design of its tiered windows reminiscent of the cathedral at St Andrews (*see p503*). Once known as the Lantern of the North, the cathedral was severely damaged in 1390 by the Wolf of Badenoch (the son of Robert II) in revenge for his excommunication by the Bishop of Moray. Worse damage came in 1576 when the Regent Moray ordered the stripping of its lead roofing. Among its remains is a Pictish cross-slab in the nave, and a basin in a corner where one of Elgin's benefactors, Andrew Anderson, was kept as a baby by his homeless mother. Next to the cathedral are the **Biblical Gardens** with all 110 plants mentioned in the Bible, while the **Elgin Museum** has anthropological displays and the **Moray Motor Museum** has over 40 vehicles.

🏛 Elgin Museum
1 High St. **Tel** 01343 543675. **Open** Apr–Oct: 10am–5pm Mon–Fri; 11am–4pm Sat. 🅿️ ♿ limited. 📷

🏛 Moray Motor Museum
Bridge St, Bishopmill. **Tel** 01343 544933. **Open** Easter–Oct: 11am–5pm daily. 🅿️ ♿

Details of the central tower of Elgin Cathedral

⑰ Aberdeen

Scotland's third largest city and Europe's offshore oil capital, Aberdeen has prospered since the discovery of petroleum in the North Sea in 1970. The sea bed has now yielded over 100 oilfields. Widely known as the Granite City, its rugged outlines are softened by sumptuous year-round floral displays in its public parks and gardens, the Duthie Park Winter Gardens being one of the largest indoor gardens in Europe. The picturesque village of Footdee, which sits at the end of the city's 2-mile (3-km) beach, has good views back to the busy harbour.

The spires of Aberdeen, rising behind the city harbour

Exploring Aberdeen
The city centre flanks the mile-long (1.5 km) Union Street ending to the east at the Mercat Cross. The cross stands in Castlegate, the one-time site of the city castle. From here the cobbled Shiprow winds southwest and passes Provost Ross's House (*see p544*) on its way to the harbour with its fish market. A bus can be taken a mile (1.5 km) north of the centre to Old Aberdeen which, with its medieval streets and wynds, has the peaceful character of a separate village. Driving is restricted in some streets.

🏛 King's College
College Bounds, Old Aberdeen. **Tel** 01224 272137. Chapel **Open** 10am–3:30pm Mon–Fri. ♿

King's College was founded in 1495 as the city's first university. The inter-denominational chapel (the only part of the college open to the public) in the past consecutively Catholic and Protestant, has a lantern tower rebuilt after a storm in 1633. Stained-glass windows by Douglas Strachan add a contemporary touch to the interior which contains a 1540 pulpit, later carved with heads of Stuart monarchs.

⬆ St Andrew's Cathedral
King St. **Tel** 01224 640119. **Open** May–Sep: 11am–4pm Tue–Fri. ♿ 📷 by appointment.

The Mother Church of the Episcopal Communion in America, St Andrew's has a memorial to Samuel Seabury, the first Episcopalian bishop in the United States, who was consecrated in Aberdeen in 1784. Coats of arms adorn the ceiling above the north and south aisles, contrasting colourfully with the white walls and pillars. They represent the American States and local Jacobite (*see p541*) families.

The elegant lantern tower of the chapel at King's College

Provost Skene's House

Guestrow. **Tel** 01224 641086. **Open** 10am–5pm Mon–Sat (limited access to upper floors). **Closed** 25 & 26, 31 Dec–2 Jan. **W** aagm.co.uk

Once the home of Sir George Skene, a 17th-century provost (mayor) of Aberdeen, the house was built in 1545. Inside, period rooms span 200 years of design. The Duke of Cumberland stayed here before the Battle of Culloden *(see p541)*.

VISITORS' CHECKLIST

Practical Information
City of Aberdeen. 220,000.
23 Union St (01224 269180).
W aberdeen-grampian.com

Transport
Guild St.

The 18th-century Parlour, with its walnut harpsichord and covered chairs by the fire, was the informal room in which the family would have tea.

The Painted Gallery has one of Scotland's most important cycles of religious art. The panels are early 17th century, though the artist is unknown.

The 17th-century Great Hall contains heavy oak dining furniture. Provost Skene's wood-carved coat of arms hangs above the fireplace.

The Regency Room typifies early 19th-century elegance. A harp dating from 1820 stands by a Grecian-style sofa and a French writing table.

The Georgian Dining Room, with its Classical design, was the main formal room in the 16th century and still has its original flagstone floor.

Entrance

Aberdeen City Centre

① Aberdeen Art Gallery
② St Nicholas Kirk
③ Provost Skene's House
④ Marischal College
⑤ St Andrew's Cathedral
⑥ Mercat Cross
⑦ Maritime Museum

For keys to map symbols *see back flap*

🏛 Art Gallery

Schoolhill. **Tel** 01224 523700.
Open 10am–5pm Tue–Sat, 2–5pm
Sun. **Closed** 25 Dec–2 Jan. ♿
W aagm.co.uk

Housed in a Neo-Classical
building, purpose-built in 1884,
the Art Gallery has a wide
range of exhibitions, with
an emphasis on
contemporary work.
A fine collection of
Aberdonian silver
can be found
among the decorative
arts on the ground floor,
and is the subject of a
video presentation. A
permanent collection
of 18th–20th-century
fine art features such
names as Toulouse-
Lautrec, Reynolds and Zoffany.
Several of the works were
bequeathed in 1900 by a local
granite merchant, Alex
Macdonald. He commissioned
many of the paintings in the
Macdonald Room, which

**Aberdonian silver in
the Art Gallery**

displays 92 self-portraits by
British artists. Occasional poetry-
readings, music recitals and
films are on offer.

🏛 St Nicholas Kirk

Union St. **Tel** 01224 643494.
Open 10am–1pm Mon–Fri. ♿
W kirk-of-st-nicholas.org.uk

Founded in the 12th century,
St Nicholas
is Scotland's largest
parish church.
Though the
present structure
dates from 1752,
many relics of earlier
times can be seen
inside. After being
damaged during the
Reformation, the
interior was divided
into two. A chapel in the East
Church contains iron rings
used to secure witches in
the 17th century, while in the
West Church there are some
embroidered panels attributed to
one Mary Jameson (1597–1644).

🏛 Maritime Museum

Shiprow. **Tel** 01224 337700.
Open 10am–5pm Tue–Sat, noon–
3pm Sun. ♿ 🚻 📷 **W** aagm.co.uk

Overlooking the harbour is
Provost Ross's House, which
dates back to 1593 and is one
of the oldest residential
buildings in the town. This
museum traces the history of
Aberdeen's seafaring tradition.
Exhibitions include ship-wrecks,
rescues, shipbuilding and the
oil installations off Scotland's
east coast.

🏛 St Machar's Cathedral

The Chanonry. **Tel** 01224 485988. **Open**
9am–5pm daily (10am–4pm winter). ♿

Dominating Old Aberdeen,
the 15th-century edifice of St
Machar's is the oldest granite
building in the city. The stonework of one arch even dates
as far back as the 14th century.
The impressive nave now serves
as a parish church and its
magnificent oak ceiling is
adorned with the coats of arms

⑱ Royal Deeside Tour

Since Queen Victoria's purchase of the
Balmoral estate in 1852, Deeside has been
best known as the summer home of the
British Royal Family, though it has been
associated with royalty since the time
of Robert the Bruce *(see p486)*. The route
follows the Dee, formerly a prolific salmon
river, through some magnificent
Grampian scenery.

④ **Muir of Dinnet
Nature Reserve**
An information
centre on the A97
provides an excellent
place from which to
explore this beautiful
mixed woodland
area, formed by the
retreating glaciers of
the last Ice Age.

⑥ **Balmoral**
Bought by Queen Victoria for
30,000 guineas in 1852, after its
owner choked to death on a
fishbone, the castle was rebuilt
in the Scottish Baronial style at
Prince Albert's request.

⑤ **Ballater**
The old railway town of
Ballater has royal warrants
on many of its shop fronts.
It grew as a 19th-century
spa town, its waters
reputedly providing a
cure for tuberculosis.

of 48 popes, emperors and princes of Christendom.

🄆 Dunkeld

Perth & Kinross. 🄯 2,500. 🄯 Birnam. 🄯 🄯 The Cross (01350 727688). 🄦 **perthshire.co.uk**

Situated by the River Tay, this ancient and charming village was all but destroyed in the Battle of Dunkeld, a Jacobite (see p541) defeat, in 1689. The **Little Houses** lining Cathedral Street were the first to be rebuilt, and are fine examples of imaginative restoration. The ruins of the 14th-century **cathedral** enjoy an idyllic setting on shady lawns beside the Tay, against a backdrop of steep and wooded hills. The choir is used as the parish church and its north wall contains a Leper's Squint: a hole through which lepers could see the altar during mass. It was while on holiday in the Dunkeld

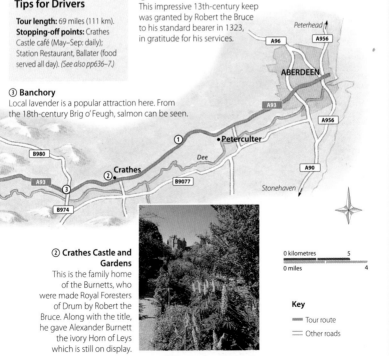

The ruins of Dunkeld Cathedral

country-side that Beatrix Potter (see p371) found the location for her Peter Rabbit stories.

🄇 Pitlochry

Perth & Kinross. 🄯 2,900. 🄯 🄯 🄯 22 Atholl Rd (01796 472215). 🄦 **perthshire.co.uk**

Surrounded by pine-forested hills, Pitlochry became famous after Queen Victoria (see p60) described it as one of the finest resorts in Europe. In early summer, salmon swim up the ladder built into the Power Station Dam, on their way to spawning grounds upriver. There is a viewing chamber here to see them. The **Power Station Visitor Centre** outlines the hydro-electric scheme that harnesses the waters of the River Tummel. The tasting tours at **Edradour Distillery** give an insight into traditional whisky-making (see p493). Scotland's famous **Festival Theatre** puts on a summer season when the programme changes daily.

🄯 **Power Station Visitor Centre**
Pitlochry. **Tel** 01796 473152. **Open** Apr–Oct: 10am–5:30pm Mon–Fri (Jul & Aug: daily). 🄯 🄯

🄯 **Festival Theatre**
Port-na-Craig. **Tel** 01796 484626. **Open** daily. 🄯 🄯 🄯

🄯 **Edradour Distillery**
Pitlochry, off A924. **Tel** 01796 472095. **Open** phone for opening hours and times of tours. 🄯 🄯 ltd. 🄯 🄯 🄦 **edradour.co.uk**

Tips for Drivers

Tour length: 69 miles (111 km). **Stopping-off points:** Crathes Castle café (May–Sep: daily); Station Restaurant, Ballater (food served all day). *(See also pp636–7.)*

① Drum Castle
This impressive 13th-century keep was granted by Robert the Bruce to his standard bearer in 1323, in gratitude for his services.

③ Banchory
Local lavender is a popular attraction here. From the 18th-century Brig o' Feugh, salmon can be seen.

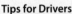

② Crathes Castle and Gardens
This is the family home of the Burnetts, who were made Royal Foresters of Drum by Robert the Bruce. Along with the title, he gave Alexander Burnett the ivory Horn of Leys which is still on display.

Peterhead

A96   A956

ABERDEEN

A93

A956

① ●Peterculter

B980   Dee

② Crathes   A90

A93   ③   B9077

Stonehaven

B974

0 kilometres   5

0 miles   4

Key
━━━ Tour route
═══ Other roads

㉑ Killiecrankie Walk

In an area famous for its scenery and historical connections, this circular walk offers typical Highland views. The route is fairly flat, though ringed by mountains, and follows the River Garry south to Loch Faskally, meandering through a wooded gorge, passing the Soldier's Leap and a Victorian viaduct. There are several ideal picnic spots along the way. Returning along the River Tummel, the walk crosses one of Queen Victoria's favourite Highland areas, before doubling back along the rivers to complete the circuit.

① Killiecrankie
A Visitor Centre provides information on the Battle of Killiecrankie, fought in 1689.

② Soldier's Leap
The Redcoat soldier Donald Macbean leapt over the river here to avoid capture by Jacobites during the 1689 battle.

⑦ Linn of Tummel
The path passes a pool beneath the Falls of Tummel and leads through a beautiful forest trail.

⑥ Coronation Bridge
Spanning the River Tummel, this footbridge was built in 1860 in honour of George IV.

Garry Bridge

Faskally House

TUMMEL FOREST PARK

③ Killiecrankie Pass
A 17th-century military road built by General Wade follows the gorge.

⑤ Memorial Arch
The workers killed in the construction of the Clunie Dam are commemorated here.

loch faskally

Pitlochry

④ Clunie Foot Bridge
This bridge crosses the artificial Loch Faskally, created by the damming of the River Tummel for hydro-electric power in the 1950s.

Tips for Walkers

Starting point: NTS Visitor Centre Killiecrankie.
Tel 0844 493 2192.
Getting there: Bus from Pitlochry or Aberfeldy.
Length: 10 miles (16 km).
Difficulty: Very easy.

Key
- ▪ ▪ Route
- ▬▬ Major road
- ▭▭ B road
- ▭▭ Minor road

0 kilometres   1
0 miles   0.5

The Three Sisters, Glencoe, in late autumn

㉒ Blair Castle

Blair Atholl, Perthshire. **Tel** 01796 481207. ⬙ Blair Atholl. **Open** Apr–Oct: 9:30am–5:30pm daily; Nov–Mar: 10am–4pm Sat & Sun. **Closed** 1 & 2 Jan, 25–27 Dec. 🅿 🅱 limited. **W** blair-castle.co.uk

This rambling, turreted castle has been altered so often in its 700-year history that it provides a unique insight into the history of Highland aristocratic life. The 18th-century wing has a display containing the gloves and pipe of Bonnie Prince Charlie *(see p539)*, who spent two days here gathering Jacobite *(see p541)* support. Family portraits cover 300 years and include paintings by such masters as Johann Zoffany and Sir Peter Lely. Sir Edwin Landseer's *Death of a Stag in Glen Tilt* (1850) was painted nearby.

In 1844 Queen Victoria visited the castle and conferred on its owners, the Dukes of Atholl, the distinction of being allowed to maintain a private army. The Atholl Highlanders still flourish.

㉓ The Cairngorms

See pp548–9.

㉔ Glencoe

Highland. ⬙ Fort William. 🚌 Glencoe. 🛈 Visit Scotland (0844 493 2222).

Renowned for its awesome scenery and savage history, Glencoe was compared by Dickens to "a burial ground of a race of giants". The precipitous cliffs of Buachaille Etive Mor and the knife-edged ridge of Aonach Eagach (both over 900 m; 3,000 ft) present a formidable challenge even to experienced mountaineers.

Against a dark backdrop of craggy peaks and the tumbling River Coe, the Glen offers superb hill-walking in the summer. Stout footwear, waterproofs and attention to safety warnings are essential. Details of routes, ranging from the easy half-hour between the **NTS Visitor Centre** and Signal Rock (from which the signal was given to commence the massacre) to a stiff 6 mile (10 km) haul up the Devil's Staircase can be had from the Visitor Centre. Guided walks are offered in summer by the NTS Ranger service.

The Massacre of Glencoe

In 1692, the chief of the Glencoe MacDonalds was five days late in registering an oath of submission to William III, giving the government an excuse to root out a nest of Jacobite *(p541)* supporters. For ten days 130 soldiers, captained by Robert Campbell, were hospitably entertained by the unsuspecting MacDonalds. At dawn on 13 February, in a terrible breach of trust, the soldiers fell on their hosts, killing some 38 MacDonalds. Many more died in their wintry mountain hideouts. The massacre, unsurprisingly, became a political scandal, though there were to be no official reprimands for three years.

Detail of *The Massacre of Glencoe* by James Hamilton

🛈 **NTS Visitor Centre**
Glencoe. **Tel** 0844 493 2222. **Open** daily. 🅿 🅱 ltd. 🄽🅃🅂 **W** nts.org.uk

㉒ The Cairngorms

Rising to a height of 1,309 m (4,296 ft), the Cairngorm mountains form the highest landmass in Britain. Cairn Gorm itself is the site of one of Britain's first ski centres. A weather station at the mountain's summit provides regular reports, essential in an area known for sudden changes of weather. Walkers should be sure to follow the mountain code without fail. The funicular railway that climbs Cairn Gorm affords superb views over the Spey Valley. Many estates in the valley have centres which introduce the visitor to Highland land use.

Strathspey Steam Railway
This track between Aviemore and Broomhill dates from 1863.

Inverness   *Nair*

A938 **Carrbridge**

B9153

Boat of Garten

A9

Aviemore ①

Coylumbridge

Beanaidh

LOCH AN EILEIN

A9   **B9152**   *Spey*

Kincraig

LOCH INSH

Feshie

Kingussie

Newtonmore

B970

Tolvah

BRAERIACH ▲
1,295 m (4,248 ft)
LOCH EINICH

Perth

Kincraig Highland Wildlife Park
Driving through this park, the visitor can see bison alongside wolves and wild boar. All of these animals were once common in the Highlands.

0 kilometres   5

0 miles   5

KEY

① **Aviemore**, the commercial centre of the Cairngorms, provides buses to the ski area 13 km (9 miles) away.

② **The Cairngorm Reindeer Centre**, provides walks in the hills among Britain's only herd of reindeer.

③ **Ben MacDhui**, is Britain's second highest peak, after Ben Nevis.

Rothiemurchus Estate
Highland cattle can be seen among many other creatures at Rothiemurchus. A visitor centre provides guided walks and illustrates life on a Highland estate.

Loch Garten Nature Reserve

Ospreys now thrive in this reserve in Abernethy Forest, which was established in 1959 to protect the first pair seen in Britain for 50 years.

Grantown-on-spey

Broomhill

A95

B970

Nethy Bridge

LOCH GARTEN

Nethy

CH LICH

② 🎿

P ▶️

CAIRN GORM

▲
1,245 m (4,084 ft)

BEN MACDHUI

▲
1,309 m (4,296 ft)

③

**C A I R N G O R M
M O U N T A I N S**

Skiing

From the Coire Cas car park, a funicular railway can be taken to the restaurant at the summit. There are 34 ski runs in all.

Flora of the Cairngorms

With mixed woodland at their base and the summits forming a sub-polar plateau, the Cairngorms present a huge variety of flora. Ancient Caledonian pines (once common in the area) survive in Abernethy Forest, while arctic flowers flourish in the heights.

The Cairngorm plateau holds little life except lichen (Britain's oldest plant), wood rush and cushions of moss campion, which is often completely covered with pink flowers.

Shady corries are important areas for alpine plants such as arctic mouse-ear, hare's foot sedge, mountain rock-cress and alpine speedwell.

Pinewoods occupy the higher slopes, revealing purple heather as they become sparser.

Mixed woodland covers the lower ground which is carpeted with heather and deergrass.

1,200 m (4000 ft)

1,000 m (3,300 ft)

800 m (2,600 ft)

600 m (2,000 ft)

400 m (1,300 ft)

200 m (650 ft)

0 m (0 ft)

An idealized section of the Cairngorm plateau

Key

▬ Major road

▬ Minor road

═ Narrow lane

• – Footpath

㉕ Road to the Isles Tour

This scenic route goes past vast mountain-corridors, breathtaking beaches of white sand and tiny villages, to the town of Mallaig, one of the ferry ports for the isles of Skye, Rum and Eigg. As well as the stunning scenery, the area is steeped in Jacobite history (see p541).

Tips for Drivers

Tour length: 45 miles (72 km).
Stopping-off points: Glenfinnan NTS Visitors' Centre (0844 493 2221) explains the Jacobite risings and serves refreshments; the Old Library Lodge, Arisaig, has good Scottish food. (See also pp636–7.)

⑦ Mallaig
The Road to the Isles ends at Mallaig, an active little fishing port with a very good harbour and one of the ferry links to Skye (see pp538–9).

⑥ Morar
The road continues through Morar, an area renowned for its white sands, and Loch Morar, rumoured to be the home of a 12-m (40-ft) monster known as Morag.

⑤ Prince's Cairn
Crossing the Ardnish Peninsula to Loch Nan Uamh, a cairn marks the spot from which Bonnie Prince Charlie finally left Scotland for France in 1746.

㉖ Oban

Argyll & Bute. ▲ 8,000. ⛴ 🚌 🚆
ℹ️ North Pier (01631 563122).
🌐 oban.org.uk

Located on the Firth of Lorne and commanding a magnificent view of the Argyll coast, the bustling port of Oban is a popular destination for travellers on their way to Mull and the Western Isles (see p533).

Dominating the skyline is McCaig's Tower, an unfinished Victorian imitation of the Colosseum in Rome. It is worth making the 10-minute climb from the town centre for the sea views alone. Attractions in the town include working centres for glass, pottery and whisky; the Oban distillery produces one of the country's finest malt whiskies (see p493). The **Scottish Sealife Sanctuary** rescues injured and orphaned seals and has displays of underwater life. Car ferries depart for Barra and South Uist, Mull, Tiree and Colonsay islands.

Dunstaffnage Castle, 3 miles (5 km) north of Oban, was the 13th-century stronghold of the MacDougalls. It has atmospheric ruins, a chapel and the "new house" where Flora MacDonald (see p539) is believed to have been imprisoned in 1746.

🌊 **Scottish Sealife Sanctuary**
Barcaldine. **Tel** 01631 720386. **Open** daily. **Closed** 25 Dec. 🅿️ ♿ 🚻 📷
🌐 sealsanctuary.co.uk

🏛️ **Dunstaffnage Castle**
Dunbeg, off A85. **Tel** 01631 562 465. **Open** daily. **Closed** Nov–Mar: Thu pm & Fri. 🅿️ 📷

㉗ Mull

Argyll & Bute. ▲ 2,700. ⛴ from Oban, Kilchoan, Lochaline. ℹ️ Main Street, Tobermory (01680 812377).

Most roads on this easily accessible Hebridean island follow the sharply indented rocky coastline, affording wonderful sea views. On a promontory to the east lies **Duart Castle**, home of the chief of Clan Maclean. Visitors can see the Banqueting Hall and State Rooms in the 13th-century keep. Its dungeons once held prisoners from a Spanish Armada galleon sunk by a

Looking out to sea across Tobermory Bay, Mull

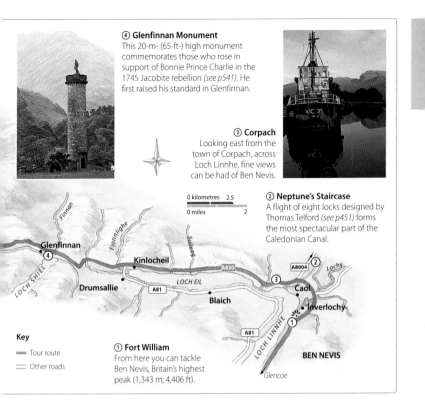

④ Glenfinnan Monument
This 20-m- (65-ft-) high monument commemorates those who rose in support of Bonnie Prince Charlie in the 1745 Jacobite rebellion (see p541). He first raised his standard in Glenfinnan.

③ Corpach
Looking east from the town of Corpach, across Loch Linnhe, fine views can be had of Ben Nevis.

② Neptune's Staircase
A flight of eight locks designed by Thomas Telford (see p451) forms the most spectacular part of the Caledonian Canal.

0 kilometres 2.5
0 miles 2

Key

▬ Tour route

═ Other roads

① Fort William
From here you can tackle Ben Nevis, Britain's highest peak (1,343 m; 4,406 ft).

Donald Maclean in 1588. The attractive riverside village of Dervaig houses a fascinating heritage centre.

Environs
From Fionnphort, a ferry goes to **Iona**, where St Columba (see p529) began his mission in Scotland in 563. North of Iona, the Isle of Staffa should be visited for its magnificent **Fingal's Cave**.

Duart Castle
Off A849, nr Craignure.
Tel 01680 812309. **Open** Apr–Oct: 10:30am– 5:30pm daily.

㉘ Loch Awe
Argyll & Bute. 🚆 🚌 Dalmally.
ℹ Inveraray (01499 302063).
🌐 loch-awe.com

One of the longest of Scotland's freshwater lochs, Loch Awe fills a 25-mile (40-km) glen in the southwestern Highlands. A short drive east of the village of Lochawe leads to the lochside remains of **Kilchurn Castle**,

The ruins of Kilchurn Castle on the shore of Loch Awe

abandoned after being struck by lightning in the 18th century. Dwarfing the castle is the huge bulk of Ben Cruachan, whose summit can be reached by the narrow Pass of Brander, in which Robert the Bruce (see p486) fought the Clan MacDougal in 1308. From the A85, a tunnel leads to the cavernous Cruachan Power Station. Near the village of Taynuilt the

preserved Lorn Furnace at Bonawe is a reminder of the iron-smelting industry that caused the destruction of much of the area's woodland in the 18th and 19th centuries.

Marked prehistoric cairns are found off the A816 between Kilmartin and Dunadd. The latter boasts a 6th-century hill fort from which the Stone of Destiny (see p486) originated.

For additional map symbols see back flap

㉙ Inveraray Castle

Inveraray, Argyll & Bute. ⛴ Dalmally.
🚌 from Glasgow. **Tel** 01499 302203.
Open Apr–Oct: 10am–5:45pm daily.
🖼 ♿ limited. 🏷 🛍 🍴
🌐 inveraray-castle.com

This multi-turreted mock Gothic palace is the family home of the powerful Clan Campbell who have been the Dukes of Argyll since 1701. The castle was built in 1745 by architects Roger Morris and William Adam on the ruins of a 15th-century castle, and the conical towers added later, after a fire in 1877. Magnificent interiors, designed by Robert Mylne in the 1770s, form a back-drop to a huge collection of Oriental and European porcelain and Regency furniture and portraits by Ramsay, Gainsborough and Raeburn. The Armoury Hall features a display of weaponry collected by the Campbells to fight the Jacobites *(see p541)*.

The pinnacled, Gothic exterior of Inveraray Castle

㉚ Auchindrain Museum

Inveraray, Argyll & Bute. **Tel** 01499 500235. 🚌 Inveraray, then bus. **Open** Apr–Oct: 10am–5pm daily (last adm: 4pm); Nov–Apr: daily, weather permitting. 🖼 🏷 ♿ limited.
🌐 auchindrain.org.uk

The first open-air museum in Scotland, Auchindrain illuminates the working lives of the kind of farming community that was typical of the Highlands until the late 19th century. Originally a township of some 20 thatched buildings, the site was communally farmed by its tenants until the last one retired in 1962. Visitors can wander through the buildings, many of which combine living space, kitchen and cattle shed under one roof. Some are furnished with box beds and

old rush lamps. The homes of Auchindrain are a fascinating memorial to the time before the transition from of subsistence to commercial farming.

An old hay turner at the Auchindrain Museum

㉛ Crarae Gardens

Crarae, Argyll & Bute. **Tel** 01546 886614 or NTS (0844 4932210). 🚌 Inveraray, then bus. **Open** 9:30am–sunset daily. Visitor Centre: **Open** Apr–Oct: 10am–5pm Thu–Mon. 🖼 ♿ limited.

Considered the most beguiling of the gardens of the West Highlands, the **Crarae Gardens** were created in the 1920s by Lady Grace Campbell. She was the aunt of explorer Reginald Farrer, whose specimens from Tibet were the beginnings of a collection of exotic plants. The gardens are nourished by the warmth of the Gulf

Stream and the high rainfall. Although there are many unusual Himalayan rhododendrons flourishing here, the gardens are also home to exotic plants from various countries including Tasmania, New Zealand and the USA. Plant collectors still contribute to the gardens, which are best seen in spring and early summer against the blue waters of Loch Fyne.

㉜ Jura

Argyll & Bute. 🏔 200. 🚢 from Kennacraig to Islay, then Islay to Jura.
ℹ Bowmore (01496 810254).

Barren, mountainous and overrun by red deer, the isle of Jura has only one road which connects the single village of Craighouse to the Islay ferry. Though walking is restricted during the stalking (deer hunting) season between August and October, the island offers superb hillwalking, especially on the slopes of the three main peaks, known as the Paps of Jura. The tallest of these is Beinn An Oir at 784 m (2571 ft). Beyond the northern tip of the isle are the notorious whirlpools of Corryvreckan. The novelist George Orwell (who came to the island to write his final novel, *1984*) nearly lost his

Lagavulin distillery, producer of one Scotland's finest malts, on Islay

Mist crowning the Paps of Jura, seen at sunset across the Sound of Islay

life here in 1946 when he fell into the water. A legend tells of Prince Breackan who, to win the hand of a princess, tried to keep his boat anchored in the whirlpool for three days, held by ropes made of hemp, wool and maidens' hair. The Prince drowned when a single rope, containing the hair of a girl who had been untrue, finally broke.

❸ Islay

Argyll & Bute. 🏔 3,500. 🚢 from Kennacraig. 🛈 The Square, Bowmore (01496 810254).
Ⓦ **visitscotland.com**

The most southerly of the Western Isles, Islay (pronounced 'Eyeluh') is the home of respected Highland single malt whiskies Lagavulin and Laphroaig. Most of the island's distilleries produce heavily peated malts with a distinctive tang of the sea. The Georgian village of Bowmore has the island's oldest distillery and a circular church designed to minimize the Devil's possible lurking-places. The **Museum of Islay Life** in Port Charlotte contains fascinating information on social and natural history. Seven miles (11 km) east of Port Ellen stands the Kildalton Cross. A block of local green stone adorned with

Old Testament scenes, it is one of the most impressive 8th-century Celtic crosses in Britain. Worth a visit for its archaeological and historical interest is the medieval stronghold of the Lords of the Isles, **Finlaggan**. Islay's beaches support a variety of bird life, some of which can be observed at the RSPB reserve at Gruinart.

🏛 **Museum of Islay Life**
Port Charlotte. **Tel** 01496 850358.
Open Apr–Oct: Mon–Sat (times vary – call to check). 🅿 ♿

❷ Kintyre

Argyll & Bute. 🏔 6,000. 🚢 Oban. 🚌 Campbeltown. 🛈 MacKinnon House, The Pier, Campbeltown (01586 552056). Ⓦ **kintyre.org**

A long, narrow peninsula stretching far south of Glasgow, Kintyre has superb views across to the islands of Gigha, Islay and

Jura. The 9 mile (14 km) Crinan Canal, opened in 1801, is a delight-ful inland waterway, its 15 locks bustling with pleasure craft in the summer. The town of Tarbert (meaning "isthmus" in Gaelic) takes its name from the neck on which it stands, which is narrow enough to drag a boat across between Loch Fyne and West Loch Tarbert. This feat was first achieved by the Viking King Magnus Barfud who, in 1198, was granted by treaty as much land as he could sail around. Travelling south past Camp-beltown, the B842 ends at the headland known as the Mull of Kintyre, which was made famous when former Beatle Paul McCartney commercialized a traditional pipe tune of the same name. Westward lies the isle of Rathlin, where Robert the Bruce (see p486) learned patience in his struggles against the English by watching a spider weaving a web in a cave.

Fishing boats and yachts moored at Tarbert harbour, Kintyre

TRAVELLERS' NEEDS

WHERE TO STAY

Whatever the budget or accommodation preferences, visitors should easily be able to find an establishment to suit their needs from the large choice given in the hotel listings on pages 560–73. These include places to stay at all price points, from modest budget venues to palatial and super-luxurious five-star establishments. All the hotels selected are among the best of their kind, with a distinctive character or exceptional qualities of hospitality, excellent facilities or good value for money. Location is another prime consideration for inclusion: all the hotels and guesthouses listed make convenient touring bases for one or more of the destinations featured in this book, or have attractive or interesting settings, which are enjoyable in their own right.

On the next few pages we outline some of the types of accommodation available across Great Britain, along with various aspects of choosing, booking and paying for your stay.

Country-House Hotels

The quintessentially British country-house hotel has proliferated in the past few decades. Individual examples vary widely, but the best are usually set in buildings of architectural or historic interest, filled with antiques or high-quality traditional furnishings. They generally have extensive grounds but are not always in deeply rural locations. Some of the best in the country are found in the Cotswolds.

Comfort, even luxury, is assured, along with good food and service – frequently with a very high price tag. Many country-house hotels also offer extensive spa or health club facilities. Some of these hotels are still owned and personally managed by resident proprietors; others belong to groups or chains.

Boutique and Designer Hotels

This fashionable, design-conscious type of hotel is found around the country. These ultra-cool temples of style revel in innovative architecture, funky decor and hip high-tech gadgetry. Many exude an air of uncluttered minimalism, and some have outstanding restaurants. Chains like **Malmaison** or **Hotel du Vin** could also be included in this category; the boutique B&B is a spin-off of this trend.

Hotel Groups

Newer hotel groups have taken the place of many of the long-established names, providing standardized accommodation at all price levels in most parts of Great Britain. The majority of chain

The front entrance of the Royal Crescent Hotel, Bath *(see p565)*

hotels lie in accessible, convenient locations. Though lacking in individuality, they are practical and efficiently run, and they usually represent good value for money. They also frequently offer bargain deals and reduced rates depending on the time of year.

Budget chains offering no-frills, motel-lodge-style accommodation include **Ibis**, **Travelodge** and **Premier Inn**; further up the scale are mid-market chains like **Holiday Inn**, **Novotel**, **Marriott** and **Radisson Blu**. Some of these hotels have corporate deals and will offer cheaper rates during the weekend.

Also found throughout the country are well-known, independently owned franchise hotels, including **Best Western** and **Pride of Britain**.

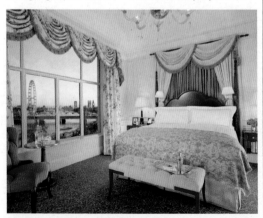

A River View suite at The Savoy, London, offers panoramic views of the Thames *(see p560)*

◀ Diagonal pedestrian crossing in Oxford Circus, London

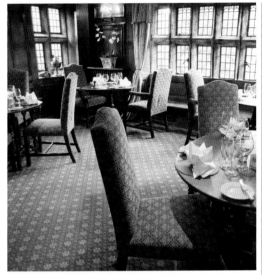
Jacobean dining area of Holdsworth House, Halifax *(see p570)*

Inns and Pubs with Rooms

The coaching inn is a familiar concept in Britain. Many of these fine old hostelries date from the 18th century, though some are even older, and often provide reliable restaurants, traditional decor and a warm and friendly atmosphere.

Other types of pubs or inns now offer accommodation and reputable food, and many have become much more welcoming to families. Britain's best inns are very comfortable and stylish and bear comparison with any good hotel. Gastropubs, informal eateries often with exceptional food, sometimes offer stylish accommodation at reasonable prices.

Guesthouses and B&Bs

The bed-and-breakfast is probably the best-known type of budget accommodation in Great Britain. These establishments are generally family-owned private homes or farmhouses. Accommodation and facilities can be simple (bedrooms may not have TV, telephones or en-suite bathrooms, for example),
but the best can be quite sophisticated. Prices include breakfast – generally a traditional British fry-up, but other options are usually available as well.

A few B&Bs are reluctant to accept credit cards or travellers' cheques or may charge a premium for doing so. It is advisable to have some alternative method of payment, preferably cash. Any regional tourist office should be able to supply a list of local registered B&Bs on request, though they
cannot make specific recommendations and may charge a fee or a commission for making bookings on your behalf. Travel websites such as www.visitengland.com serve as a good resource, as does the **London Bed and Breakfast Agency**.

Hotel Gradings

Recent but only partially successful attempts have been made to harmonize the confusing and often conflicting systems of accommodation classification used by the various tourist boards and motoring organizations, such as the AA and RAC. In England, hotel gradings are based on a system of one to five stars awarded for facilities and service: the more stars, the more luxurious you can expect your hotel to be. Guesthouses and B&Bs are also graded with one to five stars, a quality score that is based on various aspects of the accommodation, including cleanliness and hospitality. Special awards (gold and silver, ribbons, rosettes and so on) are given for excellence in certain categories, such as an exceptional breakfast or a warm welcome. Scotland and Wales have their own quality-based gradings.

The modern Champagne Bar at Gilpin Lodge, Windermere *(see p570)*

Prices and Bookings

Some hotels just quote room rates; others may quote a B&B or half-board (dinner, bed and breakfast) rate per person. Rates are generally inclusive of Value Added Tax (VAT) and service, but some top-range hotels make additional charges; most charge hefty single-person supplements.

The cost of a standard en-suite double room in a London hotel including breakfast averages £130 per night, but at the top end of the scale, a suite can cost around £3,000. The summer months and key events hike up hotel prices even further.

Outside London; expect to pay an average of £100 per night for the same. Standard B&B accommodation is typically under £50 per person per night, but again there is wide variation, with boutique B&Bs operating more like hotels. A B&B in London typically costs around £100 for a double room per night, including breakfast.

Most hotels request confirmation by email and a deposit in advance (a credit card number will generally do). Email bookings are now commonplace, and most hotels have an online booking facility on their website. Bargains can be found on sites including www.laterooms.com and www.lastminute.com. Websites such as Expedia, Kayak and Travelocity are cheaper ways of booking, especially for a room and a flight together.

The luxurious drawing room at Middlethorpe Hall, York (see p570)

A traditionally decorated bedroom at Judges Country House, Yarm *(see p570)*

Any hotel booking is a legally binding contract. If you don't show up, the full cost of your stay may be charged. Most hotels will refund your deposit if they are able to re-let the room, but some will charge a penalty, depending how close to the stay you cancel. Most travel insurance policies cover cancellation charges for pre-booked UK hotel stays of more than two days, if there is a satisfactory reason.

Watch out for hidden extras. Telephone charges from hotel rooms have a high mark-up, and rates quoted per unit do not always indicate clearly how much time you get for your money.

Roadside sign for a bed-and-breakfast

There is no need to tip staff unless they go out of their way to perform some very exceptional duty.

Self-Catering

Self-catering has many attractions, especially for families on a budget and with young children. With the arrival of the "unhotel" concept, self-catering has become a popular way to travel. Sites like **Air bnb** and **One Fine Stay** offer apartments and homes to rent directly from their owners, offering the chance to live like a local. The range of places to let for holiday rentals is huge, from luxury apartments to log cabins or converted farm buildings. Character properties are available from conservation organizations such as the **Landmark Trust**, which restores buildings of historic or architectural interest and makes them available for short-term lets, and **English Heritage** and the **National Trust** *(see p33)*, which have a number of holiday cottages on their estates. They tend to be popular, so book ahead.

Annually updated self-catering guides are a useful source of listings, and Sawdays.com is a particularly good source of information. Tourist offices can supply up-to-date regional lists and can also offer a booking service.

Confirm what is included in the price (cleaning, electricity and so on), and check whether any extra fees, deposits or insurance charges will be added to the bill.

Caravanning, Camping and Motor Homes

Most of Britain's campsites and caravan parks open only for about six months of the year (typically from Easter to

October), but you will need to make reservations in advance. Helpful organizations include the **Camping and Caravanning Club** and the **Caravan Club**, which publish lists of their member parks and operate their own grading systems.

Camping or caravanning pitches typically cost around £20 per night. For a list of sites, check www.pitchup.com, www.coolcamping.co.uk or the **Forestry Commission**.

Motor homes give greater freedom to explore at your own pace and a wider choice of places to stay, including most campsites and caravan parks. Some operators will let guests pick up their vehicle directly from an airport or ferry terminal.

Campsite in Ogwen Valley, Snowdonia

Travellers with Disabilities

All the UK's tourist boards provide information about disabled access in their accommodation and sightseeing guides. National Accessible Scheme gradings are awarded to properties approved under the **Tourism for All** initiative for various categories of disability. For information on these gradings or other advice on accommodation and travel for visitors with disabilities, contact Tourism for All. **Disability Rights UK** also publishes an annual holiday guide. The **Visit England** website has an Accessible England section detailing accessible attractions and transport, and runs the National Accessible Scheme for accommodation.

Before booking a hotel or caravan and camping site, check that it meets all your needs.

Recommended Hotels

The accommodation options in this guide have been selected across a wide range of prices for their excellent facilities, good location and value. From five-star country-house retreats to boutique hotels, humble B&Bs and character hotels with interesting and unique features. For the best of each region, look out for hotels designated as DK Choices. These are highlighted because they offer something unique – a stunning location, a compelling history or a special atmosphere. Book ahead as these are popular establishments.

DIRECTORY

Boutique and Designer Hotels

Hotel du Vin
Tel 08719 130345.
W hotelduvin.com

Malmaison
Tel 08719 430350.
W malmaison.com

Hotel Groups

Best Western
Tel 08457 767676.
W bestwestern.co.uk

Holiday Inn
W holidayinn.com

Ibis
W ibis.com

Marriott
W marriott.com

Novotel
W novotel.com

Premier Inn
W premierinn.com

Pride of Britain
Tel 08081 639084.
W prideofbritain
hotels.com

Radisson Blu
W radissonblu.com

Travelodge
W travelodge.co.uk

Guesthouses and B&Bs

London Bed and Breakfast Agency
Tel 020 7586 2768.
W londonbb.com

Self-Catering

Air bnb
W airbnb.co.uk

English Heritage
Tel 08703 331187.
W english-heritage.
org.uk

Landmark Trust
Tel 01628 825925.
W landmarktrust.org.
uk

National Trust
Tel 08448 002070.
W nationaltrust
cottages.co.uk

National Trust for Scotland
Tel 08444 932100.
W nts.org.uk

One Fine Stay
Tel 08006 124377.
W onefinestay.com

Caravanning, Camping and Motor Homes

Camping and Caravanning Club
Tel 08451 307633.
W campingand
caravanningclub.co.uk

Caravan Club
W caravanclub.co.uk

Forestry Commission
Tel 08451 308223.
W forestholidays.co.uk

Travellers with Disabilities

Disability Rights UK
Unit 12, City Forum,
250 City Road,
London, EC1V 8AF.
Tel 020 7250 3222.
W disabilityrightsuk.
org

Tourism for All
7a Pixel Mill,
44 Appleby Rd, Kendal,
Cumbria, LA9 6ES.
Tel 08451 249971.
W tourismforall.org.uk

Visit England
W visitengland.com

Tourist Information

Visit Britain
W visitbritain.com

Where to Stay

London

West End and Westminster

Lime Tree ££
B&B **Map** 18 E2
135–137 Ebury St, SW1W 9QU
Tel *020 7730 8191*
W *limetreehotel.co.uk*
Attractively furnished and comfortable, family-run B&B.

The Orange ££
Character **Map** 18 D2
37 Pimlico Rd, SW1W 8NE
Tel *020 7881 9844*
W *theorange.co.uk*
Four snug en-suite bedrooms, a rustic restaurant and free Wi-Fi.

Claridge's £££
Luxury **Map** 10 E2
49 Brook St, W1K 4HR
Tel *020 7629 8860*
W *claridges.co.uk*
Seamless service and understated luxury in a superb Art Deco hotel.

Covent Garden £££
Designer **Map** 11 B2
10 Monmouth St, WC2H 9HB
Tel *020 7806 1000*
W *firmdalehotels.com*
Designer-dressed hotel from the Firmdale stable fusing old-world style with metropolitan chic.

St James's Hotel and Club £££
Luxury **Map** 10 F4
7–8 Park Place, SW1A 1LS
Tel *020 7316 1600*
W *stjameshotelandclub.com*
Town house with its own art collection and Michelin-starred restaurant. Close to designer shops.

The Apartments by the Sloane Club £££
Designer **Map** 18 D3
52 Lower Sloane St, SW1W 8EB
Tel *020 7730 9131*

W *clubapartments.co.uk*
Stylishly refurbished Art Deco apartments with coffee machines, flat-screen TVs and 24-hour concierge service.

The Athenaeum £££
Luxury **Map** 10 E4
116 Piccadilly, W1J 7BJ
Tel *020 7499 3464*
W *athenaeumhotel.com*
An established hotel brought up to date with spacious bedrooms and family-friendly apartments.

DK Choice

The Dorchester £££
Luxury **Map** 10 D3
Park Lane, W1K 1QA
Tel *020 7629 8888*
W *thedorchester.com*
London's Art Deco grand dame overlooking Hyde Park, is the hotel of choice for A-list movie stars. The bath in which Elizabeth Taylor signed her $1m contract for *Cleopatra* (1963) is preserved, but the rest of the hotel has been gorgeously refurbished. Savour the famous and delectable afternoon tea in the dining room.

The Goring £££
Historic **Map** 18 E1
Beeston Place, SW1W 0JW
Tel *020 7396 9000*
W *thegoring.com*
A great English institution with liveried doormen, private gardens and crackling fires on winter days.

The Ritz £££
Luxury **Map** 10 F3
150 Piccadilly, W1J 9BR
Tel *020 7493 8181*
W *theritzlondon.com*
A treat with its gilded dining room and modernized yet stunning Louis XVI-style bedrooms.

Price Guide

Prices are based on one night's stay in high season for a standard double room, inclusive of service charges and taxes.

£	up to £100
££	£100–£200
£££	over £200

The Savoy £££
Luxury **Map** 11 C2
Strand, WC2R 0EU
Tel *020 7836 4343*
W *fairmont.com*
Famed for its Art Deco American bar, this is luxury at its best with elegantly decorated rooms.

The Stafford London by Kempinski £££
Character **Map** 10 F4
16–18 St James's Place, SW1A 1NJ
Tel *020 7493 0111*
W *kempinski.com*
Traditional country-house decor and an American bar.

The Wellesley £££
Luxury **Map** 10 D5
11 Knightsbridge, SW1X 7LY
Tel *020 7235 3535*
W *thewellesley.co.uk*
No expense spared, this self-consciously stylish hotel even offers free Rolls-Royce transfers.

W £££
Boutique **Map** 11 A2
10 Wardour St, W1D 6QF
Tel *020 7758 1000*
W *wlondon.co.uk*
Modern, colourful rooms set within a glass exterior.

South Kensington and Hyde Park

Hyde Park Rooms £
B&B **Map** 9 A1
137 Sussex Gardens, W2 2RX
Tel *020 7723 0225*
W *hydeparkrooms.com*
No-frills rooms, some with shared bathrooms. Good breakfasts.

Rhodes £
B&B **Map** 9 A1
195 Sussex Gardens, W2 2RJ
Tel *020 7262 0537*
W *rhodeshotel.com*
Welcoming family-run B&B with standard, contemporary rooms.

The Ampersand ££
Boutique **Map** 17 A2
10 Harrington Rd, SW7 3ER
Tel *020 7589 5895*
W *ampersandhotel.com*
Whimsical interiors inspired by music, science and nature.

View of The Savoy hotel, London, from the River Thames

Elegant bar in The Halkin by COMO

Twenty Nevern Square ££
Boutique   Map 15 C2
20 Nevern Square, SW5 9PD
Tel *020 7565 9555*
W *20nevernsquare.com*
Extravagant rooms with Colonial-
and Asian-inspired decor.

Belgraves £££
Luxury
20 Chesham Place, SW1X 8HQ
Tel *020 7858 0100*
W *thompsonhotels.com*
A taste of New York "boho" at this
bold Thompson Hotel.

Mandarin Oriental Hyde Park £££
Luxury   Map 9 C5
66 Knightsbridge, SW1X 7LA
Tel *020 7235 2000*
W *mandarinoriental.com*
Rooms with fireplaces and
mahogany furniture. Fine service.

Royal Garden £££
Rooms with a view   Map 8 D5
2–24 Kensington High St, W8 4PT
Tel *020 7937 8000*
W *royalgardenhotel.co.uk*
Appealing rooms, some with
panoramic park views.

The Capital £££
Luxury   Map 9 C5
22–24 Basil St, SW3 1AT
Tel *020 7589 5171*
W *capitalhotel.co.uk*
Intimate place with the luxury
and service of a grand hotel.

The Gore £££
Boutique   Map 8 F5
190 Queen's Gate, SW7 5EX
Tel *020 7584 6601*
W *gorehotel.com*
The Gore explodes with character.
All the bedrooms are unique.

The Halkin by COMO £££
Boutique   Map 10 D5
5 Halkin St, SW1X 7DJ
Tel *020 7333 1000*
W *comohotels.com*
Smiling service, fresh flowers,
soft lighting and exquisite beds.

The Levin £££
Boutique   Map 9 C5
28 Basil St, SW3 1AS
Tel *020 7589 6286*
W *thelevinhotel.co.uk*
A little gem, with bedrooms that
have style and charm.

Regent's Park and Bloomsbury

No. 5 Doughty Street £
Boutique   Map 4 D4
5 Doughty St, WC1N 2PL
Tel *020 7373 9120*
W *blueprintlivingapartments.com*
Modern studio and one-bedroom
apartments with all comforts, at
reasonable rates. Full kitchens.

Durrants ££
Character   Map 10 D1
26–32 George St, W1H 5BJ
Tel *020 7935 8131*
W *durrantshotel.co.uk*
A privately owned English
classic. Panelled entrance and
snug bar.

Hart House ££
Historic   Map 9 C1
51 Gloucester Place, W1U 8JF
Tel *020 7935 2288*
W *harthouse.co.uk*
Spotless rooms and excellent
cooked breakfast at this award-
winning town house B&B.

Montagu Place ££
Boutique   Map 9 C1
2–3 Montagu Place, W1H 2ER
Tel *020 7467 2777*
W *montagu-place.co.uk*
Choose from a selection of
"comfy", "swanky" or "fancy" rooms
at this intimate hotel.

Rough Luxe ££
B&B   Map 3 C3
1 Birkenhead St, WC1H 8BA
Tel *020 7837 5338*
W *roughluxe.co.uk*
A quirky and creative B&B with
original art and caring service.

The Arch ££
Designer   Map 9 C2
50 Great Cumberland Place, W1H 7FD
Tel *020 7724 4700*
W *thearchlondon.com*
Cleverly converted from a terrace
of town houses. Popular bar and
laid-back dining.

Charlotte Street £££
Boutique   Map 11 A1
15–17 Charlotte St, W1T 1RJ
Tel *020 7806 2000*
W *firmdalehotels.com*
Favourite of media folk, with lively
public areas and a private cinema.

DK Choice
The Langham £££
Luxury   Map 10 E1
1c Portland Place, W1B 1JA
Tel *020 7636 1000*
W *london.langhamhotels.co.uk*
The Langham was the largest
purpose-built hotel when it
opened in 1865. Opulent
rooms, handsome bathrooms
and a stunning spa and pool
are on offer. The Landau
restaurant is in a striking oval
room, and the cocktail bar,
Artesian, is one of the capital's
most romantic.

The City and Southwark

Fleet River Bakery Rooms £
B&B   Map 12 D1
71 Lincolns Inn Fields, WC2A 3JF
Tel *020 7691 1457*
W *fleetriverbakery.com*
Good-value studios with
kitchens. Breakfast served daily
with a hamper on Sundays.

Kennington B&B £
B&B   Map 20 F3
103 Kennington Park Rd, SE11 4JJ
Tel *020 7735 7669*
W *kenningtonbandb.com*
Affordable, comfortable family-
run townhouse B&B.

DK Choice
Andaz Liverpool Street ££
Designer   Map 13 C1
Liverpool St, EC2M 7QN
Tel *020 7961 1234*
W *london.liverpoolstreet.
andaz.com*
Two characterful bars, three
excellent restaurants and a
hidden Masonic temple
await in a refurbished palatial
old railway hotel. Bedrooms
are minimalist but comfortable.
The lobby has a room for
guests to mingle over free
refreshments.

For more information on types of hotels *see page 559*

King's Wardrobe by BridgeStreet £££
B&B   **Map** 12 F2
6 Wardrobe Place, EC4V 5AF
Tel *020 7792 2222*
w bridgestreet.com
Flagship building with well-equipped apartments ranging from studios to three bedrooms.

London Bridge £££
Boutique   **Map** 13 B4
8–18 London Bridge St, SE1 9SG
Tel *020 7855 2200*
w londonbridgehotel.com
Captivating modern lobby, smart rooms, gym and restaurants. Close to museums and galleries.

The Hoxton £££
Designer   **Map** 5 C4
81 Great Eastern St, EC2A 3HU
Tel *020 7550 1000*
w hoxtonhotels.com
The vast open-plan lobby has a real buzz. Distinctly decorated rooms. Book ahead to pay less.

The Montcalm at The Brewery London City £££
Designer   **Map** 5 B4
52 Chiswell St, EC1Y 4SA
Tel *020 7614 0100*
w themontcalmlondoncity.co.uk
Chic, modern hotel created out of a London brewery once visited by George III. Butler service.

The Rookery £££
Boutique   **Map** 4 F5
12 Peter's Ln, Cowcross St, EC1M 6DS
Tel *020 7336 0931*
w rookeryhotel.com
Three restored 18th-century houses crammed with curiosites. Rooms have antique beds. Open fires downstairs.

The Zetter Townhouse £££
Boutique   **Map** 4 E2
49–50 St John's Square, EC1V 4JJ
Tel *020 7324 4567*
w thezettertownhouse.com
Get toothpaste and champagne from the same vending machine at this cool, playful hotel.

Boundary Rooms £££
Designer   **Map** 6 D4
2–4 Boundary St, E2 7DD
Tel *020 7729 1051*
w theboundary.co.uk
Terence Conran's hotel exudes great style. Each room is different. Pick a suite with a terrace.

Shoreditch Rooms £££
Designer   **Map** 6 D4
Ebor St, E1 6AW
Tel *020 7739 5040*
w shoreditchhouse.com
An imaginatively renovated warehouse in New England style.

Comfortable furnishings at the London Bridge Hotel

Further Afield

Avo £
Boutique
82 Dalston Lane, E8 3AH
Tel *020 3490 5061*
w avohotel.com
DVDs for rent, memory foam beds and a host of thoughtful extras at this trendy hotel.

Hotel 55 £
Boutique
55 Hanger Lane, W5 3HL
Tel *020 8991 4450*
w hotel55-london.com
A stylish hotel with neutral colours, Indian art, immaculate bathrooms and a restful garden.

The Victoria Inn £
B&B
72–79 Choumert Rd, SE15 4AR
Tel *020 7639 5052*
w victoriainnpeckham.com
A gastro-pub with sunny and stylish rooms. Bunks and a jungle-themed playroom for kids.

The Westport Inn £
Historic
166 Malden Rd, NW5 4BS
Tel *020 7916 4959*
w thewestportinn.co.uk
Unwind in the traditional pub before snuggling down in one of the simple rooms. No children.

Cannizaro House £££
Historic
Westside Common, Wimbledon, SW19 4UE
Tel *020 8879 1464*
w cannizarohouse.com
A 300-year-old country house with park views and a brasserie.

Church Street Hotel £££
Character
29–33 Camberwell Church St, SE5 8TR
Tel *020 7703 5984*
w churchstreethotel.com
Colourful rooms with wrought-iron beds and Mexican art. Casual tapas dining.

Fox and Grapes £££
Boutique
9 Camp Rd, SW19 4UN
Tel *020 8619 1300*
w foxandgrapeswimbledon.co.uk
Chic getaway above a French-owned gastropub. Snug rooms.

High Road House £££
Boutique
162–170 Chiswick High Rd, W4 1PR
Tel *020 8742 1717*
w house.highroadhouse.co.uk
White, Scandinavian-inspired rooms. Brasserie downstairs.

Premier Apartments London Limehouse £££
Rooms with a view
John Nash Mews, 602 Commercial Rd, E14 7HS
Tel *0151 227 9467*
w premierapartmentslondon.com
Cheerful living areas and granite kitchens with views of Docklands.

The Alma £££
Boutique
499 Old York Road, SW18 1TF
Tel *020 8870 2537*
w almawandsworth.com
Victorian tavern, now a pub-restaurant with 23 stylish rooms.

The Downs and Channel Coast

ARUNDEL: April Cottage £
B&B
Crossbush Ln, West Sussex, BN18 9PQ
Tel *01903 885401*
w april-cottage.co.uk
Charming cottage near the wetlands. Serves good breakfasts.

BRIGHTON: Hotel Una £££
Boutique
55–56 Regency Square, East Sussex, BN1 2FF
Tel *01273 820464*
w hotel-una.co.uk
Luxurious rooms and breakfast in bed at no extra cost.

CANTERBURY: Cathedral Lodge £
Designer
The Precincts, Kent, CT1 2EH
Tel *01227 865350*
🅦 canterburycathedrallodge.org
Modern lodge and stylish
rooms in the grounds of
Canterbury Cathedral.

DK Choice

CHICHESTER:
Richmond House £
B&B
230 Oving Rd, West Sussex,
PO19 7EJ
Tel *01243 771464*
🅦 richmondhousechichester.
co.uk
This boutique B&B offers a high
level of comfort for the price.
Rooms are elegantly furnished,
one with French windows
opening onto the garden.
Choose from a comprehensive
breakfast menu. Chichester is a
10-minute walk away.

HASTINGS: Swan House ££
B&B
Hill St, East Sussex, TN34 3HU
Tel *01424 430014*
🅦 swanhousehastings.co.uk
Half-timbered 1490 guesthouse.
Serves gourmet breakfast from
local suppliers.

HEVER: Hever Castle B&B ££
Character
The Astor Wing, Hever Castle, TN8 7NG
Tel *01732 861800*
🅦 hevercastle.co.uk
Luxury B&B with access to
the castle and a golf course.
Childhood home of Anne Boleyn.

LEWES: The Shelleys ££
Boutique
135–136 High St, East Sussex, BN7 1XS
Tel *01273 472361*
🅦 the-shelleys.co.uk
Family-run 17th-century country-
house hotel with luxurious rooms.

PORTSMOUTH: Number Four
Boutique Hotel £
Boutique
69 Festing Rd, Southsea, Hampshire,
PO4 0NQ
Tel *02392 008444*
🅦 number4hotel.co.uk
This plush designer hotel is
walking distance from the town
and seafront. Quality restaurant.

PORTSMOUTH: The George £
Historic
84 Queen St, Hampshire, PO1 3HU
Tel *02392 753885*
🅦 thegeorgehotel.org.uk
Quaint rooms with wooden
beams. Public bar serves cask ales.

ROCHESTER: Sovereign £
Character
29 Medway Bridge Marina, Manor
Lane, Kent, ME1 3HS
Tel *01634 400474*
🅦 thesovereignbb.co.uk
Stay on a 1930s Rhine cruising
ship. Colourful and bright rooms.

SEAVIEW: Priory Bay Hotel £
Luxury
Priory Drive, Isle of Wight, PO34 5BU
Tel *01983 613146*
🅦 priorybay.com
Period buildings in an estate
surrounded by woodland. Yurts
and thatched cottages available.

SOUTHAMPTON: Hotel
Terravina ££
Boutique
174 Woodlands Rd, Woodlands,
Hampshire, SO40 7GL
Tel *02380 293784*
🅦 hotelterravina.co.uk
Rain showers and extras such as
fluffy bath robes on offer.

WHITSTABLE: Sleeperzzz
Guesthouse £
B&B
30 Railway Ave, Kent, CT5 1LH
Tel *01227 636975*
🅦 sleeperzzz.net
Simple and pleasant B&B near
the town centre. Bright decor
and hearty English breakfasts.

WINCHELSEA: Strand House £
Historic
Tanyards Lane, East Sussex, TN36 4JT
Tel *01797 226276*
🅦 thestrandhouse.co.uk
Old Tudor house providing full
Sussex breakfasts, packed lunches,
afternoon tea and evening meals.

WINCHESTER: Lainston
Country House ££
Luxury
Woodman Lane, Sparsholt,
Hampshire, SO21 2LT
Tel *01962 776088*
🅦 lainstonhouse.com

Picturesque exterior of the Swan House
B&B, Hastings

A 17th-century country house
with sprawling parkland, ruins of
a historic chapel and fine dining.

East Anglia

ALDEBURGH: Laurel House £
B&B
23 Lee Rd, Suffolk, IP15 5EY
Tel *07800 657545*
🅦 laurel-house.net
Supremely stylish rooms in a
Victorian house. Continental
breakfast with fresh fruit.

CAMBRIDGE: Madingley Hall £
Historic
Madingley, Cambridgeshire,
CB23 8AQ
Tel *01223 746222*
🅦 madingleyhall.co.uk
Grand 16th-century country
house with functional and
modern rooms. Superb gardens.

CAMBRIDGE: The Varsity Hotel
& Spa £
Luxury
Thompson's Lane, Cambridgeshire,
CB5 8AQ
Tel *01223 306030*
🅦 thevarsityhotel.co.uk
Situated on the River Cam with
spa, gym and roof terrace. Rooms
with picture windows.

CROMER: Captains House £
Rooms with a view
5 The Crescent, Norfolk, NR27 9EX
Tel *01263 515434*
🅦 ukcountryhotels.co.uk
Airy rooms with sea views. Fine
linen, TV and Norfolk breakfast
with home-made pastries.

KING'S LYNN: Bridge House £
B&B
Winch Rd, Gayton, Norfolk, PE32 1QP
Tel *01553 636756*
🅦 bridgehouseholidays.co.uk
Traditional, spacious rooms at
this 19th-century farmhouse
amid lawns and woodland.

LITTLE DOWNHAM: Anchor £
Boutique
25 Main St, Cambridgeshire, CB6 2ST
Tel *01353 699333*
🅦 littledownhamanchor.co.uk
Minimal but attractive rooms. The
bar serves cask ales and local gin.

LOWESTOFT: Britten House £
Rooms with a view
21 Kirkley Cliff Rd, Suffolk, NR33 0DB
Tel *01502 573950*
🅦 brittenhouse.co.uk
Birthplace and family home of
Benjamin Britten. Traditional
Victorian town house with
original features and sea views.

For more information on types of hotels *see page 559*

NORWICH: The Old Rectory ££
Luxury
103 Yarmouth Rd, Norfolk, NR7 0HF
Tel *01603 700772*
[w] oldrectorynorwich.com
Spacious Georgian country house
with a fine candlelit restaurant.

SOUTHWOLD: The Crown £
Historic
The Street, Westleton, Suffolk, IP17 3AD
Tel *01728 648777*
[w] westletoncrown.co.uk
A 12th-century coaching inn
with local ales, log fires, terraced
gardens and comfortable rooms.

**SOUTHWOLD: Sutherland
House** ££
Character
56 High St, Suffolk, IP18 6DN
Tel *01502 724544*
[w] sutherlandhouse.co.uk
Choose a room with a sleigh bed,
a fresco ceiling or a slipper bath.

Thames Valley

**BANBURY: Banbury Cross
Bed & Breakfast** £
B&B
*1 Broughton Rd, Oxfordshire,
OX16 9QB*
Tel *01295 266048*
[w] banburycrossbandb.co.uk
Award-winning B&B with
traditional rooms in a Victorian
house. Extensive breakfast menu.

**GREAT MILTON: Le Manoir aux
Quat' Saisons** £££
Luxury
Church Rd, Oxfordshire, OX44 7PD
Tel *01844 278881*
[w] manoir.com
Opulent rooms in a lush garden
setting with a Michelin-starred
restaurant and a cookery school.

DK Choice

**HENLEY-ON-THAMES:
Reachview B&B** £
B&B
*1 Cromwell Rd, Oxfordshire,
RG9 1JH*
Tel *01491 573193*
[w] reachviewbedandbreakfast.
co.uk
Choose from a double en
suite with garden views, a
sunny en-suite twin and a
double with shared bathroom
at this quiet and elegant B&B.
Luxury linen and tea- and
coffee-making facilities in the
rooms. Ideal for country and
river walks. A 10-minute stroll
rewards guests with sweeping
views of the Thames.

Grand, imposing exterior of Hope House,
Woodstock

MARLOW: Kenton House £
B&B
*4 Kenton Close, Buckinghamshire,
SL7 1DU*
Tel *01628 486536*
[w] marlow-bedandbreakfast.co.uk
Open-plan kitchen/living room
overlooking an attractive garden.
Clean rooms and huge breakfasts.

OXFORD: Keble College £
Historic
Keble College, Oxfordshire, OX1 3PG
Tel *01865 272727*
[w] keble.ox.ac.uk
Unique opportunity to stay in a
historic college building. Breakfast
is served in the Great Hall.

OXFORD: Old Bank Hotel ££
Luxury
92–94 High St, Oxfordshire, OX1 4BJ
Tel *01865 799599*
[w] oldbank-hotel.co.uk
Beautifully converted bank. Some
rooms have views of the Bodleian
Library and Radcliffe Camera.

ST ALBANS: Fleuchary House £
Boutique
*29 Upper Lattimore Rd, Hertfordshire,
AL1 3UA*
Tel *01727 766764*
[w] 29stalbans.com
Central location. Plush rooms with
tea- and coffee-making facilities.

UFFINGTON: The Fox & Hounds £
Historic
High St, Oxfordshire, SN7 7RP
Tel *01367 820680*
[w] uffingtonpub.co.uk
Beamed pub with views and
comfortable ground-floor rooms.

WANTAGE: Court Hill Centre £
Character
Court Hill, Oxfordshire, OX12 9NE
Tel *01235 760253*
[w] courthill.org.uk

Five barns converted into bunkhouses with beamed rooms.
On-site tearoom.

WINDSOR: The Old Farmhouse £
Historic
Oakley Green, Berkshire, SL44LH
Tel *01753 850411*
[w] theoldfarmhousewindsor.com
A 15th-century half-timbered
hotel in a garden setting.
Traditionally furnished rooms.

WOODSTOCK: Hope House £££
Boutique
14 Oxford St, Oxfordshire, OX20 1TS
Tel *01993 815990*
[w] hopehousewoodstock.co.uk
Italian linens, marble, gilt and
silks at this boutique hotel.

Wessex

**ABBOTSBURY: The Abbey
House** £
B&B
Church St, Dorset, DT3 4JJ
Tel *01305 871330*
[w] theabbeyhouse.co.uk
Small and friendly. Some rooms
have shared bathrooms. Kids
under 12 not allowed.

AVEBURY: The Lodge Avebury ££
B&B
High St, Wiltshire, SN8 1RF
Tel *01672 539023*
[w] aveburylodge.co.uk
Antique-filled B&B with views of
Avebury's ancient stones from the
rooms. Vegetarian fare.

BATH: Apsley House Hotel ££
B&B
*141 Newbridge Hill, Somerset,
BA1 3PT*
Tel *01225 336966*
[w] apsley-house.co.uk
A 12-roomed Georgian house with
great service and four-poster beds.

Cosy bedroom at Le Manoir aux
Quat' Saisons, Great Milton

BATH: The Queensberry ££
Boutique
Russel St, Somerset, BA1 2AF
Tel *01225 447928*
Ⓦ thequeensberry.co.uk
Gorgeous, romantic rooms and a modern Mediterranean restaurant.

DK Choice

BATH: The Royal Crescent £££
Luxury
16 Royal Crescent, Somerset, BA1 2LS
Tel *01225 823333*
Ⓦ royalcrescent.co.uk
This opulent Relais & Châteaux hotel has high-ceilinged rooms, a fantastic candlelit spa and a gourmet restaurant. Step into the very best of the Georgian era while enjoying modern amenities. Private garden cottages are also available.

BLANDFORD FORUM: The Wild Garlic ££
B&B
Blandford Rd, Iwerne Minster, Dorset, DT11 8QN
Tel *01747 811269*
Ⓦ thewildgarlic.co.uk
Dine at the restaurant run by UK *MasterChef* winner Mat Follas, then head to the B&B upstairs.

BOURNEMOUTH: Miramar ££
Rooms with a view
East Overcliff Drive, Dorset, BH1 3AL
Tel *01202 556581*
Ⓦ miramar-bournemouth.com
A large three-star hotel close to the beach. Good for families.

BOURNEMOUTH: The Chocolate Boutique Hotel ££
Boutique
5 Durley Rd, Dorset, BH2 5JQ
Tel *01202 556857*
Ⓦ thechocolateboutiquehotel.co.uk
Novelty hotel in a tree-lined area. Chocolate-themed rooms and chocolate-making lessons.

BOURNEMOUTH: Urban Beach Hotel ££
Boutique
23 Argyll Rd, Boscombe, Dorset, BH5 1EB
Tel *01202 301509*
Ⓦ urbanbeach.co.uk
Award-winning family-friendly hotel with a bistro. Near the beach.

BRIDPORT: The Bull Hotel ££
Boutique
34 East St, Dorset, DT6 3LF
Tel *01308 422878*
Ⓦ thebullhotel.co.uk
Lavish former 16th-century coaching inn bathed in modern glamour. Popular pub on site.

BRISTOL: Brooks Guesthouse £
B&B
St Nicholas St, BS1 1UB
Tel *0117 930 0066*
Ⓦ brooksguesthousebristol.com
This bright B&B behind St Nick's market is a real find. Double and triple bedrooms available.

BRISTOL: The Bristol Camper Company £
Character
Acacia Farm, Bristol Rd, Rooksbridge, BS26 2TA
Tel *0845 467 4147*
Ⓦ thebristolcampercompany.co.uk
Hire an original 1970s VW camper van and explore the West Country. Weekly or part-week hire only.

BRISTOL: Hotel du Vin ££
Boutique
The Sugar House, Lewins Mead, BS1 2NU
Tel *0117 925 5577*
Ⓦ hotelduvin.com/bristol
Classy hotel in a restored 18th-century sugar warehouse, with a bar, brasserie and romantic rooms.

BRUTON: At the Chapel ££
Boutique
High St, Somerset, BA10 0AE
Tel *01749 814 070*
Ⓦ atthechapel.co.uk
Eight simple luxury rooms in a former chapel. Enjoy freshly baked croissants for breakfast.

CORSHAM: Guyers House Hotel ££
Boutique
Pickwick, Wiltshire, SN13 0PS
Tel *01249 713399*
Ⓦ guyershouse.com
Country house with tennis, croquet and candlelit dinners.

HINTON ST GEORGE: Lord Poulett Arms £
Boutique
High St, Somerset, TA17 8SE
Tel *01460 73149*
Ⓦ lordpoulettarms.com
A 17th-century inn with lovely

chic rooms featuring antique bedheads, chandeliers, gilt mirrors and roll-top baths.

LACOCK: At the Sign of the Angel ££
B&B
6 Church St, Chippenham, Wiltshire, SN15 2LB
Tel *01249 730230*
Ⓦ lacock.co.uk
This 15th-century pub and B&B offers home-cooked meals. Antique carved beds and a fire. Ideal for a romantic weekend.

LONGLEAT: The Bath Arms ££
Boutique
Horningsham, Warminster, Wiltshire, BA12 7LY
Tel *08448 150099*
Ⓦ batharms.co.uk
Character-packed pub with 16 rooms in the heart of Longleat estate. Dog- and family-friendly. Good base for parties.

LYME REGIS: 1 Lyme Townhouse £
B&B
1 Pound St, Dorset, DT7 3HT
Tel *01297 442499*
Ⓦ hotel1lyme.com
Boutique B&B with luxurious touches and a breakfast hamper of delicious local produce.

LYME REGIS: Hotel Alexandra ££
Boutique
Pound St, Dorset, DT7 3HZ
Tel *01297 442010*
Ⓦ hotelalexandra.co.uk
Views of the beach and the Cobb (harbour). Self-catering family cottage also available.

MALMESBURY: The Rectory ££
Luxury
Crudwell, Wiltshire, SN16 9EP
Tel *01666 577194*
Ⓦ therectoryhotel.com
Boutique Cotswolds hotel in a good location with bright rooms, a walled garden and outdoor pool.

The traditional Tudor exterior of The Wild Garlic, Blandford

For more information on types of hotels *see page 559*

The modern breakfast area of
The Magdalen Chapter, Exeter

POOLE: Hotel du Vin   ££
Boutique
*The Quay, Thames St, Dorset, BH15
1JN*
Tel *01202 785570*
W *hotelduvin.com*
Virginia creeper-clad Georgian-
house hotel, with signature bistro,
wine cellar and tasting room.

SALISBURY: St Ann's House   £
B&B
33–34 St Ann St, Wiltshire, SP1 2DP
Tel *01722 335657*
W *stannshouse.co.uk*
Four-star Georgian house with
cathedral views. Close to train
station. Large breakfast menu.

**SALISBURY: Howard's House
Hotel**   £££
Boutique
Teffont Evias, Wiltshire, SP3 5RJ
Tel *01722 716392*
W *howardshousehotel.co.uk*
Classic hotel with antique head-
boards and open fires. Great for
shooting and fishing breaks.

**TAUNTON: The Mount
Somerset**   £££
Luxury
Lower Henlade, Somerset, TA3 5NB
Tel *01823 442500*
W *themountsomersethotel
andspa.com*
Regency-era country-house hotel
with spa. High ceilings, great
restaurant and expansive grounds.

TISBURY: The Beckford Arms ££
B&B
Fonthill Gifford, Wiltshire, SP3 6PX
Tel *01747 870385*
W *beckfordarms.com*
Traditional stylish pub with
simple bedrooms and two larger
lodges. Close to Stonehenge.

WELLS: The Crown at Wells   £
B&B
Market Place, Somerset, BA5 2RP
Tel *01749 673457*
W *crownatwells.co.uk*

A 15th-century coaching inn
with four four-poster beds and a
characterful pub. Family rooms.

Devon and Cornwall

**BABBACOMBE BEACH:
The Cary Arms**   £££
Boutique
South Devon, TQ1 3LX
Tel *01803 327110*
W *caryarms.co.uk*
Beachfront hotel with New
England striped linen, gastro-pub
food and activities for kids.

**BARNSTAPLE:
Broomhill Art Hotel**   ££
Designer
Muddiford, North Devon, EX31 4EX
Tel *01271 850262*
W *broomhillart.co.uk*
Six-roomed hotel in a modern
sculpture park. Weekend rates
include breakfast and dinner.

**BIGBURY-ON-SEA:
The Royal Oak**   ££
Luxury
Kingsbridge, Devon, TQ7 4AP
Tel *01548 810313*
W *theroyaloakbigbury.co.uk*
Four sumptuous rooms over a
great pub close to the beach.
Breakfast and travel cots available.

**BIGBURY-ON-SEA:
Burgh Island**   £££
Luxury
South Devon, TQ7 4BG
Tel *01548 810514*
W *burghisland.com*
Art Deco hotel on its own private
island accessible by water tractor.
Preferred by Agatha Christie.

BODMIN MOOR: Ekopod   ££
Character
*St Clether, Launceston, Cornwall,
PL15 8QJ*
Tel *01275 395447*
W *ekopod.com*
Two eco-friendly pods, each
sleeping two, with kitchen and
bathroom. Minimum four nights.

DK Choice

CAMELFORD: Belle Tents   ££
Character
*Owl's Gate, Davidstow, Cornwall,
PL32 9XY*
Tel *01840 261 556*
W *belletentscamping.co.uk*
This cluster of candy-coloured
luxury tents in a private dell
near Tintagel is a great base for
a family holiday with a twist.
Tents have beds and kitchen
areas, and there is a fire pit and

shared bar tent for the evening.
Bodmin Moor and beaches are
just a short stroll away.

CHAGFORD: Gidleigh Park £££
Luxury
Devon, TQ13 8HH
Tel *01647 432367*
W *gidleigh.com*
Tudor-house hotel famed for fine
dining. Spa suites available.
Extensive gardens with a river.

**CHILLINGTON: The White
House**   £££
Boutique
Devon, TA7 2JX
Tel *01548 580505*
W *whitehousedevon.com*
Georgian house near the coast
with slow suppers, croquet on the
lawn and modern luxury rooms.

CLOVELLY: The Red Lion   ££
Rooms with a view
The Quay, Devon, EX39 5TF
Tel *01237 431237*
W *clovelly.co.uk*
Seaside hotel overlooking
Clovelly's ancient harbour.
Nautically themed rooms and
in-room spa treatments.

DARTMOOR: Bovey Castle   £££
Luxury
*North Bovey, Dartmoor National
Park, Devon, TQ13 8RE*
Tel *08444 740077*
W *boveycastle.com*
Castle hotel with lavish furnish-
ings, a golf course and spa.

**EXETER: The Magdalen
Chapter**   £££
Luxury
Magdalen St, Devon, EX3 4HY
Tel *01392 281000*
W *themagdalenchapter.com*
Modern luxury with a Ren spa
and heated outdoor pool. The
restaurant overlooks a garden.

The classically designed Howard's House
Hotel, Salisbury

FOWEY: Upton House ££
B&B
2 Esplanade, Cornwall, PL23 1HY
Tel *01726 832732*
W upton-house.com
Eccentric Art Deco hotel with
kitsch appeal. One of the rooms
features pink flamingos.

FOWEY: The Old Quay House £££
Rooms with a view
28 Fore St, Cornwall, PL23 1AQ
Tel *01726 833302*
W theoldquayhouse.com
Modern boutique hotel
overlooking boats on the estuary.
Great terrace at the back.

LIFTON: The Arundell Arms ££
Luxury
Lifton, Devon, PL16 0AA
Tel *01566 784666*
W arundellarms.com
Country hotel ideal for fishing
and shooting. Self-catering
cottages are also available.

**MAWGAN PORTH: Bedruthan
Steps** £££
Boutique
Trenance, Cornwall, TR8 4DQ
Tel *01637 860860*
W bedruthan.com
Award-winning family hotel
with a great café, beach and
superb family facilities.

DK Choice
**MAWGAN PORTH:
The Scarlet** £££
Rooms with a view
Tredragon Rd, Cornwall, TR8 4DQ
Tel *01637 861800*
W scarlethotel.co.uk
This super-luxury hotel over-
looking the golden sands of
Mawgan Porth is the first five-
star eco hotel in the UK. Enjoy
cream teas, cider and superb
Ayurvedic spa facilities, including
a Rhassoul mud bath and a
scarlet seaweed hot-tub
experience. No children allowed.

**MOUSEHOLE: The Old
Coastguard Hotel** ££
Rooms with a view
The Parade, Cornwall, TR19 6PR
Tel *01736 731222*
W oldcoastguardhotel.co.uk
Seaside hotel in an old fishing
village, 14 classic rooms with
glorious sea views.

**MULLION: The Polurrian Bay
Hotel** £££
Boutique
Polurrian Bay, Cornwall, TR12 7EN
Tel *01326 240421*
W polurrianhotel.com
Family-friendly hotel on a cliff

overlooking the sea. Crèche,
spa, cinema room, tennis court
and indoor pool.

**NEWQUAY: Watergate Bay
Hotel** ££
Boutique
Watergate Bay, Cornwall, TR8 4AA
Tel *01637 860543*
W watergatebay.co.uk
Lavish seafront hotel with large
family rooms. Watch out for deals.

**PENZANCE: The Artist
Residence** ££
B&B
20 Chapel St, Cornwall, TR18 4AW
Tel *01736 365664*
W arthotelcornwall.co.uk
Fun and hip guesthouse in a
Georgian mansion with bright art
on the walls. Close to the seafront.

PENZANCE: The Cove £££
Boutique
Lamorna Cove, Cornwall, TR19 6XH
Tel *01736 731411*
W thecovecornwall.com
Freedom of an apartment with
the amenities of a boutique
hotel. Centred around a pool.

ROCK: St Enodoc's £££
Boutique
Rock, Cornwall, PL27 6LA
Tel *01208 863394*
W enodoc-hotel.co.uk
Designer seaside hotel with a
two-Michelin-star fish restaurant.

SALCOMBE: South Sands £££
Rooms with a view
Bolt Head, Devon, TQ8 8LL
Tel *01548 845900*
W southsands.com
Beachfront boutique hotel with
estuary views. Well placed for
exploring South Devon.

**SAUNTON: Saunton Sands
Hotel** £££
Rooms with a view
Braunton, North Devon, EX33 1LQ
Tel *01271 890 212*
W sauntonsands.co.uk
Classic family hotel overlooking
Saunton's sand dunes. Baby-
sitting, playroom and surf lessons.

ST IVES: Headland House ££
B&B
*Headland Rd, Carbis Bay,
Cornwall, TR26*
Tel *01736 796647*
W headlandhousehotel.co.uk
An Edwardian house with sea
views. Mid-afternoon cream teas.

ST MAWES: Hotel Tresanton £££
Luxury
Cornwall, TR2 5DR
Tel *01326 270055*
W tresanton.com

Estuary view of the picturesque Old Quay
House, Fowey

Super-glamorous hotel overlooking the sea. Thirty rooms
plus two small cottages.

TAVISTOCK: Hotel Endsleigh £££
Luxury
Milton Abbot, Devon, PL19 0PQ
Tel *01822 870000*
W hotelendsleigh.com
Former hunting and fishing
lodge set in Repton-designed
gardens. Country chic interiors.

ZENNOR: The Gurnard's Head ££
Boutique
Nr Zennor, Cornwall, TR26 3DE
Tel *01736 796928*
W gurnardshead.co.uk
Gastro-pub with rooms in a wild
and exciting spot. The Sunday
Sleepover includes Sunday lunch,
dinner and breakfast.

The Heart of England

BIRMINGHAM: La Tour £
Boutique
Albert St, West Midlands, B5 5JE
Tel *0121 718 8000*
W hotel-latour.co.uk
Sleek and classy hotel with
executive rooms and suites.
Classic restaurant and bar.

**BOURTON-ON-THE-WATER:
Cranbourne House** ££
B&B
*Moore Rd, Cheltenham,
Gloucestershire, GL54 2AZ*
Tel *01451 821883*
W cranbournehousebandb.co.uk
Cotswolds stone house. Rain
showers, luxury toiletries and
in-room beauty treatments.

CHALFORD: Cotswold Yurts £
Rooms with a view
Cowcombe Hill, GL6 8H
Tel *07847 517905*
W cotswoldyurts.co.uk
Yurts with a terrace, kitchen,
fire pit and compost toilet. Ask for
one with a roll-top bath.

For more information on types of hotels *see page 559*

Opulent bedroom at the luxurious Glendon Guesthouse, Matlock

CHELTENHAM: The Bradley £
Boutique
*19 Royal Parade, Bayshill Rd,
GL50 3AY*
Tel *01242 519077*
W thebradleyhotel.co.uk
Family-run Regency town house.
Antique furnished rooms with
contemporary comforts.

**CHELTENHAM: Number 4 at
Stow** ££
Boutique
*Fosseway, Stow-on-the-Wold,
Gloucestershire, GL54 1JX*
Tel *01451 830297*
W hotelnumberfour.co.uk
Housed in a 1500s building with
flagstone floors, oak beams and
pine beds. Home-baked goodies.

CHESTER: Green Bough Hotel ££
Luxury
60 Hoole Rd, CH2 3NL
Tel *01244 326241*
W chestergreenboughhotel.com
Situated in red-brick Edwardian
buildings. Top-class restaurant.

**COVENTRY: Coombe Abbey
Hotel** ££
Historic
Brinklow Rd, Warwickshire, CV3 2AB
Tel *024 7645 0450*
W coombeabbey.com
Set in a former 12th-century
abbey amid parkland, gardens
and a lake. Superb antiques.

IRONBRIDGE: Library House £
Historic
11 Severn Bank, Telford, TF8 7AN
Tel *01952 432299*
W libraryhouse.com
Next to the iconic Iron Bridge,
with fine furnishings, TV/DVD and
tea- and coffee-making facilities.

MALVERN: Cannara B&B £
B&B
147 Barnards Green Rd, WR14 3LT
Tel *01684 564418*
W cannara.co.uk
Large Victorian house with views
of Malvern Hills. Breakfast uses
locally sourced produce.

**MORETON-IN-MARSH: Railway
Cottages** £
Character
New Rd, Gloucestershire, GL56 0AS
Tel *01608 650559*
W railwaycottages.net
Restored railway cottages, some
with balconies, Jacuzzi and an
open-plan kitchen.

DK Choice

PAINSWICK: Byfield House £
Historic
Bisley St, GL6 6QQ
Tel *01452 812607*
W byfieldhouse.com
Nestled in a delightful Cotswolds
town, this historic house has
exposed stone walls and
wonderfully quirky furnishings.
Some of its intriguing features
include a medieval oak door, a
17th-century barn and an 18th-
century drawing room.

ROSS-ON-WYE: Norton House £
B&B
*Old Monmouth Rd, Whitchurch,
Herefordshire, HR9 6DJ*
Tel *01600 890046*
W norton-house.com
Traditional rooms offer old-
fashioned charm and comfort.

**SHREWSBURY: Old House
Suites** £
Historic
20 Dogpole, Shropshire, SY1 1ES
Tel *07813 610904*
W theoldhousesuites.com
Suites in a half-timbered building
built in 1480. Log fires in rooms
and breakfast in the library.

**STRATFORD-UPON-AVON:
Twelfth Night Guesthouse** £
B&B
*13 Evesham Place, Warwickshire,
CV37 6HT*
Tel *01789 414595*
W twelfthnight.co.uk
Victorian villa with bright rooms.
A short walk from Royal
Shakespeare Company theatres.

**WORCESTER: Barrington House
Bed & Breakfast** £
B&B
204 Henwick Rd, WR2 5PF
Tel *01905 422965*
W barringtonhouse.eu
Four-storey Georgian house
with a walled garden. Pretty
rooms with colour themes.

East Midlands

BAKEWELL: Hassop Hall Hotel £
Luxury
Hassop Rd, Derbyshire, DE45 1NS
Tel *01629 640488*
W hassophallhotel.co.uk
Historic hotel in picturesque
village of Hassop with com-
fortable rooms and gardens.

**BUXTON: Griff House Bed &
Breakfast** £
B&B
2 Compton Rd, Derbyshire, SK17 9DN
Tel *01298 23628*
W griffhousebuxton.co.uk
Refurbished late-Victorian
property with bright, minimalist
rooms. Breakfast includes home-
made bread and muesli.

EAST NORTON: Launde Abbey £
Character
Leicestershire, LE7 9XB
Tel *01572 717254*
W laundeabbey.org.uk
Residential retreat house with
cultivated gardens and a 12th-
century chapel. Basic rooms.

LINCOLN: The Castle Hotel ££
Boutique
Westgate, Lincolnshire, LN1 3AS
Tel *01522 538801*
W castlehotel.net
Designer rooms and bathrooms
with drench showers and full-size
bathtubs. A luxury apartment too.

DK Choice

**MATLOCK: Glendon
Guesthouse** £
B&B
*7 Knowleston Place, Derbyshire,
DE4 3BU*
Tel *01629 584732*
W glendonbandb.co.uk
This guesthouse has four-
poster, double, twin and family
en-suite rooms, and a lounge
with views of Knowleston
Gardens. Luxury touches
include Egyptian cotton linen
and towels. Home-made
sausages and free-range eggs
feature on the breakfast menu.
There is a self-catering holiday
house next door.

Sunny outdoor terrace at the Bridge Hotel, Buttermere

NORTHAMPTON: Coton Lodge £
Rooms with a view
West Haddon Rd, Guilsborough, Northamptonshire, NN6 8QE
Tel *01604 740215*
W cotonlodge.co.uk
Georgian farmhouse surrounded by gardens with rose arches.

STAMFORD: The Bull & Swan £
Boutique
St Martins, Lincolnshire, PE9 2LJ
Tel *01780 766412*
W thebullandswan.co.uk
Historic inn with chic rooms, local ales and great pub fare.

Lancashire and the Lakes

AMBLESIDE: Waterhead £
Boutique
Waterhead, Cumbria, LA22 0ER
Tel *08458 504503*
W englishlakes.co.uk
Lakeside hotel with an on-site restaurant serving modern fare.

ARMATHWAITE: Drybeck Farm £
Character
Cumbria, CA4 9ST
Tel *07854 523012*
W drybeckfarm.co.uk
"Glamping" experience in trad-itional Mongolian yurts and a gypsy caravan on a working farm.

BLACKPOOL: The Kenley £
B&B
29 St Chads Rd, Cumbria, FY1 6BP
Tel *01253 346447*
W kenleyhotel.co.uk
Boutique B&B with contemporary kitsch styling. Breakfast includes local black pudding.

BORROWDALE: Borrowdale Gates Hotel ££
Rooms with a view
Grange, Cumbria, CA12 5UQ
Tel *08458 332524*
W borrowdale-gates.com

Victorian country house in the hamlet of Grange with fell views and wooded grounds.

BOWNESS-ON-WINDERMERE: Linthwaite House £
Rooms with a view
Crook Rd, Cumbria, LA23 3JA
Tel *01539 488600*
W linthwaite.com
Views of Windermere and fells from swish country-house hotel. Stylish rooms and fine dining.

BUTTERMERE: Bridge Hotel ££
Rooms with a view
Cumbria, CA13 9UZ
Tel *01768 770252*
W bridge-hotel.com
Splendid stone hotel with cheery, floral-themed rooms and two bars.

COCKERMOUTH: Six Castlegate £
B&B
6 Castlegate, Cumbria, CA13 9EU
Tel *01900 826786*
W sixcastlegate.co.uk
Soothing decor in Georgian town house. Luxury towels and linen.

CONISTON: Bank Ground Farm £
B&B
East of the Lake, Cumbria, LA21 8AA
Tel *01539 441264*
W bankground.com
Lakefront farm with a 15th-century cottage. Tea room on site.

GRANGE OVER SANDS: Broughton House £
B&B
Field Broughton, Cumbria, LA11 6HN
Tel *01539 536439*
W broughtonhousecartmel.co.uk
Stay in yurts, wooden-floored rooms or cabins. Self-catering.

GRASMERE: Grasmere Hotel £
Boutique
Broadgate, Cumbria, LA22 9TA
Tel *01539 435277*
W grasmerehotel.co.uk
Refurbished Victorian country house with spacious rooms.

Basic double bedroom at the Waterhead hotel, Ambleside

IREBY: Overwater Hall ££
Luxury
Cumbria, CA7 1HH
Tel *01768 776566*
W overwaterhall.co.uk
An 18th-century country house with sprawling gardens and opulent rooms in floral style.

KENDAL: Crosthwaite House £
B&B
Crosthwaite, Cumbria, LA8 8BP
Tel *01539 568264*
W crosthwaitehouse.co.uk
Bright and colour-coordinated rooms and spacious lounge.

KESWICK: Oakthwaite House £
B&B
35 Helvellyn St, Cumbria, CA12 4EP
Tel *01768 772398*
W oakthwaite-keswick.com
Late Victorian stone town house in a quiet neighbourhood. Tasteful rooms and views of crags and fells.

LANCASTER: The Stork Inn £
Boutique
Corricks Lane, Conder Green, Lancashire, LA2 0AN
Tel *01524 751234*
W thestorkinn.co.uk
Whitewashed country inn with attractive rooms and tasty food.

LIVERPOOL: base2stay £
Boutique
29 Seel St, L1 4AU
Tel *01517 052626*
W base2stay.com
Boldly styled rooms in the UNESCO-protected RopeWalks area. Good value and service.

MANCHESTER: Didsbury House £
Luxury
Didsbury Park, Didsbury, M20 5LJ
Tel *0161 448 2200*
W eclectichotels.co.uk
Victorian villa in leafy suburb of Didsbury with comfortable, individually styled rooms.

MORECAMBE: Yacht Bay View Hotel £
Rooms with a view
359 Marine Rd, Lancashire, LA4 5AQ
Tel *01524 414481*
W yachtbay.co.uk
Located on Morecambe's promenade. Superior doubles and singles have sea views.

RYDAL: Cote How Organic Guesthouse ££
Historic
Cumbria, LA22 9LW
Tel *01539 432765*
W cotehow.co.uk
Characterful 16th-century country home with large rooms. Organic breakfast and afternoon tea.

For more information on types of hotels *see page 559*

ULLSWATER: Rampsbeck Country House Hotel ££
Luxury
Watermillock, Cumbria, CA11 0LP
Tel *01768 486442*
🆆 rampsbeck.co.uk
Antique-bedecked bedrooms.
Drinks on lakefront terrace.

WASDALE HEAD: Wasdale Head Inn ££
Historic
Gosforth, Cumbria, CA20 1EX
Tel *01946 726229*
🆆 wasdale.com
Famous walkers' inn surrounded
by England's highest peaks.

DK Choice
WINDERMERE: Gilpin Lodge £££
Luxury
Crook Rd, LA23 3NE
Tel *01539 488818*
🆆 thegilpin.co.uk
This supremely stylish hotel
combines a warm welcome
with haute cuisine and
contemporary comforts. The
garden suites make the most of
the sylvan environs, while other
rooms are located in the
venerable old lodge itself.

Yorkshire and the Humber Region

AMPLEFORTH: Shallowdale House ££
B&B
North Yorkshire, YO62 4DY
Tel *01439 788325*
🆆 shallowdalehouse.co.uk
Award-winning 1960s retreat
overlooking the countryside.

BARNSLEY: Holiday Inn £
Family
Barnsley Rd, Dodsworth, South Yorkshire, S75 3JT
Tel *01226 299571*
🆆 hibarnsley.com
Four-star hotel. Some rooms have
four-poster beds. Good restaurant.

BRADFORD: Dubrovnik Hotel £
Boutique
3 Oak Ave, West Yorkshire, BD8 7AQ
Tel *01274 543511*
🆆 dubrovnik.co.uk
Former mill owner's home in leafy
suburbs. Great weekend deals.

GUISBOROUGH: Gisborough Hall ££
Country House
Whitby Lane, North Yorkshire, TS14 6PT
Tel *08448 799149*
🆆 macdonaldhotels.co.uk

The pretty ivy-clad exterior of Holdsworth House, Halifax

A grand, ivy-clad Victorian
mansion. Some rooms have four-
poster beds, others roll-top baths.

HALIFAX: Holdsworth House ££
Country House
Holdsworth Rd, West Yorkshire, HX2 9TG
Tel *01422 240024*
🆆 holdsworthhouse.co.uk
Jacobean manor with some
period rooms. Breakfast made
with locally sourced produce.

HARROGATE: Balmoral ££
Boutique
Franklin Mt, North Yorkshire, HG1 5EJ
Tel *01423 508208*
🆆 balmoralhotel.co.uk
Historic hotel stylishly refurbished
in red and black. Range of
luxurious rooms and suites.

HELMSLEY: Feversham Arms ££
Luxury
1–8 High St, North Yorkshire, YO62 5AG
Tel *01439 770766*
🆆 fevershamarmshotel.com
Former coaching inn with a
glamorous swimming pool and
spa. Good, uncomplicated food.

LEEDS: Malmaison Leeds ££
Character
1 Swine Gate, West Yorkshire, LS1 4AG
Tel *0844 693 0654*
🆆 malmaison-leeds.com
Sophisticated bar, brasserie and
100 funky rooms and suites in
the city's former tramways office.

PICKERING: White Swan ££
Country House
Market Pl, North Yorkshire, YO18 7AA
Tel *01751 472288*
🆆 white-swan.co.uk
Old-fashioned inn with fireplaces
and real ales. Choose from "treat",
"vintage" and "hideaway" rooms.

SCARBOROUGH: Wrea Head Country House Hotel ££
Country House
Barmoor Lane, Scalby, North Yorkshire, YO13 0PB
Tel *01723 371 190*
🆆 wreaheadhall.co.uk
Mock-Tudor Victorian house with
panelled rooms and roll-top
baths. Popular restaurant.

WHITBY: Broom House ££
Country House
Broom House Lane, Egton Bridge, YO21 1XD
Tel *01947 895 279*
🆆 egton-bridge.co.uk
Good base for exploring the
North York moors. Comfortable,
modern rooms.

YARM: Judges Country House Hotel ££
Luxury
Kirklevington Hall, Cleveland, North Yorkshire, TS15 9LW
Tel *01642 789000*
🆆 judgeshotel.co.uk
Glorious country mansion. Period
rooms with modern amenities.

DK Choice
YORK: Middlethorpe Hall £££
Luxury
Bishopthorpe Rd, Yorkshire, YO23 2GB
Tel *01904 620176*
🆆 middlethorpe.com
Superb mansion built in
1699 amid 8 ha (20 acres)
of manicured gardens and
mature parkland. Antiques and
artworks abound in the rooms.
There are 10 bedrooms in
the house and 19 in cottages
around the delightful stable
block. Guests can dine in a
beautiful panelled dining room.

Northumbria

CROOKHAM: Coach House £
B&B
Cornhill-on-Tweed, Northumberland, TD12 4TD
Tel *01890 820293*
🆆 coachhousecrookham.com
Pleasant, comfortable rooms in a
complex of renovated 17th-
century farm buildings.

DARLINGTON: Headlam Hall ££
Country House
Headlam, County Durham, DL2 3HA
Tel *01325 730790*
🆆 headlamhall.co.uk
Grand 17th-century mansion
with impressive spa. Some rooms
have private balconies.

Enjoy afternoon tea in the drawing room at Bodysgallen Hall, Llandudno

DURHAM: Durham Marriott Hotel Royal County £
Family
Old Elvet, County Durham, DH1 3JN
Tel *0191 386 6821*
W marriott.co.uk
Convenient base to explore the city. Pool, Wi-Fi and steakhouse.

HEXHAM: Battlesteads Hotel £
Character
Wark on Tyne, Northumberland, NE48 3LS
Tel *01434 230 209*
W battlesteads.com
Pleasant and family-friendly. Real ales and a seven-course menu.

MORPETH: Macdonald Linden Hall Golf & Country Club ££
Country House
Longhorsley, Northumberland, NE65 8XF
Tel *0844 879 9084*
W macdonaldhotels.co.uk/linden
Surrounded by private grounds. Spa, health club and golf course.

DK Choice

NEWCASTLE UPON TYNE: Hotel du Vin ££
Boutique
City Rd, Northumberland, NE1 2BE
Tel *08447 364259*
W hotelduvin.com/newcastle
This friendly, stylish hotel on the banks of the River Tyne has 42 imaginatively crafted rooms with stunning bathrooms and great views. There is a bistro and wine-tasting room, as well as a courtyard for alfresco dining.

North Wales

BEAUMARIS: Ye Olde Bull's Head Inn and Townhouse ££
Character
Castle St, Isle of Anglesey, LL58 8AP
Tel *01248 810329*
W bullsheadinn.co.uk
A 15th-century inn with modern facilities and a prized restaurant.

BEDDGELERT: Sygun Fawr Country House £
Country House
Gwynedd, LL55 4NE
Tel *01766 890258*
W sygunfawr.co.uk
Rural 17th-century manor house with oak beams and fireplaces.

HARLECH: Gwrach Ynys £
B&B
Ynys, Talsarnau, Gwynedd, LL47 6TS
Tel *01766 781199*
W gwrachynys.co.uk
Quiet guesthouse overlooking Snowdonia National Park. Cosy, modern bedrooms.

LLANABER: Llwyndu Farmhouse £
Country House
Barmouth, Gwynedd, LL42 1RR
Tel *01341 280144*
W llwyndu-farmhouse.co.uk
This 17th-century farmhouse offers fine wines and local beers.

LLANDUDNO: Bodysgallen Hall ££
Luxury
Conwy, Gwynedd, LL30 1RS
Tel *01492 584466*
W bodysgallen.com
Set in a 17th-century walled garden with an award-winning restaurant and bistro. Superb spa.

LLANGOLLEN: The Wild Pheasant Hotel £
Family
Berwyn Rd, Denbighshire, LL20 8AD
Tel *01978 860629*
W wildpheasanthotel.co.uk
Charming historic rural inn with a spa. Offers gourmet breaks, rafting and off-road driving.

DK Choice

PENMAENPOOL: Penmaenuchaf Hall £££
Country House
Dolgellau, Gwynedd, LL40 1YB
Tel *01341 422129*
W penhall.co.uk
Delightful Victorian house with

8 ha (20 acres) of landscaped gardens and an oak-panelled restaurant. There is a library, drawing room and morning room for guests to relax in. Mountain-biking, fishing, walking, golf and horse-riding excursions are available as well.

PORTMEIRION: Portmeirion £££
Character
Gwynedd, LL48 6ER
Tel *01766 770000*
W portmeirion-village.com
A fantasy village built by Clough Williams-Ellis. Elegantly decorated rooms, some with sea views.

RUTHIN: Ruthin Castle Hotel ££
Historic
Denbighshire, LL15 2NU
Tel *01824 702664*
W ruthincastle.co.uk
Luxurious 13th-century castle with opulent bedrooms and a spa in the woodlands.

South and Mid-Wales

ABERGAVENNY: Clytha Arms £
Character
Clytha, Monmouthshire, NP7 9BW
Tel *01873 840206*
W clytha-arms.com
Award-winning pub-restaurant with cheerful rooms overlooking delightful grounds.

ABERYSTWYTH: Gwesty Cymru £
Boutique
19 Marine Terrace, SY23 2AZ
Tel *01970 612252*
W gwestycymru.com
Modern twist on traditional Welsh seaside boarding house. Stylish rooms with oak furniture, designer bathrooms and sea views.

CARDIFF: St David's Hotel & Spa ££
Designer
Havannah St, CF10 5SD
Tel *02920 454045*
W thestdavidshotel.com
One of the most luxurious hotels in Wales. State-of-the-art rooms have private decks overlooking the bay.

CRICKHOWELL: Gliffaes Country House ££
Country House
Powys, NP8 1RH
Tel *01874 730371*
W gliffaeshotel.com
Victorian house in grouse-filled woodland. Popular with fly-fishing enthusiasts. Fine dining.

For more information on types of hotels *see page 559*

LAMPETER: Falcondale Mansion Hotel £££
Country House
Falcondale Drive, Ceredigion, SA48 7RX
Tel *01570 422910*
W falcondalehotel.com
En-suite rooms with four-poster beds and balconies. Restaurant serves Welsh cuisine.

DK Choice

LLANTHONY: Llanthony Priory ££
Historic
Monmouthshire, NP7 7NN
Tel *01873 890487*
W llanthonyprioryhotel.co.uk
Rooms in this ruined 12th-century Augustinian priory are off a stone spiral staircase. Dining is communal, presided over by "Aunty". The hotel is a great base for walking the Black Mountains. The vaulted under-croft bar serves real ale.

ST DAVIDS: Lochmeyler Farm Guesthouse £
B&B
Llandeloy, Pembrokeshire, SA62 6LL
Tel *01348 837724*
W lochmeyler.co.uk
Quiet guesthouse on a dairy farm. Rooms in a 16th-century house and adjacent farm cottages.

TENBY: Fourcroft Hotel ££
Family
North Beach, Pembrokeshire, SA70 8AP
Tel *01834 842886*
W fourcroft-hotel.co.uk
Simple and comfortable rooms overlooking the old fishing harbour. Restaurant on site.

TINTERN: Parva Farmhouse Guesthouse ££
Rooms with a view
Chepstow, Monmouthshire, NP16 6SQ
Tel *01291 689411*
W parvafarmhouse.co.uk
Stone farmhouse and restaurant on the banks of River Wye. Homely rooms with superb views.

The Lowlands

DUNDEE: Apex City Quay Hotel & Spa ££
Rooms with a view
1 West Victoria Dock Rd, DD1 3JP
Tel *0845 365 0000*
W apexhotels.co.uk
The best hotel in Dundee sits on the waterfront. Modern rooms, some with epic views of River Tay.

EDINBURGH: Classic Guesthouse £
B&B
50 Mayfield Rd, EH9 2NH
Tel *0131 667 5847*
W classichouse.demon.co.uk
Comfortably furnished Victorian house. Free Wi-Fi and full Scottish breakfasts with vegetarian options.

EDINBURGH: Macdonald Holyrood Hotel ££
Luxury
81 Holyrood Rd, EH8 8AU
Tel *0844 879 9028*
W macdonaldhotels.co.uk
Refined rooms with a spa and pool. Acclaimed grill restaurant.

EDINBURGH: Dalhousie Castle Hotel £££
Historic
Bonnyrigg, EH19 3JB
Tel *01875 820 153*
W dalhousiecastle.co.uk
Excellent restaurant and health spa. Falconry and archery on site.

GLASGOW: Malmaison ££
Boutique
278 W George St, G2 4LL
Tel *0141 572 1000*
W malmaison.com
Set in an old church with trendy colours. Great restaurant and bar.

GLASGOW: Cameron House £££
Country House
Loch Lomond, G83 8QZ
Tel *0871 222 4681*
W devere-hotels.co.uk
Grand rooms with epic loch views. Guests arrive by seaplane.

DK Choice

GLASGOW: Hotel du Vin at One Devonshire Gardens £££
Boutique
One Devonshire Gardens, G12 0UX
Tel *08447 364 256*
W hotelduvin.com
Housed in a quintet of Victorian town houses, this famous hotel emphasizes opulence, from its spacious and unique rooms through to the whisky bar and restaurant. Service is impeccable.

PEEBLES: Cringletie House ££
Country House
Edinburgh Rd, EH45 8PL
Tel *01721 725 750*
W cringletie.com
Opulent rooms with Wi-Fi. Award-winning Sutherland Restaurant.

PERTH: Parklands ££
Rooms with a view
2 St Leonard's Bank, Perthshire, PH2 8EB
Tel *01738 622451*
W theparklandshotel.com
En-suite rooms with park views. Fine dining and informal bistro.

ST ANDREWS: Old Course Hotel £££
Luxury
Fife, KY16 9SP
Tel *01334 474371*
W oldcoursehotel.kohler.com
One of the world's greatest golf resort hotels. Excellent spa.

STIRLING: The Stirling Highland Hotel ££
Family
Spittal St, Stirlingshire, FK8 1DU
Tel *01786 272 727*
W pumahotels.co.uk/stirling
Home to an old-fashioned observatory. Near the landmark castle.

The Highlands and Islands

ABERDEEN: Malmaison Aberdeen ££
Boutique
49–53 Queens Rd, Aberdeenshire, AB15 4YP
Tel *08446 930649*
W malmaison.com
Spacious rooms with big bath-rooms and well-stocked mini bars.

ACHILTIBUIE: Summer Isles Hotel ££
Rooms with a view
Ross-shire, IV26 2YG
Tel *01854 622282*
W summerisleshotel.co.uk
Romantic hideaway with views

The cosy restaurant in the Parva Farmhouse Guesthouse, Tintern over the Summer Isles and the Hebrides. Elegant en-suite rooms. Seafood restaurant.

APPLECROSS: Applecross Inn £
Character
Wester Ross, IV54 8LR
Tel *01520 744262*
W applecross.uk.com
Whitewashed inn with views of the Isle of Skye.

ARDEONAIG: Ardeonaig Hotel & Restaurant ££
Luxury
near Killin, South of Loch Tay, FK21 8SU
Tel *01567 820400*
W ardeonaighotel.co.uk
Historic inn with comfortable rooms, African-style luxury huts and cottage suites.

ARDUAINE: Loch Melfort Hotel & Restaurant £
Rooms with a view
Oban, Argyll, PA34 4XG
Tel *01852 200233*
W lochmelfort.co.uk
A three-star hotel with views over Scotland's majestic west coast.

ARISAIG: Old Library Lodge & Restaurant £
Character
Inverness-shire, PH39 4NH
Tel *01687 450651*
W oldlibrary.co.uk
Well-run restaurant with pleasant rooms in 200-year-old stables.

AVIEMORE: Macdonald Aviemore Highland Resort ££
Character
Inverness-shire, PH22 1PN
Tel *0844 8799152*
W macdonaldhotels.co.uk
Four hotels and 18 wooden lodges for all budgets. Pool, restaurants and a 3D cinema.

BALLATER: Morvada House ££
B&B
Braemar Rd, Aberdeenshire, AB35 5RL
Tel *01339 756334*
W morvada.com
Welcoming B&B in a traditional Victorian villa. Great breakfasts.

BARRA: Castlebay Hotel ££
Rooms with a view
Castlebay, HS9 5XD
Tel *01871 810223*
W castlebay-hotel.co.uk
Charming hotel with pleasant en-suite rooms. Lovely views of Kisimul Castle and Vatersay island.

COLL: Coll Hotel ££
Rooms with a view
Ariangour, PA78 6SZ
Tel *01879 230334*
W collhotel.com
Well-appointed lochside hotel

The harbourside Plockton Inn B&B and restaurant, Plonkton

with epic views of the Treshnish Isles, Staffa, Iona and Jura. En-suite rooms and seafood eatery.

DK Choice

ERISKA: Isle of Eriska Hotel, Spa & Island £££
Luxury
Benderloch, Argyll, PA37 1SD
Tel *01631 720371*
W eriska-hotel.co.uk
An enchanting country house on a private island with grand bedrooms, fine-dining and excellent spa. Elegant self-catering lodging is also on offer. Badgers roam the grounds, and seals swim in the nearby waters.

DUNKELD: Royal Hotel £
Historic
Atholl St, Perthshire, PH8 0AR
Tel *01350 727322*
W royaldunkeld.co.uk
Good-value hotel with simple rooms and traditional decor.

FORT AUGUSTUS: The Lovat £
Family
Inverness-shire, PH32 4DU
Tel *01456 490000*
W thelovat.com
Relaxed accommodation on the southern tip of Loch Ness.

FORT WILLIAM: Inverlochy Castle £££
Luxury
Torlundy, Perthshire, PH33 6SN
Tel *01397 702177*
W inverlochycastlehotel.com
One of Scotland's finest luxury hotels decked out with antiques.

INVERNESS: No. 41 Serviced Town House £££
Boutique
41 Huntly St, Inverness-shire, IV3 5HR
Tel *01463 712255*
W no41townhouse.co.uk
Lavish accommodation with a big kitchen overlooking River Ness.

MULL: Highland Cottage ££
Luxury
24 Breadalbane St, Tobermory, Argyll, PA75 6PD
Tel *01688 302030*
W highlandcottage.co.uk
Individually styled, luxuriously furbished rooms. Innovative modern Scottish cuisine.

ORKNEY ISLANDS: The Foveran £
B&B
Kirkwall, St Ola, KW15 1SFUK
Tel *01856 872389*
W foveranhotel.co.uk
Family-run hotel with en-suite rooms and a lovely restaurant.

PITLOCHRY: East Haugh Country House Hotel & Restaurant £
B&B
by Pitlochry, Perthshire, PH16 5TE
Tel *01796 473121*
W easthaugh.co.uk
Family-run hotel. Comfortable rooms with lush fabrics and period features. Restaurant on site.

PLOCKTON: Plockton Inn & Seafood Restaurant £
Boutique
Innes St, Ross-shire, IV52 8TW
Tel *01599 544222*
W plocktoninn.co.uk
En-suite rooms with plenty of natural light. Great seafood.

SHETLAND ISLANDS: Skeoverick £
B&B
Brunatwatt, Walls, ZE2 9PJ
Tel *01595 809349*
W visitscotland.com
Welcoming B&B in a picturesque loch-side location. Spacious en-suite rooms and great breakfasts.

SPEYSIDE: Craigellachie ££
Country House
Victoria St, Banffshire, AB38 9SR
Tel *0843 1787114*
W bespokehotels.com
Delightful country house in a riverside location. Superb restaurant and the Quaich whisky bar.

For more information on types of hotels *see page 559*

WHERE TO EAT AND DRINK

Great Britain's restaurant scene is booming. Gastro-pubs, street wagons, Michelin-starred eateries and designer beach cafés, as well as a wave of celebrity chefs, are all making eating out in the UK a mouthwatering prospect. British chefs are today among the most innovative in the world, and indigenous recipes – in the best cases using local and seasonal produce, along with foraged fruit, vegetables and herbs – are worth trying. Modern approaches combine fresh produce and fresh ingredients with influences from around the world. Pub fare has perhaps undergone the greatest transformation, with a wide variety of food found in all kinds of pubs. Gastro-pubs in particular focus on quality cuisine. Whatever the budget, it is possible to eat well at most times of day in the larger towns. Less elaborate but well-prepared affordable food is available in all types of restaurants and cafés. The restaurant listings on pages 582–603 feature some of the very best places, as well as those with a steady track record.

What's on the Menu?

The choice seems endless in large cities, particularly in London. Cuisines from all over the world are represented, including Thai, Tex-Mex, Turkish, Tuscan and Tandoori, as well as their infinite variations. There are many more unusual styles of cooking, too, such as Ethiopian, Polish, Caribbean and Pacific Rim.

Outside the major cities the food scene is more limited, but creative cooking can be found in the most rural areas, and more and more AA-Rosette-awarded pubs and restaurants are popping up. Destination restaurants such as Le Manoir de Quat' Saisons are found outside major cities and are worth making a special pilgrimage for. The vague term "modern European cuisine" adopted by many restaurants disguises a diverse collection of culinary styles. The spectrum ranges from French to Asian recipes, loosely characterized by the innovative use of fresh, high-quality ingredients, that are cooked simply with a wide range of seasonings.

Nostalgic yearnings for British food have produced a revival of hearty traditional dishes such as steak and kidney pie and treacle pudding (see p581), though "Modern British" cooking adopts a lighter, more innovative approach. The likes of celebrity chef Heston Blumenthal have encouraged an experimental leaning in this style of cookery, with unexpected flavours and ingredients complementing each other, along with scientific wizardry.

Breakfast

The traditional British breakfast starts with cereal and milk followed by bacon, eggs, sausage and tomato, perhaps with fried black pudding (see p580) in the North and Scotland. It is finished off with toast and marmalade, washed down with tea. Or you can just have black coffee and fruit juice, with a croissant or selection of pastries (continental breakfast). The price of breakfast is often included in hotel and B&B tariffs in Britain.

Lunch

The most popular lunchtime food includes sandwiches, salads, baked potatoes with fillings and ploughman's lunches (see p580). A traditional Sunday lunch of roast chicken, lamb, pork or beef is served in

Bibendum, offering sophisticated French cuisine in London (see p584)

An afternoon tea including
sandwiches, cakes and scones

most pubs and restaurants.
Many establishments offer
reasonably priced set lunches
that make dining in upmarket
and Michelin-starred restaurants
much more affordable.

Afternoon Tea

No visitor should miss the
experience of a proper British
afternoon tea (see p580). Some
of the most palatial teas are
offered by country-house and
top London hotels such as the
Ritz or Browns. The area that
is best known for the classic
"cream tea" is the West Country;
these always include scones
spread with clotted cream
and jam. Wales, Scotland,
Yorkshire and the Lake District
also offer tasty teas with
regional variations; in the North
Country, a slice of apple pie or
fruitcake is served hot with
a piece of North Yorkshire
Wensleydale cheese on top.

Dinner

In the evening, grander
restaurants and hotels offer
elaborately staged meals,
sometimes billed as five or six
courses (though one may be
simply a sorbet, or coffee with
petits fours). Taster menus,
which can sometimes be up to
20 courses, are a great way to
sample the best a restaurant
has to offer, if you have the
time and budget.

In comparison with the rest of
Europe, people in the UK eat
early. Dinner is typically around
8pm in restaurants and hotels,
although it can be taken as early
as 6pm. In smaller towns and
villages, it can be difficult to find
an evening meal after 10pm.

Places to Eat

Eating venues are extremely
varied, with brasseries, bistros,
wine bars, tearooms, tapas bars
and theatre cafés competing
with the more conventional
cafés and restaurants. Many
pubs also serve excellent food,
often at reasonable prices
(see pp604–9). Some of the
finest restaurants are located
in grand hotels.

Brasseries, Bistros and Cafés

Cafés and brasseries are
popular in Britain, often staying
open all day, serving coffee,
snacks and fairly simple dishes
along with a selection of beers
and wines. Alcoholic drinks,
however, may only be
available at certain times
of day. The atmosphere is
usually young and urbane,
with decor to match.

Wine bars are similar to
brasseries but with a better
selection of wines, which may
include English varieties (see
p164). Some bars have a good
range of ciders and real ales
as well (see p578).

The charming café at Tate St Ives,
Cornwall (see p593)

Restaurants with Rooms and Hotels

Restaurants with rooms are a
new breed of small establishments offering a handful of
bedrooms and usually excellent
food. They tend to be expensive
and are usually in a rural location.

Many hotel restaurants happily
serve non-residents. They tend
to be expensive, but the best can
be unparalleled. Hotels serving
a high standard of food are also
included on pages 560–73.

Restaurant Etiquette

As a rule of thumb, the more
expensive the restaurant, the
more formal the dress code,
though very few restaurants
expect men to wear a shirt
and tie. Call ahead to check.

A total smoking ban in public
places was implemented
throughout the UK in 2007.
However, smoking outside
is still permitted.

Leith Docks in Edinburgh, a centre of good pubs, bars and restaurants

The main dining area at Porter's English Restaurant, London, serving traditional classics *(see p582)*

Alcohol

Britain's laws concerning the sale of alcohol, the "licensing laws", were once among the most restrictive in Europe. Now they are much more relaxed, with some places operating extended opening hours, especially at weekends. Some establishments, however, may only serve alcohol at set times with food. Some unlicensed restaurants operate a "Bring Your Own" policy; a corkage fee is often charged. It is illegal to sell alcohol to under 18s.

Vegetarian Food

Britain's restaurants are keen to offer vegetarian alternatives and welcome non-meat eaters. An increasing number of places in the listings serve only vegetarian meals, and most offer at least one vegetarian option. Those who want a wider choice could seek out South Indian and other restaurants that have a tradition of vegetarian cuisine.

Fast-Food and Chain Restaurants

Fast food usually costs well under £10. Apart from the ubiquitous fish and chip shop, there are many fast-food chains, as well as some more upmarket options such as Pizza Express and Yo! Sushi. Other chains offering good-value, quality food, as well as facilities for children, include Ask, Giraffe, Byron and Leon. Budget cafés, nicknamed "greasy spoons", serve inexpensive food, often in the form of endless variations of the breakfast fry-up *(see p580)*.

Booking Ahead

It is always safer to book a table before making a special trip to a restaurant; city restaurants can be very busy, and some famous establishments can be fully booked a month or more in advance. Fridays, Saturdays and Sunday lunchtimes are particularly busy. Renowned gourmet restaurants can require a booking months in advance.

Fifteen Cornwall restaurant overlooking Watergate Bay *(see p592)*

Checking the Bill

All restaurants are required by law to display their current prices outside the door. These amounts include Value Added Tax (VAT), currently at 20 per cent. Service and cover charges (if any) are also specified.

Wine is always pricey in Britain, and extras such as coffee or bottled water can be disproportionately expensive.

Service charges (usually 10–15 per cent) are often automatically added to the bill. If you feel that the service has been poor, you are entitled to subtract this service charge. If no service charge has been added, you are expected to add 10–15 per cent to the bill, but it is your decision.

Look out for additional charges: some places may leave the "total" box of credit card slips blank, hoping customers will add to the service charge. A few restaurants may also add a "cover charge" for bread and butter, and so on. Most restaurants accept credit cards.

Mealtimes

Breakfast may be as early as 6:30am in a city business hotel (most hoteliers will make special arrangements if you have to check out early for some reason) or as late as 10:30am in relaxed country-house hotels. Some hoteliers, however, insist on serving breakfast at 9am sharp. In some urban restaurants it is possible to find breakfast all day. The American concept of Sunday brunch is becoming increasingly popular in more urban hotels, restaurants and cafés.

Lunch in restaurants and pubs is usually served between noon and 2:30pm. Try to arrive in time to order the main course before 1:30pm, or you may find choice restricted. Most tourist areas have plenty of cafés, fast-food diners and coffee bars where you can have a snack at any time of day.

Traditional afternoon tea is usually served between 3pm and 5pm. Dinner is usually served from 6pm until 10pm; some places, especially Indian restaurants, stay open later. In guesthouses or small hotels, dinner may be served at a specific time. In cities, many restaurants are closed on Sunday evenings and on Mondays.

Children

The continental norm of dining out *en famille* is welcomed in Britain, and visiting a restaurant may no longer entail endless searches for a babysitter, although after 8pm, it is not usual to see small children in restaurants.

Many places welcome junior diners, and some actively encourage families, at least during the day or early evening. Formal restaurants sometimes cultivate a more adult ambience at dinnertime, and some impose age limits. If you want to take young children to a restaurant, check ahead.

Italian, Spanish, Indian, fast-food restaurants and ice-cream parlours nearly always welcome children and sometimes provide special menus or high chairs for them. Even traditional English pubs, which were once a strictly adult preserve, accommodate families and may even provide special

Organic Riverford Field Kitchen *(see p591)*

rooms or play areas. The places that welcome and cater for children are indicated in the pub guide *(see pp604–9)*.

Disabled Access

Restaurant facilities in Great Britain could be better for disabled visitors, but things are slowly improving. Modern premises usually take account of mobility problems, but it's always best to check first if you have special needs.

The website www.openbritain.com has information on accessible cafés and restaurants.

Ice-cream parlour sign

Picnics

Eating outside is becoming more popular in Britain, though it is more likely that you will find tables outside pubs (in the form of a beer garden) than outside restaurants. An inexpensive option is to make up your own

picnic; most towns have good delicatessens and bakeries where you can collect provisions. Look out for street markets to pick up fresh fruit and local cheeses at bargain prices. Department stores such as Marks & Spencer and supermarkets including Sainsbury's and Waitrose often sell an excellent range of pre-packed sandwiches and snacks; large towns usually have several sandwich bars to choose from. Your hotel or guesthouse may also be able to provide a packed lunch. Ask for it the night before.

Recommended Restaurants

The restaurants in this guide have been chosen across a wide price range for their atmosphere, location and good food. These include no-frills seafood shacks, characterful pubs, Indian curry houses, cafés and Michelin-starred restaurants in country-house estates. In a gastro-pub you can expect beautifully presented food in a warm casual pub environment. Places serving Modern British food offer dishes that are contemporary versions of traditional classics, whereas Traditional British will be hearty portions of staple fare, such as puddings, pies and stews. For the best, look out for restaurants listed as DK Choice entries. Each of these has one or more exceptional features, such as a celebrity chef, sensational food, unusual location, or a welcoming atmosphere.

Eating alfresco at Grasmere in the Lake District

The Traditional British Pub

Every country has its bars, but Britain is famous for its pubs or "public houses". Ale was brewed in England in Roman times – mostly at home – and by the Middle Ages there were inns and taverns which brewed their own. The 18th century was the heyday of the coaching inn as stage coaches brought more custom. In the 19th century came railway taverns for travellers and "gin palaces" for the new industrial workers. Today, pubs come in all styles and sizes and many cater to families, serving food as well as drink *(see pp604–7)*.

Early 19th-century coaching inn – also a social centre and post office

The Victorian Pub

A century ago, many pubs in towns and cities had smart interiors, to contrast with the poor housing of their clients.

Elaborately etched glass is a feature of many Victorian interiors.

Pub games, such as cribbage, bar billiards, pool and dominoes are part of British pub culture. Here some regular customers are competing against a rival pub's darts team.

Beer gardens outside pubs are a favourite venue for family summer treats.

Pint glasses (containing just over half a litre) are used for beer.

The Red Lion pub name is derived from Scottish heraldry *(see p30)*.

Old-fashioned cash register contributes to the period atmosphere of the bar.

Pewter tankards, seldom used by drinkers today, add a traditional touch.

What to Drink

Draught bitter is the most traditional British beer. Brewed from malted barley, hops, yeast and water, and usually matured in a wooden cask, it varies from region to region. In the north of England the sweeter mild ale is popular, and lagers served in bottles or on tap are also widely drunk. Stout, made from black malt, is another variation.

Beer pump

Draught bitter is drunk at cellar temperature.

Draught lager is a light-coloured, carbonated beer.

Guinness is a thick, creamy Irish stout.

Pavement tables, crowded with city drinkers during the summer months

A village pub, offering a waterside view and serving drinks in the garden

Bottles of spirits are ranged behind the bar.

Glass lamps imitate the Victorian style.

Wine, once rarely found in pubs, is now commonplace.

A deep-toned mahogany bar forms part of the traditional setting.

Draught beer, served from pumps or taps, comes from national and local brewers.

Optics dispense spirits in precise measures.

Mild may be served by the pint or in a half-pint tankard (as above).

Top cocktails are gin-and-tonic (right) and Pimm's.

Pub Signs

Early medieval inns used vines or evergreens as signs – the symbol of Bacchus, the Roman god of wine. Soon pubs acquired names that signalled support for monarchs or noblemen, or celebrated victories in battle. As many customers could not read, pub signs had vivid images.

The George may derive from one of the six English kings of that name, or, as here, from England's patron saint.

The Bat and Ball celebrates cricket, and may be sited near a village green where the game can be played.

The Green Man is a woodland spirit from pagan mythology, possibly the basis for the legend of Robin Hood (see p340).

The Magna Carta sign commemorates and illustrates the "great charter" signed by King John in 1215 (see p52).

The Bird in Hand refers to the ancient country sport of falconry, traditionally practised by noblemen.

The Flavours of Britain

A rich agriculture that provides meat and dairy products such as well as fruit, vegetables and cereals, gives the British table a broad scope. Traditional dishes – cooked breakfasts, roast beef, fish and chips – are famous, but there is much more on offer, varying from region to region. Many towns give their names to produce and dishes. Seasonal choices include game and seafood, while other produce can be seen at the increasingly popular farmers' markets. Britons still have a penchant for pies and puddings, and most regions have cakes and buns they can call their own. Scotland has its own distinctive cuisine (see p492).

Asparagus

Local fresh beetroot on sale at a greengrocer's shop

Central and Southern England

All tastes are catered for in the metropolis, and the surrounding countryside has long been given over to its demands. The flat lands of East Anglia provide vegetables and root crops; the South Downs have been shorn by sheep; geese have made Nottingham famous; and the county of

Kent is known as "the Garden of England" for its glorious orchards and its fields of soft fruits. From around the coast come Dover sole, Whitstable oysters (popular since Roman times) and the Cockney favourites, cockles and whelks. The game season runs from November to February, and pheasant is often on the menu.

West of England

The warmest part of England is renowned for its classic cream teas, the key ingredient provided by its dairy herds. In Cornwall, pasties have long been a staple. Once eaten by tin miners and filled with meat at one end and jam the other, to give two courses in one, they are now generally made with

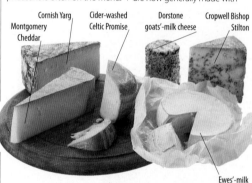

Cornish Yarg, Montgomery Cheddar

Cider-washed Celtic Promise

Dorstone goats'-milk cheese

Cropwell Bishop Stilton

Ewes'-milk Wigmore

Selection of fine, farm-produced British cheeses

Traditional British Food

Though many traditional dishes, such as Lancashire hotpot, beef Wellington and even fish and chips, can be harder to hunt down than tapas, pizza or chicken tikka masala, other reliable regulars remain. Among them are shepherd's pie (minced lamb with mashed potatoes), steak and kidney pie (beef and kidney in gravy baked in a pastry crust), or game pie and "bangers and mash" (sausages with mash potatoes and onion gravy). For pudding there is a variety of trifles, pies, tarts and crumbles, often eaten with custard, as well as a lighter summer pudding of seasonal fruit. A "full English breakfast" is a fry-up of sausages, eggs, bacon, tomatoes, mushrooms and bread, perhaps with black pudding or laverbread. Lunchtime snacks include a "Ploughman's lunch" of cheese and pickles with a "doorstep" of bread.

Dover sole This is the most tasty flatfish, best served simply grilled with lemon, spinach and new potatoes.

Display of British breads at a local farmers' market

meat and vegetables. The clear waters around the peninsula offer up such seafood as sardines, mackerel and crab in abundance, and many of the region's best restaurants specialize in fish. Bath gives its name to special biscuits and buns.

North of England

Cumberland sausage, Lancashire hotpot, Goosnargh duck and Yorkshire pudding – the names tell you exactly where the food on your plate originated. These are the staples, but restaurants these days are creating new dishes from old, such as trout with black (blood) pudding, and even being adventurous with "mushy" peas. Bradford, with its large Asian community, is one of the best places to eat Indian food.

Wales

The green grass of Wales is appreciated by sheep, who turn into fabulous lamb that is simply roasted and eaten with mint sauce – a favourite all over Britain. The grass is good for dairy products, too, including white, crumbly

A Cornish fishmonger displays a locally caught red mullet

Caerphilly. Cheese is the principal ingredient of Welsh rarebit (pronounced rabbit), made with cheese grilled on toast and occasionally augmented with beer. Look out for prize-winning Welsh Black beef – prime fillets are often accompanied by horseradish sauce. The Irish Sea provides plenty of fish, but there is also freshwater trout and salmon. A curiosity of the South Wales seashore is laver, a kind of sea spinach, which is mixed with oatmeal and fried in small cakes called *bara lawr*, or laverbread, to be served with sausage and bacon for breakfast.

British Cheeses

Caerphilly Fresh, white, mild cheese from Wales.

Cheshire Crumbly, silky and full-bodied cheese.

Cheddar Often imitated, never bettered; the best comes from the West Country.

Double Gloucester Mellow flavoured, smooth and creamy.

Sage Derby Flavoured with green veins of sage.

Stilton The king of British cheeses, a strong, blue-veined cheese with a creamy texture. Popular at Christmas.

Wensleydale Young, moist and flaky-textured, with a mild, slightly sweet flavour.

Cornish mackerel The ideal partner for this rich fish is a piquant sauce make of English gooseberries.

Roast beef Horseradish sauce is a traditional accompaniment, as are crisp Yorkshire puddings made of batter.

Welsh lamb with leeks The leek is the national vegetable of Wales, and perfectly complements roast lamb.

Where to Eat and Drink

London

West End and Westminster

Belgo Centraal £
Belgian **Map** 11 B2
50 Earlham St, WC2H 9LJ
Tel *020 7813 2233*
Bustling and quirky restaurant
with the staff dressed as monks.
Team the excellent lobster with
a delicious Trappist beer.

Food for Thought £
Vegetarian **Map** 11 B1
31 Neal St, WC2H 9PR
Tel *020 7836 0239*
Food for Thought has an
excellent vegetarian spread,
including perfectly cooked wild
mushroom gnocchi. Long queues.

Princi £
Italian **Map** 11 A2
135 Wardour St, W1F 0UT
Tel *020 7478 8888*
A stylish Milan import. Sample
handmade bread, wood-fired
pizzas and delicious pastries.

Regency Café £
Traditional British **Map** 19 A2
17–19 Regency St, SW1P 4BY
Tel *020 7821 6596* **Closed** *Sun*
A 1950s-style "caff" that was
featured in a couple of movies.
Try the heavenly hash browns
and eggs Benedict for breakfast.

Soho Joe £
Italian **Map** 11 A1
22–25 Dean St, W1D 3RY
Tel *07534 134398*
Thin-crust pizzas are the star of
the show at this great-value
Italian joint. Fantastic pastas,
burgers and sandwiches on the
menu as well. Great ambience.

Al Duca ££
Italian **Map** 11 A3
4–5 Duke of York St, SW1Y 6LA
Tel *020 7839 3090* **Closed** *Sun*
Classic Italian dishes are given a
modern twist using the freshest of
ingredients at this popular eatery.

Andrew Edmunds ££
European **Map** 11 A2
46 Lexington St, W1F 0LW
Tel *020 7437 5708*
Quirky and romantic restaurant
featuring imaginative dishes on
its daily-changing menu.

Bocca di Lupo ££
Italian **Map** 11 A2
12 Archer St, W1D 7BB
Tel *020 7734 2223*
Chef Jacob Kennedy specializes
in robust and rare regional
recipes at this small eatery.

Clos Maggiore ££
European **Map** 11 B2
33 King St, WC2E 8JD
Tel *020 7379 9696*
Modern European cooking
inspired by French regional food
in a romantic setting. Good fixed-
price pre- and post-theatre menus.

Le Deuxième ££
French **Map** 11 B2
65 Long Acre, WC2E 9JH
Tel *020 7379 0033*
The bistro-style menu at Le
Deuxième concentrates on
interesting combinations and
strong flavours.

Haozhan ££
Chinese **Map** 11 A2
8 Gerrard St, W1D 5PJ
Tel *020 7434 3838*
A world away from the standard
sweet-and-sour staples, Haozhan
serves superb cuisine made with
the finest seasonal ingredients.

Hard Rock Café ££
American **Map** 10 E4
150 Old Park Lane, W1K 1QZ
Tel *020 7514 1700*
Savour American staples at this
legendary hotel with a fascinating
collection of rock memorabilia.

Mildred's ££
Vegetarian **Map** 11 A2
45 Lexington St, W1F 9AN
Tel *020 7494 1634* **Closed** *Sun*
Inspired vegetarian cuisine fit to
convert the most confirmed
carnivore. Try porcini and ale pie.

Noura ££
Lebanese **Map** 18 E1
16 Hobart Pl, SW1W 0HH
Tel *020 7235 9444*
Classy looks and a tempting
brasserie-style menu at this
popular flagship. Exceptional
mezes and kebabs.

El Pirata ££
Tapas **Map** 10 E4
5–6 Down St, W1J 7AQ
Tel *020 7491 3810* **Closed** *Sun*
Lively restaurant, with all the
classic Spanish and Portuguese
favourites on offer. Great special
set lunch menu.

Porter's English Restaurant ££
Traditional British **Map** 11 C2
17 Henrietta St, WC2E 8QH
Tel *020 7836 6466*
Fill up on hearty English classics
such as steak and kidney
pudding, fish pie and spotted
dick. Good for families.

Terroirs ££
Mediterranean **Map** 11 B3
5 William IV St, WC2N 4DW
Tel *020 7036 0660* **Closed** *Sun*
An impressive selection of
biodynamic wines teamed with
exquisite cuisine including pork,
snails, lentils and mushrooms.
Reminiscent of a Parisian bar.

Thai Pot ££
Thai **Map** 11 B2
1 Bedfordbury, WC2N 4BP
Tel *020 7379 4580* **Closed** *Sun*
Relish Thai staples full of
fragrant flavour and fresh
ingredients at this artless refuge.
Dashes of warm colour jazz up
the contemporary decor.

Traditional British fare is served in Porter's English Restaurant, London

The Wolseley ££
European   Map 10 F3
160 Piccadilly, W1J 9EB
Tel *020 7499 6996*
A 1920s Wolseley Motor car show-room makes a stunning home for this glamorous café-restaurant. Their steak tartare is legendary.

Vasco and Piero's Pavilion ££
Italian   Map 11 A2
15 Poland St, W1F 8QE
Tel *020 7437 8774*   **Closed** *Sun*
Delicious home-made pasta used with truffles when in season. Try Umbrian specialities such as pork and lentils.

Atelier de Joël Robuchon £££
French   Map 11 B2
13–15 West St, WC2H 9NE
Tel *020 7010 8600*
Get a front row seat at the Japanese-inspired counter in this two-Michelin-starred restaurant serving fantastic French food.

Bentley's Oyster Bar and Grill
Seafood £££   Map 10 F3
11 Swallow St, W1B 4DG
Tel *020 7734 4756*   **Closed** *Sun*
Serving delectable seafood since 1916. Chef Richard Corrigan's inventive creations keep Bentley's firmly on the map.

Cecconi's £££
Italian   Map 10 F3
5a Burlington Gardens, W1S 3EP
Tel *020 7434 1500*
Sample virtuoso versions of standard dishes at Cecconi's. Gets busy at peak times so come early.

Le Caprice £££
European   Map 10 F3
Arlington House, Arlington St, SW1A 1RJ
Tel *020 7629 2239*
This restaurant offers flavourful bistro food complemented by classic decor and attentive service.

Le Gavroche £££
French   Map 10 D2
43 Upper Brook St, W1K 7QR
Tel *020 7408 0881*   **Closed** *Sun & bank hols*
Le Gavroche is a byword for luxury and exceptional haute cuisine. Great service and a well-priced set lunch.

Murano £££
European   Map 10 E3
20 Queen St, W1J 5PP
Tel *020 7495 1127*   **Closed** *Sun*
Murano serves modern European cuisine with a bias towards Italian flavours. Nothing on the menu disappoints – from the amuse-bouche to petits fours.

Elegant dining area at the sophisticated Murano, London

Nobu £££
Japanese   Map 10 E4
Metropolitan Hotel W1, 19 Old Park Lane, W1K 1LB
Tel *020 7447 4747*
Beautifully prepared sashimi, tempura and other excellent contemporary Japanese dishes. Great place for celebrity spotting.

Rules £££
Modern British   Map 11 C2
35 Maiden Lane, WC2E 7LB
Tel *020 7836 5314*
Robust British food such as rib of beef, oysters and game at London's oldest restaurant, established in 1798. Procures game from its own country estate.

The Ritz Restaurant £££
Modern British   Map 10 F3
150 Piccadilly, W1J 9BR
Tel *020 7493 8181*
The perfect place to sample exquisite classic cuisine from the seasonally changing menu. Spectacular decor.

Veeraswamy £££
Indian   Map 10 F3
Victory House, 99 Regent St, W1B 4RS
Tel *020 7734 1401*
This London institution, opened in 1926, offers contemporary and classic Indian dishes in lush interiors that evoke a palace.

South Kensington and Hyde Park

Buona Sera Jam £
Italian   Map 17 A4
289 King's Rd, SW3 5EW
Tel *020 7352 8827*
A lively trattoria that is great for families. Climb miniature ladders to reach the top-tier tables and enjoy terrific pizza and pasta.

Café Mona Lisa £
French   Map 16 E5
417 King's Rd, SW10 0LR
Tel *020 7376 5447*
Popular neighbourhood café with friendly service and warm interiors. Delicious French fare, with daily specials displayed on a chalkboard.

Jak's £
Mediterranean   Map 17 B2
77 Walton St, SW3 2HT
Tel *020 7584 3441*
Savour a range of healthy organic dishes and tempting desserts in a country-style back room.

DK Choice

Assaggi ££
Italian   Map 7 C2
39 Chepstow Pl, W2 4TS
Tel *020 7792 5501*   **Closed** *Sun*
Hidden away above a pub, this alluring restaurant is a worthy addition to the burgeoning foodie scene. The bright room reflects the vivid colours of chef Nino Sassu's native Sardinia. Sample from an extensive menu of superb regional specialities. Reservations recommended.

Byron ££
American   Map 7 C5
222 Kensington High St, W8 7RG
Tel *020 7361 1717*
Come to Byron for the best burgers in town, made from quality, freshly minced beef.

E&O ££
Asian   Map 7 A2
14 Blenheim Crescent, W11 1NN
Tel *020 7229 5454*
Amid glossy decor, E&O serves delicious tempura, sushi and specials such as pad thai.

Hunan ££
Chinese **Map** 18 D2
51 Pimlico Rd, SW1W 8NE
Tel 020 7730 5712 **Closed** *Sun*
Enjoy tapas-size portions of
Taiwanese-style Chinese food.

Kensington Place ££
Seafood **Map** 7 C4
201 Kensington Church St, W8 7LX
Tel 020 7727 3184
This famous goldfish-bowl
brasserie serves fantastic beer-
battered fish and chips.

Le Metro at the Levin Hotel
European **Map** 9 C5
28 Basil St, SW3 1AS
Tel 020 7589 6286
A genteel basement brasserie
with delectable food and the feel
of a modern European tearoom.

The Abingdon ££
European **Map** 15 C1
54 Abingdon Rd, W8 6AP
Tel 020 7937 3339
A converted pub with a refined
feel and great brasserie-style
food. Ask to be seated at a booth.

The Belvedere ££
European **Map** 7 B5
*off Abbotsbury Rd, Holland Park,
W8 6LU*
Tel 020 7602 1238
Enjoy modern European fare in
a sumptuous former ballroom
overlooking beautiful gardens.

The Markham Inn ££
Modern British **Map** 17 B2
2 Elystan St, SW3 3NS
Tel 020 7581 9139
The Markham Inn offers a
superior seasonal menu in a great
pub atmosphere. Popular with
travellers since the Victorian era.

**Apsleys, a Heinz Beck
Restaurant** £££
Italian **Map** 10 D5
*The Lanesborough Hotel, Hyde Park
Corner, SW1X 7TA*
Tel 020 7333 7254
A Venetian-style dining room
serving sumptuous Italian fare.
Try the seven-course tasting menu.

DK Choice

Bibendum £££
French **Map** 17 A2
*Michelin House, 81 Fulham Rd,
SW3 6RD*
Tel 020 7581 5817
Michelin House's Art Nouveau
stained glass makes for a
stunning backdrop to this airy
first-floor dining room. Come
for the fantastic seasonal French
cuisine and assiduous service.

**Dinner by Heston
Blumenthal** £££
Modern British **Map** 9 C5
*Mandarin Oriental Hyde Park,
66 Knightsbridge, SW1X 7LA*
Tel 020 7201 3833
London's most hyped restaurant
showcases this celebrity chef's
inspired take on classic British
cuisine. Meteoric prices, but an
unforgettable dining experience.

**Marcus Wareing at the
Berkeley** £££
Modern British **Map** 10 D5
French
*The Berkeley Hotel, Wilton Pl,
SW1X 7RL*
Tel 020 7235 1200 **Closed** *Sun*
The bright red interiors of Marcus
Wareing's dining room heightens
the dramatic and delectable
cooking from the superstar chef.

Restaurant Gordon Ramsay £££
French **Map** 17 C4
68 Royal Hospital Rd, SW3 4HP
Tel 020 7352 4441 **Closed** *Sat & Sun*
Standards remain high at this
three-Michelin-starred shrine to
haute cuisine. Very expensive,
but the menu is truly exciting.

Zuma £££
Japanese **Map** 9 B5
5 Raphael St, SW7 1DL
Tel 020 7584 1010
Popular for its robata-grilled dishes,
tempura, nigiri sushi and sashimi.
A delectable night out. Great for
celebrity spotting.

Regent's Park and Bloomsbury

Gem £
Turkish **Map** 4 F1
265 Upper St, N1 2UQ
Tel 020 7359 0405
True to its name, Gem is a great
little place serving fragrant meze
at bargain prices in a charming
white-painted room decorated
with Kurdish farm implements.

DK Choice

Golden Hind £
Traditional British **Map** 10 E1
73 Marylebone Lane, W1U 2PN
Tel 020 7486 3644 **Closed** *Sun*
A welcoming no-frills family-
run place with no alcohol
licence but a minimal corkage
fee. Established in 1914,
Golden Hind has been
expanded by its current
Greek owners. The home-
made fishcakes with the
obligatory mushy peas are
an enticing alternative to
their famous fish and chips.

Formal dining at Restaurant
Gordon Ramsay, London

Bam-Bou ££
Vietnamese **Map** 11 A1
1 Percy St, W1T 1DB
Tel 020 7323 9130 **Closed** *Sun*
Stop by for a drink in the romantic
red bar and then descend to the
candlelit restaurant to enjoy well-
crafted and innovative French-
Vietnamese dishes.

Galvin Bistrot de Luxe ££
French **Map** 1 C5
66 Baker St, W1U 7DJ
Tel 020 7935 4007
A popular high-class bistro that
serves beautifully cooked classic
French cuisine accompanied by
a wide choice of wines from all
over the World.

Ottolenghi ££
Mediterranean **Map** 4 F1
287 Upper St, N1 2TZ
Tel 020 7288 1454
Ottolenghi's designer space
is complemented by divine,
healthy cuisine served on
communal tables. Innovative
recipes of Mediterranean cuisine.

Orrery £££
French **Map** 2 D5
55–57 Marylebone High St, W1U 5RB
Tel 020 7616 8000
Outstanding modern French
cuisine, served in a converted
stable block. Grab a table by the
stylish arched windows. Great
attention to detail in every way.

Pied à Terre £££
French **Map** 3 A5
34 Charlotte St, W1T 2NH
Tel 020 7636 1178 **Closed** *Sun*
Known for its adventurous and
impeccable food. A refined yet
friendly place with a comfortable
dining room. Attentive and
dedicated staff.

Roka £££
Japanese Map 3 A5
37 Charlotte St, W1T 1RR
Tel *020 7580 6464*
Sit at the wooden counter of this goldfish-bowl restaurant to savour delicious sushi and watch the chefs at the robata grill.

The City and Southwark

Anchor and Hope £
Modern British Map 12 E4
36 The Cut, SE1 8LP
Tel *020 7928 9898* **Closed** *Sun*
Come with a large appetite for gutsy fare: braised venison, calves' brains, and pumpkin risotto.

Cây Tre £
Vietnamese Map 5 A4
301 Old St, EC1V 9LA
Tel *020 7729 8662*
Authentic and high-quality dishes, including pho and seafood platters. They also serve delicious Cornish scallops and anchovied chicken wings.

Clerkenwell Kitchen £
Modern British Map 4 E4
27–31 Clerkenwell Close, EC1R 0AT
Tel *020 7101 9959* **Closed** *Sat & Sun*
Home-style cooking with use of organic produce and attentive service. A great place for lunch.

Lahore Kebab House £
Pakistani Map 14 E1
2–10 Umberston St, E1 1PY
Tel *020 7481 9737*
Spiced curries and kebabs will set the taste buds tingling in a warehouse-style space. Bring your own bottle (BYOB).

Leon Spitalfields £
European Map 6 D5
3 Crispin Pl, E1 6DW
Tel *020 7247 4369*
Healthy "superfood" salads and Mediterranean-inspired fast food in a large and colourful space. Great option for families.

Brawn ££
French Map 6 E3
49 Columbia Road, E2 7RG
Tel *020 7729 5692*
Big, bold flavours can be found in abundance here: think venison pie, pig's trotters and ceps with Bordelaise sauce. The wine list features many organic offerings.

Champor-Champor ££
Malaysian Map 13 C4
62–64 Weston St, SE1 3QJ
Tel *020 7403 4600*
Translating as "mix and match", Champor-Champor is known for its exotic decoration and eclectic, wonderful Malaysian cuisine.

L'Anima ££
Italian Map 5 C5
1 Snowden St, EC2A 2DQ
Tel *020 7422 7000* **Closed** *Sun*
Francesco Mazzei's food is as elegant as the minimalist setting at L'Anima. Stunning regional food with fantastic wines to match.

Le Café du Marché ££
French Map 4 F5
22 Charterhouse Sq, EC1M 6DX
Tel *020 7608 1609* **Closed** *Sun*
This French hideaway offers accomplished classic cooking teamed with a simple, stylish look. Great jazz nights.

The Chancery ££
European Map 12 E1
9 Cursitor St, EC4A 1LL
Tel *020 7831 4000* **Closed** *Sun*
Fabulous hake, muntjac and slow-cooked pork belly. Reasonably priced lunch spot.

The Peasant ££
Modern British Map 4 E2
240 St John St, EC1V 4PH
Tel *020 7336 7726*
Finely executed brasserie cooking in an agreeable Victorian dining room. First-rate pub food in the cavernous bar below.

Vanilla Black ££
Vegetarian Map 12 E1
17–18 Tooks Court, EC4A 1LB
Tel *020 7242 2622* **Closed** *Sun*
Excellent vegetarian dishes in an elegant setting. Try the warm walnut panna cotta and blue Stilton dumplings.

Vinoteca ££
European Map 4 E2
7 St John St, EC1M 4AA
Tel *020 7253 8786* **Closed** *Sun*
An extensive wine list and excellent modern European fare ensure a steady crowd at this Farringdon wine bar.

Galvin La Chapelle £££
French Map 6 D5
35 Spital Sq, E1 6DY
Tel *020 7299 0400*
Housed in a converted school hall, this restaurant offers a remarkable and varied menu featuring delectable French fare. Good Sunday roast lunch menu.

Hawksmoor £££
Steakhouse Map 14 E1
157 Commercial St, E1 6BJ
Tel *020 7426 4850*
Succulent steaks prepared from traditionally reared Longhorn cattle, dry aged and cooked on a charcoal grill. Hawksmoor is, quite simply, a carnivore's delight.

DK Choice

Oxo Tower Restaurant and Brasserie £££
European Map 12 E3
Oxo Tower Wharf,
Barge House St, SE1 9GY
Tel *020 7803 3888*
The delectable cuisine and international wine list at Oxo is complemented by breathtaking eighth-floor views: colourful by day, glittering by night. Choose between the relaxed brasserie and sophisticated restaurant, both superbly run by Harvey Nichols. Picturesque terrace seating in the summer.

Further Afield

Anarkali £
Indian
303–305 King St, W6 9NH
Tel *020 8748 1760*
A Hammersmith restaurant, in a class of its own. Unique, subtle spicing and a great choice for vegetarians. Try the delicious home-made *Rafique* sauce. Delightful service.

Impressive city views at the Oxo Tower Restaurant and Brasserie, London

For more information on types of restaurants *see page 577*

Exemplary food served in a casual setting at The Curlew, Bodiam

The Greenwich Union £
Modern British
56 Royal Hill, SE10 8RT
Tel *020 8692 6258*
A local landmark, this pub showcases a unique range of beers. Menus recommend ale pairings for each delicious dish.

Emile's ££
European
98 Felsham Rd, SW15 1DQ
Tel *020 8789 3323* **Closed** *Sun*
A Putney treasure: good, simple food in an unfussy room. A blackboard, brought to the table, displays the seasonal menu.

Enoteca Turi ££
Italian
28 Putney High St, SW15 1SQ
Tel *020 8785 4449* **Closed** *Sun*
Run by a dedicated couple, this restaurant offers a convivial and relaxed atmosphere, rustic setting and wholesome food.

Indian Zing ££
Indian
236 King St, W6 0RF
Tel *020 8748 5959*
A noteworthy wine list and contemporary Indian cuisine, prepared with panache at this upmarket gem.

Jin-Kichi ££
Japanese
73 Heath St, NW3 6UG
Tel *020 7794 6158* **Closed** *Sun, bank hols & Tue after bank hol Mon*
Find a piece of Tokyo in Hampstead, with a grill, sublime sushi, well-spaced seating and efficient service.

Sam's Brasserie ££
European
11 Barley Mow Passage, W4 4PH
Tel *020 8987 0555*
Choose from a range of light salads, scrumptious roasts and

delectable desserts at this cheerful restaurant. Great for families, with activities and a kid's menu.

Singapore Garden ££
Singaporean
83 Fairfax Rd, NW6 4DY
Tel *020 7328 5314*
Sample oyster omelettes or go for the soft-shelled crabs with chillies and garlic at this Southeast Asian favourite.

Tatra ££
Polish
24 Goldhawk Rd, W12 8DH
Tel *020 8749 8193*
Located in Shepherd's Bush, Tatra blends the most appetizing tastes from Eastern Europe. Don't miss the flavoured vodka at dinner.

DK Choice

Chez Bruce £££
Modern British
2 Bellevue Rd, SW17 7EG
Tel *020 8672 0114*
Chez Bruce is renowned for its top-notch food, wine and service. The classic cuisine on offer here has French overtones with the emphasis on offal, fish and remarkable flavour combinations. Specialities include home-made charcuterie and bread, slow-cooked braises, and warm and cold salads.

Gaucho Hampstead £££
Steakhouse
64 Heath St, NW3 1DN
Tel *020 7431 8222*
This stylish chain restaurant has hearty steaks cooked on a genuine Argentine barbecue. Bright decor and cheerful ambience.

The Downs and Channel Coast

ALFRISTON: Wingrove House £
Modern British
High St, East Sussex, BN26 5TD
Tel *01323 870276*
Set in a 19th-century colonial-style house, this restaurant offers traditional English dishes. Try the delicious Sussex lamb roast.

ARUNDEL: The Bay Tree ££
European
19a–21 Tarrant St, Town Centre, West Sussex, BN18 9DG
Tel *01903 883679*
Housed in a beautiful 16th-century timber-framed building, the Bay Tree offers excellent contemporary cuisine made with high-quality organic produce.

BIDDENDEN: The West House ££
Modern British
28 High St, Ashford, TN27 8AH
Tel *01580 291341* **Closed** *Sun dinner & Mon*
Set in a 15th-century weaver's cottage, this Michelin-starred family-run restaurant offers a menu of modern British fare.

BODIAM: The Curlew £££
Modern British
Junction Rd, East Sussex, TN32 5UY
Tel *01580 861394*
Michelin-starred restaurant with a casual setting and innovative dishes such as olive oil cake.

BRIGHTON: Tookta's Café £
Thai
30 Spring St, East Sussex, BN1 3EF
Tel *01273 748071* **Closed** *Mon*
Small Thai café with endearingly chic decor and a contemporary and personal take on Thai cuisine.

BRIGHTON: 24 St Georges ££
Modern British
25 St George's Rd, East Sussex, BN2 1ED
Tel *01273 626060* **Closed** *Sun & Mon*
24 St Georges uses local, seasonal produce in regularly changing menus of delicious British food.

CANTERBURY: Kathton House ££
European
6 High St, Sturry, Kent, CT2 0BD
Tel *01227 719999* **Closed** *Sun & Mon*
Upmarket modern restaurant. Try the crab ravioli and loin fillet of Godmersham venison.

CHICHESTER: El Castizo £
Tapas
24 St Pancras, Victoria Court, West Sussex, PO19 7LT
Tel *01243 788988* **Closed** *Sun & Mon*
This affable restaurant serves traditional Spanish tapas, as well as seafood and vegetarian dishes flavoured with cheese specially imported from Spain.

CUCKFIELD: Ockenden Manor £££
European
Ockenden Ln, West Sussex, RH17 5LD
Tel *01444 416111*
Set in an attractive Elizabethan manor house, this restaurant offers excellent food and great views.

EASTBOURNE: La Locanda del Duca £
Italian
26 Cornfield Terrace, East Sussex, BN21 4NS
Tel *01323 737177*
Closed *25 & 26 Dec*
Sample a variety of truly Italian cuisine and a good selection of wines in a relaxed atmosphere.

EMSWORTH: 36 on the Quay £££
European
47 South St, Hampshire, PO10 7EG
Tel *01243 375592* **Closed** *Sun & Mon*
Overlooking the bay in the fishing village of Emsworth, 36 on the Quay serves excellent Michelin-starred European cuisine.

HASTINGS: Café Maroc £
Moroccan
37 High St, East Sussex, TN34 3ER
Tel *07500 774017* **Closed** *Mon*
This small restaurant offers authentic Moroccan cuisine with ingredients such as olives and pomegranates. Great lemon-infused chicken and desserts.

HORSHAM: The Pass at South Lodge Hotel £££
Modern British
Brighton Rd, West Sussex, RH13 6PS
Tel *01403 892235* **Closed** *Mon & Tue*
Michelin-starred restaurant in a luxurious country-house hotel. The menu features unusual flavour combinations and ingredients.

ISLE OF WIGHT: Forresters £
French
Forresters Hall, High St, Yarmouth, PO41 0PL
Tel *01983 761635* **Closed** *Mon*
Forresters is set in a beautiful building originally built for the Ancient Order of Forresters. Enjoy fantastic French cuisine and try their delicious jams and chutneys.

LYMINGTON: Egan's ££
French
24 Gosport St, Hampshire SO41 9BE
Tel *01590 676165* **Closed** *Sun & Mon*
Classical French and modern English food using locally sourced ingredients from the south coast and New Forest.

PETERSFIELD: JSW £££
Modern British
20 Dragon St, Hampshire, GU31 4JJ
Tel *01730 262030* **Closed** *Sun & Mon*
Nestled in a 17th-century coaching inn, JSW prepares simple seasonal fare. Extensive wine list.

PORTSMOUTH: Spice Merchants £
Indian
44 Osborne Rd, Southsea, PO5 3LT
Tel *023 9282 8900*
Small and convivial Indian restaurant featuring authentic recipes and the use of interesting spices. Eat in or take away.

ROCHESTER: Topes ££
Modern British
60 High St, Kent, ME1 1JY
Tel *01634 845270* **Closed** *Mon & Tue*
Set in a 15th-century building, serving excellent British food

made with fresh seasonal produce and using a blend of traditional and modern cooking.

SWANLEY: Fahims £
Indian/Bangladeshi
9 High St, Kent, BR8 8AE
Tel *01322 836164*
Great blending of herbs and spices at this authentic Indian and Bangladeshi place. Try the bargain £10 buffet on Sunday.

DK Choice

WHITSTABLE: Wheelers Oyster Bar ££
Seafood
8 High St, Kent, CT5 1BQ
Tel *01227 273311* **Closed** *Wed*
The longest-established restaurant in seaside Whitstable, Wheelers has a short menu that changes seasonally: there are just six starters, six main courses and six desserts. Dine in the Oyster Parlour, at the Seafood Bar or buy quiches and sandwiches to take away.

WINCHELSEA: The Ship £
Grill
Sea Rd, East Sussex, TN36 4LH
Tel *01797 226767*
Enjoy the picturesque views, whilst dining on the delicious grilled meats.

WINCHESTER: Bangkok Brasserie £
Thai
33 Jewry St, Hampshire, SO23 8RY
Tel *01962 86 99 66*
Closed *25 & 26 Dec*
Choose from an extensive menu of authentic Thai cuisine. Bright, modern decor and attentive staff.

WINCHESTER: Kyoto Kitchen £
Japanese
70 Parchment St, Hampshire, SO23 8AT
Tel *01962 890895*
Specializing in sushi and sashimi, Kyoto Kitchen provides a good

introduction to authentic Japanese cuisine. Great presentation and polite service.

East Anglia

DK Choice

ALDEBURGH: Regatta Restaurant £
Seafood
171 High St, Suffolk, IP15 5AN
Tel *01728 452011*
An important part of the seaside town of Aldeburgh, Regatta has a cheerful nautical theme, with a metal ship adorning the exterior. In summer the focus is on local seafood, though vegetarian and meat dishes are available. Don't miss the scallops and lobster dishes.

BURY ST EDMUNDS: Maison Bleue ££
French
30 Churchgate St, Suffolk, IP33 1RG
Tel *01284 760623* **Closed** *Sun & Mon*
Exquisitely presented French cuisine in an elegant setting. Try the line-caught salmon, wild halibut and Gressingham duck.

CAMBRIDGE: Ristorante Il Piccolo Mondo ££
Italian
85 High St, Bottisham, Cambridgeshire, CB25 9BA
Tel *01223 811434* **Closed** *Mon & Tue*
Set in a Victorian village school, this eatery offers remarkable gnocchi, risotto and pasta.

CAMBRIDGE: The Oak Bistro ££
European
6 Lensfield Rd, Cambridgeshire, CB2 1EG
Tel *01223 323361* **Closed** *Sun & bank hols*
Try the fillet of sea bream or the roasted lamb at this bistro with a great walled garden to dine in.

Dine on traditional Indian and Bangladeshi cuisine at Fahims, Swanley

For more information on types of restaurants *see page 577*

CHELMSFORD: Olio ££
Italian
37 New London Rd, Essex, CM2 0ND
Tel *01245 269174* **Closed** *Mon*
A little corner of Italy in Essex.
Speciality pizzas made with
traditional dough and topped with
artisan cheeses and meats.

COLCHESTER: Mehalah's £
Seafood
East Rd, East Mersea, Essex, CO5 8TQ
Tel *012063 82797* **Closed** *Wed*
A modest venue serving stand-
out seafood including oysters
and scallops alongside local ales.

**CROMER: Constantia Cottage
Restaurant** ££
Greek
*The High St, East Runton, Norfolk,
NR27 9NX*
Tel *01263 512017* **Closed** *Sun*
A long-established restaurant
with a cheerful ambience and
occasional live music. Try classics
such as *souvlaki* (Greek kebab)
and *stifado* (beef and onion stew).

ELY: Peacocks £
Café
*65 Waterside, Cambridgeshire,
CB7 4AU*
Tel *01353 661100* **Closed** *Mon & Tue*
An attractive award-winning tea-
room with a lush garden serving
quiches, soup and sandwiches
along with tea and cake.

HOLT: Morston Hall £££
European
Morston, Norfolk, NR25 7AA
Tel *01263 741041* **Closed** *Jan; Dec 25*
Enjoy modern European fare in a
lovely countryside setting. Good
wine list and attentive service.

**HUNTINGDON: Old Bridge
Hotel Restaurant** ££
Modern British
1 High St, Cambridgeshire, PE29 3TQ
Tel *01480 424300*
Savour premium English cuisine
in an 18th-century, ivy-clad town-

The refined orangery dining room at
Morston Hall, Holt

Key to Price Guide *see page 582*

house with scenic views. Refined
presentation and good service.

IPSWICH: Alaturka £
Turkish
9 Great Colman St, Suffolk, IP4 2AA
Tel *01473 233448*
Alaturka features modern decor
and traditional Turkish cuisine,
with some dishes cooked in clay
pots. Finish with sweet baklava.

KING'S LYNN: Market Bistro £
Modern British
*11 Saturday Market Pl, Norfolk,
PE30 5DQ*
Tel *01553 771483* **Closed** *Sun & Mon*
Serves everything from home-
smoked fish and meat to bread
and desserts. Features local
produce such as Cromer crabs.

LOWESTOFT: Desmond's £
Café
221b London Rd, Suffolk, NR33 0DS
Tel *07968 636647* **Closed** *Sun*
A pleasant café during the week,
Desmond's serves excellent
stone-baked pizza at weekends.

MALDON: El Guaca £
Mexican
122 High St, Essex, CM9 5ET
Tel *01621 852009* **Closed** *Mon*
Try classic Mexican fajitas and
nachos at this warm, friendly
and efficient Maldon joint.

NEWMARKET: Sangdao £
Thai
160 High St, Suffolk, CB8 9AQ
Tel *01638 660646*
Fragrant, spicy Thai food delicately
prepared and beautifully served.
Wines by the bottle and Thai beer.

NORWICH: Moorish Falafel Bar £
Vegetarian
17 Lower Goat Lane, Norfolk, NR2 1EL
Tel *01603 622250*
A little place with a big
reputation, offering filling falafel
burgers, salad pittas and
delicious home-made lemonade.

PETERBOROUGH: Clarke's ££
Modern British
*17 Lincoln Rd, Town Centre,
Cambridgeshire, PE1 2PB*
Tel *01733 892681* **Closed** *Mon*
Modern family-run place with
unusual items on the menu such
as strawberry gazpacho and beef
and *foie gras* slider.

**SOUTHWOLD: Sutherland
House** £££
Seafood
56 High St, Suffolk, IP18 6DN
Tel *01502 724544* **Closed** *Oct–Mar:
Mon*
The superb dining room is the
perfect setting to enjoy

acclaimed dishes such as seared
Scottish scallops and pan-fried
wild sea bass.

SWAFFHAM: Rasputin £
Russian
21–22 Plowright Pl, Norfolk, PE37 7LQ
Tel *01760 724725* **Closed** *Sun*
A surprising find in East Anglia,
serving authentic Russian food.
Modern decor with the odd
Russian flourish.

Thames Valley

ABINGDON: The White Hart ££
Gastro-pub
*Main Rd, Fyfield, Oxfordshire,
OX13 5LW*
Tel *01865 390585* **Closed** *Mon*
Timber-framed gastro-pub where
many ingredients are sourced
from the kitchen garden. Great
home-made bread and pasta.

BANBURY: Sheesh Mahal £
Indian
43 South Bar, Oxfordshire, OX16 9AB
Tel *01295 266489*
Stylish Indian restaurant housed
in a handsome mansion and
serving succulent meat dishes.

CHINNOR: Sir Charles Napier £££
European
Spriggs Alley, Oxfordshire, OX39 4BX
Tel *01494 483011* **Closed** *Sun dinner
& Mon*
This Michelin-starred pub goes
beyond pub fare to offer dishes
such as diver-caught scallops
and Iberico pork loin.

**CHIPPING NORTON:
Wild Thyme** ££
Modern British
10 New St, Oxfordshire, OX7 5LJ
Tel *01608 645060* **Closed** *Sun & Mon*
Set in an attractive old building
with window seats. Features
fantastic Cornish monkfish tails
and Tamworth pork on the menu.

COOKHAM: The White Oak ££
European
*The Pound, Maidenhead, Berkshire,
SL6 9QE*
Tel *01628 523043*
Stylish pub with a range of
choices, and an *auberge* menu
inspired by French country inns.

**GREAT MISSENDEN: La Petite
Auberge** ££
French
*107 High St, Buckinghamshire,
HP16 0BB*
Tel *01494 865370* **Closed** *Sun*
This tiny bistro has a great
atmosphere, with quintessential
French classics on the menu.

Country house setting of French fine-dining restaurant, L'Ortolan, Reading

HEMEL HEMPSTEAD:
Chiangmai Cottage £
Thai
80 High St, Town Centre,
Hertfordshire, HP1 3AQ
Tel *01442 263426*
With charmingly rustic decor, this
little place offers great pad thai
and lightly spiced dishes. Good
service and a cheerful atmosphere.

HENLEY-ON-THAMES: Shaun
Dickens at The Boathouse £££
Modern British
Station Rd, Oxfordshire, RG9 1AZ
Tel *01491 577937* **Closed** *Sun dinner*
& Mon
Savour modern British food amid a
stunning riverside setting. Try the
slow-roasted farm duck breast or
glazed Suffolk pork loin.

MARLOW: Adam Simmonds at
Danesfield House Hotel ££
European
Henley Rd, Buckinghamshire, SL7 2EY
Tel *01628 891010* **Closed** *Sun & Mon*
Set in an elegant spa hotel, this
Michelin-starred restaurant serves
outstanding food.

MARLOW: Vanilla Pod £££
French
31 West St, Buckinghamshire, SL7 2LS
Tel *01628 898101* **Closed** *Sun & Mon*
Ambitious cooking in a tranquil,
small restaurant. Knowledgeable
staff and a straightforward menu.

NEWBURY: The Halfway Bistro £
Gastro-pub
Bath Rd, West Berkshire, RG20 8NR
Tel *01488 608 115* **Closed** *Mon*
The Halfway takes pub food to a
classy level with mains such as
slow-braised beef with fresh herbs.

NEWPORT PAGNELL:
Robinsons ££
Modern British
18–20 St John St, Buckinghamshire,
MK16 8HJ
Tel *01908 611400*
Fine dining in a historic building
with a Tudor fireplace. Try the
pan-fried wild sea bass.

OXFORD: Everest £
Nepalese
147–151 Howard St, Oxfordshire,
OX4 3AZ
Tel *01865 251555*
Everest serves authentic
Nepalese cuisine prepared from
the freshest of ingredients.

READING: Mya Lacarte ££
Modern British
5 Prospect St, West Berkshire, RG4 8JB
Tel *01189 463400*
This restaurant gives an interesting
twist to traditional British cuisine
and uses seasonal ingredients.

DK Choice

READING: L'Ortolan £££
French
Church Lane, Shinfield, West
Berkshire, RG2 9BY
Tel *01189 888500* **Closed** *Sun*
Located in a former vicarage,
this acclaimed restaurant
features excellent service and a
knowledgeable sommelier,
along with outstanding cooking.
The style is modern French with
other influences interwoven
with fantastic presentation.
There are also surprisingly
affordable set lunch menus.

ST ALBANS: L'Olivo £
Italian
135 Marford Rd, Wheathampstead,
Hertfordshire, AL4 8NH
Tel *01582 834145* **Closed** *Sun & Mon*
The chic decor provides the
perfect setting for sampling
delectable southern Italian food,
from handmade pasta to seafood.

WANTAGE: Bistro 14 ££
French
14 Wallingford St, Oxfordshire,
OX12 8AX
Tel *01235 771 200* **Closed** *Mon*
A modern bistro in historic
Wantage that does elegant
variations on fish and chips and
scampi, along with a range of
grilled and roast meats.

WATFORD: Tarboush £
Lebanese
57 Market St, Hertfordshire, WD18 0PR
Tel *01923 800888*
The Middle East comes to
Watford with a shisha garden
and authentic Lebanese cuisine.

WINDSOR: Al Fassia £
Moroccan
27 St Leonard's Rd, West Berkshire,
SL4 3BP
Tel *01753 855370*
Relish home-cooked tagines
and couscous specials teamed
with beer from Casablanca at
this richly decorated restaurant.

WOODSTOCK: La Galleria ££
Italian
2 Market Pl, Town Centre, OX20 1TA
Tel *01993 813381* **Closed** *Mon*
This upmarket restaurant dishes
out traditional Italian fare amid
gorgeous white linen decor.

WOBURN: Paris House £££
Modern British
Woburn Park, London Rd,
Bedfordshire, MK17 9QP
Tel *01525 290692* **Closed** *Mon; Tue*
breakfast & lunch
Acclaimed destination restaurant.
Choose from gourmand, "surprise"
and "just desserts" menus.

Wessex

AVEBURY: The Circle Café £
Café
Wiltshire, SN8 1RF
Tel *01672 539250*
These National Trust tearooms
are great for tea and home-made
cake after a trip to the stones.

BATH: Yen Sushi £
Japanese
11–12 Bartlett St, Somerset, BA1 2QZ
Tel *01225 333313*
Thoroughly authentic *kaiten*
(conveyor belt) sushi restaurant.
Great fresh fish and Asian beer.

BATH: Demuths ££
Vegetarian
2 North Parade Passage, Somerset,
BA1 1NX
Tel *01225 446059*
Vegetarian restaurant serving
innovative and interesting
small dishes. Try the miso roast
aubergine and shallot tart.

BATH: The Bath Priory £££
Fine Dining
Weston Rd, Somerset, BA1 2XT
Tel *01225 331922*
The superb cuisine and fabulous
wines at the Bath Priory make for
an intimate fine dining experience.

For more information on types of restaurants *see page 577*

Sign outside The Wild Garlic Bar & Grill at The Talbot, Blandford Forum

BATH: The Olive Tree £££
Fine Dining
Russel St, Somerset, BA1 2QF
Tel *01225 447928* **Closed** *Mon lunch*
Friendly, classy restaurant in the Queensberry Hotel focusing on Mediterranean food and local ingredients. Great cocktail bar.

BLANDFORD FORUM: The Wild Garlic Bar & Grill at The Talbot £
Bistro
Iwene Minster, Dorset, DT11 8QN
Tel *01308 861446* **Closed** *Sun–Wed: dinner*
The Wild Garlic serves good value sandwiches and Chesil bouillabaisse. The restaurant, open select evenings, is more formal.

BOURNEMOUTH: Chez Fred £
Traditional British
10 Seamoor Rd, Dorset, BH4 9AN
Tel *01202 761023* **Closed** *Sun lunch*
Bournemouth's favourite fish-and-chips spot, with delicious gluten-free battered cod to eat in or take away.

BOURNEMOUTH: West Beach £
Seafood
Pier Approach, Dorset, BH2 5AA
Tel *01202 587785*
Kid-friendly beachfront bistro with great views. Great lobster and champagne, Scottish steak and Muddiford sea bass. Book ahead.

BOURNEMOUTH: Urban Reef Café £
Café
The Overstrand, Undercliff Drive, Boscombe, Dorset, BH5 1BN
Tel *01202 443960*
Funky beachfront bistro with a sun deck and a roaring fire in winter. Great for a lazy brunch.

BRADFORD-ON-AVON: Fat Fowl and the Roost ££
Mediterranean
Silver St, Wiltshire, BA15 1JX
Tel *01225 863111*
Tapas bar, restaurant and jazz café that serves locally sourced, seasonal food. Great live music.

BRIDPORT: Hive Beach Café £
Café
Beach Rd, Burton Bradstock, Dorset, DT6 4RF
Tel *01308 897070*
Popular café overlooking the shingle beach and honey-coloured cliffs. Great seafood and West Country ice creams.

BRIDPORT: Watchhouse Café £
Café
West Bay, Dorset DT6 4EN
Tel *01308 459330*
Breezy harbourside café serving hearty breakfasts and lunchtime pizzas from its wood-fired oven.

BRISTOL: River Cottage Canteen £
Modern British
St John's Court, Whiteladies Rd, BS8 2QY
Tel *0117 973 2458*
Local produce crafted into delicious food and served by a friendly staff. Cheerful ambience.

BRISTOL: Rocotillos £
Café
1 Queen's Rd, Clifton Triangle, Clifton, BS8 1EZ
Tel *0117 929 7207*
A 1950s-style diner on Clifton Triangle popular with students and local workers. Great burgers, chips and ice-cream milkshakes.

BRISTOL: Thali Café £
Indian
1 Regents St, Clifton, BS8 4HW
Tel *0117 974 3793*
A Bristol landmark, the Thali Café is a kitsch Indian café serving traditional *thalis*.

BRISTOL: Za Za Bazaar £
International
Harbourside, Canon's Road BS1 5UH
Tel *0117 922 0330*
The enormous all-you-can-eat buffet at Za Za Bazaar offers delicious fare from around the world. Kids under 12 eat at half price. A great bargain.

BRUTON: At the Chapel ££
Pizza
28 High St, Somerset, BA10 0AE
Tel *01749 814070*
Set in a converted chapel. Serves delicious wood-fired-oven pizzas and seasonal salads. There is also a bakery and wine store on site.

CHIPPENHAM: Lucknam Park £££
Fine Dining
Colerne, Wiltshire, SN14 8AZ
Tel *01225 742777* **Closed** *Mon*
Superb Michelin-starred and locally sourced fine dining in the 17th-century Lucknam Park Hotel.

EASTON GREY: Whatley Manor £££
Fine Dining
Malmesbury, Wiltshire, SN16 0RB
Tel *01666 822888* **Closed** *Mon & Tue*
Home to the Michelin-starred Dining Room and the brasserie Le Mazot. Legendary food and afternoon tea. Book ahead.

FROME: Meadowside Farm £
Café
46 Vallis Way, Somerset, BA11 3BA
Tel *01373 472555*
A local artisan food producer, Meadowside Farm has a café and deli serving breakfast, brunch, lunch and takeaway meals.

GLASTONBURY: Rainbow's End £
Vegetarian
17b High St, Somerset, BA6 9DP
Tel *01458 833896*
Glastonbury's original vegetarian café serves home-made cakes and meals and has a salad bar. Vegan and wheat-free meals available.

ISLE OF PURBECK: Shell Bay Seafood Restaurant ££
Seafood
Ferry Rd, Studland, Dorset, BH19 3B
Tel *01929 450363*
Arrive by boat, ferry or car to this stunning restaurant and bistro on the edge of the Isle of Purbeck. Fantastic seafood dishes.

LACOCK: The Bell £
Gastro-pub
The Wharf, Bowden Hill, Wiltshire, SS15 2PJ
Tel *01249 730308*
Country pub on the outskirts of Lacock serving award-winning drinks. Off the beaten path.

LACOCK: The Stables £
Café
High St, Wiltshire, SN15 2LQ
Tel *01249 730824*
The National Trust tearooms in the historic village of Lacock are the perfect place for a cream tea or light lunch.

LONGLEAT: The Bath Arms ££
Gastro-pub
Horningsham, Warminster, Wiltshire, BA12 7LY
Tel *0844 8150099*
Gastro-pub on the edge of the Longleat estate favoured by

hunting parties. Fantastic pub food plus a dining room that serves local cuisine and drinks.

MALMESBURY: The Rectory ££
Fine Dining
Crudwell, Wiltshire, SN16 9EP
Tel *01666 577194*
This refined Cotswold hotel has a classy dining room and a good set menu with the likes of lobster tortellini and rabbit and pea pie.

POOLE: Off Quay £
Bistro
18 High St, Dorset, BH15 1BP
Tel *01202 680014* **Closed** *Sun*
Friendly bistro-café with a light lunch menu and more extensive evening meals. Culinary inspiration drawn from the Far East and India.

POOLE: Sandbanks Beach Café £
Café
Banks Rd, Sandbanks, Dorset, BH13 7QQ
Tel *01202 708621*
Beachside café in an upmarket area that serves fish and chips, burgers, tea and cakes.

POOLE: Stormfish Restaurant ££
Seafood
16 High St, Dorset, BH15 1BP
Tel *01202 674970*
Stormfish serves delicious fresh seafood such as Goan fish curry, whole sea bass and local plaice.

PORLOCK: The Big Cheese £
Café
High St, Somerset, TA24 8PT
Tel *01643 862773*
A delightful café, purveyors of fine local cheeses. Try the cheese platters, ploughmans and coffees.

ROWDE: The Rowdey Cow Farm Café £
Café
Lower Farm, Devizes Rd, Devizes, Wiltshire, SN10 2LX
Tel *01380 829666*
Fun for the whole family, with home-made ice cream, soups and sandwiches, a good playground and grazing cows to interact with.

SALISBURY: Hox Brasserie £
Indian
155 Fisherton St, Wiltshire, SP2 7RP
Tel *01722 341600*
This restaurant and takeaway, specializing in traditional south Indian dishes, is a local favourite.

SALISBURY: Wagamama £
Asian
8–10 Bridge St, Wiltshire, SP1 2LX
Tel *01722 412165*
Japanese-inspired dining at this chain restaurant. Good for families. Takeaway is available.

SALISBURY: Charter 1227 ££
Modern British
6–7 Ox Row, The Market Place, Wiltshire, SP1 1EU
Tel *01722 333118* **Closed** *Mon*
Stylish, top-rated restaurant overlooking Salisbury's market-place. Sample delicious modern British and European fare.

SHEPTON MALLET: Kilver Court £
Café
Kilver St, Somerset, BA4 5NF
Tel *01749 340410*
The two cafés at Kilver Court serve sandwiches, flat breads and hearty food, locally sourced.

SHERBORNE: The Bakery Café £
Café
1 The Green, Dorset, DT9 3HZ
Tel *01935 813264* **Closed** *Sun*
This charming bakery offers great value and delicious bread, cakes and pizzas. Popular with kids.

SHERBORNE: The Rose and Crown at Trent £
Gastro-pub
Trent, Dorset, DT9 4SL
Tel *01935 850776* **Closed** *Mon*
A14th-century rural pub just outside Sherborne. It's worth making a detour for its fine food and charming country appeal. Fantastic Sunday lunch.

WEYMOUTH: Crab House Café £
Café
Ferrymans Way, Portland Rd, Wyke Regis, Dorset, DT4 9YU
Tel *01305 788867* **Closed** *Mon & Tue*
Glorious café overlooking Chesil beach that serves the best fresh crabs and oysters from the nearby beds. Children welcome.

WEYMOUTH: Fish 'n' Fritz £
Traditional British
9 Market St, Dorset, DT4 8DD
Tel *01305 766386*
Fish 'n' Fritz has fantastic, award-winning fish and chips to take away or snack on near the harbour. There is also a great kids' menu.

DK Choice

WRINGTON:
The Ethicurean £££
Modern British
Barley Wood Walled Garden, Somerset, BS40 5SA
Tel *01934 863713* **Closed** *Mon*
The Ethicurean is an outstanding café-restaurant overlooking the Mendip Hills. It serves dynamic and experimental organic food and is worth the trek, especially in autumn. Delicious coffee and sticky toffee apple cake.

Devon and Cornwall

BARNSTAPLE: Broomhill Art Hotel Café £
Mediterranean
Muddiford, Devon, EX31 4EX
Tel *01271 850262*
Fantastic Mediterranean slow food restaurant in a sculpture garden. Sample the freshly baked bread and artisan salamis.

BIGBURY: The Oyster Shack £
Seafood
Milburn Orchard Farm, Stakes Hill, Devon, TQ7 4BE
Tel *01548 810876*
Humble venue serving truly great local seafood with a Mediterranean twist. Bargain prices and a friendly atmosphere.

DK Choice

BUCKFASTLEIGH: Riverford Field Kitchen £
Café
Wash Barn, Devon, TQ11 0JU
Tel *01803 762074*
Get a genuine taste of the southwest: Riverford's great family-friendly restaurant serves simple weekday meals and indulgent weekend feasts. Delicious beef shin and sticky toffee pudding.

Array of fresh produce at Riverford Field Kitchen, Buckfastleigh

For more information on types of restaurants *see page 577*

BURGH ISLAND: The Pilchard £
Pub
Devon, TQ7 4BG
Tel *01548 810514*
Old smugglers' pub on this
tidal island. Delicious lunchtime
baguettes and Friday night curries.

CHAGFORD: Gidleigh Park £££
Fine Dining
Gidleigh Park, Devon, TQ13 8HH
Tel *01647 432367*
Chef Michael Caines's restaurant
has two Michelin stars and serves
modern British delights. Book at
least three months in advance.

CROYDE: Sandleigh Tea Rooms £
Café
Moor Lane, Devon, EX33 1PA
Tel *01271 890930*
These National Trust tearooms,
tucked around the corner from
the surf beach, are great for a
proper Devon cream tea.

DARTMOUTH: Rockfish £
Seafood
*8 South Embankment, Devon,
TQ6 9BH*
Tel *01803 832800*
This Mitch Tonks-run takeaway
and restaurant serves award-
winning, top-quality fish and
South Devon crab sandwiches.

DARTMOUTH: The Seahorse £££
Seafood
*4 South Embankment, Devon,
TQ6 9BH*
Tel *01803 835147*   **Closed** *Mon*
Another fantastic Mitch Tonks-
run fish restaurant specializing in
seafood with the likes of cuttlefish,
squid, turbot, sole and mussels
on the menu. Extensive wine list.

EXETER: Georgian Tea Room £
Café
*Broadway House, 35 High St,
Topsham, Devon, EX3 0ED*
Tel *01392 873465*
Retro tearoom serving classic and
traditional delights. Snack on
delicious home-made scones,
sandwiches and cream teas.

EXETER: Jack in the Green £
Gastro-pub
Rockbeare, Devon, EX5 2EE
Tel *01404 822240*
A fantastic gastro-pub with
Devon produce served in
delicious ways, with edible
flowers and at fantastic price.

EXMOUTH: River Exe Café £
Café
The Docks, Devon
Tel *07761 116103*
Book a water taxi to access this
unique floating restaurant on the
River Exe estuary with a licensed

bar and views of a friendly grey
seal. Serves locally caught seafood,
fish and chips, burgers and pizza.

FALMOUTH: Gylly Beach Café £
Café
Cliff Rd, Cornwall, TR11 4PA
Tel *01326 312884*
Stylish beach café serving big,
delicious Cornish meals. Music
and chilli every Sunday night.

FALMOUTH: The Wheelhouse £
Seafood
Upton Slip, Cornwall, TR11 3DQ
Tel *01326 318050*   **Closed** *Sun–Tue*
This unique crab and oyster bar
hands guests aprons and kitchen
rolls in case of a mess. A word-of-
mouth gem. Bookings essential.

FOWEY: Sam's on the Beach £
Café
14 Polkerris, Par, Cornwall, PL24 2TL
Tel *01726 812255*
An offshoot of Sam's Café in
Fowey, this branch is located in
the old lifeboat station. Serves
pizza, lobster and a fusion of
Cornish and Mediterranean food.

FOWEY: The Old Quay House ££
Bistro
28 Fore St, Cornwall, PL27 1AQ
Tel *01726 833302*
Upmarket but relaxed restaurant
with fabulous estuary views.
Serves local shellfish, venison,
cheeses and Modern British food.

HELSTON: Kota £
Asian
*Harbour Head, Porthleven, Cornwall,
TR13 9JA*
Tel *01326 562407*   **Closed** *Sun &
Mon; Off season: Sun–Tue*
One of the few restaurants in
Cornwall to hold a Bib Gourmand
award, Kota serves delicious Asian
fusion food not to be missed.

Beautiful estuary views from the dining
room at The Old Quay House, Fowey

HELSTON: Roskilly's Farm £
Café
*Tregellas Barton Farm, St Keverne,
Cornwall, TR12 6NX*
Tel *01326 280479*
The classic Cornish dairy farm
serves delicious ice cream, fudge
and yogurts in its ice-cream
parlour. Great for families.

ILFRACOMBE: 11 The Quay £
Café
11 The Quay, Devon, EX34 9EQ
Tel *01271 868090*
This Damien Hirst-owned chic
café-bar serves local seafood and
pasta dishes, with a more refined
dining room upstairs.

KINGSBRIDGE: The Millbrook £
Gastro-pub
South Pool, Devon, TQ7 2RW
Tel *01548 531581*   **Closed** *Dec–Feb:
Mon dinner*
Millbrook is an award-winning
traditional inn with a British menu
encouraging nose-to-tail eating.

LOOE: Squid Ink ££
Seafood
*Lower Chapel St, East Looe, Cornwall,
PL13 1AT*
Tel *01503 262674*
Friendly seafood restaurant hidden
amid Looe's narrow streets
featuring fresh catch of the day.

MAWGAN PORTH: Bedruthan
Steps Wild Café £
Brasserie
Trenance, Cornwall, TR8 4BU
Tel *01637 860860*
Sophisticated café-bar with tapas
inspired by Yotam Ottolenghi and
Hugh Fearnley-Whittingstall.
Great kids' menu and beach views.

MAWGAN PORTH:
The Scarlet £££
Fine Dining
Tredragon Rd, Cornwall, TR8 4DQ
Tel *01637 861800*
Upmarket restaurant with views
of the beach and sea. Sample
delicious Cornish food and wines.

MOUSEHOLE: The Old
Coastguard £
Modern British
*The Parade, Penzance, Cornwall,
TR19 6PR*
Tel *01736 731222*
Brasserie-style restaurant serving
plenty of fresh fish, local game
and dairy, and Sunday roast.

NEWQUAY: Fifteen Cornwall £££
Seafood
Watergate Bay, Cornwall, TR8 4AA
Tel *01637 861000*
Jamie Oliver's upmarket restaurant
serves fantastic seafood with rich
Mediterranean flavours.

The Horse and Groom beer garden, Bourton-on-the-Hill

OKEHAMPTON: Lewtrenchard Manor £££
Fine Dining
Lewdown, Devon, EX20 4PN
Tel *01566 783222*
Exquisite fine-dining restaurant in a country house on Dartmoor. Some of the best local produce cooked in innovative ways.

PADSTOW: St Petroc's ££
Fine Dining
New St, Cornwall, PL28 8EA
Tel *01841 532700*
Tucked away on a back street, St Petroc's serves Mediterranean-inspired, bistro-style dishes in a charming rustic building.

PADSTOW: The Seafood Restaurant £££
Seafood
Riverside, Cornwall, PL28 8BY
Tel *01841 532700*
Order fresh sashimi and oysters from the bar in the middle of this stunning seafood restaurant.

PENZANCE: The Victoria Inn £
Gastro-pub
Perranuthnoe, Cornwall, TR20 9NP
Tel *01736 710309* **Closed** *Mon*
A 12th-century inn serving award-winning food, fine wine, cider and Cornish lager. Good for families.

PLYMOUTH: River Cottage Canteen £
Bistro
Royal William Yard, Cornwall, PL1 3QQ
Tel *01752 252702*
Housed in the Royal Navy's former victualling depot, this bistro serves seasonal and organic food, with plenty of local fish.

PLYMOUTH: The Royal William Bakery £
Bakery
The Slaughter House, Royal William Yard, Cornwall, PL1 3RP
Tel *07880 359038*
Popular bakery serving breads, baked goods and soups in a heritage building overlooking the wharves.

ROCK: Restaurant Nathan Outlaw £££
Fine Dining
St Enodoc Hotel, Cornwall, PL27 6LA
Tel *01208 862737* **Closed** *Sun*
Outstanding two-Michelin-starred restaurant in Rock serving oysters and other Cornish delights. No children under 12.

SALCOMBE: The Winking Prawn ££
Café
North Sands, Devon, TQ8 8LD
Tel *01548 842326*
Fun beach café and barbecue restaurant overlooking North Sands. Range of seafood, snacks, ice cream and cream teas on offer.

SHALDON: Ode Café £
Café
21 Fore St, Devon, TQ14 0DE
Tel *01626 873977* **Closed** *Tue*
Stylish café serving the likes of crab cakes, ham hock, deli platters and bacon sandwiches.

ST IVES: Tate St Ives Café £
Café
Porthmeor Beach, Cornwall, TR26 1TG
Tel *01736 791122* **Closed** *Mon*
Light-meals café in the Tate St Ives modern-art gallery. Sample the luscious cakes and light bites often sourced from Cornwall.

ST IVES: Porthminster Beach Café ££
Café
Porthminster Beach, Cornwall, TR26 2EB
Tel *01736 795352*
This popular, award-winning beach café serves local food with an emphasis on seafood. Decent kids' and vegetarian menus.

ST IVES: Seagrass ££
Seafood
Fish St, Cornwall, TR26 1LT
Tel *01736 793763*
Stylish restaurant serving modern British fare especially local seafood. Great "oyster and champagne" menu. Book ahead.

TAVISTOCK: Hotel Endsleigh £££
Fine Dining
Milton Abbot, Tamar Valley, Devon, PL19 0PQ
Tel *01822 870000*
The elegant restaurant set within the luxurious Hotel Endsleigh serves delicious meals including hand-dived scallops, venison and soufflés. Good lunch deals.

TORQUAY: The Elephant £££
Fine Dining
3–4 Beacon Terrace, Devon, TQ1 2BH
Tel *01803 200044* **Closed** *Sun & Mon*
Michelin-starred restaurant and brasserie set within a two-storey Georgian townhouse. Great tasting menu. Reservations essential.

ZENNOR: The Gurnard's Head £
Pub
St Ives, Cornwall, TR26 3DE
Tel *01736 796928*
This pub with rooms serves fresh local food, with a seasonal menu. Set in a trendy dining area. Very kid-friendly, and pets are welcome.

The Heart of England

BIRMINGHAM: Purnell's £££
Modern British
55 Cornwall St, West Midlands, B3 2DH
Tel *0121 212 9799* **Closed** *Sun & Mon*
Located in a conservation area, this Michelin-starred eatery offers contemporary British cuisine.

BIRMINGHAM: Simpsons £££
French
20 Highfield Rd, Edgbaston, B15 3DU
Tel *0121 454 3434*
A stylish place where the emphasis is on high-quality ingredients and beautiful presentation.

DK Choice

BOURTON-ON-THE-HILL: Horse and Groom £
Modern British
Bourton-on-the-Hill, GL56 9AQ
Tel *01386 700413* **Closed** *Sun dinner; 25 & 31 Dec*
Horse and Groom is a multi-award-winning Gloucestershire pub where the daily-changing blackboard menu features anything from beer-battered fillet of hake to pan-fried pigeon breasts. The honey-coloured building itself is part of the draw, as is the convivial outside seating and picturesque kitchen garden. Friendly staff and beautiful surroundings.

For more information on types of restaurants *see page 577*

BOURTON-ON-THE-WATER:
The Croft Restaurant £
Traditional British
Victoria St, Gloucestershire, GL54 2BX
Tel *01451 821132*
An all-day restaurant serving full
English breakfasts through to
meaty mains: steak and ale pie,
bangers and mash, and burgers.

CHELTENHAM: Lumiere ££
Seafood
*Clarence Parade, Gloucestershire,
GL50 3PA*
Tel *01242 222200* **Closed** *Sun & Mon*
Sample innovative takes on
classic dishes, with turbot, plaice
and lobster elegantly presented.

CHELTENHAM: Prithvi ££
Indian
37 Bath Rd, Gloucestershire, GL53 7HG
Tel *01242 226229* **Closed** *Mon*
A sophisticated take on Indian
cuisine in soothing surroundings.
Also serves an amuse-bouche.

CHESTER: Upstairs at the Grill ££
Grill
70 Watergate St, Cheshire, CH1 2LA
Tel *01244 344883*
Manhattan-style steakhouse and
cocktail bar, with fantastic Welsh
steaks such as sirloin and fillet.

**CHIPPING CAMPDEN: Eight
Bells** ££
Traditional British
Church St, Gloucestershire, GL55 6JG
Tel *01386 840371*
An ancient pub, rebuilt using
original stone and timbers in the
17th century. Hearty English food
made with seasonal produce.

CIRENCESTER: Piazza Fontana £
Italian
30 Castle St, Gloucestershire, GL7 1QH
Tel *01285 643133* **Closed** *Sun*
Popular pizza joint serving up
Sardinian wine alongside pizzas
and calzones. Great tiramisu.

Traditional pizzeria Puccini's, Worcester

CIRENCESTER: Soushi £
Japanese
12 Castle St, Gloucestershire, GL7 1QA
Tel *01285 641414* **Closed** *Sun & Mon*
Take out a bento box, sample
from the sushi menu or choose
from the extensive dinner menu.

COVENTRY: Court 6 £
Asian
16 Spon St, West Midlands, CV1 3BA
Tel *2476559190* **Closed** *Sun & Mon*
A small and intimate place
dishing up Indian and Pakistani
halal food. Generous portions
and good old-fashioned service.

**IRONBRIDGE: Restaurant
Severn** ££
French
33 High St, Telford, Shropshire TF8 7AG
Tel *01952 432233* **Closed** *Mon & Tue*
Classic French food incorporating
modern British trends. Serves
produce from their farm.

MALVERN: The Inn at Welland £
Gastro-pub
*Drake St, Welland, Worcestershire,
WR13 6LN*
Tel *01684 592317* **Closed** *Mon*
Modernized country inn where
posh pub food hits the mark.
Excellent Sunday roasts, Waldorf
salad and cheese platters.

MORETON-IN-MARSH:
The Spice Room £
Indian
3 Oxford St, Gloucestershire, GL56 0LA
Tel *01608 654204*
Long-established Indian eatery
in a quintessential Cotswolds
town. Try the Jingra Roshi platter.

ROSS-ON-WYE: Eagle Inn £
Traditional British
Broad St, Herefordshire, HR9 7EA
Tel *7917466314*
A traditional friendly pub with
filling burgers and steaks. They also
do small portions of the mains.

SHREWSBURY: La Dolce Vita £
Italian
35 Hill's Lane, Shropshire, SY1 1QU
Tel *01743 249126* **Closed** *Mon & Tue*
Authentic but contemporary
Italian food. *Antipasti* are followed
by *primi* and *secondi*, as per the
true Italian eating experience.

STOW-ON-THE-WOLD:
Cutler's Restaurant ££
Modern British
*Fosseway, Cheltenham,
Gloucestershire, GL54 1JX*
Tel *01451 830297* **Closed** *Sun dinner*
Located in the boutique Number
Four Hotel, Cutler's fuses the
modern and the traditional
with elegantly served roast meat
and fish dishes.

STRATFORD-UPON-AVON:
The Opposition Bistro £
International
*13 Sheep St, Town Centre,
Warwickshire, CV37 6EF*
Tel *01789 269980* **Closed** *Sun except
bank hols*
The timber-framed interior
provides a great atmosphere for
good bistro standards such as
fishcakes and steak.

WORCESTER: Puccini's £
Italian
12 Friar St, Worcestershire, WR1 2LZ
Tel *01905 27770*
Family-run restaurant serving
hand-stretched pizza, along with
fresh pasta, risotto and fish dishes.

East Midlands

ASHBOURNE: Lighthouse ££
Modern British
*The Rose and Crown, New Rd,
Boylestone, Derbyshire, DE6 5AA*
Tel *01335 330658* **Closed** *Mon–Wed*
Elegant, classic British food with
a distinct French influence.

BAKEWELL: Piedaniel's ££
French
Bath St, Derbyshire, DE45 1BX
Tel *01629 812687* **Closed** *Sun & Mon*
Attractive dining room serving
elaborate French cuisine. Try the
crêpes suzette for dessert.

BASLOW: Fischer's £££
Modern British
Calver Rd, Derbyshire, DE45 1RR
Tel *01246 583259*
A handsome 1907 house with
a kitchen garden. Try the
Derbyshire lamb, Scottish razor
clams and Cornish shellfish dishes.

BUXTON: The Knight's Table £
Traditional British
*Leek Rd, Quarnford, Derbyshire,
SK17 0SN*
Tel *01298 23695*
Ancient Peak District pub with
open fires and stone paved floors.
Old favourites such as sausage
and mash on the menu.

DK Choice

**BUXTON: Carriages Pub &
Italian Restaurant** ££
Italian
*Newhaven, nr Hartington,
Derbyshire, SK17 0DU*
Tel *01298 84528* **Closed** *Sun
dinner, Mon & Tue*
Come to Carriages for traditional
Sicilian dishes, fresh seasonal
seafood and fine Italian wines.
The unique vintage dining

room comprises two steam rail carriages. Try the delicious Sicilian lemon ice-cream cake.

DERBY: The Exeter Arms £
Traditional British
Exeter Pl, Derbyshire, DE1 2EU
Tel *01332 605323*
Cosy pub serving well-cooked fare such as fish and chips and scampi. Good choice of ales.

GLOSSOP: Ayubowan £
Sri Lankan
46–50 High St, Derbyshire, SK13 8BH
Tel *01457 865168* **Closed** *Mon*
Authentic Sri Lankan food with a modern twist. Elegant interiors with bold Asian artworks.

ILKESTON: Durham Ox
Traditional British
Durham St, Derbyshire, DE7 8FQ
Tel *0115 854 7107* **Closed** *Mon–Wed*
An inn founded in 1780, once the town gaol. Try the lamb and mint pie or beef bourguignon.

LEICESTER: Sapori £
Italian
40 Stadon Rd, Leicestershire, LE7 7AY
Tel *0116 236 8900* **Closed** *Mon*
Sapori's head chef, from Torre del Greco in Italy, whips up fantastic handmade bread, desserts and ice cream.

LINCOLN: The Bronze Pig ££
Traditional British
6 West Parade, Lincolnshire, LN1 1JT
Tel *01522 524817* **Closed** *Sun–Tue*
Welcoming restaurant run by an Irishman and a Sicilian who give a European twist to British dishes.

MANSFIELD: BB's Italian Restaurant £
Italian
1 Bridge St, Town Centre, Nottinghamshire, NG18 1AL
Tel *01623 622940* **Closed** *Sun & Mon*
An unglamorous exterior, but great food and warm service. Delicious pizzas and puddings.

MATLOCK: Bath Matlock Balti £
Indian
256 Dale Rd, Matlock Bath, Derbyshire, DE4 3NT
Tel *01629 55069* **Closed** *Sun*
Attentive waiters serve reliably good Indian food. The setting is a spa village in the Peak District.

NORTHAMPTON: Sophia's £
Mediterranean
54 Bridge St, NN1 1PA
Tel *01604 250654* **Closed** *Sun*
Try hearty trattoria-style pasta and pizza dishes combined with unusual meat and fish mains.

Views of the Lake District at The Restaurant at the Cottage in the Wood, Braithwaite

NOTTINGHAM: La Rock ££
French
4 Bridge St, Sandiacre, Nottinghamshire, NG10 5QT
Tel *0115 939 9833* **Closed** *Mon & Tue; 26 Dec–15 Jan, 25 July–15 Aug*
Combines traditional styles with cutting-edge French cuisine. Artistic presentation.

STAMFORD: The Gallery Restaurant £
Modern British
New College Stamford, Drift Rd, Lincolnshire, PE9 1XA
Tel *01780 484340*
Fine gourmet dinners and simpler lunch specials cooked by aspiring chefs at Stamford New College.

STAMFORD: The Fat Turk ££
Turkish
162 High St, Chipping Ongar, Lincolnshire, CM5 9JJ
Tel *01277 366770* **Closed** *Sun*
Dine on meze and chicken shish kebabs at this popular Turkish place with a lamp-lit garden.

Lancashire and the Lakes

AMBLESIDE: Fellini's £
Vegetarian
Church St, Cumbria, LA22 0BT
Tel *015394 32487*
A stylish modern vegetarian restaurant attached to a small, state-of-the-art cinema.

AMBLESIDE: Zeffirellis £
Pizza
Compston Rd, Cumbria, LA22 9AD
Tel *015394 33845.*
Book ahead at this hugely popular vegetarian pizza joint. Attached cinema and jazz bar.

AMBLESIDE: Atelier ££
Mediterranean
Lake Rd, Cumbria, LA22 0AD
Tel *015394 31156* **Closed** *Sun & Mon*
Mediterranean-inspired cooking in a modern workshop.

AMBLESIDE: Eltermere Inn Restaurant ££
Modern British
Elterwater, Cumbria, LA22 9HY
Tel *015394 37207*
Local ingredients and inventive recipes provide the sustenance. Enjoy views of Elterwater Lake and Loughrigg Fell.

BOOTLE: The Byre Tearooms £
Traditional British
Millstones Barn, Millom, LA19 5TJ
Tel *01229 718757* **Closed** *Mon*
This gem of a place offers Cumbrian specialities such as pork and apple loaf, as well as home-made cakes.

BOWNESS-ON-WINDERMERE: Jintana Thai Restaurant £
Thai
Lake Rd, Cumbria, LA23 3BJ
Tel *015394 45002*
Authentic and delicious food served in an elegant and homely atmosphere.

BOWNESS-ON-WINDERMERE: Porto Restaurant £
European
3 Ash St, Cumbria, LA23 3EB
Tel *015394 48242*
Refined dining in a boutique setting. Try the Porto Pig Plate and twice-baked sticky toffee soufflé.

BOWNESS-ON-WINDERMERE: Roberto's £
Italian
8 Queens Sq, Rayrigg Rd, Cumbria, LA23 3BY
Tel *015394 43535* **Closed** *Sun*
Roberto's is a traditional bistro on the outside but with great modern Italian food inside.

BRAITHWAITE: The Restaurant at The Cottage in the Wood £
Modern British
Magic Hill, Whinlatter Forest, nr Keswick, Cumbria CA12 5TW
Tel *01768 778409* **Closed** *Sun & Mon*
A whitewashed building in the woodland serving Cumbrian produce in elegant combinations.

For more information on types of restaurants *see page 577*

Oak-beamed restaurant at The Dining Room, Grasmere

**BROUGHTON-IN-FURNESS:
The Blacksmiths Arms**   £
Pub
Broughton Mills, nr Bowness-on-Windermere, Cumbria, LA20 6AX
Tel 01229 716824
One of the Lakes' characteristic ancient inns, serving fantastic local beef and Herdwick lamb.

**BROUGHTON-IN-FURNESS:
Beswicks Restaurant**   ££
French
Langholme House, The Square, Cumbria, LA20 6JF
Tel 01229 716285 **Closed** Sun & Mon
The changing menu features up to five courses, with options for vegetarians and those with special dietary needs.

DK Choice

CARTMEL: L'Enclume   £££
Modern British
Cavendish St, Cumbria, LA11 6PZ
Tel 015395 36362
An ancient building with rough lime-washed walls and low beams is the rustic setting for some extraordinary food. Savour local cuisine, partly foraged, and presented with lots of attention to detail.

**COCKERMOUTH: Quince &
Medlar**   ££
Vegetarian
13 Castlegate, Cumbria, CA13 9EU
Tel 01900 823579 **Closed** Sun & Mon
Housed in a handsome building, serving upmarket vegetarian food such as smoked Cumberland cheese and mushroom roulade.

**GRANGE-OVER-SANDS: The
Hare and Hounds Restaurant** £
Gastro-pub
Bowland Bridge, Cumbria, LA11 6NN
Tel 015395 68333
Great gastro-pub with a cosy log fire. Try the local black pudding gâteau or lamb hot pot.

GRASMERE: Jumble Room   £
European
Ambleside, Cumbria, LA22 9SU
Tel 015394 35188   **Closed** Tue
Long-established and lavishly decorated restaurant with an eclectic menu of European fare.

GRASMERE: The Dining Room £
Modern British
Broadgate, Grasmere Village, Cumbria, LA22 9TA
Tel 015394 35217
Housed in an attractive stone-built Lakes building, this upmarket restaurant offers home-made breads, sorbets and ice cream.

**KENDAL: Baba Ganoush
Canteen**   £
Middle Eastern
Unit 4, Berrys Yard, 27 Finkle St, Cumbria, LA9 4AB
Tel 01539 731072 **Closed** Sun & Mon
Canteen-style restaurant. Great risotto, cassoulets, slow-roasted meat and vegetarian meze boards.

KESWICK: A Taste of Thailand £
Thai
Shemara Guest House, 27 Bank St, Cumbria, CA12 5JZ
Tel 017687 73936
Savour exquisitely presented northern Thai food, made using authentic ingredients, in this Lakeland guesthouse.

KESWICK: Morrels Restaurant £
Traditional British
34 Lake Rd, Cumbria, CA12 5DQ
Tel 017687 72666   **Closed** Mon
Light, modern bistro-style place. Try a starter of asparagus with walnut, and move on to braised daube of beef on root mash.

LIVERPOOL: Shiraz   £
Turkish
19 North John St, Merseyside, L2 5QU
Tel 0151 236 8325
Popular Turkish restaurant. The food is robust but well presented. Try the Turkish classic meat grills, served with a selection of salads.

MANCHESTER: The Pavilion 2 £
Bangladeshi
231 Spotland Rd, Rochdale, Lancashire, OL12 7AG
Tel 01706 526666
Specializes in *balti* curries and tandoori. Great banquet-style meals for big groups.

**MORECAMBE BAY: Aspect Bar
& Bistro**   £
Bistro
320–323 Marine Rd Central, Lancashire, LA4 5AA
Tel 01524 416404
Delicious tapas, as well as mains. Great views.

**PENRITH: Rampsbeck Country
House Hotel**   £££
Modern British
Watermillock Ullswater, Cumbria, CA11 0LP
Tel 017684 86442
A grand but spacious country-house hotel with elegant food. Try the Cartmel Valley venison.

**WINDERMERE: Grey Walls
Steakhouse and Restaurant** ££
Steakhouse
Elleray Rd, Cumbria, LA23 1AG
Tel 015394 43741   **Closed** Sun–Wed
Local ales and hearty slabs of steak are dished up at this fine place.

WINDERMERE: Hooked   ££
Seafood
Ellerthwaite Sq, Cumbria, LA23 1DP
Tel 015394 48443   **Closed** Mon
An eclectic little seafood restaurant with influences from the Mediterranean, Southeast Asia and Australia.

WINDERMERE: Miller Howe ££
European
Rayrigg Rd, Cumbria, LA23 1EY
Tel 015394 42536
Family-owned hotel with lake views. Imaginative and well-presented food.

WINDERMERE: Holbeck Ghyll £££
European
Holbeck Lane, Cumbria, LA23 1LU
Tel 015394 32375
Michelin-starred for 12 years, this is one of the best restaurants in the area. Great views.

Yorkshire and the Humber Region

ASENBY: Crab and Lobster ££
Seafood
Crab Manor, Dishforth Rd, Thirsk, North Yorkshire, YO7 3QL
Tel 01845 577286
Old-fashioned seafood diner decorated with antiques. Jazz

music on Sundays. Try their signature dish: lobster Thermidor.

BOLTON ABBEY: The Devonshire Arms Brasserie £
Modern British
Skipton, North Yorkshire, BD23 6AJ
Tel *01756 710710*
Enjoy British and French cuisine in a coaching inn dating back to 1753. Informal atmosphere.

**BOROUGHBRIDGE:
The Dining Room** £££
Modern British
20 St James Sq, North Yorkshire, YO51 9AR
Tel *01423 326426* **Closed** *Mon*
Cosy and popular brasserie with several home-made and locally sourced dishes. Fine selection of wines and champagne.

EAST WITTON: The Blue Lion £
Traditional British
nr Leyburn, North Yorkshire, DL8 4SN
Tel *01969 624273*
Housed in an old coaching inn. Try the steak as well as the kidney pudding. Extensive wine list and hand-drawn real ales at the bar.

FERRENSBY: The General Tarleton Inn ££
Seafood
Boroughbridge Rd, nr Knaresborough, North Yorkshire, HG5 0PZ
Tel *01423 340284*
This 18th-century coaching inn is renowned for its seafood Thermidor. Lots of local produce.

HALIFAX: Design House £££
Traditional British
Dean Clough Arts & Business Centre, West Yorkshire, HX3 5AX
Tel *01422 383242* **Closed** *Sun*
The three-course set lunch here is excellent value, and there is a full à la carte menu in the evening.

HARROGATE: Drum and Monkey ££
Seafood
5 Montpellier Gardens, North Yorkshire, HG1 2TF
Tel *01423 502650* **Closed** *Sun*
Locally sourced fish served in an old dining club. Try the scallops with cheese and garlic butter or the fisherman's pie.

HARROGATE: The Sportsman's Arms ££
Modern British
Wath-in-Nidderdale, Pateley Bridge, North Yorkshire, HG3 5PP
Tel *01423 711306*
A charming converted farmhouse and barn. Relish fresh, seasonal fish and seafood brought from Whitby, along with local lamb, duck and guinea fowl.

HARROGATE: The Yorke Arms £££
Modern British
Ramsgill-in-Nidderdale, Pateley Bridge, North Yorkshire, HG3 5RL
Tel *01423 755243*
Michelin-starred dining in a 17th-century shooting lodge. Seasonal meats, fish and game dishes.

**HUSTHWAITE:
The Orchard Inn** £££
Traditional British
Low St, North Yorkshire, YO61 4QA
Tel *7730036876*
Former village pub with a good early-bird menu and excellent à la carte. Great sandwiches.

ILKLEY: Box Tree £££
French
35–37 Church St, West Yorkshire, LS29 9DR
Tel *01943 608484* **Closed** *Mon*
Michelin-starred-restaurant serving modern French dishes. Don't miss the hand-dived scallops served with truffle oil.

LEEDS: Sous le Nez en Ville ££
French
The Basement, Quebec House, Quebec St, West Yorkshire, LS1 2HA
Tel *0113 244 0108* **Closed** *Sun*
Excellent, traditional French restaurant. Try the fantastic fillet steak stuffed with shallot.

LEEDS: Anthony's Restaurant £££
Modern British
The Corn Exchange, Call Lane, West Yorkshire, LS1 7BR
Tel *0113 2470995* **Closed** *Sun & Mon*
Ambitious dishes served up in a stunning location. The nine-course gourmet menu with wines is well worth the three-figure price tag.

RIPLEY: The Boar's Head £££
Modern British
Harrogate, North Yorkshire, HG3 3AY
Tel *01423 771888*
A former coaching inn with a restaurant and bistro. Seasonal fish, meat and game on offer.

**ROBINS HOOD'S BAY:
Wayfarer Bistro** £
Bistro
Station Rd, nr Whitby, North Yorkshire, YO22 4RL
Tel *01947 880240* **Closed** *Mon*
Sample excellent seafood along with chargrilled steaks and vegetarian choices.

SHEFFIELD: Zeugma £
Turkish
146 London Rd, South Yorkshire, S2 4LT
Tel *0114 2582223*
Watch *cop shish* (marinated lamb) or *kaburga* (spare ribs) cooking over charcoal. Bring your own wine for a small corkage fee.

DK Choice

SHEFFIELD: Greenhead House £££
Traditional British
84 Burncross Rd, Chapeltown, South Yorkshire, S35 1SF
Tel *0114 2469004*
Closed *Sun–Tue*
Located in a lovely 17th-century house with an open fire, intimate dining room and walled garden. The husband-and-wife team at the helm offer a traditional British menu, with delicious sea bass, quail and beef dishes.

STOKESLEY: Chapter's £££
Modern British
27 High St, Middlesbrough, North Yorkshire, TS9 5AD
Tel *01642 711888* **Closed** *Sun dinner*
Choose between gourmet dining in the stylish restaurant or more casual fare in the bar brasserie.

**SUTTON-ON-THE-FOREST:
The Rose and Crown Inn** £
Traditional British
Main St, North Yorkshire, YO61 1DP
Tel *01347 811333*
This village inn restaurant uses fantastic, locally sourced beef and fish. Try the roast on Sundays.

WHITBY: The Magpie Café £
Traditional British
14 Pier Rd, North Yorkshire, YO21 3PU
Tel *01947 602058*
Historic merchant's house turned café. Eight kinds of fish and chips.

YORK: Melton's Too £
Bistro
25 Walmgate, North Yorkshire, YO1 9TX
Tel *01904 629222*
A converted saddler's shop, this informal bistro has home-made light fare and speciality beers.

Exterior of the fish and chip favourite, The Magpie Café, Whitby

For more information on types of restaurants *see page 577*

YORK: The Blue Bicycle Restaurant ££
Seafood
34 Fossgate, North Yorkshire, YO1 9TA
Tel *01904 673990*
A former 19th-century brothel, now a restaurant with great seafood on offer.

YORKSHIRE DALES: Angel Inn £
Gastro-pub
Hetton, Skipton, North Yorkshire, BD23 6LT
Tel *01756 730263*
Angel Inn has a charming interior of wooden beams and log fires. Eat in the restaurant or in the informal bar-brasserie.

Northumbria

DURHAM: Bistro 21 ££
Bistro
Aykley Heads House, Aykley Heads, DH1 5TS
Tel *0191 384 4354*
A popular bistro in a charming 18th-century farmhouse. Enjoy alfresco dining in the courtyard during summer.

GATESHEAD: Six Restaurant £
Modern British
Baltic Centre for Contemporary Art, Gateshead Quays, South Shore Rd, Tyne and Wear, NE8 3BA
Tel *0191 4404948*
Splendid views of the Tyne from this converted flour mill. Good service in the stylish dining room.

GREAT WHITTINGTON: Queens Head Inn ££
Bistro
Corbridge, Newcastle upon Tyne, Tyne and Wear, NE19 2HP
Tel *01434 672267* **Closed** Mon
Early 17th-century coaching inn near Hadrian's Wall. The menu features local game and North Sea fish. Good range of whiskies.

HEXHAM: Valley Connection 301 £
Bangladeshi
Market Pl, Northumberland, NE46 3NX
Tel *01434 601234* **Closed** Mon
At this Bangladeshi gem, ask for Mr Daraz's *bhuna gosht* (stir-fried lamb) and *bongo po* curry (king prawns).

HEXHAM: General Havelock Inn ££
Traditional British
9 Ratcliffe Rd, Haydon Bridge, Northumberland, NE47 6ER
Tel *01434 684376* **Closed** Mon
This former riverside inn offers seasonal traditional cuisine. Ask for the chef's signature Cullen

skink, a rich smoked haddock chowder.

DK Choice

MATFEN: Matfen Hall Country House Hotel £££
Traditional British
Northumberland, NE20 0RH
Tel *0116 188 6500*
This beautifully restored 19th-century mansion has a two-AA-Rosette dining room in the library and print rooms. Less formal dining can also be found in the conservatory bistro, with pub fare served in the keeper's lodge. Matfen promises an unforgettable dining experience.

NEWCASTLE UPON TYNE: Paradiso £
Italian
1 Market Ln, Tyne and Wear, NE1 6QQ
Tel *0191 221 1240* **Closed** Sun
Stylish Italian diner with exposed brickwork and unexpected influences from Africa and Asia.

NEWCASTLE UPON TYNE: The Cherry Tree £
Modern British
9 Osborne Rd, Jesmond, NE2 2AE
Tel *0191 239 9924*
The imaginative menu features Bury black pudding, Ingram Valley lamb and grilled halibut. Good-value set lunches and early evening menus.

NEWTON AYCLIFFE: The County £
Modern British
13 The Green, Darlington, Durham, DL5 6LX
Tel *01325 312273*
Experience contemporary dining teamed with traditional modern British dishes. Range of New World wines and real ales.

NEWTON AYCLIFFE: Barcelo Redworth Hall Hotel £££
Fine Dining
Redworth, Durham, DL5 6NL,
Tel *01388 770600*
Built in 1693, the expansive Redworth Hall's elegant dining room offers an unforgettable fine dining experience.

ROMALDKIRK: The Rose and Crown Inn ££
Traditional British
Barnard Castle, Durham, DL12 9EB
Tel *01833 650213*
This 18th-century stone-built coaching inn has a classic restaurant, as well as a less formal, rustic brasserie to choose from.

YARM: Chadwick's ££
European
104b High St, Stockton-on-Tees, Durham, TS15 9AU
Tel *01642 590300* **Closed** Mon
A bustling restaurant offering pizzas and pasta at lunchtime, with a more formal evening menu. Enthusiastic staff and a good atmosphere.

North Wales

ABERDYFI: Penhelig Arms ££
Traditional British
27–29 Terrace Rd, Gwynedd, LL35 0LT
Tel *01654 767215*
Small, friendly restaurant overlooking the Dyfi Estuary. Locally sourced fish and meat. Enjoy seared scallops with champagne.

BEAUMARIS: Ye Olde Bull's Head Inn ££
Traditional British
Castle St, Isle of Anglesey, LL58 8AP
Tel *01248 810329*
This 15th-century coaching inn converted into a restaurant with

Picturesque exterior of the seafood restaurant The Blue Bicycle, York

Views over Mount Snowdon at Castle Cottage, Harlech

rooms. There is also a brasserie and popular bar.

DOLGELLAU: Bwyty Mawddach ££
Welsh
Maesygarnedd, Llanelltyd, Gwynedd, LL40 2TA
Tel *01341 424020* **Closed** *Sun dinner, Mon & Tue*
Stunning views are the perfect accompaniment to exquisite food using locally sourced ingredients.

DOLGELLAU: Penmaenuchaf Hall £££
Modern British
Penmaenpool, Gwynedd, LL40 1YB
Tel *01341 422129*
Sample award-winning cuisine. Simple but elegant food is served in a fine dining room with white linen, silver cutlery and crystal wine glasses.

HARLECH: Castle Cottage £££
Welsh
Y Llech, Gwynedd, LL46 2YL
Tel *01766 780479*
Award-winning restaurant with rooms. The traditional Welsh menu features lobster, sea bass and black bream plus venison from the Brecon Beacons.

LLANBEDROG: Glyn-Y-Weddw Arms £
Traditional British
Abersoch Rd, Pwllheli, LL53 7TH
Tel *01758 740212*
Low-key village pub serving good, locally produced food. Sip on a draught ale in their beer garden. International buffet on Saturdays.

LLANBERIS: The Gwynedd Hotel & Restaurant ££
Traditional British
Snowdonia, Gwynedd, LL55 4SU
Tel *01286 870203*
Local and seasonal cuisine meticulously served at the very foot of Mount Snowdon.

LLANDRILLO: Tyddyn Llan £££
Welsh
Llandrillo, nr Corwen, Denbighshire, LL21 0ST
Tel *01490 440264*
One of Wales's finest restaurants in a small, elegant Georgian house. The award-winning cuisine features local lamb and beef.

LLANDUDNO: The Seahorse £
Seafood
7 Church Walks, Conwy, LL30 2HD
Tel *01492 875315*
Grade II-listed Victorian dining room serving delicious locally sourced seafood such as Great Orme lobsters and Menai mussels.

LLANGEFNI: Noëlle's at Tre-Ysgawen Hall £££
Traditional British
Capel Coch, Isle of Anglesey, LL77 7UR
Tel *01248 750750*
An excellent menu and wine list. Afternoon tea is served in the hotel drawing room.

LLANGOLLEN: The Corn Mill £
Traditional British
Dee Lane, Denbighshire, LL20 8NN
Tel *01978 869555*
Family-friendly restaurant inside a heritage building. Children can fill up on haddock and chips, while the grown-ups check out the sea trout and pork belly.

DK Choice

PORTMEIRION: The Hotel Portmeirion £££
Welsh
Gwynedd, LL48 6ET
Tel *01766 772440*
The hotel's beautiful white dining room was designed by Terence Conran and overlooks a stunning estuary. Castell Deudraeth gastro-pub, another restaurant on the premises,

specializes in fresh seafood, while the Town Hall restaurant serves meals and snacks. There's something for everyone here.

PWLLHELI: Plas Bodegroes £££
Modern British
Nefyn Rd, Gwynedd, LL53 5TH
Tel *01758 612363* **Closed** *Mon*
Locally sourced meat, fish and game are used. The desserts are superb: try the rhubarb and apple with a cinnamon biscuit and elderflower custard.

RHOS-ON-SEA: Forte's Restaurant £
Café
Penrhyn Ave, Conwy, LL28 4NH
Tel *01492 877910*
An ideal lunch venue that doubles as an ice-cream parlour. Choose from a delicious range of sundaes, all made with the house ice cream.

RUTHIN: Manorhaus ££
Welsh
10 Well St, Denbighshire, LL15 1AH
Tel *01824 704830*
Stylish restaurant with rooms in a listed Georgian stone building. The seasonal menu features salt marsh Welsh lamb, Menai mussels and Welsh whiskies.

South and Mid-Wales

ABERAERON: The Hive on the Quay £
Café
Cadwgan Pl, Dyfed, SA46 0BU
Tel *01545 570445*
Enjoy harbour views while relishing grilled sardines, curried clams or ciabatta with tuna and olives. Try the home-made honey ice cream.

BRECON: Felin Fach Griffin £££
Welsh
Felin Fach, Powys, LD3 0UB
Tel *01874 620111*
Exceptional food, including squab pigeon, fresh salted cod and Welsh rib-eye. Fantastic local cheese board.

BRIDGEND: Eliot Restaurant ££
Modern British
Coed-y-Mwstwr Hotel, Coychurch, CF35 6AF
Tel *01656 860621*
The daily *table d'hôte* menu at Eliot includes duck breast with spinach and cherry port or rabbit leg stuffed with garlic and spinach pancetta. Great views.

For more information on types of restaurants *see page 577*

Sophisticated dining area at Andrew Fairlie at Gleneagles, Auchterarder

BUILTH WELLS: The Drawing Room £££
Welsh
Cwmbach, Powys, LD2 3RT
Tel *01982 552493*
A five-star restaurant with rooms in an elegant Georgian country house. Delicious Welsh black beef and lamb from local farms.

CARDIFF: Mimosa Kitchen and Bar £
Gastro-pub
Mermaid Quay, Cardiff Bay, CF10 5BZ
Tel *02920 491900*
Fashionable gastro-pub with leather seats and picture windows.

CARDIFF: Zio Piero £
Italian
126a Cowbridge Rd, Canton, CF11 9DX
Tel *02920 220269* **Closed** *Sun & Mon*
Lovely Italian pizzeria serving some of Wales's best calzones.

DK Choice

CARDIFF: Le Monde £££
Seafood
61 St Mary St, CF10 1FE
Tel *029 2038 7376*
Le Monde may be dark as a dive bar, but it has the best fish and great service. The sea bass in rock salt is a house speciality, but the atmosphere and the downtown location are what make this brasserie unmissable.

CRICKHOWELL: Nantyffin Cider Mill ££
Welsh
Brecon Rd, Powys, NP8 1SG
Tel *01873 810775* **Closed** *Mon & Tue*
Pretty country restaurant in a converted mill. Great Brecon pork and Wye Valley asparagus.

FISHGUARD: Diners' Circle ££
Welsh
Tregynon, Gwaun Valley, Pembrokeshire, SA65 9TU
Tel *01239 820531*
All food is made on the premises of this 14th-century farmhouse. Emphasis on locally reared beef and lamb.

HAVERFORDWEST: Wolfscastle Country Hotel £££
Welsh
Wolfscastle, Pembrokeshire, SA62 5LZ
Tel *01437 741225*
An old riverside vicarage with panoramic views and a menu with salmon, monkfish and halibut, as well as Welsh beef, lamb and duck.

HAY-ON-WYE: Three Cocks Hotel & Restaurant ££
Traditional British
Brecon, Powys, LD3 0SL
Tel *01497 847215* **Closed** *Sun & Mon*
Sample tasty home-made dishes prepared with local ingredients in a quiet dining room with stone fireplaces and great views of the hotel gardens.

LLANWRTYD WELLS: Lasswade Country House Hotel & Restaurant ££
Welsh
Station Rd, Powys, LD5 4RW
Tel *01591 610515*
This award-winning restaurant in an Edwardian country-house hotel is well known for its use of locally sourced, organic produce.

DK Choice

LLYSWEN: Llangoed Hall Hotel £££
Traditional British
Brecon, Powys, LD3 0YP
Tel *01874 754525*
When Sir Bernard Ashley took over this ancient hall, he set out to re-create the Edwardian country-house weekend in all its comfort and grandeur. The afternoon tea at Llangoed is a real treat, but lunch and dinner are even better, in a beautiful candlelit dining room. Book well in advance to ensure a fantastic dining experience.

MUMBLES: Verdi's ££
Café
Knab Rock, SA3 4EN
Tel *01792 369213* **Closed** *Dec–Feb*
Glass-fronted Italian café serving the best pizza this side of Naples, as well as pasta and focaccia. Tasty desserts include tiramisu and Turkish delight ice cream.

PEMBROKE: George Wheeler Restaurant ££
Welsh
Old Kings Arms Hotel, Main St, Pembrokeshire, SA71 4JS
Tel *01646 683611*
Award-winning restaurant showcasing the best of Wales's local produce. Try Welsh cockles with laver bread and bacon.

SWANSEA: Hanson at The Chelsea Restaurant ££
International
Ty Castell House, 17 St Mary St, SA1 3LH
Tel *01792 464068* **Closed** *Sun*
Award-winning fish restaurant, with great locally caught sea bass. Also try the steak and kidney pie.

SWANSEA: Patricks with Rooms ££
Welsh
638 Mumbles Rd, Mumbles, SA3 4EA
Tel *01792 360199*
This restaurant with rooms serves delicious Gower mussels with leek and laver bread, and garlic roasted rack of Welsh lamb.

The Lowlands

ABERLADY: Ducks At Kilspindie House ££
Scottish
Main St, Longniddry, EH32 0RE
Tel *01875 870 682*
Legendary Edinburgh restaurateur Malcolm Duck is the man behind this destination dining venue. There is a modern fine-dining restaurant and a relaxed bistro.

DK Choice

AUCHTERARDER: Andrew Fairlie at Gleneagles £££
Scottish
Perthshire, PH3 1NF
Tel *01764 694267* **Closed** *Sun*
The grand Gleneagles Hotel is the setting for Scotland's only two-Michelin-starred restaurant. Chef Andrew Fairlie works his magic on locally sourced produce by giving them international twists. Try the smoked lobster and roast Anjou squab.

BALQUHIDDER: Monachyle Mhor £££
Scottish
Lochearnhead, Stirling, FK19 8PQ
Tel *01877 384 622*
Chef Tom Lewis grows his own vegetables and herbs, as well as rearing livestock. The sublime five-course *table d'hôte* menu here makes the most of this produce.

BUTE: No. 29 £
Scottish
29 Gallowgate, Rothesay, PA20 0HR
Tel *01700 500685* **Closed** *Mon*
Contemporary eatery serving
creative modern cooking, with
dishes such as the delicious
crispy battered local haddock
and chips.

CUPAR: The Peat Inn £££
Pub **Map** E4
Fife, nr St Andrews, KY15 5LH
Tel *01334 840206* **Closed** *Sun & Mon*
Michelin-starred rural retreat
by chef Geoffrey Smeddle.
The menu expertly utilizes local
produce such as salmon,
langoustine and beef. Come
here to savour the multi-course
tasting menu.

DUNDEE: Jute Café Bar £
Bistro
152 Nethergate, DD1 4DY
Tel *01382 909246*
This artistic café at the Dundee
Contemporary Arts centre serves
light lunches, as well as a three-
course evening meal. Solid
cooking includes dishes such as
steak and chocolate torte.

EDINBURGH: David Bann £
Vegetarian
56–58 St Mary's St, EH1 1SX
Tel *0131 556 5888*
Stylish fine-dining restaurant
with delicious vegetarian dishes
such as leek, tarragon and
butternut squash risotto. Try
the tartlet made with Ardrahan
smoked cheese and slow-dried
tomatoes.

EDINBURGH: La Favorita £
Italian
321 Leith Walk, EH6 8SA
Tel *0131 554 2430*
A strong contender for the city's
best pizzeria, the bustling La
Favorita offers doughy delights

served with an infinite range of
toppings. Save space for an ice-
cream treat afterwards.

EDINBURGH: Orocco Pier £
International
*17 High St, South Queensferry,
EH30 9PP*
Tel *0870 118 1664*
Choose from the sumptuous pub
fare at Antico Café Bar or feast on
seafood in the Samphire Bar and
Grill. Offers sweeping views of
the Forth estuary and its bridges.

EDINBURGH: Spoon £
Café
6a Nicolson St, EH8 9DH
Tel *0131 623 1752* **Closed** *Sun*
This modern, arty café serves the
finest vegetarian breakfast in the
city, as well as a good carnivore's
version. Great place for lunch.

EDINBURGH: Centotre ££
Italian
103 George St, EH2 3ES
Tel *0131 225 1550*
Edinburgh's grandest Italian
restaurant, Centotre guarantees
authentic pasta dishes. A great
place for lunch, dinner or just
a quick snack.

**EDINBURGH: Galvin Brasserie
de Luxe** ££
Brasserie
Princes St, EH1 2AB
Tel *0131 222 8988*
This swish brasserie in the hotel
Caledonian is a real treat for lovers
of French cuisine. It features a
crustacean bar and superb wine
list. Great-value set menus.

**EDINBURGH: Kyloe Restaurant
& Grill** ££
International
1–3 Rutland St, EH1 2AE
Tel *0131 229 3402*
Choose from a variety of steak
cuts at this carnivore's heaven.

Located in the Rutland Hotel, it
offers fine views of the castle.

EDINBURGH: Stac Polly ££
Scottish
29–33 Dublin St, EH3 6NL
Tel *0131 556 2231e*
Stac Polly serves dependable
and modern Scottish cooking.
Excellent steak with black
pudding and white fish dishes.

EDINBURGH: Jeremy Wares £££
Scottish
*Macdonald Houston House Hotel,
Uphall, West Lothian, EH52 6JS*
Tel *0844 879 9043*
Jeremy Wares's signature modern
Scottish cooking in the romantic
Houston House features local
Perthshire venison, Borders lamb
and Scottish beef.

EDINBURGH: Ondine £££
Seafood
2 George IV Bridge, EH1 1AD
Tel *0131 226 1888*
Inspirational cooking based on
sustainable sourcing by chef
Roy Brett. Try the heavenly
shellfish platter served on ice
(French-style) or warmed with
garlic butter.

**EDINBURGH: Restaurant Martin
Wishart** £££
French
54 The Shore, Leith, EH6 6RA
Tel *0131 553 3557* **Closed** *Sun & Mon*
Chef Martin Wishart offers a truly
memorable experience for lovers
of French food: classic cooking
with sublime use of Scottish
ingredients. Excellent service.

**EYEMOUTH: Mackays of
Eyemouth** £
Traditional British
20–24 High St, Berwickshire, TD14 5EU
Tel *01890 751142*
Tuck into a fish supper or binge
on lobster and chips at Mackays,
while watching local fishing
boats go out to sea.

GLASGOW: Café Gandolfi £
Café
64 Albion St, G1 1NY
Tel *0141 552 6813*
A city institution and part of the
Gandolfi mini-empire. Come here
for the great breakfasts, light
lunches or substantial dinners.

**GLASGOW: The Chippy Doon
the Lane** £
Traditional British
*84 Buchanan St, McCormick Lane,
G1 3AJ*
Tel *0141 225 6650*
Relaxed restaurant serving
excellent monkfish tails, hake and
lemon sole, cod and haddock.

Outdoor tables at this popular pizzeria, La Favorita, Edinburgh

For more information on types of restaurants *see page 577*

The tasteful dining room at the Boath House, Auldearn

**GLASGOW: Malmaison
Glasgow Brasserie** ££
Brasserie
278 West George St, G2 4LL
Tel *08446 930653*
The perfectly cooked steaks are
the main attraction in this
subterranean retreat. Fish of the
day is also a good option. Choose
from a list of reasonably priced
sumptuous wines.

GLASGOW: Bistro du Vin £££
Scottish
One Devonshire Gardens, G12 0UX
Tel *08447 364256*
A fine-dining restaurant housed
in the stately Hotel du Vin. Offers
a menu featuring Scotland's
finest red meat and fish. Try the
seven-course tasting menu.

**HADDINGTON:
The Waterside Bistro** £
Scottish
1–5 Waterside, East Lothian, EH4 1 4AT
Tel *01620 825674*
Set on the banks of the River
Tyne, this welcoming, family-run
bistro serves well-sourced local
produce in cosy surroundings.
Great for families with kids.

LAUDER: Black Bull Hotel £
Traditional British
Market Pl, Berwickshire, TD2 6SR
Tel *01578 722208*
Traditional pub serving quality
food in a Georgian dining room
or a cosy bar-lounge. Dishes
include fish and chips and chunky
burgers. Good kids' menu.

**PEEBLES: Coltman's
Delicatessen & Kitchen** £
Café
71–73 High St, EH45 8AN
Tel *01721 720405*
Charming deli and restaurant with
views over the River Tweed. Offers
sandwiches, platters and dishes
with an international flavour.
Good three-course set menu.

STANLEY: Ballathie House ££
Scottish
Kinclaven, Perth, PH1 4QN
Tel *01250 883268*
Chef Scott Scorer makes the
best of Scottish produce such as
Pittenweem langoustines and
Perthshire venison by giving them
a modern twist in this elegant
restaurant. Wonderful desserts.

The Highlands
and Islands

**ABERDEEN: The Silver
Darling** £££
Seafood
*Pocra Quay, North Pier,
Aberdeenshire, AB11 5DQ*
Tel *01224 576229* **Closed** *Sun*
The Silver Darling offers fresh
seafood expertly cooked and
given a French twist by Chef
Didier Dejean. Choose from a
range of French wines, and enjoy
magnificent sea views.

**ABOYNE: At the Sign of the
Black Faced Sheep** £
Café
*Ballater Rd, Aberdeenshire,
AB34 5HN*
Tel *01339 887311*
Lovely coffee shop and food
emporium. Visitors are impressed
by the upmarket café menu of
classy sandwiches and sun-dried
tomato scones. Attractive
collection of crockery on display.

**ACHILTIBUIE: Summer
Isles Hotel** £££
Seafood
Ullapool, Ross-shire, IV26 2YG
Tel *01854 622282*
The award-winning restaurant
at the Summer Isles Hotel
delivers exceptional seafood
dishes by chef Alan White in
elegant surroundings.

APPLECROSS: Applecross Inn £
Seafood
Wester Ross, IV54 8LR
Tel *01520 744262*
Remarkable locally-caught
seafood, such as huge Applecross
prawns and plump lobster,
served in generous portions at
this restaurant and inn.

**ARDEONAIG: Ardeonaig Hotel
& Restaurant** ££
Scottish
*South Loch Tay Side, Killin,
FK21 8SU*
Tel *01567 820400* **Closed** *Mon & Tue*
Pleasantly appointed dining room
overlooking Loch Tay. Chef Ross
Miller offers an inventive menu of
dishes such as venison loin and
hay smoked salmon.

AULDEARN: Boath House £££
Scottish
Nairn, IV12 5TE
Tel *01667 454896*
The award-wining food at the
luxurious Boath House hotel is
one of its main attractions. Chef
Charlie Lockley offers a delectable
six-course tasting menu.

BADACHRO: Badachro Inn £
Pub
Gairloch, Ross-shire, IV21 2AA
Tel *01445 741255*
Friendly local pub serving bar
lunches and evening meals.
Jacket potatoes, panini and
sandwiches feature alongside
fresh shellfish, seafood, Scottish
beef and lamb.

COLL: Gannet Restaurant ££
Seafood
Ariangour, PA78 6SZ
Tel *01879 230334*
Waterfront restaurant in the Coll
Hotel, boasting fresh seafood
from around the island. Try the
lobster with fresh home-made
spaghetti.

FINDHORN: The Bakehouse £
Café
91–92 Forres, IV36 3YG
Tel *01309 691826*
Known for its vegetarian organic
produce. Meat options include
tasty pork and venison burgers.
Mouthwatering home baking.

FORT WILLIAM: Lime Tree ££
Scottish
*The Old Manse, Achintore Rd,
Inverness-Shire, PH33 6RQ*
Tel *01397 701806*
Highly praised hotel-restaurant
known for its warm welcome
and excellent food. Specialities
include pan seared Glenfinnan
venison, mackerel, west coast
crab and smoked haddock.

FORT WILLIAM: Inverlochy Castle £££
Scottish
Torlundy, Inverness-Shire, PH33 6SN
Tel *01397 702177*
The three regal dining rooms at Inverlochy Castle make for a truly memorable experience. Do not miss the hot cranachan soufflé.

GLENCOE: Clachaig Inn £
Scottish
Argyll, PH49 4HX
Tel *01855 811252*
Characterful old inn set in the centre of Glencoe. Hearty pub fare, fine ales and a range of malt whiskies to choose from.

INVERIE: The Old Forge £
Scottish
Knoydart, Mallaig, Inverness-Shire, PH41 4PL
Tel *01687 462267*
The most remote pub in the UK is a good place to try white fish and shellfish culled from around the Knoydart Peninsula.

INVERNESS: Rocpool Restaurant ££
Brasserie
1 Ness Walk, Inverness-Shire, IV3 5NE
Tel *01463 717274*
Contemporary eatery serving modern food. Relish dishes such as Parma ham salad served with balsamic roasted purple figs and baked Parmesan brûlée.

ISLE OF SKYE: The Three Chimneys £££
Scottish
Colbost, Dunvegan, IV55 8ZT
Tel *01470 511258*
Characterful converted stone croft by the self-taught, visionary chef Shirley Spear. Enjoy a superb dining experience at a spectacular location. Reserve ahead.

KILBERRY: The Kilberry Inn ££
Modern British
Tarbert, Argyll and Bute, PA29 6YD
Tel *01880 770223*   **Closed** *Mon*
This award-winning inn serves flawless dishes created with local ingredients such as surf clam with spaghetti, white wine and cream. Warm and cosy atmosphere.

DK Choice

KINLOCHLEVEN: Lochleven Seafood Café £££
Seafood
Onich, Fort William, Inverness-shire PH33 6SA
Tel *01855 821048*
A heaven for seafood lovers, Lochleven Seafood Café serves large scallops, delicious oysters

and an unparalleled shellfish platter, with refreshing white wines to ease them down. Outside tables in summer have splendid views of Loch Leven and Pap of Glencoe. Call to check opening times.

KYLESKU: Kylesku Hotel £
Scottish
Lairg, Sutherland, IV27 4HW
Tel *01971 502231*
Spacious bar-lounge in a former coaching inn. Serves quality meals including creel-caught lobster, langoustine and crab. Scottish meats and fish on offer as well.

MULL: Highland Cottage ££
Scottish
24 Breadalbane St, Tobermory, Argyll, PA75 6PD
Tel *01688 302030*
Talented chef Jo Currie delivers a menu brimming with quality local produce in this intimate dining room. Good wine list.

OBAN: Waterfront Fishouse Restaurant ££
Seafood
1 Railway Pier, PA34 4LW
Tel *01631 563110*
Plump langoustines, large king scallops and local lobster are on the menu at this waterfront restaurant. Spectacular views over the beautiful Oban bay.

PLOCKTON: Plockton Inn & Seafood Restaurant ££
Seafood
Innes St, Ross-shire, IV52 8TW
Tel *01599 544222*
Award-winning, traditional inn and restaurant in the picturesque village of Plockton, serves seafood platters, local beef, lamb and game. Also vegetarian options.

PORT APPIN: The Airds Hotel & Restaurant £££
French
Argyll and Bute, PA38 4DF
Tel *01631 730236*
The modern French fine-dining menu here uses local Scottish produce. Savour hand-dived scallops, slow-poached chicken and Mallaig halibut.

SCRABSTER: The Captain's Galley £££
Seafood
The Harbour, Caithness, KW14 7UJ
Tel *01847 894999*   **Closed** *Sun & Mon*
Set in a former ice house and salmon bothy with exposed brickwork, this place has a dozen different fresh fish on the menu.

SHETLAND ISLANDS: Frankie's Fish and Chips £
Traditional British
Brae, Shetland, ZE2 9QJ
Tel *01806 522700*
Award-winning fish-and-chip restaurant on Shetland's mainland. Fresh sustainable fish, with some unusual treats such as scallops and blue mussels.

TROON: MacCallum's of Troon Oyster Bar ££
Seafood
Harbourside, Ayrshire, KA10 6DH
Tel *01292 319339*   **Closed** *Mon*
Seafood restaurant known for its exemplary dishes and oysters. Delicacies include lemon sole with capers, prawn tempura and Cullen skink (thick fish soup).

TYNDRUM: The Real Food Café £
Café
Perthshire, FK20 8RY
Tel *01838 400235*
Arguably the best fish and chips in Scotland. Enjoy a large or small fish supper, and sample excellent coffee and cakes.

Enjoy views across the North Sea at Frankie's Fish and Chips, Shetland

For more information on types of restaurants *see page 577*

British Pubs

No tour of Britain could be complete without some exploration of its public houses. These are a great social institution, descendants of centuries of hostelries, ale houses and stagecoach halts. Some have colourful histories or fascinating contents, and occupy a central role in the community, staging quiz games and folk dancing. Many of those listed below are lovely buildings, or have attractive settings. Most serve a variety of beers, spirits and wine by the glass.

A "free house" is independent and will stock several leading regional beers, but most pubs are "tied" – this means that they are owned by a brewery and only stock that brewery's selection.

Many pubs offer additional attractions such as live music and beer gardens with picnic tables. Traditional pub food and more varied gastropub cuisine is often served at lunchtime, and increasingly, in the evenings as well. Traditional pub games take many forms, including cribbage, shove ha'penny, skittles, dominoes and darts.

London

Bloomsbury: Lamb
94 Lamb's Conduit St, WC1.
Tel *020 7405 0713.* **Map** *3 C5*
Unspoilt Victorian pub with lovely cut-glass "snob screens" and theatrical photographs. Small courtyard at the rear.

City: Black Friar
174 Queen Victoria St, EC4.
Tel *020 7236 5474.* **Map** *12 F2*
Eccentric inside and out, with intriguing Art Nouveau decor. Attentive service.

City: Ye Olde Cheshire Cheese
145 Fleet St EC4.
Tel *020 7353 6170.* **Map** *12 E1*
Authentic 17th-century inn that evokes shades of Dickens's London. Its stark glory is best enjoyed in front of the open fires.

Hammersmith: Dove
19 Upper Mall, W6. **Tel** *020 8748 9474.*
One of west London's most attractive riverside pubs – you can watch rowing crews from the terrace.

Hampstead: Spaniards Inn
Spaniards Lane, NW3.
Tel *020 8731 8406.*
Famous Hampstead landmark dating from the 16th century, once part of a tollgate.

Kensington: Windsor Castle
114 Campden Hill Rd, W8.
Tel *020 7243 8797.* **Map** *7 C4*
A civilized Georgian inn with oak furnishings and open fires. The walled garden attracts well-heeled crowds in summer. Hearty English food.

Southwark: George Inn
77 Borough High St, SE1.
Tel *020 7407 2056.* **Map** *13 B4*
Quaint coaching inn with unique galleried courtyard. Rooms ramble upstairs and downstairs, and the overspill sits outside. Morris dancers may be seen performing here at times *(see p124).*

The Downs and Channel Coast

Alciston: Rose Cottage Inn
Alciston nr Polegate.
Tel *01323 870377.*
In a creeper-covered cottage, this rural Sussex pub is decorated in classic rustic style, with beamed ceilings and open fireplaces. The local ales and busy kitchen add to its warmth.

Brighton: Market Inn
Market St, BN1 1HH. **Tel** *01273 329483.*
Once home to the Prince of Wales's chimney sweep, it is now something of a Brighton institution, spilling out onto The Lanes in the summer months.

Charlton: The Fox Goes Free
Charlton nr Chichester.
Tel *01243 811461.*
This lovely 16th-century inn serves local ales and cider straight from barrels. Full à la carte menu and great selection of bar meals. Live music on Wednesdays.

Ditchling: The Bull Hotel
2 High St, BN6 8TA. **Tel** *01273 843147.*
Housed in a 14th-century building, the main bar is large, rambling and pleasantly traditional with characterful old wooden floorboards, beams and furniture, and a blazing fire.

Faversham: White Horse Inn
The Street, Boughton. **Tel** *01227 751343.*
Chaucer gave this place a passing mention in *The Canterbury Tales.* Among hop gardens and orchards, this genial country pub resounds with echoes from the past. Thirteen en suite bedrooms.

Isle of Wight: The Wight Mouse Inn
Newport Rd, Chale. **Tel** *01983 730431.*
This pub draws in the locals with its range of real ales. Jazz music on Thursdays.

Lewes: Six Bells Inn
Chiddingly, nr Lewes. **Tel** *01825 872227.*
Once a stopover for stagecoaches, this cosy drop-in now does a fine job of reviving weary ramblers and thirsty locals. Supposedly haunted by a grey cat and one Sara French, hanged in 1852 after serving her husband a pie seasoned with arsenic.

Romsey: The Star Inn
East Tytherley, nr Romsey.
Tel *01794 340225.*
Popular watering hole on the edge of the New Forest, overlooking the village cricket pitch. The rivers Test and Dunn are nearby. Overnight accommodation available.

Rye: The Mermaid
Mermaid St. **Tel** *01797 223065.*
Dating from 1136, this is one of the country's oldest inns. Constructed from old ship timbers, The Mermaid is an evocative slice of England's nautical history. Sit by the open fire and spot the celebrities having a quiet drink.

Walliswood: The Scarlett Arms
Walliswood Green Rd.
Tel *01306 627243.*
Handsome inn with flagstone bar, wooden benches and a grand inglenook fireplace. The staff make the experience all the more congenial. Occasional live music.

East Anglia

Cambridge: The Boathouse
14 Chesterton Rd. **Tel** *01223 460905.*
This riverside pub boasts a natty
nautical theme and exceedingly
comfortable armchairs. The
beer garden is always warm and
toasty, courtesy of heaters, allowing
you to watch the river flow all year
around.

Itteringham: The Walpole Arms
The Common. **Tel** *01263 587258.*
Oak-beamed inn that has been
serving locally brewed ales since the
1700s. The restaurant is also highly
regarded.

Kings Lynn: The Lord Nelson
Walsingham Rd, Burnham Thorpe.
Tel *01328 738241.*
This watering hole was once one of
Lord Nelson's favourite haunts. Kick
back on any of the old highbacked
benches, and wait for the attentive
staff to take your order. Private
functions are held in the handsome,
flagstoned Victory Barn. Quiz
Tuesday lunchtime.

Norfolk: Red Lion
Wells Rd, Stiffkey. **Tel** *01328 830552.*
The oldest parts of the simple bars
have a few beams, aged flooring tiles
or bare boards, and big open fires.
A back gravel terrace has seats and
tables for enjoying the bar food on a
sunny day, and some pleasant walks
are nearby. Real ale and 30 malt
whiskies are available.

Norwich: The Fat Cat
49 W End St. **Tel** *01603 624364.*
Rightly famed for its extensive real
ale selection, The Fat Cat is full of
attractions, starting with the well-
stocked bar and the lively local
clientele.

Ringstead: The Gin Trap Inn
6 High St. **Tel** *01485 525264.*
Close to the Norfolk coastline and
just on the edge of the Ringstead
Downs nature reserve, this classic
country pub features hand-pumped
real ales and cosy log fires. The
restaurant has a devoted following.
Overnight accommodation available.
Quiz every other Sunday.

Southwold: The Crown Hotel
High St. **Tel** *01502 722275.*
The pub remains the star of this
converted hotel, though the chic
restaurant is becoming a firm local
favourite. Excellent selection of
wines at the bar.

Stowmarket: The Buxhall Crown
Mill Rd, Buxhall. **Tel** *01449 736521.*
Local real ales take pride of place in
this old village pub that also does a

roaring trade in home-cooked food
with locally sourced ingredients.
Good list of wine by the glass.

Suffolk: The Six Bells at
Bardwell *Bardwell, Bury St Edmunds.*
Tel *01359 250820.*
This village green charmer,
dating from the 1500s, offers
superb food and peaceful
accommodation.

Walden: Queen's Head Inn
High St, Littlebury, Saffron Walden.
Tel *01799 522251.*
Attractive coaching inn with a
relaxed, family ambience. Stocks a
decent selection of ales and has a
heady wine list. There are six en
suite rooms.

Thames Valley

Aylesbury: The King's Head
*Kings Head Passage, Market Sq,
Buckinghamshire.* **Tel** *01280 817156.*
A small oasis in the heart of a
pretty market town, this airy
pub has award-winning
food and ales and a courtyard
for whiling away long summer
afternoons.

Bedford: The Park
98 Kimbolton Rd, Bedfordshire.
Tel *01234 273929.*
This warm and friendly pub has
traditional features such as oak
beams and old fireplaces. Good,
wholesome food on offer.

Chipping Norton: The Falkland
Arms
*Great Tew, Chipping Norton,
Oxfordshire.* **Tel** *01608 683653.*
Award-winning cask ales and a
wonderful atmosphere. You can try
beer tasters before you buy at this
traditional gem of a place.

Faringdon: The Trout Inn
*Tadpole Bridge, Buckland Marsh, nr
Faringdon.* **Tel** *01367 870382.*
Always busy and bustling, this
17th-century pub boasts a river-front
garden where customers can savour
local dishes.

Great Hormead: The Three Tuns
High Street, Hertfordshire.
Tel *01763 289405.*
A traditional thatched and beamed
village pub with a cosy open fire in
winter and a patio in summer. Hearty
and reasonably priced food.

Leighton Buzzard: The Five Bells
*Station Road, Stanbridge,
Bedfordshire.*
Tel *01525 210224.*
A traditional pub surrounded by
picturesque countryside. Locally

sourced pub classics are served with
barbecues in the summer months.
Seasonal cask ales and fine wines.

Newbury: The Monument
Northbrook St, Berkshire.
Tel *01635 41964.*
The busiest pub around, there are
different events every night of the
week and a wide range of pub
games. There is also a beer garden.

Oxford: The Bear Inn
6 Alfred St. **Tel** *01865 728164.*
The oldest pub in Oxford (1242) is
famed for its quirky collection of ties
that dates back to the early 1900s,
representing clubs in the Oxford
area. The pub serves real ale and
good home-cooked food.

Oxford: The White Horse
52 Broad St. **Tel** *01865 204801.*
This cosy pub has loads of character,
with pictures of old sports stars on
the walls and a great range of beers.

Watton-at-Stone: The Bull
113 High St, Herts. **Tel** *01920 831032.*
Sit around the open-hearth fire at
this 14th-century inn, or in the
picturesque garden.

Wessex

Abbotsbury: Ilchester Arms
Market St, Dorset. **Tel** *01305 871243.*
A prominent landmark in this quaint
village, the 18th-century stone Grade
II listed inn features a deluxe
conservatory.

Bath: The Bell
103 Walcot St, Bath, Avon.
Tel *01225 460426.*
Splendid little pub, with billiards, live
music and organic beers. Soak in the
friendly atmosphere while tucking
into tasty sandwiches and snacks.

Bridport: Shave Cross Inn
Shave Cross, Marshwood Vale, Dorset.
Tel *01308 868358.*
Award-winning inn with
fine ales as well as English,
Caribbean and international food.
Five rooms.

Pensford: Carpenter's Arms
Stanton Wick, nr Pensford, Somerset.
Tel *01761 490202.*
Overlooking the lovely Chew Valley,
this welcoming pub is set among a
row of small miners' cottages. It has
an excellent menu and a
comprehensive wine list.

Salisbury: Haunch of Venison
1 Minster St, Salisbury, Wiltshire.
Tel *01722 411313.*
The severed, mummified hand of
an 18th-century card player is on

display (along with more pleasant antiques) at this 650-year-old pub. The restaurant is a must-visit for a good meal. Keep an eye out for the resident ghost.

Salisbury: The New Inn
41/47 New St, Wiltshire.
Tel *01722 326662.*
The low-beamed ceilings and intimate interior lighting here are offset by fine views of the cathedral spire opposite. The menu is broad and vegetarian-friendly.

Devon and Cornwall

Dawlish: The Mount Pleasant
Mount Pleasant Rd, Dawlish Warren, Devon. **Tel** *01626 863151.*
This pub is renowned for its views over Exmouth from the dining area. Drinkers visit once and become loyal customers for years. The warm ambience makes a winning combination with super value for money.

Exeter: The Bridge Inn
Bridge Hill, Topsham, Devon.
Tel *01392 873862.*
With its pink exterior, you can't miss this riverside pub, which has been run by the same family since 1899. Its several separate rooms with fireplaces are truly snug in winter, while the garden is gorgeous on sunny days. A pub with no bar, they serve drinks and bar snacks through a hatch in the corridor.

Falmouth: Pandora Inn
Restronguet Creek, Mylor Bridge, nr Falmouth, Cornwall. **Tel** *01326 372678.*
Medieval pub with a thatched roof by the waterside. Full of cosy corners, low wooden ceilings, panelled walls and a variety of maritime memorabilia.

Knowstone: Masons Arms Inn
Devon.
Tel *01398 341231.*
An atmospheric Grade II listed cottage that is full of character. The decor includes farm tools and a bread-oven fireplace. Delicious restaurant food and friendly hosts.

Lynton: Fox and Goose
Parracombe, Barnstaple.
Tel *01598 763239.*
A friendly and welcoming pub/B&B with very good food and beer. The log fire, plank ceiling and assorted mounted antlers and horns give a proper Exmoor feel to the place. Serves real ale and local cider.

Newton Abbot: Two Mile Oak
Totnes Rd. **Tel** *01803 812411.*
An old coaching inn with a beamed

lounge and an alcove just for two. A mix of wooden tables and chairs, and a fine winter log fire.

Penzance: The Pirate Inn
Alverton Rd, Alverton, Cornwall.
Tel *01736 366094.*
Recommended by the local youth hostel, this is a friendly stop for a beer and sandwich. Visitors often invest in the souvenir T-shirts sold here.

Porthleven: Harbour Inn
Commercial Rd, Cornwall.
Tel *01326 573876.*
Watch the sun go down and sip a top-quality pint as you sit by Porthleven's harbour. Two hundred years old, this pub retains its original character, the modern sofas and coffee tables notwithstanding.

Saltash: Rod and Line
Church Rd, Tideford, Cornwall.
Tel *01752 851323.*
This friendly old Cornish pub is set just off the main A38 road. Popular with locals, it has a single bar with a log fire. The interesting menu features local seafood.

Tiverton: The White Ball Inn
Bridge St, Devon.
Tel *01884 251525.*
Although the decor is slightly generic, there is an unusual visible well with a glass top. Vertigo sufferers should not look down.

The Heart of England

Alderminster: The Bell
Warwickshire. **Tel** *01789 450414.*
Smart 18th-century coach inn just 6.4 km (4 miles) out of Stratford-upon-Avon, The Bell also boasts a high-class restaurant. Great views over Stour Valley from the garden and conservatory.

Armscote: The Fuzzy Duck
Imington Rd, Devon. **Tel** *01608 682293.*
This atmospheric bar-restaurant (and B&B) is perfect for a light supper or relaxing drink. Sit in the vast lawns during summer. The bar has an open fire in winter.

Ashleworth: Queen's Arms
The Village, Gloucestershire.
Tel *01452 700395.*
Sixteenth-century inn with a noticeable Victorian makeover, this pub features wood-beamed ceilings and antique furnishings. The fantastic kitchen serves traditional pub food as well as more international flavours.

Bickley Moss: Cholmondeley Arms
Malpas, Cheshire. **Tel** *01829 720300.*
The menu in this family-friendly pub includes the very best of traditional local cuisine. Children will adore the desserts – baked syrup sponge, black cherry Pavlova, bakewell tart, ice creams and sorbets. Accommodation is also available.

Bretforton: Fleece Inn
Near Evesham. **Tel** *01386 831173.*
This real ale pub with its half-timbered façade is also a National Trust property. Beautifully located in the Vale of Evesham. Rooms available. Parking in village square.

Farnborough: Inn at Farnborough
Near Banbury. **Tel** *01295 690615.*
Classy inn in a Grade II listed free house from the 1700s, this inn serves delicious local cuisine, including sumptuous organic steak burgers. Large garden and conservatory.

Shrewsbury: Armoury
Welsh Bridge, Victoria Quay.
Tel *01743 340525.*
This converted 18th-century warehouse, with views over the river, is a popular open-plan venue. Go early if you want to enjoy a leisurely sit-down meal.

Welford-on-Avon: The Bell Inn
Nr Stratford-upon-Avon, Warwickshire.
Tel *01789 750353.*
This lovely 17th-century country pub serves wonderful real ale and traditional bar food. The Bell Inn lies just a short distance southwest of Stratford-upon-Avon. There is a delightful seating area in the garden.

Wenlock Edge: Wenlock Edge Inn
Hilltop, nr Much Wenlock, Shropshire.
Tel *01746 785678.*
This award-winning pub is popular with walkers – there is a comprehensive selection of maps and guidebooks on stand-by. A fairly homely affair, Wenlock Edge Inn serves good bar food and ales. Three rooms are available on a bed and breakfast basis.

East Midlands

Alderwasley: The Bear Inn
Belper, Derbyshire. **Tel** *01629 822585.*
Friendly country pub with real olde-worlde charm, The Bear Inn serves a good range of real ales and delicious cuisine. Popular with locals and visitors alike. Ten rooms are also available.

Bakewell: Packhorse Inn
Main St, Little Longstone.
Tel *01629 640471.*
This has been a welcome stop for
weary travellers since 1787. The pub
sits off what is known today as the
Monsal Trail, a popular route with
walkers, runners, and cyclists. Great
real ales and locally sourced food.

Grimsthorpe: Black Horse
Grimsthorpe Bourne, Lincolnshire.
Tel *01778 591093.*
Nestled just below Grimsthorpe
Castle, this early 18th-century inn
has been renovated into a high-class
pub-eaterie. Lovers of the outdoors
will enjoy the rambling grounds and
lakeside nature trail. Return to enjoy
the cosy atmosphere of the bar and
spend the night in one of the three
charmingly old-fashioned rooms.

Hathersage: Plough Inn
Leadmill Bridge, Hope Valley, Derbyshire.
Tel *01433 650319.*
Enjoying an idyllic location on the
banks of River Derwent, the
16th-century Plough Inn is set on
nine acres of private parklands and
offers the perfect summer stop off.
Fabulous food, great views and six
en suite rooms.

Lyddington: Old White Hart
51 Main St, Rutland. **Tel** *01572 821 703.*
Charming country inn with an
award-winning à la carte menu.
The Old White Hart has lovingly
retained the oak-beamed ceilings,
exposed brick walls and open fires
of the renovated 17th-century
stone building.

Mumby: Red Lion
Hogsthorpe Rd, Lincolnshire.
Tel *01507 490391.*
Run by the local Bateman's Brewery,
this pub is an excellent choice to
sample the flavours of Lincolnshire.
On the menu are traditional dishes
prepared with locally sourced
ingredients.

Nottingham: Cock and Hoop
25 High Pavement, Nottingham.
Tel *0115 852 3231.*
This traditional Victorian Ale
House offers a friendly, civilised
retreat where punters can enjoy
superb real ale and excellent
wines. The restaurant serves
excellent British home cooking.
Small dogs welcome.

Stamford: The George of Stamford
71 St Martins, Lincolnshire.
Tel *01780 750750.*
One of England's most famous
coaching inns, the George's bar,
restaurant and rooms are all rich in
history. Other than the award-
winning restaurant menu, there are
also more informal pub food choices
served in the ivy-covered courtyard
and in the York Bar.

Lancashire and The Lakes

Ambleside: The Britannia Inn
Elterwater, Cumbria. **Tel** *015394 37210.*
This traditional inn began life
as a farmhouse and cobbler's.
Standing on the village green
and surrounded by stunning
scenery, it is a delightful place to
unwind in after a day's walk. There
are also nine en suite rooms.

Clitheroe: The Shireburn Arms
Hurst Green, Lancashire.
Tel *01254 826678.*
Located in a picturesque village, this
characterful 17th-century inn was
one of author JRR Tolkien's favourite
haunts. The Shireburn Arms takes its
name from the family who built
Stonyhurst College and nearby
almshouses.

Downham: Assheton Arms
Downham, Lancashire.
Tel *01200 441227.*
Previously known as The George and
Dragon, this pub was renamed
following the elevation of the local
squire, Ralph Assheton, to Lord
Clitheroe. Facing the old church in a
pretty village of stone cottages, it
has even been featured in films and
television series. Specialities on the
menu include seafood and stone-
cooked steaks.

Hawkshead: Queen's Head Hotel
Main St, Cumbria. **Tel** *01539 436271.*
Situated at the heart of one
of the prettiest Lake District
villages, the superb food ranges
from simple sandwiches at the bar
to full meals at the restaurant.
William Wordsworth was schooled
in this village.

Hawkshead: Tower Bank Arms
Near Sawrey, Hawkshead, Cumbria.
Tel *01539 436334.*
Standing in a picturesque
village, this 17th-century inn
is very close to Hill Top, where
the legendary children's
book author Beatrix Potter
once lived. It even features in
one of her well-known stories,
The Tale of Jemima Puddle-Duck.
Three letting rooms.

Liverpool: Ship and Mitre
133 Dale St, Merseyside.
Tel *0151 236 0859.*
Close to the city centre, this
traditional pub has a reputation
for serving a wide range of
real ales. Hot food served daily.
Pub quiz on Thursdays.

Lonsdale: Snooty Fox Tavern
Main St, Kirkby Lonsdale, Cumbria.
Tel *01524 271308.*
A listed Jacobean coaching
inn in the centre of the
town, the Snooty Fox lies in
the picturesque Lune Valley.
Its rambling bars and
cobbled courtyard exude a
quaint charm.

Manchester: Lass o'Gowrie
36 Charles St. **Tel** *0161 273 6932.*
Famous for its cask ales, this lively
pub is popular with students. The
menu offers a range of freshly
cooked food. Entertainment comes
in the form of live music and
comedy nights.

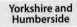

Yorkshire and Humberside

Askrigg: Kings Arms
Market Place, N Yorks. **Tel** *01969 650113.*
Fans of James Herriot's *All Creatures
Great and Small* will recognize this as
"The Drover's Arms". There is a broad
menu of appetizing food and five
real ales on tap in the bar.

Driffield: Wellington Inn
19 The Green, Lund, Driffield, E Yorks.
Tel *01377 217294.*
Just north of the minster town
of Beverley, this attractive pub
overlooks a charming village
green. Its fine food and friendly
service have won it an enviable
reputation.

Flamborough: The Seabirds
Tower St, Flamborough, E Yorks.
Tel *01262 850242.*
Near the bird sanctuary
(see pp404–5) on the chalk
cliffs of Flamborough Head,
this pub is popular with both
locals and walkers. The specialities
on the menu revolve around
fish, but a range of other dishes
is on offer too.

Lancaster: The Game Cock Inn
*The Green Austwick, via Lancaster, N
Yorks.* **Tel** *01524 251226.*
Close to the Yorkshire "Three Peaks",
this 17th-century coaching inn is the
focal point of the tiny village. The
award-winning food is home-
cooked by a French chef, and the
menus offer a range of options –
everything from a simple snack to an
elaborate dinner. Dog friendly and
rooms available.

Leyburn: The Blue Lion
E Witton, Leyburn, N Yorks.
Tel *01969 624273.*
An 18th-century coaching and
drover's inn within a charming
Wensleydale village, it retains many

original features. Open fires warm the rooms in winter. The food is traditional, but often with an unusual twist.

Pickering: New Inn
Cropton, Pickering, N Yorks.
Tel 01751 417330.
With an award-winning bewery in the backyard, it's no wonder that this popular pub on the edge of the Moors can get busy. The warren of rooms includes several characterful dining areas. Brewery tours are available.

Skipton: The Red Lion Hotel
By the Bridge, Burnsall, N Yorks.
Tel 01756 720204.
Before the bridge was built across the Wharfe at Burnsall, this 16th-century inn used to operate a ferry across the river. Today, it has a reputation for fine food and its generous range of real ales and wine. Dogs welcome.

Northumbria

Barnard Castle: The Morritt Arms
Greta Bridge, Barnard Castle, Co Durham. Tel 01833 627232.
Located between Carlisle and London, this 17th-century stone farmhouse eventually became a coaching inn. Dickens stayed here while writing *Nicholas Nickleby*. A mural by local artist John Gilroy depicts Dingley Dell from *The Pickwick Papers*.

Consett: Lord Crewe Arms
Blanchland, nr Consett, Co Durham.
Tel 01434 675469.
Built in 1160 as the abbot's house, this delightful hotel faces an unusual enclosed cobbled square at the heart of a very pretty village. Dine in the formal restaurant or opt for the more casual style and menu at the bar. Dog friendly. Accommodation available.

Cornhill on Tweed: Black Bull
Etal Village, Northumb. Tel 01890 820200.
Close to the Norman castle in this attractive estate village, the award-winning Black Bull is famous as the only thatched pub in Northumberland. Ingredients for the home-cooked food are sourced locally wherever possible and the menu always includes tasty vegetarian options.

Craster: Jolly Fisherman
Haven Hill, nr Alnwick, Northumb.
Tel 01665 576461.
Unassuming local pub with lovely sea views. Home-made crab soup and seafood are specialities.

Hedley on the Hill: The Feathers Inn
Stocksfield, Northumb.
Tel 01661 843607.
This family-run pub is popular with foodies, and serves traditional British fare. There is always a good selection of vegetarian dishes too and at least four guest ales on tap at the bar.

Hexham: Dipton Mill Inn
Dipton Mill Rd, Northumb.
Tel 01434 606577.
Originally an 18th-century mill, this family-run pub lies beside Dipton Burn in a wooded valley. The characterful bar stocks a range of beers brewed next door, and serves home-made food.

Kielder Water: The Pheasant Inn
Stannersburn, Falstone, Northumb.
Tel 01434 240382.
This 17th-century farmhouse has functioned as a pub for the last 250 years. Popular with visitors to Kielder Water and the surrounding forest. Meals are served at the bar, with the dining room opening for Sunday lunch and evening dinner.

Newton: Cook and Barker Inn
Morpeth, Northumberland.
Tel 01665 575234.
Once a forge, the inn got its name from its first proprietors, a Captain Cook who married a Miss Barker. Dine à la carte in the restaurant, where the original fireplace and well remain. Hearty pub meals are available at the bar. Accommodation available.

Seahouses: The Olde Ship Hotel
Northumb. Tel 01665 720200.
Situated above the tiny fishing harbour with a view across Farne Islands. Interesting nautical memorabilia decorate the bars. Pleasant beer garden. Accommodation is also available.

North Wales

Capel Curig: Bryn Tyrch Hotel
Conwy. Tel 01690 720223.
Pretty country inn in the heart of Snowdonia National Park, this is a popular stop-off point for walkers and climbers. Traditional Welsh cuisine. Great views of Mt Snowdon from the bar.

Ganllwyd: Tyn-y-groes
Dolgellau, Gwynedd. Tel 01341 440275.
Picturesque 16th-century inn in the heart of the Snowdonia National Park, Tyn-y-groes hotel and pub offers a friendly base for walking, mountain biking and fishing in the park.

Glanwydden: Queen's Head
Llandudno. Tel 01492 546570.
This bustling village pub has a reputed bar menu. Tables at the Queen's Head fill quickly so it is wise to arrive early. Great range of real ales.

Maentwrog: Grapes Hotel
Blaenau Ffestiniog, Gwynedd.
Tel 01766 590365.
Said to be haunted, this Grade II listed coaching inn serves fine ales and home-made cuisine in a stunning setting. Pitch pine pews, exposed stone walls and a roaring fire in winter all add to the effect.

Holywell: The Black Lion
Babell, Holywell, Flintshire.
Tel 01352 720239.
The Black Lion can trace its roots back to the 13th century. Today this quiet country pub, near the A55, is popular with diners and Real Ale enthusiasts.

Mold: Glasfryn
Raikes Lane, Sychdyn, Mold.
Tel 01352 750500.
Pretty village pub known for its theatre-going clientele (Theatre Clwyd is just next door), Glasfryn is a converted farmhouse pub with a warm welcome. Good menu and wine list.

Nant Gwynant: Pen-y-Gwryd
Gwynedd. Tel 01286 870211.
Hotel with a bustling pub in the shadow of Mt Snowdon. It is here that the 1953 Everest team holed up here while training for the ultimate ascent. Popular with walkers for its prime location, it also serves great food and drink.

Overton Bridge: Cross Foxes Inn
Erbistock, Wrexham, Clwyd.
Tel 01978 780380.
Fabulous food in a fabulous setting, Cross Foxes Inn, on the banks of the River Dee, is a very welcoming 18th-century coaching inn with a distinctive dining room. Good choice of real ales.

South and Mid-Wales

Aberaeron: Harbourmaster
Pen Cei, Ceredigion. Tel 01545 570755.
Fabulous hotel-pub overlooking the town's picturesque harbour. This blue-washed building serves tasty seafood such as Cardigan Bay crab and lobster, Aberaeron mackerel and several other such freshly caught delicacies in its restaurant. Also has 13 rooms.

Aberystwyth: Halfway Inn
Devils Bridge Rd, Pisgah.
Tel *01970 880631.*
Halfway between Aberystwyth and Devil's Bridge (hence the name), this large inn has steadily built a strong reputation for its fine food and fabulous real ale. Designated restaurant area away from the bar.

Brecon: Griffin at Felin Fach
Felin Fach, Brecon. **Tel** *01874 602111.*
Comfy leather sofas piled with soft cushions, roaring log fires in winter and a gorgeous garden for summer drinking and dining, the Griffin has it all. Food and ales are locally sourced (many ingredients are home-grown) and there's a great choice of fine wines, sherries and spirits too. Seven beautifully furnished and comfortable rooms complete the picture.

East Aberthaw: Blue Anchor
Barry, S Glamorgan. **Tel** *01446 750329.*
This refurbished, thatched pub in the seaside town of Barry is just 16 km (10 miles) from Cardiff, Blue Anchor has a friendly little bar as well as an elegant restaurant serving superior cuisine. Estuary walks nearby.

Hay-on-Wye: The Pandy Inn
Dorstone, Herefordshire.
Tel *01981 550273.*
A picturesque pub with rooms just over the border in Herefordshire, The Pandy Inn boasts a long and illustrious history. Supposedly the oldest pub in the county, it played host to Oliver Cromwell during the 17th-century Civil War. The restaurant seats 50 and serves wholesome, filling and tasty food. Dogs welcome.

Pembroke Ferry: Ferry Inn
Pembroke Dock. **Tel** *01646 682947.*
This early 17th-century inn serves delicious seafood in a prime location overlooking the harbour. Ferry Inn has an extensive waterfront terrace, which is a perfect setting for languid summer dining. Check out the specials board for locally caught fish.

Penallt: Boat Inn
Lone Lane. **Tel** *01600 712615.*
With a stunning location on the banks of River Wye, the beer garden of Boat Inn is a great place to relax with a chilled drink on a warm summer's day. Bar food is available. Access is via a footbridge.

Tintern: The Rose & Crown Inn
Monmouth Rd, Monmouthshire.
Tel *01291 689254.*
On the banks of the River Wye, in a

designated Area of Outstanding Natural Beauty, the Rose & Crown dates back to at least 1835. Walkers and dogs welcome.

Usk: Nag's Head
Twyn Sq. **Tel** *01291 672820.*
Atmospheric village pub with an extensive menu that is very reasonably priced for the size of the portions. The warmly welcoming establishment places an emphasis on the home-made food, but there is also a bustling bar area.

The Lowlands

Edinburgh: Café Royal Circle Bar
West Register St.
Tel *0131 556 1884.*
This atmospheric pub features tiled portraits of Scottish worthies and ornate chandeliers. Sink back into one of the comfortable leather chairs for a drink before making your way to the oyster bar and restaurant.

Elie: Ship Inn
The Harbour, Fife. **Tel** *01333 330 246.*
Quayside pub with nautical decor and attractive views. Summer barbecues.

Glasgow: Horseshoe
17–19 Drury St.
Tel *0141 248 6368.*
Busy Victorian pub with a long bar and plenty of period features. Good value bar snacks. Karaoke in the evenings.

Isle of Whithorn: Steam Packet
Isle of Whithorn, Dumfries & Galloway.
Tel *01988 500 334.*
Superb setting on a lovely harbour. Pleasant eating areas and a good selection of real ales. Boat trips from the harbour.

The Highlands and Islands

Applecross: Applecross Inn
Shore St, Wester Ross, Highland.
Tel *01520 744262.*
Spectacularly located beyond Britain's highest mountain pass, this pub overlooks the Isle of Skye. Local seafood is served, and there is music once a week in season.

Dundee: Fishermans Tavern
10–16 Fort St, Broughty Ferry, Tayside.
Tel *01382 775941.*
Choose between award-winning real ales and the extensive selection of malts, or savour a little of both. Good seafront and views of the Tay Rail Bridge. Rooms available.

Isle of Skye: Praban Bar at Eilean Iarmain. Isle Ornsay, Isle of Skye.
Tel *01471 833332.*
Welcoming hotel bar. Lots of malts and good bar food. Gorgeous setting.

Loch Lomond: Oak Tree Inn
Balmaha, (E side). **Tel** *01360 870357.*
Traditional stone inn with a well-stocked bar, restaurant and B&B. Sit by the roaring fires in winter and snack on the tasty bar food that is served all day.

Portsoy: The Shore Inn
The Old Harbour, Banffshire.
Tel *01261 842831.*
A 300-year-old seafaring inn nestled in a picturesque harbour. Traditional cask ale and a real open fire.

Ullapool: Ferry Boat Inn
Shore St, Highland. **Tel** *01854 612366.*
Good whiskies, bar lunches and fine views over the harbour. Coal fires and big windows overlooking the loch.

SHOPPING IN BRITAIN

While the West End of London (see pp152–5) is undeniably the most exciting place to shop in Britain, many of the regional towns and cities offer nearly as wide a range of goods. Moreover, regional shopping can be less stressful, less expensive, and remarkably varied, with craft studios, farm shops, street markets and factory outlets adding to the enjoyment of bargain-hunting. Britain is famous for its country clothing: wool, waxed cotton and tweed are all popular, along with classic prints such as Liberty or Laura Ashley and tartan. Other particularly British goods include antiques, floral soaps and scents, porcelain, glass and local crafts.

Antiques stall at Bermondsey Market

Shopping Hours

In general, shops in Britain open during the week from 9am or 10am, and close after 5pm or 6pm. Many town centre shops open on Sundays. Some stores open late for two evenings a week – Thursday and Friday in London's West End – while village shops may close at lunch-time, or for one afternoon each week. Market days vary from town to town.

How to Pay

Most large shops all over the UK accept well-known credit cards such as Access and VISA. Charge cards such as American Express or Diners Club are acceptable in some places, but markets and some small shops do not take credit cards. Traveller's cheques can be used in larger stores, though exchange rates for non-sterling cheques may be poor. Take your passport with you for identification. Few places accept cheques drawn on foreign banks. Cash is still the most popular way to pay for small purchases.

Rights and Refunds

If something you buy is defective, you are entitled to a refund, provided you have kept your receipt as proof of purchase and return the goods in the same condition as when you bought them, preferably in the same packaging. This may not always apply to sale goods clearly marked as seconds, imperfect, or shop-soiled. Inspect these carefully before you buy. You do not have to accept a credit note in place of a cash refund.

Annual Sales

Sales take place during January, and in June and July, when nearly every shop cuts prices to get rid of old stock. But you may find special offers at any time of the year. Some shops begin winter sales just before Christmas. Department stores and fashion houses have some excellent bargains for keen shoppers; one of the most prestigious sales is at Harrods (see p101), where queues form long before opening time.

Sign for the Lanes, Brighton (see p179)

VAT and Tax-Free Shopping

Value added tax (VAT) is charged on most goods and services sold in Britain – exceptions are food, books and children's clothes. It is usually included in the advertised price. Visitors from outside the European Union who stay less than three months may claim this tax back. Take your passport with you when you go shopping. You must complete a form in the shop when you buy goods and give a copy to the customs authorities when you leave the country. You may have to show your goods as proof of purchase. If you arrange to have goods shipped from the store, VAT should be deducted before you pay.

Out-of-Town Shopping Centres

These large complexes, built in the style of North American malls, have also opened around Britain. The advantages of car access and cheap parking are undeniable, and most centres are accessible by public transport too. The centres usually feature popular high street stores, with facilities such as cafés, crèches, restaurants and cinemas.

Department Stores

A few big department stores, such as Harrods, are only found in London, but others have provincial branches. John Lewis, for example, has shops all over the country. It sells a huge range of fabrics, clothing and household items, combining quality service with good value. Marks & Spencer, with branches

A traditional shop front in Stonegate, York *(see p408)*

in most major towns and cities in Britain, is famed for its good-value clothing and pre-prepared food. Debenhams and British Home Stores (BHS) are other well-known general stores with inexpensive clothing and home furnishings. Habitat is a reputable supplier of modern furniture. The sizes of all these stores, and the range of stock they carry, differs from region to region.

Clothes Shops

Once again, the larger cities such as London, Manchester, Birmingham and Bristol have the widest range, from *haute couture* to cheap and cheerful items ready-made. Shopping for clothing in the regions, however, can often be less tiring. Many towns popular with tourists – Oxford, Bath and York for instance – have independently owned clothes shops where you are likely to receive a more personal service. Or you could try one of the chain stores in any high street such as Laura Ashley or Next for smart, reasonably priced clothes, and Topshop, Oasis and H&M for younger and cheaper fashions.

Supermarkets and Foodshops

Supermarkets are a good way to shop for food. The range and quality of items is usually excellent. Several large chains compete for market share, and as a result prices are generally lower than in smaller shops. Sainsbury, Tesco, Asda, Morrisons and Waitrose are some of the national names.

Local Teesdale cheeses

The smaller town-centre shops such as bakeries, green-grocers or farm shops, may give you a more interesting choice of regional produce, and a more personal service.

Souvenir, Gift and Museum Shops

Buying presents is a must for most travellers. Most reputable, large stores can arrange freight of high-value items. If you want to buy things you can carry back in your suitcase, the choice is wide. You can buy attractive,

The Mustard Shop *(see p205)*, Norwich

well-made, portable craft items all over the country, especially in areas tourists are likely to visit. For slightly more unusual presents, have a look in museum shops and the gifts available in National Trust *(see p33)* and English Heritage *(see p623)* properties.

Second-Hand and Antique Shops

Britain's long history means there are many interesting artifacts to be found. A visit to any of Britain's stately homes will reveal a passion for antiques. Most towns have an antique or bric-a-brac (miscellaneous second-hand items) shop or two. Look for auctions – tourist information centres *(see pp620–21)* can help you to locate them. You may like to visit a car boot sale or charity shop in the hope of picking up a bargain.

Book stall, Hay-on-Wye, Wales *(see p465)*

Markets

Large towns and cities usually have a central covered market which operates most weekdays, selling everything from fresh produce to pots and pans. The information under each town entry in this guide lists market days. Many towns hold weekly markets in the main square, while Farmers' Markets have become increasingly popular and are a good place to source fresh, organic produce from British farms.

ENTERTAINMENT IN BRITAIN

London is without a doubt the entertainment capital of Britain *(see pp156–9)*, with a whole wealth of shows, films and concerts to choose from, but many regional theatres, opera houses and concert halls also have varied programmes. Edinburgh, Manchester, Leeds, Birmingham, and Bristol in particular have a lot to offer and there are a number of summer arts festivals around the country such as those at Bath and Aldeburgh *(see pp66–7)*. Ticket prices vary but are usually cheaper outside the capital and when booked in advance.

Sources of Information

In London, check the listings magazines, such as *Time Out*, or the *Evening Standard*, London's evening newspaper (both free). All of the highbrow newspapers *(see p631)* provide comprehensive arts reviews and listings of the cultural events and shows throughout the country. Local newspapers, libraries, or tourist offices *(see p621)* can supply details of regional events. Specialist magazines such as *NME* give up-to-date news of the pop music scene and are available from any newsagent.

Theatres

Britain has an enduring theatrical tradition dating back to Shakespeare *(see pp328–9)* and beyond. All over the country, amateurs and professionals tread the boards in auditoriums, pubs, clubs and village halls. Production and performance standards are generally high, and British actors have an international reputation. London is the place to enjoy theatre at its most varied and glamorous *(see p156)*. The West End alone has more than 50 theatres *(see p157)* ranging from elaborate Edwardian, to Modernist-style buildings such as the National Theatre on the South Bank.

In Stratford-upon-Avon, the Royal Shakespeare Company presents a year-round programme of Shakespeare, as well as avant-garde and experimental plays. Bristol also has a long dramatic tradition, the Theatre Royal *(see p260)* is the oldest working theatre in Britain. Some of the best productions outside the capital can be found at the West Yorkshire Playhouse in Leeds, the Royal Exchange in Manchester *(see p376)* and the Traverse in Edinburgh. Open-air theatre ranges from the free street entertainment found in many city centres, to student performances on the grounds of university colleges, or a

Street entertainer

production at Cornwall's clifftop amphitheatre, the Minack Theatre *(see p280)*. Every fourth year, York also stages a series of open-air medieval mystery plays called the York Cycle.

Perhaps the liveliest theatrical tradition in Britain is the Edinburgh Festival *(see p513)*. Ticket availability varies from show to show. For a midweek matinee, you may be able to buy a ticket at the door, but for the more popular West End shows tickets may have to be booked weeks or months in advance. You can book through agencies and some travel agents, and most hotels will organize tickets for you. Booking fees are often charged. Beware of tickets offered by touts *(see p71)* – these may be counterfeit. There are no age restrictions in Britain's theatres.

Music

A diverse musical repertoire can be found in a variety of venues. Church choral music is a national tradition, and many churches and cathedrals host concerts. London, Manchester, Birmingham, Liverpool, Bristol and Bournemouth all have their own excellent orchestras. Major cities also have grand opera houses.

Rock, jazz, folk and country-and-western concerts are staged periodically in pubs and clubs. Wales has a strong musical tradition; northern England is known for its booming brass and silver bands; and Scotland has its famous bag-pipers *(see p484)*.

The Buxton Opera House, the Midlands

The multiplex Vue West End cinema, Leicester Square, London

Cinemas

The latest films can be seen in any large town. Check the local papers or the tourist office to find out what is on.

Luxurious multi-screen cinemas are now taking over from the local, single-screen cinemas. In larger cities a more diverse range of films is often on offer including foreign-language productions. These tend to be shown at arts or repertory cinemas. Mainstream English-speaking films are usually shown by the big chains. Age limits apply to certain films. Young children are allowed to see any feature film which is graded with a U (universal) or PG (parental guidance) certificate. Cinema prices vary widely; some are cheaper at off-peak times, such as Mondays or afternoons. For new releases it is advisable to book in advance.

Clubs

Most cities have some sort of club scene, though London has the most famous venues (see p159). These may feature live music, discos, or DJ or dance performances. Some insist on dress codes or members only, and most have doormen, or "bouncers". Apart from the major cities, Brighton and Bristol also have lively clubs.

Dance

This covers a multitude of activities: everything from classical ballet and house music to traditional English Morris dancing or the Scottish Highland fling, which you may come upon in pubs and villages around the country.

Dance halls are rarer than they were, but ballroom dancing is alive and well. Other dance events you may find are ceilidhs (pronounced kay-lee), which is Celtic dancing and music; dinner or tea dances and square dancing.

Birmingham is home to the Birmingham Royal Ballet and is the best place to see performances outside London. Avant-garde contemporary dance is also performed.

Gay

Most large communities will have some gay meeting places, mostly bars and clubs. You can find out about them from publications such as the free *Pink Paper* or *Gay Times* on sale in some newsagents, and in gay bars and clubs. London's gay life is centred around Soho (see p84) with its many European-style cafés and bars. Outside London, the most active gay scenes are in Manchester and Brighton. Gay Pride is the largest free outdoor festival in Europe.

Three revellers, Gay Pride Festival

Children

London offers children a positive goldmine of fun, excitement and adventure, though it can be expensive. From the traditional sights to something more unusual such as a discovery centre, London has a wide range of activities, many interactive, to interest children of all ages. The weekly magazine *Time Out* has details of children's events.

Outside London, activities for children range from nature trails to fun fairs. Your local tourist office or the local library will have information on things to do with children.

Pirate Ship, Chessington World of Adventures, Surrey

Theme Parks

Theme parks in Britain are enjoyed by children of all ages. Alton Towers has conventional rides plus a motor museum. Chessington World of Adventures is a huge complex south of London. Based on a zoo, it includes nine themed areas, such as Forbidden Kingdom and Pirates Cove. Legoland is fantastic for younger children. Thorpe Park is a large, watery theme park with roller-coasters. Not for the faint-hearted, it is aimed at older children and adults.

Alton Towers
Alton, Staffordshire. **Tel** 0871 222 3330.
W altontowers.com

Chessington World of Adventures
Leatherhead Rd, Chessington, Surrey.
Tel 0871 663 4477.
W chessington.co.uk

Legoland
Winkfield Rd, Windsor, Berkshire.
Tel 0871 222 2001.
W legoland.co.uk

Thorpe Park
Staines Rd, Chertsey, Surrey. **Tel** 0871
663 1673. W thorpepark.com

SPECIALIST HOLIDAYS AND OUTDOOR ACTIVITIES

Britain offers a wide variety of special interest holidays and courses, where you can learn a new sport or skill, practise an activity you enjoy, or simply have fun and meet people. If you prefer less structured activities, there are numerous options to choose from, such as walking in Britain's national parks, pony trekking in Wales, surfing in Cornwall or skiing in Scotland. There are also several spectator sports for those who like to watch rather than participate, including Premier League football, test match cricket and historic horse races.

Arvon Foundation writing week at Totleigh Barton in Devon

Special Interest Holidays

There are a number of special interest holidays and residential courses available in Great Britain. One advantage of this type of vacation is that you can attend a course alone, and yet have plenty of congenial company – most people are delighted to meet others who share their interests. Whatever your passion, you are likely to come across a holiday package that suits your needs.

Centres such as **Wye Valley Art Centre** in Gloucestershire and **West Dean College**, West Sussex, offer engaging, resid-ential courses in arts and crafts. These can range from familiar activities such as drawing and painting to more esoteric subjects such as mosaic art and glass engraving. Those interested in writing can enroll at the **Arvon Foundation**, which organizes week-long courses in fiction, poetry, songwriting and TV drama at four rural retreats in Devon, Shropshire, West Yorkshire and Invernesshire. The **Ashburton**

Cookery School in Devon and **Cookery at the Grange** in Somerset offer fun cookery courses with lots of hands-on involvement. Non-carnivores might try the Vegetarian Society's **Cordon Vert School** in Cheshire, which has innovative cookery courses catering to chefs at all levels – from complete beginners to talented amateurs.

Companies such as **Hidden Britain Tours**, **Inscape Tours** and the **Back-Roads Touring Company** provide themed holidays. History lovers can opt for a tour of King Arthur's Country or Shakespeare's England. Other tours designed for motor enthusiasts, garden lovers or fans of rock and roll are also available.

The prices of such holidays include expert guidance, transport, entry fees to attractions and accommodation, which could be anything from a farm-house to a medieval castle.

Walking

Walking is a popular activity in Britain and a network of long-distance footpaths and shorter routes criss-crosses the country (see pp40–41). It is also an excellent way to experience the spectacular variety of the British landscape, either by yourself or with a group. An advantage is that most routes are away from major tourist sites and often pass through picturesque villages that are off the beaten track.

The **Ramblers' Association** is Britain's main walking body, and its website provides useful information on most routes and walking areas. It also publishes a range of books, including *Walk Britain*, which lists many good walks as well as suitable hotels, bed and breakfasts and hostels along the way.

There is no shortage of companies providing guided and self-guided holidays for walkers. The cost of these holiday packages should cover accommodation, transport and detailed route guides.

Walking on Holyhead Mountain near South Stack Anglesey, Wales

Ramblers' Countrywide Holidays offers guided group walks through some of the country's most splendid landscapes. **Sherpa Expeditions** has a variety of self-led walks. Pick a challenging 15-day coast-to-coast walk, or a more leisurely ramble along South Downs Way. Individual companies will advise you on the level of fitness required and the type of clothing and footwear that will be needed.

If you are planning to walk on your own, especially in remote areas, remember that it is essential to not only be well equipped, but to also leave details of your route with someone.

Mountain biking in Yorkshire

Cycling

The country's tranquil lanes, bridleways and designated tracks are perfect for cyclists who want to explore the back roads of Britain. Depending on your level of fitness, you may opt for demanding routes through mountainous areas such as the magnificent West Highland Way in Scotland *(see p498)*. Those who would like to take it easy can enjoy a relaxed tour along Devon's lanes and take the opportunity to stop off for a sinfully rich cream tea.

Country Lanes offers a good variety of guided holidays in small groups around the Ωwest of England. The price includes an experienced leader, high quality bicycle equipment, accommodation, meals and entry to attractions along the way.

Compass Holidays and **Wheely Wonderful Cycling** concentrate on self-led tours, with routes throughout the country. They also provide bicycles, accommodation, detailed route maps, (including details of pubs, cafés and places of interest along the way) and appropriate luggage transport. Such self-guided bicycling holidays are ideal for families or groups of friends.

If you wish to organize your own cycling holiday, you may contact the **Cyclists' Touring Club**, which is Britain's main recreational cycling body, and **Sustrans**, the organization that formed the National Cycle Network. Both can provide a wealth of information about cycling in the country, including advice on matters such as bringing a bike into Britain, taking your bike on the train and the rules of the road. *Cycling in the UK*, the official guide book for the National Cycle Network, has route details and maps for many of the best rides, and also offers tips on how to hire a bike and what to do along the way.

Horse Riding and Pony Trekking

There are good riding centres in most parts of Britain, but certain areas are especially suitable for this invigorating activity. The best of these locations include the New Forest *(see p172)*, the South Downs *(see p185)*, the Yorkshire Dales National Park *(see pp388–90)* and the Brecon Beacons on the border between Wales and England *(see pp472–3)*.

Pony trekking holidays are also becoming very popular, and generally include basic training, a guide, meals and accommodation. These vacations are perfect for novice riders and children since the ponies are very well-trained and rarely proceed above a canter. The **British Horse Society** has all the information on where to ride as well as a list of approved riding schools that offer training. You can also consult the **Equine**

Horse riding on a country bridleway *(see p41)*

Tourism website for information on riding centres and horse-riding holidays. National park information offices can also provide details of the many equestrian centres that organize riding holidays in or around national parks.

Golf

Over a quarter of Britain's 2,000-odd golf clubs are in Scotland, which is unsurprising given that the ancient game was invented here. The first formal club was established in Edinburgh in 1744.

Today, the best known clubs are Carnoustie and St Andrews in Scotland, Royal St George's in England and Celtic Manor in Wales. These high-profile clubs only admit players above a certain handicap. Most other clubs, however, are more relaxed and welcome visitors.

Green fees vary greatly, as do the facilities offered by various clubs. Some clubs may ask to see a valid handicap certificate before they allow a player on the course. Failing that, a letter of introduction from a home club may be sufficient.

Specialist operators such as **Golf Vacations UK** and **Great Golf Holidays** can smooth the way to the first hole considerably by booking golf packages. They will organize travel and accommodation, reserve tee times and pay the green fees. They will also help you get temporary membership of a club if required.

If you wish to go it alone, the **Golf Club of Great Britain** can provide information on where to play. They also have an affiliated website for nonresidents of the UK.

Surfing

The best areas for surfing are in the West Country and South Wales. Tuition is available at many resorts, and equipment can be hired.

The Cornwall-based **British Surfing Association** runs its own surf school with professional coaching catering to a range of abilities, from novices to advanced competition surfers. Other companies that offer good surfing courses include **Surf South West** in Devon and the **Welsh Surfing Federation Surf School** in South Wales.

Sailing in Cardigan Bay, Welsh coast

Boating and Sailing

The British are extremely enthusiastic about boating and sailing. The network of rivers, lakes and canals ensures an abundance of boating sites. Many excellent choices are available – the Isle of Wight and the south coast are full of pleasure crafts. Several inland areas such as the Lake District (see pp358–73) are among the most widely favoured. Canal cruising is also very popular (see p641) and the Norfolk Broads (see p202) provide one of the best inland boating experiences. Check with the **Broads Authority** for details.

Many sailing courses are available. The **Royal Yachting Association** can provide lists of approved courses and training centres around Britain. One of the most trusted is Dorset's **Weymouth & Portland National Sailing Academy**, which has a range of courses to suit all ages and levels of ability. The **Falmouth School of Sailing** in Cornwall is a privately owned

sailing and powerboat school, which conducts lessons in the enclosed, safe waters of the Fal Estuary. Courses include basic "taster sessions", one-to-one tuition for adults and children, as well as group lessons.

Skiing

Facilities for skiing are limited in the UK, especially since the weather is rather unreliable. However, skiing enthusiasts can head for Scotland, which has a range of challenging slopes. **Ski Scotland**, the official ski site of the Scottish Tourist Board, has information about ski packages, accommodation, up-to-date weather conditions and details of the main ski areas, including the Cairngorms and the Nevis Range. **Snowsport Scotland**, the governing body for all Scottish snowsports, provides information on other snow-based activities such as Nordic skiing and snowboarding.

Fishing

Fishing, both on the sea and in rivers, is one of Britain's most popular participation sports. Regulations, however, are strict and can be rather complicated. It is advisable to check for details about rod licences, close seasons and other restrictions at tourist offices or tackle shops, or with the **Angling Trust** in Leominster.

The best game fishing (trout and salmon) is in the West Country, the Northeast, Wales and Scotland. Also, there are several websites with links to specialist operators who arrange fishing holidays.

Anglers fishing from the pier at Portsmouth Harbour

Spectator sports

Football (soccer) is a passion for a large section of the population. The English Premier League is run by the **Football Association** and is home to some of the world's top clubs, including **Manchester United** (see p379), **Arsenal FC** and **Chelsea FC**. The domestic football season runs from August to May. Tickets for Premier League games can be expensive and difficult to obtain, but it is worth attempting to get hold of returned or unsold tickets directly from the clubs.

The main tennis event of the year is Wimbledon, which is held at the **All England Lawn Tennis Club (AELTC)** in London. This two-week event takes place in the last week of June and the first week of July. The tournament sparks off a period of tennis fever in England, especially when British players such as Andy Murray progress in the competition. Most tickets for Centre Court are allocated by a public ballot. Check the official website of the AELTC for details on how to procure tickets. Around 6,000 tickets are available on the day of play (payment by cash only), except for the final four days of the tournament.

Rugby Football is administered by the **Rugby Football Union** and also has a good following. Games are played in cities such as Edinburgh, London and Cardiff.

Cricket, the English national game, is played from April to September. Tickets for country matches are relatively cheap. International test matches are played on historic grounds such as **Surrey County Cricket Club's** ground at the Oval in London, and the **Yorkshire County Cricket Club** situated at Headingley in Leeds.

Both steeplechasing and flat-racing are very popular, and betting is big business. The Grand National is the best-known steeplechase and runs at **Aintree Racecourse** in early April. The main flat-race meeting is **Royal Ascot**, which takes place in Berkshire towards the end of June.

DIRECTORY

Special Interest Holidays

Arvon Foundation
42A Buckingham Palace Rd, London SW1.
Tel 020 7324 2554.
W arvonfoundation.org

Ashburton Cookery School
Old Exeter Rd, Ashburton, Devon TQ13. Tel 01364 652784. W ashburton cookeryschool.co.uk

Back-Roads Touring Company
107 Power Rd, London W4. Tel 020 8987 0990.
W backroadstouring. co.uk

Cookery at the Grange
The Grange, Whatley, Frome, Somerset BA11.
Tel 01373 836579.
W cookeryatthegrange. co.uk

Cordon Vert School
The Vegetarian Society, Parkdale, Dunham Rd, Altrincham, Cheshire WA14. Tel 0161 9252015.
W cordonvert.co.uk

Hidden Britain Tours
28 Chequers Rd, Basingstoke, Hampshire RG21 7PU. Tel 01256 814222. W hidden britaintours.co.uk

Inscape Tours
12a Castlebar Hill, London W5. Tel 020 8566 7539.
W inscapetours.co.uk

West Dean College
West Dean, Chichester, W Sussex PO18. Tel 01243 811301. W westdean. org.uk

Wye Valley Art Centre
Llandogo, Monmouthshire NP25.
Tel 01594 530214.
W wyearts.co.uk

Walking

Ramblers' Association
2nd Floor, Camelford Hse, 87–90 Albert Embankment, London SE1. Tel 020 7339 8500.
W ramblers.org.uk

Ramblers' Countrywide Holidays
Lemsford Mill, Lemsford Village AL8. Tel 01707 331133. W ramblers countrywide.co.uk

Sherpa Expeditions
81 Craven Gdns, Wimbledon, London SW19. Tel 020 8577 2717. W sherpa-walking-holidays.co.uk

Cycling

Compass Holidays
Cheltenham Spa Railway Station, Queens Rd, Cheltenham, Gloucestershire GL51. Tel 01242 250642. W compass-holidays.com

Country Lanes
Brokenhurst New Forest.
Tel 01590 622627.
W countrylanes.co.uk

Cyclists' Touring Club
Parklands, Railton Rd, Guildford GU2.
Tel 0844 736 8450.

Sustrans
National Cycle Network Centre, 2 Cathedral Sq, College Green, Bristol BS1. Tel 01179 268893.
W sustrans.org.uk

Wheely Wonderful Cycling
Petchfield Farm, Elton, Ludlow, Shropshire SY8.
Tel 01568 770755.

Horse Riding and Pony Trekking

British Horse Society
Abbey Park, Stareton, Kenilworth, Warwickshire CV8. Tel 0844 848 1666.
W bhs.org.uk

Equine Tourism
Holt Ball, Luccombe, Somerset TA24.
Tel 01643 862785.
W equinetourism.co.uk

Golf

Golf Club of Great Britain
338 Hook Rd, Chessington, Surrey KT9.
Tel 020 8391 4666.
W golfclubgb.co.uk

Golf Vacations UK
Tel 01228 598098.
W golfvacationsuk.com

Great Golf Holidays
Tel 01637 879991.
W greatgolfholidays. com

Surfing

British Surfing Association
The International Surfing Centre, Fistral Beach, Newquay, Cornwall TR7.
Tel 01637 876474.
W sup-surfing.org.uk

Surf South West
PO Box 39, Croyde, N Devon EX33. Tel 01271 890400. W surf southwest.com

Welsh Surfing Federation Surf School
The Barn, The Croft, Llangennith, Swansea SA3. Tel 01792 386426.
W wsfsurfschool.co.uk

Boating and Sailing

Broads Authority
Yare House, 62–64 Thorpe Rd, Norwich NR1. Tel 01603 610734. W broads-authority.gov.uk

Falmouth School of Sailing
Grove Place, Falmouth, Cornwall TR11. Tel 01326 211311. W falmouth-school-of-sailing.co.uk

Royal Yachting Association
RYA House, Ensign Way, Southampton, Hampshire SO31. Tel 023 8060 4100.
W rya.org.uk

Weymouth & Portland National Sailing Academy
Osprey Quay, Portland, Dorset DT5. Tel 01305 866 000. W wpnsa.org.uk

Skiing

Ski Scotland
W ski.visitscotland.com

Snowsport Scotland
Caledonian House, South Gyle, Edinburgh EH12.
Tel 0131 625 4405.
W snowsportscotland. org

Fishing

Angling Trust
6 Rainbow St, Leominster, Herefordshire HR6 8DQ.
Tel 0844 770 0616.
W anglingtrust.net

Fishing Net
W fishingnet.com

Fishing UK
W fishing.co.uk

Spectator Sports

Aintree Racecourse
Ormskirk Rd, Aintree, Liverpool L9. Tel 0151 523 2600. W aintree.co.uk

All England Lawn Tennis Club (AELTC)
Church Rd, Wimbledon, SW19. Tel 020 8944 1066.
W wimbledon.org

Arsenal FC
Emirates Stadium, 2 Gilders Way, Highbury, London N5. Tel 020 7619 5000. W arsenal.com

Chelsea FC
Stamford Bridge, Fulham Rd, London SW6.
Tel 0871 984 1955.
W chelseafc.com

Football Association
16 Lancaster Gate, London W2. Tel 0844 980 8200. W thefa.com

Manchester United
Sir Matt Busby Way, Old Trafford, Manchester M16.
Tel 0161 868 8000.
W manutd.com

Royal Ascot
Ascot Racecourse, Ascot, Berkshire SL5. Tel 0844 346 3000. W ascot.co.uk

Rugby Football Union
Rugby Rd, Twickenham, Middlesex TW1. Tel 020 8892 8877. W rfu.com

Surrey County Cricket Club
The Kia Oval, Kennington, London SE11. Tel 0844 375 1845. W kiaoval.com

Yorkshire County Cricket Club
Headingley Carnegie Cricket Ground, Leeds LS6. Tel 0871 971 1222.
W yorkshireccc.com

SURVIVAL
GUIDE

PRACTICAL INFORMATION

Every year, millions of people from all over the world seek out what the British often take for granted: the country's ancient history, colourful pageantry, spectacularly varied countryside and wonderful coastline. The range of facilities on offer to visitors in Britain has improved considerably over the past few years. Be aware that prices vary within Britain, and regional differences can be very noticeable. London, not surprisingly, is the most expensive city, and the knock-on effect extends to most of southern England, Britain's most affluent region. Food, accommodation, entertainment, transport and consumer items in shops are generally cheaper in other parts of the country. It is always advisable to plan your trip before you travel and to enjoy Britain fully, it is important to be aware of the basics of British life: when to visit, what to take, how to get around, where to find information and what to do if things go wrong.

Weymouth Beach, Dorset, on a busy public holiday weekend

When to Go

Britain's temperate climate does not produce many temperature extremes (see p72). However, weather patterns shift constantly, and the climate can vary widely in places only a short distance apart. Since it is impossible to predict rain or shine reliably in any season, be sure to pack a mix of warm and cool clothes and an umbrella, irrespective of when you plan to visit. Always get an up-to-date weather forecast before you set off on foot to remote mountain areas or moorland. Walkers can be surprised by the weather, and the Mountain Rescue services are often called out due to unexpectedly severe conditions. Weather reports can be found on television and radio, as well as in newspapers. They can also be provided by phone services (see p630).

A sign for the Mountain Rescue

Britain's towns and cities are all-year destinations, but many attractions are open only between Easter and October. The main family holiday months, July and August, and public holidays (see p69) are always busy, and some hotels are full around Christmas. Spring and autumn offer a good compromise between reasonably good weather and a relative lack of crowds.

Visas and Passports

A valid passport is required to enter Britain. Visitors from the European Union (EU), the United States, Canada, New Zealand and Australia do not need visas to enter the country. Visit www.ukvisas.gov.uk to check your visa status. Visas can be arranged online at www.fco.gov.uk. When you arrive at any British air- or seaport, you will find separate queues at immigration control – one set for EU nationals, and another for everyone else.

Residents of the EU are allowed to work in Britain with no permit, while the Youth Mobility Scheme offers places to young people from other participating countries who wish to experience life in the UK. North American students can get a Blue Card through their university. This enables them to work for up to six months, but it must be obtained before arrival in Britain. BUNAC (see p624) is a student club that organizes exchange schemes for students to work abroad.

Customs Information

Britain is part of the European Union, so anyone who arrives here from a member country can pass through a blue channel. However, random checks are still being made to detect entry of prohibited goods, particularly drugs, indecent material and weapons. Never, under any circumstances, carry luggage or parcels through customs for someone else. For most EU members there is no limit to the amount of excise goods (such as tobacco or alcohol) that can be brought into Britain, provided these are for your own use. This legislation does not apply to some new member states; check if you are unsure.

Travellers entering from outside the EU have to pass through customs channels. Go through the green channel if you have nothing to declare over the customs allowances, and use the red channel if you have goods to declare. If you are unsure of importation restrictions, go through the red channel. On departure, non-EU residents can apply for a VAT refund on goods bought in Britain (see p610).

Britain is free of rabies, and no live animals may be imported without a permit. Any animals found will be impounded and may be destroyed.

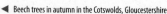
◀ Beech trees in autumn in the Cotswolds, Gloucestershire

Tourist Information

Tourist information is available in many towns and public places, including airports and main rail and coach stations, and some places of historical interest. Look out for the tourist information symbol, which can indicate anything from a large and busy central tourist bureau to a simple kiosk or even simply an information board in a parking area.

Tourist offices will be able to help you on almost anything in their area, including places of interest and guided walks. Both the regional and national tourist boards produce comprehensive lists of local attractions and registered accommodation options. A range of leaflets is generally available for free at tourist offices, but a charge may be made for more detailed maps and booklets. For route planning, consider the excellent large-format motoring atlases produced by both the RAC and the AA *(see p637)*. For rural exploration, Ordnance Survey maps are ideal (www. ordnancesurvey.co.uk).

The most common English tourist information sign

It's wise to book accommodation well in advance of your visit. **VisitBritain** is a good resource for this. Out of season, you should have few problems booking transport, restaurants or even theatre performances at short notice, but in the high season, if you have set your heart on a luxury hotel, popular West End show or specific tour, you should try to book in advance. Contact VisitBritain in your country, or see a travel agent for advice and general information.

Opening Hours

Outside of London and other main cities, many businesses and shops still close on Sundays, even though trading is legal. During the week, opening hours are generally from 9 or 10am until 5 or 5:30pm. Shop hours may include a late opening one evening a week, usually Thursday. In big city centres, particularly London, shops are generally open longer – often until 7pm and seven days a week.

Museums in London tend to operate late opening hours one day a week, while those outside the capital may be less flexible, sometimes closing in the morning or for one day a week, often on Mondays.

On public holidays, also known as bank holidays in Britain, banks, offices and some shops, restaurants and attractions often close, and transport networks run a limited service.

DIRECTORY

Customs and Immigration

UK Border Agency
🆆 ukba.homeoffice.gov.uk/customs-travel

Home Office
Border & Immigration Agency, Lunar House, 40 Wellesley Rd, Croydon, Surrey. **Tel** 0870 606 7766. 🆆 **ind.homeoffice. gov.uk**
For information on import or export restrictions, visit 🆆 hmrc.gov.uk

Embassies and Consulates

Australian High Commission
Australia House, Strand, London WC2.
Tel 020 7379 4334.
🆆 uk.embassy.gov.au

Canadian High Commission
Macdonald House, Grosvenor Square, London W1.
Tel 020 7258 6600.
🆆 canada.gc.ca

New Zealand High Commission
New Zealand House, 80 Haymarket, London SW1.
Tel 020 7930 8422.
🆆 nzembassy.com

United States Embassy
24 Grosvenor Sq, London W1.
Tel 020 7499 9000.
🆆 usembassy.org.uk

International Tourist Information

VisitBritain Australia
🆆 visitbritain.com

VisitBritain Canada
🆆 visitbritain.com

VisitBritain Ireland
🆆 enjoyengland.ie

VisitBritain USA
🆆 visitbritain.com

Regional Tourist Boards

Cumbria
Tel 01539 822222.
🆆 golakes.co.uk

East of England
Tel UK: 0333 320 4202; International: +44 1953 888021. 🆆 **visiteastof england.com**

East Midlands
🆆 discover eastmidlands.com

London
Tel 0870 156 6366.
🆆 visitlondon.com

Northumbria
🆆 visitnortheast england.com

Northwest
🆆 visitnorthwest.com

Scotland
Tel 0845 859 1006.
🆆 visitscotland.com

Southeast
🆆 visitsoutheast england.com

Southwest
Tel 0117 230 1262.
🆆 swtourism.org.uk

Wales
Tel 0870 830 0306.
🆆 visitwales.co.uk

Yorkshire and the Humber Region
🆆 yorkshire.com

A Cotswolds church, one of hundreds of parish churches open to the public free of charge

eligibility will be required when purchasing a ticket. Visitors from overseas may buy a Great British Heritage Pass, which gives access to more than 600 sights including Stonehenge (see pp266–7) and Warwick Castle (see pp326–7). The pass is also available as a Family Pass. Families of two adults and up to three children, aged 5–15, can benefit. The pass can be bought from VisitBritain offices abroad. In the UK, it is sold at the Britain Visitor Centre in Lower Regent Street in London, as well as at some ports of entry and tourist information centres across Britain (see p621).

Public Conveniences

Although some old-style supervised public toilets still exist, these have been largely replaced by the modern, free-standing, coin-operated "superloos". Main railway stations usually have toilet facilities for which there is sometimes a small charge. Young children should never use these toilets on their own.

Tipping, Etiquette and Smoking

In Britain it is the norm to tip taxi drivers and waiting staff in restaurants. Between 10 and 15 per cent is standard. Many restaurants automatically add a service charge to the bill, so do check before leaving a tip. It is not customary to leave a tip when buying a drink in a pub or bar.

Smoking is now forbidden in all of Britain's public indoor spaces, including pubs, restaurants, nightclubs, transport systems, taxis, theatres and cinemas. For advice on smoking-related issues, contact **ASH** (Action on Smoking and Health). It is illegal to buy cigarettes if you are under the age of 18.

Age restrictions also apply in pubs and bars, where you must be over 18 to be served. Some bars are for over-21s only, and patrons may be asked for identification before being served.

Admission Prices

Admission fees for museums and sights vary widely, from a nominal 50p to in excess of £10 for the more popular attractions. Many of the major national museums are free, although donations are encouraged. The same is true of a few local authority museums and art galleries. Some sights are in private hands, run either as a commercial venture or on a charitable basis. Stately homes open to the public may still belong to the gentry who have lived there for centuries; a charge is usually made to offset the enormous costs of upkeep. Many of these houses, such as Woburn Abbey (see p234), have added safari parks or garden centres to attract larger numbers of visitors.

Great British Heritage Pass

Britain's thousands of small parish churches are among the country's greatest architectural treasures. None of these churches charges an entrance fee, although you may find that some are locked because of vandalism. Increasingly, many of the great cathedrals expect a donation from visitors.

Reductions are often available for groups, senior citizens, children and students. Proof of

Travellers with Special Needs

The facilities on offer for disabled visitors to Britain are steadily improving. Recently designed or newly renovated buildings and public spaces now offer lifts and ramps for wheelchair access (this information is given in the headings for each entry in this guide); specially designed toilets; grab rails; and, for the hearing-impaired, earphones. Buses are also becoming increasingly accessible, and, if given advance notice, train, ferry or bus staff will help any disabled passengers. Ask a travel agent about the Disabled Persons Railcard, which entitles you to discounted rail fares.

Many banks, theatres and museums now provide aids for the visually or hearing-impaired. Specialist tour operators, such as **Tourism for All**, cater for physically handicapped visitors.

If renting a car, Hertz (see p637) offers hand-controlled vehicles for hire at no extra cost. In order to use any of the disabled parking spaces, you need to display a special badge in your car.

For more general information on facilities for disabled travellers, contact **RADAR**. This association also publishes two books that carry a wealth of information for disabled holiday-makers: *Holidays in Britain and Ireland* and *There and Back*. The latter is a comprehensive guide to non-local travel. It pays particular attention to the links between the different methods of transport, whether by air, rail, road or sea.

Travelling with Children

Britain offers a wealth of activities and fun days out for those travelling with children. The VisitBritain website *(see p621)* is a great resource for offering ideas, tips and useful information for the family.

Peak holiday times – Easter, July and August – and half-term school holidays have most to offer in terms of entertainment for children. There is always something child-friendly going on at Christmas, too, like pantomimes and winter skating rinks. It is worth checking the websites of individual museums and art galleries, because these often host child-centred events at key times of year. A couple of useful websites for information on things to do with children are dayoutwiththekids.co.uk and letsgowiththekids.co.uk.

Discounts for children or family tickets are available for travel, theatre shows and other forms of entertainment.

Choose a hotel that welcomes children, or opt for

The Natural History Museum, a great day out for the whole family

self-catering quarters with hard-wearing furnishings and lots of room in which to run around. Many hotels now provide baby-sitting or baby-listening services, and may offer reductions or even free accommodation for very young children *(see pp556–73)*.

Restaurants are also becoming more welcoming of tiny patrons, and many provide high chairs and special menus *(see pp574–603)*. Italian eateries are often the most friendly and informal, but even the traditional British pub, once resolutely child-free, has relented, with beer gardens and family rooms. Under-18s are not permitted near the bars, nor are they allowed to buy or consume

alcohol. The over-16s however, are permitted to consume wine, beer or cider with a table meal provided the alcohol is bought by an adult.

Baby-changing facilities are often provided at larger shops, department stores and shopping centres, as well as at most large museums and art galleries. For those who don't want to travel with all the paraphernalia necessary for their offspring (baby food, nappies, sunscreen), many shops will deliver everything you need for your trip directly to your accommodation if you order online – try johnlewis.com, mothercare.com, or tesco.com.

The privately owned, admission-charging Hever Castle *(see p193)*

International Student Identity Card

Student Travellers

Full-time students in possession of a valid International Student Identity Card (ISIC) are often entitled to discounts on things such as travel, entrance fees and sports facilities. North American students can also get medical cover, although it may be very basic *(see p627)*. ISICs can be purchased from **STA Travel**, the **National Union of Students** or online. Proof of student status is required.

A **Hostelling International** card enables you to stay in Britain's youth hostels. Outside of term time, inexpensive accommodation is also available at many of the university halls of residence, such as the **University of London**. This is a good way of staying in city centres on a tight budget. Those who are exploring the wilder regions of Britain can find affordable sleeping quarters in camping barns (dormitory-style bunkhouses). Though spartan, they cost very little. The YHA website (www.yha.org.uk) has a full list of camping barns across Britain.

US and Canadian students interested in working in Britain should contact **BUNAC**.

Lorna Doone Cottage and National Trust Information Centre, Somerset

English Heritage and The National Trust

Many of Britain's historic buildings, parks and gardens, not to mention vast tracts of countryside and coastline, are cared for by associations such as **English Heritage** [EH], the **National Trust** [NT] or the **National Trust for Scotland** [NTS]. Entrance fees for these sights are often quite steep, so if you wish to visit several of them during your stay, it may be worth taking out an annual membership, which allows free access to any of these properties for a calendar year. Be aware that many may be closed in winter.

Many of the National Trust's properties are "listed", meaning that they are recognized as having special architectural or historical interest and are therefore protected from alterations and demolition. This guide identifies EH, NT and NTS properties at the beginning of each entry.

ENGLISH HERITAGE

The sign and symbol of English Heritage

Electricity

The voltage in Britain is 220/240 AC, 50 Hz. Electrical plugs have three rectangular pins and take fuses of 3, 5 and 13 amps.

Visitors from abroad will need an adaptor for appliances that have been brought from home, such as portable computers, hairdryers and phone chargers. Most hotels will have two-pronged European-style sockets for shavers only.

Clock at the Royal Observatory, Greenwich *(see p129)*

Time

During the winter months, Britain is on Greenwich Mean Time (GMT), which is five hours ahead of Eastern Standard Time and 10 hours behind Sydney. From about the middle of March until October, the clocks go forward one hour to British Summer Time (BST).

To check the correct time, contact the Speaking Clock service by dialling 123.

Conversion Chart

Britain is officially metric, in line with the rest of Europe. However, imperial measures are still in use, especially for road distances, which are measured in miles. Imperial pints and gallons are 20 per cent larger than US measures.

Imperial to Metric

1 inch = 2.5 centimetres
1 foot = 30 centimetres
1 mile = 1.6 kilometres
1 ounce = 28 grams
1 pound = 454 grams
1 pint = 0.6 litres
1 gallon = 4.6 litres

Metric to Imperial

1 millimetre = 0.04 inch
1 centimetre = 0.4 inch
1 metre = 3 feet 3 inches
1 kilometre = 0.6 mile
1 gram = 0.04 ounce
1 kilogram = 2.2 pounds

Responsible Travel

Like many European countries, Britain is aware of the need to be greener and is making a concerted effort to reduce emissions and waste. While most rubbish is still sent to landfill sites, there are recycling campaigns in every town and city, and the amounts of household waste are gradually diminishing.

Many holiday properties across the country publish their green policies, showing how they minimize energy use. Some lodgings even offer discounts to guests arriving by public transport or on foot, particularly in heavily congested areas such as national parks. These themselves vary in the environmental schemes they operate, but all are committed to encouraging green tourism.

The **Green Tourism Business Scheme** is a national scheme that has vetted 1,500 places to stay in England, Scotland and Wales, from small B&Bs

Colourful stalls at a farmers' market

to luxury five-star hotels, as well as about 500 visitor attractions. The scheme requires owners to provide details on more than 145 criteria, ranging from energy and waste control to use of local produce and transport. A qualified environmental auditor visits each property and allocates an award based on the standards met. There are also more than 20 regional accommodation certification schemes across Britain, including **Green Leaf** (New Forest).

Another green accommodation solution is the great outdoors. Campsites are located across Britain, and pitches are available from as little as £4.50 per night. Note, however, that sites are often fairly far from the main towns and may not be served by public transport.

Organic and fair-trade products can be bought at most supermarkets. Many towns and cities hold a weekly food market, and farmers' markets are also on the increase. These stock locally sourced produce, and shopping here is a great way to give back to the local economy. Visit www.farmersmarkets.net to find your nearest farmers' market. When in rural areas, look out for farm shops that stock fresh products from local farms. "Slow Food" fairs are held occasionally across the country. These tend to last several days and are a great opportunity for small vendors to set up stalls and for visitors to sample food from sustainable sources.

DIRECTORY

Student Travellers

BUNAC
Priory House, 6 Wrights Lane, London W8 6TA.
Tel 020 7870 9570.
W bunac.org

Hostelling International
Tel 01707 324170.
W hihostels.com

National Union of Students
Tel 0845 521 0262.
W nus.org.uk

STA Travel
Unit 7, Kensington Arcade, 125 Kensington High St, London W8 5SF.
Tel 0871 702 9824.
W statravel.co.uk

University of London
Malet St, London WC1.
Tel 020 7862 8880.
W housing.lon.ac.uk

Heritage Organizations

English Heritage
Tel 0870 333 1181.
W english-heritage. org.uk

National Trust
Tel 0844 800 1895.
W national trust.org.uk

National Trust for Scotland
Hermiston Quay, 5 Cultins Rd, Edinburgh EH11 4DF.
Tel 0844 493 2100.
W nts.org.uk

Religious Organizations

Baptist
London Baptist Assn, 235 Shaftesbury Ave, London WC2. Tel 020 7692 5592.
W londonbaptist.org.uk

Buddhist
Buddhist Society, 58 Eccleston Sq, London SW1. Tel 020 7834 5858.
W thebuddhist society. org

Church of England
Great Smith St, London SW1.
Tel 020 7898 1000.
W cofe.anglican.org

Evangelical Alliance
176 Copenhagen Street, London N1 0ST.
Tel 020 7520 3830.
W eauk.org

Jewish
Liberal Jewish Synagogue, 28 St John's Wood Rd, London NW8.
Tel 020 7286 5181.
W ljs.org

Muslim
Islamic Cultural Centre, 146 Park Rd, London NW8. Tel 020 7724 3363.
W iccuk.org

Quakers
Friends House, 173–177 Euston Rd, London NW1.
Tel 020 7663 1000.
W quaker.org.uk

Roman Catholic
Westminster Cathedral, Victoria St, London SW1.
Tel 020 7798 9055.
W westminster cathedral.org.uk

United Synagogue (Orthodox)
Adler House, 735 High Rd, North Finchley, London N12.
Tel 020 8343 8989.
W theus.org.uk

Responsible Travel

Green Business
W green-business. co.uk

Green Leaf Tourist Scheme
W www.thenewforest. co.uk/accommodation/ green-leaf-accommodation.aspx

Green Tourism Business Scheme
W green-business. co.uk

Personal Security and Health

Britain is a densely populated country that, like any other, has its share of social problems. However, it is very unlikely that you will come across any violence. If you do encounter difficulties, do not hesitate to contact the police for help. Britain's National Health Service can be relied upon for both emergency and routine treatment. Note that you may have to pay if your country has no reciprocal arrangement with Britain.

Police car

Ambulance

Fire engine

Police

The sight of a traditional bobby walking the streets is now less common than that of the police patrol car, but the old-fashioned police constable does still exist, particularly in rural areas and crowded city centres.

Unlike in many other countries, the police force in Britain does not carry guns, although 10 per cent of the London Metropolitan police are armed.

If you are lost, ask a policeman or woman – they are courteous, approachable and helpful. Traffic wardens may also be able to help you with directions. If you have been the victim of a robbery or an assault, contact the police by dialling 999. All Britain's major cities have community police support officers who patrol the city streets working alongside the police. They are able to deal with anti-social behaviour, can offer advice on crime prevention and can also help you with directions and information.

Lost and Stolen Property

If you lose anything or have anything stolen, report it at the nearest police station as soon as you are able. A written report from the local police is required to make a claim on your insurance for any theft. All of the main bus and rail stations have lost-property offices.

Crime

Britain is not a dangerous place for visitors, and it is most unlikely that your stay will be blighted by crime. Due to terrorist threats, there are occasional security alerts, especially on the Underground, but these are mainly false alarms often due to people accidentally leaving a bag or parcel unattended.

Always co-operate with the authorities if your bag has to be searched or if you are asked to evacuate a building.

What to be Aware of

Make sure that your possessions are adequately insured before you arrive in Britain, and never leave them unattended in public places. Keep your valuables concealed (particularly mobile phones), especially in crowded places. Pickpockets love markets, busy shops and all modes of transport during rush hour. Keep handbags on your lap, never on the floor or on the back of your chair. It is advisable not to carry too much cash or jewellery with you. Take what you need for the day, and leave the rest in your hotel safe instead. It is also advisable not to leave any valuables on display in your hotel room.

At night, try to avoid deserted and poorly lit places such as back streets and car parks.

Begging is an increasingly common sight in many British cities, and foreign visitors are frequent targets for hard-luck stories. Requests for money are usually polite, but any abuse should be reported to the police immediately.

Female police constable   Traffic police officer   Male police constable

Women Travellers

It is not unusual in Britain for women to travel unaccompanied or to visit a bar or restaurant with a group of female friends. However, caution is advisable in deserted places, especially after dark. Always summon a licensed taxi (*see pp642–3*) and do not walk through a quiet area at night, especially if you are not familiar with the district. Try to avoid using train carriages where there is just one other passenger or a group of young men.

It is illegal to carry any offensive weapons such as knives, guns and even tear gas around with you, even for self-defence. However, personal alarms are allowed.

Pharmacy sign

In an Emergency

The police, fire and ambulance services are on call 24 hours a day and can be reached by dialling 999. Along the coastal areas, this number will also put you in touch with Britain's voluntary coastguard rescue service, the Royal National Lifeboat Institute. Calls are free from any public or private phone, but they should be made only in real emergencies.

Pharmacies

You can buy a wide range of over-the-counter drugs in Britain. **Boots** (www.boots.com) is the best-known chemist, with branches in most towns. Many medicines, however, are available only with a doctor's prescription. If you are likely to need medication, either bring your own or get your doctor to write out the generic (as opposed to the brand) name of the drug. If you are entitled to an NHS prescription, you will be charged a standard rate; if not, you will be charged the full cost of the drug. Do ask for a receipt

Royal National Lifeboat
Institute logo

for any insurance claim. Some pharmacies are open until midnight; contact your local hospital for a list. You can call the **NHS 111 Service** a 24-hour helpline or go to a hospital casualty department any time. In an emergency, dial 999 for an ambulance.

Health Insurance

It is sensible to take out travel insurance to cover cancellation or curtailment of your holiday, theft or loss of money and possessions, and the cost of any medical treatment, which may include emergency hospital care, repatriation and specialists' fees. This is particularly important for visitors from outside the European Union. Emergency medical treatment in a British NHS casualty ward is free, but any kind of additional medical care could prove very expensive.

Those with a European Health Insurance Card (EHIC) are entitled to free treatment under the NHS. This applies to visitors from EU and European Economic Area (EEA) countries, as well as some Commonwealth countries, such as Australia and New Zealand. Be aware, though, that certain benefits covered by medical insurance will not be included. North American and Canadian health plans or student identity cards (*see p624*) may give you some protection against costs, but do always check the small print.

If you need to see a dentist while staying in Britain, be aware that you will have to pay. The cost varies, depending on your entitlement to NHS treatment and whether you can find an NHS dentist to treat you (many dental practices no longer take on NHS patients). Emergency dental treatment is available in some hospitals, but if you prefer to be seen by a private dentist, try looking in the Yellow Pages (*see p630*).

Banking and Currency

The high-street banks usually offer the best rates of currency exchange, though commission fees may vary. However, if you do find yourself having to use one of the many privately owned bureaux de change that are found at nearly every major airport, train station and tourist area, take care to check the commission and minimum charges before completing any transaction.

Customers using ATMs outside a branch of Lloyds TSB

Bureaux De Change

Private bureaux de change may be more conveniently located and have more flexible opening hours than banks. However, rates of exchange vary and commission charges can be high, so it is always worth shopping around.

Exchange International, **Travelex**, **American Express** and **Chequepoint** all have branches throughout Britain and usually offer good exchange facilities. Marks & Spencer (www.marksand spencer.com) has bureaux de change in more than 110 of its stores across the UK. They charge no commission on foreign-currency travellers' cheques and only 1 per cent on sterling travellers' cheques.

Banks

Every large town and city in Britain has a branch of at least one of these five high-street banks: Barclays, Lloyds TSB, HSBC, NatWest and Royal Bank of Scotland.

Banking hours vary but the majority are open 9am to 5:30pm Monday to Friday. Most main branches open on Saturday mornings, too. All banks close on public holidays (*see p69*).

If you run out of funds, it is possible to have money wired from your country to your nearest British bank. Branches of Travelex and American Express will also do this for you. North American visitors can get cash dispatched through **Western Union** to a bank or post office. Remember to take along your passport as proof of identity.

ATMs

Most banks have a cash dispenser, or ATM, from which you can obtain money with a credit card and your personal identification number (PIN). Cash machines can also be found in some supermarkets, post offices, petrol stations, train stations and London Underground stations. Some of the most modern ATMs have on-screen instructions in several languages. Some make a charge for cash withdrawals (typically £1.50 per transaction). American Express cards may be used at all cash-dispensing machines, but there is a 2 per cent handling charge for each transaction.

There have been some incidences of card crime at ATMs; be vigilant and cover the keypad with your hand when entering your PIN.

Credit Cards

Credit cards are widely used throughout Britain. Indeed, a credit card is necessary in order to rent a car and for some hotel bookings. However, many small shops, guesthouses, markets and cafés may not accept them, so always check in advance of your purchase. Cards that are accepted are usually displayed on the windows of the establishment. Britain uses the "chip and PIN" system instead of a signature on a credit slip. You will need a four-digit PIN, so ask your bank for one before you leave.

A credit card allows you to obtain cash advances up to your credit limit at any bank and cash dispenser displaying the appropriate card sign. You will be charged the credit card company's interest rate for obtaining cash, and this will appear on your statement with the amount advanced. You will probably also incur a currency-exchange fee.

British Banks

These high-street banks have branches in most of Britain's towns and cities. Many will also offer currency-exchange facilities, but proof of identity may be required.

The Royal Bank of Scotland logo

NatWest — National Westminster logo

HSBC logo

BARCLAYS — Barclays Bank logo

Lloyds TSB logo

DIRECTORY

American Express
Tel 01273 696 933.
ⓦ americanexpress.co.uk

Chequepoint
Tel 020 7244 1252.
ⓦ chequepoint.com

Exchange International
Tel 020 7630 1107.

Travelex
ⓦ travelex.co.uk

Western Union
Tel 0808 234 9168.
ⓦ westernunion.co.uk

Currency

Britain's currency is the pound sterling (£), which is divided into 100 pence (p). There are no exchange controls in Britain, so you may bring in and take out as much cash as you like. Scotland has its own pound sterling notes. These represent the same value as an English note and can be used elsewhere in Britain, although it is usually with reluctance. The Scottish £1 note will not be accepted outside Scotland.

A Scottish one pound (£1) bank note

Travellers' cheques are the safest alternative to carrying large amounts of cash, but are not always accepted. Keep receipts from your travellers' cheques separate from the cheques themselves. This makes it easier to obtain a refund if they are lost or stolen. Some high-street banks issue travellers' cheques free of commission to their account holders. When changing money, ask for smaller notes, since these are easier to use.

Bank Notes

English notes are produced in denominations of £5, £10, £20 and £50. Some shops may refuse the larger notes, so always get small denominations.

£50 note

£20 note

£10 note

£5 note

Coinage

Coins currently in use are £2, £1, 50p, 20p, 10p, 5p, 2p and 1p.

2 pounds (£2)

1 pound (£1)

50 pence (50p)

20 pence (20p)

10 pence (10p)

5 pence (5p)

2 pence (2p)

1 penny (1p)

Communications and Media

With constantly improving telecommunication systems and email, staying in touch and making plans while travelling has never been easier. The telephone system in Britain is efficient and inexpensive. Charges depend on when, where and for how long you talk. The cheapest time to call is between 7pm and 8am Monday to Friday and throughout the weekend. Local calls made on public payphones, however, are charged at a fixed rate per minute.

Round-the-clock Internet access at the Europe-wide chain easyInternetcafe

Public Telephones

You can use a payphone with coins or a card. All payphones accept 10p, 20p, 50p and £1 pieces; the newer ones also accept £2 coins. The minimum cost of a call is 60p. Phone cards are more convenient than coins and can be bought from newsagents and post offices. If you use a credit card, note that it carries a minimum charge and that your calls will be charged at a higher rate.

Useful Dialling Codes

The following services exist to help you find or reach a specific phone number. You will be charged more for enquiries if calling from a mobile phone.

BT Directory Enquiries
Tel 118 500
(charge applies).

International Directory Enquiries
Tel 118 505
(charge applies).

International Operator
Tel 155
(freephone).

Operator Assistance
Tel 100.

Overseas Calls
Tel 00 followed by country code: Australia (61), Canada (1), Ireland (353), New Zealand (64), South Africa (27), United States (1).

Yellow Pages
Tel 118 247 (charge applies).
w yell.com
Provides services in any area, as well as maps and driving directions.

Mobile Phones

Mobile phones are widespread in Britain, and every high street has at least one mobile-phone shop, the most common being **Vodafone**, **O2**, **Carphone Warehouse**, **Orange** and **Phones4U**. The UK network uses the 900 or 1800 GSM system, so visitors from the United States (where the system is 800 or 1900 MHz band) will need to acquire a tri- or quad-band set. Contact your service provider for details. You may need to inform your network operator in advance of your trip, so that the "roaming" facility can be enabled. When abroad, you will be charged for the calls you receive, as well as for the calls you make; in addition, you have to pay a substantial premium for the international leg of the call.

It is easier and cheaper to purchase a SIM card locally and top it up with credit. This will allow you to use the local mobile-phone networks, though you can only do this if your handset is not "locked" to a specific network.

Alternatively, you could buy a brand-new phone and top up with a pay-as-you-go card. Make sure the phone you buy can accept international calls. Check that your insurance policy covers you in case your phone gets stolen, and keep your network operator's helpline number handy for emergencies.

Internet

Most cities and towns now have some form of public access to computers and the Internet, including specially adapted payphones in the street. Many hotels include Internet facilities as part of their service, and free Internet access is often available at libraries, though you may have to book a time slot. Many cafés now offer free Wi-Fi (wireless) Internet access, so you can use your laptop computer.

Internet cafés usually charge for computer use by the minute. Internet access is generally very cheap, but it is most reasonable during off-peak times. However, charges can build up quickly, especially when including the cost of printing.

VoIP (Voice over Internet Protocol) is a way of communicating telephonically via your computer. Most Internet cafés will have at least one such system installed. In order to use it, you will need a Skype account (free to set up), a set of headphones and a microphone (usually provided by the café). It is free to call other Skype accounts. Calling land lines and mobiles is very cheap, but you need to buy Skype credits using credit/debit cards or PayPal.

Postal Services

Stamps can be bought at many outlets, including supermarkets and petrol stations. When writing to a British address, always include the postcode, which can be obtained from **Royal Mail**. Within the UK, letters and postcards can be sent either first or second class; second-class mail is cheaper and takes a day or two longer. The price of postage depends on the size and weight of your letter. For more details, visit the Royal Mail website or take your letter/parcel to any post office, where they will weigh it and give you the price of postage.

Large urban post office branches have a *poste restante* service where letters can be collected. Corre-spondence should be sent to the recipient at *Poste Restante*, followed by the address of the relevant post office branch. To collect your post, you will have to show your passport or other form of identification. Post is kept for one month. London's main post office is in William IV Street, WC2. The American Express office on Haymarket also has a *poste restante* service for customers.

Main post office branches offer all the mail services available. In more isolated areas, there are often small branches in newsagents, grocery stores and general information centres. In many villages, the post office is also the only shop.

Post offices are usually open from 9am to 5:30pm Monday to Friday, and until 12:30pm on Saturday.

Post boxes can be found throughout cities, towns and villages in Britain. They may be either free-standing boxes or wall safes, but they are always painted bright red. Collections are usually made several times a day during weekdays (less often on Saturdays and Sundays). The last collection time of the day is marked on the box.

Air letters go by Royal Mail's airmail service anywhere in the world; the cost depends on the destination. On average, it takes three days for them to reach cities in Europe, and four to six days for other destinations. Royal Mail also offers an express airmail service called **Airsure**, available from all post office branches. Mail goes on the first available flight to the country of destination. **Parcelforce Worldwide** offers courier-style services to most

Post box

destinations and is comparable in price to **DHL**, **Crossflight**, **Expressair** or **UPS**.

Newspapers and Magazines

British national newspapers fall into two categories: quality papers, such as *The Times*, *The Daily Telegraph* and *The Guardian*; and those heavy on gossip, such as *The Sun* or the *Daily Mirror*. The weekend newspapers, more expensive than dailies, are packed with supplements of all kinds, including sections on the arts, entertainment, travel, listings and reviews. Free newspapers, with an emphasis on news and celebrity gossip, are given away, morning and evening, at main railway stations in major cities such as London and Manchester.

Specialist periodicals on just about every topic are available from newsagents. For in-depth analysis of current events, buy *The Economist*, *New Statesman* or *The Spectator*, while *Private Eye* offers a satirical look at public figures. A few foreign magazines and newspapers are available in large towns, often at main train stations, but mostly in London. One of the most popular is the *International Herald Tribune*, available on the day of issue.

Television and Radio

The state-run BBC (British Broad-casting Corporation) has 10 digital TV channels, 17 radio channels and a reputation for making some of the world's best television. Its commercial rivals include ITV, Channel 4

Some of Britain's national newspapers

and Five. ITV is liked for its soap operas and game shows; Channel 4 offers art films, documentaries and offbeat chat shows; and Five relies on US imports and TV movies.

There are also 20–40 free-to-air digital TV channels (depending on area), including Sky News and BBC World, and many homes and hotels have hundreds of British and international channels via digital subscription services.

The BBC's radio stations range from pop music (Radio 1) to the middle-brow Radio 4. There are many local commercial radio stations.

Full TV and radio schedules appear in newspapers and listings magazines, as well as online and in the *Radio Times*, a weekly publication.

TRAVEL INFORMATION

Britain is an international gateway for both air and sea traffic, which translates into a variety of options in terms of travel. Visitors enjoy a large selection of air carriers linking Britain to the rest of Europe, North America and Australasia. Coach travel is a cheap, if rather slow, form of transport from Europe, while travelling by train has been transformed thanks to the Channel Tunnel. It takes less than two and a half hours from

Paris to London on Eurostar. Travelling within Britain is also easy. There is an extensive network of roads to all parts of the country, and hiring a car can be a convenient way of travelling around. The railway network is efficient and far-reaching, especially around London. Travelling by coach is the cheapest option. The coach network reaches most areas but can be slow. If time is short, air travel is possible if expensive.

Eurostar trains at St Pancras International Station, London

Travelling Around Britain

Choosing the best form of transport depends on where and when you want to go, although the quickest and most convenient methods are generally also the most expensive. The **Transport Direct** website offers a number of alternative ways of getting to your chosen destination.

Distances between any two points within mainland Britain are relatively small, so air travel usually makes sense only between the extremes, such as London to Edinburgh.

Train travel is the best option if you want to visit Britain's major cities, though fares, especially at peak times, can be expensive. If you plan to do much travelling within Britain, invest in a rail pass (see p638). You can buy one before you arrive in the UK since several schemes cater for overseas visitors. **BritRail** has several options on offer, from a few days' to two weeks' worth of rail travel.

Coaches (see p640) cover a wide number of UK destinations and are cheaper than trains, but they take longer and may be less comfortable.

For a touring holiday, hiring a car (see p637) is easier than relying on public transport. Car rental can be arranged at major airports, large train stations and city centre outlets. Small local firms often undercut the large operators in price but may not be as reliable or convenient. To get the best deals, book from abroad.

For detailed exploration of smaller areas, such as Britain's national parks, you may prefer more leisurely forms of transport such as bike, narrowboat or horse. Sometimes there are picturesque local options, like the rowing-boat ferry between Southwold and Walberswick on the Blyth Estuary (see p206). Larger car ferries travel to Britain's islands.

Taxis (see p642) are available at all main coach and train stations; without a car you will avoid the stress of driving in congested city centres.

Green Travel

With congestion charges in London and limited parking throughout the urban areas, driving in British cities is not recommended. Instead, make use of the country's extensive public transport network.

Covering a lot of ground without a car is possible, although this does take careful planning to ensure you catch all of your connections. Most areas are served by trains and/or buses, and services tend to be fairly regular. Travelling around the countryside without private transport, however, can be difficult, because bus services can be infrequent (particularly on Sundays). It may be sensible to hire a car.

Trains in Britain can be overcrowded at peak times, and they are often expensive, although booking tickets in advance can bring the cost down. The GroupSave ticket scheme allows discounted rail travel for groups of three or four, and various other discounts are available with a travel card.

The National Trust (see p624) offers some incentives, including discounted entry, to those who use public transport when visiting some of their sites.

The National Cycle Network provides more than 20,000 km (12,430 miles) of cycle paths across Britain. A bike can be taken on most off-peak trains, but you may have to book a spot for it. Check before you travel.

For more information on environmentally friendly travel options, contact **Sustrans**.

Arriving by Sea, Rail and Coach

Irrespective of how you are travelling from Europe, you will have to cross the English Channel or the North Sea. Ferry services operate from a huge number of ports on the European mainland and have good link-ups with international coaches, with services from most European cities to Britain. The Channel Tunnel means there is a non-stop rail link between Europe and Britain. Prices between the ferries and the tunnel services remain competitive, and both options are good green alternatives to flying.

Ferry Services from Europe

A complex network of car and passenger ferry services links over a dozen British ports to many ports in northern and southern Europe.

Ferries can be convenient and economical for those travelling by car or on foot. Fares vary greatly according to the season, time of travel and duration of stay. Early booking means big savings – a Dover–Calais return crossing can cost as little as £22. The shortest crossings are not always the cheapest, since you often pay a premium for the speed of the journey.

Crossing Times

Crossing times vary from just over an hour on the shortest routes to a full 24 hours on services from Spain and Scandinavia. If you take an overnight sailing, it is often worth paying extra for sleeping quarters to avoid feeling exhausted when you arrive. **DFDS** runs fast Seacat (catamaran) services between Dover and Boulogne, in France, taking just under an hour. Catamarans can carry vehicles and lack the dip and sway of a conventional ship, so may be less painful for those who tend to get seasick.

Seaport Bureaucracy

Visitors from outside the EU should allow plenty of time for immigration control and customs clearance at British seaports (*see p620*).

Channel Tunnel

Thanks to the Channel Tunnel, there is access to Britain via **Eurostar** and **Eurotunnel** from the French and Belgian high-speed rail networks. In France and Belgium, trains reach speeds of up to 186 mph (300 km/h). The cost is comparable to flying but the train is much more convenient and much less environmentally damaging. Typically, a ticket from London to Paris costs about £99 but can be as low as £59. Passengers on buses and cars get on to a freight train run by Eurotunnel that takes 35 minutes to travel between Calais and

Eurotunnel logo

Folkestone. For those travelling by rail there are about 40 scheduled passenger-only Eurostar services, operated by the French, Belgians and British. They run direct services from Brussels, Paris, Lille and Calais to Ashford, Ebbsfleet and St Pancras in London. There are two passenger tunnels and one service tunnel, both lying 25–45 m (82–147 ft) below the sea bed.

International Coach Travel

Although coach (bus) travel is considerably cheaper than other forms of travel, it is not the most comfortable. If you have a lot of spare time and want to stop off en route, however, it can be convenient. Once you have paid for your ticket, you will not have to pay extra for the ferry or the Channel Tunnel.

Ferry arriving at Dover

Arriving by Air

Britain has about 130 licensed airports, only a handful of which deal with long-haul traffic. The largest one, London's Heathrow, is the world's busiest international airport and one of Europe's main routing points for international air travel. Heathrow is served by most of the world's leading airlines, with direct flights from nearly all the major cities. Other international airports include Gatwick, Stansted, Manchester, Glasgow, Newcastle, Birmingham and Edinburgh. Smaller airports, such as London City, Bristol, Norwich and Cardiff, have daily flights to European destinations. Strict anti-terrorist measures are in force at all airports.

A British Airways 747 jet at Heathrow Airport

British Airports

Most of Britain's largest and best-known airports are run by the British Airports Authority (BAA); the rest are either owned by a local authority or in private hands. BAA airports offer up-to-date facilities, including 24-hour banking, shops, cafés, hotels and restaurants. Security is strict at all British airports, and it is important never to leave your luggage unattended.

For visitors to London, Heathrow, Gatwick or Stansted are equally convenient. If you plan to visit northern England, there are now many flights going to Birmingham, Newcastle and Manchester, while for Scotland you can fly to Glasgow or Edinburgh.

Heathrow has five terminals and other airports have two. Before you fly, check with the airport from which terminal your flight leaves.

During severe weather conditions in the winter months, your flight may be diverted to another airport. If this happens, the airline will organize transportation back to your original destination.

British Airways has flights to most of the world's important destinations. Other British international airlines include **Virgin Atlantic**, with routes to the USA and the Far East, and **Flybe**, which flies to Western Europe.

American airlines offering scheduled services to Britain include **Delta**, **US Air**, **United Airlines** and **American Airlines**. From Canada, the main carrier is **Air Canada**. From Australasia, the national carriers **Qantas** and **Air New Zealand** vie with several Far Eastern rivals, including Emirates.

Britain imposes an airport tax on all departing passengers. This is currently £13 for domestic and EU routes, and up to £94 for non-EU and long-haul flights. It is included in the price of the ticket.

Transport from the Airport

Britain's international airports lie some way from the city centres, but transport to and from them is efficient. The most convenient form of door-to-door travel is a taxi, but it is also the most expensive. In addition, taxis can be slow if there is road congestion. This is also a problem with buses or coaches, although they are a lot cheaper.

Heathrow and Newcastle airports are linked to the city centres by the Underground (see p643), which is efficient, quick and cheap. Visitors to London arriving at Heathrow can also

Airport	ℹ Information	Distance to City Centre	Taxi Fare to City Centre	Public Transport to City Centre
Heathrow	08443 351 801	23 km (14 miles)	£40–£45	Rail: 15 mins Tube: 45 mins
Gatwick	08448 920 322	45 km (28 miles)	£75	Rail: 30 mins Bus: 70 mins
Stansted	08443 351 803	60 km (37 miles)	£80	Rail: 45 mins Bus: 75 mins
Manchester	08712 710 711	16 km (10 miles)	£15–£16	Rail: 15 mins Bus: 30 mins
Birmingham	08712 220 072	13 km (8 miles)	£12–£15	Bus: 30 mins
Newcastle	08718 821 121	8 km (5 miles)	£10–£12	Metro: 20 mins Bus: 20 mins
Glasgow	08444 815 555	13 km (8 miles)	£12–£15	Bus: 20 mins
Edinburgh	08444 81 89 89	13 km (8 miles)	£17–£18	Bus: 25 mins

Terminal 5 at Heathrow Airport

take the Heathrow Express, the fast train to Paddington Station (www.heathrowexpress.com or 0845 600 1515). Trains run every 15 minutes from 5am until around midnight, taking 15 minutes from Terminals 1, 2 and 3, and 21 minutes from Terminal 5. Terminal 4 requires a change of train and takes a total of 23 minutes. Those arriving at Gatwick can take the Gatwick Express to London Victoria (www.gatwick express.com or 0845 850 15 30). Trains run every 15 minutes and take 30 minutes. Stansted and Manchester also have regular express trains that are not too expensive and are a reliable method for travelling into the heart of the city.

Signs for express railway services to London

National Express coaches (see p640) provide direct connections from major airports (London's Heathrow, Gatwick and Stansted, Luton, Birmingham, Liverpool, Manchester, Coventry, East Midlands and Bristol) to many British destinations. They also have a regular service between Gatwick and Heathrow.

Choosing a Ticket

Finding the right flight at the right price can be difficult. Promotional fares do come up, and it is always worth checking with the airlines. Cheap deals are often available from package operators and are advertised in newspapers and travel magazines. Even if you enjoy independent travel, it may be worth considering a package, since sometimes car rental or rail travel is included, and this can be cheaper than arranging it yourself once in Britain.

Fares are usually seasonal, the most expensive falling between June and September. The best deals can be had from November to April, excluding Christmas – if you want to travel then, be sure to book well in advance. APEX (Advance Purchase Excursion) fares are often the best value, though they must be booked up to a month ahead and are subject to restrictions. Charter flights offer even cheaper seats but are not usually flexible.

Budget airlines such as **easyJet** and **Ryanair** offer exceptionally cheap flights if booked long enough in advance. Always buy discount fares from a reputable operator, and do not part with any cash until you have seen your ticket and ensured your seat has been confirmed.

Students, the under-26s, senior citizens and frequent travellers may obtain a discount through student travel agencies. Children also travel at cheaper rates.

Travelling Within Britain by Air

Internal air travel in Britain only makes sense over long distances, where it can save a great deal of time – for example, London to Scotland, or to one of the many offshore islands. Fares can be expensive, but if you book well ahead, they can be up to three times cheaper than if you just turn up at the airport. The British Airways shuttle flights that operate between London and cities such as Glasgow, Edinburgh and Manchester are very popular with business travellers. At peak times of the day, flights leave every hour, while at other times there is usually a flight every two hours. Even on domestic flights, security is strict. Never leave your bags unattended.

DIRECTORY

Air Travel

Air Canada
Tel 0871 220 1111.

Air New Zealand
Tel 0800 028 4149.

American Airlines
Tel 0844 499 7300.

British Airways
Tel 0844 493 0787.

Delta Airlines
Tel 0871 221 1222.

EasyJet
w easyjet.com

Flybe
w flybecom

Qantas
Tel 020 8600 4300.

Ryanair
w ryanair.com

United Airlines
Tel 0871 781 6774.
w united.com

US Airways
Tel 08456 003 300.
w usairways.com

Virgin Atlantic
Tel 08448 747 747.

Travelling Around by Car

The most startling difference for most foreign motorists is that in Britain you drive on the left, with corresponding adjustments at roundabouts and junctions. Distances are measured in miles. Once you adapt, rural Britain is an enjoyable place to drive, though traffic density in towns and at busy holiday times can cause long delays – public holiday weekends near the south coast can be particularly horrendous. An extensive network of toll-free motorways and trunk roads has now cut travelling time to most parts of the country.

The A30 dual carriageway going through Cornwall

What You Need

To drive in Britain you need a current driving licence with an international driving permit, if required. You must also carry proof of ownership or a rental agreement in your vehicle, plus any insurance documents.

Roads in Britain

Rush hour can last from 8 to 9:30am and from 5 to 7pm on weekdays in the cities; at these times, traffic can grind to a halt.

A good touring map is vital for driving in the country. The AA or RAC motoring atlases are fairly straightforward to use. For exploration of more rural areas, the Ordnance Survey series is the best. Motorways are marked with an "M" followed by their identifying number. "A" roads, sometimes dual carriageways (that is, with two

lanes in each direction), are main routes, while "B" roads are secondary roads. The latter are often less congested and more enjoyable. Rural areas are criss-crossed by a web of tiny lanes.

Road Signs

Signs are mostly standardized in line with Europe. Directional signs are colour-coded: blue for motorways, green for major routes and white for minor routes. Brown signs indicate places of interest. Advisory or warning signs are usually triangles in red and white, with easy-to-understand pictograms. Watch for electronic notices on motorways that warn of roadworks, accidents or patches of fog.

Level crossings, found at railway lines, often have automatic barriers. If the lights

are flashing red, it means a train is coming and you must stop.

The UK Highway Code Manual, available online at the Department of Transport website, is an up-to-date guide to all the current British driving regulations and traffic signs.

Rules of the Road

Speed limits are 20–40 mph (50–65 km/h) in built-up areas and 70 mph (110 km/h) on motorways or dual carriageways. Look out for speed signs on other roads. It is compulsory to wear seatbelts in Britain, and further laws govern children. Drink-driving penalties are severe; see the UK Highway Code Manual for legal limits. It is illegal to use a mobile phone while driving.

Parking

Parking meters operate during working hours (usually 8am–6:30pm Mon–Sat). Be sure to keep a supply of coins for them. Some cities have "park and ride" schemes, where you can take a bus from an out-of-city car park into the centre. Other towns have parking schemes where you buy a card at the tourist office or newsagents, fill in your parking times and display it on your dashboard. Avoid double red or yellow lines at all times; single lines sometimes mean you can park in the evenings and at weekends, but check carefully. Traffic wardens will not hesitate to ticket, clamp or tow away your car. If in doubt, find a car park. Outside urban areas and popular tourist zones, parking

Distance Chart												
LONDON						**10 Distance in miles**						
492 / 792	ABERDEEN					10 Distance in kilometres						
111 / 179	411 / 658	BIRMINGHAM										
114 / 182	490 / 784	88 / 101	BRISTOL									
150 / 240	493 / 789	102 / 163	44 / 70	CARDIFF								
74 / 118	563 / 901	185 / 296	189 / 302	228 / 365	DOVER							
372 / 600	121 / 194	290 / 464	369 / 590	373 / 597	442 / 707	EDINBURGH						
170 / 272	565 / 904	164 / 262	75 / 120	120 / 192	244 / 342	444 / 710	EXETER					
198 / 317	792 / 492	90 / 144	161 / 258	165 / 264	270 / 432	214 / 342	237 / 380	LIVERPOOL				
184 / 294	333 / 533	81 / 130	162 / 258	173 / 277	257 / 411	213 / 341	238 / 381	34 / 54	MANCHESTER			
274 / 438	228 / 365	204 / 326	288 / 461	301 / 482	343 / 549	107 / 171	364 / 582	155 / 248	131 / 210	NEWCASTLE		
56 / 90	473 / 757	63 / 101	70 / 112	104 / 166	129 / 206	353 / 565	141 / 226	153 / 245	144 / 230	254 / 406	OXFORD	
194 / 310	307 / 491	129 / 206	217 / 347	231 / 397	264 / 422	186 / 297	292 / 467	97 / 155	65 / 104	82 / 131	174 / 278	YORK

is much easier. Look out for signs with a blue "P", indicating parking spaces. Never leave any valuables or luggage in your car: thefts are common, especially in cities.

Petrol

Large supermarkets often have the best deals; look out for branches of Asda, Morrisons or Sainsbury's with petrol stations. Motorway service areas and rural or isolated regions are generally more expensive. Petrol is sold in three grades: diesel, LRP (lead replacement petrol) and unleaded. Most modern cars in Britain use unleaded petrol, and any vehicle you hire will probably do too. Unleaded and diesel are cheaper than LRP. Most petrol stations in Britain are self-service, but the instructions at pumps are easy to follow.

Breakdown Services

Britain's major motoring organizations are the **AA** (Automobile Association) and the **RAC** (Royal Automobile Club). They provide a comprehensive 24-hour breakdown service for members, as well as many other motoring services. Both offer reciprocal assistance for members of overseas motoring organizations – before arrival, check with your own group to see if you are covered. You can contact the AA or RAC from the roadside SOS phones found on motorways. **Green Flag** is the other major rescue service in Britain.

Most car-hire agencies have their own cover, and their charges include membership of the AA, the RAC or Green Flag.

A small petrol station in Goathland, North Yorkshire

Be sure to ask the rental company for the service's emergency number.

If you are not a member of an affiliated organization, you can still call out a rescue service, although it will be expensive. Always follow the advice given on your insurance policy or rental agreement. If you have an accident that involves injury or another vehicle, call the police as soon as possible *(see p627)*.

The Environmental Transport Association gives advice on reducing the impact of carbon emissions, as well as offering a number of ethical breakdown services.

Car Hire

Hiring a car in Britain can be expensive. Details of car-hire companies at Britain's airports are on the VisitBritain website *(see p621)*. One of the most competitive national companies is **Autos Abroad**, but small local firms may undercut even these rates. Other reputable car-hire companies include **Avis**, **Hertz**, **Europcar** and **Budget**. It is illegal to drive without third-party insurance, and it is advisable to take out fully comprehensive insurance. Many companies prefer you to leave a credit card number; if not, you may have to part with a substantial cash deposit. You need your driving licence and a passport when you hire. Most companies will not hire cars to novice drivers, and may have age limits (normally 21–74). Automatic cars are also usually available for hire. If you are touring Britain for three weeks or more, you may find a leasing arrangement cheaper than hiring. Remember to add VAT and insurance costs when you check hire rates.

Hitchhiking

It is not advisable to hitchhike in Britain, and there is a risk in hitchhiking alone, especially for a woman. If you must, stand near a busy exit road junction.

Directory

Breakdown

AA
Tel 0800 085 2721.
W theaa.com

Environmental Transport Association
W eta.co.uk

Green Flag
Tel 0845 246 2766.
W greenflag.com

RAC
Tel 08448 913 111.
W rac.co.uk

Car Hire

Autos Abroad
Tel 0844 826 6536.
W autosabroad.com

Avis
Tel 0844 581 0147.
W avis.co.uk

Budget
Tel 0844 544 3470.
W budget.co.uk

Europcar
Tel 0871 384 9900.
W europcar.co.uk

Hertz
W hertz.co.uk

National Car Rentals
W nationalcar.co.uk

General Information

AA Disabled Line
Tel 0800 262 050.

AA Road Watch
Tel 0906 888 4322.

Department of Transport
W dft.gov.uk

DVLA
W dvla.gov.uk

Weather
W metoffice.gov.uk/weather

In rural or walking areas like the Lake District, tired hikers may well be offered a lift. It is illegal to hitch on motorways or their approach roads.

Lift-sharing is now a common practice. The small-ads magazine *Loot* (sold in London, Manchester and Bristol, and also available online) has a large section for lift-seekers.

Travelling Around by Rail

Britain has a privatized rail network that covers the whole of the country, serving more than 2,500 stations. Divided into regional sections, the system is generally efficient and reliable. Parts of the network are occasionally closed for repairs, mostly at weekends, so check with your local station or online before travelling. Journeys across the country may involve a number of changes, since most lines radiate from London, which has seven major terminals. There is also a rail link with continental Europe on Eurostar, from King's Cross St Pancras station in London and Ebbsfleet and Ashford in Kent *(see p632)*.

The concourse at Liverpool Street Station, London

Tickets

Large travel agents and all railway stations sell train tickets. First-class tickets cost about one-third more than standard fares, and buying a return fare is generally significantly cheaper than buying two singles.

Allow plenty of time to buy your ticket, and always ask about any special offers or reduced fares. An Advance ticket is often cheaper than one bought on the day, but there may be restrictions on your ability to change or cancel your journey.

Consumers can buy tickets directly from the rail provider, National Rail or a third-party website. Thetrainline.com is the most popular of these and worth checking first. At raileasy. co.uk, you may find discounted tickets in advance. National Express's **East Coast** system covers the whole of the UK. It charges no booking fees and sometimes offers discounts if your journey uses its network.

Inspectors can levy on-the-spot fines if you do not have a valid ticket, so buy a ticket before boarding the train at all times. Ticket offices in rural areas may close at weekends, but small branch lines have a conductor on board who sells tickets. Many stations have automatic ticket machines.

Rail Passes

If you plan to do much train travelling around Britain, buy a rail pass. This can be purchased from many agents abroad, such as **Rail Europe** or **Cie Tours International**. National Rail's All Line Rail Rover gives adults unlimited travel throughout England,

Scotland and Wales for seven or 14 days. For many trips, a Family & Friends Railcard or Network Railcard saves one-third on adult and 60 per cent off kids' (aged 5–15) fares. A Young Person's Railcard offers discounts to 16- to 25-year-olds or full-time students attending a UK educational establishment. The Senior Rail Card entitles those over the age of 60 to a discount of one-third on most fares. There are special passes for London transport, too, and a pass that covers London, Oxford, Canterbury and Brighton. Children aged five to 15 pay half fare; those under the age of five travel free. Disabled travellers qualify for many discounts.

Keep a passport-sized photograph handy for buying passes. If you have a pass, make sure you always show it when you buy a ticket.

General Tips

Britain's fastest and most comfortable trains are those on the mainline routes. These are very popular services and get booked up quickly. It is always advisable to reserve your seat in advance, especially if you want to travel at peak times, such as Friday evenings. Mainline trains have dining cars and air-conditioning, and they are fast – travelling to Edinburgh from London, for example, takes just over four hours.

Porters are rare on British stations, although trolleys are often available for passengers to help themselves. If you are disabled and need help, call **National Rail Enquiries** to book Passenger Assistance at least 24 hours ahead of your journey. A yellow line above a train window indicates a first-class

Mainline train at platform

Reconditioned steam trains on the tracks in North Yorkshire

Trains sometimes split en route, each section proceeding to different destinations, so always check which section you should be on. Trains stop for only a minute at each station, and doors close 30 seconds before the train is due to depart, so gather your belongings in advance and be ready to get on and off.

Some stations are a little way from town centres, but they are usually well signposted and mostly on a bus route. Trains on Sundays and public holidays can be slower and less frequent than normal.

Scenic Train Rides

After motor transport made many rural railways redundant in the mid-20th century, some picturesque sections of track, as well as many old steam engines, were rescued and restored to working order by enthusiasts. These services are often privately run; the local tourist office, railway station ticket office or travel agents will provide you with more information. This is one of the best ways to enjoy Britain's spectacular scenery. Most of the lines are short – around 20 miles (32 km) – but cover some of the prettiest parts of the country. Lines include the Ffestiniog Railway *(see pp456–7)* in North Wales; the North York Moors Railway *(see p398)*; the Strathspey Steam Railway in the Cairngorm Mountains of the Scottish Highlands *(see p548)* and the La'l Ratty Railway in Cumbria *(see p368)*.

compartment. Note that even if the train is full, you cannot sit in the first-class area without paying the full fare.

National Rail Network

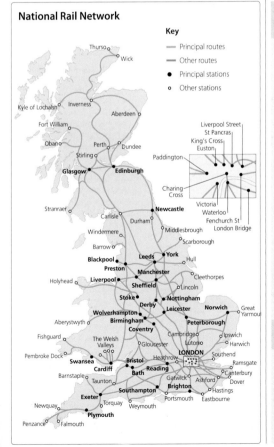

Key

— Principal routes
— Other routes
● Principal stations
○ Other stations

Thurso
Wick
Kyle of Lochalsh
Inverness
Fort William
Oban
Perth
Dundee
Aberdeen
Stirling
Glasgow **Edinburgh**
Stranraer
Carlisle
Newcastle
Durham
Windermere
Middlesbrough
Barrow
Scarborough
Blackpool
Leeds **York**
Preston
Hull
Holyhead
Liverpool **Manchester**
Cleethorpes
Sheffield
Lincoln
Stoke
Derby **Nottingham**
Aberystwyth
Wolverhampton **Leicester** **Norwich**
Birmingham
Great Yarmouth
Coventry
Peterborough
Fishguard
The Welsh Valleys
Cambridge Ipswich
Gloucester
Luton Harwich
Pembroke Dock
LONDON
Southend
Swansea
Heathrow
Ramsgate
Cardiff
Bristol
Reading
Bath
Canterbury
Barnstaple
Gatwick Ashford Dover
Taunton
Brighton
Hastings
Southampton
Newquay
Exeter
Portsmouth Eastbourne
Torquay Weymouth
Plymouth
Penzance Falmouth

Liverpool Street
St Pancras
King's Cross
Euston
Paddington
Charing Cross
Victoria
Waterloo
Fenchurch St
London Bridge

Travelling Around by Coach

In Britain, the word "coach" refers to a long-distance express bus and one used for sightseeing excursions. What the British refer to as "buses" covers those vehicles that operate on regular routes with scheduled stops around or between villages, towns and cities. Many coach services duplicate rail routes but are generally cheaper. Journey times, however, are longer and much less predictable on crowded roads. Modern coaches are comfortable, sometimes with refreshments and toilets on board. Some city-to-city routes, especially at weekends, are so popular that it is a good idea to buy a reserved journey ticket, which guarantees you a seat. For ideas on visits to make, consult the VisitBritain website.

A coach tour on the Royal Mile, Edinburgh

National Coach Network

There are many regional coach companies, but the largest British coach operator is **National Express**, with a nationwide network of more than 1,200 destinations *(see pp20–23)*. Always book ahead for the more popular routes. The company offers a number of discounts, such as their £5 Funfares (50p booking fee), which are available online, to over 50 destinations. **Megabus** offers tickets for destinations all over Britain from as little as £1 (50p booking fee). As you would expect, you will need to book early, and the less popular destinations and travel times have the best deals.

The **Oxford Tube** and **Oxford Espress** run frequent, wheelchair-friendly services between Oxford and London, while **Scottish Citylink** is a major operator running regular services between London, the north and Scotland. Some services run from Heathrow, Gatwick and Stansted airports. Allow plenty of time to buy your ticket before boarding.

Discounts are available for full-time students and anyone under 25. The over-50s can also qualify for a discount coach card, saving up to 30 per cent on many fares.

Coach Tours

A range of coach tours, covering all interests, age groups and destinations, is available. Some include a tour guide. They may last anything from a couple of hours to two weeks or more, touring coast or countryside and visiting places of interest. Some are highly structured, organizing every break en route; others leave you to sightsee or shop at your own pace. You can opt for a prearranged route, or commission your own itinerary for a group. Visit the **Enjoy England** website for inspiration on planned tours.

Any large town will have a selection of coach companies. Check the local Yellow Pages *(see p630)* or ask at your hotel or local tourist office. You can also book coach trips direct from overseas through a specialist travel agent.

Seaside resorts and tourist sites are destinations for many day trips, especially in high season. In some of the more popular rural areas, such as the Lake District, special small coaches operate for ease of movement. You can book these in advance, or just turn up before the coach leaves, although the tour is likely to be fully booked, especially in high season. The local tourist information point or travel agent will be able to tell you where these trips leave from, the cost and may even sell you tickets. It is customary to tip the guide after your tour.

Regional Buses

Regional bus services are run by a number of companies, some private and some operated by local authorities. Services to remote areas tend to be sporadic and expensive, with some buses running just once a week and many isolated villages having no service at all. Only a few rural buses are equipped for wheelchairs.

As a rule, the further you get from a city, the fewer the buses

A National Express coach

and the more expensive the fare. On the plus side, local buses can be a pleasant and often sociable way of travelling around Britain's lovely countryside.

Most buses run with just one operator – the driver. All drivers prefer you to have the correct fare, so always keep a selection of coins handy. Some routes do not operate on Sundays and public holidays; those that do offer a much reduced service. Always check your routes, schedules and fare prices at the local tourist office or bus station before you depart on a bus to avoid becoming stranded somewhere remote with no return transport.

DIRECTORY

Enjoy England
w visitengland.com

VisitBritain
w visitbritain.com

Travelling Around by Coach

Megabus
Tel 0871 266 3333.
w megabus.com

National Express
Tel 08717 81 81 78.
w nationalexpress.com

Oxford Bus Company
Tel 01865 785400.
w oxfordbus.co.uk

Oxford Tube
Tel 01865 772250.
w stagecoachbus.com/oxfordshire

Scottish Citylink
Tel 0871 266 3333.
w citylink.co.uk

Victoria Coach Station
Tel 020 7027 2541.
w tfl.gov.uk/vcs

Travelling Britain's Coasts and Waterways

Caledonian MacBrayne
Tel 0800 066 5000.
w calmac.co.uk

Canal & River Trust
Tel 03030 40 40 40 (head office).
w canalrivertrust.org.uk

Travelling Britain's Coasts and Waterways

Britain has thousands of miles of inland waterways and hundreds of islands scattered along its beautiful coastline. Cruising along a canal in the Midlands countryside or travelling on one of the small local ferries to a remote Scottish island are both wonderful experiences. Canal boats can be hired, and scores of ferries run between Britain's offshore islands. For information on Britain's canals, rivers and lakes and to book accommodation, a boat or a hotel boat, visit the Waterscape website.

A barge on the Welsh Backs, Bristol

Canals

As industrial production grew in the 18th century, it became vital to find a cheap and effective way of transporting heavy loads. Canals fulfilled this need, and a huge network was built, linking most industrial areas in the north and sea ports.

The arrival of the railways and their immediate success for freight made most canals redundant, but there are still some 3,200 km (2,000 miles) left, most in the old industrial heartland of the Midlands.

Today these canals lure travellers who are content to cruise on old-fashioned, slow narrowboats, taking their time to enjoy the views and the canalside inns, originally built to satisfy the bargees' thirsts and to supply stabling for the barge horses. These canal holidays can be very relaxing if you have the time.

If you wish to hire a narrowboat, you can book with a specialist travel firm or contact **Canal & River Trust**.

Local Ferries

Britain's local ferries can offer anything from a 10-minute river journey to a 7-hour sea cruise.

Many of Scotland's ferries are operated by **Caledonian MacBrayne**. They sail to lots of different destinations, such as the Isle of Skye to the Kyle of Lochalsh, or the 5-hour journey from Oban to Lochboisdale in the Western Isles. They offer a variety of different ticket types, from unlimited rover tickets for a specific period of time, to island-hop passes or all-inclusive coach tour and ferry tickets. Not all the island ferries take cars.

River ferries make an interesting alternative to the more usual forms of transport. The ferry across the Mersey, between the cities of Liverpool and Birkenhead, is still used by many commuters. London's river trips, such as the one that runs from Westminster to Tower Bridge, offer a different perspective on the city and make a change from tubes, buses and cars. Local tourist information centres can give you information about ferries in their area.

A car ferry travelling from Oban to Lochboisdale

Travelling within Cities

Urban public transport in Britain is efficient and can be fun – children love London's double-decker buses. Fares are good value, especially compared to the expense of parking a car. Most of the larger cities have good bus services. London, Newcastle and Glasgow also have an underground system, while Blackpool, Manchester and Nottingham have trams. Taxis are available at every train station and at ranks near hotels and city centres. The best way to see many cities is on foot, but whatever transport you opt for, try to avoid the rush hours, from 8am to 9:30am and 5pm to 6:30pm.

Double-decker buses on the Strand, in London

Local Buses

Buses come in all shapes and sizes, with automatic doors and comfortable interiors. They include driver-operated double-deckers, the Routemaster buses and even smaller single-deckers that are able to weave in and out of traffic more easily. The old "big red bus" with a conductor still exists in London, but only as Heritage route numbers 9 and 15 (through the West End and the City respectively).

On most buses you pay the driver as you enter. They will not always accept notes, so keep a few pound coins handy. Credit cards and cheques are not accepted. The fare depends on the distance you travel. If you are exploring a city by bus, a daily pass is a good idea. Many of the larger cities have daily or weekly passes that can be used on all public transport in that city; these can often be bought from newsagents. Check with the tourist office for schedules and fares.

Night services are available only in major cities, from about 11pm until early morning. Day passes are valid on these until 4:30am.

In London, night buses are prefixed with the letter "N", and most of them pass through Trafalgar Square. Be on your guard when travelling alone late at night, when there may be few other passengers on board, and sit downstairs, near the driver.

At some stops, called request stops, the driver will not halt unless you signal that you want to get on or off. If you want to board, raise your arm as the bus approaches; if you want to get off, ring the bell once before your stop. Destinations are shown on the front of buses. If you are not sure which stop you need, ask the driver or conductor to alert you and stay on the lower deck. Always keep your ticket until the end of the journey in case an inspector gets on board. They can impose an on-the-spot fine if you are without a valid ticket.

Cities have bus lanes, intended to bypass car traffic jams during the rush hours. These can be effective, but your journey could still take a long time. Schedules are hard to keep to, so regard timetables as advisory.

Driving in Cities

Driving in city centres is increasingly discouraged. London has a congestion charge – if you drive or park within the congestion zone from Monday to Friday (7am to 6pm), you will be charged a £9–12 fee to pay before midnight that day at a newsagent, petrol station or post office. Not paying the charge will lead to a large fine. See **Transport for London**'s website for more information. Other cities are considering similar steps to keep drivers out of the centres. Parking in city centres is also strictly controlled to prevent congestion (see p636).

Taxis

In large towns, taxis can be found at taxi ranks and train stations. Some operate by radio, so you have to phone. The local Yellow Pages (see p630), pubs, restaurants and hotels will all have a list of taxi numbers. Prices are usually regulated. Always ask the price before you start your journey if there is no taxi meter. If you are not sure of the correct fare, ask the local tourist information point.

The famous London black cabs are almost as much of an institution as the big red buses. These are the safest cabs to use in London since all the drivers are licensed and have undergone strict tests. All licensed cabs must display a "For hire" sign, which is lit up whenever they are free. The newer cab designs are equipped to carry wheelchairs. If a cab stops for you in London, it must by law take you anywhere within a radius of 6 miles (10 km) so long as it is within the Metropolitan Police District. This includes most of London and Heathrow Airport. All licensed cabs have meters that start ticking as soon as the driver accepts your custom. The fare

One of London's black cabs

will increase minute by minute or for each 311 m (1,020 ft) travelled. Most drivers expect a tip of between 10 and 15 per cent of the fare. If you have a complaint, note the serial number found in the back of the cab.

Do not use unlicensed minicabs – they may be mechanically unsound or even uninsured. Never accept an unbooked minicab ride in the street.

Guided Bus Tours

Most major tourist cities offer sightseeing bus tours. Weather permitting, a good way to see the cities is from a traditional open-topped double-decker bus. Private tours can be arranged with many companies. Contact the local tourist information centre for more details.

Trams

Trams are making a comeback throughout Britain in clean, energy- efficient and more modern guises. One of the best tram schemes in Britain is Manchester's Metrolink. The oldest tramway is in Blackpool, which opened in 1885.

London Underground

The Underground network in London, known as the Tube, has more than 270 stations, each of

A tram along Blackpool's famous promenade

Cycling

Cycling is one of the greenest ways of getting around town. Even modest towns have somewhere you can hire bikes (see tfl.gov.uk for London, or cyclehireinfo.com for the rest of the UK). Cyclists may not use motorways or their approach roads, nor can they ride on pavements, footpaths or pedestrianized zones. Many city roads have cycle lanes and their own traffic lights. You can take a bike on most trains; see the **National Rail** website for more information. Never leave your bike unlocked, and always wear a helmet.

Cyclists stopped at a red light on a London street

which is marked with the London Underground logo. The only other cities with an underground system are Newcastle and Glasgow. Newcastle's system is limited to the city centre, while Glasgow's skirts around the centre. Both are clean and efficient, running the same hours as London's.

London tube trains run every day, except Christmas Day, from about 5:30am until just after midnight. Fewer trains run on Sundays and bank holidays. Note that the tube can get very crowded during rush hour.

The 11 tube lines are colour-coded and maps called Journey Planners are posted at every tube station, while maps of the central section are displayed in each train.

Most tube journeys between central destinations in London can be completed with only one or two changes of line. Smoking is not permitted on the Underground.

Tickets are purchased at the station, but many travellers use an Oyster card, an electronic card that can be topped up for use on buses, trains and the tube. Using an Oyster card is, by far, the cheapest way of travelling on

A London Underground sign outside a station

An Oyster card

London Transport's tubes and buses. For information on how to get one, see the Transport for London website. Oyster cards can be purchased from abroad. There are similar electronic card schemes in other major British cities, such as Oxford.

Walking in Cities

Once you get used to traffic on the left, Britain's cities can be safely and enjoyably explored on foot. Instructions written on the road will tell you from which direction you can expect the traffic to come.

There are two types of pedestrian crossing: striped zebra crossings and push-button crossings at traffic lights. At a zebra crossing, traffic should stop for you, but at push-button crossings, cars will not stop until the lights change in your favour. More and more cities and towns are creating traffic-free zones in the city centre for pedestrians.

DIRECTORY

National Rail
Tel 08457 48 49 50 (enquiries).
W nationalrail.co.uk

Transport for London
Tel 0343 222 1234
(voice-activated service).
W tfl.gov.uk

General Index

Acknowledgments

Dorling Kindersley would like to thank the following people whose contributions and assistance have made the preparation of this book possible.

Main Contributor
Michael Leapman was born in London in 1938 and has been a professional journalist since he was 20. He has worked for most British national newspapers and now writes about travel and other subjects for several publications, among them *The Independent, Independent on Sunday, The Economist* and *Country Life*. He has written 11 books, including the award-winning *Companion Guide to New York* (1983, revised 1995) and *Eyewitness Travel Guide to London*. In 1989 he edited the widely praised *Book of London*.

Additional Contributors
Amanda Clark, Paul Cleves, Laura Dixon, Damian Harper, James Henderson, Lucy Juckes, John Lax, Marcus Ramshaw, Nick Rider, Victoria Trott.

Additional Illustrations
Christian Hook, Gilly Newman, Paul Weston.

Design and Editorial
Managing Editor Georgina Matthews
Senior Art Editor Sally Ann Hibbard
Deputy Editorial Director Douglas Amrine
Deputy Art Director Gaye Allen
Production David Proffit
Picture Research Ellen Root, Rhiannon Furbear, Susie Peachey
DTP Designer Ingrid Vienings
Map Co-ordinators Michael Ellis, David Pugh
Researcher Pippa Leahy
Revisions Team Emma Anacootee, Eliza Armstrong, Sam Atkinson, Chris Bagshaw, Moerida Belton, Lydia Baillie, Josie Barnard, Sonal Bhatt, Hilary Bird, Louise Boulton, Julie Bowles, Nick Bruno, Roger Bullen, Robert Butt, Chloe Carleton, Divya Chowfin, Deborah Clapson, Louise Cleghorn, Elspeth Collier, Gary Cross, Cooling Brown Partnership, Lucy Cowie, Deshphal Singh Dabas, Caroline Elliker, Guy Dimond, Nicola Erdpresser, Mariana Evmolpidou, Danny Farnham, Joy Fitzsimmons, Fay Franklin, Ed Freeman, Janice Fuscoe, Richard Hammond, John Harrison, Mohammed Hassan, Charlie Hawkings, Andy Hayes, Kaberi Hazarika, Martin Hendry, Andrew Heritage, Shobhna Iyer, Annette Jacobs, Gail Jones, Rupanki Kaushik, Steve Knowlden, Nic Kynaston, Esther Labi, Kathryn Lane, Pippa Leahy, Carly Madden, Alison McGill, Caroline Mead, James Mills Hicks, Rebecca Milner, Kate Molan, Elaine Monaghan, Natalie Morrison, Mary Ormandy, Catherine Palmi, Helen Peters, Marianne Petrou, Chez Picthall, Clare Pierotti, Andrea Powell, Mani Ramaswamy, Mark Rawley, Jake Reimann, Carolyn Ryden, David Roberts, Sands Publishing Solutions, Mary Scott, Azeem Siddiqui, Claire Smith, Meredith Smith, Alison Stace, Gillian Thomas, Hugh Thompson, Simon Tuite, Conrad Van Dyk, Karen Villabona, Mary Villabona, Christian Williams, Alice Wright.

Additional Photography
Max Alexander, Peter Anderson, Apex Photo Agency: Stephen Bere, Deni Bown, June Buck, Simon Burt, Lucy Claxton, Michael Dent, Philip Dowell, Tim Draper, Mike Dunning, Chris Dyer, Andrew Einsiedel, Gaizka Elordi, Philip Enticknap, Jane Ewart, DK Studio/Steve Gorton, Frank Greenaway, Alison Harris, Stephen Hayward, John Heseltine, Sean Hunter, Ed Ironside, Dave King, Neil Mersh, Robert O'Dea, Ian O'Leary, Stephen Oliver, Vincent Oliver, Roger Phillips, Kim Sayer, Karl Shone, Chris Stevens, Jim Stevenson, Clive Streeter, Harry Taylor, Conrad Van Dyk, David Ward, Mathew Ward, Alan Williams, Stephen Wooster, Nick Wright, Colin Yeates.

Photographic and Artwork Reference
Christopher Woodward of the Building of Bath Museum, Franz Karl Freiherr von Linden, Gendall Designs, NRSC Air Photo Group, The Oxford Mail and Times, and Mark and Jane Rees.

Photography Permissions
Dorling Kindersley would like to thank the following for their assistance and kind permission to photograph at their establishments: Banqueting House (Crown copyright by kind permission of Historic Royal Palaces); Cabinet War Rooms; Paul Highnam at English Heritage; Dean and Chapter Exeter Cathedral; Gatwick Airport Ltd; Heathrow Airport Ltd; Thomas Woods at Historic Scotland; Provost and Scholars Kings College; Cambridge; London Transport Museum; Madame Tussaud's; National Museums and Galleries of Wales (Museum of Welsh Life); Diana Lanham and Gayle Mault at the National Trust; Peter Reekie and Isla Roberts at the National Trust for Scotland; Provost Skene House; Saint Bartholmew the Great; Saint James's Church; London St Paul's Cathderal; Masters and Wardens of the Worshipful Company of Skinners; Provost and Chapter of Southwark Cathderal; HM Tower of London; Dean and Chapter of Westminster; Dean and chapter of Worcetser Cathedral and all the other churches, museums, hotels, restaurants, shops, galleries and sights too numerous to thank individually.

Key
a = above; b = below/bottom; c = centre; f = far; l = left; r = right, t = top.

Works of art have been reproduced with the permission of the following copyright holders: © ADAGP, Paris and DACS, London 2011: 175tr; © Alan Bowness, Hepworth Estate 281bl; *Fish* Constantin Brancusi © ADAGP, Paris and DACS, London 2011 © The Estate of Patrick Heron/DACS, London 2011: 244cl; © David Hockney: *The First Marriage (A Marriage of Styles I)* 1962, oil on canvas 1829–2140 mm, 95tr; *The Other Side* 1990-93, oil on 2 canvases, 72 x 132 in, 415t; © Estate of Stanley Spencer/DACS, London 2011 239t; © Cy Twombly 125clb; © Angela Verren-Taunt/DACS, London 2011: 281br.
The work of Henry Moore, *Large Two Forms*, 1966, illustrated on page 417b *Recumbent Figure* 1938 illustrated on page 95c has been reproduced by permission of the Henry Moore Foundation.
The publisher would like to thank the following individuals, companies and picture libraries for permission to reproduce their photographs:
Abbot Hall Art Gallery and Museum, Kendal: 374br(d); **Aberdeen Art Galleries** 544cla; **Aberdeen and Grampian Tourist Board** 483cr; **Action Plus:** 71t; 484ca; David Davies 71cra; Peter Tarry 70cla, 71bl; **Airport Express Alliance: 687c;** Printed by kind permission of **Mohamed Al Fayed:** 101tr; **Alamy Images:** Peter Adams Photography 14b, 418; BANANA PANCAKE 220, 434-5; Gina Calvi 377tl; CBW 334; Bertrand Collet 492cla; Greg Balfour Evans 24; f8 images 598br; gkphotography 581tl; Nick Higham 379tr; Bjanka Kadic 325tl; B. O'Kane 635tl; andy lane 100cl; LOOK Die Bildagentur 180-1; Jeremy Pardoe 616bc; parkerphotography 11ca; The Photolibrary Wales 581cl; Seb Rogers 615cl; Neil Setchfield 580cl; Nick Turner 461bc; Andrew Wiard 65crb; **American Museum,** Bath: 265ca; **Ancient Art and Architecture Collection:** 46cb, 48cla, 48cb, 49cra, 49clb, 50cb, 50br, 52clb, 55cra, 239br, 443ca; **APEX Photo Agency:** Nick Gregory 287tl; **The Archive & Business Records Centre,** University of Glasgow: 487tr; **T & R Annan and Sons:** 522br(d); **Ashmolean Museum,** Oxford: 51tc; **Barnaby's Picture Library:** 64ca; **Beamish Open Air Museum:** 574bl; **Boath House:** 602tl; **Bodysgallen Hall:** 571tl; **Bridge Hotel:** 569tl; **Bridgeman Art Library, London and New York:** 239tl, 191tc; Agnew and Sons, London 327tl; Bibliotheque Nationale, Paris *Neville Book of Hours* 326t(d); Birgmingham City Museums and Gallery 323tl; Bonham's, London, *Portrait of Lord Nelson with Santa Cruz Beyond,* Lemeul Francis Abbot 58cb(d); Bradford Art Galleries and Museums 53clb; City of Bristol Museums and Art Galleries 260c; British Library, London, *Pictures and Arms of English Kings and Knights* 8t(d), 43t(d); *The Kings of England from Brutus to Henry* 34bl(d), *Stowe manuscript* 44ca(d); *Calendar Anglo-Saxon Miscellany* 50–1t(d), 50–1c(d), 50–1b(d), *Decrees of Kings of Anglo-Saxon and Norman England* 51cb, 53bl(d), *Portrait of Chaucer,* Thomas Occleve 53br(d), *Portrait of Shakespeare,* Droeshurt 55bl(d), *Chronicle of Peter of Langtoft* 289bl(d), *Lives and Miracles of St Cuthbert,* 423cl(d), 423cr(d), *Lindisfarne Gospels* 423br(d), *Commendatio Lamentabilis intransitu Edward IV* 440bc(d), *Histoire du Roy d'Angleterre Richard II* 541bl; Christies, London 449tc; Claydon House, Bucks, *Florence Nightingale,* Sir William Blake Richmond 166tr; Department of Environment, London 52tr; City of Edinburgh Museums and Galleries, *Chief of Scottish Clan,* Eugene

Deveria 488bl(d); Fitzwilliam Museum, University of Cambridge, *George IV as Prince Regent*, Richard Cosway 183tc, 216bl, Giraudon/Musee de la Tapisserie, with special authorization of the city of Bayeux 51br,185bc; Guildhall Library, Corporation of London, *The Great Fire*, Marcus Willemsznik 57bl(d), *Bubbler's Melody* 58bc(d), *Triumph of Steam and Electricity*, The Illustrated London News 61tc(d), *Great Exhibition, The transept from Dickenson's Comprehensive Pictures* 60–1, *A Balloon View of London as seen from Hampstead* 109c(d); Harrogate Museum and Art Gallery, North Yorkshire 392tl; Holburne Museum and Crafts Study Centre, Bath 57tl; Imperial War Museum, *London Field Marshall Montgomery*, J Worsley 35cb(d); Kedleston Hall, Derbyshire 32br; Lambeth Palace Library, London, *St Alban's Chronicle* 53tc; Lever Brothers Ltd, Cheshire 353cra; Lincolnshire County Council, Usher Gallery, Lincoln, *Portrait of Mrs Fitzherbert after Richard Cosway* 183tc; London Library, *The Barge Tower from Ackermann's World in miniature*, F Scol ert 59tc; Manchester Art Gallery, UK, *Etruscan Vase Painters* 1871, Sir Lawrence Alma-Tadema 378bc; Manchester City Art Galleries 377bc; David Messum Gallery, London 451br; National Army Museum, London, *Bunker's Hill*, R Simkin 58ca; National Gallery, London, *Mrs Siddons the Actress*, Thomas Gainsborough 167cra; National Museet, Copenhagen 50ca; Phillips, the International Fine Art Auctioneers, *James I*, John the Elder Decritz 56bl(d); Private Collections: 34ca(d), 52–3, 59ca, 59bl, 60clb, Vanity Fair 61br, 167tl, *Armada: map of the Spanish and British Fleets*, Robert Adam 297tl, 426b; Royal Geographical Society, London 167cr(d); Smith Art Gallery and Museum, Stirling 501bl; Tate Gallery, London 60b, 101ca, 208tl, 355crb, 397bl, *Miniature of Mary Queen of Scots*, by a follower of Francois Clouet 515br, 541tr(d); Walker Art Gallery, Liverpool 382cla; Westminster Abbey, London, *Henry VII Tomb effigy*, Pietro Torrigiano 34br(d), 44bc(d); The Trustees of the Weston Park Foundation, *Portrait of Richard III*, Italian School 53ca(d); Christopher Wood Gallery, London, *High Life Below Stairs*, Charles Hunt 33c(d); **BFI London IMAX Cinema Waterloo:** Richard Holttum 157c; **British Airways:** Adrian Meredith 634cla; **British Library Board:** *Cotton Faustina BVII folio 85* 53crb, 113cl; © The British Museum: 46c, 47crb, 77tl, 110–11 all except 111tr and 111bl; © The Bronte Society: 416 all; **Cadogen Management:** 88bl; **CADW – Welsh Historic Monuments (Crown Copyright),** 478tl; **Camera Press:** Cecil Beaton 96bc; **Cardiff City Council:** 476tr, 477tl, 477cr; **Fkb Carlson:** 579bl; **Castle Cottage:** 599tl; **Castle Howard Estate Ltd:** 402ca; **Colin de Chaire:** 201c; **Chapter Hotels:** 566tl; **Trustees of the Chatsworth Settlement:** 339br; **Museum of Childhood, Edinburgh:** 514bl; **Bruce Coleman Ltd:** 39br; Stephen Bond 298cl; Jane Burton 39tr; Mark N. Boulton 39cl; Patrick Clement 38clb; Sir Jeremy Grayson 39bc; Harald Lange 38bc; Gordon Langsbury 549t; George McCarthy 39bl, 246bl, 289br; Paul Meitz 532cra; Dr. Eckart Pott 38bl, 532t; Hans Reinhard 38clb, 39tc; N Schwiatz 39clb; Kim Taylor 39tl, 532cra; Konrad Wothe 532ca; **Collections:** Liz Stares 34tr, Yuri Lewinski 377tl; **Burton Constable:** 406tr; **Corbis:** Atlantide Phototravel 98; Richard Bowden/Loop Images 348-9; Matt Cheetham/Loop Images 554-5; Neale Clark/Robert Harding World Imagery 460; Kathy Collins 310; Ashley Cooper 15tl; Alan Copson/info@awl-images.com/JAI 384, 480-1; Alan Copson/JAI 74-5; Alan Copson/Robert Harding World Imagery 2-3; Julian Elliott/Robert Harding World Imagery 618-9; Eurasia Press/Steven Vidler 441br; Krista Ewert/Design Pics/Design Pics 194; Nigel Hicks/Purestock/Superstock 300-1; Craig Joiner/LOOP IMAGES/Loop Images 242-3; John Heseltine 115br; Angelo Hornak 121tc; Eric Nathan/Loop Images 160-1; Ocean 80, 494; VIEW/HUFTON & CROW 522cr; Sebastian Wasek/Loop Images 250; York & Son/English Heritage/Acaid 8-9; **Joe Cornish:** 407b; **Doug Corrance:** 489b; **The Cottage in the Wood:** 595tr; **John Crook:** 175b; **The Curlew:** 586tl; **Design Musuem:** Amelia Webb 121bl; **EasyEverything:** James Hamilton 630tr; **1805 Club:** 35tc; **1853 Bradford:** 415t; **The Dining Room at the Oak Bank Hotel:** 596tl; **Dreamstime.com:** Steve Allen 439bc; Andyfox0c0uk 10cla; Anizza 12bc; Anthony Baggett 154tr; Gail Johnson 16tr; Hans Klamm 16bl; **Empics ltd:** Nigel French 70bl; Tony Marshall 70ca; **English Heritage:** 130b, 212cb, 213cb, 253br, 267bc, 354br, 355bc, 423tr, 423tl; Avebury Museum 46cla; Devizes Museum 46br, drawing by Frank Gardiner 427clb; Salisbury Museum 46tr, 46bc; Skyscan Balloon Photography 47tl, 266crb; 398tl; 427cla **English Life Publications Ltd, Derby:** 346tr, 347tl, 347bc; **Et Archive:** 45tc, 45cr, 56clb, 57clb, 62crb, 166clb; Bodleian Library, Oxford 52cb; British Library, London 52cla; Devizes Museum 46cl, 47bc; Imperial War Museum, London 62clb(d), 63br; Labour Party Archives 64bc; London Museum 47cla; Magdalene College 54cla; National Maritime

Museum, London 43b; Stoke Museum Staffordshire Polytechnic 45bc; **Mary Evans Picture Library:** 578tr, 44br, 45tl, 45cl, 45clb, 45br, 48bl, 48br, 50clb, 51ca, 55tl, 55crb, 55br, 57crb, 58bl, 59br, 62ca, 63ca, 63cb, 63cr, 83br, 108tc, 124br, 166cl, 167br, 191cr, 193cl, 199br, 210crb, 226bl, 232br, 236c, 235cb, 235bc, 235br, 238bl, 283tr, 340bc, 353t, 353cla, 424tl, 451tl, 486br, 503bl, 516bl, 518clb, 519tr, 539br. **Fahims:** 587br; **Chris Fairclough:** 299br, 356br; **Andrew Fairlie at Gleneagles:** 600tl; **Falkirk Wheel:** 505bl; **La Favorita:** 601bl; **Paul Felix:** 239ca; **Ffotograff** © Charles Aithie: 439tl; **Fifteen Cornwall:** 576bc; **Fishbourne Roman Villa:** 49tc; **Louis Flood:** 488bc; **Foreign and British Bible Society:** Cambridge University Library 441cl; **Fotolia:** Zechal 276; **Fotomas Index:** 109cra; **Frankie's Fish & Chips:** 603br. **Garden Picture Library:** J S Sira 31cra; John Glover 31br; Steven Wooster 30–1t; **Getty Images:** 45cra, 65cr, 625tc; Gonzalo Azumendi 106; Mike Caldwell 452-3; Alan Copson 221bc; Bill Heinsohn 528; joe daniel price 444; Terry Roberts Photography 536-7; Matthew Stockman 70crb; Travel Ink 677tc; WireImage/Samir Hussein 65tr; **Gilpin Lodge:** 557br; **Glasgow Museums:** Burrell Collection 524–5 all except 524tl; Art Gallery & Museum, Kelvingrove 523tr, 535br, 547b(d); Saint Mungo Museum of Religious Life and Art 521tl; **Glendon Guest House:** 568tl; **John Glover:** 66cr, 164cb, 209br; **The Halkin by COMO:** 561tl; **Robert Harding Picture Library:** 186t, 552t, 64cra, 626cr; Jan Baldwin 291bl; M H Black 292tl; Michael Botham 40crb; C Bowman 613cr; Nelly Boyd 378tl; Lesley Burridge 308tr; Martyn F Chillman 309bc; 204br, 329ca; Nigel Francis 223br; Robert Francis 70–1b; Paul Freestone 230b; Sylvain Gradadom 303tc; Brian Harrison 533br; Van der Hars 542cra; Michael Jenner 49br, 533cla; Christopher Nicholson 257tl; B O'Connor 41ca; Jenny Pate 165bc; Rainbird Collection 51crb; Roy Rainsford 41br, 172tl, 302clb, 342cr, 372t, 390tl, 479b; Walter Rawling 29tl; Michael Short 309br; James Strachen 388bl; Julia K Thorne 490bl; Adina Tovy 651, 490br; Andy Williams 182br, 238br, 350cl, 436tr; Adam Woolfitt 28tc, 48tr, 49crb, 291cra, 309bl, 443bl, 548tr; **Harewood House:** 414c; **Paul Harris:** 66cl, 305bl(d), 342bl, 371b, 615tr; **Harrogate International Centre:** 393br; **Crown** copyright is reproduced with the permission of the Controller of HMSO: 77br, 122br, 122tr; **Cathedral Church of the Blessed Virgin Mary and St Ethelbert in Hereford:** 320bc; **Hertfordshire County Council:** Bob Norris 62–3, 63clb; **John Heseltine:** 111tr, 254tr, 255tl, 473tl; **Historic Royal Palaces (Crown Copyright):** 4crb, 30cl, 123tl, 177 all; **Historic Scotland (Crown Copyright):** 501cra, 510tr, 510cl; **Holdsworth House:** 557tl, 570tc; **Peter Hollings:** 352clb; **Barry J. Holmes/Glastonbury:** 67tr; **Neil Holmes:** 264cla, 290tr, 375bc, 433tl, 433cra, 455br; **Hope House:** 564tc; **Angelo Hornak Library:** 410bc, 410br; **The Horse and Groom:** 593tl; Reproduced by permission of the **Clerk of Records, House of Lords:** 487bl; **Howard's House Hotel:** 566br; **Hulton-Deutsch Collection:** 30ca, 35cl, 57ca, 58cl, 60c, 61crb, 62tc, 62bl, 63tc, 64bl, 166cla, 173tl, 237bc, 304tr, 352cla, 353crb, 354bl, 381br, 401bc, 403bc, 441tr, 499br, 540bl; **Hunterian Art Gallery:** 523bc; **Hutchison Library:** Bernard Gerad 485tl; **Hutton in the Forest:** Lady Inglewood 362tr. **The Image Bank, London:** Colin Molyneux 473bl; Trevor Wood 290bl; Simon Wilkinson 184br; Terry Williams 116tc; **Images Colour Library:** 38cla, 47cr, 225br, 238tr, 254cla, 255br, 340tr, 342cla, 343tr, 357cr, 638cl; Horizon/Robert Estall 442cb; Landscape Only 41cr, 252bl, 369t, 443br; **Imperial War Museum North:** 379t; **Ironbridge Museum:** 319bl; **ISIC:** 624tl; **Jarrold Publishers:** 217tc, 308bc; **Michael Jenner:** 344bl, 532bc; **Jorvik Viking Centre,** York: 409tc; **Judges Country House:** 558bl. **Frank Lane Picture Agency:** 404br(d); W Broadhurst 258bl; Michael Callan 246clb; **Andrew Lawson:** 31cb, 248br, 249tl, 249tr, 249br; **Leeds Castle Enterprises:** 169b; **Leighton House, Royal Borough of Kensington:** 126crb; **Lincolnshire County Council:** Usher Gallery, Lincoln: c 1820 by William Ilbery 345bl; **Llangolen International Musical Eisteddfod** 454cra; **London Ambulance Service:** 626cra; **London Bridge Hotel:** 562tr; **London Transport Museum:** 84tl; **Longleat House:** 270tl; **The Lowry Collection,** Salford: *Coming From the Mill*, 1930, L.S. Lowry 375tr. **Madame Tussauds:** 108bl; **Magna:** 417br; **The Magpie Cafe:** 597br; **Maldom Millenium Trust:** 213tr; **Mansell Collection, London:** 35clb, 56cla, 59crb, 265tr, 353clb, 406br; **Nick Meers:** 26t; **Metro-politan Police Service:** 679t; **Middlethorpe Hall:** 558tr; **Archie Miles:** 244ca; **Simon Miles:** 356tr; **Minack Theatre:** Murray King 280bl; **Mirror Syndication International:** 78br, 91bc; **Morston Hall:** 588bl; **Murano:** 583tr; **Museum of London:** 48crb, 117tr; **National Express Ltd:** 640bl; **National Fishing Heritage Centre,** Grimsby: 407c; **National Gallery,** London: 77tl, 86–7 all; **National Gallery Of Scotland:** *The Reverend Walker Skating on Duddingston Loch*, Sir Henry Raeburn 508c(d); **National Library Of Wales:** 440tr, 443cr(d), 471crb; **National Museum Of Film and Television,** Bradford: 415c; Board of Trustees of the

National Museums and Galleries on Merseyside: Liverpool Museum 383tc; Maritime Museum 381cla; Walker Art Gallery 350bc, 382tr, 382br, 383cl; National Museums Liverpool: Mills Media 361br; National Museums of Scotland: 515bl; National Museum of Wales: 440cla; By courtesy of the National Portrait Gallery, London: First Earl of Essex, Hans Peter Holbein 355tr(d); National Tramway Museum, Crich: 343cr; National Trust Photographic Library: 395tl, 395br, 397tr, 624bl; Bess of Hardwick (Elizabeth, Countess of Shrewsbury), Anon 338tr(d); Mathew Antrobus 306br, 394cl, 395bl; Oliver Benn 33br, 282c, 297bl, 394br; John Bethell 283cr, 283bl, 283br, 307tr; Nick Carter 259br; Prudence Cumming 271bl Martin Dohrn 54crb; Andreas Von Einsiedel 33bl, 306clb, 307cra; Roy Fox 275tr; Geoffry Frosh 293tl; Jerry Harpur 248tr, 248bc; Derek Harris 248clb; Nadia MacKenzie 32cla; Nick Meers 270cb, 271tl, 324bl, 676bl; Rob Motheson 296tr; Ian Shaw 464t; Richard Surman 307bl, 366clb; Rupert Truman 307bl, 383br; Andy Tryner 306bl; Charlie Waite 396t; Jeremy Whitaker 307bc, 464b; Mike Williams 306cla, 396c; George Wright 248crb, 296cla; National Trust For Scotland: 482br, 504bc, 512bl, 526tr, 527tl, 527br; Lindsey Robertson 527bl; National Waterways Museum at Gloucester: 305bc, 305br; NHPA: Martin Garwood 399cla; Daniel Heuclin 286cl; Nature Photographers: Andrew Cleave 246cla; E A James 39cla; Hugh Miles 425cra; Owen Newman 39ca; William Paton 532crb; Paul Sterry 38crb, 38br, 39cb, 39crb, 238cl, 259cra, 532cla; Roger Tidman 201br; Network Photographers: Laurie Sparham 484bl; New Shakespeare Theatre Co: 157tl; Norfolk Museums Service: Norwich Castle Museum 205br; Old Quay House: 567tr, 592bc; Orient Express Hotels: Paul Wilkinson 564br; L'Ortolan: 589tl; Oxford Scientific Films: Okapia 286clb; OXO Tower Restaurant/ Harvey Nichols: 585br; 'PA' News Photo Library: John Stillwell 65cr; Palace Theatre Archive: 156cl; Parva Farmhouse Guesthouse: 572; Photos Horticultural: 165cr, 165cra, 165cb, 165cb, 248cla, 249crb; Planet Earth Pictures: David Phillips 31cra; Plockton Inn: 573tr; Popperfoto: 35br, 64cb, 64br, 164tr, 207tr, 288cl, 448clb; AFP/ Eric Feferber 65bc; SG Forester 71br; Porter's English Restaurant: 576tc, 582bl; Port Merion Ltd: 458cr, 458cl; The Post Office: 511bl; Press Association: Martin Keene 66bl; Public Record Office (Crown Copyright): 52b; Puccini's: 594bl. Restaurant Gordon Ramsay: 584tr; Rob Reichenfeld: 179b, 179cr, 304br, 610bc; RBS Group: 628bl, 628cb; Rex Features Ltd: 35ca, 240c, 613clb; Barry Beattie 263c; Peter Brooke 35bc, 682br; Nils Jorgensen 34cb; Eileen Kleinman 665br; Hazel Murray 65tl; Tess, Renn-Burrill Productions 273bl; Tim Rooke 68cr, 70tr; Sipa/Chesnot 35bc; The Ritz, London: 85tl; Riverford Field Kitchen: 577tc, 591br; Royal Academy Of Arts, London: 88cla; Royal Collection © 1995 Her Majesty Queen Elizabeth II: The Family of Henry VIII, Anon 42(d), 89cr, 90tr, 90clb, 91tl, 240br, 241tl(d), 241tr, George IV, in full Highland dress, Sir David Wilkie 489tc; David Cripps 91cr; Royal Crecent Hotel, Bath: 556cra; Royal Pavilion, Art Gallery and Museums, Brighton: 182cla, 182cra, 183cl, 183cr; Royal Botanic Gardens, Kew: 78ca; Royal Shakespeare Theatre Company: 329tl; Donald Cooper 331cl(d). St. Alban's Museums: Verulamium Museum 236bl; St. Pauls Cathedral: Sampson Lloyd 118cla, 118c, 119tc; Sartaj Balti House: Clare Carnegie 415br; The Savoy: 556bl, 560bl; Scottish National Gallery of Modern Art: Roy Lichtenstein In the Car 509cl; Scottish National Portrait Gallery: on loan from the collection of the Earl of Roseberry, Execution of Charles I, Unknown Artist 56–7; Shakespeare Birthplace Trust: Amy Murrell 302bl; Sidmouth Folk Festival: Derek Brooks 293br; Skyscan Balloon Photo-graphy: 266tr; John Snocken: 31cr/crb; Southbank Press Office: 158tl; Sporting Pictures: 70bc, 70br, 362bc; STA Travel Group: 622cr; Still Moving Pictures: Doug Corrance 552b; Wade Cooper 487br; Derek Laird 486cla; Robert Lees 69t; STB 548br, 549cr, Paisley Museum 519br, Paul Tomkins 533tr; SJ Whitehorn 499tl; David Tarn: 393tl; Tony Stone Images: 578–9; Rex A.Butcher 85cr; Richard Elliott 68b; Rob Talbot

357cla; Superstock: Adam Burton/Robert Harding Picture Library 358; Malcome Park/Loop Images 168; Prisma 411bl; Lizzie Shepherd/ Robert Harding Picture Library 112; Swan House/Fotoseeker: Grant Scott 563bc; © Tate Britain: 77bl, 95all, ; © Tate Modern: 125tr, 125cr, 125br; © Tate St. Ives: 281cr, 281clb, 281br; Rob Talbot: 357crb; TKTS Leicester Square: 159cr; Transport for London: 643crb; Troika Photos Limited: Michael Walter 632cla; Tuille House Museum, Carlisle: 362cl; Urbis: 376c; courtesy of the Board of Trustees of the Victoria And Albert Museum, London: 76br, 102–103 all; Vue 613tl; The View from the Shard: 121cr; Charlie Waite: 553t; © Wales Tourist Board: 437cr, 438bl, 442–3, 472br, 473cra, 473br; Roger Vitos 472tr, 472cb; The Wallace Collection, London: 108br; David Ward: 529b, 547t; Frederick Warne & Co: 371tc(d); © Warwick Castle: 327cra; Courtesy of the Trustees of The Wedgwood Museum, Barlaston, Staffordshire, England: 315bc; West Midlands Police: 626bl, 626br, 626tr; Dean and Chapter of Westminster: 96cla, 97bl; Tony Middleton 96clb; Jeremy Whitaker: 232cla, 233tl, 233bl; Whitworth Art Gallery, University of Manchester: courtesy of Granada Television . Arts Foundation 378c; The Wild Garlic: 565br, 590tl; Christopher Wilson: 408bl; Wilton House Trust: 269br; Woburn Abbey – by kind permission of the Marquess of Tavistock and Trustees of the Bedford Estate: 54–5, 234tl; Photo © Woodman-sterne, Watford, UK: Jeremy Marks 119cra. York Castle Museum: 409crb; York Art Gallery: 411c; Dean & Chapter York Minster: Peter Gibson 413cla, 413ca, 413cr; Jim Korshaw 410tr; York Minster (Chapter of York): 413cl/c/bc; Yorkshire Sculpture Park: Jerry Hardman Jones 417t. ZEFA: 68tl, 158cr, 267tr, 273tr, 490cra, 611tl, 636tr; Bob Croxford 67br; Weir 201tr.

Front Endpaper: Alamy Images: Peter Adams Photography Ltd Rtr; BANANA PANCAKE Rbr; CBW Rcra; Corbis: Neale Clark/Robert Harding World Imagery Lcb; Kathy Collins Rcl; Alan Copson/info@awl-images. com/JAI Rca; Krista Ewert/Design Pics/Design Pics Rcrb; Ocean Rcb; Sebastian Wasek/Loop Images Lbc; Fotolia: Zechal Lcbl; Getty Images: Bill Heinsohn Lcla; joe daniel price Lclb; Superstock: Adam Burton/Robert Harding Picture Library Rtc; Malcom Park/Loop Images Rbc..

Back Endpaper: Corbis: Atlantide Phototravel Lbl; Ocean Lbr; Getty Images: Gonzalo Azumendi Ltl; Superstock: Lizzie Shepherd/Robert Harding Picture Library Rbl.

Jacket: Front main image and spine – Alamy Images: eye35.pix

All other images © Dorling Kindersley. For further information see www.DKimages.com

Special Editions of DK Travel Guides

DK Travel Guides can be purchased in bulk quantities at discounted prices for use in promotions or as premiums. We are also able to offer special editions and personalized jackets, corporate imprints, and excerpts from all of our books, tailored specifically to meet your own needs.

To find out more, please contact:

in the United States SpecialSales@dk.com

in the UK TravelSpecialSales@uk.dk.com

in Canada DK Special Sales at general@ tourmaline.ca

in Australia business.development@pearson. com.au

Central London

**Regent's Park and
Bloomsbury**
See pp106–111

REGENT'S
PARK

GLOUCESTER PLACE
MARYLEBONE ROAD
EUSTON ROAD
GOWER STR
TOTTENHAM COURT ROA

BAKER STREET
HARLEY STREET
PORTLAND PLACE
GREAT PORTLAND STREET
MORTIMER ST

MARYLEBONE

WIGMORE STREET
OXFORD STREET
REGENT ST
WARDOUR ST

BROOK STREET

SOHO

MARBLE
ARCH

BAYSWATER ROAD

PARK LANE

MOUNT ST

PICADILLY
CIRCUS

SHAFTES

KENSINGTON

HYDE PARK

MAYFAIR

Round
Pond

SERPENTINE ROAD

Serpentine

PICCADILLY

ST JAMES'S STREET
PALL MALL

THE M

GARDENS

ROTTEN ROW

**GREEN
PARK**

**ST
JAMES'S
PARK**

KENSINGTON PALACE GDNS

KENSINGTON ROAD

KNIGHTSBRIDGE

KNIGHTSBRIDGE

HYDE
PARK
CORNER

**Buckingham
Palace**

West

KENSINGTON

EXHIBITION ROAD

BROMPTON ROAD

GROSVENOR PLACE

BUCKINGHAM GATE

ST RE

**Victoria and
Albert Museum**

LOWER
GROSVENOR
PLACE

VICTORIA

WESTM

VAUXHALL BRIDGE

**South Kensington
and Hyde Park**
See pp98–105

**West End and
Westminster**
See pp80–97